THE POLICE OFFICERS MANUAL

Thirteenth Edition

1994

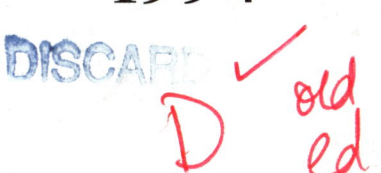

1st Ed.	Arthur W. Rogers and Clifford R. Magone	1932
2nd Ed.	Arthur W. Rogers and Clifford R. Magone	1944
3rd Ed.	Clifford R. Magone	1955
4th Ed.	William C. Bowman, Q.C.	1964
5th Ed.	Clay M. Powell, Q.C.	1974
6th Ed.	Clay M. Powell, Q.C. and Gary P. Rodrigues	1976
7th Ed.	Gary P. Rodrigues	1978
8th Ed.	Gary P. Rodrigues	1980
9th Ed.	Gary P. Rodrigues	1982
10th Ed.	Gary P. Rodrigues	1983
11th Ed.	Gary P. Rodrigues	1989
12th Ed.	Gary P. Rodrigues	1991
13th Ed.	Gary P. Rodrigues	1993

THE POLICE OFFICERS MANUAL

Thirteenth Edition - 1994

BY
Gary P. Rodrigues, B.A., LL.B.
of the Ontario Bar

with the assistance of

Kevin Bryson, B.A.

CARSWELL
Thomson Professional Publishing

© 1993 Thomson Canada Limited

All rights reserved. No part of this publication may be reproduced, stored in a retrieval system, or transmitted, in any form or by any means, electronic, mechanical, photocopying, recording, or otherwise, without the prior written permission of the publisher.

This publication is designed to provide accurate and authoritative information. It is sold with the understanding that the publisher is not engaged in rendering legal, accounting or other professional advice. If legal advice or other expert assistance is required, the services of a competent professional should be sought. The analysis contained herein should in no way be construed as being either official or unofficial policy of any governmental body.

The paper used in this publication meets the minimum requirements of American National Standard for Information Sciences — Permanence of Paper for Printed Library Materials, ANSI Z39.48-1984.

Canadian Cataloguing in Publication Data

The National Library of Canada has catalogued this publication as follows:

Main entry under title:

Police officers manual

Editor: 1974-1976, C. M. Powell.
Editor: 1976-   , G. P. Rodrigues.
ISSN 0822-465X
ISBN 0-459-55234-1 (13th ed.)

1. Police — Canada — Handbooks, manuals, etc.
2. Criminal law — Canada — Handbooks, manuals, etc.
3. Evidence, Criminal — Canada — Handbooks, manuals, etc.
I. Rodrigues, Gary P., 1946-   . II. Powell, Clay M., 1936-   .

KE8809.8.P6P6   345.7100883632
KF9219.8.P65P6

Typesetting: Video Text Inc., Barrie, Ontario

CARSWELL
Thomson Professional Publishing

One Corporate Plaza,
2075 Kennedy Road
Scarborough,
Ontario M1T 3V4

Customer Service:
Toronto 1-416-609-3800
Elsewhere in Canada/U.S. 1-800-387-5164
Fax 1-416-298-5094

PREFACE

The police officer in the 1990's must continuously adapt to changes of all kinds, including changes in the criminal law itself that occur with such frequency that one is sometimes left in doubt as to what is an offence.

Originally published in 1932, The Police Officers Manual is expressly designed to be of help in such situations. Organized like a dictionary, it provides a clear statement of offences, notes on relevant procedure and evidence, and sample forms of charges. The current edition incorporates the many changes in the Criminal Code that have been enacted since the publication of the previous edition. These include the creation of new offences, changes in the rules of evidence, and even changes in terminology such as the introduction of the term "mental disorder" in place of "insanity".

Scarborough
November, 1993

Gary P. Rodrigues

TABLE OF CONTENTS

A Posteriori	1
A Priori	1
Ab Initio	1
Abandon	1
Abatement	1
Abduction	1
1. Definition of "abduction"	2
2. Abduction of unmarried person under 16 — section 280(1)	2
3. Abduction of person under 14 — section 281	3
4. Abduction in contravention of custody order — section 282(1)	4
5. Abduction whether or not custody order — section 283(1)	5
6. Removal of child from Canada for sexual purpose. See SEXUAL ASSAULT, 7.	
Abet	6
Abortifacient	6
Abortion and Miscarriage	7
1. Definitions	7
2. Constitutional validity	7
3. Supplying or procuring drugs or instruments — section 288	7
4. Advertising means of causing abortion or miscarriage — section 163(2)(c) and 169	8
Absente Reo	9
Absolute Liability	9
Abuse of Process	9
Accessory After the Fact	10
Accident	12
Accomplice	12
Accused	13
Acquittal	13
Act	13
1. General	13
2. Act of God	13
3. Criminal Act	14
4. Acts and omissions causing danger to the person. See BODILY HARM AND ACTS AND OMISSIONS CAUSING DANGER TO THE PERSON	
5. Acts or omissions likely to cause mischief. See MISCHIEF, 7.	
Action	14

Actus Non Facit Reum Nisi Meens Sit Rea	14
Actus Reus	14
Ad	14
Addiction	14
Adjournment	14
1. General	15
2. Adjournment sie die	15
3. Adjournment of preliminary inquiry	15
4. Adjournment of trial following the amending of a defective indictment or count	15
Advertisement	16
Advertising Offences	16
1. Advertising means of restoring sexual virility or curing veneral disease — section 163(2)(d) and 169	16
2. Advertisement in the likeness of a bank note or security. See CURRENCY OFFENCES, 10	
3. Advertising counterfeit money or tokens of value. See CURRENCY OFFENCES, 14	
4. Advertising means of causing abortion or miscarriage. See ABORTION AND MISCARRIAGE, 4.	
5. Advertising reward and immunity. See MISLEADING JUSTICE, 10.	
Affidavit	17
Affirmation	17
1. Definition	17
2. Giving evidence	17
3. Making an affidavit or deposition	18
4. Young offenders	18
Age	18
1. Effect of being under 12 years of age	18
2. Effect of being 12 years of age or more but under 18 years of age	19
3. Transfer to ordinary court	19
4. Proof of age	19
5. Time when specified age attained	20
6. Inference of age from appearance	20
7. Mistake of age in sexual offences	20
8. Testimony of a complainant under the age of 18 years	21
Agent	22
Aircraft Offences	22
1. Definition of "aircraft"	23
2. Hijacking — section 76	23

TABLE OF CONTENTS

    3. Endangering safety of aircraft or airport.................... 24
    4. Offensive weapons and explosive substances — section 78(1).. 27
    5. Dangerous operation of aircraft — section 249(1)(c) and (2)... 27
    6. Dangerous operation causing bodily harm — section 249(3)... 28
    7. Dangerous operation causing death — section 249(4)......... 29
    8. Unsafe aircraft — section 251(1)(b)........................ 29
    9. Failing to stop at scene of accident — section 252(1)......... 30
    10. Operation of aircraft while impaired or with more than 80 mg of alcohol in blood — section 253 and 255(1)............... 31
    11. Impaired operation causing bodily harm — section 255(2)..... 36
    12. Impaired operation causing death — section 255(3).......... 37
    13. Failure or refusal to provide sample — section 254(3) and 255(1)... 37
    14. Operation of aircraft while disqualified — section 259(4)...... 40
    15. Setting fire to aircraft. See ARSON, 3.
Alias.. 41
Alibi.. 41
    1. Definition... 41
    2. Evidence.. 41
Alien.. 42
Allocutus.. 42
Alternative Measures... 42
Amendment.. 42
    1. Definition... 42
    2. Restrictions on the amendment of an indictment or a count thereof.. 42
    3. Amendment of an allegation that does not conform to the evidence... 43
    4. Amendment of a count that charges an offence under the wrong federal Act....................................... 43
    5. Amendment of a count that fails to state or defectively states the essential elements of the offence........................ 43
    6. Amendment of a count that is defective in substance.......... 43
    7. Amendment of a charge that is defective in form............. 44
    8. Amendment of a mistake in the heading of an indictment...... 44
    9. Procedure following the amendment of an indictment or a count thereof... 44
Ammunition... 44
Amphetamines... 44
Analysis... 45
Animal Offences... 45
    1. Injuring or endangering cattle............................ 45

TABLE OF CONTENTS

2. Injuring or endangering animals other than cattle	46
3. Cruelty to animals	47
4. Owning or having custody of animal or bird while prohibited — section 446(5) and (6)	50
5. Assisting at cock fight — section 446(1)(d) and (2)	51
6. Keeping cockpit — section 447(1)	52
Animus	53
Ante	53
Appearance Notice	53
1. Definition	53
2. Issued in circumstances when arrest without warrant not permitted	53
3. Issued after arrest without warrant	54
4. Failure to appear or to comply with appearance notice	54
5. Period for which appearance notice continues in force	55
6. Proof of issue	55
7. Signature of accused	55
8. Valid if issued on a holiday	55
9. Effect of new information charging the same offence or an included offence	55
Approved Container	55
Approved Instrument	55
Approved Screening Device	56
Arraignment	56
Arrest	56
1. What constitutes "arrest"	57
2. What constitutes "detention"	57
3. What constitutes "imprisonment"	58
4. Right to life, liberty and security of the person	58
5. Right not to be arbitrarily detained or imprisoned	58
6. Rights of person arrested	58
7. Habeas corpus	59
8. Citizen's authority to arrest	59
9. Peace officer's authority to arrest without a warrant	60
10. Peace officer's authority to arrest with a warrant	63
11. Arrested person detained in custody to be brought before a justice	64
12. Use of force in making an arrest	64
13. Arrest of wrong person	65
14. Arrest of young persons	65
15. Arrest pursuant to provincial statutes	66
16. Arrest pursuant to municipal by-laws	66

Arson	66
1. Disregard for human life — section 433(a)	66
2. Causing bodily harm — section 433(b)	67
3. Damage to property — section 434	68
4. Own property — section 434.1	68
5. For fraudulent purpose — section 435(1)	69
6. Negligence — section 436(1)	69
7. Possession of incendiary material — section 436.1	70
8. False alarm of fire — section 437	71
As Soon as Practicable	71
Assassination	72
Assault	72
1. Assault	72
2. Assault with a weapon — section 267(1)(a)	74
3. Assault causing bodily harm — section 267(1)(b)	74
4. Aggravated assault	75
5. Unlawfully causing bodily harm — section 269	75
6. Torture — section 269.1(1)	76
7. Assaulting a public officer or a peace officer — section 270(1)(a) and (2)	77
8. Assault with intent to resist arrest — section 270(1)(b) and (2)	78
9. Assault during execution of process or making a distress or seizure — section 270(1)(c)(i) and (2)	79
10. Assault with intent to rescue thing taken under lawful process — section 270(1)(c)(ii) and (2)	80
11. Assault by trespasser	80
Assisting Deserter	81
1. Canadian Forces deserter — section 54	81
2. R.C.M.P. deserter	82
Association	83
Assumpsit	83
Attempts	83
Audi Alteram Partem	85
Authorization	85
Automatism	85
1. Definitions	85
2. Distinction between insane and non-insane automatism	85
3. Evidence	85
Automobile Master Key	86
Autopsy	86
Autrefois Acquit	86

Autrefois Convict	86
Averments	86
Bailee	86
Ballistics	86
Bank-note	87
Barbiturates	88
Barrel-Length	88
Battery	88
Bench	88
Bench Warrant	88
Benzedrine	89
Best Evidence Rule	89
Bestiality	89
Bet	89
Bias	89
Bigamy	90
Bill of Rights	91
Binding Over to Keep the Peace	92
1. Binding over to keep the peace	92
2. Binding over to keep the peace where fear of sexual violence	94
Board	95
Bodily Harm and Acts and Omissions Causing Danger to the Person	95
1. Definitions	96
2. Discharging a firearm, air gun or air pistol with intent — section 244	96
3. Administering poison or other destructive or noxious thing — section 245	97
4. Overcoming resistance to commission of offence	98
5. Traps likely to cause bodily harm — section 247(1)	99
6. Interferring with transportation facilities — section 248	100
7. Assault with a weapon or causing bodily harm. See ASSAULTS, 3.	
8. Unlawfully causing bodily harm. See ASSAULTS, 5.	
9. Causing bodily harm by criminal negligence. See CRIMINAL NEGLIGENCE, 3.	
10. Causing bodily harm by arson. See ARSON, 2.	
Body	100
Bona Fide	100
Boundary Lines	101
1. Definition of "boundary line"	101
2. Interfering with boundary lines of land — section 442	101

TABLE OF CONTENTS

    3. Interfering with international, provincial, county or municipal boundary lines — section 443(1)(a) 101
    4. Boundary marks placed by land surveyors — section 443(1)(b) 102
Breach of Contract 103
Breach of Probation Order 104
Breach of the Peace 105
Break 105
Breaking and Entering 106
    1. Breaking and entering with intent — section 348(1)(a) 106
    2. Breaking and entering and committing offence — section 348(1)(b) 107
    3. Breaking out — section 348(1)(c) 107
    4. Being unlawfully in dwelling-house — section 349(1) 108
    5. Possession of break-in instrument — section 351(1) 109
    6. Being in disguise — section 351(2) 110
    7. Possession of instruments or breaking into coin-operated device or currency exchange device — section 352 110
    8. Automobile master keys 111
    9. Records of sales of automobile master keys 112
Bruise 113
Building Damage 114
Business 114
Burking 114

Cadaver 114
Caliber 115
Canadian Forces 115
Capias Ad Satisfaciendum (CA. SA.) 115
Carbon Monoxide 115
Caspar's Rule 115
Cattle 115
Causa Causans 115
Causa Effectiva 115
Causa Sine Qua Non 115
Cause 115
Caveat 115
Certificate of Citizenship 116
    1. Definition of "certificate of citizenship" 116
    2. Fraudulent use of certificate of citizenship 116
Certificate of Naturalization 117
    1. Definition of "certificate of naturalization" 117

TABLE OF CONTENTS

2. Fraudulent use of certificate of naturalization	117
Certiorari	118
Cesui Que Trust	118
Charter of Rights and Freedoms	118
1. General	118
2. Fundamental freedoms	119
3. Democratic rights	119
4. Mobility rights	119
5. Legal rights	119
6. Equity rights	120
7. Official language rights and minority education rights	120
8. Reasonable limits	121
Chaste Character	121
Cheque	121
Child	121
Child Pornography	121
Chilled Shot	122
Choke	122
Choking	122
Civil Aircraft	122
Clip	122
Cocaine	122
Commencement	122
Common Law	122
Company	123
Complainant	123
Complaint	123
Compos Mentis	123
Computer Offences	123
1. Definitions	123
2. Unauthorized use of computer	124
3. Damage not more than $50. See MISCHIEF, 6.	
Concealing Dead Body of Child	125
Consensus Ad Idem	126
Consent to Prosecute	126
Conspiracy	127
1. Conspiracy to commit murder — section 465(1)(a)	127
2. Conspiracy to prosecute innocent person — section 465(1)(b)	127
3. Conspiracy to commit an indictable offence — section 465(1)(c)	128
4. Conspiracy to commit an offence punishable on summary conviction — section 465(1)(d)	129

5. Conspiracies deemed to occur in Canada	129
6. Conspiracy in restraint of trade	129
7. Husband and wife	130
8. Definition of "seditious conspiracy". See SEDITION, 1.	
Contempt of Court	130
1. Definition	130
2. General	130
3. Preliminary inquiry	131
4. Exhibits	131
5. Failure to attend or remain in attendance at court	132
Control of Drugs	132
1. Definitions	132
2. Trafficking in a controlled drug — Food and Drugs Act, section 39(1) and (3)	134
3. Possession of controlled drug for trafficking Food and Drugs Act, section 39(2) and (3)	135
4. Failure to disclose previous prescriptions — Food and Drugs Act, section 38.1(1) and (2)	135
Conveyance	136
Copy	136
Coram	136
Corporations	136
1. General	137
2. Service of process on a municipal corporation	137
3. Service of process on corporations other than municipal corporations	137
4. Appearance by corporation	137
5. Non-appearance by corporation	137
6. Notice of indictment	138
7. Punishment	138
8. Offences by officers and employees of corporations	139
Corpus Delecti	139
Corrupting Morals	139
1. Definition of "obscene"	140
2. Making, printing, publishing, distributing, circulating or having in possession obscene matter — section 163(1)(a) and 169	140
3. Selling, exposing to public view or having in possession obscene matter — section 163(2)(a) and 169	141
4. Offences in connection with crime comics — section 163(1)(b) and 169	142
5. Exhibiting disgusting objects or indecent show — section 163(2)(b) and 169	143

TABLE OF CONTENTS

    6. Making, printing, publishing or possessing for purpose of publication child pornography — section 163.1(2)............ 143
    7. Importing, distributing, selling or possessing for purpose of distribution or sale child pornography — section 163.1(3)...... 144
    8. Possession of child pornography — section 163.1(4).......... 145
    9. Tied sale — section 165 and 169.......................... 146
    10. Printing or publishing indecent matter — section 166(1)(a) and 169... 147
    11. Printing or publishing particulars of matrimonial proceedings — section 166(1)(b) and 169............................. 148
    12. Presenting or giving immortal theatrical performance — section 167(1) and 169................................... 149
    13. Taking part or appearing in immoral theatrical performance — section 167(2) and 169................................... 149
    14. Mailing obscene matter — section 168 and 169.............. 150
    15. Parent or guardian procuring sexual activity — section 170.... 151
    16. Householder permitting sexual activity — section 171......... 155
    17. Corrupting children — section 172(1)..................... 155
Corruption.. 156
    1. Of judges, members of Parliament, and members of provincial legislatures... 156
    2. Of persons employed in the administration of criminal law..... 157
    3. Frauds on the government............................... 158
    4. Breach of trust by public officer — section 122.............. 161
    5. Municipal corruption.................................... 162
    6. Influencing municipal official — section 123(2).............. 163
    7. Selling office — section 124(a)........................... 163
    8. Purchasing office — section 124(b)....................... 163
    9. Influencing appointments — section 125(a)................. 164
    10. Negotiating appointments — section 125(b)................. 164
    11. Keeping a place for dealing in offices — section 125(c)....... 165
Costs... 165
Counsel... 165
Counselling Commission of Offence Which is not Committed......... 165
Counselling or Aiding Suicide................................... 166
Count... 167
Courts.. 167
    1. General... 167
    2. Court of criminal jurisdiction............................. 168
Cranial Sutures.. 168
Cranium.. 169

Credit Cards	169
1. Definition of "credit card"	169
2. Credit card offences	169
Criminal Harassment	171
Criminal Interest Rate	172
1. Definitions	172
2. Receiving interest at a criminal rate	174
Criminal Law	175
Criminal Negligence	175
1. Definition of "criminal negligence"	175
2. Causing death by criminal negligence — section 220	176
3. Causing bodily harm by criminal negligence — section 221	176
Criminal Records	177
Cius Est Dare Eius Est Disponere	178
Cuius Est Solum, Eius Est Usque Ad Caelum Et Ad Inferos	178
Culpa	178
Curia	178
Currency Offences	178
1. Definitions	178
2. Making counterfeit money — section 449	179
3. Possession of counterfeit money — section 450	180
4. Possession of filings or clippings — section 451	181
5. Uttering or exporting counterfeit money	181
6. Fraudulently uttering coins — section 453	182
7. Slugs and tokens — section 454	183
8. Clipping or uttering clipped coin	184
9. Defacing current coin or uttering defaced coin	185
10. Making advertisement in likeness of bank note or security — section 457(1)	185
11. Publishing or printing likeness of bank note or security — section 457(2)	186
12. Making, having or dealing in instruments for counterfeiting — section 458	187
13. Conveying instruments for coining or metals out of mint — section 459	188
14. Advertising counterfeit money or tokens of value — section 460(1)(a)	189
15. Trafficking or dealing in counterfeit money or tokens of value — section 460(1)(b)	190
16. Sufficiency of count	190
Current	190

TABLE OF CONTENTS

Custody	191
1. Custody of a child	191
2. Custody of a young offender	191
Cut	191
Cutis Anserina	191
Cyanosis	191
D.O.A.	191
Dactylography	192
Damnum Sine (or Absque) Injuria	192
Dangerous Offender	192
Day	193
De	193
Death	193
Deciduous Teeth	194
Defences	194
1. Definition of a "defence"	194
2. Common law defences	194
3. Presumption of innocence	194
4. Failure to prove essential elements	194
Dehors	195
Delegated Legislation	195
Delegatus Non Potest Delegare	195
Delirium	195
Delusion	195
Dementia	195
Deportation	195
Deposition	195
Diatoms	196
Dictum (Dicta)	196
Diminished Responsibility	196
Diplomatic or Consular Officer	196
Diptera	196
Disobedience	196
1. Disobeying a statute — section 126(1)	196
2. Disobeying order of court — section 127(1)	197
Disorderly Conduct	197
1. Indecent acts — section 173(1)	198
2. Exposure — section 173(2)	201
3. Nudity — section 174(1)	202
4. Causing a disturbance — section 175(1)(a)	203
5. Indecent exhibition — section 175(1)(b)	204

	TABLE OF CONTENTS	xix

    6. Loitering and obstructing — section 175(1)(c).............. 204
    7. Disturbing the occupants of a dwelling-house — section 175(1)(d)... 205
    8. Obstructing officiating clergyman........................ 206
    9. Disturbing religious worship............................. 207
   10. Trespassing at night — section 177....................... 208
   11. Stink or stench bombs — section 178..................... 209

Disorderly Houses.. 209
    1. Definitions.. 210
    2. Keeping a gaming house — section 201(1)................ 210
    3. Keeping a betting house — section 201(1)................ 211
    4. Found in gaming house or betting house — section 201(2)(a)... 212
    5. Allowing premises to be used as gaming house or betting house — section 201(2)(b)................................... 213
    6. Betting, pool-selling and book-making — section 202(1) and (2).. 213
    7. Placing bets on behalf of others.......................... 218
    8. Pari-mutuel betting..................................... 219
    9. Violation or non-compliance with race-track regulations...... 220
   10. Lotteries and games of chance prohibited by law............ 221
   11. Cheating at play — section 209.......................... 224
   12. Keeping common bawdy-house — section 210(1)............ 224
   13. Being an inmate or being found in a common bawdy-house.... 225
   14. Having charge or control of place used for common bawdy-house — section 210(2)(c)............................... 226
   15. Transporting person to bawdy-house — section 211.......... 227
   16. Search and seizure in disorderly houses. See SEARCH AND SEIZURE, 10. See PROCURING and PROSTITUTION

Disposition Process.. 227
Disqualification... 227
Distinguishing Mark... 228
Distress.. 228
Document.. 228
Documentary Evidence....................................... 229
    1. Hearsay evidence...................................... 229
    2. Production of documents................................ 229
    3. Authentication... 229
    4. Public and judicial documents........................... 230
    5. Records kept in financial institutions...................... 234
    6. Business records....................................... 236
    7. Ancient documents..................................... 238
    8. Attested documents.................................... 238

TABLE OF CONTENTS

Dominus Litus 238
Donatio 238
Double Action 238
Drowning 238
Drug Offences 239
    1. Definition of "drug" 239
    2. Drug for causing abortion or miscarriage 239
    3. Drug for restoring sexual virility or curing venereal diseases 239
    4. Drug for obtaining illicit sexual intercourse 240
    5. Causing death in commission of offences 240
    6. Administering noxious thing 240
    7. Drug for overcoming resistance to commission of offence 240
    8. Narcotic drugs 240
    9. Controlled drugs and restricted drugs 240
Duelling 241
    1. Definition of "duelling" 241
    2. Killing or attempting to kill a person in a duel 241
    3. Offences in connection with duelling — section 71 241
Dum Se Bene Gesserint 241
Duplicity 241
Duties Tending to Preservation of Life 242
    1. Parent, foster parent, guardian or head of family 242
    2. Married person 243
    3. Person under the charge of another person 244
    4. Duties of persons undertaking acts 245
    5. Abandoning child — section 218 245
    6. Definition 246
Dwelling-House 246

Ei Qui Affirmat, Non Ei Qui Negat, Incumbit Probatio 246
Ejector 246
Ejusdem Generis 246
Elections Document 246
Electrocution 247
Electromagnetic, Acoustic, Mechanical or Other Device 247
Electronic Surveillance 247
Embalming 247
Embolus 247
Embryo 248
Employers Offences 248
    1. Refusing to employ union members — section 425(a) 248
    2. Intimidation of employees — section 425(b) 249

3. Conspiring to refuse to employ — section 425(a) and (c)	249
4. Conspiring to intimidate — section 425(b) and (c)	250
Enactment	250
Entrapment	250
Entry	251
Eo Instanti	251
Escape	251
Escapes and Rescues	251
1. Prison breach	251
2. Escaping lawful custody — section 145(1)(a)	252
3. Being at large without lawful excuse — section 145(1)(b)	253
4. Failure to attend at court when at large on undertaking or recognizance — section 145(2)(a)	254
5. Failure to attend at court after appearing before court, justice or judge — section 145(2)(b)	254
6. Failure to comply with condition of undertaking or recognizance — section 145(3)	255
7. Failure to appear or to comply with summons — section 145(4)	256
8. Failure to appear or to comply with appearance notice or promise to appear — section 145(5)	257
9. Permitting or assisting escape	258
10. Rescue or permitting escape	259
11. Assisting prisoner of war to escape	260
See also ACCESSORY AFTER THE FACT	
Essential Averments	261
Et Al	261
Et Seq	261
Every One	262
Evidence	262
1. Definition	262
2. Direct evidence	262
3. Circumstantial evidence	262
4. Character evidence	262
5. Expert evidence	263
6. Handwriting	264
7. Hearsay	264
8. Dying declarations	264
9. Self-incrimination	265
10. Admissions by the accused	265
11. Confessions	265
12. Evidence of accomplices	267

TABLE OF CONTENTS

13. Corroboration	267
14. Husband and wife	267
15. Burden of proof	269
16. Application of provincial rules of evidence	269
Ex.	269
Excavation	270
Exceptio Confirmat (or Probat) Regulum	270
Exchequer Bill	270
Exchequer Bill Paper	271
Exeat	271
Execution of Process	271
1. Execution of process — section 129(c)	271
2. Assault with intent to rescue thing taken under lawful process. See ASSAULTS, 10	
3. Misconduct in the execution of a process. See PEACE OFFICER, 2.	
Exhibit	272
Exhibitionism	272
Exhumation	272
Explosive Substances	272
1. Definition of "explosive substances"	272
2. Breach of duty of care	273
3. Using explosives (causing injury with intent) — section 81(1) and (2)	273
4. Possession without lawful excuse — section 82	275
5. Explosive substances on aircraft. See AIRCRAFT OFFENCES, 3.	
Expose	276
Extractor	276
Extradition	276
1. Definition	276
2. From Canada to other Commonwealth countries	276
3. From Canada to countries that are not members of the Commonwealth	278
4. To Canada from other Commonwealth countries	280
5. To Canada from countries that are not members of the Commonwealth	281
Factum	282
False Document	282
False Imprisonment	282
False Pretences	282

1. Definition of a "false pretence"...........................	283
2. Obtaining anything that may be the object of theft — section 362(1)(a) and (2)(a), (b).................................	283
3. Obtaining credit — section 362(1)(b) and (3)..............	284
4. False statement in writing — section 362(1) and (3).........	285
5. Obtaining execution of valuable security by fraud — section 363..	286
6. Fraudulently obtaining food and lodging — section 364(1).....	286
7. Witchcraft..	287
8. Sufficiency of count...................................	289
Falsification of Books and Documents............................	289
1. Book, paper, writing, valuable security or document..........	289
2. Employment record — section 398.......................	289
3. Statement or return of public officer — section 399..........	291
4. Prospectus — section 400(1)............................	291
5. Obtaining carriage by false billing — section 401(1).........	292
6. Trader or businessman failing to keep accounts — section 402(1)..	292
7. Sufficiency of count...................................	293
Federal Court...	293
Feigned Marriage...	293
Felo De Se...	294
Felony...	294
Fetus..	294
Fiat..	294
Fieri Facias (Fi. Fa.)..	294
Financial Institution...	295
Fine...	295
Fingerprints..	295
Firearm..	296
Firearms and Weapons Offences.................................	297
Firearms Offences	
1. Using firearm during commission of indictable offence........	298
2. Pointing a firearm — section 86(1).......................	299
3. Careless use of firearm — section 86(2)...................	300
4. Storing, displaying, handling or transporting firearm contrary to regulation — section 86(3)...........................	301
5. Transfer of firearm to person under 16 years — section 93(1)...	302
6. Wrongful delivery of firearms, ammunition or explosive substances — section 94................................	303
7. Making automatic firearm — section 95.1..................	304

8. Acquisition of firearm without firearms acquisition certificate — section 97(3) 305
9. Delivery of firearm to person without firearms acquisition certificate — section 97(1) 306
10. Possession of firearm, ammunition, explosive substance or firearms acquisition certificate while prohibited 307
11. Finding firearm — section 104(1) and (5) 308
12. Tampering with serial number 309
13. False statements to procure firearms acquisition certificate, registration certificate or permit — section 113(1) 310
14. Tampering with firearms acquisition certificate, registration certificate or permit — section 113(2) 311
15. Failure to comply with conditions or permit — section 113(3).. 312
16. Failure to deliver up revoked certificates or permits — section 113(4) 313
17. Records of transactions in firearms 313
18. Business person reporting loss, destruction or theft 314
19. Carrying on business in firearms or ammunition without permit 315
20. Handling, storing, displaying, advertising or selling by mail order of firearms or ammunition 316
21. Handling, shipping, storage and transportation of firearms and ammunition 317

Weapons Offences

22. Possession of weapon or imitation for dangerous purpose — section 87 318
23. Possession of weapon at public meeting — section 88 319
24. Carrying concealed weapon — section 89 319
25. Possession of prohibited weapon — section 90(1) 320
26. Prohibited weapon in motor vehicle — section 90(2) 322
27. Possession of unregistered restricted weapon — section 91(1).. 323
28. Possession of restricted weapon elsewhere than at place authorized — section 91(2) 324
29. Restricted weapon in motor vehicle — section 91(3) 325
30. Wrongful delivery of offensive weapons, ammunition or explosive substances — section 94 326
31. Importing or delivering prohibited weapon or part of prohibited weapon — section 95 327
32. Delivery of restricted weapon to person without permit — section 96(1) 329
33. Importation of restricted weapon by person without permit — section 96(3) 330

TABLE OF CONTENTS

34. Possession of offensive weapon, ammunition, explosive substance or firearms acquisition certificate while prohibited — section 103(10)..331
35. Finding weapon — section 104(1) and (5)..................332
36. Losing or mislaying restricted weapon — section 104(2) and (5)...333
37. Records of transactions in restricted or prohibited weapons.....334
38. Carrying on business in restricted weapons or ammunition without permit..335
39. Business person reporting loss, destruction or theft...........336
40. Handling, storing, displaying, advertising or selling by mail order of restricted weapon or ammunition..................337
41. Handling or storing of prohibited weapon..................338
42. Handling, shipping, storing and transportation of prohibited weapon...339

Fixed Platform..340
Flight...340
Floater..340
Fontanelles..340
Forcible Confinement...341
Forcible Entry and Detainer.....................................341
  1. Committing forcible entry...............................341
  2. Committing forcible detainer.............................342
Forensic...343
Forgery and Related Offences...................................343
  1. Forgery..344
  2. Uttering forged document — section 368(1)...............345
  3. Exchequer bill paper, revenue paper and bank note paper — section 369(a)..346
  4. Instrument, writing or material adapted and intended to be used in forgery — section 369(b)........................346
  5. Seal of public body or authority — section 369(c)............347
  6. Counterfeit proclamation, order, regulation or appointment — section 370..347
  7. Drawing or using documents without authority..............348
  8. Obtaining anything by instrument based on forged document — section 375...348
  9. Counterfeiting stamp...................................349
10. Counterfeiting mark — section 376(2).....................349
11. Damaging documents...................................350
12. False certified copies...................................351

TABLE OF CONTENTS

    13. False certificate or declaration — section 378(c) 352
    14. Sufficiency of count 352
Form of Marriage 352
Forthwith 352
Forum 352
Fraud 353
    1. Fraud — section 380(1) 353
    2. Frauds affecting public market price — section 380(2) 354
    3. Using mails to defraud — section 381 355
    4. Fraudulent manipulation of stock exchange transactions — section 382 356
    5. Gaming in stocks or merchandise — section 383(1) 356
    6. Broker reducing stock by selling for his own account — section 384 357
    7. Fraudulent concealment of title documents — section 385(1) ...358
    8. Fraudulent registration of title — section 386 359
    9. Fraudulent sale of real property — section 387 359
    10. Misleading receipt 360
    11. Fraudulent disposal of goods on which money advanced 360
    12. Fraudulent receipts under Bank Act 361
    13. Disposal of property to defraud creditors 362
    14. Fraud in relation to fares 363
    15. Fraudulently obtaining transportation — section 393(3) 363
    16. Fraud in relation to minerals 364
    17. Fraud in relation to mines 365
    18. Sufficiency of count 366
Fraudulent Conversion 366
Fugitive Offender 366
Functus Officio 366

Games 366
Gangrene 366
Garrotting 366
Gauge 367
Genetic Markers 367
Gestation 367
Goods 367
Government 367
Governor General 367
Gravamen 367
Grey Ring 367
Guardian 368

TABLE OF CONTENTS

Habeas Corpus..368
Habendum et Tenendum.......................................368
Hallucination..368
Hanging..368
Hard Labour...368
Hashish..369
Hate Propaganda..369
    1. Definitions...369
    2. Advocation genocide — section 318(1).................369
    3. Public incitement of hatred — section 319(1)..........370
    4. Wilful promotion of hatred — section 319(2)..........371
    5. Seizure of material....................................372
Hearsay..373
    1. General..373
    2. Hearsay exceptions...................................373
    3. Dying declarations....................................373
    4. Declaration against interest..........................373
    5. Declarations in the course of duty....................374
    6. Former testimony.....................................374
Hemorrhage...375
Her Majesty...375
Herein...375
Heroin...375
High Seas, Offence On...375
Highway...376
Homicide..376
    1. Definitions...376
    2. Murder..377
    3. Manslaughter...381
    4. Infanticide...382
    5. Killing unborn child in act of birth — section 238(1)........383
    6. Attempt to commit murder — section 239.............383
    7. Accessory after fact to murder........................383
Hostage Taking..384
    1. Offence of hostage taking.............................384
    2. Offence deemed to be committed in Canada..........385
Hypostasis...386

Ibid..386
Idem...386
Identification of Criminals.....................................386
    1. Bertillon Signaletic System...........................387

xxviii   TABLE OF CONTENTS

    2. Use of force..387
    3. Publication of results..................................387
    4. Liability under the Identification of Criminals Act............387
Ignoramus..387
Ignorantia Juris Non (Haud, Neminem) Excusat....................388
Impeding Attempt to Save Life..................................388
In...388
In Absentia...389
Incapable..389
Inciting to Mutiny..389
Included Offences...390
Indicia...390
Indictable Offences..390
Indictment...391
Informant..391
Informations and Indictments..................................391
    1. Informations and indictments............................391
    2. Information to launch criminal proceedings.................392
    3. Contents of an information or indictment...................392
    4. Information to obtain a search warrant.....................393
Infra..393
Injuria Absque (or Sine) Damno................................393
Injuria Non Excusat Injurium..................................393
Injury...393
Inquest..394
Inter..394
Intercept...394
Interception of Communications................................394
Internationally Protected Person................................395
    1. Definition of "internationally protected person".............395
    2. Threatening to commit offence against internationally
       protected person — section 424...........................395
    3. Attack on premises, residence or transport of internationally
       protected person — section 431...........................396
    4. Offence deemed to be committed in Canada.................396
Intimidation..398
    1. Intimidation of a person — section 423(1).................398
    2. Intimidation of Parliament or legislature — section 51........399
Intra Vires...399
Ipse Dixit..400
Ipso Facto...400
Issuance of Process..400

TABLE OF CONTENTS

Item 400

Judges Notes 400
Judicial Notice 400
    1. Definition 400
    2. Statutes 401
    3. Regulations 401
Judicial Proceeding 401
Jurat 401
Juries 402
    1. General 402
    2. Coroner's Jury 403
Jurisdiction 403
    1. Definition 403
    2. Absolute jurisdiction 403
    3. Original and appellate jurisdiction 404
    4. Territorial jurisdiction 404
Jus 404
Justification or Excuse 404
Juvenile Delinquent 404

Keeper 405
Kidnapping 405
Knowing 406

Laceration 406
Lands 407
Law of Canada 407
Law of Nations 407
Lawful Process 407
Legal Proceeding 407
Lex 407
Libel 407
    1. Publishing a blasphemous libel 407
    2. Publishing a defamatory libel 408
    3. Extortion by libel 413
    4. Definition of "seditious libel". See SEDITION, 1.
Lieutenant Governor in Council 413
Limitation Periods 414
Lis Pendens 414
Lividity 414
Local Registrar of Firearms 414
Loco Citato (Loc. Cit.) 414

TABLE OF CONTENTS

Lumber 415
Lumbering Equipment 415

Mala Fide 415
Malicious Prosecution 415
Malum (Mala) In Se 416
Mandamus 416
Marihuana 416
Mark 416
May 416
Mens Rea 416
Mental Disorder 416
Mescaline 416
Military 417
Miscarriage 417
Mischief 417
   1. Mischief in relation to property 417
   2. Mischief causing danger to life — section 430(2) 417
   3. Mischief in relation to testamentary instruments — section 430(3) 418
   4. Mischief in relation to property worth more than $1,000 — section 430(3) 419
   5. Mischief in relation to other property — section 430(4) .. 420
   6. Mischief in relation to data 420
   7. Acts or omissions likely to cause mischief — section 430(5.1) 421
   8. Public mischief. See MISLEADING JUSTICE, 7.
Misleading Justice 422
   1. Perjury 422
   2. False statements — section 134 423
   3. Witness giving contradictory evidence — section 136(1) . 424
   4. Fabricating evidence — section 137 425
   5. Offences relating to affidavits 426
   6. Obstructing justice 427
   7. Public mischief 428
   8. Compounding indictable offence — section 141(1) 430
   9. Corruptly taking reward for recovery of goods — section 142 .. 430
   10. Advertising reward and immunity 431
Modus Operandi 432
Moot Case or Moot Point 432
Mora 432
Moto Proprio 432

TABLE OF CONTENTS

Motor Vehicles and Vehicles Generally 432
    1. Definitions of "motor vehicle" 432
    2. Dangerous operation of motor vehicle — section 249(1)(a) and (2) 432
    3. Dangerous driving causing bodily harm — section 249(3) 433
    4. Dangerous driving causing death — section 249(4) 434
    5. Failing to stop at scene of accident — section 252(1) 435
    6. Operation of motor vehicle while impaired or with more than 80 mg. of alcohol in blood — section 253 and 255(1) 436
    7. Impaired driving causing bodily harm — section 255(2) 441
    8. Impaired driving causing death — section 255(3) 441
    9. Failure or refusal to provide sample — section 254(5) and 255(1) 442
    10. Operation of motor vehicle while disqualified — section 259(4) 445
    11. Taking motor vehicle without consent. See THEFT AND OFFENCES RESEMBLING THEFT, 10.

Multifarious or Multiplicitous 446
Municipal Official 446
Municipality 446
Mutatis Mutandis 446
Mutilation 446
Mutiny 446

N.A. 446
Narcotic Addict 446
Narcotics 447
    1. Definitions 447
    2. Possessing of narcotic — Narcotic Control Act, Section 3(1) and (2) 447
    3. Trafficking — Narcotic Control Act, Section 4(1) and (3) 448
    4. Possession for purpose of trafficking — Narcotic Control Act, Section 4(2) and (3) 448
    5. Importing and exporting — Narcotic Control Act, Section 5(1). 449
    6. Cultivation of opium poppy or marihuana — Narcotic Control Act, Section 6(1) and (2) 449
    7. Failure to disclose previous prescriptions — Narcotic Control Act, Section 3.1(1) and (2) 450
    8. Prosecutions for narcotic offences 450
    9. Search and seizure of narcotics. See SEARCH AND SEIZURE, 14.

TABLE OF CONTENTS

Ne Exeat Regno 451
Neat Cattle 451
Neglect in Childbirth 451
Nembutal 452
Nemo 452
Newly-Born Child 452
Newspaper 452
Night 452
Nihil (Nil) 452
Nisi 453
Nolens Volens 453
Nolle Prosequi 453
Nolo Contendere 453
Non 453
Nonfeasance 453
Noscitur A Sociis 453
Nota Bene (N.B.) 453
Novus Actus Interveniens 453
Nuclear Material 453
    1. Definition of "nuclear material" 453
    2. Offence deemed to be committed in Canada 454
Nude 456
Nuisances 456
    1. Common nuisance 456
    2. Spreading false news — section 181 457
    3. Neglect of or indignity to dead human body — section 182 457
Nulla Bona 458
Nulla Poena Sine Lege 458
Nullity 458
Nunc Pro Tunc 458

Oaths 458
Obiter 459
Observing People 459
    1. Observation 459
    2. General characteristics 460
    3. Specific characteristics 460
    4. Changeable characteristics 464
Obstructing 464
Obturation 464
Offences 464
Offender 465

TABLE OF CONTENTS

Offensive Weapon 466
Office 466
Officer in Charge 466
Official 466
Omission 466
Omnia Praesumuntur Contra Spoliatorem 466
Omnia Praesmuntur Rite Esse Acta 467
Onus 467
Op. Cit. 467
Open Court 467
Opening in Ice 467
Operate 468
Opium 468
Ordinary Court 468

PCP 469
Paraffin Test 469
Pardon 469
Parent 469
Pari Passu 469
Particeps Criminis 469
Particulars 469
Parties to Offences 470
Passim 470
Passport Offences 470
    1. Definition of "passport" 470
    2. Forgery of passport — section 57(1)(a) 471
    3. Uttering forged passport — section 57(1)(b) 471
    4. False statement to procure passport — section 57(2) 472
    5. Possession of forged passport — section 57(3) 473
    6. Possession of passport obtained by false statement — section 57(3) 474
    7. Sufficiency of count 474
Pathology 474
Peace Officer 475
    1. Definition of "peace officer" 475
    2. Misconduct in the execution of a process — section 128 476
    3. Resisting or obstructing peace officer — section 129(a) 476
    4. Omitting to assist peace officer — section 129(b) 477
    5. Personating a peace officer 477
    6. Assaulting a peace officer. See ASSAULT, 7.

7. Neglect by a peace officer. See UNLAWFUL ASSEMBLIES AND RIOTS, 5.

Pedophilia 478
Pendente Lite 478
Per 478
Period of Probation 479
Permanent Cavity 479
Person 479
Persona Designata 479
Persona (Non) Grata 479
Personal Property 479
Personation 479
   1. Definition of "personation" 480
   2. With intent to gain property or advantage 480
   3. With intent to cause disadvantage — section 403(c) 481
   4. At an examination — section 404 481
   5. Acknowledging instrument in false name — section 405 482
   6. Sufficiency of count 483
   7. Personating a peace officer. See PEACE OFFICER, 5.
   8. Personating a public officer. See PUBLIC OFFICER, 4.
   9. Unlawful use of military uniforms or certificates. See PUBLIC STORES, 6.

Photographic Film 483
Photography 483
Piracy 483
   1. Definition of "piracy" 483
   2. Piracy by law of nations 483
   3. Offences in connection with Canadian ships. See also VESSELS AND RELATED OFFENCES 484

Place 485
Plea Bargaining 486
Pleadings 486
Polygamy 486
Possession 487
   1. Definition of "possession" 487
   2. Attributed possession 488
   3. Property obtained by crime - Having in possession — section 354(1) and 355 488
   4. Property obtained by crime - Bringing into Canada — section 357 490
   5. Mail — section 356(1)(b) 491

TABLE OF CONTENTS   XXXV

For specific offences of possession, see BREAKING AND ENTERING, CONTROLLED DRUGS, CURRENCY OFFENCES, EXPLOSIVE SUBSTANCES, FIREARMS AND WEAPONS OFFENCES, NARCOTICS, PASSPORT OFFENCES, PROCEEDS OF CRIME, RESTRICTED DRUGS, AND TRADEMARK OFFENCES.

Post Mortem 491
Power of Attorney 492
Practitioner 492
Pre-Hearing Conference 492
Preliminary Inquiry 492
Prescription 493
Prima Facie 493
Primer 493
Printing or Publishing 493
Prison 493
Private Communication 494
Prize Fights 494
Pro 495
Proceedings 495
Proceeds of Crime 496
    1. Definitions 496
    2. Laundering proceeds of crime 497
Process 498
Proclamations 498
    1. Definition of "proclamation" 499
    2. Effective day of proclamations 499
    3. Judicial notice 499
    4. Counterfeit proclamation. See FORGERY AND RELATED OFFENCES, 6.
    5. Proclamation and related offences. See UNLAWFUL ASSEMBLIES AND RIOTS, 3 and 4.
Procuring 499
    1. Definition of "procuring" 499
    2. Procuring offences 500
    3. Living on avails of prostitution 503
    4. Offence in relation to juvenile prostitution — section 212(4) 504
    5. Supplying or procuring drugs or instrument. See ABORTION AND MISCARRIAGE, 3.
    6. Parent or guardian procuring sexual activity. See CORRUPTING MORALS, 15.

See also COUNSELLING COMMISSION OF OFFENCE WHICH IS NOT COMMITTED.

Prohibited Act...504
Prohibited Weapons..504
Promise to Appear...512
    1. Definitions..512
    2. Contents of promise to appear.........................512
    3. Attendance for purposes of Identification of Criminals Act.....513
    4. Valid if issued on holiday.............................513
    5. Signature of accused..................................513
    6. Period for which appearance notice continues in force........513
    7. Failure to comply with promise to appear..............513
Propellant..513
Property..513
Proprio Motu..514
Prostitution...514
    1. Definitions..514
    2. Offence in relation to prostitution.....................514
    See also Procuring, 3 and 4.
Provincial Court Judge..515
Proviso...515
Provocation...516
Psychosis...516
Public Department...516
Public Officer...516
    1. Definition of "public officer".........................516
    2. Resisting or obstructing public officer — section 129(a).......517
    3. Omitting to assist public officer — section 129(b)............517
    4. Personating a public officer...........................518
    5. Assaulting a public officer. See ASSAULT, 7.
Public Place..519
Public Stores...519
    1. Definitions..519
    2. Applying or removing marks without authority..........520
    3. Unlawful transactions in public stores — section 417(2).......520
    4. Selling defective stores to the government — section 418(1)....521
    5. Being a party to the selling of defective stores to the government...522
    6. Unlawful use of military uniforms or certificates.............522
    7. Buying military stores from member of Canadian Forces or from deserter — section 420(1)........................524
    8. Sufficiency of count...................................524

Public Switched Telephone Network	525
Publishing Offences	525
1. Publishing evidence of sexual activity	525
2. Publishing report of admission or confession tendered at preliminary inquiry — section 542(2)	526
3. Publishing obscene matter. See CORRUPTING MORALS, 2.	
4. Publishing crime comic. See CORRUPTING MORALS, 4.	
5. Publishing child pornography. See CORRUPTING MORALS, 6.	
6. Publishing indecent matter. See CORRUPTING MORALS, 10.	
7. Publishing particulars of matrimonial proceedings. See CORRUPTING MORALS, 11.	
8. Publishing or printing the likeness of bank note or security. See CURRENCY OFFENCES, 11.	
9. Publishing report on proceedings under the Young Offenders Act. See YOUNG OFFENDERS, 9.	
Puisne Judge	526
Punitive Damages	526
Putative	527
Qua	527
Quaere	527
Qualified Medical Practitioner	527
Qualified Technician	527
Quantum Meruit	527
Quasi	527
Question	527
Quia Timet	528
Quid Pro Quo	528
Quo Jure?	528
Quo Warranto	528
Quorum	528
Radio-Based Telephone Communication	528
Radiocommunication	528
Rape	529
Ratio Decidendi	529
Recognizance	529
1. Definitions	529
2. Recognizance entered into before an officer in charge	530
3. Recognizance entered into before a justice or a judge	530
4. Contents of a recognizance	531
5. Attendance for purposes of Identification of Criminals Act	531

6.	Valid if issued on a holiday	531
7.	Acknowledging recognizance using false name	531
8.	Failure to comply with the terms of a recognizance	532
9.	Recognizance of witness	532
10.	Recognizance of appellant	532
11.	Recognizance of continuing effect	533
12.	Effect of subsequent arrest	533
13.	Surety	533
14.	Committal	536
15.	Procedure on default	537

Record 539
Recovery 539
Recrimination 539
Rectum 539
Regina 539
Regulation 539
Release 539

1. Release from custody by a peace officer 540
2. Release from custody by either a peace officer or an officer in charge 540
3. Release from custody by an officer in charge 542
4. Release by a justice 544
5. Release by a judge 548
6. Release from imprisonment 550

See also APPEARANCE NOTICE, PROMISE TO APPEAR, SUMMONS, RECOGNIZANCE and UNDERTAKING.

Remand 550
Remanet 550
Repeal 550
Replication 551
Reports 551
Res 551
Rescue 552
Resistance 552
Respondeat Superior 552
Restitutio in Integrum 552
Restricted Drugs 552

1. Definitions 553
2. Possession of restricted drug — Food and Drugs Act, Section 47(1) 554
3. Trafficking in a restricted drug — Food and Drugs Act, Section 48(1) and (3) 555

TABLE OF CONTENTS

    4. Possession of restricted drug for trafficking — Food and Drugs Act, Section 48(2) and (3)....................................556
Restricted Weapons...556
Revenue Paper...561
Rex...561
Rifle..561
Rifling..561
Rigor Mortis...561
Rim Fire..561
Robbery and Extortion..562
    1. Robbery..562
    2. Stopping mail with intent to rob or search — section 345......563
    3. Extortion...564
Royal Warranty..565
Rule of Law...565

S...566
Sabotage..566
Sadism...567
Sale..567
Scienter..567
Scilicet (SC.)...567
Scintilla of Evidence..567
Search and Seizure...567
    1. Unreasonable search and seizure.........................567
    2. Admissibility of illegally obtained evidence.................568
    3. Search warrants.......................................568
    4. Telewarrants..570
    5. Execution of search warrants............................572
    6. Firearms and other offensive weapons.....................573
    7. Obscene publications...................................576
    8. Timber...576
    9. Disorderly houses......................................577
    10. Precious metals.......................................578
Second Offence..578
Secret Commissions..579
Secretor..580
Sed Quaere...580
Sedative..580
Sedition..580
    1. Definitions..580
    2. Seditious offences.....................................581

TABLE OF CONTENTS

- 3. Offences in relation to members of military forces 582
- Segmentation 583
- Self-Defence 583
- Sell 583
- Semen 583
- Sex Chromatin 584
- Sexual Assault 584
  - 1. Sexual assault 584
  - 2. Sexual assault — With a weapon — section 272(a) 586
  - 3. Sexual assault — Threats to a third party — section 272(b) . 587
  - 4. Sexual assault — Causing bodily harm — section 272(c) 587
  - 5. Sexual assault — Party to the offence — section 272(d) 588
  - 6. Aggravated sexual assault 588
  - 7. Removal of child from Canada 588
  - 8. Evidence of sexual activity 590
  - 9. Consent 593
- Sexual Offences 593
  - 1. Sexual interference — section 151 594
  - 2. Invitation to sexual touching — section 152 597
  - 3. Sexual exploitation 598
  - 4. Incest 599
  - 5. Anal intercourse — section 159(1) 600
  - 6. Bestiality 601
  - 7. Compulsion to commit bestiality — section 160(2) 601
  - 8. Bestiality in presence of or by a child — section 160(3) .. 602
  - 9. Order of Prohibition — section 161 603
  - 10. Person convicted of sexual offence. See VAGRANCY, 2.
  - 11. Parent or guardian procuring sexual activity. See CORRUPTING MORALS, 15.
  - 12. Householder permitting sexual activity. See CORRUPTING MORALS, 16.
  - 13. Corrupting children. See CORRUPTING MORALS, 17.
- Shall 604
- Ship 604
- Shock 604
- Sic 605
- Simpliciter 605
- Sine Die 605
- Sine Parole 605
- Sine Qua Non 605
- Singeing 605
- Situs 605

Slot Machine	605
Smudging	605
Sponte Sua	605
Stamp	605
Stare Decisis	606
Statements	606
Status Quo	606
Statutory Declarations	606
Steal	606
Stillbirth	606
Strangulation	606
Strychnine	607
Sub	607
Subpoena	607
1. Subpoena (Ad testificandum)	607
2. Subpoena (Duces tecum)	607
3. When subpoena issued	607
4. How subpoena issued	607
5. Who may issue subpoena	608
6. Contents of subpoena	608
7. Effect of subpoena	608
8. Service of subpoena	608
9. Proof of service	609
10. Where subpoena effective	609
Sui Generis	609
Sui Juris	609
Summary Conviction	609
Summary Conviction Court	610
Summary Trial	610
Summons	610
1. Definition	610
2. Issue of summons	611
3. Period for which summons continues in force	611
4. Valid if issued on a holiday	612
5. Service of summons on a corporation	612
6. Where summons effective	612
7. Failure to appear or to comply with summons	612
8. Contents of summons	613
9. Service of summons	613
10. Proof of Service	613
Superior Court	613
Suppressio Veri Suggestio Falsi	614

TABLE OF CONTENTS

Supra..614
Surplusage..614

Telecommunication Offences...614
    1. Definition of "telecommunication"................................614
    2. Instrument or device to obtain service without payment —
       section 327..614
    3. Telegram, cablegram or radio message in false name — section
       371..616
    4. False messages — section 372(1)..................................616
    5. Indecent telephone calls — section 372(2)........................617
    6. Harassing telephone calls — section 372(3).......................617
    7. Sufficiency of count...617
    8. Theft of telecommunication service. See THEFT, 4.
    See also WIRETAPPING OFFENCES.

Temperature Plateau..618
Temporary Cavity...618
Territorial Division...618
Testamentary Instrument..618
Theatre..618
Theft and Offences Resembling Theft....................................618
    1. Theft..619
    2. Theft by bailee of things under seizure..........................621
    3. Electricity and gas..622
    4. Telecommunications...623
    5. Theft by husband or wife...623
    6. Assisting theft by husband or wife...............................624
    7. Theft by person required to account..............................625
    8. Theft by person holding power of attorney........................626
    9. Misappropriation of money held under direction...................626
    10. Taking motor vehicle or vessel without consent — section
        335...627
    11. Criminal breach of trust — section 336..........................628
    12. Public servant refusing to deliver property — section 337.......628
    13. Theft of cattle — section 338(2)................................629
    14. Fraudulently taking cattle or defacing brand....................630
    15. Lumber and lumbering equipment..................................631
    16. Dealing in marked lumbering equipment — section
        339(2)..632
    17. Destroying documents of title — section 340....................633
    18. Fraudulent concealment — section 341...........................633
    19. Theft from mail — section 356(1)(a).............................634

20. Sufficiency of count...................................635
21. Credit card offences. See CREDIT CARDS, 2.

Threats...635
   1. Uttering threats relating to persons — section 264.1(1)(a) and (2)..635
   2. Uttering threats relating to property — section 264.1(1)(b) and (3)..636
   3. Uttering threats relating to animals — section 264.1(1)(c) and (3)..637

Three-Card Monte..637

Time..638
   1. Computation of time.....................................638
   2. Holiday..639
   3. Month..639
   4. Year...640
   5. Standard time..640
   6. Local time...641

Trace Evidence..641
Trade Combination...641
Trade-Mark Offences...641
   1. Definitions..641
   2. Forging a trade-mark — section 407 and 412(1)............642
   3. Passing off — section 408 and 412(1).....................643
   4. Possession of instruments for forging trade-mark — section 409(1) and 412(1)......................................644
   5. Defacing, concealing or removing trade-mark — section 410(a) and 412(1).......................................645
   6. Using bottle or siphon bearing trade-mark — section 410(b) and 412(1).......................................646
   7. Reconditioned goods — section 411 and 412(1).............646
   8. Falsely claiming royal warrant — section 413..............647
   9. Sufficiency of count....................................647

Trading Stamp Offences..647
   1. Definition of "trading stamps"..........................648
   2. Issuing trading stamps — section 427(1)..................648
   3. Giving to purchaser of goods — section 427(2)............649

Trafficking...649

Treason and Other Offences Against the Queen's Authority and Person..650
   1. High treason...650
   2. Treason..652
   3. Alarming Her Majesty the Queen — section 49(a)...........654

4. Causing bodily harm to Her Majesty the Queen — section 49(b)	655
5. Assisting alien enemy to leave Canada	655
6. Omitting to prevent treason — section 50(1)(b) and (2)	656
Trial	656
Trial Court	656
Trial, Place of	656
Trustee	657
Uberrimae Fidei	657
Ubi Jus, Ibi Remedium	657
Ultra Vires	657
Umbilical Cord	658
Undertaking	658
1. Definition	658
2. Undertaking of appellant	658
3. Undertaking of prosecutor other than the Attorney General	659
4. Period for which undertaking continues in force	659
5. Valid if given on a holiday	659
6. Failure to comply with an undertaking	659
Unfit to Stand Trial	659
Unlawful Assemblies and Riots	660
1. Unlawful assembly	660
2. Rioting	661
3. Reading proclamation	662
4. Offences relating to proclamation	662
5. Neglect by peace officer — section 69	663
Unlawful Drilling	663
1. Orders prohibiting unlawful drilling	663
2. Contravention of orders prohibiting unlawful drilling — section 70(3)	664
Unlawful Solemnization of Marriage	664
1. Pretending to solemnize marriage	664
2. Solemnizing a marriage contrary to law — section 295	665
Unusquisque Spondet Peritiam Artis Suae	665
Utter	665
Vagal Inhibition	666
Vagina	666
Vagrancy	666
1. Supporting oneself by gaming or crime	666
2. Person convicted of sexual offence	667
Valuable Security	668

TABLE OF CONTENTS

Vehicle Identification Number.................................668
Venir de Novo..669
Venire Facias..669
Venue..669
Verba Chartarum Fortius Accipiuntur Contra Proferentum........669
Verba Ita Sunt Intelligenda Ut Res Magis Valeat Quam Pereat..........669
Verbatim...670
Vessels and Related Offences.................................670
    1. Definition of "vessel"..................................670
    2. Dangerous operation of vessel — section 249(1)(b) and (2)....670
    3. Dangerous operation causing bodily harm — section 249(3)...671
    4. Dangerous operation causing death — section 249(4).........672
    5. Failure to keep watch on person towed — section 250(1).......673
    6. Towing person after dark — section 250(2).................673
    7. Unseaworthy vessel — section 251(1)(a)....................674
    8. Failing to stop at scene of accident — section 252(1).........675
    9. Operation of vessel while impaired or with more than 80 mg. of alcohol in blood — section 253 and 255(1)...............676
   10. Impaired operation causing bodily harm — section 255(2).....681
   11. Impaired operation causing death — section 255(3)..........681
   12. Failure or refusal to provide sample — section 254(5) and 255(1)...682
   13. Operation of vessel while disqualified — section 259(4).......685
   14. Preventing or impeding the saving of a vessel — section 438(1)..686
   15. Making fast a vessel or boat to a marine signal — section 439(1)..686
   16. Altering, removing or concealing marine signal — section 439(2)..687
   17. Public harbours — section 440...........................688
   18. Seizing control of ship or fixed platform — section 78.1(1).....688
   19. Endangering safety of ship or fixed platform — section 78.1(2)(a)...689
   20. False communication endangering safe navigation — section 78.1(3)..690
   21. Threats causing damage or injury on ship or fixed platform — section 78.1(4)..691
   22. Taking vessel without consent. See THEFT AND OFFENCES RESEMBLING THEFT, 10.
   23. Setting fire to vessel. See ARSON, 3.
Vi Et Armis..691
Viability..691

Vice Versa	691
Vide	691
Videlicet (or VIZ)	692
View	692
Vigilantibus Non Dormientibus Lex Succurrit	692
Vinculum Juris	692
Virtual Cooling Time	692
Vis Major	692
Vital	692
Vive Voice	692
Viz	692
Voir Dire	692
Volenti Non Fit Injuria	693
Warrants	693
1. Definition of a "warrant"	693
2. Warrant for the arrest of an accused	693
3. Warrant for the committal of an accused	694
4. Warrant to convey an accused before a justice	696
5. Warrant for a witness	696
6. Warrant to arrest an absconding witness	696
7. Warrant remanding a prisoner	697
8. Warrant of committal of witness for refusing to be sworn or to give evidence	697
9. Warrant of committal on conviction by a judge	698
10. Warrant of committal on conviction by a summary conviction court	698
11. Warrant of committal for failure to furnish recognizance to keep the peace	698
12. Warrant of committal of witness for failure to enter into recognizance	699
13. Warrant of committal for contempt	700
14. Warrant of committal in default of payment of the costs of an appeal	700
15. Warrant of committal on forfeiture of a recognizance	701
16. Warrant for tracking device	701
17. Warrant for number recorder	701
Waschhaut	702
Weapon	702
Whiplash Injury	702
Wilfully	702
Wired Informant	703

Wiretapping Offences 703
   1. Interception of private communication — section 184(1) 703
   2. Interception of radio-based telephone communication — section 184.5(1) 706
   3. Possession of devices for interception — section 191(1) 707
   4. Disclosure of information from private communication — section 193(1) 708
   5. Disclosure of information received from interception of radio-based telephone communications — section 193.1(1) 710

Witnesses 711
   1. Definition of "witness" 711
   2. Appearance before a justice or provincial court judge 711
   3. At other trials of indictable offences 712
   4. Witness in prison 712
   5. Material Witness 713
   6. Adverse witness 713
   7. Previous statements in writing 714
   8. Previous oral statements 714
   9. Pervious conviction 714
   10. Incriminating questions and answers to such questions 715

Wound 715
Wounded Offenders 716
Wreck 716
   1. Definition of "wreck" 716
   2. Offences in relation to wreck 717
   3. Preventing or impeding the saving of wreck — section 438(2) .. 718

Writing 718

Young Offenders 719
   1. Definitions 719
   2. Application of the Young Offenders Act 719
   3. Application of the Criminal Code 720
   4. Procedure on arrest 720
   5. Notice to parents, relatives or friends 720
   6. Detention of a young person 721
   7. Jurisdiction 721
   8. Prosecution and trials of young persons 721
   9. Dispositions 721
   10. Protection of privacy of young persons 722

A

A POSTERIORI. The method of reasoning based on experience, experiment or observation, in which one proceeds from effects to causes. "From the effect to the cause" (Latin).

A PRIORI. The method of reasoning from abstract ideas to their consequences. "From the cause to the effect" (Latin).

AB INITIO. From the beginning (Latin).

ABANDON. 1. In general, "to give up or renounce; to desert; leave without help" (Sharp v. Sharp (1962), 38 W.W.R. 257 (B.C. S.C.)). 2. For the purpose of Part VIII of the Criminal Code (Offences Against the Person and Reputation), "abandon" includes: (a) A wilful omission to take charge of a child by a person who is under a legal duty to do so, and (b) dealing with a child in a manner that is likely to leave that child exposed to risk without protection (s. 214). *For abandoning child, see DUTIES TENDING TO PRESERVATION OF LIFE. For abandoning animal in captivity, see ANIMAL OFFENCES, 3.*

Abandonment. 1. The relinquishing of an interest or claim (Jowitt's Dictionary of English Law). 2. The giving up of something to which one is entitled (Goldberg v. Employers' Liability Assurance Corp., [1922] 1 W.W.R. 529 (Alta. S.C.)).

ABATEMENT. 1. A reduction or a rebate. 2. The interruption or termination of an action or proceeding. Criminal proceedings are not abated either by the death of the prosecutor or by the death of the sovereign, but proceedings are terminated on the death of the accused (Jowitt's Dictionary of English Law).

ABDUCTION

1. *Definition of "abduction"*
2. *Abduction of unmarried person under 16*
3. *Abduction of person under 14*
4. *Abduction in contravention of custody order*
5. *Abduction whether or not custody order*
6. *Removal of child from Canada for sexual purpose. See SEXUAL ASSAULT, 7.*

See also KIDNAPPING.

1. Definition of "abduction". The taking, enticing away, concealing, detaining, receiving or harbouring of any person (s. 284 and s. 285).

2. Abduction of unmarried person under 16 — Section 280(1)

Every one who — without lawful authority — takes or causes to be taken — an unmarried person under the age of 16 years — out of the possession of and against the will of — the parent or guardian of that person or of any other person who has the lawful care or charge of that person — is guilty of an indictable offence.

Included offences. Attempts (s. 660 and s. 662(1)(b)).

Punishment. Imprisonment for a term not exceeding 5 years (s. 280(1)).

Release. Initial decision to release made by officer in charge or justice (s. 498).

Election. Accused may elect trial by judge and jury, judge alone, or provincial court judge (s. 536).

Defences. 1. No one shall be found guilty of this offence if the court is satisfied that the taking, enticing away, concealing, detaining, receiving or harbouring of any young person was necessary to protect the young person from danger of imminent harm or if the person charged with the offence was escaping from danger of imminent harm or if the person charged with the offence was escaping from danger of imminent harm (s. 285).
2. It is not a defence to any charge of abduction that a young person consented to or suggested any conduct of the accused (s. 286).

Evidence. 1. The wife or husband of a person charged with this offence is a competent and compellable witness for the prosecution without the consent of the accused (Canada Evidence Act, s. 4(2)).
2. The courts have held that the phrase "takes or causes to be taken" requires that the accused participate in the removal of the unmarried person, either directly through physical involvement or by inducement or enticement. An accused has been acquitted of an offence under s. 280 where he did nothing to encourage a girl to leave her home, but merely permitted her to remain at his home (R. v. Johnson (1977), 37 C.C.C. (2d) 352 (Sask. Dist. Ct.)).
3. The courts have also held that the phrase "against the will" in s. 280 includes consent that has been obtained by fraud (R. v. Cox (1969), 5 C.R.N.S. 395 (Ont. C.A.)).

4. An accused will be convicted even when the unmarried person under 16 plays an active part, if it is proved that the taking was against the will of the parent or guardian (R. v. Langevin (1962), 38 C.R. 421 (Ont. C.A.)).
See also AGE.

Informations

A.B., on or about the —— day of ——, 19 ——, at the —— of ——, in the said (territorial division), did without lawful authority take [OR cause to be taken] C.D., an unmarried person under the age of 16 years, out of the possession of and against the will of E.F., her [OR his] father [OR mother OR guardian OR (specify other person)] then having the lawful care or charge of her [OR him], to wit: (specify the particulars of the offence), contrary to s. 280 of the Criminal Code of Canada.

3. Abduction of person under 14 — Section 281

Every one who — not being the parent or guardian or person having the lawful care or charge of a person under the age of 14 years — unlawfully takes or entices away or conceals or detains or receives or harbours that person — with intent to deprive a parent or guardian, or any other person who has the lawful care or charge of that person, of the possession of that person — is guilty of an indictable offence.

Intent. Intention to deprive parent, guardian or person having lawful care and charge of possession.

Included offences. Attempts (s. 660 and s. 662(1)(b)).

Punishment. Imprisonment for a term not exceeding 10 years (s. 281).

Release. Initial decision to release made by justice (s. 515(1)).

Election. Accused may elect trial by judge and jury, judge alone, or provincial court judge (s. 536).

Defences. 1. No one shall be found guilty of this offence if he establishes that the taking, enticing away, concealing, detaining, receiving or harbouring of any young person was done with the consent of the parent, guardian or other person having the lawful possession, care or charge of that young person (s. 284).
2. *See also Defences under* **2**, *above.*

Evidence. 1. The word "detains" means "withhold" and applies to the situation where one parent intentionally withholds a child from

the other parent with lawful custody of the child (Re Bigelow and R. (1982), 69 C.C.C. (2d) 204 (Ont. C.A.)).
2. *See also Evidence, item 1., under* **2**, *above.*

Informations

A.B., not being the parent, guardian or person having the lawful care or charge of C.D., a person under the age of 14 years, on or about the —— day of ——, 19 ——, at the —— of ——, in the said (territorial division), did unlawfully take [OR entice away OR conceal OR detain OR receive OR harbour] C.D. with intent to deprive E.F., the parent [OR guardian OR person having the lawful care or charge] of C.D., of the possession of C.D., to wit: (specify the particulars of the offence), contrary to s. 281 of the Criminal Code of Canada.

4. Abduction in contravention of custody order — Section 282(1)

Every one who — being the parent or guardian or person having the lawful care or charge of a person under the age of 14 years — takes or entices away or conceals or detains or receives or harbours that person — in contravention of the custody provisions of a custody order in relation to that person made by a court anywhere in Canada — with intent to deprive a parent or guardian or any other person who has the lawful care or charge of that person, of the possession of that person — is guilty of either an indictable offence or an offence punishable on summary conviction.

Intent. Intention to deprive parent, guardian or person having lawful care and charge of possession.

Limitation period. No proceedings in respect of offences that are declared to be punishable on summary conviction shall be instituted more than 6 months after the time when the subject matter of the proceedings arose (s. 786(2) and s. 785(1)).

Included offences. Attempts (s. 660 and s. 662(1)(b)).

Punishment. On indictment, imprisonment for a term not exceeding 10 years (s. 282(1)(a)). On summary conviction, a fine not exceeding $2,000, or 6 months' imprisonment, or both (s. 282(1)(b) and s. 787(1)).

Release. Initial decision to release made by peace officer (s. 497).

Election. On indictment, accused may elect trial by judge and jury, judge alone or provincial court judge (s. 536). On summary conviction, no election.

Defences. 1. *See Defences under* **2**, *above.*
2. *See also Defences, item 1., under* **3**, *above.*

Evidence. 1. Where a count charges an offence under s. 282(1) and the offence is not proven only because the accused did not believe that there was a valid custody order but the evidence does prove an offence under s. 283, the accused may be convicted of an offence under s. 283 (s. 282(2)).
2. The courts have held that, in the absence of a custody order, both parents have an equal joint lawful right to possession (R. v. Kosowan (1980), 54 C.C.C. 571 (Man. Co. Ct.)).
3. *See also Evidence, item 1. , under* **2**, *above.*

Informations

A.B., being the parent [OR guardian OR person having the lawful care or charge] of C.D., a person under the age of 14 years, on or about the —— day of ——, 19 ——, at the —— of ——, in the said (territorial division), did take [OR entice away OR conceal OR detain OR receive OR harbour] C.D. in contravention of the custody provisions of a custody order in relation to C.D. made by (specify the name of the court) at (specify the location of the court) on (specify the date that the order was made), with intent to deprive E.F., the parent [OR guardian OR person having the lawful care or charge] of C.D., of the possession of C.D., to wit: (specify the particulars of the offence), contrary to s. 282 of the Criminal Code of Canada.

5. Abduction whether or not custody order — Section 283(1)

Every one who — being the parent or guardian or person having the lawful care or charge of a person under the age of 14 years — takes or entices away or conceals or detains or receives or harbours that person — whether or not there is a custody order in relation to that person made by a court anywhere in Canada — with intent to deprive a parent or guardian, or any other person who has the lawful care or charge of that person, of the possession of that person — is guilty of either an indictable offence or an offence punishable on summary conviction.

Intent. Intention to deprive parent, guardian or person having lawful care or charge of possession.

Limitation period. No proceedings in respect of offences that are declared to be punishable on summary conviction shall be instituted more than 6 months after the time when the subject matter of the proceedings arose (s. 786(2) and s. 785(1)).

Consent to prosecute. No proceedings may be commenced without the consent of the Attorney General or counsel instructed by him for that purpose (s. 283(2)).

Included offences. Attempts (s. 660 and s. 662(1)(b)).

Punishment. On indictment, imprisonment for a term not exceeding 10 years (s. 283(1)(a)). On summary conviction, a fine not exceeding $2,000, or 6 months' imprisonment, or both (s. 283(1)(b) and s. 787(1)).

Release. Initial decision to release made by peace officer (s. 497).

Election. On indictment, accused may elect trial by judge and jury, judge alone, or provincial court judge (s. 536). On summary conviction, no election.

Defences. 1. *See Defences under* **2**, *above.*
2. *See also Defences, item 1., under* **3**, *above.*

Evidence. 1. The courts have held that the custody order referred to in s. 283 means a subsisting court order and not one that had expired at the time of the offence (R. v. Reynolds (1984), 11 C.C.C. (3d) 248 (N.W.T. S.C.)).
2. *See also Evidence, item 1., under* **2**, *above.*

Informations

A.B., being the parent [OR guardian OR person having the lawful care or charge] of C.D., a person under the age of 14 years, on or about the —— day of ——, 19 ——, at the —— of ——, in the said (territorial division), did take [OR entice away OR conceal OR detain OR receive OR harbour] C.D., whether or not there was a custody order in relation to that person made by a court anywhere in Canada, with intent to deprive E.F., the parent [OR guardian OR person who has the lawful care or charge of] C.D., of the possession of C.D., to wit: (specify the particulars of the offence), contrary to s. 283 of the Criminal Code of Canada.

ABET. To encourage or set on; to maintain or patronise (Jowitt's Dictionary of English Law).

Abettor. An instigator; one who promotes or procures a crime to be committed (Jowitt's Dictionary of English Law).

ABORTIFACIENT. A substance or instrument used to procure an abortion by causing the death of the fetus or by stimulating uterine contractions which result in the expulsion of the fetus (Jaffe, A Guide to Pathological Evidence, 2nd ed.).

ABORTION AND MISCARRIAGE

1. *Definitions*
2. *Constitutional validity*
3. *Supplying or procuring drugs or instruments*
4. *Advertising means of causing abortion or miscarriage*

1. Definitions

"Abortion". The intentional expulsion or removal of an unborn child from the womb (other than for the purpose of producing a live birth or removing a dead fetus). *See also MISCARRIAGE.*

2. Constitutional validity

The Supreme Court of Canada has held that s. 287 of the Criminal Code (procuring miscarriage, woman procuring her own miscarriage, therapeutic abortion) infringes the right to "security of the person" that is guaranteed by s. 7 of the Canadian Charter of Rights and Freedoms and has rendered s. 287 invalid. No prosecutions should therefore be initiated pursuant to this section of the Criminal Code until it has been amended or re-enacted by the federal Parliament.

3. Supplying or procuring drugs or instruments — Section 288

Every one who — unlawfully supplies or procures — a drug or other noxious thing or an instrument or thing — knowing that it is intended to be used or employed to procure the miscarriage of a female person — whether or not she is pregnant — is guilty of an indictable offence.

Intent. Knowledge of intended use or employment.

Included offences. Attempts (s. 660 and s. 662(1)(b)).

Punishment. Imprisonment for a term not exceeding 2 years (s. 288).

Release. Initial decision to release made by officer in charge or justice (s. 498).

Election. Accused may elect trial by judge and jury, judge alone, or provincial court judge (s. 536).

Informations

A.B., on or about the —— day of ——, 19 ——, at the —— of ——, in the said (territorial division), did unlawfully supply [OR procure] a drug [OR noxious thing OR instrument] to [OR for] C.D., knowing it was intended to be used [OR employed] to procure the miscarriage of C.D. [OR E.F.], a female person, to wit: (specify the particulars of the offence), contrary to s. 288 of the Criminal Code of Canada.

4. Advertising means of causing abortion or miscarriage — Section 163(2)(c) and section 169

Every one who — knowingly — without lawful justification or excuse — offers to sell or advertises or publishes an advertisement of, or has for sale or disposal — any means or instructions or medicine or drug or article — intended or represented as a method of causing abortion or miscarriage — is guilty of either an indictable offence or an offence punishable on summary conviction.

Intent. Knowingly.

Limitation period. No proceedings in respect of offences that are declared to be punishable on summary conviction shall be instituted more than 6 months after the time when the subject matter of the proceedings arose (s. 786(2) and s. 785(1)).

Included offences. Attempts (s. 660 and s. 662(1)(b)).

Punishment. On indictment, imprisonment for a term not exceeding 2 years (s. 169(a)). On summary conviction, a fine not exceeding $2,000, or 6 months' imprisonment, or both (s. 169(b) and s. 787(1)).

Release. Initial decision to release made by peace officer (s. 497).

Election. On indictment, accused may elect trial by judge and jury, judge alone, or provincial court judge (s. 536). On summary conviction, no election.

Defences. No person shall be convicted of this offence if the public good was served by the acts that are alleged to constitute the offence and if the acts alleged did not extend beyond what served the public good (s. 163(3)).

Evidence. 1. It is a question of law whether an act served the public good and whether there is evidence that the act alleged went beyond what served the public good, but it is a question of fact whether the

acts did or did not extend beyond what served the public good (s. 163(4)).
2. For the purposes of this offence, the motives of an accused are irrelevant (s. 163(5)).

Informations

A.B., on or about the —— day of —— 19 ——, at the —— of ——, in the said (territorial division), did knowingly without lawful justification or excuse, offer to sell [OR advertise OR publish an advertisement of OR have for sale OR have for disposal] means [OR instructions OR medicine OR a drug OR an article] intended [OR represented] as a method of causing an abortion [OR miscarriage], to wit: (specify the particulars of the offence), contrary to s. 163(2) of the Criminal Code of Canada.

ABSENTE REO. In the absence of the accused (Latin).

ABSOLUTE LIABILITY. 1. In criminal law, absolute liability is liability for specified conduct or results independently of intention or other mental factors. In respect of such an offence, the Crown is relieved of the burden of proving mens rea. 2. The term used to describe offences where it is not open to the accused to exculpate himself by showing that he was free of fault (R. v. Sault St. Marie (1978), 40 C.C.C. (2d) 353 (S.C.C.)).

ABUSE OF PROCESS. Pursuant to this doctrine, a court of competent jurisdiction has inherent power to prevent the abuse of its process by staying or dismissing an action. This power is to be exercised in favour of an accused only where a real injustice will result, and such cases are rare. In Canadian courts, there has been uncertainty as to the existence of such a doctrine, but the enactment of the Canadian Charter of Rights and Freedoms as part of the Constitution of Canada is expected to provide a statutory basis for the doctrine.

Specifically, the Charter provides as follows:

(i) Anyone whose rights or freedoms, as guaranteed by the Charter, have been infringed or denied may apply to a court of competent jurisdiction to obtain such remedy as the court considers appropriate and just in the circumstances (Charter, s. 24(1)).

(ii) Where a court concludes that evidence was obtained in a manner that infringed or denied any rights or freedoms guaranteed by the Charter, the evidence shall be excluded if it is established that, having regard to all the circumstances, the admission of it in the proceedings would bring the administration of justice into disrepute (Charter, s. 24(2)).

(iii) However, the Charter guarantees the rights and freedoms set out in it subject only to such limits prescribed by law as can be demonstrably justified in a free and democratic society (Charter, s. 1).

ACCESSORY AFTER THE FACT

Definitions. An accessory after the fact to an offence is one who, knowing that a person has been a party to the offence, receives, comforts or assists that person for the purpose of enabling that person to escape (s. 23(1)). However, no married person whose spouse has been a party to an offence is an accessory after the fact to that offence by receiving, comforting or assisting the spouse for the purpose of enabling the spouse to escape (s. 23(2)).

Statements of offences

Except where otherwise expressly provided by law, the following provisions apply in respect of persons who are accessories after the fact to the commission of offences, namely:

Section 240

Every one who — is an accessory after the fact to murder — is guilty of an indictable offence. *See also HOMICIDE, 7.*

Section 463(a)

Every one who — is an accessory after the fact — to the commission of an indictable offence — for which, on conviction, an accused is liable to be sentenced to death or to imprisonment for life — is guilty of an indictable offence.

Section 463(b)

Every one who — is an accessory after the fact — to the commission of an indictable offence — for which, on conviction, an accused is liable to imprisonment for 14 years or less — is guilty of an indictable offence.

Section 463(c)

Every one who — is an accessory after the fact — to the commission of an offence punishable on summary conviction — is guilty of an offence punishable on summary conviction.

Section 463(d)

Every one who — is an accessory after the fact — to the commission of an offence for which the offender may be prosecuted by indictment — or for which he is punishable on summary conviction — is guilty of either an indictable offence or an offence punishable on summary conviction.

Limitation period. No proceedings in respect of offences that are declared to be punishable on summary conviction shall be instituted more than 6 months after the time when the subject matter of the proceedings arose (s. 786(2) and s. 785(1)).

Indictment. Any one who is charged with being an accessory after the fact to any offence may be indicted, whether or not the principal or any other party to the offence has been indicted or convicted or is or is not amenable to justice (s. 592).

Punishment. Every one who is an accessory after the fact to the commission of an indictable offence for which, on conviction, an accused is liable to be sentenced to death or to imprisonment for life, is liable to imprisonment for a term not exceeding 14 years (s. 463(a)).

Every one who is an accessory after the fact to the commission of an indictable offence for which, on conviction, an accused is liable to imprisonment for 14 years or less, is liable to imprisonment for a term that is one-half of the longest term to which a person who is guilty of that offence is liable (s. 463(b)).

Every one who is an accessory after the fact to the commission of an offence punishable on summary conviction is liable to a fine not exceeding $2,000, or 6 months' imprisonment, or both (s. 463(c) and s. 787(1)).

Every one who is an accessory after the fact to the commission of an offence for which the offender may be prosecuted by indictment or for which he is punishable on summary conviction is liable either — to imprisonment for a term not exceeding one-half of the longest term to which a person who is guilty of that offence is liable, or — to a fine not exceeding $2,000, or 6 months' imprisonment, or both (s. 463(d) and s. 787(1)).

Evidence. 1. The courts have held that an accessory after the fact is not a party to the offence (R. v. Vinette (1974), 19 C.C.C. (2d) 1 (S.C.C.)).

2. To be convicted of the offence of being an accessory after the fact to an offence, it must be proven that the accessory knew that a crime had been committed by the principal offender, that the accessory

desired to help the principal offender escape justice and that the accessory committed some positive act or omission to aid the offender in escaping justice (Young v. R. (1950), 10 C.R. 142 (Que. C.A.)).

3. Mere failure to disclose information has been held by the courts not to be enough to make one an accessory (R. v. Semenick (1955), 21 C.R. 202 (B.C. C.A.)).

Informations

A.B., on or about the —— day of ——, 19 ——, at the —— of ——, in the said (territorial division), knowing that C.D. had been a party to the offence of (specify the offence to which C.D. had been a party), did receive [OR comfort OR assist] C.D. for the purpose of enabling C.D. to escape, to wit: (specify the particulars of the offence), contrary to s. 463 of the Criminal Code of Canada.

ACCIDENT. 1. An unlooked-for mishap or an untoward event which is not expected or designed. An occurrence cannot be called an accident unless it is due neither to design nor to the negligence of the person responsible for the accident (Jowitt's Dictionary of English Law). 2. In criminal law, an effect is said to be accidental when the act by which it is caused is not done with the intention of causing it, and when its occurrence, as a consequence of such act, is not so probable that a person of ordinary prudence ought, in the circumstances in which it is done, to take reasonable precautions against it (Stephen, Digest of Criminal Law, Art. 294). 3. Proof that an event occurred naturally may negate its criminal character: e.g., in the appropriate circumstances, an accident may be a complete defence to murder (R. v. Tennant (1975), 31 C.R.N.S. 1 (Ont. C.A.), but in other circumstances, the defence of accident may merely reduce a charge of murder to manslaughter (R. v. Hughes (1942), 78 C.C.C. 257 (S.C.C.)). *See also MOTOR VEHICLES AND VEHICLES GENERALLY, 5.*

ACCOMPLICE. 1. "Accomplice" is used chiefly in relation to the rule of evidence that the judge must warn the jury of the danger of convicting on the uncorroborated evidence of an accomplice. When two or more persons participate in the commission of an offence, each one is an accomplice of the other or others. An accessory is an accomplice (Glanville Williams, Textbook of Criminal Law). 2. When considering whether a witness is an accomplice in a particular case, accomplice means an accomplice in the crime charged. It does not mean the accomplice of an accused in some other crime (R. v. Quiring (1974), 27 C.R.N.S. 367 (Sask. C.A.)).

ACCUSED. For the purposes of the Criminal Code, "accused" includes a person to whom a peace officer has issued an appearance notice under s. 496 of the Code, and a person arrested for a criminal offence (s. 493).

To accuse. The courts have held that to accuse, in ordinary parlance, in the form of "to accuse a person of", means to charge with the crime or fault of, etc. This may be done by laying an information against the person. The person so charged is said to be the person accused. The expression "to accuse" is used to denote the bringing of a charge against one before some court or officer. The expression "threatening to prosecute" is deemed equivalent to "threatening to accuse". "Prosecuting" would be "accusing" (R. v. Kempel (1900), 3 C.C.C. 481 (Ont. C.A.)).

ACQUITTAL. Discharge from prosecution on a verdict of not guilty, or on a successful plea of pardon, or of autrefois acquit, or of autrefois convict. The term applies to offences tried on indictment. Acquittal is a bar to any subsequent prosecution for the same offence (Jowitt's Dictionary of English Law).

ACT

1. *General*
2. *Act of God*
3. *Criminal act*
4. *Acts and omissions causing danger to the person. See BODILY HARM AND ACTS AND OMISSIONS CAUSING DANGER TO THE PERSON*
5. *Acts or omissions likely to cause mischief. See MISCHIEF, 7.*

---

1. General. For the purpose of the Criminal Code, "act" includes:
   (i) An Act of Parliament
   (ii) An Act of the legislature of the former Province of Canada
   (iii) An Act of the legislature of a province
   (iv) An Act or ordinance of the legislature of a province, territory or place in force at the time that province, territory or place became a province of Canada (s. 2).

2. Act of God. An event which happens independently of human action, such as a storm or an earthquake. The courts have held that an accused may use the defence of an act of God to certain charges, such as pollution offences; however the test requires an unusual operation of nature to which no person has contributed and which can be neither foreseen nor prevented (R. v. North Canadian Enterprises Ltd. (1974), 20 C.C.C. (2d) 242 (Ont. Prov. Ct.)).

3. Criminal act. The external manifestation of one's will which is prerequisite to criminal responsibility. There can be no crime without some act, either affirmative or negative, and an omission or failure to act may constitute an "act" for the purpose of criminal law (Black's Law Dictionary).

ACTION. 1. A suit brought in a court. 2. Conduct or behaviour, something done.

ACTUS NON FACIT REUM NISI MENS SIT REA. "An act does not make a person guilty unless he has a guilty mind" (Latin).

ACTUS REUS. 1. A criminal act (Latin). 2. "Not just the criminal act but all the external elements of the offence." External elements are those parts of the offence that are not in the accused's mind. They generally include some conduct by the accused and sometimes require a specific result to follow from his conduct (Glanville Williams, Textbook on Criminal Law).

AD. At; by; for; near; on account of; to; until; upon; with relation to; concerning (Latin). *Ad diem.* At the day appointed (Latin). *Ad hoc.* For this purpose; for a particular purpose (Latin). An ad hoc committee is a committee formed for a special or particular purpose. *Ad idem.* At one (Latin). Parties are said to be ad idem when they are in agreement with one another. *Ad infinitum.* Forever; without limit (Latin). *Ad litem.* For the lawsuit (Latin). A guardian ad litem is sometimes appointed to advise a child in particular legal proceedings only.

ADDICTION. A severe psychological and physical dependence on a drug such as alcohol or a narcotic. Sudden abstinence from the drug will result in withdrawal symptoms (Jaffe, A Guide to Pathological Evidence, 2nd ed.).

ADJOURNMENT

1. *General*
2. *Adjournment sie die*
3. *Adjournment of preliminary inquiry*
4. *Adjournment of trial following the amending of a defective indictment or count*

1. General. A putting off or postponing to another time or place. The hearing of a case may be adjourned.

The principle is that the granting or refusal of an adjournment lies in the discretion of the trial judge and, unless shown not to have been decided judicially or to have been decided on wrong principles, the exercise of the discretion will not be disturbed on appeal (R. v. Johnson (1973), 21 C.R.N.S. 375 (B.C. C.A.)).

Reasonable speed is required in the disposition of criminal matters. A request for an adjournment should be made in good faith and not for the purpose of delay. Delay may result in the unavailability of witnesses or in forgetfulness by witnesses. Regard is given to requests for adjournments made by counsel to fit the case in with other engagements, but long delays are to be avoided.

2. Adjournment sie die. An adjournment without a fixed day for another hearing, or generally.

3. Adjournment of preliminary inquiry. A justice may adjourn a preliminary inquiry where it appears that the accused has been deceived or misled by:

(a) any irregularity or defect in the substance or form of the summons or warrant;

(b) any variance between the charge set out in the summons or warrant and the charge set out in the information;

(c) any variance between the charge set out in the summons, warrant or information and the evidence adduced by the prosecution at the inquiry (s. 547 and s. 546).

4. Adjournment of trial following the amending of a defective indictment or count. Where, in the opinion of the court, the accused has been misled or prejudiced in his defence, by a variance, error or omission in an indictment or a count therein, the court may, if it is of the opinion that the misleading or prejudice may be removed by an adjournment, adjourn the proceedings to a specified day or sitting of the court and may make such an order with respect to the payment of costs resulting from the necessity for amendment as it considers desirable (s. 601(5)).

Where the offence is a summary conviction offence, the accused is entitled to an adjournment in the same circumstances (s. 795 and s. 601(5)).

ADVERTISEMENT. 1. A public notice or announcement of a thing (Jowitt's Dictionary of English Law). 2. "Advertisement" includes any representation by any means whatever for the purpose of promoting directly or indirectly the sale or disposal of any food, drug, cosmetic or device (Food and Drugs Act, s. 2).

ADVERTISING OFFENCES

1. *Advertising means of restoring sexual virility or curing venereal disease*
2. *Advertisement in the likeness of a bank note or security. See CURRENCY OFFENCES, 10.*
3. *Advertising counterfeit money or tokens of value. See CURRENCY OFFENCES, 14.*
4. *Advertising means of causing abortion or misscarriage. See ABORTION AND MISCARRIAGE, 4.*
5. *Advertising reward and immunity. See MISLEADING JUSTICE, 10.*

1. Advertising means of restoring sexual virility or curing venereal disease — Section 163(2)(d) and section 169

Every one who — knowingly — without lawful justification or excuse — advertises or publishes an advertisement — of any means or instructions or medicine or drug or article — intended or represented as a method for restoring sexual virility or curing venereal diseases or diseases of the generative organs — commits either an indictable offence or an offence punishable on summary conviction.

Intent. Knowingly.

Limitation period. No proceedings in respect of offences that are declared to be punishable on summary conviction shall be instituted more than 6 months after the time when the subject matter of the proceedings arose (s. 786(2) and s. 785(1)).

Included offences. Attempts (s. 660 and s. 662(1)(b)).

Punishment. On indictment, imprisonment for a term not exceeding 2 years (s. 169(a)). On summary conviction, a fine not exceeding $2,000, or 6 months' imprisonment, or both (s. 169(b) and s. 787(1)).

Release. Initial decision to release made by peace officer (s. 497).

Election. On indictment, accused may elect trial by judge and jury, judge alone, or provincial court judge (s. 536). On summary conviction, no election.

Defences. No person shall be convicted of this offence if the public good was served by the acts that are alleged to constitute the offence and if the acts alleged did not extend beyond what served the public good (s. 163(3)).

Evidence. 1. For these purposes, it is a question of law whether an act served the public good and whether there is evidence that the act alleged went beyond what served the public good, but it is a question of fact whether the acts did or did not extend beyond what served the public good (s. 163(4)).
2. For the purposes of this offence, the motives of an accused are irrelevant (s. 163(5)).

Informations

A.B., on or about the —— day of ——, 19 ——, at the —— of ——, in the said (territorial division), knowingly and without lawful excuse, did advertise [OR publish an advertisement] of means [OR instructions OR medicine OR a drug OR an article] intended [OR represented] as a method for restoring sexual virility [OR curing venereal diseases OR curing diseases of the generative organs], to wit: (specify the particulars of the offence), contrary to s. 163(2) of the Criminal Code of Canada.

AFFIDAVIT. A written statement in the name of a person, called the deponent, who makes it and signs and swears (or affirms) as to its truth before either a Notary Public or a Commissioner of Oaths. *See also AFFIRMATION and MISLEADING JUSTICE, 5.*

AFFIRMATION

1. *Definition*
2. *Giving evidence*
3. *Making an affidavit or deposition*
4. *Young offenders*

1. Definition. A solemn declaration that the declarant will tell the truth; the alternative to taking an oath.

2. Giving evidence. Where a person called or desiring to give evidence objects, on grounds of conscientious scruples, to take an oath, or is objected to as incompetent to take an oath, such person may make the following affirmation:

> "I do solemnly affirm that the evidence to be given by me shall be the truth, the whole truth, and nothing but the truth" (Canada Evidence Act, s. 14(1)).

Upon the person making such solemn affirmation, his evidence shall be taken and have the same effect as if taken under oath (Canada Evidence Act, s. 14(2)).

3. Making an affidavit or deposition. Where a person required or desiring to make an affidavit or deposition in a proceeding or on an occasion whereon or concerning a matter respecting which an oath is required or is lawful, whether on the taking of office or otherwise, refuses or is unwilling to be sworn, on grounds of conscientious scruples, the court or judge, or other officer or person qualified to take affidavits or depositions, shall permit such person, instead of being sworn, to make his solemn affirmation in the words following, namely: "I, A.B., do solemnly affirm, etc."; and this solemn affirmation shall be of the same force and effect as if such person had taken an oath in the usual form (Canada Evidence Act, s. 15(1)).

Any witness who evidence is admitted or who makes an affirmation is liable to indictment and punishment for perjury in all respects as if he had been sworn (Canada Evidence Act, s. 15(2)).

4. Young offenders. In any proceedings under the Young Offenders Act, where the evidence of a child or a young person is taken, it shall be taken only after the youth court judge or the justice, as the case may be, has (a) in all cases, if the witness is a child, and (b) where he deems it necessary, if the witness is a young person, instructed the child or young person as to the duty of the witness to speak the truth and the consequences of failing to do so (Young Offenders Act, s. 60).

AGE

1. *Effect of being under 12 years of age*
2. *Effect of being 12 years of age or more but under 18 years of age*
3. *Transfer to ordinary court*
4. *Proof of age*
5. *Time when specified age attained*
6. *Inference of age from appearance*
7. *Mistake of age in sexual offences*
8. *Testimony of a complainant under the age of 18 years*

1. Effect of being under 12 years of age. No person shall be convicted of an offence in respect of an act or omission on his part while that person was under the age of 12 years (s. 13).

2. Effect of being 12 years of age or more but under 18 years of age. A youth court has exclusive jurisdiction in respect of any offence committed by a person in this age group and such person shall be dealt with as provided in the Young Offenders Act (Young Offenders Act, s. 5(1)).

3. Transfer to ordinary court. In the case of a young person 14 years of age or more who has committed an indictable offence (other than an offence that is in the absolute jurisdiction of a provincial court judge), a youth court shall, on application of the young person or the young person's counsel or the Attorney General or the Attorney General's agent, after affording both parties and the parents of the young person an opportunity to be heard, determine, in accordance with subsection (1.1), whether the young person should be proceeded against in ordinary court (Young Offenders Act, s. 16(1)).

In making the determination referred to in s. 16(1), the youth court shall consider the interest of society, which includes the objectives of affording protection to the public and rehabilitation of the young person, and determine whether those objectives can be reconciled by the youth court. If the court is of the opinion that those objectives cannot be so reconciled, protection of the public shall be paramount and the court shall order that the young person be proceeded against in ordinary court in accordance with the law ordinarily applicable to an adult charged with the offence (Young Offenders Act, s. 16 (1.1.)).

4. Proof of age

Testimony of parent. In any proceedings under the Young Offenders Act, the testimony of a parent as to age of a person of whom he is a parent is admissible as evidence of the age of that person (Young Offenders Act, s. 57(1)).

Birth or baptismal certificate. In any proceedings under the Young Offenders Act, a birth or baptismal certificate or a copy thereof purporting to be certified under the hand of the person in whose custody those records are held is evidence of the age of the person named in the certificate or copy (Young Offenders Act, s. 57(2)(a)).

Record of incorporated society. In any proceedings under the Young Offenders Act, an entry or record of an incorporated society that has had the control or care of the person alleged to have committed the offence in respect of which the proceedings are taken at or about the time the person came to Canada, is evidence of the age of that person, if the entry or record was made before the time when the offence is alleged to have been committed (Young Offenders Act, s. 57(2)(b)).

The Criminal Code has a similar provision. In any proceedings to which the Criminal Code applies, an entry or record of an incorporated society or its officers who have had the control or care of a child or young person at or about the time the child or young person was brought to Canada is evidence of the age of the child or young person if the entry or record was made before the time when the offence is alleged to have been committed (s. 658(1)).

Other evidence. In the absence, before a youth court, of any such certificate, copy, entry or record of an incorporated society, or in corroboration of any such certificate, copy, entry, or record, the youth court may receive and act on any other information relating to age that it considers reliable (Young Offenders Act, s. 57(3)).

5. Time when specified age attained. A person shall be deemed not to have attained a specified number of years of age until the commencement of the anniversary, of the same number, of the day of his birth (Interpretation Act, s. 30).

6. Inference of age from appearance. In the absence of either evidence, or by way of corroboration of other evidence, a jury, judge, justice or provincial court judge, as the case may be, may infer the age of a child or young person from his appearance (s. 658(2)).

In any proceedings under the Young Offenders Act, a youth court may draw inferences as to the age of a person from a person's appearance or from statements made by that person in direct examination or cross examination (Young Offenders Act, s. 57(4)).

7. Mistake of age in sexual offences. With respect to sexual offences involving a person under the age of 14 years, it is not a defence to a charge that the accused believed that the complainant was 14 years of age or more at the time the offence was alleged to have been committed unless the accused took all reasonable steps to ascertain the age of the complainant (s. 150.1(4)).

With respect to sexual offences involving a person over the age of 14 years but under the age of 18 years, it is not a defence to a charge that the accused believed that the complainant was 18 years of age or more at the time the offence was alleged to have been committed unless the accused took all reasonable steps to ascertain the age of the complainant (s. 150.1(5)).

8. Testimony of a complainant under the age of 18 years. For the purposes of s. 486(1) and (2.3) and for greater certainty, the "proper administration of justice" includes ensuring that the interests of witnesses under the age of 14 years are safeguarded in proceedings in which the accused is charged with a sexual offence, an offence against any of ss. 271, 272 and 273 or an offence in which violence against the person is alleged to have been used, threatened or attempted (s. 486(1.2)). In proceedings referred to in s. 486(1.1), the presiding judge, provincial court judge or justice may, on application of the prosecutor or a witness who, at the time of the trial or preliminary hearing, is under the age of 14 years, order that a support person of the witness' choice be permitted to be present and to be close to the witness while testifying. (s. 486(1.1)). The presiding judge, provincial court judge or justice shall not permit a witness in the proceedings referred to in s. 486 (1.1) to be a support person unless the presiding judge, provincial court judge or justice is of the opinion that the proper administration of justice so requires (s. 486(1.3)). The presiding judge, provincial court judge or justice may order that the support person and the witness not communicate with each other during the testimony of the witness (s. 486(1.4)).

For certain offences, at the time of the trial or preliminary inquiry, the presiding judge or justice may order that a complainant under the age of 18 years testify outside the courtroom or behind a screen or other device that would allow the complainant not to see the accused. This may be done if the judge or justice is of the opinion that the exclusion is necessary to obtain a full and candid account of the acts complained of from the complainant (s. 486(2.1)). Where such an order is made, arrangements must be made for the accused, the judge or justice, and the jury to watch the testimony of the complainant by means of closed-circuit television or otherwise. Further, the accused must be permitted to communicate with counsel while watching the testimony (s. 486(2.2)). In proceedings referred to in s. 486(1.1), the accused shall not personally cross-examine a witness who at the time of the proceedings is under the age of 14 years, unless the presiding judge, provincial court judge or justice is of the opinion that the proper administration of justice requires the accused to personally conduct the cross-examination and, where the accused is not personally conducting the cross-examination, the presiding judge, provincial court judge or justice shall appoint counsel for the purpose of conducting the cross-examination (s. 486(2.3)).

In such cases, the presiding judge or justice may make an order directing that the identity of the complainant or witness, and any information that could disclose the identity of the complainant or witness, shall not be published in any document or broadcast in any way. Such an order may be made on the motion of the presiding judge or justice, or shall be made on application by the complainant, by the prosecutor or by a witness under the age of 18 years (s. 486(3)). It should also be noted that the presiding judge or justice is required to inform the complainant and every witness under the age of 18 years in such cases of their right to make an application for such an order at the first reasonable opportunity (s. 486(4)).

The offences for which such an order may be made include the following:

1. Sexual interference. (s. 151)
2. Invitation to sexual touching. (s. 152)
3. Sexual exploitation. (s. 153)
4. Incest. (s. 155)
5. Anal intercourse. (s. 159)
6. Compulsion to commit bestiality. (s. 160(2))
7. Bestiality in presence of or by child. (s. 160(3))
8. Parent or guardian procuring sexual activity. (s. 170)
9. Householder permitting sexual activity. (s. 171)
10. Corrupting children. (s. 172)
11. Indecent acts. (s. 173)
12. Sexual assault. (s. 271)
13. Sexual assault with a weapon, threats to a third party, or causing bodily harm. (s. 272)
14. Aggravated sexual assault. (s. 273)
15. Extortion. (s. 346)
16. Criminal interest rate. (s. 347)

AGENT. A person who acts on behalf of another person (the principal) by his authority, express or implied (Jowitt's Dictionary of English Law). *See also SECRET COMMISSIONS.*

Agency. The status of an agent, or the relationship between him and his principal (Jowitt's Dictionary of English Law).

AIRCRAFT OFFENCES

1. *Definition of "aircraft"*
2. *Hijacking*
3. *Endangering safety of aircraft or airport*
4. *Offensive weapons and explosive substances*
5. *Dangerous operation of aircraft*
6. *Dangerous operation causing bodily harm*
7. *Dangerous operation causing death*
8. *Unsafe aircraft*
9. *Failing to stop at scene of accident*

10. *Operation of aircraft while impaired or with more than 80 mg of alcohol in blood*
11. *Impaired operation causing bodily harm*
12. *Impaired operation causing death*
13. *Failure or refusal to provide sample*
14. *Operation of aircraft while disqualified*
15. *Setting fire to aircraft. See ARSON, 3.*

1. Definition of "aircraft"

1. Any machine used or designed for navigation of the air but does not include a machine designed to derive support in the atmosphere from reactions against the earth's surface of air expelled from the machine (Aeronautics Act, s. 12).
2. For the purposes of Part VIII of the Criminal Code (Offences Against the Person and Reputation), "aircraft" does not include a machine designed to derive support in the atmosphere primarily from reactions against the earth's surface of air expelled from the machine (s. 214).

2. Hijacking — Section 76

Every one who — unlawfully — by force or threat thereof, or by any other form of intimidation — seizes or exercises control of an aircraft — with intent — either to cause any person on board the aircraft to be confined or imprisoned against his will — or to cause any person on board the aircraft to be transported against his will to any place other than the next scheduled place of landing of the aircraft — or to hold any person on board the aircraft for ransom or to service against his will — or to cause the aircraft to deviate in a material respect from its flight plan — is guilty of an indictable offence.

Intent. Intention to cause confinement, imprisonment, transportation, hold for ransom or service against will; to cause deviation from flight plan.

Included offences. Attempts (s. 660 and s. 662(1)(b)).

Punishment. Imprisonment for life (s. 76).

Release. Initial decision to release made by justice (s. 515(1)).

Election. Accused may elect trial by judge and jury, judge alone, or provincial court judge (s. 536).

Informations

A.B., on or about the —— day of ——, 19——, at the —— of ——, in the said (territorial division), unlawfully, by force [OR threat of force OR (specify form of intimidation)] did seize [OR exercise control of] an aircraft with intent to cause C.D., a person on board the aircraft, to be confined [OR imprisoned] against his will, to wit: (specify the particulars of the offence), contrary to s. 76(a) of the Criminal Code of Canada.

A.B., on or about the —— day of ——, 19——, at the —— of ——, in the said (territorial division), unlawfully, by force [OR threat of force OR (specify form of intimidation)] did seize [OR exercise control of] an aircraft with intent to cause C.D., a person on board the aircraft, to be transported against his will to a place other than the next scheduled landing place of the aircraft, to wit: (specify the particulars of the offence), contrary to s. 76(b) of the Criminal Code of Canada.

A.B., on or about the —— day of ——, 19——, at the —— of ——, in the said (territorial division), unlawfully, by force [OR threat of force OR (specify form of intimidation)] did seize [OR exercise control of] an aircraft with intent to hold C.D., a person on board the aircraft, for ransom [OR to service against his will], to wit: (specify the particulars of the offence), contrary to s. 76(c) of the Criminal Code of Canada.

A.B., on or about the —— day of ——, 19——, at the —— of ——, in the said (territorial division), unlawfully, by force [OR threat of force OR (specify form of intimidation)] did seize [OR exercise control of] an aircraft with intent to cause the aircraft to deviate in a material respect from its flight plan, to wit: (specify the particulars of the offence), contrary to s. 76(d) of the Criminal Code of Canada.

3. Endangering safety of aircraft or airport

Section 77(a)

Every one who — on board an aircraft in flight — commits an act of violence against a person — that is likely to endanger the safety of the aircraft — is guilty of an indictable offence.

Section 77(b)

Every one who — using a weapon — commits an act of violence against a person at an airport serving international civil aviation — that causes or is likely to cause serious injury or death — and that endangers or is likely to endanger safety at the airport — is guilty of an indictable offence.

Section 77(c)

Every one who — causes damage to an aircraft in service — that renders the aircraft incapable of flight — or that is likely to endanger the safety of the aircraft in flight — is guilty of an indictable offence.

Section 77(d)

Every one who — places or causes to be placed on board an aircraft in service — anything that is likely to cause damage to the aircraft that will render it incapable of flight — or that is likely to endanger the safety of the aircraft in flight — is guilty of an indictable offence.

Section 77(e)

Every one who — causes damages to or interferes with the operation of — any air navigation facility — where the damage or interference is likely to endanger the safety of an aircraft in flight — is guilty of an indictable offence.

Section 77(f)

Every one who — using a weapon, substance or device — destroys or causes serious damage — to the facilities of an airport serving international civil aviation — or to any aircraft not in service located there — or causes disruption of services of the airport — that endangers or is likely to endanger safety at the airport — is guilty of an indictable offence.

Section 77(g)

Every one who — endangers the safety of an aircraft in flight — by communicating to any other person — any information that the person knows to be false — is guilty of an indictable offence.

Included offences. Attempts (s. 660 and s. 662(1)(b)).

Punishment. Imprisonment for life (s. 77).

Release. Initial decision to release made by justice (s. 515(1)).

Election. Accused may elect trial by judge and jury, judge alone, or provincial court judge (s. 536).

Informations

A.B., on or about the —— day of ——, 19——, at the —— of ——, in the said (territorial division), did commit an act of violence against a person on board an aircraft in flight that was likely to endanger the safety of the aircraft, to wit: *(specify the particulars of the offence)*, contrary to s. 77(a) of the Criminal Code of Canada.

A.B., on or about the —— day of ——, 19——, at the —— of ——, in the said (territorial division), using a weapon, did commit an act of violence against a person at an airport serving international civil aviation that caused [OR was likely to cause] serious injury [OR death] that endangered [OR was likely to endanger] safety at the airport, to wit: *(specify the particulars of the offence)*, contrary to s. 77(b) of the Criminal Code of Canada.

A.B., on or about the —— day of ——, 19——, at the —— of ——, in the said (territorial division), did cause damage to an aircraft in service that rendered the aircraft incapable of flight [OR was likely to endanger the safety of the aircraft in flight], to wit: *(specify the particulars of the offence)*, contrary to s. 77(c) of the Criminal Code of Canada.

A.B., on or about the —— day of ——, 19——, at the —— of ——, in the said (territorial division), did place [OR cause to be placed] on board an aircraft in service a *(specify the thing placed on board)* which was likely to cause damage to an aircraft that would render it incapable of flight [OR was likely to endanger the safety of an aircraft in flight], to wit: *(specify the particulars of the offence)*, contrary to s. 77(d) of the Criminal Code of Canada.

A.B., on or about the —— day of ——, 19——, at the —— of ——, in the said (territorial division), did damage to [OR interfere with the operation of] an air navigation facility, which damage [OR interference] was likely to endanger the safety of an aircraft in flight, to wit: *(specify the particulars of the offence)*, contrary to s. 77(e) of the Criminal Code of Canada.

A.B., on or about the —— day of ——, 19——, at the —— of ——, in the said (territorial division), using a weapon [OR substance OR device] did destroy [OR cause serious damage] to the facilities of an airport serving international civil aviation [OR to any aircraft not in service located there [OR did cause disruption of services of the airport] that endangered [OR was likely to endanger] safety at the airport, to wit: *(specify the particulars of the offence)*, contrary to s. 77(f) of the Criminal Code of Canada.

A.B., on or about the —— day of ——, 19——, at the —— of ——, in the said (territorial division), did endanger the safety of an aircraft in flight by communicating information that the person knew to be false to C.D., to wit: *(specify the particulars of the offence), contrary to s. 77(g) of the Criminal Code of Canada.*

4. Offensive weapons and explosive substances — Section 78(1)

Every one who — other than a peace officer engaged in the execution of his duty — takes on board a civil aircraft — an offensive weapon or any explosive substance — either without the consent of the owner or operator of the aircraft or of a person duly authorized by either of them to consent thereto — or with such consent without complying with all terms and conditions on which the consent was given — is guilty of an indictable offence.

Included offences. Attempts (s. 660 and s. 662(1)(b)).

Punishment. Imprisonment for a term not exceeding 14 years (s. 78).

Release. Initial decision to release made by justice (s. 515(1)).

Election. Accused may elect trial by judge and jury, judge alone, or provincial court judge (s. 536).

Definitions. See CIVIL AIRCRAFT.

Informations

A.B., on or about the —— day of ——, 19——, at the —— of ——, in the said (territorial division), did take on board a civil aircraft an offensive weapon [OR an explosive substance] without the consent of the owner [OR the operator OR C.D., a person duly authorized by the owner (OR the operator) to consent thereto] to wit: (specify the particulars of the offence), contrary to s. 78(1)(a) of the Criminal Code of Canada.

A.B., on or about the —— day of ——, 19——, at the —— of ——, in the said (territorial division), did take on board a civil aircraft an offensive weapon [OR an explosive substance] without the consent of the owner [OR the operator OR C.D., a person duly authorized by the owner (OR the operator) to consent thereto] but without complying with the terms [OR conditions] on which consent was given, to wit: (specify the particulars of the offence), contrary to s. 78(1)(b) of the Criminal Code of Canada.

5. Dangerous operation of aircraft — Section 249(1)(c) and (2)

Every one who — operates an aircraft — in a manner that is dangerous to the public — having regard to all the circumstances — including the nature and condition of that aircraft or the place or air space in or through which the aircraft is operated — is guilty

of an of either an indictable offence or an offence punishable on summary conviction.

Limitation period. No proceedings in respect of offences that are declared to be punishable on summary conviction shall be instituted more than 6 months after the time when the subject matter of the proceedings arose (s. 786(2) and s. 785(1)).

Included offences. Attempts (s. 660 and s. 662(1)(b)).

Punishment. On indictment, imprisonment for a term not exceeding 5 years (s. 249(2)(a)). On summary conviction, a fine not exceeding $2,000, or 6 months' imprisonment, or both (s. 249(2)(b) and s. 787(1)).

In addition to any other punishment that may be imposed, the court may make an order prohibiting the offender from operating an aircraft during any period not exceeding 3 years (s. 259(2)(c)).

Release. Initial decision to release made by peace officer (s. 497).

Election. On indictment, accused may elect trial by judge and jury, judge alone, or provincial court judge (s. 536). On summary conviction, no offence.

Informations

A.B., on or about the —— day of ——, 19——, at the —— of ——, in the said (territorial division), did operate an aircraft in a manner dangerous to the public, to wit: (specify the particulars of the offence), contrary to s. 249(1)(c) of the Criminal Code of Canada.

6. Dangerous operation causing bodily harm — Section 249(3)

Every one who — commits the offence of dangerous operation of an aircraft (s. 249(1)(c)) — and thereby causes bodily harm to any other person — is guilty of an indictable offence.

Included offences. Attempts (s. 660 and s. 662(1)(b)); dangerous operation of aircraft.

Punishment. Imprisonment for a term not exceeding 10 years (s. 249(3)).

In addition to any other punishment that may be imposed, the court may make an order prohibiting the offender from operating an aircraft during any period not exceeding 10 years (s. 259(2)(b)).

Release. Initial decision to release made by justice (s. 515(1)).

AIRCRAFT OFFENCES

Election. Accused may elect trial by judge and jury, judge alone, or provincial court judge (s. 536).

Informations

A.B., on or about the —— day of ——, 19——, at the —— of ——, in the said (territorial division), did operate an aircraft in a manner dangerous to the public, thereby causing bodily harm to C.D., to wit: (specify the particulars of the offence), contrary to s. 249(3) of the Criminal Code of Canada.

7. Dangerous operation causing death — Section 249(4)

Every one who — commits the offence of dangerous operation of an aircraft (s. 249(1)(c)) — and thereby causes the death of any other person — is guilty of an indictable offence.

Included offences. Attempts (s. 660 and s. 662(1)(b)); dangerous operation of aircraft.

Punishment. Imprisonment for a term not exceeding 14 years (s. 249(4)).

In addition to any other punishment that may be imposed, the court may make an order prohibiting the offender from operating an aircraft during any period not exceeding 10 years (s. 259(2)(b)).

Release. Initial decision to release made by justice (s. 515(1)).

Election. Accused may elect trial by judge and jury, judge alone, or provincial court judge (s. 536).

Informations

A.B., on or about the —— day of ——, 19——, at the —— of ——, in the said (territorial division), did operate an aircraft in a manner dangerous to the public, thereby causing the death of C.D., to wit: (specify the particulars of the offence), contrary to s. 249(4) of the Criminal Code of Canada.

8. Unsafe aircraft — Section 251(1)(b)

Every one who — knowingly — either sends an aircraft on a flight or operates an aircraft — that is not fit and safe for flight — and thereby endangers the life of any person — is guilty of an indictable offence.

Intent. Knowingly.

Consent to prosecute. No proceedings shall be instituted under s. 251 without the written consent of the Attorney General of Canada (s. 251(3)).

Included offences. Attempts (s. 660 and s. 662(1)(b)).

Punishment. Imprisonment for a term not exceeding 5 years (s. 251(1)).

In addition to any other punishment that may be imposed, the court may make an order prohibiting the offender from operating an aircraft during any period not exceeding 3 years (s. 259(2)(c)).

Release. Initial decision to release made by officer in charge or justice (s. 498).

Election. Accused may elect trial by judge and jury, judge alone, or provincial court judge (s. 536).

Defences. An accused shall not be convicted where he establishes that (i) he used all reasonable means to ensure that the aircraft was fit and safe for flight, or (ii) to send or operate the aircraft while it was not fit and safe for flight was, under the circumstances, reasonable and justifiable (s. 251(2)(b)).

Informations

A.B., on or about the —— day of ——, 19 ——, at the —— of ——, in the said (territorial division), did knowingly send an aircraft on a flight [OR did knowingly operate an aircraft], that was not fit and safe for flight, thereby endangering the life of C.D., to wit: (specify the particulars of the offence), contrary to s. 251(1)(b) of the Criminal Code of Canada.

9. Failing to stop at scene of accident — Section 252(1)

Every one who — has the care or charge or control of an aircraft — that is involved in an accident with — either another person — or a vehicle or a vessel or another aircraft — and with intent to escape civil or criminal liability — fails to stop, where possible, his aircraft — and fails to give his name and address — and, where any person has been injured or appears to require assistance, fails to offer assistance — is guilty of either an indictable offence or an offence punishable on summary conviction.

Intent. Intention to escape civil or criminal liability.

Limitation period. No proceedings in respect of offences that are declared to be punishable on summary conviction shall be instituted

more than 6 months after the time when the subject matter of the proceedings arose (s. 786(2) and s. 785(1)).

Included offences. Attempts (s. 660 and s. 662(1)(b)).

Punishment. On indictment, imprisonment for a term not exceeding 2 years (s. 252(1)). On summary conviction, a fine not exceeding $2,000, or 6 months' imprisonment, or both (s. 252(1) and s. 787(1)).

In addition to any other punishment that may be imposed, the court may make an order prohibiting the offender from operating an aircraft during any period not exceeding 3 years (s. 259(2)(c)).

Release. Initial decision to release made by peace officer (s. 497).

Election. On indictment, accused may elect trial by judge and jury, judge alone, or provincial court judge (s. 536). On summary conviction, no election.

Evidence. Evidence that an accused failed to stop, where possible, his aircraft, offer assistance where any person had been injured or appeared to require assistance and give his name and address is, in the absence of evidence to the contrary, proof of an intent to escape civil or criminal liability (s. 252(2)).

Informations

A.B., on or about the —— day of ——, 19——, at the —— of ——, in the said (territorial division), having the care [OR charge OR control] of an aircraft that was involved in an accident with C.D. [OR a vehicle (OR a vessel OR an aircraft) in the charge of C.D.], did, with intent to escape civil or criminal liability, fail to stop his aircraft and give his name and address [and offer assistance to C.D. (OR E.F.), a person who was injured in the accident], to wit: (specify the particulars of the offence), contrary to s. 252(1) of the Criminal Code of Canada.

10. Operation of aircraft while impaired or with more than 80 mg of alcohol in blood — Section 253 and section 255(1)

Every one who — either operates or assists in the operation of an aircraft — or has the care or control of an aircraft — whether it is in motion or not — either while his ability to operate the aircraft is impaired by alcohol or a drug — or having consumed alcohol in such a quantity that the concentration thereof in his blood exceeds 80 mg of alcohol in 100 ml of blood — is guilty of either an indictable offence or an offence punishable on summary conviction.

Limitation period. No proceedings in respect of offences that are declared to be punishable on summary conviction shall be instituted

more than 6 months after the time when the subject matter of the proceedings arose (s. 786(2) and s. 785(1)).

Included offences. Attempts (s. 660 and s. 662(1)(b)).

Punishment. On indictment, imprisonment for a term not exceeding 5 years (s. 255(1)(b)). On summary conviction, imprisonment for a term not exceeding 6 months (s. 255(1)(c)).

Whether on indictment or on summary conviction, liable to the following minimum punishment namely:

  (i) for a first offence, to a fine of not less than $300,
  (ii) for a second offence, to imprisonment for not less than 14 days, and
  (iii) for each subsequent offence, to imprisonment for not less than 90 days (s. 255(1)(a)).

In addition to any other punishment that may be imposed, the court shall make an order prohibiting the offender from operating an aircraft (a) for a first offence, during a period of not more than 3 years and not less than 3 months; (b) for a second offence, during a period of not more than 3 years and not less than 6 months; and (c) for each subsequent offence, during a period of not more than 3 years and not less than one year (s. 259(1)).

Release. Initial decision to release made by peace officer (s. 497).

Election. On indictment, accused may elect trial by judge and jury, judge alone, or provincial court judge (s. 536). On summary conviction, no election.

Breath samples. Where a peace officer believes on reasonable and probable grounds that a person is committing, or at any time within the preceding 2 hours has committed, as a result of the consumption of alcohol, an offence under s. 253 (operation of aircraft while impaired or with more than 80 mg of alcohol in blood), the peace officer may, by demand made to that person forthwith or as soon as practicable, require that person to provide then or as soon thereafter as is practicable such samples of the person's breath as in the opinion of a qualified technician are necessary to enable proper analysis to be made in order to determine the concentration, if any, of alcohol in the person's blood, and to accompany the peace officer for the purpose of enabling such samples to be taken (s. 254(3)(a)).

Where samples of the breath of the accused have been taken pursuant to a demand made under s. 254(3), evidence of the results of the analyses so made is (in the absence of evidence to the contrary) proof of the concentration of alcohol in the blood of the accused at the time of the alleged offence if the following conditions are met: (i) at the time each sample was taken, the person taking the sample offered to provide to the accused a specimen of the breath of the accused in an approved container for his own use, and, at the request of the accused made at that time, such a specimen was thereupon provided to the accused; (ii) each sample was taken as soon as practicable after the time of the alleged offence and, in the case of the first sample, not later than 2 hours after that time, with an interval of at least 15 minutes between the times when the samples were taken; (iii) each sample was received from the accused directly into an approved container or approved instrument operated by a qualified technician; and (iv) an analysis of each sample was made by means of an approved instrument operated by a qualified technician (s. 258(1)(c)).

However, the result of an analysis of a sample of the breath of the accused (other than a sample taken pursuant to a s. 254(3) demand) may be admitted in evidence notwithstanding that, before the accused gave the sample, he was not warned that he need not give the sample or that the result of the analysis of the sample might be used in evidence (s. 258(1)(b)).

Blood samples. Where a peace officer believes on reasonable and probable grounds that a person is committing, or at any time within the preceding 2 hours has committed, as a result of the consumption of alcohol, an offence under s. 253 (operation of aircraft while impaired or with more than 80 mg alcohol in blood), the peace officer may, by demand made to that person forthwith or as soon as practicable, require that person to provide then or as soon thereafter as is practicable, where the peace officer has reasonable and probable grounds to believe that, by reason of any physical condition of the person, (i) the person may be incapable of providing a sample of his breath, or (ii) it would be impracticable to obtain a sample of his breath, such samples of the person's blood as in the opinion of a qualified medical practitioner or qualified technician taking the samples are necessary to enable proper analysis to be made in order to determine the concentration, if any, of alcohol in the person's blood, and to accompany the peace officer for the purpose of enabling such samples to be taken (s. 254(3)(b)).

Samples of blood may be taken pursuant to a s. 254(3) demand only if the samples are taken by or under the direction of a qualified medical practitioner who is satisfied that the taking of such samples would not endanger the life or health of the person from whom those samples are taken (s. 254(4)).

Where a justice is satisfied, on an information on oath in Form 1 or on an information on oath submitted to the justice pursuant to s. 487.1 by telephone or other means of telecommunications, that there are reasonable grounds to believe that (a) a person has, within the preceding 2 hours, committed, as a result of the consumption of alcohol, an offence under s. 253 (operation of aircraft while impaired or with more than 80 mg alcohol in blood) and that person was involved in an accident resulting in the death of another person or in bodily harm to himself or herself or to any other person, and (b) a qualified medical practitioner is of the opinion that (i) by reason of any physical or mental condition of the person that resulted from the consumption of alcohol, the accident or any other occurrence related to or resulting from the accident, the person is unable to consent to the taking of samples of his blood and (ii) the taking of samples of blood from the person would not endanger the life or health of the person, the justice may issue a warrant authorizing a peace officer to require a qualified medical practitioner to take, or to cause to be taken by a qualified technician under the direction of the qualified medical practitioner, such samples of the blood of the person as in the opinion of the person taking the samples are necessary to enable a proper analysis to be made in order to determine the concentration, if any, of alcohol in his blood (s. 256(1)). For the purposes of s. 256, an information on oath submitted by telephone or other means of telecommunication shall include a statement of the circumstances that make it impracticable for the peace officer to appear personally before a justice (s. 487.1(4)(a)), a statement setting out the offence alleged to have been committed and identifying the person from whom blood samples are to be taken (s. 256(3)) and a statement as to any prior application for a warrant in respect of the same matter, of which the peace officer has knowledge (s. 487.1(4)(d)). Where a warrant issued pursuant to s. 256(1) is executed, the peace officer shall, as soon as practicable thereafter, give a copy or, in the case of a warrant issued by telephone or other means of telecommunication, a facsimile of the warrant to the person from whom the samples were taken (s. 256(5)).

No qualified medical practitioner or qualified technician is guilty of an offence only by reason of his refusal to take a sample of blood from a person for the purposes of s. 254 or s. 256 and no qualified medical practitioner is guilty of an offence only by reason of his refusal to cause to be taken by a qualified technician under his direction a sample of blood from a person for such purposes (s. 257(1)).

No qualified medical practitioner by whom or under whose direction a sample of blood is taken from a person pursuant to a demand made under s. 254(3) or a warrant issued under s. 256 and no qualified technician acting under the direction of a qualified medical practitioner incurs any criminal or civil liability for anything necessarily done with reasonable care and skill in the taking of such a sample of blood (s. 257(2)).

Where a sample of the blood of the accused has been taken pursuant to a demand made under s. 254(3) or otherwise with the consent of the accused or pursuant to a warrant issued under s. 256, evidence of the result of the analysis is (in the absence of evidence to the contrary) proof of the concentration of alcohol in the blood of the accused at the time of the alleged offence if the following conditions are met: (i) at the time the sample was taken, the person taking the sample took an additional sample of the blood of the accused and one of the samples was retained, to permit an analysis thereof to be made by or on behalf of the accused and, at the request of the accused made within 3 months from the taking of the samples, one of the samples was ordered to be released; (ii) both such samples were taken as soon as practicable after the time of the alleged offence and in any event not later than 2 hours after that time; (iii) both such samples were taken by a qualified medical practitioner or a qualified technician under the direction of a qualified medical practitioner; (iv) both samples were received from the accused directly into, or placed directly into, approved containers that were subsequently sealed; and (v) an analysis was made by an analyst of at least one of the samples that was contained in a sealed approved container (s. 258(1)(d)). However, the result of an analysis of a sample of blood of the accused (other than a sample taken pursuant to a s. 254(3) demand) may be admitted in evidence notwithstanding that, before the accused gave the sample, he was not warned that he need not give the sample or that the result of the analysis of the sample might be used in evidence (s. 258(1)(b)).

Other evidence. Physical evidence of impaired operation or impaired care or control should be obtained from the investigating officer and, if possible, one or more civilian witnesses, i.e., that (i) he staggered or was unsteady on his feet, (ii) his breath smelled of an alcoholic beverage, (iii) his speech was slurred, (iv) his eyes were bloodshot, and (v) his operation of the aircraft was erratic.

An accused shall be deemed to have had the care or control of an aircraft where it is proved that the accused occupied the seat or position ordinarily occupied by a person who operates an aircraft or who assists in the operation of an aircraft, unless the accused establishes that he did not occupy that seat or position for the purpose of setting the aircraft in motion or assisting in the operation of the aircraft, as the case may be (s. 258(1)(a)).

The result of an analysis of the urine or other bodily substance of the accused (other than a sample of breath or blood taken pursuant to a s. 254(3) demand) may be admitted in evidence notwithstanding that, before the accused gave the sample, he was not warned that he need not give the sample or that the result of the analysis of the sample might be used in evidence (s. 258(1)(b)).

Evidence that the accused, without reasonable excuse, failed or refused to comply with a demand for samples made to him by a peace officer under s. 254 is admissible and the court may draw an inference therefrom adverse to the accused (s. 258(3)).

Informations

A.B., on or about the —— day of ——, 19——, at the —— of ——, in the said (territorial division), while his ability to operate an aircraft was impaired by alcohol [OR a drug], did operate [OR assist in the operation of OR have the care or control of] an aircraft, to wit: (specify the particulars of the offence), contrary to s. 253 of the Criminal Code of Canada.

A.B., on or about the —— day of ——, 19——, at the —— of ——, in the said (territorial division), did operate [OR assist in the operation of OR have the care or control of] an aircraft, having consumed alcohol in such a qualtity that the concentration thereof in the blood of A.B. exceeded 80 mg of alcohol in 100 ml of blood, to wit: (specify the particulars of the offence), contrary to s. 253 of the Criminal Code of Canada.

11. Impaired operation causing bodily harm — Section 255(2)

Every one who — commits the offence of operation of an aircraft while impaired (s. 253(a)) — and thereby causes bodily harm to any other person — is guilty of an indictable offence.

Included offences. Attempts (s. 660 and s. 662(1)(b)); operation of aircraft while impaired.

Punishment. Imprisonment for a term not exceeding 10 years (s. 255(2)).

In addition to any other punishment that may be imposed, the court may make an order prohibiting the offence from operating an aircraft during any period not exceeding 10 years (s. 259(2)(b)).

Release. Initial decision to release made by justice (s. 515(1)).

Election. Accused may elect trial by judge and jury, judge alone, or provincial court judge (s. 536).

Informations

A.B., on or about the —— day of ——, 19——, at the —— of ——, in the said (territorial division), while his ability to operate an aircraft was impaired by alcohol *[OR a drug]*, did operate *[OR assist in the operation of OR have the care or control of]* an aircraft, thereby causing bodily harm to C.D., to wit: *(specify the particulars of the offence)*, contrary to s. 255(2) of the Criminal Code of Canada.

12. Impaired operation causing death — Section 255(3)

Every one who — commits the offence of operation of an aircraft while impaired (s. 253(a)) — and thereby causes the death of any other person — is guilty of an indictable offence.

Included offences. Attempts (s. 660 and s. 662(1)(b)); operation of aircraft while impaired.

Punishment. Imprisonment for a term not exceeding 14 years (s. 255(3)).

In addition to any other punishment that may be imposed, the court may make an order prohibiting the offender from operating an aircraft during any period not exceeding 10 years (s. 259(2)(b)).

Release. Initial decision to release made by justice (s. 515(1)).

Election. Accused may elect trial by judge and jury, judge alone, or provincial court judge (s. 536).

Informations

A.B., on or about the —— day of ——, 19——, at the —— of ——, in the said (territorial division), while his ability to operate an aircraft was impaired by alcohol *[OR a drug]*, did operate *[OR assist in the operation of OR have the care or control of]* an aircraft, thereby causing the death of C.D., to wit: *(specify the particulars of the offence)*, contrary to s. 255(3) of the Criminal Code of Canada.

13. Failure or refusal to provide sample — Section 254(3) and section 255(1)

Every one who — without reasonable excuse — fails or refuses to comply with a demand — made to him by a peace officer under

s. 254 — is guilty of either an indictable offence or an offence punishable on summary conviction.

Intent. Intentional non-compliance.

Authority to test. Where a peace officer reasonably suspects that a person who is operating or assisting in the operation of an aircraft or who has the care or control of an aircraft, whether it is in motion or not, has alcohol in his body, the peace officer may, by demand made to that person, require that person to provide forthwith such a sample of his breath as in the opinion of the peace officer is necessary to enable a proper analysis of his breath to be made by means of an approved screening device and, where necessary, to accompany the peace officer for the purpose of enabling such a sample of his breath to be taken (s. 254(2)). Where a peace officer believes on reasonable and probable grounds that a person is committing, or at any time within the preceding 2 hours has committed, as a result of the consumption of alcohol, an offence under s. 253 (operation of aircraft while impaired or with more than 80 mg of alcohol in blood), the peace officer may, by demand made to that person forthwith or as soon as practicable, require that person to provide then or as soon thereafter as is practicable (a) such samples of the person's breath as in the opinion of a qualified technician (or (b) where the peace officer has reasonable and probable grounds to believe that, by reason of any physical condition of the person, (i) the person may be incapable of providing a sample of his breath, or (ii) it would be impracticable to obtain a sample of his breath, such samples of the person's blood, as in the opinion of a qualified medical practitioner or qualified technician taking the samples) are necessary to enable proper analysis to be made in order to determine the concentration, if any, of alcohol in the person's breath (or blood), and to accompany the peace officer for the purpose of enabling such samples to be taken (s. 254(3)).

Limitation period. No proceedings in respect of offences that are declared to be punishable on summary conviction shall be instituted more than 6 months after the time when the subject matter of the proceedings arose (s. 786(2) and s. 785(1)).

Included offences. Attempts (s. 660 and s. 662(1)(b)).

Punishment. On indictment, imprisonment for a term not exceeding 5 years (s. 255(1)(b)). On summary conviction, imprisonment for a term not exceeding 6 months (s. 255(1)(c)).

Whether on indictment or on summary conviction, liable to the following minimum punishment namely:

(i) for a first offence, to a fine not less than $300;
(ii) for a second offence, to imprisonment for not less than 14 days; and
(iii) for each subsequent offence, to imprisonment for not less than 90 days (s. 255(1)(a)).

In addition to any other punishment that may be imposed, the court shall make an order prohibiting the offender from operating an aircraft (a) for a first offence, during a period of not more than 3 years and not less than 3 months; (b) for a second offence, during a period of not more than 3 years and not less than 6 months; and (c) for each subsequent offence, during a period of not more than 3 years and not less than one year (s. 259(1)).

Release. Initial decision to release made by peace officer (s. 497).

Election. On indictment, accused may elect trial by judge and jury, judge alone, or provincial court judge (s. 536). On summary conviction, no election.

Evidence. With respect to a s. 254(2) demand, proof is necessary that (i) there was in fact a demand, (ii) the accused was either operating or assisting in the operation of an aircraft or had the care or control of an aircraft, (iii) a peace officer formed a suspicion that the accused had alcohol in his body, and (iv) the suspicion was a reasonable one. A demand, not a request, must be made to the accused and it is usually made in the words of the section itself; for example, "I demand that you provide such a sample of your breath as is necessary to enable a proper analysis of your breath to be made by means of an approved screening device", or "I demand that you accompany me to [specify where] for the purpose of enabling you to provide such a sample of your breath as is necessary to enable a proper analysis of your breath to be made by means of an approved screening device". An "approved screening device" is a device of a kind that is designed to ascertain the presence of alcohol in the blood of a person and that is approved for the purposes of s. 254 by order of the Attorney General of Canada (s. 254(1)).

With respect to a s. 254(3) demand, proof is necessary that (i) there was in fact a demand, (ii) a peace officer formed a belief that the accused was committing or had committed within the 2 preceding hours an offence under s. 253 (operation of aircraft while impaired or with more than 80 mg of alcohol in blood), and (iii) the officer had reasonable and probable grounds for his belief. The belief must be formulated within 2 hours after the time of the operation or the care or control. A demand, not a request, must be made to the accused and is usually made in the words of the section itself; for example, "I demand that you accompany me to [specify where] to enable you to provide such samples of your breath as are necessary to enable proper analysis to be made in order to determine the concentration, if any, of alcohol in your blood". That demand must be made forthwith or as soon as practicable after the peace officer has formed the belief referred to above. The words "as soon as practicable" mean that as long as there is reasonable justification for any delay after the belief is formed, the demand will be a proper one.

Before making either a s. 254(2) demand or a s. 254(3) demand, the officer must inform the accused of his right to retain and instruct counsel without delay (Canadian Charter of Rights and Freedoms, s. 10(b)).

Proof is necessary that there was in fact a failure or refusal. There is no significant difference between the words "failure" and "refusal". The qualified technician is entitled to determine what a suitable sample of breath is and anything less than that offered by the accused, such as short puffs of air, can constitute a refusal. The failure or refusal can be to fail or refuse to accompany the officer or to provide a sample or to do both.

What is a reasonable excuse? The burden is on the accused at trial to show that there was a reasonable excuse. A refusal by an officer to give the accused a reasonable opportunity to attempt to communicate with a solicitor in private before complying with the demand may be a reasonable excuse.

Informations

A.B., on or about the —— day of ——, 19——, at the —— of ——, in the said (territorial division), without reasonable excuse, did fail [OR refuse] to comply with a demand made to A.B. by C.D., a peace officer, under s. 254(2) [OR s. 254(3)] of the Criminal Code, to wit: (specify the particulars of the offence), contrary to s. 254(5) of the Criminal Code of Canada.

14. Operation of aircraft while disqualified — Section 259(4)

Every one who — operates an aircraft in Canada — while he is disqualified from doing so — is guilty of either an indictable offence or an offence punishable on summary conviction.

Limitation period. No proceedings in respect of offences that are declared to be punishable on summary conviction shall be instituted

more than 6 months after the time when the subject matter of the proceedings arose (s. 786(2) and s. 785(1)).

Included offences. Attempts (s. 660 and s. 662(1)(b)).

Punishment. On indictment, imprisonment for a term not exceeding 2 years (s. 259(4)(a)). On summary conviction, a fine not exceeding $2,000, or 6 months' imprisonment, or both (s. 259(4)(b) and s. 787(1)).

In addition to any other punishment that may be imposed, the court may make an order prohibiting the offender from operating an aircraft during any period not exceeding 3 years (s. 297).

Release. Initial decision to release made by peace officer (s. 497).

Election. On indictment, no election, absolute jurisdiction of provincial court judge (s. 553). On summary conviction, no election.

Definitions. *See DISQUALIFICATION.*

Informations

A.B., on or about the —— day of ——, 19——, at the —— of ——, in the said (territorial division), did operate an aircraft in Canada while he was disqualified from doing so, to wit: (specify the particulars of the offence), contrary to s. 259(4) of the Criminal Code of Canada.

ALIAS. Otherwise, i.e., otherwise called or otherwise known as (Latin). In a criminal context, the false names which a person may have used at different times; an assumed name.

ALIBI

1. *Definition*	2. *Evidence*

1. Definition. 1. Elsewhere (Latin). 2. An accused person is said to have an alibi when he alleges that, at the time when the offence with which he was charged was committed, he was at a place so far distant from the place where the offence was committed as to make it impossible to be the guilty party.

2. Evidence. 1. The courts have held that, where alibi evidence is presented by the defence, the trial judge must instruct the jury that, if the alibi evidence raises a reasonable doubt as to the guilt of the accused, he is to be acquitted (R. v. O'Leary (1982), 1 C.C.C. (3d) 182 (N.B. C.A.)). 2. The courts have held that failure to disclose an alibi at a sufficiently early time to permit it to be investigated, is a fact which may be considered in determining the weight to be attached to the alibi evidence (R. v. Dunbar (1982), 28 C.R. (3d) 324 (Ont. C.A.)).

ALIEN. The subject of a foreign state. *See also TREASON AND OTHER OFFENCES AGAINST THE QUEEN'S AUTHORITY AND PERSON, 5.*

ALLOCUTUS. The demand put to a person convicted of treason or felony whether he has anything to say why the court should not proceed to judgment against him (Latin).

ALTERNATIVE MEASURES. For the purposes of the Young Offenders Act, "alternative measures" means measures other than judicial proceedings under the Act used to deal with a young person alleged to have committed an offence (Young Offenders Act, s. 2(1)).

AMENDMENT

1. *Definition*
2. *Restrictions on the amendment of an indictment or a count thereof*
3. *Amendment of an allegation that does not conform to the evidence*
4. *Amendment of a count that charges an offence under the wrong federal Act*
5. *Amendment of a count that fails to state or defectively states the essential elements of the offence*
6. *Amendment of a count that is defective in substance*
7. *Amendment of a charge that is defective in form*
8. *Amendment of a mistake in the heading of an indictment*
9. *Procedure following the amendment of an indictment or a count thereof*

1. Definition. The alteration of a writ, pleading, indictment or other document, to correct some error or defect in the original or to raise a new claim or allegation (Oxford, A Concise Dictionary of Law).

2. Restrictions on the amendment of an indictment or a count thereof. The question whether an order to amend an indictment or a count thereof should be granted or refused is a question of law (s. 601(6)). In considering whether or not an amendment should be made, the court shall consider:

(a) the matters disclosed by the evidence taken on the preliminary inquiry;
(b) the evidence taken on trial, if any;
(c) the circumstances of the case;
(d) whether the accused has been misled or prejudiced in his defence by any variance, error or omission; and
(e) whether, having regard to the merits of the case, the proposed amendment can be made without injustice being done (s. 601(4)).

3. Amendment of an allegation that does not conform to the evidence. A court may, on the trial of an indictment, amend the indictment or a count therein, or a particular that is furnished under s. 587 (*see PARTICULARS*), to make the indictment, count or particular conform to the evidence, where there is a variance (s. 601(2)).

The courts have amended the following things in an indictment:

(i) an error with respect to the date (R. v. MacKay (1947), 2 C.R. 412 (N.S. C.A.));
(ii) the name of the victim (R. v. Faulkner (1911), 19 C.C.C. 47 (B.C. C.A.)); and
(iii) details of the property that was the subject of the offence (R. v. Powell (1965), 4 C.C.C. 349 (B.C. C.A.)).

4. Amendment of a count that charges an offence under the wrong federal Act. A court shall, at any stage of the proceedings, amend the indictment or a count therein as may be necessary where it appears that the indictment has been preferred under a particular Act of Parliament, instead of another Act of Parliament (s. 601(3)(a)).

5. Amendment of a count that fails to state or defectively states the essential elements of the offence. A court shall, at any stage of the proceedings, amend the indictment, or a count therein as may be necessary, where it appears that the indictment or a count thereof fails to state or states defectively anything that is requisite to constitute the offence or does not negative an exception that should be negatived. It should be noted however that such amendment can only be ordered if the matters alleged in the proposed amendment are disclosed by the evidence taken on the preliminary inquiry or on the trial (s. 601(3)(b)(i) and (ii)).

6. Amendment of a count that is defective in substance. A court shall, at any stage of the proceedings, amend the indictment, or a count therein as may be necessary, where it appears that the indictment or a count thereof is in any way defective in substance, if and only if the matters to be alleged in the proposed amendment are disclosed by the evidence on the preliminary inquiry or on the trial (s. 601(3)(b)(iii)).

7. Amendment of a charge that is defective in form. A court shall, at any stage of the proceedings, amend the indictment or a count therein as may be necessary where it appears that the indictment or a count thereof is in any way defective in form (s. 601(3)(c)).

8. Amendment of a mistake in the heading of an indictment. A mistake in the heading of an indictment shall be corrected as soon as it is discovered but, whether corrected or not, is not material (s. 601(8)).

9. Procedure following the amendment of an indictment or a count thereof. An order to amend an indictment or a count therein shall be endorsed on the indictment as part of the record and the proceedings shall continue as if the indictment or count had been originally preferred as amended (s. 601(7)).

Where, in the opinion of the court, the accused has been misled or prejudiced in his defence by a variance, error or omission in an indictment or a count therein, the court may, if it is of the opinion that the misleading or prejudice may be removed by an adjournment, adjourn the proceedings to a specified day or sittings of the court, and may make such an order with respect to the payment of costs resulting from the necessity for amendment as it considers desirable (s. 601(5)).

AMMUNITION. An explosive of any class when enclosed in a case or contrivance or otherwise adapted or prepared so as to form:

  (i) a cartridge or charge for small arms, cannon, any other weapon, or for blasting.
 (ii) any safety or other fuse for blasting or shells
(iii) any tube for firing explosives
(iv) a percussion cap, detonator, shell, torpedo, war rocket or other contrivance other than a firework. (Explosives Act Regulations, C.R.C. 1978, c. 599, s. 13(1)).

AMPHETAMINES. The group of drugs which includes amphetamine sulphate, methylamphetamine and dextroamphetamine. The amphetamines are central nervous system stimulants which in therapeutic doses cause elevation of mood, alertness, increase in mental ability and reduction of appetite. In toxic doses they cause restlessness, irritability, hallucinations and panic states. Brain hemorrhage may be a terminal event (Jaffe, A Guide to Pathological Evidence, 2nd ed.).

ANALYSIS. The resolution of a thing into its elements or component parts (Jowitt's Dictionary of English Law).

Chemical analysis. Chemical analysis is the separation of compounds and elements into their constituent substances for the purpose of determining their nature (qualitative analysis) or the proportion (quantitative analysis) of the constituents; also, the determination of the nature or proportion of one or more constituents of a substance, whether separated out or not (Webster's New World Dictionary).

Analyst. 1. A person who makes an analysis or who analyzes. 2. For the purposes of ss. 254 to 262, "analyst" means a person designated by the Attorney General as an analyst for the purposes of s. 262 (s. 254(1)). 3. For the purposes of the Narcotic Control Act, "analyst" means a person designated as an analyst under the Food and Drugs Act or under the Narcotic Control Act (Narcotic Control Act, s. 2). 4. For the purposes of the Food and Drugs Act, "analyst" means any person designated as an analyst under s. 28, which states that the Minister may designate any person as an analyst for the purpose of the enforcement of the Food and Drugs Act (Food and Drugs Act, s. 2 and s. 28).

ANIMAL OFFENCES

1. *Injuring or endangering cattle*
2. *Injuring or endangering animals other than cattle*
3. *Cruelty to animals*
4. *Owning or having custody of animal or bird while prohibited*
5. *Assisting at cock fight*
6. *Keeping cockpit*

1. Injuring or endangering cattle

Section 444(a)

Every one who — wilfully — kills or maims or wounds or poisons or injures cattle — is guilty of an indictable offence.

Section 444(b)

Every one who — wilfully — places poison in such a position that it may easily be consumed by cattle — is guilty of an indictable offence.

Intent. Wilfully.

Included offences. Attempts (s. 660 and s. 662(1)(b)).

Punishment. Imprisonment for a term not exceeding 5 years (s. 444).

Release. Initial decision to release made by officer in charge or justice (s. 498).

Election. Accused may elect trial by judge and jury, judge alone, or provincial court judge (s. 536).

Evidence. No person shall be convicted of this offence where he proves that he acted with legal justification or excuse and with colour of right (s. 429(2)).

Informations

A.B., on or about the —— day of ——, 19——, at the —— of ——, in the said (territorial division), did wilfully kill [OR maim OR wound OR poison OR injure] certain cattle, to wit: (specify the particulars of the offence), contrary to s. 444(a) of the Criminal Code of Canada.

A.B., on or about the —— day of ——, 19——, at the —— of ——, in the said (territorial division), did wilfully place poison in such a position as to be easily consumed by certain cattle, to wit: (specify the particulars of the offence), contrary to s. 444(b) of the Criminal Code of Canada.

2. Injuring or endangering animals other than cattle

Section 445(a)

Every one who — wilfully and without lawful excuse — kills or maims or wounds or poisons or injures — dogs or birds or animals that are not cattle and are kept for a lawful purpose — is guilty of an offence punishable on summary conviction.

Section 445(b)

Every one who — wilfully and without lawful excuse — places poison in such a position that it may easily be consumed — by dogs

or birds or animals that are not cattle and are kept for a lawful purpose — is guilty of an offence punishable on summary conviction.

Intent. Wilfully.

Limitation period. No proceedings in respect of offences that are declared to be punishable on summary conviction shall be instituted more than 6 months after the time when the subject matter of the proceedings arose (s. 786(2) and s. 785(1)).

Included offences. Attempts (s. 660 and s. 662(1)(b)).

Punishment. A fine not exceeding $2,000, or 6 months' imprisonment, or both (s. 445 and s. 787(1)).

Release. Initial decision to release made by peace officer (s. 497).

Election. No election, summary conviction offence.

Evidence. 1. The words "kept for a lawful purpose" refer to domesticated or domestic animals and do not apply to stray animals (R. v. Deschamps (1978), 43 C.C.C. (2d) 45 (Ont. Prov. Ct.)).
2. *See also Evidence under* **1**, *above.*

Informations

A.B., on or about the —— day of ——, 19——, at the —— of ——, in the said (territorial division), did wilfully and without lawful excuse kill [OR maim OR wound OR poison OR injure] a dog [OR a bird OR (specify animal other than cattle)], that was kept for a lawful purpose to wit: (specify the particulars of the offence), contrary to s. 445(a) of the Criminal Code of Canada.

A.B., on or about the —— day of ——, 19——, at the —— of ——, in the said (territorial division), did wilfully and without lawful excuse place poison in such a position as to be easily consumed by dogs [OR birds OR (specify animals other than cattle)] that were kept for a lawful purpose, to wit: (specify the particulars of the offence), contrary to s. 445(b) of the Criminal Code of Canada.

3. Cruelty to animals

Section 446(1)(a) and (2)

Every one who — wilfully causes or, being the owner, wilfully permits to be caused — unnecessary pain or suffering or injury — to an animal or bird — commits an offence punishable on summary conviction.

Section 446(1)(b) and (2)

Every one who — by wilful neglect — causes damage or injury to animals or birds — while they are being driven or conveyed — commits an offence punishable on summary conviction.

Section 446(1)(c) and (2)

Every one who — being the owner or the person having the custody or control of a domestic animal or bird or an animal or a bird wild by nature that is in captivity — abandons it in distress — or wilfully neglects or fails to provide suitable and adequate food and water and shelter and care for it — commits an offence punishable on summary conviction.

Section 446(1)(d) and (2)

Every one who — in any manner — encourages or aids or assists — at the fighting or baiting of animals or birds — commits an offence punishable on summary conviction.

Section 446(1)(e) and (2)

Every one who — wilfully — without reasonable excuse — administers a poisonous or an injurious drug or substance — to a domestic animal or bird or an animal or a bird wild by nature that is kept in captivity — or being the owner of such an animal or bird — wilfully permits a poisonous or an injurious drug or substance to be administered to it — commits an offence punishable on summary conviction.

Section 446(1)(f) and (2)

Every one who — promotes or arranges or conducts or assists in or receives money for or takes part in — any meeting or competition or exhibition or pastime or practice or display or event — at or in the course of which captive birds are liberated by hand or trap or contrivance or any other means — for the purpose of being shot when they are liberated — commits an offence punishable on summary conviction.

Section 446(1)(g) and (2)

Every one who — being the owner or occupier, or person in charge of any premises — permits the premises or any part thereof — to be used for a purpose mentioned in s. 446(1)(f) above — commits an offence punishable on summary conviction.

Intent. Wilfully (s. 446(1)(a), (b), (c) and (e)).

Limitation period. No proceedings in respect of offences that are declared to be punishable on summary conviction shall be instituted more than 6 months after the time when the subject matter of the proceedings arose (s. 786(2) and s. 785(1)).

Included offences. Attempts (s. 660 and s. 662(1)(b)).

Punishment. A fine not exceeding $2,000, or 6 months' imprisonment, or both (s. 446(2) and s. 787(1)).

In addition to any other sentence that may be imposed for this offence, the court may make an order prohibiting the accused from owning or having the custody or control of an animal or bird during any period not exceeding 2 years (s. 446(5)).

Release. Initial decision to release made by peace officer (s. 497).

Election. No election, summary conviction offence.

Evidence. 1. For the purposes of proceedings under s. 446(1)(a) or (b) above, evidence that a person failed to exercise reasonable care or supervision of an animal or bird thereby causing it pain, suffering, damage or injury is, in the absence of any evidence to the contrary, proof that such pain, suffering, damage or injury was caused or was permitted to be caused wilfully or was caused by wilful neglect, as the case may be (s. 446(3)).
2. For the purposes of proceedings under s. 446(1)(d) above, evidence that an accused was present at the fighting or baiting of animals or birds is, in the absence of any evidence to the contrary, proof that he encouraged, aided or assisted at the fighting or baiting (s. 446(4)).
3. *See also Evidence under* **1**, *above.*

Informations

A.B., on or about the —— day of ——, 19——, at the —— of ——, in the said (territorial division), did wilfully cause [OR being the owner, did wilfully permit to be caused] unnecessary pain [OR suffering OR injury] to a bird [OR an animal], to wit: (specify the particulars of the offence), contrary to s. 446(1)(a) of the Criminal Code of Canada.

A.B., on or about the —— day of ——, 19——, at the —— of ——, in the said (territorial division), by wilful neglect did cause damage [OR injury] to animals [OR birds] while they were being driven [OR conveyed], to wit: (specify the particulars of the offence), contrary to s. 446(1)(b) of the Criminal Code of Canada.

A.B., on or about the —— day of ——, 19——, at the —— of ——, in the said (territorial division), being the owner [OR the person having the custody or control] of a domestic animal [OR bird OR an animal OR a bird wild by nature that was in captivity] did abandon it in distress [OR wilfully neglect (OR fail) to provide suitable and adequate food and water and shelter and care for such animal (OR bird)], to wit: (specify the particulars of the offence), contrary to s. 446(1)(c) of the Criminal Code of Canada.

A.B., on or about the —— day of ——, 19——, at the —— of ——, in the said (territorial division), did encourage [OR aid OR assist] at the fighting [OR baiting] of an animal [OR bird], to wit: (specify the particulars of the offence), contrary to s. 446(1)(d) of the Criminal Code of Canada.

A.B., on or about the —— day of ——, 19——, at the —— of ——, in the said (territorial division), did wilfully and without reasonable excuse, administer [OR being the owner thereof did permit to be administered] a poisonous [OR an injurious] drug [OR substance] to a domestic animal [OR bird OR an animal OR a bird wild by nature that was kept in captivity], to wit: (specify the particulars of the offence), contrary to s. 446(1)(e) of the Criminal Code of Canada.

A.B., on or about the —— day of ——, 19——, at the —— of ——, in the said (territorial division), did promote [OR arrange OR conduct OR assist in OR receive money for OR take part in] any meeting [OR competition OR exhibition OR pastime OR practice OR display OR event] at [OR in the course of] which captive birds were liberated by hand [OR trap OR contrivance OR (specify other means)] for the purpose of being shot while they were liberated, to wit: (specify the particulars of the offence), contrary to s. 446(1)(f) of the Criminal Code of Canada.

A.B., on or about the —— day of ——, 19——, at the —— of ——, in the said (territorial division), being the owner [OR occupier OR person in charge] of (specify the premises) did permit the said [OR part of the said] premises to be used for any meeting [OR competition OR exhibition OR pastime OR practice OR display OR event] at [OR in the course of] which captive birds were liberated for the purpose of being shot while they were liberated, to wit: (specify the particulars of the offence), contrary to s. 446(1)(g) of the Criminal Code of Canada.

4. Owning or having custody of animal or bird while prohibited — Section 446(5) and (6)

Every one who — having been convicted of an offence under s. 446(1) (cruelty to animals) — and having been prohibited by an order of the court from owning or having the custody or control of

ANIMAL OFFENCES 51

an animal or bird during any period not exceeding 2 years — is in breach of such order — is guilty of an offence punishable on summary conviction.

Limitation period. No proceedings in respect of offences that are declared to be punishable on summary conviction shall be instituted more than 6 months after the time when the subject matter of the proceedings arose (s. 786(2) and s. 785(1)).

Included offences. Attempts (s. 660 and s. 662(1)(b)).

Punishment. A fine not exceeding $2,000, or 6 months' imprisonment, or both (s. 446(6) and s. 787(1)).

Release. Initial decision to release made by peace officer (s. 497).

Election. No election, summary conviction offence.

Evidence. See Evidence under **1**, *above.*

Informations

A.B., on or about the —— day of ——, 19——, at the —— of ——, in the said (territorial division), did own [OR have the custody (OR control)] of an animal [OR bird] while prohibited from doing so by an order of the court made under s. 446(5) of the Criminal Code, to wit: (specify the particulars of the offence), contrary to s. 446(6) of the Criminal Code of Canada.

5. Assisting at cock fight — Section 446(1)(d) and (2)

Every one who — in any manner — encourages or aids or assists at — the fighting or baiting of animals or birds — is guilty of an offence punishable on summary conviction.

Limitation period. No proceedings in respect of offences that are declared to be punishable on summary conviction shall be instituted more than 6 months after the time when the subject matter of the proceedings arose (s. 786(2) and 785(1)).

Included offences. Attempts (s. 660 and s. 662(1)(b)).

Punishment. A fine not exceeding $2,000, or 6 months' imprisonment, or both (s. 446(2) and s. 787(1)).

Release. Initial decision to release made by peace officer (s. 497).

Election. No election, summary conviction offence.

Evidence. See Evidence under **1**, *above.*

Informations

A.B., on or about the —— day of ——, 19——, at the —— of ——, in the said (territorial division), did encourage [OR aid OR assist at] the fighting [OR baiting] of animals [OR birds], to wit: (specify the particulars of the offence), contrary to s. 446(1)(d) of the Criminal Code of Canada.

6. Keeping cockpit — Section 447(1)

Every one who — builds or makes or maintains or keeps a cockpit — on premises that he owns or occupies — is guilty of an offence punishable on summary conviction.

Every one who — allows a cockpit to be built or made or maintained or kept — on premises that he owns or occupies — is guilty of an offence punishable on summary conviction.

Limitation period. No proceedings in respect of offences that are declared to be punishable on summary conviction shall be instituted more than 6 months after the time when the subject matter of the proceedings arose (s. 786(2) and s. 785(1)).

Included offences. Attempts (s. 660 and s. 662(1)(b)).

Punishment. A fine not exceeding $2,000, or 6 months' imprisonment, or both (s. 447(1) and s. 787(1)).

Release. Initial decision to release made by peace officer (s. 497).

Election. No election, summary conviction offence.

Evidence. A peace officer who finds cocks in a cockpit or on premises where a cockpit is located shall seize them and take them before a justice who shall order them to be destroyed (s. 447(2)).

Informations

A.B., on or about the —— day of ——, 19——, at the —— of ——, in the said (territorial division), did build [OR make OR maintain OR keep] a cockpit on premises that he owned [OR occupied], to wit: (specify the particulars of the offence), contrary to s. 447(1) of the Criminal Code of Canada.

A.B., on or about the —— day of ——, 19——, at the —— of ——, in the said (territorial division), did allow a cockpit to be built [OR made OR maintained OR kept] on premises that he owned [OR occupied] to wit: (specify the particulars of the offence), contrary to s. 447(1) of the Criminal Code of Canada.

ANIMUS. An intent or intention (Latin). ***Animus furandi.*** The intent to steal (Latin). ***Animus possidendi.*** The intention of remaining (Latin). ***Animus quo.*** The intent with which (Latin). ***Animus recipiendi.*** The intention of receiving (Latin). ***Animus restituendi.*** The intention of restoring (Latin). ***Animus revertendi.*** The intention of returning (Latin). ***Animus revocandi.*** The intention to revoke (Latin).

ANTE. Before (Latin). ***Ante litem motam.*** Before litigation was initiated; before the controversy arose (Latin), (when the declarant had no motive not to tell the truth).

APPEARANCE NOTICE

1. *Definition*
2. *Issued in circumstances when arrest without warrant not permitted*
3. *Issued after arrest without warrant*
4. *Failure to appear or to comply with appearance notice*
5. *Period for which appearance notice continues in force*
6. *Proof of issue*
7. *Signature of accused*
8. *Valid if issued on a holiday*
9. *Effect of new information charging the same offence or an included offence*

1. Definition. A notice in Form 9 issued by a peace officer (s. 493). The appearance notice is issued to a person not yet charged with an offence. The notice sets out the name of the accused and the substance of the offence that the accused is alleged to have committed. The appearance notice requires the accused to attend court at a time and place stated therein and to attend thereafter as required by the court in order to be dealt with according to law (s. 501(1)). An appearance issued by a peace officer may, where the accused is alleged to have committed an indictable offence, require the accused to appear at a time and place stated therein (a police station) for the purposes of the Identification of Criminals Act (s. 501(3)). Finally, the appearance notice sets out the text of s. 145(5) and s. 502 which state that failure to attend at court in accordance with the appearance notice is an offence and failure to attend at a police station in accordance with the appearance notice will result in the issue of a warrant for his arrest, even where the appearance notice states defectively the substance of the alleged offence (s. 145(6)).

2. Issued in circumstances when arrest without warrant not permitted. A peace officer may issue an appearance notice in certain circumstances where the peace officer is not permitted to arrest a person without warrant, i.e. for the following offences: (1) an indictable offence for which the jurisdiction of a provincial court judge to try an offence is absolute (s. 553); (2) an offence for which a person may be presented by indictment or for which he is punishable on summary conviction; or (3) an offence punishable on summary conviction (s. 495(2)(d)). The circumstances referred to include any case where a peace officer believes, on reasonable grounds, that the public interest may be satisfied without so arresting the person (s. 495(2)(d)), and where the peace officer has no reasonable grounds to believe that the person will fail to attend in court (s. 495(2)(e)). In determining whether the public interest is or is not likely to be satisfied, the peace officer is to consider the need to establish the identity of the person, the need to secure or preserve evidence of or relating to the offence, and the need to prevent the continuation or repetition of the offence or the commission of another offence (s. 495(2)(d)(i), (ii) and (iii)).

3. Issued after arrest without warrant. Unless there is a reason to detain a person in custody, a peace officer shall, as soon as practicable, either release a person from custody with the intention of compelling his appearance by way of a summons or issue an appearance notice to a person without warrant for the following offences: (1) an indictable offence for which the jurisdiction of a provincial court judge to try the offence is absolute (s. 553); (2) an offence for which the person may be prosecuted by indictment or for which he is punishable on summary conviction; or (3) an offence punishable on summary conviction (s. 497(1)). A peace officer may detain the person in custody in the following circumstances: (1) where he believes on reasonable grounds that it is necessary in the public interest, having regard to all the circumstances including the need to establish the identity of the person, the need to secure or preserve evidence of or relating to the offence, or the need to prevent the continuation or repetition of the offence or the commission of another offence (s. 497(1)(f)); (2) where he believes on reasonable grounds that, if the person is released by him from custody, the person will fail to attend in court in order to be dealt with according to law (s. 497(1)(g)); or (3) where the person has been arrested without warrant for an indictable offence alleged to have been committed in Canada outside the province in which he was arrested (s. 497(2) and s. 503(3)).

4. Failure to appear or to comply with appearance notice. It is an offence to fail to appear or to comply with an appearance notice. *For particulars of this offence, see ESCAPES AND RESCUES.*

5. Period for which appearance notice continues in force. An appearance notice continues in force until the trial of the person and, if found guilty, until a sentence is imposed on the accused unless, at the time the accused is determined to be guilty, the court, judge or justice orders that the accused be taken into custody pending sentence (s. 523(1)).

6. Proof of issue. The issue of an appearance notice by any peace officer may be proved by the oral evidence, given under oath, of the peace officer who issued it or by the peace officer's affidavit made before a justice or other person authorized to administer oaths or take affidavits (s. 501(5)).

7. Signature of accused. An accused shall be requested to sign in duplicate his appearance notice and, whether or not he complies with that request, one of the duplicates shall be given to the accused. However, if the accused fails or refuses to sign, the lack of his signature does not invalidate the appearance notice (s. 501(4)).

8. Valid if issued on a holiday. An appearance notice may be issued on a holiday (s. 20).

9. Effect of new information charging the same offence or an included offence. An appearance notice applies in respect of a new information charging the same offence or an included offence that is received after the appearance notice has been issued (s. 523(1.1)).

APPROVED CONTAINER. For the purposes of ss. 254 to 258, "approved container" means
    (a) in respect of breath samples, a container of a kind that is designed to receive a sample of the breath of a person for analysis and is approved as suitable for the purposes of s. 258 by order of the Attorney General of Canada; and
    (b) in respect of blood samples, a container of a kind that is designed to receive a sample of blood of a person for analysis and is approved as suitable for the purposes of s. 258 by order of the Attorney General of Canada (s. 254(1)).
    Containers approved as suitable for this purpose include the following:
    Vacutainer XF947 (SI/85-199 (Gaz. 27/11/85, p. 4690)).

APPROVED INSTRUMENT. For the purposes of ss. 254 to 258, "approved instrument" means an instrument of a kind that is designed to receive and make an analysis of a sample of the breath of a person in order to measure the concentration of alcohol in the blood of that person and is approved as suitable for the purposes of s. 258 by order of the Attorney General of Canada (s. 254(1)).

Instruments approved as suitable for this purpose include the following:

Breathalyzer, Model 800
Breathalyzer, Model 900
Breathalyzer, Model 900A
Intoximeter Mark IV
Alcolmeter AE-DI
Intoxilyzer 4011AS
Alcotest 7110
Intoxilyzer 5000 C

(SI/85-201 (Gaz. 27/11/85, p. 4692); SI/92-105 (Gaz. 17/6/92, p. 2577); SI/92-167 (Gaz. 23/9/92, p. 3807)).

APPROVED SCREENING DEVICE. For the purposes of ss. 254 to 258, "approved screening device" means a device of a kind that is designed to ascertain the presence of alcohol in the blood of a person and that is approved for the purposes of s. 254 by order of the Attorney General of Canada (s. 254(1)).

Devices approved as suitable for this purpose are:

A.L.E.R.T., Model J3A
Alcolmeter S-L2
Alco-Sûr
Alcotest 7410 PA3

(SI/85-200 (Gaz. 27/11/85, p. 4691); SI/88-136 (Gaz. 28/9/88, p. 4074); SOR/93-263 (Gaz. 2/6/93, p. 2403)).

ARRAIGNMENT. The arraignment of a prisoner consists of calling on him by name, reading to him the indictment, demanding of him whether he is guilty or not guilty and entering his plea (Jowitt's Dictionary of English Law).

ARREST

1. *What constitutes arrest*
2. *What constitutes detention*
3. *What constitutes imprisonment*
4. *Right to life, liberty and security of the person*
5. *Right not to be arbitrarily detained or imprisoned*
6. *Rights of person arrested*
7. *Habeas corpus*
8. *Citizen's authority to arrest*

9. *Peace officer's authority to arrest without a warrant*
10. *Peace officer's authority to arrest with a warrant*
11. *Arrested person detained in custody to be brought before a justice*
12. *Use of force in making an arrest*
13. *Arrest of wrong person*
14. *Arrest of young persons*
15. *Arrest pursuant to provincial statutes*
16. *Arrest pursuant to municipal by-laws*

1. What constitutes "arrest"

In general an arrest is constituted by a physical seizure or touching of the arrested person's body, with a view to his detention.

However, there is no need for an actual seizing or touching to constitute an arrest. There may be an arrest by mere words, by saying "I arrest you" without any touching, provided that the accused submits and goes with the officer.

An arrest is constituted when any form of words is used, which, in the circumstances of the case, is calculated to bring to the accused's notice, and does so, that he is under compulsion, and he thereafter submits to compulsion. It all depends on the circumstances of the particular case whether a person has been arrested.

No formula will suit every case and it may well be that different procedures might have to be followed with different persons, depending on their age, intellectual qualities, physical or mental disabilities. There is no magic formula; only the obligation to make it plain to the suspect by what is said and done that he is no longer a free man (Archbold, Criminal Pleading, Evidence and Practice).

2. What constitutes "detention"

A restraint of liberty other than arrest. There is a "detention" when a police officer or other agent of the State assumes control over a person by a demand or a direction which may have significant legal consequences and which prevents or impedes access to counsel.

Detention may be effected without the application or threat of application of physical restraint if the person concerned submits or acquiesces in the deprivation of liberty and reasonably believes that the choice to do otherwise does not exist.

An example of the detention of a person is a demand to accompany the police officer to a police station and to submit to a breathalyzer test (R. v. Therens (1985), 18 C.C.C. (3d) 481 (S.C.C.)).

3. What constitutes "imprisonment"

The term imprisonment is most commonly used to refer to confinement or detention in a prison as a punishment. The term also refers to the restraint of a person's liberty of movement (David M. Walker, The Oxford Companion to Law).

4. Right to life, liberty and security of the person

The Canadian Charter of Rights and Freedoms provides that every one has the right to life, liberty and security of the person and the right not to be deprived thereof except in accordance with the principles of fundamental justice (Charter of Rights and Freedoms, s. 7).

5. Right not to be arbitrarily detained or imprisoned

The Canadian Charter of Rights and Freedoms provides that everyone has the right not to be arbitrarily detained or imprisoned (Charter of Rights and Freedoms, s. 9).

6. Rights of person arrested

Every one has the right on arrest or detention to be informed promptly of the reasons therefore (Charter of Rights and Freedoms, s. 10(a)).

Every one has the right on arrest or detention to retain and instruct counsel without delay (Charter, s. 10(b)).

Every one has the right on arrest or detention to be informed of his right to retain and instruct counsel without delay (Charter, s. 10(b)). The right to instruct counsel means the right to consult in private without interference or without being overheard. If that right is not given to a person, the courts have held that his right to counsel has been denied (R. v. Penner (1973), 12 C.C.C. (2d) 468 (Man. C.A.)).

The failure by a police officer to respect these rights may have the effect of helping the arrested person avoid the punishment that he may deserve. This is because the Charter of Rights and Freedoms provides as follows:

1. Where a court concludes that evidence was obtained in a manner that infringed or denied any rights or freedoms guaranteed by the Charter, the evidence shall be excluded if it is established that, having regard to all the circumstances, the admission of it in the proceedings

would bring the administration of justice into disrepute (Charter, s. 24(2)).

2. Every one whose rights or freedoms, as guaranteed by the Charter, have been infringed or denied may apply to a court of competent jurisdiction to obtain such remedy as the court considers appropriate and just in the circumstances (Charter, s. 24(1)).

3. In short, it isn't worth it to deny a person being arrested his rights under the Charter.

7. Habeas corpus

The Charter of Rights and Freedoms provides that everyone has the right on arrest or detention to have the validity of the detention determined by way of habeas corpus and to be released if the detention is not lawful (Charter of Rights and Freedoms, s. 10(c)). *See also HABEAS CORPUS.*

8. Citizen's authority to arrest

Person found committing an indictable offence. Anyone may arrest without warrant any person that he finds committing either an indictable offence (s. 494(1)(a)) or a hybrid offence (Interpretation Act, s. 34(1)(a)).

The courts have held that the person carrying out the arrest must have witnessed the commission of the offence himself (R. v. Dean (1966), 47 C.R. 311 (Ont. C.A.); R. v. Kelly (1970), 4 C.C.C. 191 (Ont. C.A.); R. v. Vance (1980), 10 C.R. (3d) 1 (Y.T. C.A.)).

Person found committing a criminal offence on or in relation to property. Anyone who is the owner of property, or a person in the lawful possession of property, may arrest without warrant a person whom he finds committing a criminal offence on or in relation to that property (s. 494(2)(a)). A person authorized by the owner, or a person authorized by a person in lawful possession of property, has the same authority to arrest (s. 494(2)(b)).

Fresh pursuit. Anyone may arrest without warrant any person that he believes on reasonable grounds has committed a criminal offence and is escaping from and is being freshly pursued by persons who have lawful authority to arrest that person (s. 494(1)(b)).

The courts have held that the term "criminal offence" includes both indictable and summary conviction offences (R. v. Dean (1966), 47 C.R. 311 (Ont. C.A.)).

Person found committing a breach of the peace. Every one who witnesses a breach of the peace is justified in interfering to prevent the continuance or renewal thereof and may detain any person who commits or is about to join in or to renew the breach of the peace, for the purpose of giving him into the custody of a peace officer, if he uses no more force than is reasonably necessary to prevent the continuance or renewal of the breach of the peace or than is reasonably proportioned to the danger to be apprehended from the continuance or renewal of the breach of the peace (s. 30).

The courts have held that, in order to commit "a breach of the peace", one must commit an offence (Frey v. Fedoruk, [1950] S.C.R. 517).

Duty of citizen making an arrest. Anyone other than a peace officer who arrests a person without warrant shall forthwith deliver the person arrested to a peace officer (s. 494(3)). By "forthwith" is meant as soon as is reasonably practical under all the circumstances (R. v. Cunningham and Ritchie (1979), 49 C.C.C. (2d) 390 (Man. Co. Ct.)).

It is the duty of every one who arrests a person, with or without a warrant, to give notice to that person, where it is feasible to do so, of (a) the process or warrant under which he makes the arrest, or (b) the reason for the arrest (s. 29(2)). Failure to comply with this duty does not of itself deprive the person who makes the arrest of protection from criminal responsibility (s. 29(3)).

9. Peace officer's authority to arrest without a warrant

Authority to arrest of a private citizen. A peace officer has all the powers of arrest of a private citizen (R. v. Huff (1980), 50 C.C.C. (2d) 324 (Alta. C.A.)). A peace officer is also given special powers of arrest because of his status as a peace officer.

Person who has committed an indictable offence. A peace officer may arrest without warrant a person who has committed an indictable offence (s. 495(1)(a)).

Person believed to have committed an indictable offence. A peace officer may also arrest without warrant a person who the peace officer believes, on reasonable grounds, has committed an indictable offence (s. 495(1)(a)).

The courts held that a peace officer may acquire his belief through information received from others (R. v. Biron, [1976] 2 S.C.R. 56). A peace officer must take into account all of the information available to him; he may disregard only what he has good reason for believing is not reliable (A.G. Que. v. Chartier, [1979] 1 S.C.R. 195).

Person about to commit an indictable offence. A peace officer may arrest without warrant a person who, on reasonable grounds, the peace officer believes is about to commit an indictable offence (s. 495(1)(a)).

The offence need not be commenced or even attempted. The courts have held that an arrest under s. 495(1)(a) was legal where a peace officer believed that an impaired person was about to enter a motor vehicle and drive it away, thus committing the offence of impaired driving (R. v. Beaudette (1957), 118 C.C.C. 295 (Ont. C.A.)).

A peace officer or an officer in charge having the custody of a person who has been arrested without warrant as a person about to commit an indictable offence shall release that person unconditionally as soon as practicable after he is satisfied that the continued detention of that person is no longer necessary in order to prevent the commission by him of an indictable offence (s. 503(4)).

Person found committing a "criminal" offence. A peace officer may arrest without warrant a person whom he finds committing a criminal offence (s. 495(1)(b)). A criminal offence includes both an indictable offence and a summary conviction offence (R. v. Biron, [1976] 2 S.C.R. 56).

Summary conviction offence. The power of a peace officer to arrest a person without warrant with regard to a summary conviction offence is restricted to a person that the peace officer finds committing such an offence (s. 495(1)(b)).

Person for whom valid warrant outstanding. A peace officer may arrest without warrant a person in respect of whom he has reasonable grounds to believe that a warrant of arrest or committal is in force within the territorial jurisdiction in which the person is found (s. 495(1)(c)).

Accused person in breach of interim release orders. A peace officer may arrest without warrant an accused who the peace officer believes on reasonable grounds has contravened or is about to contravene any summons, appearance notice, promise to appear, undertaking or recognizance that was issued or given to him or entered into by him (s. 524(2)(a)).

A peace officer may arrest without warrant an accused who the peace officer believes on reasonable grounds has committed an indictable offence after any summons, appearance notice, promise to appear, undertaking or recognizance was issued or given to him or entered into by him (s. 524(2)(b)).

A peace officer may arrest without warrant an accused who has been released from custody by a judge and who the peace officer believes on reasonable grounds has contravened or is about to contravene the undertaking or recognizance on which he has been released (s. 525(6)(a)).

A peace officer may arrest without warrant an accused who has been released from custody by a judge and who the peace officer believes on reasonable grounds has, after his release from custody on his undertaking or recognizance, committed an indictable offence (s. 525(6)(b)).

Person keeping common gaming house or found therein. A peace officer may, whether or not he is acting under a warrant, take into custody any person whom he finds keeping a common gaming house and any person whom he finds therein and shall bring those persons before a justice having jurisdiction, to be dealt with according to the law (s. 199(2)).

Duty of peace officer making an arrest without a warrant. It is the duty of every one who arrests a person, whether with or without a warrant, to give notice to that person, where it is feasible to do so, of (a) the process or warrant under which he makes the arrest, or (b) the reason for the arrest (s. 29(2)). Failure to comply with this duty does not of itself deprive the person who makes the arrest of protection from criminal responsibility (s. 29(3)).

Breach of the peace. Every peace officer who witnesses a breach of the peace and every one who lawfully assists him is justified in arresting any person whom he finds committing the breach of the peace or who, on reasonable grounds, he believes is about to join in or renew the breach of the peace (s. 31(1)).

Every peace officer is justified in receiving into custody any person who is given into his charge as having been a party to a breach of the peace by one who has, or who on reasonable grounds he believes has, witnessed a breach of the peace (s. 31(2)).

Limitation on peace officer's authority to arrest without a warrant. A peace officer's power to arrest without a warrant is restricted by s. 495(2) which provides that the peace officer shall not arrest a person for certain offences where the public interest may be satisfied without an arrest and where he has no reasonable grounds to believe that the accused will fail to attend in court.

The offences referred to in s. 495(2) include: 1. an indictable offence within the absolute jurisdiction of a provincial court judge (s. 553); 2. an offence for which the person may be prosecuted by indictment or for which he is punishable on summary conviction; and 3. an offence punishable on summary conviction.

Limitation on peace officer's authority to arrest with warrant. In determining whether the public interest may be satisfied without an arrest, the peace officer must have regard to all the circumstances, including the need to establish the identity of the person, secure or preserve evidence of or relating to the offence, or prevent the continuation or repetition of the offence or the commission of another offence (s. 495(2)).

Release by peace officer of person arrested without warrant by him. Unless it is in the public interest to do otherwise, a peace officer, having the custody of a person arrested by him without a warrant for less serious offences shall, as soon as practicable, either release the person from custody with the intention of compelling his appearance by way of a summons, or issue an appearance notice to the person and then release him. The less serious offences referred to include an indictable offence within the absolute jurisdiction of a provincial court judge (s. 553), an offence for which the person may be prosecuted by indictment or for which he is punishable on summary conviction, or an offence punishable on summary conviction (s. 497). It would be in the public interest to detain the person in custody where it is necessary to establish the identity of the person, to secure or preserve evidence of or relating to the offence, or to prevent the continuation or repetition of the offence or the commission of another offence (s. 497(1)(f)).

Release by peace officer of person arrested without warrant by him. A peace officer having the custody of a person who has been arrested without warrant as a person about to commit an indictable offence shall release that person unconditionally as soon as practicable after he is satisfied that the continued detention of that person in custody is no longer necessary in order to prevent the commission by him of an indictable offence (s. 503(3)).

10. Peace officer's authority to arrest with a warrant.

What is a warrant for arrest. A warrant for arrest is a written order of a court, commanding peace officers in the jurisdiction of the court, to forthwith arrest the person named in the warrant, for the offence set out in the warrant, for the purpose of bringing the person before the court to be dealt with according to law (Form 7).

Duties of peace officer making an arrest with a warrant. It is the duty of every one who executes a process or warrant to have it with him, where it is feasible to do so, and to produce it when requested to do so (s. 29(1)).

It is the duty of every one who arrests a person, whether with or without a warrant, to give notice to that person, where it is feasible to do so of (a) the process or warrant under which he makes the arrest or (b) the reason for the arrest (s. 29(2)).

The failure to comply with these duties does not of itself deprive a person who executes a process or warrant of protection from criminal responsibility (s. 29(3)).

When an arrest is made by a peace officer pursuant to a warrant, but without possession of the warrant, the duty of the arresting officer imposed by s. 29(2) is fully discharged by the peace officer telling the arrested person that the reason for his arrest is the existence of an outstanding warrant for his arrest (Gamracy v. R., [1974] S.C.R. 604).

11. Arrested person detained in custody to be brought before a justice

A peace officer who arrests any person, with or without warrant, or who receives an arrested person, and has detained that person, shall take him before a justice (a) where one is available, within a period of 24 hours, as soon as it is practical and without unreasonable delay, or (b) where one is not available, as soon as possible, unless the peace officer or officer in charge releases the suspect beforehand (s. 503(1)).

12. Use of force in making an arrest

A peace officer who is proceeding lawfully to arrest, with or without warrant, any person for an offence for which that person may be arrested without warrant, is justified, if the person to be arrested takes flight to avoid arrest, in using as much force as is necessary to prevent the escape by flight, unless the escape can be prevented by reasonable means in a less violent manner (s. 25(4)).

Every one lawfully assisting the peace officer has the same authority as the peace officer to use force in making an arrest (s. 25(4)).

Every one who is authorized by law to use force is criminally responsible for any excess thereof according to the nature and quality of the act that constitutes the excess (s. 26).

13. Arrest of wrong person

Protection from criminal responsibility. Where a person is authorized to execute a warrant to arrest believes, in good faith and on reasonable grounds, that the person whom he arrests is the person named in the warrant, he is protected from criminal responsibility in respect thereof to the same extent as if that person were the person named in the warrant (s. 28(1)).

Where a person is authorized to execute a warrant to arrest, every one who, being called upon to assist him, believes that the person in whose arrest he is called upon to assist is the person named in the warrant, is protected from criminal responsibility in respect thereof to the same extent as if that person were the person named in the warrant (s. 28(2)(a)).

Where a person is authorized to execute a warrant to arrest, every keeper of a prison who is required to receive and detain a person who he believes has been arrested under the warrant, is protected from criminal responsibility in respect thereof to the same extent as if that person were the person named in the warrant (s. 28(2)(b)).

14. Arrest of young persons

Young persons have rights and freedoms in their own right, including those stated in the Canadian Charter of Rights and Freedoms or in the Canadian Bill of Rights (Young Offenders Act, s. 3(1)(f)).

In particular, every young person who is arrested or detained shall, forthwith on his arrest or detention, be advised by the arresting officer or the officer in charge, as the case may be, of his right to be represented by counsel and shall be given an opportunity to obtain counsel (Young Offenders Act, s. 11(2)).

Application of Criminal Code. Except to the extent that they are inconsistent with or excluded by the Young Offenders Act, all the provisions of the Criminal Code apply, with such modifications as the circumstances require, in respect of offences alleged to have been committed by young persons (Young Offenders Act, s. 51).

Designated place of detention. A young person who is arrested and detained with or without a warrant shall, be detained in a place of temporary detention designated as such by the Lieutenant Governor in Council of the appropriate province or his delegate or in a place within a class of such places so designated (Young Offenders Act, s. 7(1)).

Certain proceedings may be taken before justices. Any proceedings that may be carried out before a justice under the Criminal Code, other than a plea, a trial or an adjudication, may be carried out before such justice in respect of an offence alleged to have been committed by a young person, and any process that may be issued by a justice under the Criminal Code may be issued by such justice in respect of an offence alleged to have been committed by a young person (Young Offenders Act, s. 6).

15. Arrest pursuant to provincial statutes

A number of provincial statutes provide for arrests with or without a warrant for certain offences. Reference should be made to the statute creating the offence in order to ascertain the powers of arrest available to a peace officer.

16. Arrest pursuant to municipal by-laws

As a general rule, there is no power to arrest for an offence created by a municipal by-law.

ARSON

1. *Disregard for human life*
2. *Causing bodily harm*
3. *Damage to property*
4. Own property
5. *For fraudulent purpose*
6. *Negligence*
7. *Possession of incendiary material*
8. *False alarm of fire*

1. Disregard for human life — Section 433(a)

Every person who — intentionally or recklessly — causes damage — by fire or explosion — to property — whether or not that person owns the property — where the person knows that or is reckless with respect to whether the property is inhabited or occupied — is guilty of an indictable offence.

Intent. 1. "Intentionally or recklessly" causes damage to property; and, 2. "knows that or is reckless with respect to whether the property is inhabited or occupied".

Included offences. Attempts (s. 660 and s. 662(1)(b)).

Punishment. Imprisonment for life (s. 433).

Release. Initial decision to release made by justice (s. 515(1)).

Election. Accused may elect trial by judge and jury, judge alone, or provincial court judge (s. 536).

Evidence. It is not necessary that the person who caused the damage be the owner of the property (s. 433).

Informations

A.B., on or about the —— day of ——, 19——, at the —— of ——, in the said (territorial division), intentionally [OR recklessly] did cause damage by fire [OR explosion] to property, where A.B. knew that [OR was reckless with respect to whether] the property was inhabited [OR occupied], to wit: (specify the particulars of the offence), contrary to s. 433(a) of the Criminal Code of Canada.

2. Causing bodily harm — Section 433(b)

Every person who — intentionally or recklessly — causes damage — by fire or explosion — to property — where the fire or explosion causes bodily harm to another person — is guilty of an indictable offence.

Intent. Intentionally or recklessly.

Included offences. Attempts (s. 660 and s. 662(1)(b)).

Punishment. Imprisonment for life (s. 433).

Release. Initial decision to release made by justice (s. 515(1)).

Election. Accused may elect trial by judge and jury, judge alone, or provincial court judge (s. 536).

Evidence. It is not necessary that the person who caused the damage be the owner of the property (s. 433).

Informations

A.B., on or about the —— day of ——, 19——, at the —— of ——, in the said (territorial division), intentionally [OR recklessly] did cause damage by fire [OR explosion] to property where the fire [OR explosion] causes bodily harm to C.D., to wit: (specify the particulars of the offence), contrary to s. 433(b) of the Criminal Code of Canada.

ARSON

3. Damage to property — Section 434

Every person who — intentionally or recklessly — causes damage — by fire or explosion — to property that is not wholly owned by that person — is guilty of an indictable offence.

Intent. Intentionally or recklessly.

Included offences. Attempts (s. 660 and s. 662(1)(b)).

Punishment. Imprisonment for a term not exceeding 14 years (s. 434).

Release. Initial decision to release made by justice (s. 515(1)).

Election. Accused may elect trial by judge and jury, judge alone, or provincial court judge (s. 536).

Informations

A.B., on or about the —— day of ——, 19——, at the —— of ——, in the said (territorial division), did intentionally [OR recklessly] cause damage by fire [OR explosion] to property not wholly owned by A.B., to wit: (specify the particulars of the offence), contrary to s. 434 of the Criminal Code of Canada.

4. Own property — Section 434.1

Every person who — intentionally or recklessly — causes damage — by fire or explosion — to property — that is owned in whole or in part by that person — where the fire or explosion seriously threatens the health, safety or property of another person — is guilty of an indictable offence.

Intent. Intentionally or recklessly.

Included offences. Attempts (s. 660 and s. 662(1)(b)).

Punishment. Imprisonment for a term not exceeding 14 years (s. 434.1).

Release. Initial decision to release made by justice (s. 515(1)).

Election. Accused may elect trial by judge and jury, judge alone, or provincial court judge (s. 536).

Informations

A.B., on or about the —— day of ——, 19——, at the —— of ——, in the said (territorial division), did intentionally [OR recklessly] cause damage by fire [OR explosion] to property owned in whole [OR in part] by A.B. thereby threatening the health [OR safety OR property] of C.D., to wit: (specify the particulars of the offence), contrary to s. 434.1 of the Criminal Code of Canada.

5. For fraudulent purpose — Section 435(1)

Every person who — with intent to defraud any other person — causes damage — by fire or explosion — to property — is guilty of an indictable offence.

Intent. Intent to defraud any other person.

Included offences. Attempts (s. 660 and s. 662(1)(b)).

Punishment. Imprisonment for a term not exceeding 10 years (s. 435(1)).

Release. Initial decision to release made by justice (s. 515(1)).

Election. Accused may elect trial by judge and jury, judge alone, or provincial court judge (s. 536).

Evidence. 1. It is irrelevant whether or not the person who caused the damage owns, in whole or in part, the property (s. 435(1)).
2. The fact that the person charged with the offence was the holder of or was named as a beneficiary under a policy of fire insurance relating to the property in respect of which the offence is alleged to have been committed is a fact from which intent to defraud may be inferred by the court (s. 435(2)).

Sufficiency of count. No count that alleges false pretences, fraud or any attempt or conspiracy by fraudulent means is insufficient by reason only that it does not set out in detail the nature of the false pretence, fraud or fraudulent means (s. 586).

Informations

A.B., on or about the —— day of ——, 19——, at the —— of ——, in the said (territorial division), did with intent to defraud C.D. cause damage by fire [OR explosion] to property, to wit: (specify the particulars of the offence), contrary to s. 435(1) of the Criminal Code of Canada.

6. Negligence — Section 436(1)

Every person who — either owns property in whole or in part or controls property — as a result of a marked departure in the standard of care that a reasonably prudent person would use to prevent or control the spread of fires or to prevent explosions —

is a cause of a fire or explosion in that property — that causes bodily harm to another person or damage to property — is guilty of an indictable offence.

Included offences. Attempts (s. 660 and s. 662(1)(b)).

Punishment. Imprisonment for a term not exceeding 5 years (s. 436(1)).

Release. Initial decision to release made by justice (s. 515(1))

Election. Accused may elect trial by judge and jury, judge alone, or provincial court judge (s. 536).

Evidence. The fact that a person has failed to comply with any law respecting the prevention or control of fires or explosions in the property is a fact from which a marked departure from the standard of care may be inferred by the court (s. 436(2)).

Informations

A.B., on or about the —— day of ——, 19——, at the —— of ——, in the said (territorial division), being the owner [OR part owner OR person in control] of (specify property owned or controlled), did cause a fire [OR explosion] in the said property, as a result of a marked departure from the standard of care that a reasonably prudent person would use to prevent or control the spread of fires [OR explosions], that caused bodily harm to C.D. [OR damage to property], to wit: (specify the particulars of the offence), contrary to s. 436(1) of the Criminal Code of Canada.

7. Possession of incendiary material — Section 436.1

Every person who — possesses — any incendiary material or incendiary device or explosive substance — for the purpose of committing arson — is guilty of an indictable offence.

Intent. For the purpose of committing arson.

Included offences. Attempts (s. 660 and s. 662(1)(b)).

Punishment. Imprisonment for a term not exceeding five years (s. 436.1).

Release. Initial decision to release made by officer in charge or justice (s. 498).

Election. Accused may elect trial by judge and jury, judge alone, or provincial court judge (s. 536).

Informations

A.B., on or about the —— day of ——, 19——, at the —— of ——, in the said (territorial division), did have in his possession incendiary material [OR an incendiary device OR an explosive substance] for the purpose of committing an offence under s. 433 [OR s. 434 OR s. 435 OR s. 436] of the Criminal Code, to wit: (specify the particulars of the offence), contrary to s. 436.1 of the Criminal Code of Canada.

8. False alarm of fire — Section 437

Every one who — wilfully — without reasonable cause — by outcry or ringing bells or using a fire alarm or telephone or telegraph — or in any other manner — makes or circulates or causes to be made or circulated — an alarm of fire — is guilty of an indictable offence or an offence punishable on summary conviction.

Intent. Wilfully.

Limitation period. No proceedings in respect of offences that are declared to be punishable on summary conviction shall be instituted more than 6 months after the time when the subject matter of the proceedings arose (s. 786(2) and s. 785(1)).

Included offences. Attempts (s. 660 and s. 662(1)(b)).

Punishment. On indictment, imprisonment for a term not exceeding 2 years (s. 437(a)). On summary conviction, a fine not exceeding $2,000, or 6 months' imprisonment, or both (s. 437(b) and s. 787(1)).

Release. Initial decision to release made by peace officer (s. 497).

Election. On indictment, accused may elect trial by judge and jury, judge alone, or provincial court judge (s. 536). On summary conviction, no election.

Informations

A.B., on or about the —— day of ——, 19——, at the —— of ——, in the said (territorial division), wilfully and without reasonable cause, did not make [OR circulate OR cause to be made OR cause to be circulated] an alarm of fire by outcry [OR ringing bells OR using a fire alarm (OR telephone OR telegraph) OR (specify other manner in which the alarm was made), to wit: (specify the particulars of the offence), contrary to s. 437 of the Criminal Code of Canada.

AS SOON AS PRACTICABLE. The courts have held that these words mean "as soon as possible having regard for the practical requirements of the situation". The words do not require that all else be dropped in order to accomplish the end; some idea of reasonableness and practicality is implied (R. v. Fitzpatrick (1978), 2 M.V.R. 216 (Alta. T.D.)).

ASSASSINATIION. A murder committed without direct provocation or cause of resentment given to the murdered by this victim. The murder may have been committed for hire, or for personal, social or political reasons (Black's Law Dictionary). *See also HOMICIDE.*

ASSAULT

1. *Assault*
2. *Assault with a weapon*
3. *Assault causing bodily harm*
4. *Aggravated assault*
5. *Unlawfully causing bodily harm*
6. *Torture*
7. *Assaulting a public officer or a peace officer*
8. *Assault with intent to resist arrest*
9. *Assault during execution of process or making a distress or seizure*
10. *Assault with intent to rescue thing taken under lawful process*
11. *Assault by trespasser*

See also SEXUAL ASSAULT and THREATS.

1. Assault

Definition of offence

Section 265(1)(a)

Every one who — without the consent of another person, applies force intentionally to that other person — directly or indirectly — commits an assault.

Section 265(1)(b)

Every one who — by an act or a gesture — attempts or threatens to apply force to another person — if he has, or causes that other person to believe on reasonable grounds that he has, present ability to effect his purpose — commits an assault.

Section 265(1)(c)

Every one who — while openly wearing or carrying a weapon or an imitation thereof — accosts or impedes another person or begs — commits an assault.

This definition applies to all forms of assault, including sexual assault, sexual assault with a weapon, threats to a third party or causing bodily harm and aggravated sexual assault (s. 265(2)).

Statement of offence — Section 266

Every one who — commits an assault — is guilty of an indictable offence or an offence punishable on summary conviction.

Limitation period. No proceedings in respect of offences that are declared to be punishable on summary conviction shall be instituted more than 6 months after the time when the subject matter of the proceedings arose (s. 786(2) and s. 785(1)).

Included offences. Attempts (s. 660 and s. 662(1)(b)).

Punishment. On indictment, imprisonment for 5 years (s. 266(a)). On summary conviction, a fine not exceeding $2,000, or 6 months' imprisonment, or both (s. 266(b) and s. 787(1)).

Release. Initial decision to release made by peace officer (s. 497).

Election. On indictment, accused may elect trial by judge and jury, judge alone, or provincial court judge (s. 536). On summary conviction, no election.

Evidence. 1. No consent is obtained where the complainant submits or does not resist by reason of (a) the application of force to the complainant or to a person other than the complainant; (b) threats or fear of the application of force to the complainant or to a person other than the complainant; (c) fraud; or (d) the exercise of authority (s. 265(3)).
2. Where an accused alleges that he believed that the complainant consented to the conduct that is the subject matter of the charge, a judge, if satisfied that there is sufficient evidence and that, if believed by the jury, the evidence would constitute a defence, shall instruct the jury, when reviewing all the evidence relating to the determination of the honesty of the accused's belief, to consider the presence or absence of reasonable grounds for that belief (s. 265(4)).
3. The wife or husband of a person charged with this offence where the complainant or victim is under the age of 14 years is a competent and compellable witness for the prosecution without the consent of the person charged (Canada Evidence Act, s. 4(4)).

Informations

A.B., on or about the —— day of ——, 19——, at the —— of ——, in the said (territorial division), did commit an assault on C.D., to wit: (specify the details of the assault committed), contrary to s. 266 of the Criminal Code of Canada.

2. Assault with a weapon — Section 267(1)(a)

Every one who — in committing an assault — carries or uses or threatens to use — a weapon or an imitation thereof — is guilty of an indictable offence.

Included offences. Attempts (s. 660 and s. 662(1)(b)); assault.

Punishment. Imprisonment for a term not exceeding 10 years (s. 267(1)).

Release. Initial decision to release made by justice (s. 515(1)).

Election. Accused may elect trial by judge and jury, judge alone, or provincial court judge (s. 536).

Evidence. See Evidence under **1**, *above.*

Informations

A.B., on or about the —— day of ——, 19——, at the —— of ——, in the said (territorial division), while committing an assault on C.D., did carry [OR use OR threaten to use] a weapon [OR an imitation of a weapon], to wit: (specify the particulars of the offence), contrary to s. 267(1)(a) of the Criminal Code of Canada.

3. Assault causing bodily harm — Section 267(1)(b)

Every one who — in committing an assault — causes bodily harm to the complainant — is guilty of an indictable offence.

Included offences. Attempts (s. 660 and s. 662(1)(b)); assault.

Punishment. Imprisonment for a term not exceeding 10 years (s. 267(1)).

Release. Initial decision to release made by justice (s. 515(1)).

Election. Accused may elect trial by judge and jury, judge alone, or provincial court judge (s. 536).

Definitions. See BODILY HARM; COMPLAINANT.

Evidence. See Evidence under **1**, *above.*

Informations

A.B., on or about the —— day of ——, 19——, at the —— of ——, in the said (territorial division), while committing an assault against C.D., did cause bodily harm to C.D., to wit: (specify the particulars of the offence), contrary to s. 267(1)(b) of the Criminal Code of Canada.

4. Aggravated assault

Definition of offence — Section 268(1)

Every one who — wounds or maims or disfigures or endangers the life of — the complainant — commits an aggravated assault.

Statement of offence — Section 268(2)

Every one who — commits an aggravated assault — is guilty of an indictable offence.

Included offences. Attempts (s. 660 and s. 662(1)(b)); assault.

Punishment. Imprisonment for a term not exceeding 14 years (s. 268(2)).

Release. Initial decision to release made by justice (s. 515(1)).

Election. Accused may elect trial by judge and jury, judge alone, or provincial court judge (s. 536).

Evidence. See Evidence under **1**, *above.*

Informations

A.B., on or about the —— day of ——, 19——, at the —— of ——, in the said (territorial division), did commit an aggravated assault on C.D., to wit: (specify the particulars of the offence), contrary to s. 268(2) of the Criminal Code of Canada.

5. Unlawfully causing bodily harm — Section 269

Every one who — unlawfully — causes bodily harm — to any person — is guilty of an indictable offence.

Included offences. Attempts (s. 660 and s. 662(1)(b)).

Punishment. Imprisonment for a term not exceeding 10 years (s. 269).

Release. Initial decision to release made by justice (s. 515(1)).

Election. Accused may elect trial by judge and jury, judge alone, or provincial court judge (s. 536).

Definitions. *See BODILY HARM.*

Evidence. *See Evidence under* **1**, *above.*

Informations

A.B., on or about the —— day of ——, 19——, at the —— of ——, in the said (territorial division), did unlawfully cause bodily harm to C.D., to wit: (specify the particulars of the offence), contrary to s. 269 of the Criminal Code of Canada.

6. Torture — Section 269.1(1)

Every official or every person acting at the instigation of or with the consent or acquiescence of an official, who — inflicts torture on any other person — is guilty of an indictable offence.

Included offences. Attempts (s. 660 and s. 662(1)(b)).

Punishment. Imprisonment for a term not exceeding 14 years (s. 269.1(1)).

Release. Initial decision to release made by justice (s. 515(1)).

Election. Accused may elect trial by judge and jury, judge alone, or provincial court judge (s. 536).

Definitions. For these purposes, "official" means (a) a peace officer; (b) a public officer; (c) a member of the Canadian Forces; or (d) any person who may exercise powers, pursuant to a law in force in a foreign state, that would, in Canada be exercised by a person referred to above, whether the person exercises powers in Canada or outside Canada (s. 269.1(2)).

"Torture" means any act or omission by which severe pain or suffering, whether physical or mental, is intentionally inflicted on a person (a) for a purpose including obtaining from the person or from a third person information or a statement, punishing the person for an act that the person or a third person has committed or is suspected of having committed, and intimidating or coercing the person or a third person, or (b) for any reason based on discrimination of any kind, but does not include any act or omission arising only from, inherent in or incidental to a lawful sanctions (s. 269.1(2)).

Defences. It is no defence to a charge under this section that the accused was ordered by a superior or a public authority to perform the act or omission that forms the subject matter of the charge or that the act or omission is alleged to have been justified by exceptional circumstances, including a state of war, a threat of war, internal political instability or any other public emergency (s. 269.1(3)).

Evidence. In any proceedings over which Parliament has jurisdiction, any statement obtained as a result of the commission of this offence is inadmissible in evidence except as evidence that the statement was so obtained (s. 269.1(4)).

Informations

A.B., being an official [OR C.D., being a person acting at the instigation of or with the consent or acquiescence of A.B.], on or about the —— day of ——, 19——, at the —— of ——, in the said (territorial division), did inflict torture on E.F., to wit: (specify the particulars of the offence), contrary to s. 269.1(1) of the Criminal Code of Canada.

7. Assaulting a public officer or a peace officer — Section 270(1)(a) and (2)

Every one who — assaults — a public officer or peace officer engaged in the execution of his duty — or a person acting in aid of such an officer — is guilty of either an indictable offence or an offence punishable on summary conviction.

Limitation period. No proceedings in respect of offences that are declared to be punishable on summary conviction shall be instituted more than 6 months after the time when the subject matter of the proceedings arose (s. 786(2) and s. 785(1)).

Included offences. Attempts (s. 660 and s. 662(1)(b)); assault.

Punishment. On indictment, imprisonment for a term not exceeding 5 years (s. 270(2)(a)). On summary conviction, a fine not exceeding $2,000, or 6 months' imprisonment, or both (s. 270(2)(b) and s. 787(1)).

Release. Initial decision to release made by peace officer (s. 497).

Election. On indictment, accused may elect trial by judge and jury, judge alone, or provincial court judge (s. 536). On summary conviction, no election.

Evidence. 1. The officer must be engaged in the execution of his duty at the time of the assault. An officer cannot be said to be acting in the execution of his duty when acting far in excess of his duty and authority.

2. *See also Evidence, items 1. and 2., under* **1**, *above.*

Informations

A.B., on or about the —— day of ——, 19——, at the —— of ——, in the said (territorial division), did assault C.D., a public officer [OR peace officer OR person acting in aid of E.F., a public (OR peace) officer], engaged in the execution of his duty, to wit: (specify the particulars of the offence), contrary to s. 270(1)(a) of the Criminal Code of Canada.

8. Assault with intent to resist arrest — Section 270(1)(b) and (2)

Every one who — assaults a person — with intent to resist or prevent the lawful arrest or detention of himself or another person — is guilty of either an indictable offence or an offence punishable on summary conviction.

Intent. Intention to resist or prevent lawful arrest or detention.

Limitation period. No proceedings in respect of offences that are declared to be punishable on summary conviction shall be instituted more than 6 months after the time when the subject matter of the proceedings arose (s. 786(2) and s. 785(1)).

Included offences. Attempts (s. 660 and s. 662(1)(b)); assault.

Punishment. On indictment, imprisonment for a term not exceeding 5 years (s. 270(2)(a)). On summary conviction, a fine not exceeding $2,000, or 6 months' imprisonment, or both (s. 270(2)(b) and s. 787(1)).

Release. Initial decision to release made by peace officer (s. 497).

Election. On indictment, accused may elect trial by judge and jury, judge alone, or provincial court judge (s. 536). On summary conviction, no election.

Evidence. See Evidence, items 1. and 2., under **1**, *above.*

Informations

A.B., on or about the —— day of ——, 19——, at the —— of ——, in the said (territorial division), did assault C.D., with intent to resist [Or prevent] the lawful arrest [OR detention] of A.B. [OR E.F.], to wit: (specify the particulars of the offence), contrary to s. 270(1)(b) of the Criminal Code of Canada.

9. Assault during execution of process or making a distress or seizure — Section 270(1)(c)(i) and (2)

Every one who — assaults a person — who is engaged in the lawful execution of a process against lands or goods — or who is engaged in making a lawful distress or seizure — is guilty of either of an indictable offence or an offence punishable on summary conviction.

Limitation period. No proceedings in respect of offences that are declared to be punishable on summary conviction shall be instituted more than 6 months after the time when the subject matter of the proceedings arose (s. 786(2) and s. 785(1)).

Included offences. Attempts (s. 660 and s. 662(1)(b)).

Punishment. On indictment, imprisonment for a term not exceeding 5 years (s. 270(2)(a)). On summary conviction, a fine not exceeding $2,000, or 6 months' imprisonment, or both (s. 270(2)(b) and s. 787(1)).

Release. Initial decision to release made by peace officer (s. 497).

Election. On indictment, accused may elect trial by judge and jury, judge alone, or provincial court judge (s. 536). On summary conviction, no election.

Evidence. See Evidence, items 1. and 2., under **1**, *above.*

Informations

A.B., on or about the —— day of ——, 19——, at the —— of ——, in the said (territorial division), did assault C.D., a person engaged in the lawful execution of a process against the lands [OR goods] of A.B. [OR E.F.], to wit: (specify the particulars of the assault as well as the particulars of the process being lawfully executed), contrary to s. 270(1)(c)(i) of the Criminal Code of Canada.

A.B., on or about the —— day of ——, 19——, at the —— of ——, in the said (territorial division), did assault C.D., a person engaged in making a lawful distress [OR seizure], to wit: (specify the particulars of the assault as well as the particulars of the lawful distress or seizure), contrary to s. 270(1)(c)(i) of the Criminal Code of Canada.

10. Assault with intent to rescue thing taken under lawful process — Section 270(1)(c)(ii) and (2)

Every one who — assaults a person — with intent to rescue anything taken under a lawful process or distress or seizure — is guilty of either an indictable offence or an offence punishable on summary conviction.

Intent. Intention to rescue anything taken lawfully.

Limitation period. No proceedings in respect of offences that are declared to be punishable on summary conviction shall be instituted more than 6 months after the time when the subject matter of the proceedings arose (s. 786(2) and s. 785(1)).

Included offences. Attempts (s. 660 and s. 662(1)(b)); assault.

Punishment. On indictment, imprisonment for a term not exceeding 5 years (s. 270(2)(a)). On summary conviction, a fine not exceeding $2,000, or 6 months' imprisonment, or both (s. 270(2)(b) and s. 787(1)).

Release. Initial decision to release made by peace officer (s. 497).

Election. On indictment, accused may elect trial by judge and jury, judge alone, or provincial court judge (s. 536). On summary conviction, no election.

Evidence. See Evidence, items 1. and 2., under **1**, *above.*

Informations

A.B., on or about the —— day of ——, 19——, at the —— of ——, in the said (territorial division), did assault C.D., with intent to rescue property that had been taken under a lawful process [OR distress OR seizure], to wit: (specify the particulars of the offence), contrary to s. 270(1)(c)(ii) of the Criminal Code of Canada.

11. Assault by trespasser

Defence of personal property. Every one who is in peaceable possession of personal property, and every one lawfully assisting him, is justified (a) in preventing a trespasser from taking it, or (b) in taking it from a trespasser who has taken it, if he does not strike or cause bodily harm to the trespasser (s. 38(1)).

Where a person who is in peaceable possession of personal property lays hands upon it, a trespasser who persists in attempting to keep it or take it from him or from anyone lawfully assisting him shall be deemed to commit an assault without justification or provocation (s. 38(2)).

Defence of house or real property. Every one who is in peaceable possession of a dwelling-house or real property, and every one lawfully assisting him or acting under his authority, is justified in using force to prevent any person from trespassing on the dwelling-house or real property, or to remove a trespasser therefrom, if he uses no more force than is necessary (s. 41(1)).

A trespasser who resists an attempt by a person who is in peaceable possession of a dwelling-house or real property or a person lawfully assisting him or acting under his authority to prevent his entry or to remove him, shall be deemed to commit an assault without justification or provocation (s. 41(2)).

ASSISTING DESERTER

1. *Canadian Forces deserter*	2. *R.C.M.P. deserter*

1. Canadian Forces deserter — Section 54

Every one who — aids or assists or harbours or conceals — a person who he knows is a deserter or absentee without leave from the Canadian Forces — is guilty of an offence punishable on summary conviction.

Intent. Knowledge of status.

Consent to prosecute. No proceedings shall be instituted under s. 54 without the consent of the Attorney General of Canada (s. 54).

Limitation period. No proceedings in respect of offences that are declared to be punishable on summary conviction shall be instituted more than 6 months after the time when the subject matter of the proceedings arose (s. 786(2) and s. 785(1)).

Included offences. Attempts (s. 660 and s. 662(1)(b)).

Punishment. A fine not exceeding $2,000, or 6 months' imprisonment, or to both (s. 54 and s. 787(1)).

Release. Initial decision to release made by peace officer (s. 497).

Election. No election, summary conviction offence.

Informations

A.B., on or about the —— day of ——, 19——, at the —— of ——, in the said (territorial division), did aid [OR harbour OR conceal] C.D., knowing the said C.D. to be a deserter [OR absent without leave] from the Canadian Forces, to wit: (specify the particulars of the offence), contrary to s. 54 of the Criminal Code of Canada.

2. R.C.M.P. deserter

Section 56(a)

Every one who — wilfully — persuades or counsels — a member of the Royal Canadian Mounted Police — to desert or absent himself without leave — is guilty of an offence punishable on summary conviction.

Section 56(b)

Every one who — wilfully — aids or assists or harbours or conceals — a member of the Royal Canadian Mounted Police — who he knows is a deserter or absentee without leave — is guilty of an offence punishable on summary conviction.

Section 56(c)

Every one who — wilfully — aids or assists — a member of the Royal Canadian Mounted Police — to desert or absent himself without leave — knowing that the member is about to desert or absent himself without leave — is guilty of an offence punishable on summary conviction.

Intent. Wilfully; knowledge of status.

Limitation period. No proceedings in respect of offences that are declared to be punishable on summary conviction shall be instituted more than 6 months after the time when the subject matter of the proceedings arose (s. 786(2) and s. 785(1)).

Included offences. Attempts (s. 660 and s. 662(1)(b)).

Punishment. A fine not exceeding $2,000, or 6 months' imprisonment, or to both (s. 56 and s. 787(1)).

Release. Initial decision to release made by peace officer (s. 497).

Election. No election, summary conviction offence.

ASSOCIATION. For the purposes of s. 204, "association" means an association incorporated by or pursuant to an Act of Parliament or of the legislature of a province, having as its purpose or one of its purposes the conduct of horse-races (s. 204(11)). *See also BILL OF RIGHTS.*

ASSUMPSIT. "He undertook" (a form of pleading used to enforce contractual promises) (Latin).

ATTEMPTS

Definition of "attempt" — Section 24(1)

Every one who — having an intent to commit an offence — does or omits to do anything — for the purposes of carrying out the intention — is guilty of an attempt to commit the offence — whether or not it was possible under the circumstances to commit the offence.

Statements of offences

Except where otherwise expressly provided by law, the following provisions apply in respect of persons who attempt to commit offences, namely:

Section 463(a)

Every one who — attempts to commit — an indictable offence — for which on conviction, an accused is liable to be sentenced to death or to imprisonment for life — is guilty of an indictable offence.

Section 463(b)

Every one who — attempts to commit — an indictable offence — for which, on conviction, an accused is liable to imprisonment 14 years or less — is guilty of an indictable offence.

Section 463(c)

Every one who — attempts to commit — an offence punishable on summary conviction — is guilty of an offence punishable on summary conviction.

Section 463(d)

Every one who — attempts to commit — an offence for which the offender may be prosecuted by indictment — or for which he is punishable on summary conviction — is guilty of either an indictable offence or an offence punishable on summary conviction.

Intent. Intention to commit offence.

Limitation period. No proceedings in respect of offences that are declared to be punishable on summary conviction shall be instituted more than 6 months after the time when the subject matter of the proceedings arose (s. 786(2) and s. 785(1)).

Punishment. Every one who attempts to commit an indictable offence for which, on conviction, an accused is liable to be sentenced to death or to imprisonment for life is liable to imprisonment for a term not exceeding 14 years (s. 463(a)).

Every one who attempts to commit an indictable offence for which, on conviction, an accused is liable to imprisonment for 14 years or less is liable to imprisonment for a term that is one-half of the longest term to which a person who is guilty of that offence is liable (s. 463(b)).

Every one who attempts to commit an offence punishable on summary conviction is liable to a fine not exceeding $2,000, or 6 months' imprisonment, or both (s. 463(c) and s. 787(1)).

Every one who attempts to commit an offence for which the offender may be prosecuted by indictment or for which he is punishable on summary conviction is liable either to imprisonment for a term not exceeding one-half of the longest term to which a person who is guilty of that offence is liable, or to a fine not exceeding $2,000, or 6 months' imprisonment, or both (s. 463(d) and s. 787(1)).

Evidence. 1. The question whether an act or omission by a person who has an intent to commit an offence is or is not mere preparation to commit the offence, and too remote to constitute an attempt to commit the offence, is a question of law (s. 24(2)).

2. Mere preparation does not constitute an attempt. The person must, with the intention of committing the offence, commence to perform some act or series of acts that would result in its commission if he were not interrupted. For example, where a person in preparation for burning down a building has placed inflammable substances against it, then lights a match for the purpose of starting a fire and the wind blows the match out, or the police seize him, or he is deterred from his purpose by some other outside influence, he is guilty of attempted arson. It is doubtful that he would be guilty in these circumstances if he simply changed his mind and desisted, and such charge of mind were not brought about by the approach of others and consequent fear of detection, or by the elements or some other outside influence.

Informations

A.B., on or about the —— day of ——, 19——, at the —— of ——, in the said *(territorial division)*, did attempt to *(specify the particulars of the offence attempted)*.

AUDI ALTERAM PARTEM. "Hear the other side" (Latin).

AUTHORIZATION. For the purposes of Part VI of the Criminal Code (Invasion of Privacy), "authorization" means an authorization to intercept a private communication given under s. 186, s. 184.2(3), s. 184.3(6), s. 188(2) or (s. 183).

AUTOMATISM

1. *Definitions*
2. *Distinction between insane and non-insane automatism*
3. *Evidence*

1. Definitions. 1. Under the doctrine of (non-insane) automatism, a person who by reason of impaired consciousness lacks the mental state necessary for the crime charged can be acquitted in the ordinary way, his condition not being regarded as a disease of the mind. The main instances of automatism are sleepwalking, concussion, involuntary intoxication, epilepsy, hypoglycaemia and dissociative states (Glanville Williams, Textbook of Criminal Law).
2. Unconscious, involuntary behaviour; the state of a person who, though capable of action, is not conscious of what he is doing (Rabey v. R. (1980), 15 C.R. (3d) 225 (S.C.C.)).

2. Distinction between insane and non-insane automatism. The courts have held that "insane automatism" or "insanity" arises from a malfunctioning of the mind caused by something internal, having its source in the accused's psychological or emotional make-up or in organic pathology. "Non-insane automatism" arises from a malfunctioning of the mind which is transient, having been caused by an external factor (Rabey v. R. (1980), 15 C.R. (3d) 225 (S.C.C.)).

3. Evidence. 1. The courts have held that it is a question of law whether there is evidence to support the defence of automatism but, if there is evidence, the judge must instruct the jury on this defence (R. v. Sproule (1975), 30 C.R.N.S. 56 (Ont. C.A.)).

2. To establish a defence of automatism, the accused, either by cross-examination of the prosecution witness or by evidence called on his own behalf or by both means combined, is required to place before the court such material as will make the defence a viable issue and one fit and proper to be presented to a jury (R. v. Szymusiak (1972), 19 C.R.N.S. 373 (Ont. C.A.)).

AUTOMOBILE MASTER KEY. For the purposes of s. 353, "automobile master key" includes a key, pick, rocker key or other instrument designed or adapted to operate the ignition or other switches or locks of a series of motor vehicles (s. 353(5)). *See also BREAKING AND ENTERING, 8.*

AUTOPSY. A dissection of the body after death to determine the cause of death, sometimes the identity of the deceased and to study the changes in the tissues caused by disease or violence; the term often includes any subsequent microscopic or chemical examination. Also, necropsy, postmortem (Jaffe, A Guide to Pathological Evidence, 2nd ed.).

AUTREFOIS ACQUIT. In criminal law, the name of a special plea in which an accused states that he has already been lawfully acquitted of the offence with which he has been charged (s. 607).

AUTREFOIS CONVICT. In criminal law, the name of a special plea in which an accused states that he has already been lawfully convicted of the offence with which he has been charged (s. 607).

AVERMENTS. *See ESSENTIAL AVERMENTS.*

B

BAILEE. A person to whom goods are entrusted for a specific purpose without any intention of transferring the ownership to him. *See also THEFT AND OFFENCES RESEMBLING THEFT, 2.*

BALLISTICS

Definition. The science of gun examination; the study of the behaviour of projectiles, or of projectiles in motion. In criminal cases, it is used to determine whether a particular bullet was fired from a particular gun, the firing capacity of a weapon and its fireability.

External ballistics. The behaviour of projectiles in flight.

Internal ballistics. The behaviour of projectiles with the weapon from which they were fired.

Terminal ballistics. The behaviour of projectiles when striking the target.

Wound ballistics. The mechanism of wound production by projectiles.

Bullet comparisons. Bullets are manufactured with certain general physical properties and characteristics, i.e., shape (round nose, flat point, etc.), weight expressed in grains (1 grain = .065 grams or 1 gram = 15.43 grains), caliber (or diameter), cannelures (grooves and crimps), composition (lead, alloys, etc.), and base contour (flat, hollow, etc.). After firing, these properties may remain intact and can be used to indicate the nature of the firearm in which they were intended to be used by comparing the fired bullet with a known bullet.

Additional markings found on a discharged bullet may be used to identify the type and make of the gun from which the bullet was fired, i.e., caliber, the number, width and depth of lands and grooves, the twist (direction of pitch, left or right), and pitch (angle of spiral from horizontal).

In addition, the firearm itself may scratch the bullet or mark it in some other way so as to permit the identification of the individual weapon from which it was fired.

Case comparisons. When an automatic weapon or a semi-automatic weapon is fired, a shell casing is ejected. When a shell casing is found at the scene of the crime, it may be compared with a known shell casing. Shell casings are manufactured with certain physical properties and characteristics, i.e., trade mark or manufacturer's name, shape (rimmed, rimless, straight or bottle-necked), caliber and composition (brass, copronickel, etc.).

Individual characteristics of the shell casing may include firing pin indentations (shape, filemarks, etc.), breech face markings (file or machining marks), extractor marks or ejector marks.

BANK-NOTE. For the purposes of the Criminal Code, "bank-note" includes any negotiable instrument (a) issued by or on behalf of a person carrying on the business of banking in or out of Canada, (b) issued under the authority of Parliament or under the lawful authority of the government of a state other than Canada, intended to be used as money or as the equivalent of money, immediately upon issue or at some time subsequent thereto, and includes bank bills and bank post bills (s. 2). *See also CURRENCY OFFENCES, 10, 11.*

BARBITURATES. A group of drugs used as sedatives, hypnotics and anaesthetics. They include thiopental (ultra-short acting), pentobarbital (short acting), amobarbital (intermediate) and phenobarbital (long acting) (Jaffe, A Guide to Pathological Evidence, 2nd ed.).

BARREL-LENGTH. For the purposes of paragraph (d) of the definition "prohibited weapon" and paragraph (b)(i) of the definition "restricted weapon" in s. 84(1) of the Criminal Code, the length of a barrel of a firearm means (a) in the case of a revolver, the distance from the muzzle of the barrel to the breach end immediately in front of the cylinder; and (b) in any other case, the distance from the muzzle of the barrel to and including the chawmber, but not including the length of any part or accessory including parts or accessories designed or intended to suppress the muzzle flash or reduce recoil (s. 84(1.1)).

BATTERY. 1. Beating and wounding. In law, this includes every touching or laying hold, however trifling, of another's person or clothes, in an angry, revengeful, rude, insolent or hostile manner (Jowitt's Dictionary of Criminal Law). 2. The actual offer to use force to the injury of another person is assault; the use of it is battery, which always includes an assault. Hence, the two forms are commonly combined in the term "assault and battery" (Black's Law Dictionary). *For criminal proceedings, see ASSAULT.*

BENCH. A term used to describe judges collectively, or the judges of a particular court (David M. Walker, The Oxford Companion to Law).

BENCH WARRANT. A warrant issued by the court itself (from the bench) for the arrest of a person. Although the term "bench warrant" continues to be used, references to a bench warrant are not to be found in the Criminal Code except for the marginal note to s. 597(1) which provides for the issuance of a warrant for arrest in Form 7 of a person against whom an indictment has been preferred and who either did not appear or remain in attendance at his trial.

BENZEDRINE. A brand of amphetamine sulphate (Smith, Kline and French Laboratories) (Jaffe, A Guide to Pathological Evidence, 2nd ed.).

BEST EVIDENCE RULE. A rule of evidence applying only to documents, which requires that, if an original document is available in your hands, you must produce it, i.e., that evidence should be the best that the nature of the case will allow (R. v. Swartz (1977), 37 C.C.C. (2d) 409 (Ont. C.A.)).

BESTIALITY. The crime of persons having carnal intercourse with animals or beasts.

BET. 1. An agreement between two or more persons that a sum of money or other valuable thing, to which all jointly contribute, shall become the sole property of one or some of them on the happening in the future of an event at present uncertain, or according as a question disputed between them is settled one way or the other. Also, a contract by which two or more parties agree that a sum of money, or other thing, shall be paid or delivered to one of them on the happening of an uncertain event (Black's Law Dictionary). 2. For the purposes of Part VII of the Criminal Code, "bet" means a bet that is placed on any contingency or event that is to take place in or out of Canada, and without restricting the generality of the foregoing, includes a bet that is placed on any contingency relating to a horse-race, fight, match or sporting event that is to take place in or out of Canada (s. 197(1)).

BIAS. 1. With regard to anyone acting in a judicial capacity, this means anything which tends or may be regarded as tending to cause such person to decide a case otherwise than on the evidence (Jowitt's Dictionary of English Law). 2. Bias, or the reasonable apprehension of bias, disqualifies a judge from hearing a case. Some usual grounds upon which a judge may be disqualified to sit on a trial or appeal are these: a pecuniary relationship in the outcome of the litigation; a family relationship or close friendship with a litigant or a witness; the expression by the judge of views reflecting bias regarding a litigant or the matter to be litigated; a previous professional connection with the litigant or, in some cases, the litigant. But a judge, apparently disqualified, may sit if the situation is such that there is no other way in which the trial or appeal may be heard (the rule of necessity), or, if, knowing of the judge's disqualification, all parties to the litigation consent (Wilson, A Book for Judges).

BIGAMY

Definition of offence — Section 290(1)(a) and (b)

Every one who — in Canada — either being married, goes through a form of marriage with another person — or knowing that another person is married, goes through a form of marriage with that person — or on the same day or simultaneously, goes through a form of marriage with more than one person — commits bigamy.

Every one who — being a Canada citizen resident in Canada — leaves Canada with intent to do anything mentioned above — and, pursuant thereto, does outside of Canada anything mentioned above in such circumstances — commits bigamy.

Statement of offence — Section 291(1)

Every one who — commits bigamy — is guilty of an indictable offence.

Included offences. Attempts (s. 660 and s. 662(1)(b)).

Punishment. Imprisonment for a term not exceeding 5 years (s. 291(1)).

Release. Initial decision to release made by officer in charge or justice (s. 498).

Election. Accused may elect trial by judge and jury, judge alone, or provincial court judge (s. 536).

Defences. 1. No person commits bigamy by going through a form of marriage if: (a) that person in good faith and on reasonable grounds believes that his spouse is dead; (b) the spouse of that person has been continuously absent from him for 7 years immediately preceding the time when he goes through the form of marriage, unless he knew that his spouse was alive at any time during those 7 years; (c) that person has been divorced from the bond of the first marriage; or (d) the former marriage has been declared void by a court of competent jurisdiction (s. 290(2)).
2. Where a person is alleged to have committed bigamy, it is not a defence that the parties would, if unmarried, have been incompetent to contract marriage under the law of the place where the offence is alleged to have been committed (s. 290(3)).

Evidence. 1. Every marriage or form of marriage shall, for the purpose of this offence, be deemed to be valid unless the accused establishes that it was invalid (s. 290(4)).

2. No act or omission on the part of an accused who is charged with bigamy invalidates a marriage or form of marriage that is otherwise valid (s. 290(5)).

3. For the purposes of this offence, a certificate of marriage issued under the authority of law is evidence of the marriage or form of marriage to which it relates without proof of the signature or official character of the person by whom it purports to be signed (s. 291(2)).

4. The wife or husband of a person charged with this offence is a competent and compellable witness for the prosecution without the consent of the accused (Canada Evidence Act, s. 4(2)).

Informations

A.B., on or about the —— day of ——, 19——, at the —— of ——, in the said (territorial division), being then already married [OR knowing her to be then married] did go through a form of marriage with C.D., and did thereby commit bigamy, to wit: (specify the particulars of the offence), contrary to s. 291(1) of the Criminal Code of Canada.

BILL OF RIGHTS. The Canadian Bill of Rights is a statute of the federal Parliament. It provides that in Canada there have existed and shall continue to exist without discrimination by reason of race, national origin, colour, religion or sex, the following human rights and fundamental freedoms, namely:

(a) the right of the individual to life, liberty, security of the person and enjoyment of property, and the right not to be deprived thereof except by due process of law;

(b) the right of the individual to equality before the law and the protection of the law;

(c) freedom of religion;

(d) freedom of speech;

(e) freedom of assembly and association; and

(f) freedom of the press (Bill of Rights, s. 1).

The Bill of Rights further provides that every law of Canada shall, unless it is expressly declared by Act of Parliament that it shall operate notwithstanding the Canadian Bill of Rights, be so construed and applied as not to abrogate, abridge or infringe or to authorize the abrogation, abridgment or infringement of any of the rights or freedoms herein recognized and declared, and in particular, no law of Canada shall be construed or applied so as to:

(a) authorize or effect the arbitrary detention, imprisonment or exile of any person;

(b) impose or authorize the imposition of cruel and unusual treatment or punishment;

(c) deprive a person who has been arrested or detained of the right to be informed promptly of the reason for his arrest or detention, of the right to retain and instruct counsel without delay, or of the remedy by way of habeas corpus for the determination of the validity of his detention and for his release if the detention is not lawful;

(d) authorize a court, tribunal, commission, board or other authority to compel a person to give evidence if he is denied counsel, protection against self-crimination or other constitutional safeguards;

(e) deprive a person of the right to a fair hearing in accordance with the principles of fundamental justice for the determination of his rights and obligations;

(f) deprive a person charged with a criminal offence of the right to be presumed innocent until proved guilty according to law in a fair and public hearing by an independent and impartial tribunal, or of the right to reasonable bail without just cause; or

(g) deprive a person of the right to the assistance of an interpreter in any proceedings in which he is involved or in which he is a party or a witness, before a court, commission, board or other tribunal, if he does not understand or speak the language in which such proceedings are conducted (Bill of Rights, s. 2).

The Canadian Bill of Rights has generally been given a narrow interpretation by the courts and has never played a critical role with respect to the criminal law of Canada. By contrast, the Charter of Rights and Freedoms does form part of the Constitution of Canada and is expected to produce many radical changes in our criminal law in coming years.

BINDING OVER TO KEEP THE PEACE

1. *Binding over to keep the peace*
2. *Binding over to keep the peace where fear of sexual violence*

1. Binding over to keep the peace

Laying an information. Any person who fears that another person will cause personal injury to him or his spouse or child or will damage his property may lay an information before a justice (s. 810(1)).

A justice who receives such an information shall cause the parties to appear before him or before a summary conviction court having jurisdiction in the same territorial division. (s. 810(2)).

Statement of offence — Section 811

Every one who — being bound by a recognizance under s. 810 — commits a breach of the recognizance — is guilty of an offence punishable on summary conviction.

Limitation period. No proceedings in respect of offences that are declared to be punishable on summary conviction shall be instituted more than 6 months after the time when the subject matter of the proceedings arose (s. 786(2) and s. 785(1)).

Included offences. Attempts (s. 660 and s. 662(1)(b)).

Punishment. A fine not exceeding $2,000, or 6 months' imprisonment, or both (s. 811 and s. 787(1)).

Release. Initial decision to release made by peace officer (s. 497).

Election. No election, summary conviction offence.

Evidence. The justice or the summary conviction court before which the parties appear may, if satisfied by the evidence adduced that the informant has reasonable grounds for his fears, (a) order that the defendant enter into a recognizance with or without sureties, to keep the peace and be of good behaviour for any period that does not exceed 12 months, and comply with such other reasonable conditions prescribed in the recognizance as the court considers desirable for securing the good conduct of the defendant; or (b) commit the defendant to prison for a term not exceeding 12 months if he fails or refuses to enter into the recognizance (s. 810(3)).

Before making such an order, the justice or the summary conviction court shall consider whether it is desirable, in the interests of the safety of the defendant or of any other person, to include as a condition of the recognizance that the defendant be prohibited from possessing any firearm or any ammunition or explosive substance for any period of time specified in the recognizance and that the defendant surrender any firearms acquisition certificate that the accused possesses and, where the justice or summary conviction court decides that it is not desirable, in the interests of the safety of the defendant or of any other person, for the defendant to possess any of those things, the justice or summary conviction court may add the appropriate condition to the recognizance (s. 810(3.1)).

Informations

A.B., on or about the —— day of ——, 19——, at the —— of ——, in the said (territorial division), did utter certain words [OR do such things] so as to cause fear on the part of C.D. that A.B. would cause personal injury to C.D. [OR the spouse of C.D. OR the children of C.D.], to wit: (specify the particulars of the offence), contrary to s. 811 of the Criminal Code of Canada.

A.B., on or about the —— day of ——, 19——, at the —— of ——, in the said (territorial division), did utter certain words [OR do such things] so as to cause fear on the part of C.D. that A.B. will damage the property of C.D., to wit: (specify the particulars of the offence), contrary to s. 811 of the Criminal Code of Canada.

2. Binding over to keep the peace where fear of sexual violence

Laying an information. Any person who fears on reasonable grounds that another person will commit an offence under ss. 151, 152, 155, 159, 160(2), 160(3), 170, 171, 173(2), 271, 272 or 273, in respect of one or more persons who are under the age of 14 years, may lay an information before a provincial court judge, whether or not the person or persons in respect of whom it is feared that the offence will be committed are named (s. 810.1(1)).

A provincial court judge who receives such an information shall cause the parties to appear before the provincial court judge (s. 810.1(2)).

Statement of offence — Section 811

Every one who — being bound by a recognizance under s. 810.1 — commits a breach of the recognizance — is guilty of an offence punishable on summary conviction.

Limitation period. No proceedings in respect of offences that are declared to be punishable on summary conviction shall be instituted more than 6 months after the time when the subject matter of the proceedings arose (s. 786(2) and s. 785(1)).

Included offences. Attempts (s. 660 and s. 662(1)(b)).

Punishment. A fine not exceeding $2,000, or 6 months' imprisonment, or both (s. 811 and s. 787(1)).

Release. Initial decision to release made by peace officer (s. 497).

Election. No election, summary conviction offence.

Evidence. The provincial court judge before whom the parties appear may, if satisfied by the evidence adduced that the informant has reasonable grounds for the fear, order the defendant to enter into a recognizance and comply with the conditions fixed by the provincial court judge, including a condition prohibiting the defendant from engaging in any activity that involves contact with persons under the age of 14 years and prohibiting the defendant from attending a public park or public swimming area where persons under the age of 14 years are present or can reasonably be expected to be present, or a daycare centre, schoolground, playground or community centre, for any period fixed by the provincial court judge that does not exceed 12 months (s. 810.1(3)).

Informations

A.B., on or about the —— day of ——, 19——, at the —— of ——, in the said (territorial division), with utter certain words [OR do such things] so as to cause fear on the part of C.D. that A.B. would commit an offence under s. 151 [OR 152 OR 155 OR 159 OR 160(2) OR 160(3) OR 170 OR 171 OR 173(2) OR 271 OR 272 OR 273], in respect of one or more persons who were under the age of 14 years, to wit: (specify the particulars of the offence), contrary to s. 811 of the Criminal Code of Canada.

BOARD. 1. A body of persons, statutory or otherwise, having delegated to them certain powers or elected for certain purposes. 2. For the purposes of the Criminal Records Act, "Board" means the National Parole Board (Criminal Records Act, s. 2(1)).

BODILY HARM AND ACTS AND OMISSIONS CAUSING DANGER TO THE PERSON

1. *Definitions*
2. *Discharging a firearm, air gun or air pistol with intent*
3. *Administering poison or other destructive or noxious thing*
4. *Overcoming resistance to commission of offence*
5. *Traps likely to cause bodily harm*
6. *Interfering with transportation facilities*
7. *Assault with a weapon or causing bodily harm. See ASSAULTS, 3.*
8. *Unlawfully causing bodily harm. See ASSAULTS, 5.*
9. *Causing bodily harm by criminal negligence. See CRIMINAL NEGLIGENCE, 3.*
10. *Causing bodily harm by arson. See ARSON, 2.*

1. Definitions

Bodily harm. For the purposes of ss. 267, 269 and 272, "bodily harm" means any hurt or injury to the complainant that interferes with the health or comfort of the complainant and that is more than merely transient or trifling in nature (s. 267(2)).
See also COMPLAINANT.

2. Discharging a firearm, air gun or air pistol with intent — Section 244

Every one who — with intent — either to wound or maim or disfigure any person — or to endanger the life of any person — or to prevent the arrest or detention of any person — discharges a firearm or air gun or air pistol at any person — whether or not that person is the one intended to be harmed — is guilty of an indictable offence.

Intent. Intention to wound, maim, disfigure, endanger life, or prevent arrest or detention.

Included offences. Attempts (s. 660 and s. 662(1)(b)).

Punishment. Imprisonment for a term not exceeding 14 years (s. 244).

Release. Initial decision to release made by justice (s. 515(1)).

Election. Accused may elect trial by judge and jury, judge alone, or provincial court judge (s. 536).

Evidence. 1. To constitute "wounding", there must be breaking of the skin.
2. To "maim" a man is to injure any part of his body so as to deprive him of the use of that part of his body. The courts have held that the breaking of a man's leg was a sufficient injury to amount to maiming (R. v. Schultz (1962), 38 C.R. 76 (Alta. C.A.)).
3. To "disfigure" a man is to do him some external injury that may detract from his physical appearance. The courts have held that "disfigure" denotes more than a temporary marring of the figure or appearance of a person (R. v. Innes (1972), 7 C.C.C. (2d) 544 (B.C. C.A.)).
4. The courts have held that the intent to endanger life is different from the intent to murder (R. v. Boomhower (1974), 27 C.R.N.S. 188 (Ont. C.A.)).

Informations

A.B., on or about the —— day of ——, 19——, at the —— of ——, in the said (territorial division), with intent to wound [OR maim OR disfigure OR endanger the life of OR prevent the arrest (OR detention) of] C.D., did discharge a firearm [OR air gun OR air pistol] at C.D. [OR E.F., another person], to wit: (specify the particulars of the offence), contrary to s. 244 of the Criminal Code of Canada.

3. Administering poison or other destructive or noxious thing — Section 245

Every one who — administers or causes to be administered to any person — or causes any person to take — poison or any other destructive or noxious thing — is guilty of an indictable offence.

Included offences. Attempts (s. 660 and s. 662(1)(b)).

Punishment. Imprisonment for a term not exceeding 14 years, if he intends thereby to endanger the life of or to cause bodily harm to that person (s. 245(a)). Imprisonment for a term not exceeding 2 years, if he intends thereby to aggrieve or annoy that person (s. 245(b)).

Release. With intent to endanger life or to cause bodily harm, initial decision to release made by justice (s. 515(1)). With intent to aggrieve or annoy, initial decision to release made by officer in charge or justice (s. 498).

Election. Accused may elect trial by judge and jury, judge alone, or provincial court judge (s. 536).

Evidence. The courts have held that a "noxious thing" is any substance which, in light of all the circumstances attendant upon its administration, is capable of effecting or, in the normal course of events, will effect one of the defined consequences. Even an innocuous substance may in some circumstances come within the section (R. v. Burkholder (1977), 34 C.C.C. (2d) 214 (Alta. C.A.)).

Informations

A.B., on or about the —— day of ——, 19——, at the —— of ——, in the said (territorial division), did administer to C.D. [OR cause to be administered to C.D. OR cause C.D. to take] poison [OR a destructive (OR noxious) thing] with intent thereby to endanger the life of [OR cause bodily harm to OR grieve OR annoy] C.D., to wit: (specify the particulars of the offence), contrary to s. 245 of the Criminal Code of Canada.

4. Overcoming resistance to commission of offence

Section 246(a)

Every one who — with intent to enable or assist himself or another person to commit an indictable offence — attempts, by any means, to choke or suffocate or strangle another person — or by any means calculated to choke or suffocate or strangle, attempts to render another person insensible or unconscious or incapable of resistance — is guilty of an indictable offence.

Section 246(b)

Every one who — administers, or causes to be administered to any person — or attempts to administer to any person — or causes or attempts to cause any person to take — a stupefying or overpowering drug or matter or thing — is guilty of an indictable offence.

Intent. Intention to enable or assist in commission of indictable offence (s. 246(a)).

Included offences. Attempts (s. 660 and s. 662(1)(b)).

Punishment. Imprisonment for life (s. 246).

Release. Initial decision to release made by justice (s. 515(1)).

Election. Accused may elect trial by judge and jury, judge alone, or provincial court judge (s. 536).

Informations

A.B., on or about the —— day of ——, 19——, at the —— of ——, in the said (territorial division), with intent to enable [OR assist] himself [OR E.F.] to commit the indictable offence of (specify), did attempt to choke [OR suffocate OR strangle] C.D., to wit: (specify the particulars of the offence), contrary to s. 246(a) of the Criminal Code of Canada.

A.B., on or about the —— day of ——, 19——, at the —— of ——, in the said (territorial division), with intent to enable [OR assist] himself [OR E.F.] to commit the indictable offence of (specify), did attempt to render C.D. insensible [OR unconscious OR incapable of resistance] by a means calculated to choke [OR suffocate OR strangle] C.D., to wit: (specify the particulars of the offence), contrary to s. 246(a) of the Criminal Code of Canada.

A.B., on or about the —— day of ——, 19——, at the —— of ——, in the said (territorial division), with intent to enable [OR assist] himself [OR E.F.] to commit the indictable offence of (specify), did administer [OR cause to be administered OR attempt to administer] to C.D., a stupefying [OR overpowering] drug [OR matter OR thing], to wit: (specify the particulars of the offence), contrary to s. 246(b) of the Criminal Code of Canada.

A.B., on or about the —— day of ——, 19——, at the —— of ——, in the said (territorial division), with intent to enable [OR assist] himself [OR E.F.] to commit the indictable offence of (specify), did cause [OR attempt to cause] C.D. to take a stupefying [OR overpowering] drug [OR matter OR thing], to wit: (specify the particulars of the offence), contrary to s. 246(b) of the Criminal Code of Canada.

5. Traps likely to cause bodily harm — Section 247(1)

Every one who — with intent to cause death or bodily harm to persons, whether ascertained or not — sets or places or causes to be set or placed — a trap or device or other thing whatever that is likely to cause death or bodily harm to persons — is guilty of an indictable offence.

Intent. Intention to cause death or bodily harm, whether ascertained or not.

Included offences. Attempts (s. 660 and s. 662(1)(b)).

Punishment. Imprisonment for a term not exceeding 5 years (s. 247(1)).

Release. Initial decision to release made by officer in charge or justice (s. 498).

Election. Accused may elect trial by judge and jury, judge alone, or provincial court judge (s. 536).

Evidence. 1. Any person in occupation or possession of a place where such a trap or device has been set or placed, who knowingly and wilfully permits it to remain at that place, is deemed to have placed it there with intent to cause death or bodily harm to persons (s. 247(2)). 2. Once it has been shown that the land occupier knowingly and wilfully permitted the trap or device on his land, the courts have held that the offence is one of absolute liability (R. v. Besse (1975), 26 C.C.C. (2d) 140 (B.C. Prov. Ct.)).

Informations

A.B., on or about the —— day of ——, 19——, at the —— of ——, in the said (territorial division), with intent to cause death [OR bodily harm] to C.D. [OR persons], did set [OR place OR cause to be set (OR placed)] a trap

[OR device OR (specify some other thing likely to cause death or bodily harm to persons)] that was likely to cause death or bodily harm to C.D. [OR persons], to wit: (specify the particulars of the offence), contrary to s. 247(1) of the Criminal Code of Canada.

6. Interfering with transportation facilities — Section 248

Every one who — with intent to endanger the safety of any person — places anything on or does anything to — any property that is used for or in connection with the transportation of persons or goods by land or water or air — that is likely to cause death or bodily harm to persons — is guilty of an indictable offence.

Intent. Intention to endanger safety.

Included offences. Attempts (s. 660 and s. 662(1)(b)).

Punishment. Imprisonment for life (s. 248).

Release. Initial decision to release made by justice (s. 515(1)).

Election. Accused may elect trial by judge and jury, judge alone, or provincial court judge (s. 536).

Informations

A.B., on or about the —— day of ——, 19——, at the —— of ——, in the said (territorial division), with intent to danger the safety of C.D., did place a (specify the thing placed) upon property that was used for [or in connection with] the transportation of persons [OR goods] by land [OR water OR air], that was likely to cause death [OR bodily harm] to C.D. [OR E.F.], to wit: (specify the particulars of the offence), contrary to s. 248 of the Criminal Code of Canada.

A.B., on or about the —— day of ——, 19——, at the —— of ——, in the said (territorial division), with intent to endanger the safety of C.D., did (specify the thing done) to property that was used for [OR in connection with] the transportation of persons [OR goods] by land [OR water OR air], that was likely to cause death [OR bodily harm] to C.D. [OR E.F.], to wit: (specify the particulars of the offence), contrary to s. 248 of the Criminal Code of Canada.

BODY. 1. A person; also the main part of a human body — the trunk. 2. In relation to written instruments, the main part.

BONA FIDE. "In good faith" or "genuine" (Latin).

BOUNDARY LINES

1. *Definition of boundary line*
2. *Interfering with boundary lines of land*
3. *Interfering with international, provincial, county or municipal boundary lines*
4. *Boundary marks placed by land surveyors*

1. Definition of "boundary line". The imaginary line that divides two pieces of property. The line is generally, but not necessarily, marked or indicated on the surface of the land by a wall, fence, ditch or other object.

2. Interfering with boundary lines of land — Section 442

Every one who — wilfully — pulls down or defaces or alters or removes — anything planted or set up as the boundary line or part of the boundary line of land — is guilty of an offence on summary conviction.

Intent. Wilfully.

Limitation period. No proceedings in respect of offences that are declared to be punishable on summary conviction shall be instituted more than 6 months after the time when the subject matter of the proceedings arose (s. 786(2) and s. 785(1)).

Included offences. Attempts (s. 660 and s. 662(1)(b)).

Punishment. A fine not exceeding $2,000, or 6 months' imprisonment, or both (s. 442 and s. 787(1)).

Release. Initial decision to release made by peace officer (s. 497).

Election. No election, summary conviction offence.

Evidence. No person shall be convicted of this offence where he proves that he acted with legal justification or excuse and with colour of right (s. 429(2)).

3. Interfering with international, provincial, county or municipal boundary lines — Section 443(1)(a)

Every one who — wilfully — pulls down or defaces or alters or removes — a boundary mark lawfully placed to mark an

international or provincial or county or municipal boundary — is guilty of an indictable offence.

Intent. Wilfully.

Included offences. Attempts (s. 660 and s. 662(1)(b)).

Punishment. Imprisonment for a term not exceeding 5 years (s. 443(1)).

Release. Initial decision to release made by officer in charge or justice (s. 498).

Election. Accused may elect trial by judge and jury, judge alone, or provincial court judge (s. 536).

Evidence. See Evidence under **2**, *above.*

4. Boundary marks placed by land surveyors — Section 443(1)(b)

Every one who — wilfully — pulls down or defaces or alters or removes — a boundary mark lawfully placed by a land surveyor to mark any limit or boundary or angle of a concession or range or lot or parcel of land — is guilty of an indictable offence.

Intent. Wilfully.

Exception. A land surveyor does not commit this offence where, in his operations as a land surveyor, (a) he takes up, when necessary, a boundary mark and carefully replaces it as it was before he took it up; or (b) he takes up a boundary mark in the course of surveying for a highway or other work that, when completed, will make it impossible or impracticable for that boundary mark to occupy its original position, and he establishes a permanent record of the original position sufficient to permit that position to be ascertained (s. 443(2)).

Included offences. Attempts (s. 660 and s. 662(1)(b)).

Punishment. Imprisonment for a term not exceeding 5 years (s. 443(1)).

Release. Initial decision to release made by officer in charge or justice (s. 498).

Election. Accused may elect trial by judge and jury, judge alone, or provincial court judge (s. 536).

Evidence. See Evidence under **2**, *above.*

BREACH OF CONTRACT

Section 422(1)

Every one who — wilfully — breaks a contract — knowing or having reasonable cause to believe — that the probable consequences of doing so, whether alone or in combination with others, will be — either to endanger human life — or to cause serious bodily injury — or to expose valuable property, real or personal, to destruction or serious injury — or to deprive the inhabitants of a city or place or part thereof, wholly or to a great extent, of their supply of light or power or gas or water — or to delay or prevent the running of a locomotive engine or tender or freight or passenger train or car, on a railway that is a common carrier — is guilty of either an indictable offence or an offence punishable on summary conviction.

Intent. Wilfully with knowledge or reasonable cause to believe in probable consequence of breach.

Exceptions. No person wilfully breaks a contract by reason only that, (a) being the employee of an employer, he stops work as a result of the failure of his employer and himself to agree upon any matter relating to his employment, or (b) being a member of an organization of employees formed for the purpose of regulating relations between employers and employees, he stops work as a result of the failure of the employer and a bargaining agent acting on behalf of the organization to agree on any matter relating to the employment of members of the organization, if, before the stoppage of work occurs, all steps provided by law with respect to the settlement of industrial disputes are taken and any provision for the final settlement of industrial disputes are taken and any provision for the final settlement of differences, without stoppage of work, contained in or by law deemed to be contained in a collective agreement is complied with and effect given thereto (s. 422(2)).

Consent to prosecute. No proceedings shall be instituted for this offence without the consent of the Attorney General (s. 422(3)).

Limitation period. No proceedings in respect of offences that are declared to be punishable on summary conviction shall be instituted more than 6 months after the time when the subject matter of the proceedings arose (s. 786(2) and s. 785(1)).

Included offences. Attempts (s. 660 and s. 662(1)(b)).

Punishment. On indictment, imprisonment for a term not exceeding 5 years (s. 422(1)(f)). On summary conviction, a fine not exceeding $2,000, or 6 months' imprisonment, or both (s. 422(1)(g) and s. 787(1)).

Release. Initial decision to release made by peace officer (s. 497).

Election. On indictment, accused may elect trial by judge and jury, judge alone, or provincial court judge (s. 536). On summary conviction, no election.

Informations

A.B., on or about the —— day of ——, 19——, at the —— of ——, in the said (territorial division), wilfully did break a contract knowing *[OR having reasonable cause to believe]* that the probable consequences of doing so would be to endanger human life *[OR to cause bodily injury OR to expose valuable property to destruction (OR to serious injury) OR to deprive the inhabitants of a city (OR a place OR part of a city OR part of a place) wholly (OR to a great extent) of their supply of light (OR power OR gas OR water) OR to delay (OR prevent) the running of a locomotive engine (OR tender OR freight train OR passenger train OR car) on a railway that was a common carrier]*, to wit: *(specify the particulars of the offence)*, contrary to s. 422(1) of the Criminal Code of Canada.

BREACH OF PROBATION ORDER

Section 740(1)

An accused who — is bound by a probation order — and wilfully fails or refuses to comply with that order — is guilty of an offence punishable on summary conviction.

Intent. Wilfully.

Jurisdiction. An accused charged with this offence may be tried and punished by any court having jurisdiction to try that offence in the place where the offence is alleged to have been committed, or in the place where the accused is found, is arrested or is in custody (s. 740(2)).

Consent to prosecute. Where the place where the accused is found, is arrested or is in custody is outside the province in which the offence is alleged to have been committed, no proceedings in respect of that offence shall be instituted in that place without the consent of the Attorney General of that province (s. 740(2)).

Included offences. Attempts (s. 660 and s. 662(1)(b)).

Punishment. A fine not exceeding $2,000, or 6 months' imprisonment, or both (s. 740(1) and s. 787(1)).

In addition to any punishment that may be imposed for this offence, the court that made the probation order may, on application by the prosecutor, require the accused to appear before it and, after hearing the prosecutor and the accused may either:

(i) revoke the order and impose any sentence that could have been imposed for the offence for which the probation order was imposed if the passing of sentence had not been suspended (s. 738(4)(d)); or

(ii) make such changes in or additions to the conditions prescribed in the order as the court deems desirable, or extend the period for which the order is to remain in force for such period, not exceeding one year, as the court deems desirable (s. 738(4)(e)).

Release. Initial decision to release made by peace officer (s. 497).

Election. No election, summary conviction offence.

Informations

A.B., on or about the —— day of ——, 19——, at the —— of ——, in the said (territorial division), being a person bound by a probation order made (specify where and when the order was made), did wilfully fail [OR refuse] to comply with that order, to wit: (specify the particulars of the offence), contrary to s. 740(1) of the Criminal Code of Canada.

BREACH OF THE PEACE. 1. Any act which tends to disturb the quiet and tranquillity of the realm or the ordinary peaceful state of the country: a riot, a disturbance, a fight or affray or assault. 2. There is a breach of the peace whenever harm is actually done or is likely to be done to a person, or in his presence to his property, or a person is in fear of being so harmed through an assault, an affray, riot, unlawful assembly or other disturbance (R. v. Lefebvre (1982), 1 C.C.C. (3d) 241 (B.C. Co. Ct.), affirmed 15 C.C.C. (3d) 503 (B.C. C.A.)).

BREAK. For the purposes of Part IX (Offences Against Rights of Property), "break" means (a) to break any part, internal or external, or (b) to open any thing that is used or intended to be used to close or to cover an internal or external opening (s. 321).

BREAKING AND ENTERING

1. *Breaking and entering with intent*
2. *Breaking and entering and committing offence*
3. *Breaking out*
4. *Being unlawfully in dwelling-house*
5. *Possession of break-in instrument*
6. *Being in disguise*
7. *Possession of instruments for breaking into coin-operated device or currency exchange device*
8. *Automobile master keys*
9. *Records of sales of automobile master keys*

1. Breaking and entering with intent — Section 348(1)(a)

Every one who — breaks and enters a place — with intent to commit an indictable offence therein — is guilty of an indictable offence.

Intent. Intention to commit indictable offence.

Included offences. Attempts (s. 660 and s. 662(1)(b)); attempted theft (s. 322, s. 334, s. 660 and s. 662(1)(b)); and, being unlawfully in a dwelling-house with intent to commit indictable offence (s. 349).

Punishment. Imprisonment for life, if the offence is committed in relation to a dwelling-house (s. 348(1)(d)). Imprisonment for a term not exceeding 14 years, if the offence is committed in relation to a place other than a dwelling-house (s. 348(1)(e)).

Release. Initial decision to release made by justice (s. 515(1)).

Election. Accused may elect trial by judge and jury, judge alone, or provincial court judge (s. 536).

Definitions. See PLACE.

Evidence. 1. Evidence that an accused broke and entered a place or attempted to break and enter a place is, in the absence of evidence to the contrary, proof that he broke and entered the place, or attempted to do so, as the case may be, with intent to commit an indictable offence therein (s. 348(2)(a)).
2. Evidence that an accused broke out of a place is, in the absence of evidence to the contrary, proof that he broke out after committing an indictable offence therein, or after entering with intent to commit an indictable offence therein (s. 348(2)(b)).
3. For these purposes, a person enters as soon as any part of his body or any part of an instrument that he uses is within any thing that is being entered (s. 350(a)).

4. For these purposes, a person shall be deemed to have broken and entered if he obtained entrance by a threat or artifice or by collusion with a person within, or if he entered without lawful justification or excuse, the proof of which lies on him, by a permanent or temporary opening (s. 350(b)).

Informations

A.B., on or about the —— day of ——, 19——, at the —— of ——, in the said (territorial division), did break and enter a place with intent to commit therein the indictable offence of (specify the indictable offence), to wit: (specify the particulars of the break-in and entry), contrary to s. 348(1)(a) of the Criminal Code of Canada.

2. Breaking and entering and committing offence — Section 348(1)(b)

Every one who — breaks and enters a place — and commits an indictable offence therein — is guilty of an indictable offence.

Included offences. Attempts (s. 660 and s. 662(1)(b)).

Punishment. Imprisonment for life, if the offence is committed in relation to a dwelling-house (s. 348(1)(d)). Imprisonment for a term not exceeding 14 years, if the offence is committed in relation to a place other than a dwelling-house (s. 348(1)(e)).

Release. Initial decision to release made by justice (s. 515(1)).

Election. Accused may elect trial by judge and jury, judge alone, or provincial court judge (s. 536).

Evidence. *See Evidence under* **1**, *above.*

Informations

A.B., on or about the —— day of ——, 19——, at the —— of ——, in the said (territorial division), did break and enter a place and did commit therein the indictable offence of (specify the indictable offence committed), to wit: (specify the particulars of the break-in and entry), contrary to s. 348(1)(b) of the Criminal Code of Canada.

3. Breaking out — Section 348(1)(c)

Every one who — breaks out of a place after — either committing an indictable offence therein — or entering the place with intent to

commit an indictable offence therein — is guilty of an indictable offence.

Intent. Intention to commit indictable offence.

Included offences. Attempts (s. 660 and s. 662(1)(b)).

Punishment. Imprisonment for life, if the offence is committed in relation to a dwelling-house (s. 348(1)(d)). Imprisonment for a term not exceeding 14 years, if the offence is committed in relation to a place other than a dwelling-house (s. 348(1)(e)).

Release. Initial decision to release made by justice (s. 515(1)).

Election. Accused may elect trial by judge and jury, judge alone, or provincial court judge (s. 536).

Evidence. See Evidence under **1**, *above.*

Informations

A.B., on or about the —— day of ——, 19——, at the —— of ——, in the said (territorial division), did break out of a place after having committed therein the indictable offence of (specify the indictable offence committed), to wit: (specify the particulars of the breaking-out), contrary to s. 348(1)(c) of the Criminal Code of Canada.

A.B., on or about the —— day of ——, 19——, at the —— of ——, in the said (territorial division), did break out of a place after having entered the place with the intention to commit therein the indictable offence of (specify the indictable offence), to wit: (specify the particulars of the breaking-out), contrary to s. 348(1)(c) of the Criminal Code of Canada.

4. Being unlawfully in dwelling-house — Section 349(1)

Every one who — without lawful excuse — enters or is in a dwelling-house — with intent to commit an indictable offence therein — is guilty of an indictable offence.

Intent. Intention to commit indictable offence.

Included offences. Attempts (s. 660 and s. 662(1)(b)).

Punishment. Imprisonment for a term not exceeding 10 years (s. 349(1)).

Release. Initial decision to release made by justice (s. 515(1)).

Election. Accused may elect trial by judge and jury, judge alone, or provincial court judge (s. 536).

Evidence. 1. For the purposes of this offence, the proof of lawful excuse lies on the accused (s. 349(1)).
2. Evidence that an accused, without lawful excuse, entered or was in a dwelling-house is, in the absence of any evidence to the contrary, proof that he entered or was in the dwelling-house with intent to commit an indictable offence therein (s. 349(2)).
3. *See also Evidence, items 3. and 4., under* **1**, *above.*

Informations

A.B., on or about the —— day of ——, 19——, at the —— of ——, in the said (territorial division), without lawful excuse, did enter [OR was in] the dwelling-house of C.D. with intent to commit therein the indictable offence of (specify the indictable offence), to wit: (specify the particulars of the offence), contrary to s. 349(1) of the Criminal Code of Canada.

5. Possession of break-in instrument — Section 351(1)

Every one who — without lawful excuse — has in his possession — any instrument suitable for the purpose of breaking into any place or motor vehicle or vault or safe — under circumstances that give rise to a reasonable inference that the instrument has been used or is or was intended to be used for any such purpose — is guilty of an indictable offence.

Included offences. Attempts (s. 660 and s. 662(1)(b)).

Punishment. Imprisonment for a term not exceeding 10 years (s. 351(1)).

Release. Initial decision to release made by justice (s. 515(1)).

Election. Accused may elect trial by judge and jury, judge alone, or provincial court judge (s. 536).

Definitions. See PLACE.

Evidence. 1. For the purposes of this offence, the proof of lawful excuse lies on the accused (s. 351(1)).
2. It must be proved that the accused was in possession of the instrument.
3. The essential elements of this offence, that is, possession of the instrument by the accused, its suitability for breaking into any place, etc., and the circumstances giving rise to the inference of its proposed use, must be proved before the accused is required to discharge the burden of proving a lawful excuse for the possession of the instrument.

Informations

A.B., on or about the —— day of ——, 19——, at the —— of ——, in the said (territorial division), without lawful excuse, did have in his possession an instrument suitable for breaking into a place [OR motor vehicle OR vault OR safe] under circumstances that gave rise to a reasonable inference that the instrument had been used [OR was intended to be used OR had been intended to be used] for breaking into a place [OR motor vehicle OR vault OR safe], to wit: (specify the particulars of the offence), contrary to s. 351(1) of the Criminal Code of Canada.

6. Being in disguise — Section 351(2)

Every one who — with intent to commit an indictable offence — either has his face masked or coloured — or is otherwise disguised — is guilty of an indictable offence.

Intent. Intention to commit indictable offence.

Included offences. Attempts (s. 660 and s. 662(1)(b)).

Punishment. Imprisonment for a term not exceeding 10 years (s. 351(2)).

Release. Initial decision to release made by justice (s. 515(1)).

Election. Accused may elect trial by judge and jury, judge alone, or provincial court judge (s. 536).

Informations

A.B., on or about the —— day of ——, 19——, at the —— of ——, in the said (territorial division), with intent to commit the indictable offence of (specify the indictable offence), did have his face masked [OR coloured], to wit: (specify the particulars of the offence), contrary to s. 351(2) of the Criminal Code of Canada.

A.B., on or about the —— day of ——, 19——, at the —— of ——, in the said (territorial division), with intent to commit the indictable offence of (specify the indictable offence), was disguised, to wit: (specify the particulars of the offence), contrary to s. 351(2) of the Criminal Code of Canada.

7. Possession of instruments for breaking into coin-operated device or currency exchange device — Section 352

Every one who — without lawful excuse — has in his possession — any instrument suitable for breaking into a coin-operated device or a currency exchange device — under circumstances that give rise

to a reasonable inference that the instrument has been used or is or was intended to be used for breaking into a coin-operated device or a currency exchange device — is guilty of an indictable offence.

Included offences. Attempts (s. 660 and s. 662(1)(b)).

Punishment. Imprisonment for a term not exceeding 2 years (s. 352).

Release. Initial decision to release made by officer in charge or justice (s. 498).

Election. Accused may elect trial by judge and jury, judge alone, or provincial court judge (s. 536).

Evidence. For the purposes of this offence, the proof of lawful excuse lies on the accused (s. 352).

Informations

A.B., on or about the —— day of ——, 19——, at the —— of ——, in the said (territorial division), without lawful excuse, did have in his possession an instrument suitable for breaking into a currency exchange device under circumstances that gave rise to a reasonable inference that the instrument had been used [OR was (OR had been) intended to be used] for breaking into a currency exchange device, to wit: (specify the particulars of the offence), contrary to s. 352 of the Criminal Code of Canada.

A.B., on or about the —— day of ——, 19——, at the —— of ——, in the said (territorial division), without lawful excuse, did have in his possession an instrument suitable for breaking into a coin-operated device under circumstances that gave rise to a reasonable inference that the instrument had been used [OR was (OR had been) intended to be used] for breaking into a coin-operated device, to wit: (specify the particulars of the offence), contrary to s. 352 of the Criminal Code of Canada.

8. Automobile master keys

Section 353(1)(a)

Every one who — sells or offers for sale or advertises — in a province — an automobile master key — otherwise than under the authority of a licence issued by the Attorney General of that province — is guilty of an indictable offence.

Section 353(1)(b)

Every one who — purchases or has in his possession — in a province — an automobile master key — otherwise than under the

authority of a licence issued by the Attorney General of that province — is guilty of an indictable offence.

Included offences. Attempts (s. 660 and s. 662(1)(b)).

Punishment. Imprisonment for a term not exceeding 2 years (s. 353(1)).

Release. Initial decision to release made by officer in charge or justice (s. 498).

Election. Accused may elect trial by judge and jury, judge alone, or provincial court judge (s. 536).

Definitions. See *AUTOMOBILE MASTER KEY*.

Evidence. A licence issued by the Attorney General of a province as described above may contain such terms and conditions relating to the sale, offering for sale, advertising, purchasing or having in possession of an automobile master key as the Attorney General of that province may prescribe (s. 353(2)).

Informations

A.B., on or about the —— day of ——, 19——, at the —— of ——, in the said (territorial division), did sell [OR offer for sale OR advertise] in the Province of (specify), an automobile master key without the authority of a licence issued by the Attorney General of that Province, to wit: (specify the particulars of the offence), contrary to s. 353(1) of the Criminal Code of Canada.

A.B., on or about the —— day of ——, 19——, at the —— of ——, in the said (territorial division), did purchase [OR have in his possession] in the Province of (specify), an automobile master key without the authority of a licence issued by the Attorney General of that Province, to wit: (specify the particulars of the offence), contrary to s. 353(1) of the Criminal Code of Canada.

9. Records of sales of automobile master keys

Duty — Section 353(3)

Every one who — sells an automobile master key — is required to keep a record of the transaction showing the name and address of the purchaser and particulars of the licence issued to the purchaser as described in s. 353(1)(b) — and is required to produce such record for inspection at the request of a peace officer.

Statement of offence — Section 353(4)

Every one who — fails to comply with these requirements — is guilty of an offence punishable on summary conviction.

Limitation period. No proceedings in respect of offences that are declared to be punishable on summary conviction shall be instituted more than 6 months after the time when the subject matter of the proceedings arose (s. 786(2) and s. 785(1)).

Included offences. Attempts (s. 660 and s. 662(1)(b)).

Punishment. A fine not exceeding $2,000, or 6 months' imprisonment, or both (s. 353(4) and s. 787(1)).

Release. Initial decision to release made by peace officer (s. 497).

Election. No election, summary conviction offence.

Definitions. See AUTOMOBILE MASTER KEY.

Informations

A.B., on or about the —— day of ——, 19——, at the —— of ——, in the said (territorial division), having sold an automobile master key, did fail to keep a record of the transaction showing the name and address of the purchaser and the particulars of the licence issued to the purchaser as described in s. 353(1)(b) of the Criminal Code, to wit: (specify the particulars of the offence), contrary to s. 353(4) of the Criminal Code of Canada.

A.B., on or about the —— day of ——, 19——, at the —— of ——, in the said (territorial division), having sold an automobile master key, did fail to produce for inspection at the request of C.D., a peace officer, the record of that transaction required by law to be kept by anyone who sells an automobile master key, to wit: (specify the particulars of the offence), contrary to s. 353(4) of the Criminal Code of Canada.

BRUISE. A hemorrhage into the tissues beneath the skin; usually caused by violence but may be spontaneous in certain disorders of the blood. During life the colour of bruises changes gradually, giving a rough indication of their ages (Jaffe, A Guide to Pathological Evidence, 2nd ed.).

BUILDING DAMAGE

Section 441

Every one who — wilfully and to the prejudice of a mortgagee or an owner — either pulls down or demolishes or removes all or any part of a dwelling-house or other building of which he is in possession or occupation — or severs from the freehold any fixture fixed therein or thereto — is guilty of an indictable offence.

Intent. Wilfully.

Included offences. Attempts (s. 660 and s. 662(1)(b)).

Punishment. Imprisonment for a term not exceeding 5 years (s. 441).

Release. Initial decision to release made by officer in charge or justice (s. 498).

Election. Accused may elect trial by judge and jury, judge alone, or provincial court judge (s. 536).

Evidence. No person shall be convicted of this offence where he proves that he acted with legal justification or excuse and with colour of right (s. 429(2)).

BUSINESS. For the purposes of s. 30 of the Canada Evidence Act, "business" means any business, profession, trade, calling, manufacture or undertaking of any kind carried on in Canada or elsewhere whether for profit or otherwise, including any activity or operation carried on or performed in Canada or elsewhere by any government, by any department, branch, board, commission or agency of any government, by any court or other tribunal or by any other body or authority performing a function of government (Canada Evidence Act, s. 30(12)).

BURKING. A homicidal form of traumatic asphyxia employed by Burke and Hare in which one of the assailants sat on the victim's chest (Jaffe, A Guide to Pathological Evidence, 2nd ed.).

C

CADAVER. A dead body, a corpse (Jaffe, A Guide to Pathological Evidence, 2nd ed.).

CALIBER. The inside diameter of the barrel of a firearm. In rifled barrels it is the distance from land to land (Jaffe, A Guide to Pathological Evidence, 2nd ed.).

CANADIAN FORCES. For the purposes of the Criminal Code, the armed forces of Her Majesty raised by Canada (s. 2).

CAPIAS AD SATISFACIENDUM (CA. SA.). "Take in satisfaction". The opening words of a writ empowering the arrest of a debtor.

CARBON MONOXIDE. A toxic gas produced by the incomplete combustion of organic materials. It combines with hemoglobin, thus preventing the carriage of oxygen, and producing a state of asphyxia. Carbon monoxide is an important constituent of motor exhaust gas and coal gas (Jaffe, A Guide to Pathological Evidence, 2nd ed.).

CASPAR'S RULE. "At a tolerably similar temperature the degree of putrefaction present in a body after lying in the open air for one week corresponds to that found in a body after lying in water for two weeks or after lying in the earth in the usual manner for eight weeks": Johann Ludwig Caspar 1786-1864 (Jaffe, A Guide to Pathological Evidence, 2nd ed.).

CATTLE. For the purposes of the Criminal Code, "cattle" means neat cattle or an animal of the bovine species by whatever technical or familiar name it is known, including any horse, mule, ass, pig, sheep or goat (s. 2). *See also ANIMAL OFFENCES, SEARCH AND SEIZURE, 12 and THEFT AND OFFENCES RESEMBLING THEFT, 13 and 14.*

CAUSA CAUSANS. The immediate cause (Latin).

CAUSA EFFECTIVA. Effective cause (Latin).

CAUSA SINE QUA NON. Indispensable cause (Latin).

CAUSE. For the purposes of Part II of the Canada Evidence Act, "cause" includes a proceeding against a criminal (Canada Evidence Act, s. 44).

CAVEAT. Caution or a warning (Latin). ***Caveat actor.*** "Let the doer beware" (Latin). ***Caveat emptor.*** "Let the buyer beware" (Latin). ***Caveat venditor.*** "Let the seller beware" (Latin).

CERTIFICATE OF CITIZENSHIP

1. *Definition of "certificate of citizenship"*
2. *Fraudulent use of certificate of citizenship*

1. Definition of "certificate of citizenship". For the purposes of s. 58, this expression means a certificate of citizenship as defined by the Canadian Citizenship Act (s. 58(2)).

2. Fraudulent use of certificate of citizenship

Section 58(1)(a)

Every one who — while in or out of Canada — uses a certificate of citizenship — for a fraudulent purpose — is guilty of an indictable offence.

Section 58(1)(b)

Every one who — while in or out of Canada — being a person to whom a certificate of citizenship has been granted — knowingly — parts with the possession of that certificate — with intent that it should be used for a fraudulent purpose — is guilty of an indictable offence.

Intent. Intention to use for fraudulent purpose (s. 58(1)(a)); knowingly part with possession with intention to use for fraudulent purpose (s. 58(1)(b)).

Included offences. Attempts (s. 660 and s. 662(1)(b)).

Punishment. Imprisonment for a term not exceeding 2 years (s. 58(1)).

Release. Initial decision to release made by officer in charge or justice (s. 498).

Election. Accused may elect trial by judge and jury, judge alone, or provincial court judge (s. 536).

Sufficiency of count. No count that alleges false pretences, fraud or any attempt or conspiracy by fraudulent means is insufficient by reason that it does not set out in detail the nature of the false pretence, fraud or fraudulent means (s. 586).

Informations

A.B., on or about the —— day of ——, 19——, at the —— of ——, in the said (territorial division), did use a certificate of citizenship for a fraudulent purpose, to wit: (specify the particulars of the offence), contrary to s. 58(1)(a) of the Criminal Code of Canada.

A.B., on or about the —— day of ——, 19——, at the—— of ——, in the said (territorial division), being a person to whom a certificate of citizenship had been granted under the provisions of the Canadian Citizenship Act, did knowingly part with possession of that certificate to C.D. with intent that it be used for a fraudulent purpose, to wit: (specify the particulars of the offence), contrary to s. 58(1)(b) of the Criminal Code of Canada.

CERTIFICATE OF NATURALIZATION

1. Definition of "certificate of naturalization"
2. Fraudulent use of certificate of naturalization

1. Definition of "certificate of naturalization". For the purposes of s. 58, this expression means a certificate of naturalization as defined by the Canadian Citizenship Act (s. 58(2)).

2. Fraudulent use of certificate of naturalization

Section 58(1)(a)

Every one who — while in or out of Canada — uses a certificate of naturalization — for a fraudulent purpose — is guilty of an indictable offence.

Section 58(1)(b)

Every one who — while in or out of Canada — being a person to whom a certificate of naturalization has been granted — knowingly — parts with the possession of that certificate — with intent that it should be used for a fraudulent purpose — is guilty of an indictable offence.

Intent. Intention to use for fraudulent purposes (s. 58(1)(a)); knowingly part with possession with intention to use for fraudulent purpose (s. 58(1)(b)).

Included offences. Attempts (s. 660 and s. 662(1)(b)).

Punishment. Imprisonment for a term not exceeding 2 years (s. 58(1)).

Release. Initial decision to release made by officer in charge or justice (s. 498).

Election. Accused may elect trial by judge and jury, judge alone, or provincial court judge (s. 536).

Sufficiency of count. No count that alleges false pretences, fraud or any attempt or conspiracy by fraudulent means is insufficient by reason only that it does not set out in detail the nature of the false pretence, fraud or fraudulent means (s. 586).

Informations

A.B., on or about the —— day of ——, 19——, at the —— of ——, in the said (territorial division), did use a certificate of naturalization for a fraudulent purpose, to wit: (specify the particulars of the offence), contrary to s. 58(1)(a) of the Criminal Code of Canada.

A.B., on or about the —— day of ——, 19——, at the —— of ——, in the said (territorial division), being a person to whom a certificate of naturalization has been granted, did knowingly part with the possession of that certificate with intent that it should be used for a fraudulent purpose, to wit: (specify the particulars of the offence), contrary to s. 58(1)(b) of the Criminal Code of Canada.

CERTIORARI. An original writ which is issued out of a superior court, addressed to judges or officers of inferior courts, commanding them to certify or to return the records of a cause pending before an inferior court, to the end that justice may be done.

CESTUI QUE TRUST. "A person for whom another is trustee; a beneficiary" (Norman French).

CHARTER OF RIGHTS AND FREEDOMS

1. *General*
2. *Fundamental freedoms*
3. *Democratic rights*
4. *Mobility rights*
5. *Legal rights*
6. *Equality rights*
7. *Official language rights and minority education rights*
8. *Reasonable limits*

1. General. The Constitution Act, 1982, includes a Canadian Charter of Rights and Freedoms. In the Preamble of the Charter, it states that "Canada is founded upon principles that recognize the supremacy of

God and the rule of law". The rights and freedoms guaranteed by the Charter are:

2. Fundamental freedoms. Everyone has the following fundamental freedoms:

(a) freedom of conscience and religion;
(b) freedom of thought, belief, opinion and expression, including freedom of the press and other media of communication;
(c) freedom of peaceful assembly; and
(d) freedom of association (Charter, s. 2).

3. Democratic rights. Specifically, the Charter provides for the right of every citizen to vote or run for the House of Commons and the provincial legislative assembly, and the right to elections at least every 5 years, though in time of real or apprehended war, invasion or insurrection, the life of a federal or provincial House may be prolonged by a two-thirds vote of the Commons or legislative assembly (Charter, ss. 3, 4 and 5).

4. Mobility rights. The Charter provides for the right of every citizen to enter, remain in and leave Canada, and to move to, and earn a living in, any province subject to certain limitations, notably to provide for "affirmative action" programs for the socially or economically disadvantaged (Charter, s. 6).

5. Legal rights. Everyone has the right to life, liberty and security of the person and the right not to be deprived thereof except in accordance with the principles of fundamental justice (Charter, s. 7).

Everyone has the right to be secure against unreasonable search or seizure (Charter, s. 8).

Everyone has the right not to be arbitrarily detained or imprisoned (Charter, s. 9).

Everyone has the right on arrest or detention: (a) to be informed promptly of the reasons therefor; (b) to retain and instruct counsel without delay and to be informed of that right; and (c) to have the validity of the detention determined by way of habeas corpus and to be released if the detention is not lawful (Charter, s. 10).

Any person charged with an offence has the right: (a) to be informed without unreasonable delay of the specific offence; (b) to be tried within a reasonable time; (c) not to be compelled to be a witness in proceedings against that person in respect of the offence; (d) to be presumed innocent until proven guilty according to law in a fair and public hearing by an independent and impartial tribunal; (e) not to be denied reasonable bail without just cause; (f) except in the case of an offence under military law tried before a military tribunal, to the benefit of trial by jury where the maximum punishment for the offence is imprisonment for 5 years or a more severe punishment; (g) not to be found guilty on account of any act or omission unless, at the time of the act or omission, it constituted an offence under Canadian or international law or was criminal according to the general principles of law recognized by the community of nations; (h) if finally acquitted of the offence, not to be tried for it again and, if finally found guilty and punished for the offence, not to be tried or punished for it again; and (i) if found guilty of the offence and if the punishment for the offence has been varied between the time of commission and the time of sentencing, to the benefit of the lesser punishment (Charter, s. 11).

Everyone has the right not to be subjected to any cruel and unusual treatment or punishment (Charter, s. 12).

A witness who testifies in any proceedings has the right not to have any incriminating evidence so given used to incriminate that witness in any other proceedings, except in a prosecution for perjury or for the giving of contradictory evidence (Charter, s. 13).

A party or witness in any proceedings who does not understand or speak the language in which the proceedings are conducted or who is deaf has the right to the assistance of an interpreter (Charter, s. 14).

6. Equality rights. The Charter also provides that every individual is equal before and under the law and has the right to the equal protection and equal benefit of the law without discrimination and, in particular, without discrimination based on race, national or ethnic origin, colour, religion, sex, age or mental or physical disability (Charter, s. 15(1)). This provision does not preclude any law, program or activity that has as its object the amelioration of conditions of disadvantaged individuals or groups including those that are disadvantaged because of race, national or ethnic origin, colour, religion, sex, age or mental or physical disability (Charter, s. 15(2)).

These equality rights provisions did not come into effect until 3 years after the Charter came into force.

7. Official language rights and minority language education rights. The Charter also includes additional rights regarding the use of the

French and English languages in Canada (Charter, ss. 15, 16, 17, 18, 19, 20, 21, 22 and 23).

8. Reasonable limits. The Canadian Charter of Rights and Freedoms guarantees the rights and freedoms set out in it subject only to such reasonable limits prescribed by law as can be demonstrably justified in a free and democratic society (Charter, s. 1).

CHASTE CHARACTER. This expression does not of necessity mean an intact hymen, although previous chaste character is usually proved by a medical examination disclosing a recently ruptured hymen or bruises on the genitals. Chaste character does not mean chaste reputation. A girl who had submitted some time previously to illicit intercourse but who had since then rehabilitated herself in character could be said to be of chaste character, so of course any married woman might be of chaste character.

CHEQUE. For the purposes of ss. 362 and 364, "cheque" includes, in addition to its ordinary meaning, a bill of exchange drawn on any institution that makes it a business practice to honour bills of exchange or any particular kind thereof drawn on it by depositors (s. 362(5) and s. 364(3)).

CHILD. 1. For the purposes of s. 172, "child" means a person who is or appears to be under the age of 18 years (s. 172(3)). 2. For the purposes of Part VIII (Offences Against the Person and Reputation), "child" includes an adopted child and an illegitimate child (s. 214). 3. For the purposes of the Young Offenders Act, "child" means a person who is or, in the absence of evidence to the contrary, appears to be under 12 years of age (Young Offenders Act, s. 2(1)). 4. A child becomes a human being within the meaning of the Criminal Code when it has completely proceeded, in a living state, from the body of its mother whether or not (a) it has breathed, (b) it has an independent circulation, or (c) the navel string is severed (s. 223(1)). 5. A child under the age of 12 years cannot be convicted of a criminal offence in any proceedings (Mewett, Introduction to the Criminal Process).

CHILD PORNOGRAPHY. For the purposes of s. 163.1, "child pornography" means (a) a photographic, film, video or other visual representation, whether or not it was made by electronic or mechanical means, (i) that shows a person who is or is depicted as being under the age of 18 years and is engaged in or is depicted as engaged in explicit sexual activity, or (ii) the dominant characteristic of which is the depiction, for a sexual purpose, of a sexual organ or the anal region of a person under the age of 18 years; or (b) any written material or visual representation that advocates or counsels sexual activity with a person under the age of 18 years that would be an offence under the Criminal Code. (s. 163.1(1)).

CHILLED SHOT. Especially hardened shot pellets (Jaffe, A Guide to Pathological Evidence, 2nd ed.).

CHOKE. Amongst other things, a constriction in the muzzle end of a shotgun barrel which narrows the area of scatter of shotgun pellets (Jaffe, A Guide to Pathological Evidence, 2nd ed.).

CHOKING. A form of asphyxia caused by the obstruction of the upper air passages (Jaffe, A Guide to Pathological Evidence, 2nd ed.).

CIVIL AIRCRAFT. For the purposes of s. 78, "civil aircraft" means all aircraft other than aircraft operated by the Canadian Forces, a police force in Canada or persons engaged in the administration or enforcement of the Customs Act or the Excise Act (s. 78(2)).

CLIP. A removable magazine of a firearm containing unfired cartridges. Also, "cartridge clip" (Jaffe, A Guide to Pathological Evidence, 2nd ed.).

COCAINE. An alkaloid from the leaves of the Erythroxylon trees native to Peru and Bolivia. Systemically cocaine is a cerebral stimulant, topically a local anaesthetic. Used illicitly it is usually snuffed in the form of a white powder (Jaffe, A Guide to Pathological Evidence, 2nd ed.).

COMMENCEMENT. When used with reference to an enactment, "commencement" means the time at which the enactment comes into force (Interpretation Act, s. 35).

COMMON LAW. That part of the law of England formulated, developed and administered by the old common law courts, based originally on the common customs of the country, and unwritten. Under the Criminal Code, almost all offences for which a prosecution can take place have been codified. Charges can no longer be laid for common law offences which have not been so codified except for contempt of court (s. 9).

COMPANY. For the purposes of s. 400, "company" means a syndicate, body corporate or company, whether existing or proposed to be created (s. 400(2)).

COMPLAINANT. For the purposes of the Criminal Code, "complainant" means the victim of an alleged offence (s. 2).

COMPLAINT. For the purpose of Part XXVII (Summary Convictions), an "information" includes a "complaint" (s. 785(1)). There is a difference between a complaint and an information; a complaint is made when a person is liable to have an order made against him, and an information is laid when the person is liable to imprisonment, fine or penalty.

COMPOS MENTIS. "Of sound mind" (Latin).

COMPUTER OFFENCES

1. *Definitions*
2. *Unauthorized use of computer*
3. *Damage not more than $50. See MISCHIEF, 6.*

1. Definitions

"Computer program". For the purposes of s. 342.1, "computer program" means data representing instructions or statements that, when executed in a computer system, causes the computer to perform a function (s. 342.1(2)).

"Computer service". For the purposes of s. 342.1, "computer service" includes data processing and the storage or retrieval of data (s. 342.1(2)).

"Computer system". For the purposes of s. 342.1, "computer system" means a device that, or a group of interconnected or related devices one or more of which, (a) contains computer programs or other data, and (b) pursuant to computer programs, performs logic and control, and may perform any other function (s. 342.1(2)).

"Data". For the purposes of s. 342.1 "data" means representations of information or of concepts that are being prepared or have been prepared in a form suitable for use in a computer system (s. 342.1(2)).

"Electro-magnetic, acoustic, mechanical or other device". For the purposes of s. 342.1, this expression means any device or apparatus that is used or is capable of being used to intercept any function of a computer system, but does not include a hearing aid used to correct subnormal hearing of the user to not better than normal hearing (s. 342.1(2)).

"Function". For the purposes of s. 342.1 "function" includes logic, control, arithmetic, deletion, storage and retrieval and communication or telecommunication to, from or within a computer system (s. 342.1(2)).

"Intercept". Fo the purposes of s. 342.1, "intercept" includes listen to or record a function of a computer system, or acquire the substance, meaning or purport thereof (s. 342.1(2)).

2. Unauthorized use of computer

Section 342.1(1)(a)

Every one who — fraudulently and without colour of right — obtains, directly or indirectly — any computer service — is guilty of either an indictable offence or an offence punishable on summary conviction.

Section 342.1(1)(b)

Every one who — fraudulently and without colour of right — by means of an electro-magnetic or acoustic or mechanical or other device — intercepts or causes to be intercepted, directly or indirectly — any function of a computer system — is guilty of either an indictable offence or an offence punishable on summary conviction.

Section 342.1(1)(c)

Every one who — fraudulently and without colour of right — uses or causes to be used, directly or indirectly — a computer system — with intent to commit either of the above offences or the offence of mischief in relation to data or a computer system (s. 430) — is guilty of either an indictable offence or an offence punishable on summary conviction.

Intent. Fraudulently.

Limitation period. No proceedings in respect of offences that are declared to be punishable on summary conviction shall be instituted

more than 6 months after the time when the subject matter of the proceedings arose (s. 786(2) and s. 785(1)).

Included offences. Attempts (s. 660 and s. 662(1)(b)).

Punishment. On indictment, imprisonment for a term not exceeding 10 years (s. 342.1(1)). On summary conviction, a fine not exceeding $2,000, or 6 months' imprisonment, or both (s. 342.1(1) and s. 787(1)).

Release. Initial decision to release made by peace officer (s. 497).

Election. On indictment, accused may elect trial by judge and jury, judge alone, or provincial court judge (s. 536). On summary conviction, no election.

Sufficiency of count. No count that alleges false pretences, fraud or any attempt or conspiracy by fraudulent means is insufficient by reason only that it does not set out in detail the nature of the false pretence, fraud or fraudulent means (s. 586).

Informations

A.B., on or about the —— day of ——, 19——, at the —— of ——, in the said (territorial division), did, fraudulently and without colour of right, obtain, directly [OR indirectly], a computer service, to wit: (specify the particulars of the offence), contrary to s. 342.1(1)(a) of the Criminal Code of Canada.

A.B., on or about the —— day of ——, 19——, at the —— of ——, in the said (territorial division), did, fraudulently and without colour of right, by means of an electro-magnetic [OR acoustic OR mechanical OR (specify other type of device)] device, intercept [OR cause to be intercepted] directly [OR indirectly], a function of a computer system, to wit: (specify the particulars of the offence), contrary to s. 342.1(1)(b) of the Criminal Code of Canada.

CONCEALING DEAD BODY OF CHILD

Section 243

Every one who — in any manner — disposes of the dead body of a child — with intent to conceal the fact that its mother has been delivered of it — whether the child died before or during or after birth — is guilty of an indictable offence.

Intent. Intention to conceal fact that mother has been delivered of it.

Included offences. Attempts (s. 660 and s. 662(1)(b)).

Punishment. Imprisonment for a term not exceeding 2 years (s. 243).

Release. Initial decision to release made by officer in charge or justice (s. 498).

Election. Accused may elect trial by judge and jury, judge alone, or provincial court judge (s. 536).

Informations

A.B., on or about the —— day of ——, 19——, at the —— of ——, in the said (territorial division), did dispose of the dead body of the child of A.B. [OR C.D.] with intent to conceal the fact that A.B. [OR C.D.] had been delivered of it, to wit: (specify the particulars of the offence), contrary to s. 243 of the Criminal Code of Canada.

CONSENSUS AD IDEM. "Agreement as to the same thing; the common consent necessary for a binding contract" (Latin).

CONSENT TO PROSECUTE. The consent of the Attorney General of a province to prosecute is required in the following Criminal Code offences: witness giving contradictory evidence (s. 136); publishing reports of judicial proceedings (s. 166); corrupting children (s. 172); nudity (s. 174); fraudulently concealing title documents (s. 385); criminal breach of contract (s. 422); and an offence, other than one listed in section 469 committed outside of the province but in Canada (s. 478(3)).

The consent of the Attorney General of Canada to prosecute is required in the following Criminal Code offences: assisting a deserter (s. 54); judicial officer taking a bribe (s. 119); unseaworthy vessel and unsafe aircraft (s. 251); and, offences on the territorial sea of Canada where the accused is not a Canadian citizen (s. 477).

For procedure in obtaining consent to prosecute it is suggested that senior police officers or the Crown prosecutor be consulted. It is further suggested that a practical method is to prepare a draft Information and submit it to the Crown prosecutor for transmission to the Attorney General. Consent to prosecute may be endorsed thereon and the Information may then be sworn.

CONSPIRACY

1. *Conspiracy to commit murder*
2. *Conspiracy to prosecute innocent person*
3. *Conspiracy to commit an indictable offence*
4. *Conspiracy to commit an offence punishable on summary conviction*
5. *Conspiracies deemed to occur in Canada*
6. *Conspiracy in restraint of trade*
7. *Husband and wife*
8. *Definition of "seditious conspiracy". See SEDITION, 1.*

1. Conspiracy to commit murder — Section 465(1)(a)

Every one who — conspires with any one — either to commit murder — or to cause another person to be murdered — whether in Canada or not — is guilty of an indictable offence.

Included offences. Attempts (s. 660 and s. 662(1)(b)).

Punishment. A maximum term of imprisonment for life (s. 465(1)(a)).

Release. Initial decision to release may only be made by superior court judge (s. 522).

Election. Superior court (with jury) exclusive, except where accused elects superior court trial without jury with consent of Attorney General (s. 473) (s. 469).

Evidence. See **5**, below.

Informations

A.B., on or about the —— day of ——, 19——, at the —— of ——, in the said (territorial division), did conspire with C.D. to commit murder [OR to cause E.F. to be murdered], to wit: (specify the particulars of the offence), contrary to s. 465(1)(a) of the Criminal Code of Canada.

2. Conspiracy to prosecute innocent person — Section 465(1)(b)

Every one who — conspires with any one — to prosecute a person for an alleged offence — knowing that he did not commit that offence — is guilty of an indictable offence.

Intent. Knowledge that person innocent.

Included offences. Attempts (s. 660 and s. 662(1)(b)).

Punishment. Imprisonment for a term not exceeding 10 years, if the alleged offence is one for which, on conviction, the person would be liable to be sentenced to death or to imprisonment for life or for a term not exceeding 14 years (s. 465(1)(b)(i)). Imprisonment for a term not exceeding 5 years, if the alleged offence is one for which, on conviction, that person would be liable to imprisonment for less than 14 years (s. 465(1)(b)(ii)).

Release. If alleged offence is one for which, on conviction, the person would be liable to be sentenced to death or to imprisonment for life or for a term not exceeding 14 years, initial decision to release made by justice (s. 515(1)). If alleged offence is one for which, on conviction, the person would be liable to imprisonment for less than 14 years, initial decision to release made by officer in charge or justice (s. 498).

Election. Accused may elect trial by judge and jury, judge alone, or provincial court judge (s. 536).

Evidence. See **5**, *below.*

Informations

A.B., on or about the —— day of ——, 19——, at the —— of ——, in the said (territorial division), did conspire with C.D. to prosecute E.F. for an alleged offence, knowing that he did not commit that offence, to wit: (specify the particulars of the offence), contrary to s. 465(1)(b) of the Criminal Code of Canada.

3. Conspiracy to commit an indictable offence — Section 465(1)(c)

Every one who — conspires with any one — to commit an indictable offence (other than conspiracy to commit murder (s. 465(1)(a)) and conspiracy to prosecute an innocent person (s. 465(1)(b)) — is guilty of an indictable offence.

Included offences. Attempts (s. 660 and s. 662(1)(b)).

Punishment. The same punishment as that to which an accused who is guilty of that offence would, upon conviction, be liable (s. 465(1)(c)).

Evidence. See **5**, *below.*

Informations

A.B., on or about the —— day of ——, 19——, at the —— of ——, in the said (territorial division), did conspire with C.D. to commit the indictable offence of (specify the indictable offence), to wit: (specify the particulars of the conspiracy), contrary to s. 465(1)(c) of the Criminal Code of Canada.

4. Conspiracy to commit an offence punishable on summary conviction — Section 465(1)(d)

Every one who — conspires with any one — to commit an offence punishable on summary conviction — is guilty of an offence punishable on summary conviction.

Limitation period. No proceedings in respect of offences that are declared to be punishable on summary conviction shall be instituted more than 6 months after the time when the subject matter of the proceedings arose (s. 786(2) and s. 785(1)).

Included offences. Attempts (s. 660 and s. 662(1)(b)).

Punishment. A fine not exceeding $2,000, or 6 months' imprisonment, or both (s. 465(1)(d) and s. 787(1)).

Release. Initial decision to release made by peace officer (s. 497).

Election. No election, summary conviction offence.

Evidence. See **5**, *below.*

Informations

A.B., on or about the —— day of ——, 19——, at the —— of ——, in the said (territorial division), did conspire with C.D. to commit the offence of (specify the offence punishable on summary conviction), such offence being punishable on summary conviction, to wit: (specify the particulars of the conspiracy), contrary to s. 465(1)(d) of the Criminal Code of Canada.

5. Conspiracies deemed to occur in Canada.

1. Every one who, while in Canada, conspires with any one to do anything referred to in s. 465(1) (i.e., to commit murder, to prosecute an innocent person, to commit an indictable offence, to commit an offence punishable on summary conviction) in a place outside Canada that is an offence under the laws of that place shall be deemed to have conspired to do that thing in Canada (s. 465(3)).
2. Every one who, while in a place outside Canada, conspires with any one to do anything referred to in s. 465(1) in Canada shall be deemed to have conspired in Canada to do that thing (s. 465(4)).

6. Conspiracy in restraint of trade

Definition. An agreement between two or more persons to do or to procure to be done any unlawful act in restraint of trade (s. 466(1)).

This definition is subject to certain exceptions that were made necessary when acts that were formerly unlawful became lawful.

Exceptions. 1. The purposes of a trade union are not, by reason only that they are in restraint of trade, unlawful (s. 466(2)).
2. No person is to be convicted of the offence of conspiracy by reason only that he refuses to work with a workman or for an employer (s. 467(1)(a)).
3. No person is to be convicted of the offence of conspiracy by reason only that he does any act or causes any act to be done for the purpose of a trade combination, unless such act is an offence expressly punishable by law (s. 467(1)(b)).

For these purposes, "trade combination" means any combination between masters or workmen or other persons for the purpose of regulating or altering the relations between masters or workmen, or the conduct of a master or workman in or in respect of his business, employment or contract of employment or service (s. 467(2)).

7. Husband and wife

A husband and wife cannot be found guilty of conspiring together as in law they are considered as one person. To be convicted of conspiracy, it would be necessary for there to be a third party to their agreement.

CONTEMPT OF COURT

1. *Definition*	4. *Exhibits*
2. *General*	5. *Failure to attend or remain in attendance at court*
3. *Preliminary inquiry*	

1. Definition. Any act which is calculated to embarrass, hinder or obstruct a court in the administration of justice, or which is calculated to lessen its authority or its dignity.

2. General. The common law powers of a court to punish for contempt of court is preserved by the Criminal Code (s. 9). Contempts are of two kinds, direct and constructive.

Direct contempts are those committed in the immediate view and presence of the court (such as insulting language or acts of violence) or so near the presence of the court as to obstruct or interrupt the due and orderly course of proceedings. These are punishable summarily. They are also called "criminal contempts".

Constructive (or indirect) contempts are those which arise from matters not occurring in or near the presence of the court, but which tend to obstruct or defeat the administration of justice, and the term is chiefly used with reference to the failure or refusal of a party to obey a lawful order, injunction or decree of a court laying upon him a duty of action or forbearance. Constructive contempts were formerly called "consequential contempts".

Contempts are also classed as civil or criminal. The former are those quasi contempts which consist in the failure to do something which the party is ordered by the court to do for the benefit or advantage of another party to the proceedings before the court, while criminal contempts are acts done in disrespect of the court or its process or which obstruct the administration of justice or tend to bring the court into disrespect.

3. Preliminary inquiry. Where a person, being present at a preliminary inquiry and being required by the justice to give evidence, either (a) refuses to be sworn, or (b) having been sworn, refuses to answer the questions that are put to him, or (c) fails to produce any writings that he is required to produce, or (d) refuses to sign his deposition, without offering a reasonable excuse for his failure or refusal, the justice may adjourn the inquiry and may, by warrant in Form 20, commit the person to prison for a period not exceeding 8 clear days or for the period during which the inquiry is adjourned, whichever is the lesser period (s. 545(1)).

Where such a person is brought before the justice on the resumption of the adjourned inquiry and again refuses to do what is required of him, the justice may again adjourn the inquiry for a period not exceeding 8 clear days and commit him to prison for the period of adjournment or any part thereof, and may adjourn the inquiry and commit the person to prison from time to time until the person consents to do what is required of him (s. 545(2)).

4. Exhibits. A judge of a superior court of criminal jurisdiction or a court of criminal jurisdiction may, on summary application on behalf of the accused or the prosecutor, after 3 days' notice to the accused or prosecutor, as the case may be, order the release of any exhibit for the purpose of a scientific or other test or examination, subject to such terms as appear to be necessary or desirable to ensure the safeguarding of the exhibit and its preservation for use at the trial (s. 605(1)).

Every one who fails to comply with the terms of such an order is guilty of contempt of court and may be dealt with summarily by the judge or provincial court judge who made the order or before whom the trial of the accused takes place (s. 605(2)).

5. Failure to attend or to remain in attendance at court. A person who, being required by law to attend or remain in attendance for the purpose of giving evidence, fails, without lawful excuse, to attend or remain in attendance accordingly, is guilty of contempt of court (s. 708(1)).

A court, judge, justice or provincial court judge may deal summarily with a person who is guilty of such a contempt of court and that person is liable to a fine not exceeding $100 or to imprisonment for a term not exceeding 90 days or to both, and may be ordered to pay the costs that are incident to the service of any process and to his detention, if any (s. 708(2)).

CONTROLLED DRUGS

1. *Definitions*
2. *Trafficking in a controlled drug*
3. *Possession of controlled drug for trafficking*
4. *Failure to disclose previous prescriptions*

1. Definitions

"Controlled drug". For the purposes of Part III of the Food and Drugs Act, this expression means any drug or other substance included in Schedule G (Food and Drugs Act, s. 38). At present, Schedule G includes the following drugs:

> Amphetamine and its salts
> Androisoxazole
> Androstanolone
> Androstenediol and its derivatives
> Barbituric acid and its salts and derivatives
> Benzphetamine and its salts
> Bolandiol and its derivatives
> Bolasterone
> Bolazine
> Boldenone and its derivatives
> Bolenol
> Butorphanol and its salts

Calusterone
Chlorphentermine and its salts
Clostebol and its derivatives
Diethylpropion and its salts
Drostanolone and its derivatives
Enestebol
Epitiostanol
Ethylestrenol
Fluoxymesterone
Formebolone
Furazabol
4-Hydroxy-19-nortestosterone and its derivatives
Mebolazine
Mesabolone
Mesterolone
Metandienone
Metenolone and its derivatives
Methamphetamine and its salts
Methandriol
Methaqualone and its salts
Methylphenidate and its salts
Methyltestosterone and its derivatives
Metribolone
Mibolerone
Nalbuphine and its salts
Nandrolone and its derivatives
Norboletone
Norclostebol and its derivatives
Norethandrolone
Oxabolone and its derivatives
Oxandrolone
Oxymesterone
Oxymetholone
Phendimetrazine and its salts
Phenmetrazine and its salts
Phentermine and its salts
Prasterone
Quinbolone
Stanozolol
Stenbolone and its derivatives
Testosterone and its derivatives
Thiobarbituric acid and its salts and derivatives

Tibolone
Tiomesterone
Trenbolone and its derivatives
Zeranol

(As amended by SOR/71-357; SOR/71-460; SI/73-47; SI/77-112; SOR/77-824; SOR/78-426; SOR/79-756; SOR/81-85; SI/84-66; SOR/92-387)

Schedule G is amended by the Governor in Council (Food and Drugs Act, s. 45(2)).

See also POSSESSION; TRAFFICKING.

2. Trafficking in a controlled drug — Food and Drugs Act, section 39(1) and (3)

Every one who — traffics — in a controlled drug — or any substance represented or held out by him to be a controlled drug — is guilty of either an indictable offence or an offence punishable on summary conviction.

Punishment. On indictment, imprisonment for a term not exceeding 10 years (Food and Drugs Act, s. 39(3)(b)). On summary conviction, imprisonment for a term not exceeding 18 months (Food and Drugs Act, s. 39(3)(a)).

Release. Initial decision to release made by peace officer (s. 497).

Election. On indictment, accused may elect trial by judge and jury, judge alone, or provincial court judge (s. 536). On summary conviction, no election.

Evidence. 1. No exception, exemption, excuse or qualification prescribed by law is required to be set out or negatived, as the case may be, in an information or indictment for this offence (Food and Drugs Act, s. 41(1)).
2. The burden of proving that an exception, exemption, excuse or qualification prescribed by law operates in favour of the accused is on the accused, and the prosecutor is not required, except by way of rebuttal, to prove that the exception, exemption, excuse or qualification does not operate in favour of the accused, whether or not it is set out in the information or indictment (Food and Drugs Act, s. 41(2)).

Informations

A.B., on or about the —— day of ——, 19——, at the —— of ——, in the said (territorial division), did traffic in a controlled drug [OR a substance represented or held out by him to be a controlled drug], to wit: (specify the particulars of the offence), contrary to s. 39 of the Food and Drugs Act.

3. Possession of controlled drug for trafficking — Food and Drugs Act, section 39(2) and (3)

Every one who — has in his possession — any controlled drug — for the purpose of trafficking — is guilty of an indictable offence or an offence punishable on summary conviction.

Punishment. On indictment, imprisonment for a term not exceeding 10 years (Food and Drugs Act, s. 39(3)(b)). On summary conviction, imprisonment for a term not exceeding 18 months (Food and Drugs Act, s. 39(3)(a)).

Release. Initial decision to release made by peace officer (s. 497).

Election. On indictment, accused may elect trial by judge and jury, judge alone, or provincial court judge (s. 536). On summary conviction, no election.

Evidence. See Evidence under **2**, *above.*

Informations

A.B., on or about the —— day of ——, 19——, at the —— of ——, in the said (territorial division), did have in his possession a controlled drug for the purpose of trafficking, to wit: (specify the particulars of the offence), contrary to s. 39 of the Food and Drugs Act of Canada.

4. Failure to disclose previous prescriptions — Food and Drugs Act, section 38.1(1) and (2)

Every one who — at any time — seeks or obtains from a practitioner — a controlled drug or a prescription for a controlled drug — unless he discloses to that practitioner particulars of every controlled drug or prescription for a controlled drug issued to him by a different practitioner within the preceding 30 days — is guilty of either an indictable offence or an offence punishable on summary conviction.

Punishment. On indictment, a fine not exceeding $5,000 or to imprisonment for a term not exceeding 3 years (Food and Drugs Act, s. 38.1(2)(a)). On summary conviction
  (a) for a first offence, a fine not exceeding $1,000 or to imprisonment for a term not exceeding 6 months, and
  (b) for a subsequent offence, a fine not exceeding $2,000 or to imprisonment for a term not exceeding one year (Food and Drugs Act, s. 38.1(2)(b)).

Release. Initial decision to release made by peace officer (s. 497).

Election. On indictment, accused may elect trial by judge and jury, judge alone, or provincial court judge (s. 536). On summary conviction, no election.

Definitions. *See PRACTITIONER; PRESCRIPTION.*

Informations

A.B., on or about the —— day of ——, 19——, at the —— of ——, in the said (territorial division), did seek [OR obtain] a controlled drug [OR a prescription for a controlled drug] from C.D., a practitioner, without disclosing to C.D. particulars of every controlled drug or prescription for a controlled drug issued to him by a different practitioner within the preceding 30 days, to wit: (specify the particulars of the offence), contrary to s. 38.1 of the Food and Drugs Act of Canada.

CONVEYANCE. For the purposes of the Narcotic Control Act, "conveyance" includes any aircraft, vessel, motor vehicle or other conveyance of any description whatever (Narcotic Control Act, s. 2).

COPY. For the purposes of s. 30 of the Canada Evidence Act, "copy", in relation to any record, includes a print, whether enlarged or not, from a photographic film of such record (Canada Evidence Act, s. 30(12)).

CORAM. "In the presence of" (Latin). ***Coram judice.*** "Before a properly constituted court" (Latin).

CORPORATIONS

1. *General*
2. *Service of process on a municipal corporation*
3. *Service of process on corporation other than municipal corporations*
4. *Appearance by corporation*

5. *Non-appearance by corporation*
6. *Notice of indictment*
7. *Punishment*
8. *Offences by officers and employees of corporations*

1. General. A corporation may be directly charged with a criminal offence. The Criminal Code expressly states that the expressions "every one", "person", "owner", and similar expressions include Her Majesty and public bodies, bodies corporate, societies, companies and inhabitants of counties, parishes, municipalities or other districts in relation to the acts and things that they are capable of doing and owning respectively (s. 2). The liability of a corporation would generally be in addition to and not a substitute for the individual liability of the person who was the "directing mind" responsible for the criminal offence (Canadian Dredge and Dock Co. Ltd. v. R. (1985), 45 C.R. (3d) 289 (S.C.C.)).

In the case of a corporation, criminal proceedings are initiated by means of a summons.

2. Service of process on a municipal corporation. Where any summons, notice or other process is required to be or may be served on a municipal corporation, and no other method of service is provided, such service may be affected by delivery to the mayor, warden, reeve or other chief officer of the corporation, or to the secretary, treasurer or clerk of the corporation (s. 703.2).

3. Service of process on corporations other than municipal corporations. Where any summons, notice or other process is required to be or may be served on a corporation, and no other method of service is provided, such service may be affected by delivery to the manager, secretary, or other executive officer of the corporation or of a branch thereof (s. 703.2).

4. Appearance by corporation. An accused corporation shall appear by counsel or agent (s. 556(1) and s. 620).

5. Non-appearance by corporation. Where an accused corporation does not appear pursuant to a summons and service of the summons on the corporation is proved, a provincial court judge may proceed with the trial of the charge in the absence of the accused corporation if the charge is one over which he has absolute jurisdiction. If the charge is not one over which he has absolute jurisdiction, the provincial court judge shall hold a preliminary inquiry in the absence of the accused corporation (s. 556(2)).

Where a corporation does not appear in the court in which an indictment is found and plead within the time specified in a notice of an indictment, the presiding judge may, on proof by affidavit of service of the notice, order the clerk of the court to enter a plea of not guilty on behalf of the corporation. The plea has the same force and effect as if the corporation has appeared by its counsel or agent and pleaded that plea (s. 622).

6. Notice of indictment. Where an indictment is found against a corporation, the clerk of the court shall cause a notice of the indictment to be served upon the corporation (s. 621(1)). The notice shall set out the nature and purport of the indictment and advise that, unless the corporation appears and pleads within 7 days after service of the notice, a plea of not guilty will be entered for the accused by the court. Further, the notice shall advise that the trial of the indictment will be proceeded with as though the corporation had appeared and pleaded (s. 621(2)).

7. Punishment. A corporation that is convicted of an offence is liable to be fined in lieu of any imprisonment that is prescribed as punishment for that offence. Except where otherwise provided by law, the amount of the fine is in the discretion of the court where the offence is an indictable offence. Where the offence is a summary conviction offence, the fine imposed by the court may not exceed $25,000 (s. 719).

Where a fine imposed on a corporation is not paid forthwith, the prosecutor may, by filing the conviction, enter as a judgment the amount of the fine and costs, if any, in the superior court of the province in which the trial is held. That judgment is enforceable against the corporation in the same manner as if it were a judgment rendered against the corporation in that court in civil proceedings (s. 720).

Where the court proceeds with the trial of a corporation that has not appeared and pleaded and convicts the corporation, the court may make inquiries and hear evidence with respect to previous convictions of the corporation. If any such conviction is proved, the court may impose a greater sentence than it would otherwise have done. In such a case, the court may proceed whether or not the corporation was notified that a greater punishment would be sought (s. 665(4)).

After conviction for an offence under s. 121 (frauds on the government), s. 124 (selling or purchasing office) and s. 418 (selling defective stores to the government), the person so convicted has no capacity to contract with the government, receive any benefit under a contract with the government and any other person, or to hold office in or under the government (s. 748(3)). This section of the Criminal Code refers to Her Majesty, but the meaning in this case is the government. Applications may be made for the restoration of these capacities in the appropriate circumstances (s. 748(4) and s. 748(5)). Needless to say, where a conviction is set aside on appeal, any disability imposed by the section is removed (s. 748(6)).

8. Offences by officers and employees of corporations. In appropriate circumstances, the officers and employees of a corporation may also be charged with having committed offences by or on behalf of a corporation. One such offence is that of "selling defective stores to Her Majesty", i.e. to the government. For this offence, the Criminal Code expressly provides that it is an indictable offence for a director, an officer, an agent or an employee to either (a) knowingly take part in the fraud, or (b) not inform the responsible government, or a department thereof, of a fraud that the person knows or has reason to expect is being committed or has been or is about to be committed (s. 418(2)).

CORPUS DELECTI. The body or essential nature of a crime. It is often used incorrectly to designate the corpse in a case of homicide (Jaffe, A Guide to Pathological Evidence).

CORRUPTING MORALS

1. *Definition of "obscene"*
2. *Making, printing, publishing, distributing, circulating or having in possession obscene matter*
3. *Selling, exposing to public view or having in possession obscene matter*
4. *Offences in connection with crime comics*
5. *Exhibiting disgusting objects or indecent show*
6. *Making, printing, publishing or possessing for purpose of publication child pornography*
7. *Importing, distributing, selling or possessiong for purpose of distribution or sale child pornography*
8. *Possession of child pornography*
9. *Tied sale*
10. *Printing or publishing indecent matter*
11. *Printing or publishing particulars of matrimonial proceedings*
12. *Presenting or giving immoral theatrical performance*
13. *Taking part or appearing in immoral theatrical performance*
14. *Mailing obscene matter*
15. *Parent or guardian procuring sexual activity*
16. *Householder permitting sexual activity*
17. *Corrupting children*

1. Definition of "obscene". For the purposes of the Criminal Code any publication a dominant characteristic of which is the undue exploitation of sex, or of sex and any one or more of the following subjects, namely, crime, horror, cruelty and violence, shall be deemed to be obscene (s. 163(8)).

2. Making, printing, publishing, distributing, circulating or having in possession obscene matter — Section 163(1)(a) and section 169

Every one who — makes or prints or publishes or distributes or circulates — or has in his possession for the purpose of publication or distribution or circulation — any obscene written matter or picture or model or phonograph record or other thing whatever — is guilty of either an indictable offence or an offence punishable on summary conviction.

Limitation period. No proceedings in respect of offences that are declared to be punishable on summary conviction shall be instituted more than 6 months after the time when the subject matter of the proceedings arose (s. 786(2) and s. 785(1)).

Included offences. Attempts (s. 660 and s. 662(1)(b)).

Punishment. On indictment, imprisonment for a term not exceeding 2 years (s. 169(a)). On summary conviction, a fine not exceeding $2,000, or 6 months' imprisonment, or both (s. 169(b) and s. 787(1)).

Release. Initial decision to release made by peace officer (s. 497).

Election. On indictment, accused may elect trial by judge and jury, judge alone, or provincial court judge (s. 536). On summary conviction, no election.

Defences. No person shall be convicted of this offence if the public good was served by the acts that are alleged to constitute the offence and if the acts alleged did not extend beyond what served the public good (s. 163(3)).

Evidence. 1. It is a question of law whether an act served the public good and whether there is evidence that the act alleged went beyond what served the public good, but it is a question of fact whether the acts did or did not extend beyond what served the public good (s. 163(4)).
2. For the purposes of this offence, the motives of an accused are irrelevant (s. 163(5)).

Informations

A.B., on or about the —— day of ——, 19——, at the —— of ——, in the said (territorial division), did make [OR print OR publish OR distribute OR circulate OR have in his possession for the purpose of publication (OR distribution OR circulation)] obscene written matter [OR an obscene picture OR an obsence model OR an obscene phonograph OR (specify any other obscene thing)], to wit: (specify the particulars of the offence), contrary to s. 163(1)(a) of the Criminal Code of Canada.

3. Selling, exposing to public view or having in possession obscene matter — Section 163(2)(a) and section 169

Every one who — knowingly — without lawful justification or excuse — sells or exposes to public view or has in his possession for such a purpose — any obscene written matter or picture or model or phonograph record or other thing whatever — is guilty of either an indictable offence or an offence punishable on summary conviction.

Intent. Knowingly.

Limitation period. No proceedings in respect of offences that are declared to be punishable on summary conviction shall be instituted more than 6 months after the time when the subject matter of the proceedings arose (s. 786(2) and s. 785(1)).

Included offences. Attempts (s. 660 and s. 662(1)(b)).

Punishment. On indictment, imprisonment for a term not exceeding 2 years (s. 169(a)). On summary conviction, a fine not exceeding $2,000, or 6 months' imprisonment, or both (s. 169(b) and s. 787(1)).

Release. Initial decision to release made by peace officer (s. 497).

Election. On indictment, accused may elect trial by judge and jury, judge alone, or provincial court judge (s. 536). On summary conviction, no election.

Defences. *See Defences, under* **2**, *above.*

Evidence. *See Evidence, under* **2**, *above.*

Sufficiency of count. No count for selling or exhibiting an obscene book, pamphlet, newspaper or other written matter is insufficient by reason only that it does not set out the writing that is alleged to be obscene (s. 584(1)).

Informations

A.B., on or about the —— day of ——, 19——, at the —— of ——, in the said (territorial division), knowingly, without lawful justification or excuse, did sell [OR expose to public view OR have in his possession for the purpose of sale], obscene written matter [OR an obscene picture OR an obscene model OR an obscene phonograph record OR (specify any other obscene thing)], to wit: (specify the particulars of the offence), contrary to s. 163(2)(a) of the Criminal Code of Canada.

4. Offences in connection with crime comics — Section 163(1)(b) and section 169

Every one who — either makes or prints or publishes or distributes or sells — or has in his possession for the purpose of publication or distribution or circulation — a crime comic — is guilty of either an indictable offence or an offence punishable on summary conviction.

Limitation period. No proceedings in respect of offences that are declared to be punishable on summary conviction shall be instituted more than 6 months after the time when the subject matter of the proceedings arose (s. 786(2) and s. 785(1)).

Included offences. Attempts (s. 660 and s. 662(1)(b)).

Punishment. On indictment, imprisonment for 2 years (s. 169(a)). On summary conviction, a fine not exceeding $2,000, or 6 months' imprisonment, or both (s. 169(b) and s. 787(1)).

Release. Initial decision to release made by peace officer (s. 497).

Election. On indictment, accused may elect trial by judge and jury, judge alone, or provincial court judge (s. 536). On summary conviction, no election.

Definitions. For these purposes, "crime comic" means a magazine, periodical or book that exclusively or substantially comprises matter depicting pictorially either (a) the commission of crimes, real or fictitious; or (b) events connected with the commission of crimes, real or fictitious, whether occurring before or after the commission of the crime (s. 163(7)).

Defences. See Defences, under 2, above.

Evidence. See Evidence, under 2, above.

5. Exhibiting disgusting objects or indecent show — Section 163(2)(b) and section 169

Every one who — knowingly — without lawful justification or excuse — publicly exhibits — a disgusting object or an indecent show — is guilty of either an indictable offence or an offence punishable on summary conviction.

Intent. Knowingly.

Limitation period. No proceedings in respect of offences that are declared to be punishable on summary conviction shall be instituted more than 6 months after the time when the subject matter of the proceedings arose (s. 786(2) and s. 785(1)).

Included offences. Attempts (s. 660 and s. 662(1)(b)).

Punishment. On indictment, imprisonment for 2 years (s. 169(a)). On summary conviction, a fine not exceeding $2,000, or 6 months' imprisonment, or both (s. 169(b) and s. 787(1)).

Release. Initial decision to release made by peace officer (s. 497).

Election. On indictment, accused may elect trial by judge and jury, judge alone, or provincial court judge (s. 536). On summary conviction, no election.

Defences. See Defences, under 2, above.

Evidence. See Evidence, under 2, above.

6. Making, printing, publishing or possessing for purpose of publication child pornography — Section 163.1(2)

Every person who — makes or prints or publishes or possesses — for the purpose of publication — any child pornography — is guilty of either an indictable offence or an offence punishable on summary conviction.

Intent. For the purpose of publication.

Limitation period. No proceedings in respect of offences that are declared to be punishable on summary conviction shall be instituted more than 6 months after the time when the subject matter of the proceedings arose (s. 786(2) and s. 785(1)).

Included offences. Attempts (s. 660 and s. 662(1)(b)).

Punishment. On indictment, imprisonment for a term not exceeding 10 years (s. 163.1(2)(a)). On summary conviction, a fine not exceeding $2,000, or 6 months' imprisonment, or both (s. 163.1(2)(b) and s. 787(1)).

Release. Initial decision to release made by peace officer (s. 497).

Election. On indictment, accused may elect trial by judge and jury, judge alone, or provincial court judge (s. 536). On summary conviction, no election.

Definitions. *See CHILD PORNOGRAPHY.*

Defences. 1. It is not a defence to a charge under s. 163.1(2) in respect of a visual representation that the accused believed that a person shown in the representation that is alleged to constitute child pornography was or was depicted as being 18 years of age or more unless the accused took all reasonable steps to ascertain the age of that person and took all reasonable steps to ensure that, where the person was 18 years of age or more, the representation did not depict that person as being under the age of 18 years (s. 163.1(5)).
2. Where the accused is charged with an offence under s. 163.1(2), (3) or (4), the court shall find the accused not guilty if the representation or written material that is alleged to constitute child pornography has artistic merit or an educational, scientific or medical purpose (s. 163.1(6)).
3. *See also Defences under* **2**, *above.*

Evidence. *See Evidence under* **2**, *above.*

Informations

A.B., on or about the —— day of ——, 19——, at the —— of ——, in the said (territorial division), knowingly, did make [OR print OR publish OR possess] for the purpose of publication any child pornography, to wit: (specify the particulars of the offence), contrary to s. 163.1(2) of the Criminal Code of Canada.

7. Importing, distributing, selling or possessing for purpose of distribution or sale child pornography — Section 163.1(3)

Every person who — imports or distributes or sells or possesses — for the purpose of distribution or sale — any child pornography — is guilty of either an indictable offence or an offence punishable on summary conviction.

Intent. For the purpose of distribution or sale.

Limitation period. No proceedings in respect of offences that are declared to be punishable on summary conviction shall be instituted more than 6 months after the time when the subject matter of the proceedings arose (s. 786(2) and s. 785(1)).

Included offences. Attempts (s. 660 and s. 662(1)(b)).

Punishment. On indictment, imprisonment for a term not exceeding 10 years (s. 163.1(3)(a)). On summary conviction, a fine not exceeding $2,000, or 6 months' imprisonment, or both (s. 163.1(3)(b) and s. 787(1)).

Release. Initial decision to release made by peace officer (s. 497).

Election. On indictment, accused may elect trial by judge and jury, judge alone, or provincial court judge (s. 536). On summary conviction, no election.

Definitions. See CHILD PORNOGRPAHY.

Defences. 1. *See Defences, item 2, under* **6**, *above.*
2. *See also Defences under* **2**, *above.*

Evidence. See Evidence under **2**, *above.*

Informations

A.B., on or about the —— day of ——, 19——, at the —— of ——, in the said (territorial division), did import [OR distribute OR sell OR possess] for the purpose of distribution [or sale] any child pornography, to wit: (specify the particulars of the offence), contrary to s. 163.1(3) of the Criminal Code of Canada.

8. Possession of child pornography — Section 163.1(4)

Every person who — possesses — any child pornography — is guilty of either an indictable offence or an offence punishable on summary conviction.

Limitation period. No proceedings in respect of offences that are declared to be punishable on summary conviction shall be instituted more than 6 months after the time when the subject matter of the proceedings arose (s. 786(2) and s. 785(1)).

Included offences. Attempts (s. 660 and s. 662(1)(b)).

Punishment. On indictment, imprisonment for a term not exceeding 5 years (s. 163.1(4)(a)). On summary conviction, a fine not exceeding $2,000, or 6 months' imprisonment, or both (s. 163.1(4)(b) and s. 787(1)).

Release. Initial decision to release made by peace officer (s. 497).

Election. On indictment, accused may elect trial by judge and jury, judge alone, or provincial court judge (s. 536). On summary conviction, no election.

Definitions. *See CHILD PORNOGRAPHY.*

Defences. 1. *See Defences, item 2., under* **6***, above.*
2. *See also Defences under* **2***, above.*

Evidence. *See Evidence under* **2***, above.*

Informations

A.B., on or about the —— day of ——, 19——, at the —— of ——, in the said (territorial division), did possess any child pornography, to wit: (specify the particulars of the offence), contrary to s. 163.1(4) of the Criminal Code of Canada.

9. Tied sale — Section 165 and section 169

Every one who — refuses to sell or supply to any other person — copies of any publication — for the reason only that the other person refuses to purchase or acquire for him copies of any other publication that the other person is apprehensive may be obscene or a crime comic — is guilty of either an indictable offence or an offence punishable on summary conviction.

Limitation period. No proceedings in respect of offences that are declared to be punishable on summary conviction shall be instituted more than 6 months after the time when the subject matter of the proceedings arose (s. 786(2) and s. 785(1)).

Included offences. Attempts (s. 660 and s. 662(1)(b)).

Punishment. On indictment, imprisonment for a term not exceeding 2 years (s. 169(a)). On summary conviction, a fine not exceeding $2,000, or 6 months' imprisonment, or both (s. 169(b) and s. 787(1)).

Release. Initial decision to release made by peace officer (s. 497).

Election. On indictment, accused may elect trial by judge and jury, judge alone, or provincial court judge (s. 536). On summary conviction, no election.

10. Printing or publishing indecent matter — Section 166(1)(a) and section 169

Every one who — being a proprietor or an editor or a master printer or a publisher — prints or publishes in relation to any judicial proceedings — any indecent matter or indecent medical or surgical or physiological details — being matter or details that, if published, are calculated to injure public morals — is guilty of either an indictable offence or an offence punishable on summary conviction.

Exceptions. This offence does not apply to a person who:

(a) prints or publishes any matter for use in connection with any judicial proceedings or communicates it to persons who are concerned in the proceedings;

(b) prints or publishes a notice or report pursuant to the directions of a court; or

(c) prints or publishes any matter in a volume or part of a genuine series of law reports that does not form part of any other publication and consists solely of reports of proceedings in courts of law, or in a publication of a technical character that is bona fide intended for circulation among members of the legal or medical professions (s. 166(4)).

Consent to prosecute. No proceedings for an offence under s. 166 shall be commenced without the consent of the Attorney General (s. 166(3)).

Limitation period. No proceedings in respect of offences that are declared to be punishable on summary conviction shall be instituted more than 6 months after the time when the subject matter of the proceedings arose (s. 786(2) and s. 785(1)).

Included offences. Attempts (s. 660 and s. 662(1)(b)).

Punishment. On indictment, imprisonment for a term not exceeding 2 years (s. 169(a)). On summary conviction, a fine not exceeding $2,000, or 6 months' imprisonment, or both (s. 169(b) and s. 787(1)).

Release. Initial decision to release made by peace officer (s. 497).

Election. On indictment, accused may elect trial by judge and jury, judge alone, or provincial court judge (s. 536). On summary conviction, no election.

Informations

A.B., on or about the —— day of ——, 19——, at the —— of ——, in the said (territorial division), being the proprietor [OR editor OR master printer OR publisher] of (specify) did print [OR publish] in relation to a judicial proceeding indecent matter [OR indecent medical details OR indecent surgical details OR indecent physiological details] that, when published, were calculated to injure public morals, to wit: (specify the particulars of the offence), contrary to s. 166(1)(a) of the Criminal Code of Canada.

11. Printing or publishing particulars of matrimonial proceedings — Section 166(1)(b) and section 169

Every one who — being a proprietor or an editor or a master printer or a publisher — prints or publishes — in relation to any judicial proceedings for dissolution of marriage or nullity of marriage or judicial separation or restitution of conjugal rights — any particulars other than — the names and addresses and occupations of the parties and witnesses — and a concise statement of the charges and defences and countercharges in support of which evidence has been given — and submissions on a point of law arising in the course of the proceedings, and the decision of the court in connection therewith — and the summing up of the judge and the finding of the jury and the judgment of the court and the observations that are made by the judge in giving judgment — is guilty of either an indictable offence or an offence punishable on summary conviction.

Exceptions. See Exceptions, under **10**, above.

Consent to prosecute. No proceedings for an offence under s. 166 shall be commenced without the consent of the Attorney General (s. 166(3)).

Limitation period. No proceedings in respect of offences that are declared to be punishable on summary conviction shall be instituted more than 6 months after the time when the subject matter of the proceedings arose (s. 786(2) and s. 785(1)).

Included offences. Attempts (s. 660 and s. 662(1)(b)).

Punishment. On indictment, imprisonment for a term not exceeding 2 years (s. 169(a)). On summary conviction, a fine not exceeding $2,000, or 6 months' imprisonment, or both (s. 169(b) and s. 787(1)).

Release. Initial decision to release made by peace officer (s. 497).

CORRUPTING MORALS — 149

Election. On indictment, accused may elect trial by judge and jury, judge alone, or provincial court judge (s. 536). On summary conviction, no election.

12. Presenting or giving immoral theatrical performance — Section 167(1) and section 169

Every one who — being the lessee or manager or agent or person in charge of a theatre — presents or gives or allows to be presented or given therein — an immoral or indecent or obscene performance or entertainment or representation — is guilty of either an indictable offence or an offence punishable on summary conviction.

Limitation period. No proceedings in respect of offences that are declared to be punishable on summary conviction shall be instituted more than 6 months after the time when the subject matter of the proceedings arose (s. 786(2) and s. 785(1)).

Included offences. Attempts (s. 660 and s. 662(1)(b)).

Punishment. On indictment, imprisonment for a term not exceeding 2 years (s. 169(a)). On summary conviction, a fine not exceeding $2,000, or 6 months' imprisonment, or both (s. 169(b) and s. 787(1)).

Release. Initial decision to release made by peace officer (s. 497).

Election. On indictment, accused may elect trial by judge and jury, judge alone, or provincial court judge (s. 536). On summary conviction, no election.

Informations

A.B., on or about the —— day of ——, 19——, at the —— of ——, in the said (territorial division), being the lessee [OR manager OR agent OR person in charge] of a theatre, did present [OR give OR allow to be presented OR allow to be given] therein an immoral [OR indecent OR obscene] performance [OR entertainment OR representation] to wit: (specify the particulars of the offence), contrary to s. 167(1) of the Criminal Code of Canada.

13. Taking part or appearing in immoral theatrical performance — Section 167(2) and section 169

Every one who — takes part or appears as an actor or a performer or an assistant in any capacity — in an immoral or indecent or obscene performance or entertainment or representation in a

theatre — is guilty of an indictable offence or an offence punishable on summary conviction.

Limitation period. No proceedings in respect of offences that are declared to be punishable on summary conviction shall be instituted more than 6 months after the time when the subject matter of the proceedings arose (s. 786(2) and s. 785(1)).

Included offences. Attempts (s. 660 and s. 662(1)(b)).

Punishment. On indictment, imprisonment for a term not exceeding 2 years (s. 169(a)). On summary conviction, a fine not exceeding $2,000, or 6 months' imprisonment, or both (s. 169(b) and s. 787(1)).

Release. Initial decision to release made by peace officer (s. 497).

Election. On indictment, accused may elect trial by judge and jury, judge alone, or provincial court judge (s. 536). On summary conviction, no election.

Informations

A.B., on or about the —— day of ——, 19——, at the —— of ——, in the said (territorial division), did take part [OR appear] as an actor [OR a performer OR an assistant], in an immoral [OR indecent OR obscene] performance [OR entertainment OR representation] in a theatre, to wit: (specify the particulars of the offence), contrary to s. 167(2) of the Criminal Code of Canada.

14. Mailing obscene matter — Section 168 and section 169

Every one who — makes use of the mails — for the purpose of transmitting or delivering — anything that is obscene or indecent or immoral or scurrilous — is guilty of either an indictable offence or an offence punishable on summary conviction.

Intent. Intention to use for proscribed purpose.

Exceptions. This offence does not apply to a person who makes use of the mails for transmitting or delivering:

(a) any matter printed or published for use in connection with any judicial proceedings or communicated to persons who are concerned in the proceedings;

(b) a notice or report printed or published pursuant to directions of a court; or

(c) matter printed or published in a volume or part of a genuine series of law reports that does not form part of any other publication and consists solely of reports of proceedings in courts of law, or in a publication of a technical character that is bona fide intended for circulation among members of the legal or medical professions (s. 168 and s. 166(4)).

Limitation period. No proceedings in respect of offences that are declared to be punishable on summary conviction shall be instituted more than 6 months after the time when the subject matter of the proceedings arose (s. 786(2) and s. 785(1)).

Included offences. Attempts (s. 660 and s. 662(1)(b)).

Punishment. On indictment, imprisonment for a term not exceeding 2 years (s. 169(a)). On summary conviction, a fine not exceeding $2,000, or 6 months' imprisonment, or both (s. 169(b) and s. 787(1)).

Release. Initial decision to release made by peace officer (s. 497).

Election. On indictment, accused may elect trial by judge and jury, judge alone, or provincial court judge (s. 536). On summary conviction, no election.

Informations

A.B., on or about the —— day of ——, 19——, at the —— of ——, in the said (territorial division), did make use of the mails for the purpose of transmitting [OR delivering] (specify the thing transmitted or delivered), that was obscene [OR indecent OR immoral OR scurrilous], to wit: (specify the particulars of the offence), contrary to s. 168 of the Criminal Code of Canada.

15. Parent or guardian procuring sexual activity — Section 170

Every one who — being the parent or guardian of a person under the age of 18 years — procures that person — for the purpose of engaging in any sexual activity prohibited by the Criminal Code — with a person other than the parent or guardian — is guilty of an indictable offence.

Intent. Intention to procure for proscribed purpose.

Included offences. Attempts (s. 660 and s. 662(1)(b)).

Punishment. Imprisonment for a term not exceeding 5 years, if the person procured for that purpose is under the age of 14 years, or imprisonment for a term not exceeding 2 years, if the person so procured is 14 years of age or more but under the age of 18 years (s. 170).

Release. If the person procured is under the age of 14 years, initial decision to release made by justice (s. 515(1)). If the person procured is 14 years of age or more but under the age of eighteen, initial decision to release made by officer in charge or justice (s. 498).

Election. Accused may elect trial by judge and jury, judge alone, or provincial court judge (s. 536).

Defences. It is not a defence to a charge under this offence that the accused believed that the complainant was 18 years of age or more at the time the offence is alleged to have been committed unless the accused took all reasonable steps to ascertain the age of the complainant (s. 150.1(5)).

Evidence. 1. Age must be proven in order to determine the appropriate punishment. In the absence of other evidence, or by way of corroboration of other evidence, the age of a child or young person may be inferred from his or her appearance (s. 658(2)).
2. The wife or husband of a person charged with this offence is a competent and compellable witness for the prosecution without the consent of the person charged (Canada Evidence Act, s. 4(2)).
3. Where an accused is charged with this offence, no corroboration is required for a conviction and the judge shall not instruct the jury that it is unsafe to find the accused guilty in the absence of corroboration (s. 274).
4. The rules relating to evidence of recent complaint are abrogated with respect to this offence (s. 275).
5. In proceedings in respect of this offence, evidence that the complainant has engaged in sexual activity, whether with the accused or with any other person, is not admissible to support an inference that, by reason of the sexual nature of that activity, the complainant (a) is more likely to have consented to the sexual activity that forms the subject-matter of the charge; or (b) is less worthy of belief (s. 276(1)). No evidence shall be adduced by or on behalf of the accused that the complainant has engaged in sexual activity other than the sexual activity that forms the subject-matter of the charge, whether with the accused or with any other person, unless the judge, provincial court judge or justice determines, in accordance with the procedures set out in ss. 276.1 and 276.2, that the evidence (a) is of specific instances of sexual activity; (b) is relevant to an issue at trial;o and (c) has significant probative value that is not substantially outweighed by the danger of prejudice to the proper administration of justice (s. 276(2)).

In determining whether evidence is admissible under s. 276(2), the judge, provincial court judge or justice shall take into account (a) the interests of justice, including the right of the accused to make a full answer and defence; (b) society's interest in encouraging the reporting of sexual assault offences; (c) whether there is a reasonable prospect that the evidence will assist in arriving at a just determination in the case; (d) the need to remove from the fact-finding process any discriminatory belief or bias; (e) the risk that the evidence may unduly arouse sentiments of prejudice, sympathy or hostility in the jury; (f) the potential prejudice to the complainant's personal dignity and right of privacy; (g) the right of the complainant and of every individual to personal security and to the full protection and benefit of the law; and (h) any other factor that the judge, provincial court judge or justice considers relevant (s. 276(3)).

Application may be made to the judge, provincial court judge or justice by or on behalf of the accused for a hearing under s. 276.2 to determine whether evidence is admissible under s. 276(2) (s. 276.2(1)).

An application referred to in s. 276.1(1) must be made in writing and set out (a) detailed particulars of the evidence that the accused seeks to adduce, and (b) the relevance of that evidence to an issue at trial, and a copy of the application must be given to the prosecutor and to the clerk of the court l(s. 276.1(2)). The judge, provincial court judge or justice shall consider the application with the jury and the public excluded (s. 276.1(3)). Where the judge, provincial court judge or justice is satisfied (a) that the application was made in accordance with s. 276.1(2), (b) that a copy of the application was given to the prosecutor and to the clerk of the court at least 7 days previously, or such shorter interval as the judge, provincial court judge or justice may allow where the interests of justice so require, and (c) that the evidence sought to be adduced is capable of being admissible under s. 276(2), the judge, provincial court judge or justice shall grant the application and hold a hearing under s. 276.2 to determine whether the evidence is admissible under s. 276(2) (s. 276.1(4)).

At a hearing to determine whether evidence is admissible under s. 276(2), the jury and the public shall be excluded (s. 276.2(1)). The complainant is not a compellable witness at the hearing (s. 276.2(2)). At the conclusion of the hearing, the judge, provincial court judge or justice shall determine whether the evidence, or any part thereof, is admissible under s. 276(2) and shall provide reasons for that determination, and (a) where not all of the evidence is to be admitted, the reasons must state the part of the evidence that is to be admitted;

(b) the reasons must state the factors referred to in s. 276(3) that affected the determination; and (c) where all or any part of the evidence is to be admitted, the reasons must state the manner in which that evidence is expected to be relevant to an issue at trial (s. 276.2(3)). The reasons provided under s. 276.2(3) shall be entered in the record of the proceedings or, where the proceedings are not recorded, shall be provided in writing (s. 276.2(4)).

No person shall publish in a newspaper, as defined in s. 297, or in a broadcast, any of the following: (a) the contents of an application made under s. 276.1; (b) any evidence taken, the information given and the representations made at an application under s. 276.1 or at a hearing under s. 276.2; (c) the decision of a judge, provincial court judge or justice under s. 276.1(4), unless the judge, provincial court judge or justice, after taking into account the complainant's right of privacy and the interests of justice, orders that the decision may be published; and (d) the determination made and the reasons provided under s. 276.2, unless (i) that determination is that evidence is admissible, or (ii) the judge, provincial court judge or justice, after taking into account the complainant's right of privacy and the interests of justice, orders that the determination and reasons may be published (s. 276.3(1)).

For definitions, see NEWSPAPER. Every person who contravenes s. 276.3(1) is guilty of an offence punishable on summary conviction (s. 276.3(2)).

Where evidence is admitted at trial pursuant to a determination made under s. 276.2, the judge shall instruct the jury as to the uses that the jury may and may not make of that evidence (s. 276.4).

For the purposes of ss. 675 and 676, a determination made under s. 276.2 shall be deemed to be a question of law (s. 276.5).

6. In proceedings in respect of this offence, evidence of sexual reputation, whether general or specific, is not admissible for the purpose of challenging or supporting the credibility of the complainant (s. 277).

Informations

A.B., on or about the —— day of ——, 19——, at the —— of ——, in the said (territorial division), being the parent [OR guardian] of C.D., a person under the age of 18 years, did procure C.D. to engage in prohibited sexual activity with E.F., to wit: (specify the particulars of the offence), contrary to s. 170 of the Criminal Code of Canada.

16. Householder permitting sexual activity — Section 171

Every one who — being the owner or occupier or manager of premises — or being another person having control of premises or assisting in the management or control of premises — knowingly — permits a person under the age of 18 years — to resort to or to be in or upon the premises — for the purpose of engaging in any sexual activity prohibited by the Criminal Code — is guilty of an indictable offence.

Intent. Knowingly.

Included offences. Attempts (s. 660 and s. 662(1)(b)).

Punishment. Imprisonment for a term not exceeding 5 years if the person in question is under the age of 14 years, or imprisonment for a term not exceeding 2 years if the person in question is 14 years of age or more but under the age of 18 years (s. 171).

Release. Initial decision to release made by officer in charge or justice (s. 498).

Election. Accused may elect trial by judge and jury, judge alone, or provincial court judge (s. 536).

Defences. See Defences under **15**, *above.*

Evidence. See Evidence under **15**, *above.*

Informations

A.B., on or about the —— day of ——, 19——, at the —— of ——, in the said (territorial division), being the owner [OR the occupier OR the manager OR a person having control of premises OR a person assisting in the management (OR control)], of premises knowingly did permit C.D., a person under the age of 18 years to resort to [OR to be in OR to be upon the premises] for the purpose of engaging in prohibited sexual activity with E.F., to wit: (specify the particulars of the offence), contrary to s. 171 of the Criminal Code of Canada.

17. Corrupting children — Section 172(1)

Every one who — in the home of a child — participates in adultery or sexual immorality — or indulges in habitual drunkenness or any other form of vice — and thereby endangers the morals of the child — or renders the home an unfit place for the child to be in — is guilty of an indictable offence.

Consent to prosecute. No proceedings shall be commenced for this offence without the consent of the Attorney General, unless they are instituted by or at the instance of a recognized society for the protection of children or by an officer of a juvenile court (s. 172(4)).

Included offences. Attempts (s. 660 and s. 662(1)(b)).

Punishment. Imprisonment for a term not exceeding 2 years (s. 172(1)).

Release. Initial decision to release made by officer in charge or justice (s. 498).

Election. Accused may elect trial by judge and jury, judge alone, or provincial court judge (s. 536).

Definitions. See CHILD.

Defences. See Defences under **15**, above.

Evidence. See Evidence under **15**, above.

CORRUPTION

1. *Of judges, members of Parliament, and members of provincial legislatures*
2. *Of persons employed in the administration of criminal law*
3. *Frauds on the government*
4. *Breach of trust by public officer*
5. *Municipal corruption*
6. *Influencing municipal official*
7. *Selling office*
8. *Purchasing office*
9. *Influencing appointments*
10. *Negotiating appointments*
11. *Keeping a place for dealing in offices*

1. Of judges, members of Parliament and members of provincial legislatures

Accepting bribes — Section 119(1)(a)

Every one who — being the holder of a judicial office — or being a member of Parliament or of the legislature of a province — corruptly — either accepts or obtains — or agrees to accept — or attempts to obtain — any money or valuable consideration or office or place or employment — for himself or another person — in respect of anything done or omitted or to be done or omitted by him in his official capacity — is guilty of an indictable offence.

Offering bribes — Section 119(1)(b)

Every one who — gives or offers — corruptly — to a person who holds a judicial office or is a member of Parliament or of the legislature of a province — any money or valuable consideration or office or place or employment — in respect of anything done or omitted or to be done or omitted by him in his official capacity — for himself or another person — is guilty of an indictable offence.

Intent. Corruptly.

Jurisdiction. When committed by the holder of a judicial office, triable only in a superior court of criminal jurisdiction (s. 468 and s. 469 (c)).

Consent to prosecute. No proceedings against a person who holds a judicial office shall be instituted under s. 119 without the consent in writing of the Attorney General of Canada (s. 119(2)).

Included offences. Attempts (s. 660 and s. 662(1)(b)).

Punishment. Imprisonment for a term not exceeding 14 years (s. 119(1)).

Release. Under s. 119(1)(a), initial decision to release may only be made by superior court judge (s. 522). Under s. 119(1)(b), initial decision to release made by justice (s. 515(1)).

Election. Under s. 119(1)(a), superior court (with jury) exclusive, except where accused elects superior court trial without jury with consent of Attorney General (s. 473) (s. 469). Under s. 119(1)(b), accused may elect trial by judge and jury, judge alone, or provincial court judge (s. 536).

2. Of persons employed in the administration of criminal law

Accepting bribes — Section 120(a)

Every one who — being a justice or police commissioner or peace officer or public officer or officer of a juvenile court — or being employed in the administration of criminal law — corruptly — either accepts or obtains — or agrees to accept — or attempts to obtain — for himself or any other person — any money or valuable consideration or office or place or employment — with intent — either to interfere with the administration of justice — or to procure or facilitate the commission of an offence — or to protect from detection or punishment a person who has committed or who intends to commit an offence — is guilty of an indictable offence.

Offering bribes — Section 120(b)

Every one who — gives or offers — corruptly — to a person who is a justice or police commissioner or peace officer or public officer or officer of a juvenile court — or who is employed in the administration of criminal law — any money or valuable consideration or office or place or employment — with intent that the person should — either interfere with the administration of justice — or procure or facilitate the commission of an offence — or protect from detection or punishment a person who has committed or who intends to commit an offence — is guilty of an indictable offence.

Intent. Corruptly.

Included offences. Attempts (s. 660 and s. 662(1)(b)).

Punishment. Imprisonment for a term not exceeding 14 years (s. 120).

Release. Initial decision to release made by justice (s. 515(1)).

Election. Accused may elect trial by judge and jury, judge alone, or provincial court judge (s. 536).

Informations

A.B., on or about the —— day of ——, 19——, at the —— of ——, in the said (territorial division), being a justice [OR a police commissioner OR a peace officer OR a public officer OR an officer of a juvenile court OR employed in the administration of criminal law] corruptly did accept [OR did obtain OR did agree to accept OR did attempt to obtain] for himself [OR for C.D.] money [OR valuable consideration OR an office OR a place OR employment] with intent to interfere with the administration of justice [OR with intent to procure or facilitate the commission of an offence OR with intent to protect from detection (OR punishment) E.F. who has committed (OR who intends to commit) an indictable offence], to wit: (specify the particulars of the offence), contrary to s. 120(a) of the Criminal Code of Canada.

3. Frauds on the government

In connection with the transaction of business or a claim against Her Majesty or a benefit bestowed by Her Majesty — Section 121(1) and (3)

Section 121(1)(a)

Every one who — directly or indirectly — either gives or offers or agrees to give or offer to an official or to any member of his family, or to any one for the benefit of an official — or being an official, demands or accepts or offers or agrees to accept from any person for himself or another person — a loan or reward or advantage or benefit of any kind — as consideration for cooperation or assistance or exercise of influence or an act or omission in connection with — either the transaction of business with or any matter of business relating to the government — or a claim against Her Majesty of any benefit that Her Majesty is authorized or is entitled to bestow — whether or not, in fact, the official is able to cooperate or render assistance or exercise influence or do or omit to do what is proposed, as the case may be — is guilty of an indictable offence.

Section 121(1)(d)

Every one who — having or pretending to have influence with the government or with a minister of the government or an official — demands or accepts or offers or agrees to accept for himself or another person — a reward or advantage or benefit of any kind — as consideration for cooperation or assistance or exercise of influence or an act or omission in connection with — either the transaction of business with or any matter of business relating to the government — a claim against Her Majesty or any benefit that Her Majesty is authorized or is entitled to bestow — or the appointment of any person including himself to an office — is guilty of an indictable offence.

Section 121(1)(e)

Every one who — gives or offers or agrees to give or offer — to a minister of the government or an official — a reward or advantage or benefit of any kind — as consideration for cooperation or assistance or exercise of influence or an act or omission in connection with — either the transaction of business with or any matter of business relating to the government — or a claim against Her Majesty or any benefit that Her Majesty is authorized or is entitled to bestow — or the appointment of any person, including himself, to an office — is guilty of an indictable offence.

In connection with dealings of any kind — Section 121(1) and (3)

Section 121(1)(b)

Every one who — having dealings of any kind with the government — either pays a commission or reward to — or confers an advantage or benefit of any kind on — either an employee or official of the government with which he deals — or to any member of his family — or to any one for the benefit of the employee or official — with respect to those dealings — unless he has the consent in writing of the head of the branch of government with which he deals — is guilty of an indictable offence.

Section 121(1)(c)

Every one who — being an official or employee of the government — demands or accepts or offers or agrees to accept — from a person who has dealings with the government — a commission or reward or advantage or benefit of any kind directly or indirectly — by himself or through a member of his family or through any one for his benefit — unless he has the consent in writing of the head of the branch of government that employs him or of which he is an official — is guilty of an indictable offence.

In connection with tenders — Section 121(1)(f) and (3)

Every one who — having made a tender to obtain a contract with the government — gives or offers or agrees to give or offer — to another person who has made a tender or to a member of his family, or to another person for the benefit of that person — a reward or advantage or benefit of any kind — as consideration for the withdrawal of the tender of that person — is guilty of an indictable offence.

Every one who — having made a tender to obtain a contract with the government — demands or accepts or offers or agrees to accept — from another person who has made a tender — a reward or advantage or benefit of any kind — as consideration for the withdrawal of his tender — is guilty of an indictable offence.

Contractor subscribing to election fund — Section 121(2) and (3)

Every one who — in order to obtain or retain a contract with the government — or as a term of any such contract, whether express or implied — directly or indirectly subscribes or gives, or agrees to subscribe or give — to any person — any valuable consideration — either for the purpose of promoting the election of a candidate or a class or party of candidates to Parliament or the legislature of a

province — or with intent to influence or affect in any way the result of an election conducted for the purpose of electing persons to serve in Parliament or the legislature of a province — is guilty of an indictable offence.

Included offences. Attempts (s. 660 and s. 662(1)(b)).

Punishment. Imprisonment for a term not exceeding 5 years (s. 121(3)).

Release. Initial decision to release made by officer in charge or justice (s. 498).

Election. Accused may elect trial by judge and jury, judge alone, or provincial court judge (s. 536).

Evidence. For the purposes of this offence, the proof of consent lies on the accused (s. 121(1)(b) and (c)).

Informations

A.B., on or about the —— day of ——, 19——, at the —— of ——, in the said (territorial division), directly [OR indirectly] did give [OR offer OR agree to give (OR offer)] to C.D., an official [OR a member of the family of E.F., an official, OR for the benefit of E.F., an official], a loan [OR a reward OR an advantage OR a benefit] as consideration for cooperation [OR assistance OR the exercise of influence OR an act OR an omission] in connection with the transaction of business with the government [OR any matter of business relating to the government OR a claim against Her Majesty OR any benefit that Her Majesty is entitled to bestow], to wit: (specify the particulars of the offence), contrary to s. 121(1)(a) of the Criminal Code of Canada.

4. Breach of trust by public officer — Section 122

Every official who — in connection with the duties of his office — commits fraud or a breach of trust — whether or not the fraud or breach of trust would be an offence if it were committed in relation to a private person — is guilty of an indictable offence

Included offences. Attempts (s. 660 and s. 662(1)(b)).

Punishment. Imprisonment for a term not exceeding 5 years (s. 122).

Release. Initial decision to release made by officer in charge or justice (s. 498).

Election. Accused may elect trial by judge and jury, judge alone, or provincial court judge (s. 536).

Sufficiency of count. No count that alleges false pretences, fraud or any attempt or conspiracy by fraudulent means is insufficient by reason only that it does not set out in detail the nature of the false pretence, fraud or fraudulent means (s. 586).

Informations

A.B., an official on or about the —— day of ——, 19——, at the —— of ——, in the said (territorial division), did commit fraud [OR a breach of trust] in connection with the duties of his office, to wit: (specify the particulars of the offence), contrary to s. 122 of the Criminal Code of Canada.

5. Municipal corruption

Corrupting of a municipal official — Section 123(1)(a)

Every one who — gives or offers or agrees to give or offer — to a municipal official — a loan or reward or advantage or benefit of any kind — as consideration for the official — either to abstain from voting at a meeting of the municipal council or a committee thereof — or to vote in favour of or against a measure or motion or resolution — or to aid in procuring or preventing the adoption of a measure or motion or resolution — or to perform or fail to perform an official act — is guilty of an indictable offence.

Being a corrupt municipal official — Section 123(1)(b)

Every one who — being a municipal official — demands or accepts or offers or agrees to accept from any person — a loan or reward or advantage or benefit of any kind — as consideration for the official — either to abstain from voting at a meeting of the municipal council or a committee thereof — or to vote in favour of or against a measure or motion or resolution — or to aid in procuring or preventing the adoption of a measure or motion or resolution — or to perform or fail to perform an official act — is guilty of an indictable offence.

Included offences. Attempts (s. 660 and s. 662(1)(b)).

Punishment. Imprisonment for a term not exceeding 5 years (s. 123(1)).

Release. Initial decision to release made by officer in charge or justice (s. 498).

Election. Accused may elect trial by judge and jury, judge alone, or provincial court judge (s. 536).

Definitions. See MUNICIPAL OFFICIAL.

6. Influencing municipal official — Section 123(2)

Every one who — either by suppression of the truth, in the case of a person who is under a duty to disclose the truth — or by threats or deceit — or by any unlawful means — influences or attempts to influence — a municipal official — either to abstain from voting at a meeting of the municipal council or a committee thereof — to vote in favour of or against a measure or motion or resolution — or to aid in procuring or preventing the adoption of a measure or motion or resolution — or to perform or fail to perform an official act — is guilty of an indictable offence.

Included offences. Attempts (s. 660 and s. 662(1)(b)).

Punishment. Imprisonment for a term not exceeding 5 years (s. 123(2)).

Release. Initial decision to release made by officer in charge or justice (s. 498).

Election. Accused may elect trial by judge and jury, judge alone, or provincial court judge (s. 536).

Definitions. See MUNICIPAL OFFICIAL.

7. Selling office — Section 124(a)

Every one who — purports to sell or agrees to sell — an appointment to or resignation from an office — or a consent to any such appointment or resignation — or receives or agrees to receive — a reward or profit from the purported sale thereof — is guilty of an indictable offence.

Included offences. Attempts (s. 660 and s. 662(1)(b)).

Punishment. Imprisonment for a term not exceeding 5 years (s. 124).

Release. Initial decision to release made by officer in charge or justice (s. 498).

Election. Accused may elect trial by judge and jury, judge alone, or provincial court judge (s. 536).

8. Purchasing office — Section 124(b)

Every one who — either purports to purchase — or gives a reward or profit for the purported purchase of — any such

appointment or resignation or consent — or agrees or promises to do so — is guilty of an indictable offence.

Included offences. Attempts (s. 660 and s. 662(1)(b)).

Punishment. Imprisonment for a term not exceeding 5 years (s. 124).

Release. Initial decision to release made by officer in charge or justice (s. 498).

Election. Accused may elect trial by judge and jury, judge alone, or provincial court judge (s. 536).

9. Influencing appointments — Section 125(a)

Every one who — receives or agrees to receive or gives or procures to be given — directly or indirectly — a reward or advantage or benefit or any kind — as consideration for cooperation or assistance or exercise of influence to secure the appointment of any person to an office — is guilty of an indictable offence.

Included offences. Attempts (s. 660 and s. 662(1)(b)).

Punishment. Imprisonment for a term not exceeding 5 years (s. 125).

Release. Initial decision to release made by officer in charge or justice (s. 498).

Election. Accused may elect trial by judge and jury, judge alone, or provincial court judge (s. 536).

10. Negotiating appointments — Section 125(b)

Every one who — solicits or recommends or negotiates in any matter — with respect to an appointment to or resignation from an office — in expectation of a direct or indirect reward or advantage or benefit — is guilty of an indictable offence.

Included offences. Attempts (s. 660 and s. 662(1)(b)).

Punishment. Imprisonment for a term not exceeding 5 years (s. 125).

Release. Initial decision to release made by officer in charge or justice (s. 498).

Election. Accused may elect trial by judge and jury, judge alone, or provincial court judge (s. 536).

11. Keeping a place for dealing in offices — Section 125(c)

Every one who — without lawful authority — keeps a place for transacting or negotiating any business relating to — either the filling of vacancies in offices — or the sale or purchase of offices — or appointments to or resignations from offices — is guilty of an indictable offence.

Included offences. Attempts (s. 660 and s. 662(1)(b)).

Punishment. Imprisonment for a term not exceeding 5 years (s. 125).

Release. Initial decision to release made by officer in charge or justice (s. 498).

Election. Accused may elect trial by judge and jury, judge alone, or provincial court judge (s. 536).

Evidence. For the purposes of this offence, the proof of lawful excuse lies on the accused (s. 125(c)).

COSTS. For the purposes of s. 809, "costs" includes the costs and charges, after they have been ascertained, of committing and conveying to prison the person against whom costs have been rewarded (s. 809(5)).

COUNSEL. For the purposes of the Criminal Code, "counsel" means a barrister or solicitor, in respect of the matters or things that barristers and solicitors, respectively, are authorized by the law of a province to do or perform in relation to legal proceedings (s. 2).

Counselling. For the purposes of the Criminal Code, "counselling" includes procuring, soliciting or inciting (s. 22(3)).

COUNSELLING COMMISSION OF OFFENCE WHICH IS NOT COMMITTED

Section 464(a)

Except where otherwise expressly provided by law

every one who — counsels another person — to commit an indictable offence — if the offence is not committed — is guilty of an indictable offence.

Section 464(b)

Except where otherwise expressly provided by law

every one who — counsels another person — to commit an offence punishable on summary conviction — if the offence is not committed — is guilty of an offence punishable on summary conviction.

Limitation period. No proceedings in respect of offences that are declared to be punishable on summary conviction shall be instituted more than 6 months after the time when the subject matter of the proceedings arose (s. 786(2) and s. 785(1).

Included offences. Attempts (s. 660 and s. 662(1)(b)).

Punishment. On indictment, the same punishment to which a person who attempts to commit the counselled offence is liable (s. 464(a)). On summary conviction, a fine not exceeding $2,000, or 6 months' imprisonment, or both (s. 464(b) and s. 787(1)).

Election. On indictment, accused may elect trial by judge and jury, judge alone, or provincial court judge (s. 536). On summary conviction, no election.

Informations

A.B., on or about the —— day of ——, 19——, at the —— of ——, in the said (territorial division), did counsel C.D. to commit the offence of (specify the offence), to wit: (specify the particulars of the counselling) contrary to s. 464 of the Criminal Code of Canada.

COUNSELLING OR AIDING SUICIDE

Section 241(a)

Every one who — counsels a person — to commit suicide — whether suicide ensues or not — is guilty of an indictable offence.

Section 241(b)

Every one who — aids or abets a person — to commit suicide — whether suicide ensues or not — is guilty of an indictable offence.

Included offences. Attempts (s. 660 and s. 662(1)(b)).

Punishment. Imprisonment for a term not exceeding 14 years (s. 241).

Release. Initial decision to release made by justice (s. 515(1)).

Election. Accused may elect trial by judge and jury, judge alone, or provincial court judge (s. 536).

Informations

A.B., on or about the —— day of ——, 19——, at the —— of ——, in the said (territorial division), did counsel C.D. to commit suicide, to wit: (specify the particulars of the offence), contrary to s. 241(a) of the Criminal Code of Canada.

A.B., on or about the —— day of ——, 19——, at the —— of ——, in the said (territorial division), did aid [OR abet] C.D. to commit suicide, to wit: (specify the particulars of the offence), contrary to s. 241(b) of the Criminal Code of Canada.

COUNT. A charge in an information or indictment (s. 2).

COURTS

1. *General* 2. *Court of criminal jurisdiction*

See also ORDINARY COURT, TRIAL COURT and YOUTH COURT

1. General. There are several kinds of courts for criminal trials. Unless the section specifies two justices, one justice of the peace can try summary conviction cases. A provincial court judge has the power of two justices and therefore may try any summary conviction offence required to be tried by two justices of the peace.

Where an accused is before a justice of the peace other than a provincial court judge and is charged with an offence over which a provincial court judge has absolute jurisdiction (i.e., "s. 553 offences"), the justice is required to remand the accused to appear before a provincial court judge (s. 536(1)).

If the offence is not a "s. 553 offence" and is not an offence triable only in a superior court (s. 469), the justice shall, after the information has been read to the accused, put him to an election as follows:

"You have the option to elect to be tried by a provincial court judge without a jury and without having had a preliminary inquiry or you may elect to have a preliminary inquiry and to be tried by a judge without a jury; or you may elect to have a preliminary inquiry and to be tried by a court composed of a judge and jury. If you do not elect now, you shall be deemed to have elected to have a preliminary inquiry and to be tried by a court composed of a judge and jury. How do you elect to be tried?" (s. 536(2)).

Where an accused elects to have a preliminary inquiry, the justice has the power to hold a preliminary inquiry to determine whether the accused should be committed for trial (s. 536(4)).

A provincial court judge has power under Part XIX of the Code to try, in some cases with and in some cases without the consent of the accused, certain indictable offences. This Part, called "Indictable Offences — Trial Without Jury" or "The Summary Trials Part" is not to be confused with a summary conviction. When a provincial court judge has jurisdiction to try the accused without his consent, it is indicated by stating that the provincial court judge has absolute jurisdiction. If there is no indication as to what court the accused may be tried by, the provincial court judge may try the accused if he consents to be so tried. If, however, the accused elects to be tried by a court composed of a judge and jury or by a judge without a jury, the provincial court judge proceeds to hold a preliminary inquiry. If the provincial court judge commits the accused for trial, the accused may re-elect, if the offence is not one of those mentioned in s. 469 which are triable only at the Assizes, to be tried in a manner different from his first election.

The General Sessions of the Peace is a jury court presided over by a county court judge sitting as Chairman of the General Sessions of the Peace for the trial of all criminal cases except murder and other offences specified in s. 469.

The Assizes and General Sessions are courts of jail delivery. All persons in jail awaiting trial should be brought before these courts. The Assizes can try any indictable offence but the offences mentioned in s. 469 must be tried there. The Assizes are presided over by a judge of a superior court of criminal jurisdiction.

2. Court of criminal jurisdiction. For the purposes of the Criminal Code, "court of criminal jurisdiction" means (a) a court of general or quarter sessions of the peace, when presided over by a superior court judge, or in the Province of Quebec, the Court of Quebec, the municipal court of Montreal and the municipal court of Quebec, (b) a provincial court judge or judge acting under Part XIX of the Criminal Code (Indictable Offence — Trial without Jury) and (c) in the Province of Ontario, the Ontario Court of Justice (s. 2).

CRANIAL SUTURES. The fibrous lines of union between the bones of the vault of the skull. The gradual disappearance of the cranial sutures is one of the anatomical features upon which an estimate of the age of skeletal remains may be based (Jaffe, A Guide to Pathological Evidence, 2nd ed.).

CRANIUM. That part of the skull which encloses the brain (Jaffe, A Guide to Pathological Evidence, 2nd ed.).

CREDIT CARDS

1. *Definition of "credit card"*	2. *Credit card offences*

1. Definition of "credit card". For the purposes of Part IX of the Criminal Code (Offences Against Rights of Property), "credit card" means any card, plate, coupon book or other device issued or otherwise distributed for the purpose of being used (a) on presentation to obtain, on credit, money, goods, services or any other thing of value, or (b) in an automated teller machine, a remote service unit or a similar automated banking device to obtain any of the services offered through the machine, unit or device (s. 321).

2. Credit card offences

Section 342(1)(a)

Every one who — steals — a credit card — is guilty of either an indictable offence or an offence punishable on summary conviction.

Section 342(1)(b)

Every one who — forges or falsifies — a credit card — is guilty of either an indictable offence or an offence punishable on summary conviction.

Section 342(1)(c)

Every one who — has in his possession or uses or deals in any other way with — a credit card that he knows was obtained — either by the commission in Canada of an offence — or by an act or omission anywhere that, if it had occurred in Canada, would have constituted an offence — is guilty of either an indictable offence or an offence punishable on summary conviction.

Section 342(1)(d)

Every one who — uses a credit card — that he knows has been revoked or cancelled — is guilty of either an indictable offence or an offence punishable on summary conviction.

Intent. Knowledge of how card obtained (s. 342(1)(c)); knowledge of revokation or cancellation (s. 342(1)(d)).

Jurisdiction. An accused who is charged with this offence may be tried and punished by any court having jurisdiction to try that offence in the place where the offence is alleged to have been committed or in the place where the accused is found, is arrested or is in custody (s. 342(2)).

Consent to prosecute. Where the place where the accused is found, is arrested or is in custody is outside the province in which the offence is alleged to have been committed, no proceedings in respect of that offence shall be commenced in that place without the consent of the Attorney General of that province (s. 342(2)).

Limitation period. No proceedings in respect of offences that are declared to be punishable on summary conviction shall be instituted more than 6 months after the time when the subject matter of the proceedings arose (s. 786(2) and s. 785(1)).

Included offences. Attempts (s. 660 and s. 662(1)(b)).

Punishment. On indictment, imprisonment for a term not exceeding 10 years (s. 342(1)(e)). On summary conviction, a fine not exceeding $2,000 or 6 months' imprisonment, or both (s. 342(1)(f) and s. 787(1)).

Release. Initial decision to release made by peace officer (s. 497).

Election. On indictment, accused may elect trial by judge and jury, judge alone, or provincial court judge (s. 536). On summary conviction, no election.

Evidence. For these purposes, the offence of having in possession is complete when a person has, alone or jointly with another person, possession of or control over anything mentioned in s. 342 or when he aids in concealing or disposing of it, as the case may be (s. 358).

Sufficiency of count. No count that alleges false pretences, fraud or any attempt or conspiracy by fraudulent means is insufficient by reason only that it does not set out in detail the nature of the false pretence, fraud or fraudulent means (s. 586).

Informations

A.B., on or about the —— day of ——, 19——, at the —— of ——, in the said (territorial division), did steal a credit card, to wit: (specify the particulars of the offence), contrary to s. 342(1)(a) of the Criminal Code of Canada.

A.B., on or about the —— day of ——, 19——, at the —— of ——, in the said (territorial division), did forge [OR falsify] a credit card, to wit: (specify the particulars of the offence), contrary to s. 342(1)(b) of the Criminal Code of Canada.

A.B., on or about the —— day of ——, 19——, at the —— of ——, in the said (territorial division), did have in his possession [OR use OR deal] with a credit card that he knew was obtained by the commission in Canada of an offence [OR by an act (OR omission) anywhere that, if it had occurred in Canada, would have constituted an offence], to wit: (specify the particulars of the offence), contrary to s. 342(1)(c) of the Criminal Code of Canada.

A.B., on or about the —— day of ——, 19——, at the —— of ——, in the said (territorial division), did use a credit card that he knew had been revoked [OR cancelled], contrary to s. 342(1)(d) of the Criminal Code of Canada.

CRIMINAL HARASSMENT

Prohibition — Section 264(1) and (2)

No person shall — without lawful authority — and knowing that another person is harassed — or recklessly as to whetr the other person is harassed — engage in conduct consisting of — repeatedly following from place to place the other person or anyone known to them — or repeatedly communicating with, either directly or indirectly, the other person or anyone known to them — or besetting or watching the dwelling-house, or place where the other person, or anyone known to them, resides, works, carries on business or happens to be — or engaging in threatening conduct directed at the other person or any member of their family — that causes that other person reasonably, in all the circumstances, to fear for their safety or the safety of anyone known to them.

Statement of offence — Section 264(3)

Every person who — contravenes s. 264 — is guilty of either an indictable offence or an offence punishable on summary conviction.

Intent. Knowledge of harassment or recklessness as to harassment.

Limitation period. No proceedings in respect of offences that are declared to be punishable on summary conviction shall be instituted more than 6 months after the time when the subject matter of the proceedings arose (s. 786(2) and s. 785(1)).

Punishment. On indictment, imprisonment for a term not exceeding 5 years (s. 264(3)(a)). On summary conviction, a fine not exceeding $2,000, or 6 months' imprisonment, or both (s. 264(3)(b) and s. 787(1)).

Release. Initial decision to release made by peace officer (s. 497).

Election. On indictment, accused may elect trial by judge and jury, judge alone, or provincial court judge (s. 536). On summary conviction, no election.

Informations

A.B., on or about the —— day of ——, 19——, at the —— of ——, in the said (territorial division), did, without lawful authority and knowing that another person was harassed *[OR reckless as to whether the other person was harassed]*, engage in conduct consisting of repeatedly following from place to place the other person *[OR anyone known to them OR repeatedly communicating with, either directly or indirectly, the other person (OR anyone known to them) OR besetting (OR watching) the dwelling-house (OR place) where the other person (OR anyone known to them) resides (OR works OR carries on business OR happens to be) OR engaging in threatening conduct directed at the other person (OR any member of their family)]*, that causes that other person reasonably in all the circumstances, to fear for their safety *[Or the safety of anyone known to them]*, to wit: (specify the particulars of the offence), contrary to s. 264(3) of the Criminal Code of Canada.

CRIMINAL INTEREST RATE

1. *Definitions*   2. *Receiving interest at a criminal rate*

1. Definitions

"Criminal rate". For the purposes of s. 347, "criminal rate" means an effective annual rate of interest calculated in accordance with generally accepted actuarial practices and principles that exceeds 60 per cent on the credit advanced under an agreement or arrangement (s. 347(2)).

"Credit advanced". For the purposes of s. 347, "credit advanced" means the aggregate of the money and the monetary value of any goods, services or benefits actually advanced or to be advanced under

an agreement or arrangement minus the aggregate of any required deposit balance and any fee, fine, penalty, commission and other similar charge or expense directly or indirectly incurred under the original or any collateral agreement or arrangement (s. 347(2)).

"Insurance charge". For the purposes of s. 347, "insurance charge" means the cost of insuring the risk assumed by the person who advances or is to advance credit under an agreement or arrangement, where the face amount of the insurance does not exceed the credit advanced (s. 347(2)).

"Interest". For the purposes of s. 347, "interest" means the aggregate of all charges and expenses, whether in the form of a fee, fine, penalty, commission or other similar charge or expense or in any other form, paid or payable for the advancing of credit under an agreement or arrangement, by or on behalf of the person to whom the credit is or is to be advanced, irrespective of the person to whom any such charges and expenses are or are to be paid or payable, but does not include any repayment of credit advanced or any insurance charge, official fee, overdraft charge, required deposit balance or, in the case of a mortgage transaction, any amount required to be paid on account of property taxes (s. 347(2)).

"Official fee". For the purposes of s. 347, "official fee" means a fee required by law to be paid to any governmental authority in connection with perfecting any security under an agreement or arrangement for the advancing of credit (s. 347(2)).

"Overdraft charge". For the purposes of s. 347, "overdraft charge" means a charge not exceeding $5 for the creation of or increase in an overdraft, imposed by a credit union or caisse populaire, the membership of which is wholly or substantially comprised of natural persons, or a deposit-taking institution, the deposits in which are insured, in whole or in part, by the Canada Deposit Insurance Corporation or guaranteed, in whole or in part, by the Quebec Deposit Insurance Board (s. 347(2)).

"Required deposit balance". For the purposes of s. 347, "required deposit balance" means a fixed or an ascertainable amount of the money actually advanced or to be advanced under an agreement or arrangement that is required, as a condition of the agreement or arrangement, to be deposited or invested by or on behalf of the person to whom the advance is or is to be made and that may be available, in the event of his defaulting in any payment, to or for the benefit of the person who advances or is to advance the money (s. 347(2)).

2. Receiving interest at a criminal rate

Section 347(1)(a)

Notwithstanding any Act of the Parliament of Canada

every one who — enters into an agreement or arrangement — to receive interest at a criminal rate — is guilty of either an indictable offence or an offence punishable on summary conviction.

Section 347(1)(b)

Notwithstanding any Act of the Parliament of Canada

every one who — receives a payment or partial payment of interest — at a criminal rate — is guilty of either an indictable offence or an offence punishable on summary conviction.

Exceptions. This offence does not apply to any transaction to which the Tax Rebate Discounting Act applies (s. 347(8)).

Consent to prosecute. No proceedings shall be commenced under this section without the consent of the Attorney General (s. 347(7)).

Limitation period. No proceedings in respect of offences that are declared to be punishable on summary conviction shall be instituted more than 6 months after the time when the subject matter of the proceedings arose (s. 786(2) and s. 785(1)).

Included offences. Attempts (s. 660 and s. 662(1)(b)).

Punishment. On indictment, imprisonment for a term not exceeding 5 years (s. 347(1)(c)). On summary conviction, a fine of not more than $25,000 or to imprisonment for a term not exceeding 6 months or to both (s. 347(1)(d)).

Release. Initial decision to release made by peace officer (s. 497).

Election. On indictment, accused may elect trial by judge and jury, judge alone, or provincial court judge (s. 536). On summary conviction, no election.

Evidence. 1. Where a person receives a payment or partial payment of interest at a criminal rate, he shall, in the absence of evidence to the contrary, be deemed to have knowledge of the nature of the payment and that it was received at a criminal rate (s. 347(3)).
2. In any proceedings under s. 347, a certificate of a Fellow of the Canadian Institute of Actuaries stating that he has calculated the effective annual rate of interest on any credit advanced under an

agreement or arrangement and setting out the calculations and the information on which they are based is, in the absence of evidence to the contrary, proof of the effective annual rate without proof of the signature or official character of the person appearing to have signed the certificate (s. 347(4)).

The certificate shall not be received in evidence unless the party intending to produce it has given to the accused or defendant reasonable notice of that intention together with a copy of the certificate (s. 347(5)).

An accused or a defendant against whom a certificate is produced may, with leave of the court, require the attendance of the actuary for the purposes of cross-examination (s. 347(6)).

Informations

A.B., on or about the —— day of ——, 19——, at the —— of ——, in the said (territorial division), did enter into an agreement [OR arrangement] to receive interest at a criminal rate, to wit: (specify the particulars of the offence), contrary to s. 347(1)(a) of the Criminal Code of Canada.

A.B.,, on or about the —— day of ——, 19——, at the —— of ——, in the said (territorial division), did receive a payment [OR partial payment] of interest at a criminal rate, to wit: (specify the particulars of the offence), contrary to s. 347(1)(b) of the Criminal Code of Canada.

CRIMINAL LAW. 1. A law enacted with a view to a public purpose such as public peace, order, security, health or morality (Reference re section 5(a) of Dairy Industry Act ((Margarine Case), [1949] S.C.R. 1 at 50, affirmed [1951] A.C. 179 (P.C.); Proprietary Articles Trade Assn. v. A.G. Can. (1931), 55 C.C.C. 241 (P.C.)). 2. The Constitution Act, 1867 s. 91(27), grants Parliament the exclusive power to enact criminal law in Canada.

CRIMINAL NEGLIGENCE

1. *Definition of "criminal negligence"*
2. *Causing death by criminal negligence*
3. *Causing bodily harm by criminal negligence*

1. Definition of "criminal negligence". Every one is criminally negligent who either (a) in doing anything, or (b) in omitting to do anything that it is his duty to do, shows wanton or reckless disregard for the lives or safety of other persons (s. 219(1)). The term "duty" as it is used in this definition refers to a duty that is imposed by law (s. 219(2)).

2. Causing death by criminal negligence — Section 220

Every one who — by criminal negligence — causes death — to another person — is guilty of an indictable offence.

Exceptions. No person commits this offence unless the death occurs within one year and one day from the time of the occurrence of the last event by means of which he caused or contributed to the cause of death (s. 227).

Included offences. Where a count charges an offence under s. 220 that arises out of the operation of a motor vehicle or the navigation or operation of a vessel or aircraft, and the evidence does not prove such offence but does prove an offence under s. 249 (dangerous operation of motor vehicles, vessels and aircraft), the accused may be convicted of an offence under s. 249 (s. 662(5)).

Punishment. Imprisonment for life (s. 220).

Release. Initial decision to release made by justice (s. 515(1)).

Election. Accused may elect trial by judge and jury, judge alone, or provincial court judge (s. 536).

Evidence. The wife or husband of a person charged with this offence where the complainant or victim is under the age of 14 years is a competent and compellable witness for the prosecution without the consent of the person charged (Canada Evidence Act, s. 4(4)).

Informations

A.B., on or about the —— day of ——, 19——, at the —— of ——, in the said (territorial division), by criminal negligence, did cause death to C.D., to wit: (specify the particulars of the offence), contrary to s. 220 of the Criminal Code of Canada.

3. Causing bodily harm by criminal negligence — Section 221

Every one who — by criminal negligence — causes bodily harm — to another person — is guilty of an indictable offence.

Included offences. *See Included offences under* **2**, *above*.

Punishment. Imprisonment for a term not exceeding 10 years (s. 221).

Release. Initial decision to release made by justice (s. 515(1)).

Election. Accused may elect trial by judge and jury, judge alone, or provincial court judge (s. 536).

Evidence. *See Evidence under* **2**, *above.*

Informations

A.B., on or about the —— day of ——, 19——, at the —— of ——, in the said (territorial division), by criminal negligence, did cause bodily harm to C.D., to wit: (specify the particulars of the offence), contrary to s. 221 of the Criminal Code of Canada.

CRIMINAL RECORDS. The Parliament of Canada has enacted An Act to provide for the relief of persons who have been convicted of offences and have subsequently rehabilitated themselves, R.S.C. 1985, c. C-47, that is commonly known as the Criminal Records Act. This Act provides that a person who has been convicted of an offence under an Act of Parliament or a regulation made under an Act of Parliament may apply to the National Parole Board for a pardon in respect of that offence and a Canadian offender within the meaning of the Transfer of Offenders Act, R.S.C. 1985, c. T-15, who has been transferred to Canada under that Act may apply to the Board for a pardon in respect of the offence of which the offender has been found guilty (Criminal Records Act, s. 3(1)).

The pardon (a) is evidence of the fact (i) that, in the case of a pardon for an offence referred to in s. 4(a), the Board, after making inquiries, was satisfied that the applicant for the pardon was of good conduct, and (ii) that, in the case of any pardon, the conviction in respect of which the pardon is granted or issued should no longer reflect adversely on the applicant's character; and (b) unless the pardon is subsequently revoked or ceases to have effect, vacates the conviction in respect of which it is granted and, without restricting the generality of the foregoing, removes any disqualification to which the person so convicted is, by reason of the conviction, subject by virtue of the provisions of any Act of Parliament, other than s. 100 or 259 of the Criminal Code, or of a regulation made under an Act of Parliament (Criminal Records Act, s. 5).

There are different provisions as to the time such an application for a pardon can be considered by the National Parole Board, which vary with the nature of the offence committed and the penalty imposed (Criminal Records Act, s. 4-s. 4.3).

CUIUS EST DARE EIUS EST DISPONERE. "He who gives can also direct the disposition of the gift" (Latin).

CUIUS EST SOLUM, EIUS EST USQUE AD CAELUM ET AD INFEROS. "Whoever owns the soil owns up to the sky and down to the centre of the earth" ("to heaven and hell") (Latin).

CULPA. Fault (Latin).

CURIA. A court of justice (Latin). *Curia advisari vult*. "The court takes time for consideration" ("wishes to be advised") (Latin).

CURRENCY OFFENCES

1. *Definitions*
2. *Making counterfeit money*
3. *Possession of counterfeit money*
4. *Possession of filings or clippings*
5. *Uttering or exporting counterfeit money*
6. *Fraudulently uttering coins*
7. *Slugs and tokens*
8. *Clipping or uttering clipped coin*
9. *Defacing current coin or uttering defaced coin*
10. *Making advertisement in likeness of bank note or security*
11. *Publishing or printing likeness of bank note or security*
12. *Making, having or dealing in instruments for counterfeiting*
13. *Conveying instruments for coining or metals out of mint*
14. *Advertising counterfeit money or tokens of value*
15. *Trafficking or dealing in counterfeit money or tokens of value*
16. *Sufficiency of count*

See also FORGERY AND RELATED OFFENCES

1. Definitions

"Counterfeit money". For the purposes of Part XII of the Criminal Code, "Offences Relating to Currency", "counterfeit money" includes

(a) a false coin or false paper money that resembles or is apparently intended to resemble or pass for a current coin or current paper money,

(b) a forged bank note or forged blank bank note, whether complete or incomplete

(c) a genuine coin or genuine paper money that is prepared or altered to resemble or pass for a current coin or current paper money of a higher denomination,

(d) a current coin from which the milling is removed by filing or cutting the edges and on which new milling is made to restore its appearance

(e) a coin cased with gold, silver or nickel, as the case may be, that is intended to resemble or pass for a current gold, silver or nickel coin, and

(f) a coin or a piece of metal or mixed metals washed or coloured by any means with a wash or material capable of producing the appearance of gold, silver or nickel and that is intended to resemble or pass for a current gold, silver or nickel coin (s. 448).

"Counterfeit token of value". For the purposes of Part XII of the Criminal Code, "counterfeit token of value" means a counterfeit excise stamp, postage stamp or other evidence of value, by whatever technical, trivial or deceptive designation it may be described, and includes genuine coin or paper money that has no value as money (s. 448).

See also CURRENT; UTTER.

2. Making counterfeit money — Section 449

Every one who — makes or begins to make — counterfeit money — is guilty of an indictable offence.

Included offences. Attempts (s. 660 and s. 662(1)(b)).

Punishment. Imprisonment for a term not exceeding 14 years (s. 449).

Release. Initial decision to release made by justice (s. 515(1)).

Election. Accused may elect trial by judge and jury, judge alone, or provincial court judge (s. 536).

Evidence. 1. Every offence relating to counterfeit money or counterfeit tokens of value shall be deemed to be complete notwithstanding that the money or tokens of value in respect of which the proceedings are taken are not finished or perfected or do not copy exactly the money or tokens of value that they are apparently intended to resemble or for which they are apparently intended to pass (s. 461(1)).
2. Counterfeit money, counterfeit tokens of value and anything that is used or is intended to be used to make counterfeit money or counterfeit tokens of value belong to Her Majesty (s. 462(1)).
3. A peace officer may seize and detain (a) counterfeit money, (b) counterfeit tokens of value, and (c) machines, engines, tools, instruments, materials or things that have been used or that have been adapted and are intended for use in making counterfeit money or

counterfeit tokens of value, and anything seized shall be sent to the Minister of Finance to be disposed of or dealt with as he may direct, but anything that is required as evidence in any proceedings shall not be sent to the Minister until it is no longer required in those proceedings (s. 462(2)).

Informations

A.B., on or about the —— day of ——, 19——, at the —— of ——, in the said (territorial division), did make [OR begin to make] counterfeit money, to wit: (specify the particulars of the offence), contrary to s. 449 of the Criminal Code of Canada.

3. Possession of counterfeit money — Section 450

Every one who — without lawful justification or excuse — either buys or receives or offers to buy or receive — or has in his custody or possession — or introduces into Canada — counterfeit money — is guilty of an indictable offence.

Included offences. Attempts (s. 660 and s. 662(1)(b)).

Punishment. Imprisonment for a term not exceeding 14 years (s. 450).

Release. Initial decision to release made by justice (s. 515(1)).

Election. Accused may elect trial by judge and jury, judge alone, or provincial court judge (s. 536).

Evidence. 1. For the purposes of this offence, the proof of lawful excuse lies on the accused (s. 450).
2. *See also Evidence under* **2***, above.*

Informations

A.B., on or about the —— day of ——, 19——, at the —— of ——, in the said (territorial division), without lawful justification or excuse, did buy [OR receive OR offer to buy OR offer to receive] counterfeit money, to wit: (specify the particulars of the offence), contrary to s. 450(a) of the Criminal Code of Canada.

A.B., on or about the —— day of ——, 19——, at the —— of ——, in the said (territorial division), without lawful justification or excuse, did have in his custody [OR did have in his possession] counterfeit money, to wit: (specify the particulars of the offence), contrary to s. 450(b) of the Criminal Code of Canada.

A.B., on or about the —— day of ——, 19——, at the —— of ——, in the said (territorial division), without lawful justification or excuse, did introduce into Canada counterfeit money, to wit: (specify the particulars of the offence), contrary to s. 450(c) of the Criminal Code of Canada.

4. Possession of filings or clippings — Section 451

Every one who — without lawful justification or excuse — has in his custody or possession — either gold or silver filings or clippings — or gold or silver bullion — or gold or silver in dust or solution or otherwise — produced or obtained by impairing or diminishing or lightening a current gold or silver coin — knowing that it has been so produced or obtained — is guilty of an indictable offence.

Intent. Knowledge of nature and origins of subject-matter.

Included offences. Attempts (s. 660 and s. 662(1)(b)).

Punishment. Imprisonment for a term not exceeding 5 years (s. 451).

Release. Initial decision to release made by officer in charge or justice (s. 498).

Election. Accused may elect trial by judge and jury, judge alone, or provincial court judge (s. 536).

Evidence. For the purposes of this offence, the proof of lawful excuse lies on the accused (s. 451).

Informations

A.B., on or about the —— day of ——, 19——, at the —— of ——, in the said (territorial division), without lawful justification or excuse, did have in his custody or possession gold [OR silver] filings [OR clippings OR bullion OR in dust OR in solution OR (specify)], produced or obtained by impairing [OR diminishing OR lightening] a current gold [OR silver] coin, knowing that it has been so produced [OR obtained], to wit: (specify the particulars of the offence), contrary to s. 451 of the Criminal Code of Canada.

5. Uttering or exporting counterfeit money

Section 452(a)

Every one who — without lawful justification or excuse — either utters or offers to utter counterfeit money — or uses counterfeit money as if it were genuine — is guilty of an indictable offence.

Section 452(b)

Every one who — without lawful justification or excuse — exports or sends or takes counterfeit money out of Canada — is guilty of an indictable offence.

Included offences. Attempts (s. 660 and s. 662(1)(b)).

Punishment. Imprisonment for a term not exceeding 14 years (s. 452).

Release. Initial decision to release made by justice (s. 515(1)).

Election. Accused may elect trial by judge and jury, judge alone, or provincial court judge (s. 536).

Evidence. 1. For the purposes of this offence, the proof of lawful excuse lies on the accused (s. 452).
2. *See also Evidence under* **2**, *above.*

Informations

A.B., on or about the —— day of ——, 19——, at the —— of ——, in the said (territorial division), without lawful justification or excuse, did utter [OR offer to utter OR use as if it were genuine] counterfeit money, to wit: (specify the particulars of the offence), contrary to s. 452(a) of the Criminal Code of Canada.

A.B., on or about the —— day of ——, 19——, at the —— of ——, in the said (territorial division), without lawful justification or excuse, did export [OR send OR take] counterfeit money out of Canada, to wit: (specify the particulars of the offence), contrary to s. 452(b) of the Criminal Code of Canada.

6. Fraudulently uttering coins — Section 453

Every one who — with intent to defraud — knowingly utters — either a coin that is not current — or a piece of metal or mixed metals — that resembles in size or figure or colour a current coin for which it is uttered — is guilty of an indictable offence.

Intent. Intention to defraud; knowingly.

Included offences. Attempts (s. 660 and s. 662(1)(b)).

Punishment. Imprisonment for a term not exceeding 2 years (s. 453).

Release. Initial decision to release made by officer in charge or justice (s. 498).

Election. Accused may elect trial by judge and jury, judge alone, or provincial court judge (s. 536).

Informations

A.B., on or about the —— day of ——, 19——, at the —— of ——, in the said (territorial division), with intent to defraud, knowingly did utter a coin that was not current, to wit: (specify the particulars of the offence), contrary to s. 453(a) of the Criminal Code of Canada.

A.B., on or about the —— day of ——, 19——, at the —— of ——, in the said (territorial division), with intent to defraud, knowingly did utter a piece of metal [OR mixed metals] that resembles in size [OR figure OR colour] a current coin for which it was uttered, to wit: (specify the particulars of the offence), contrary to s. 453(b) of the Criminal Code of Canada.

7. Slugs and tokens — Section 454

Every one who — without lawful excuse — either manufactures or produces or sells — or has in his possession — anything that is intended to be fraudulently used — in substitution for a coin or token of value that any coin or token-operated device is designed to receive — is guilty of an offence punishable on summary conviction.

Intent. Intention to use item fraudulently.

Limitation period. No proceedings in respect of offences that are declared to be punishable on summary conviction shall be instituted more than 6 months after the time when the subject matter of the proceedings arose (s. 786(2) and s. 785(1)).

Included offences. Attempts (s. 660 and s. 662(1)(b)).

Punishment. A fine not exceeding $2,000, or 6 months' imprisonment, or both (s. 454 and s. 787(1)).

Release. Initial decision to release made by peace officer (s. 497).

Election. No election, summary conviction offence.

Evidence. For the purposes of this offence, the proof of lawful excuse lies on the accused (s. 454).

Informations

A.B., on or about the —— day of ——, 19——, at the —— of ——, in the said (territorial division), without lawful justification or excuse, did manufacture [OR produce OR sell OR have in his possession] (specify the thing), that was intended to be fraudulently used in substitution for a coin [OR token of value] that a coin [OR token-operated] device was designed to receive, to wit: (specify the particulars of the offence), contrary to s. 454 of the Criminal Code of Canada.

8. Clipping or uttering clipped coin

Section 455(a)

Every one who — impairs or diminishes or lightens — a current gold or silver coin — with intent that it should pass for a current gold or silver coin — is guilty of an indictable offence.

Section 455(b)

Every one who — utters — a current gold or silver coin — knowing that it has been impaired or diminished or lightened with intent to pass for a current gold or silver coin — is guilty of an indictable offence.

Intent. Intention that item pass for current coin.

Included offences. Attempts (s. 660 and s. 662(1)(b)).

Punishment. Imprisonment for a term not exceeding 14 years (s. 455).

Release. Initial decision to release made by justice (s. 515(1)).

Election. Accused may elect trial by judge and jury, judge alone, or provincial court judge (s. 536).

Informations

A.B., on or about the —— day of ——, 19——, at the —— of ——, in the said (territorial division), did impair [OR diminish OR lighten] a current gold [OR silver] coin with intent that it should pass for a current gold [OR silver] coin, to wit: (specify the particulars of the offence), contrary to s. 455(a) of the Criminal Code of Canada.

A.B., on or about the —— day of ——, 19——, at the —— of ——, in the said (territorial division), did utter a current gold [OR silver] coin, knowing that it had been impaired [OR diminished OR lightened] with intent to pass for a current gold [OR silver] coin, to wit: (specify the particulars of the offence), contrary to s. 455(b) of the Criminal Code of Canada.

CURRENCY OFFENCES

9. Defacing current coin or uttering defaced coin

Section 456(a)

Every one who — defaces a current coin — is guilty of an offence punishable on summary conviction.

Section 456(b)

Every one who — utters a current coin — that has been defaced — is guilty of an offence punishable on summary conviction.

Limitation period. No proceedings in respect of offences that are declared to be punishable on summary conviction shall be instituted more than 6 months after the time when the subject matter of the proceedings arose (s. 786(2) and s. 785(1)).

Included offences. Attempts (s. 660 and s. 662(1)(b)).

Punishment. A fine not exceeding $2,000, or 6 months' imprisonment, or both (s. 456 and s. 787(1)).

Release. Initial decision to release made by peace officer (s. 497).

Election. No election, summary conviction offence.

Informations

A.B., on or about the —— day of ——, 19——, at the —— of ——, in the said (territorial division), did deface a current coin [OR utter a current coin that had been defaced], to wit: (specify the particulars of the offence), contrary to s. 456 of the Criminal Code of Canada.

10. Making advertisement in likeness of bank note or security — Section 457(1)

Every one who — designs or engraves or prints or in any manner makes or executes or issues or distributes or circulates or uses — any business or professional card or notice or placard or circular or handbill or advertisement — in the likeness or appearance of — either a current bank note or current paper money — or any obligation or security of a government or a bank — is guilty of an offence punishable on summary conviction.

Limitation period. No proceedings in respect of offences that are declared to be punishable on summary conviction shall be instituted more than 6 months after the time when the subject matter of the proceedings arose (s. 786(2) and s. 785(1)).

Included offences. Attempts (s. 660 and s. 662(1)(b)).

Punishment. A fine not exceeding $2,000, or 6 months' imprisonment, or both (s. 457(1) and s. 787(1)).

Release. Initial decision to release made by peace officer (s. 497).

Election. No election, summary conviction offence.

Informations

A.B., on or about the —— day of ——, 19——, at the —— of ——, in the said (territorial division), did design [OR engrave OR print OR make OR execute OR issue OR distribute OR circulate OR use] a business card [OR a professional card OR a notice OR a placard OR a circular OR a handbill OR an advertisement] in the likeness [OR appearance] of a current bank note [OR current paper money OR an obligation (OR security) of a government (OR bank)], to wit: (specify the particulars of the offence), contrary to s. 457(1) of the Criminal Code of Canada.

11. Publishing or printing likeness of bank note or security — Section 457(2)

Every one who — publishes or prints — anything in the likeness or appearance of — either all or part of a current bank note or current bank money — or all or part of any obligation or security of a government or a bank — is guilty of an offence punishable on summary conviction.

Limitation period. No proceedings in respect of offences that are declared to be punishable on summary conviction shall be instituted more than 6 months after the time when the subject matter of the proceedings arose (s. 786(2) and s. 785(1)).

Included offences. Attempts (s. 660 and s. 662(1)(b)).

Punishment. A fine not exceeding $2,000, or 6 months' imprisonment, or both (s. 457(2) and s. 787(1)).

Release. Initial decision to release made by peace officer (s. 497).

Election. No election, summary conviction offence.

Evidence. No person shall be convicted of this offence where it is established that, in publishing or printing anything to which s. 457(2) applies:

(a) no photography was used at any stage for the purpose of publishing or printing it, except in connection with processes necessarily involved in transferring a finished drawing or sketch to a printed surface;

(b) except for the word "Canada", nothing having the appearance of a word, letter or numeral was a complete word, letter or numeral;

(c) no representation of a human face or figure was more than a general indication of features, without detail;

(d) no more than one colour was used; and

(e) nothing in the likeness or appearance of the back of a current bank note or current paper money was published or printed in any form (s. 457(3)).

Informations

A.B., on or about the —— day of ——, 19——, at the —— of ——, in the said (territorial division), did publish [OR print] (specify the thing published or printed) in the likeness [OR appearance] of all [OR part of] a current bank note [OR current paper money OR an obligation (OR a security) of a government (OR a bank)], to wit: (specify the particulars of the offence), contrary to s. 457(2) of the Criminal Code of Canada.

12. Making, having or dealing in instruments for counterfeiting — Section 458

Every one who — without lawful justification or excuse — either makes or repairs — or begins or proceeds to make or repair — or buys or sells — or has in his custody or possession — any machine or engine or tool or instrument or material or thing — that he knows has been used or that he knows is adapted and intended for use in making counterfeit money or counterfeit tokens of value — is guilty of an indictable offence.

Intent. Knowledge of previous, adapted or intended use.

Included offences. Attempts (s. 660 and s. 662(1)(b)).

Punishment. Imprisonment for a term not exceeding 14 years (s. 458).

Release. Initial decision to release made by justice (s. 515(1)).

Election. Accused may elect trial by judge and jury, judge alone, or provincial court judge (s. 536).

Evidence. For the purposes of this offence, the proof of lawful excuse lies on the accused (s. 458).

Informations

A.B., on or about the —— day of ——, 19——, at the —— of ——, in the said (territorial division), without lawful justification or excuse, did make [OR repair OR begin to make OR begin to repair OR proceed to make OR proceed to repair OR buy OR sell OR have in his custody OR have in his possession] a machine [OR an engine OR a tool OR an instrument OR material OR a thing] that he knew had been used [OR that he knew was adapted and intended for use] in making counterfeit money [OR counterfeit tokens of value], to wit: (specify the particulars of the offence), contrary to s. 458 of the Criminal Code of Canada.

13. Conveying instruments for coining or metals out of mint — Section 459

Every one who — without lawful justification or excuse — knowingly — conveys out of any of Her Majesty's mints in Canada — either any machine or engine or tool or instrument or material or thing used or employed in connection with the manufacture of coins — or a useful part of any such thing — or coin or bullion or metal or a mixture of metals — is guilty of an indictable offence.

Intent. Knowingly.

Included offences. Attempts (s. 660 and s. 662(1)(b)).

Punishment. Imprisonment for a term not exceeding 14 years (s. 459).

Release. Initial decision to release made by justice (s. 515(1)).

Election. Accused may elect trial by judge and jury, judge alone, or provincial court judge (s. 536).

Evidence. For the purposes of this offence, the proof of lawful excuse lies on the accused (s. 459).

Informations

A.B., on or about the —— day of ——, 19——, at the —— of ——, in the said (territorial division), without lawful justification or excuse, knowingly did convey out of Her Majesty's mints in Canada, a machine [OR part of a machine OR an engine OR part of an engine OR a tool OR a part of a tool OR an instrument OR part of an instrument OR material OR thing] used or employed in connection with the manufacture of coins, to wit: (specify the particulars of the offence), contrary to s. 459(a) [OR (b)] of the Criminal Code of Canada.

A.B., on or about the —— day of ——, 19——, at the —— of ——, in the said (territorial division), without lawful justification or excuse, knowingly *did convey out of Her Majesty's mints in Canada, coin [OR bullion OR metal OR a mixture of metals], to wit: (specify the particulars of the offence), contrary to s. 459(c) of the Criminal Code of Canada.*

14. Advertising counterfeit money or tokens of value — Section 460(1)(a)

Every one who — by an advertisement or any other writing — either offers to sell or procure or dispose of counterfeit money or counterfeit tokens of value — or offers to give information with respect to the manner in which or the means by which counterfeit money or counterfeit tokens of value may be sold or procured or disposed of — is guilty of an indictable offence.

Included offences. Attempts (s. 660 and s. 662(1)(a)).

Punishment. Imprisonment for a term not exceeding 5 years (s. 460(1)).

Release. Initial decision to release made by officer in charge or justice (s. 498).

Election. Accused may elect trial by judge and jury, judge alone, or provincial court judge (s. 536).

Evidence. 1. No person shall be convicted of this offence in respect of genuine coin or genuine paper money that has no value as money unless, at the time when the offence is alleged to have been committed, he knew that the coin or paper money had no value as money and he had a fraudulent intent in his dealings with or with respect to the coin or paper money (s. 460(2)).
2. *See also Evidence under* **2**, *above.*

Informations

A.B., on or about the —— day of ——, 19——, at the —— of ——, in the said (territorial division), did by an advertisement [OR a writing] offer to sell [OR procure OR dispose of] counterfeit money [OR counterfeit tokens of value], to wit: (specify the particulars of the offence), contrary to s. 460(1)(a) of the Criminal Code of Canada.

A.B., on or about the —— day of ——, 19——, at the —— of ——, in the said (territorial division), did by an advertisement [OR a writing] offer to give information with respect to the manner in which [OR the means by which] counterfeit money [OR counterfeit tokens of value] may be sold [OR procured OR disposed of], to wit: (specify the particulars of the offence), contrary to s. 460(1)(a) of the Criminal Code of Canada.

15. Trafficking or dealing in counterfeit money or tokens of value — Section 460(1)(b)

Every one who — either purchases or obtains or negotiates or otherwise deals with counterfeit tokens of value — or offers to negotiate with a view to purchasing or obtaining counterfeit tokens of value — is guilty of an indictable offence.

Included offences. Attempts (s. 660 and s. 662(1)(b)).

Punishment. Imprisonment for a term not exceeding 5 years (s. 460(1)).

Release. Initial decision to release made by officer in charge or justice (s. 498).

Election. Accused may elect trial by judge and jury, judge alone, or provincial court judge (s. 536).

Evidence. 1. *See Evidence under* **14**, *above.*
2. *See also Evidence under* **2**, *above.*

Informations

A.B., on or about the —— day of ——, 19——, at the —— of ——, in the said (territorial division), did purchase [OR obtain OR negotiate OR deal with] counterfeit tokens of value, to wit: (specify the particulars of the offence), contrary to s. 460(1)(b) of the Criminal Code of Canada.

A.B., on or about the —— day of ——, 19——, at the —— of ——, in the said (territorial division), did offer to negotiate with a view to purchasing [OR obtaining] counterfeit tokens of value, to wit: (specify the particulars of the offence), contrary to s. 460(1)(b) of the Criminal Code of Canada.

16. Sufficiency of count

No count that alleges false pretences, fraud or any attempt or conspiracy by fraudulent means is insufficient by reason only that it does not set out in detail the nature of the false pretence, fraud or fraudulent means (s. 586).

CURRENT. For the purposes of Part XII of the Criminal Code (Offences Relating to Currency), "current" means lawfully current in Canada or elsewhere by virtue of a law, proclamation or regulation in force in Canada or elsewhere as the case may be (s. 448).

CUSTODY

1. *Custody of a child*   2. *Custody of a young offender*

1. Custody of a child. The charge of a child's person, coupled with the right to determine the matter of his or her up bringing.

2. Custody of a young offender

Open custody. Required residence in some place such as a residential centre, group home or wilderness camp, where a young offender may be required to live under supervision and be subject to control but not kept in close confinement.

Secure custody. By contrast, this expression refers to detention in close confinement and is used only as a last resort in the case of young offenders (Mewett, Introduction to the Criminal Process).

CUT. 1. A wound caused by a sharp object, usually of metal or glass. The wound is longer than deep and tends to gape. Its edges are usually not contused, distinguishing it from a split. Also incised wound, slash and slice (Jaffe, A Guide to Pathological Evidence, 2nd ed.). 2. To dilute a drug, usually by an admixture of starch or milk sugar (Jaffe, A Guide to Pathological Evidence, 2nd ed.).

CUTIS ANSERINA. A roughening of the skin caused by the contraction of the erector muscles of the hairs. In the living person it is caused by fear or exposure to cold; in the cadaver it is a manifestation of rigor mortis. The presence of cutis anserina in a body recovered from water was at one time regarded as an indication that death had occurred in the water. This view is no longer held. Also goose lesh and goose pimples (Jaffe, A Guide to Pathological Evidence, 2nd ed.).

CYANOSIS. A bluish or grey discolouration of the skin and mucous membranes due to the presence of insufficiently oxygenated blood (Jaffe, A Guide to Pathological Evidence, 2nd ed.).

D

D.O.A. The abbreviation for "dead on arrival" (Jaffe, A Guide to Pathological Evidence, 2nd ed.).

DACTYLOGRAPHY. The recording of fingerprints as an aid in identification (Jaffe, A Guide to Pathological Evidence, 2nd ed.).

DAMNUM SINE (or ABSQUE) INJURIA. "Loss without legal cause of action" (Latin).

DANGEROUS OFFENDER

Definition. The Criminal Code provides that a court may find an offender to be a "dangerous offender" and may thereupon impose a sentence of detention in a penitentiary for an indeterminate period, in lieu of any other sentence that might be imposed for the offence for which the offender has been convicted. This may be done where, following the conviction of a person for an offence but before the offender is sentenced therefor, the following things are established to the satisfaction of the court:

(a) that the offence for which the offender has been convicted is a serious personal injury offence as defined in para. (a) of the definition in s. 752 and the offender constitutes a threat to the life, safety or physical or mental well-being of other persons on the basis of evidence establishing either a pattern of repetitive behaviour by the offender, of which the offence for which he has been convicted forms a part, showing a failure to restrain his behaviour and a likelihood of his causing death or injury to other persons, or inflicting severe psychological damage on other persons, through failure in the future to restrain his behaviour, or a pattern of persistent aggressive behaviour by the offender, of which the offence for which he has been convicted forms a part, showing a substantial degree of indifference on the part of the offender respecting the reasonably foreseeable consequences to other persons of his behaviour, or any behaviour by the offender, associated with the offence for which he has been convicted, that is of such a brutal nature as to compel the conclusion that his behaviour in the future is unlikely to be inhibited by normal standards of behavioural restraint, or

(b) that the offence for which the offender has been convicted is a serious personal injury offence as defined in para. (b) of the definition in s. 752 and the offender, by his conduct in any sexual matter including that involved in the commission of the offence for which he has been convicted, has shown a failure to control his sexual impulses and a likelihood of his causing injury, pain or other evil to other persons through failure in the future to control his sexual impulses (s. 753).

Serious personal injury offence. 1. Para. (a) of the definition in s. 752 provides that a "serious personal injury offence" means an indictable offence (other than high treason, treason, first degree murder or second degree murder) involving either the use or attempted use of violence against another person, or conduct endangering or likely to endanger the life or safety of another person or inflicting or likely to inflict severe psychological damage upon another person, and for which the offender may be sentenced to imprisonment for 10 years or more. 2. Para. (b) of the definition in s. 752 provides that a "serious personal injury offence" means an offence or attempt to commit an offence mentioned in s. 271 (sexual assault), s. 272 (sexual assault with a weapon, threats to a third party or causing bodily harm) or s. 273 (aggravated sexual assault).

DAY. For the purposes of the Criminal Code, "day" means the period between 6 o'clock in the forenoon and 9 o'clock in the afternoon of the same day (s. 2).

DE. From; after; during; about; on account of (Latin). ***De bene esse.*** "Conditionally" (Latin). ***De facto.*** "In fact" (Latin). ***De jure.*** "By right" or "from the law" (Latin). ***De minimis non curat lex.*** "The law does not concern itself with trifles" (Latin). ***De novo.*** "Anew" (Latin).

DEATH. The permanent cessation of all vital functions (Jaffe, A Guide to Pathological Evidence, 2nd ed.).

Crib death. Sudden death in apparently well infants, usually between the 3rd and 12th months of life, with negative or minimal autopsy findings. Also, cot death; sudden infant death syndrome (S.I.D.S.) (Jaffe, A Guide to Pathological Evidence, 2nd ed.).

Molecular death. The permanent loss by the cell of its functional integrity. The earliest manifestation of molecular death appears to be an irreversible change in the selective permeability of the cell membrane. Also, "cellular death" (Jaffe, A Guide to Pathological Evidence, 2nd ed.).

Somatic death. The permanent cessation of respiration and circulation. Absence of response to external stimuli, of spontaneous muscular movements and lack of brain function as determined by the electroencephalograph have recently been added to the criteria on which the definition of somatic death had been based. Somatic death marks the extinction of the biological and legal personality. Also, clinical death (Jaffe, A Guide to Pathological Evidence, 2nd ed.).

DECIDUOUS TEETH. The first dentition of the child consisting of 20 teeth. Also "milk teeth" (Jaffe, A Guide to Pathological Evidence, 2nd ed.).

DEFENCES

1. *Definition of a defence*
2. *Common law defences*
3. *Presumption of innocence*
4. *Failure to prove essential elements*

See also JUSTIFICATION OR EXCUSE.

1. Definition of a "defence"

1. Any claim which, if accepted, would necessitate an acquittal. 2. A claim for an acquittal which requires the discharge of an evidentiary burden by the accused (Eric Colvin, Principles of Criminal Law). 3. A defence is any answer which defeats the charge on the facts, or any means or argument on the law which has the same effect (Knoll, Criminal Law Defences) (R. v. Romer; R. v. Johnson; R. v. Farrell (1914), 23 C.C.C. 235 (Que. Police Ct.)).

2. Common law defences. Every rule and principle of the common law that renders any circumstance a justification or excuse for an act or a defence to a charge continues in force and applies in respect of proceedings for any Criminal Code offence or federal offence, except insofar as they are altered by or are inconsistent with the Criminal Code or any other federal Act (s. 8(3)).

3. Presumption of innocence. Any person charged with an offence has the right to be presumed innocent until proven guilty according to law in a fair and public hearing by an independent and impartial tribunal (Canadian Charter of Rights and Freedoms, s. 11(d)). Where an enactment creates an offence and authorizes a punishment to be imposed in respect of that offence, a person shall not be deemed guilty of that offence until he is either convicted or discharged pursuant to s. 736 of the Criminal Code (s. 6(1)(a)).

4. Failure to prove essential elements. In all criminal prosecutions there must be, at the close of the case for the prosecution, sufficient evidence on all essential elements of the offence which ultimately must be proved by the prosecution, such that a trier of fact (the judge or judge and jury), on all the evidence and properly instructed, could find the accused guilty beyond a reasonable doubt. The prosecution must prove all these elements beyond a reasonable doubt in order to obtain a conviction (Patrick J. Knoll, Criminal Law Defences). A defence in this sense could be simply that the Crown has not proved its case (Eric Colvin, Principles of Criminal Law).

DEHORS. "Outside the scope of" or "foreign to" (French).

DELEGATED LEGISLATION. Rules, orders and regulations on particular subjects made pursuant to an act of Parliament or a provincial legislature, a Cabinet, a Minister of the Crown, a municipality or some other person or body, other than Parliament or a provincial legislature. Such rules, orders and regulations have the same effect as if they were enacted by Parliament or a provincial legislature.

DELEGATUS NON POTEST DELEGARE. "A delegate cannot delegate" (Latin).

DELIRIUM. A state of mental disorientation, usually temporary (Jaffe, A Guide to Pathological Evidence, 2nd ed.).

DELUSION. A false belief, contrary to reality, which cannot be corrected by reasoning (Jaffe, A Guide to Pathological Evidence, 2nd ed.).

DEMENTIA. An irreversible mental deterioration, the end result of many intoxications or nervous disorders (Jaffe, A Guide to Pathological Evidence, 2nd ed.).

DEPORTATION. The deportation of aliens from Canada rests wholly with the Immigration Department under the provisions of the Immigration Act.
    When a fugitive escapes to a foreign country it is sometimes possible to have the immigration authorities of the foreign country arrest the fugitive and deport him. This action will only be taken, of course, when the fugitive is an alien in the country to which he has escaped, has entered the country illegally or has a criminal record. In other cases extradition proceedings must be taken.

DEPOSITION. For the purposes of the Fugitive Offenders Act, "deposition" includes every affidavit, affirmation or statement made upon oath (Fugitive Offenders Act, s. 2).

DIATOMS. One-celled microscopic algae possessing a siliceous wall. Their presence in the lungs and bone marrow of bodies recovered from water has been used in the diagnosis of drowning (Jaffe, A Guide to Pathological Evidence, 2nd ed.).

DICTUM (DICTA). "Thing(s) said" (Latin).

DIMINISHED RESPONSIBILITY. A state bordering on but not amounting to insanity, i.e., where an accused is suffering from infirmity or aberration of mind or impairment of intellect to such an extent as not to be fully accountable for his actions (Walker, The Oxford Companion to Law).

DIPLOMATIC OR CONSULAR OFFICER. This expression includes an ambassador, envoy, minister, chargé d'affaires, counsellor, secretary, attaché, consul-general, consul, vice-consul, pro-consul, consular agent, acting consul-general, acting consul, acting vice-consul, acting consular agent, high commissioner, permanent delegate, adviser, acting high commissioner and acting permanent delegate (Interpretation Act, s. 35).

DIPTERA. The name given to an order of insects consisting of the true flies, mostly possessing a single pair of wings. The order includes the species Calliphora vomitoria which infests recently dead bodies and the larvae of which feed upon the tissues (Jaffe, A Guide to Pathological Evidence, 2nd ed.).

DISOBEDIENCE

1. *Disobeying a statute*	2. *Disobeying order of court*

1. Disobeying a statute — Section 126(1)

Every one who — without lawful excuse — contravenes an Act of Parliament — either by wilfully doing anything that it forbids — or by wilfully omitting to do anything that it requires to be done — unless a punishment is expressly provided by law — is guilty of an indictable offence.

Intent. Wilfully.

Included offences. Attempts (s. 660 and s. 662(1)(b)).

Punishment. Imprisonment for a term not exceeding 2 years (s. 126(1)).

Release. Initial decision to release made by officer in charge or justice (s. 498).

Election. Accused may elect trial by judge and jury, judge alone, or provincial court judge (s. 536).

Informations

A.B., on or about the —— day of ——, 19——, at the —— of ——, in the said (territorial division), without lawful excuse, did contravene an Act of Parliament by wilfully doing a thing it forbids [OR by wilfully omitting to do a thing it requires to be done], to wit: (specify the particulars of the offence), contrary to s. 126 of the Criminal Code of Canada.

2. Disobeying order of court — Section 127(1)

Every one who — without lawful excuse — disobeys a lawful order — made by a court of justice or by a person or body of persons authorized by any Act to make or give the order — other than an order for the payment of money — unless a punishment or other mode of proceeding is expressly provided by law — is guilty of an indictable offence.

Included offences. Attempts (s. 660 and s. 662(1)(b)).

Punishment. Imprisonment for a term not exceeding 2 years (s. 127(1)).

Release. Initial decision to release made by officer in charge or justice (s. 498).

Election. Accused may elect trial by judge and jury, judge alone, or provincial court judge (s. 536).

Informations

A.B., on or about the —— day of ——, 19——, at the —— of ——, in the said (territorial division), without lawful excuse, did disobey a lawful order made by a court of justice [OR by a person (OR body of persons) authorized by statute to make (OR give) the order], to wit: (specify the particulars of the offence), contrary to s. 127 of the Criminal Code of Canada.

DISORDERLY CONDUCT

1. *Indecent acts*
2. *Exposure*
3. *Nudity*
4. *Causing a disturbance*
5. *Indecent exhibition*
6. *Loitering and obstructing*

7. *Disturbing the occupants of a dwelling-house*
8. *Obstructing officiating clergyman*
9. *Disturbing religious worship*
10. *Trespassing at night*
11. *Stink or stench bombs*

See also *VAGRANCY*.

1. Indecent acts — Section 173(1)

Every one who — wilfully — does an indecent act — either in a public place in the presence of one or more persons — or in any place with intent thereby to insult or offend any person — is guilty of an offence punishable on summary conviction.

Intent. Wilfully; intention to insult or offend.

Limitation period. No proceedings in respect of offences that are declared to be punishable on summary conviction shall be instituted more than 6 months after the time when the subject matter of the proceedings arose (s. 786(2) and s. 785(1)).

Included offences. Attempts (s. 660 and s. 662(1)(b)).

Punishment. A fine not exceeding $2,000, or 6 months' imprisonment, or both (s. 173(1) and s. 787(1)).

Release. Initial decision to release made by peace officer (s. 497).

Election. No election, summary conviction offence.

Evidence. 1. It is essential that the offence should have been committed "wilfully".
2. Where an accused is charged with this offence no corroboration is required for a conviction and the judge shall not instruct the jury that it is unsafe to find the accused guilty in the absence of corroboration (s. 274).
3. The rules relating to evidence of recent complaint are hereby abrogated with respect to this offence (s. 275).
4. In proceedings in respect of this offence, evidence that the complainant has engaged in sexual activity, whether with the accused or with any other person, is not admissible to support an inference that, by reason of the sexual nature of that activity, the complainant (a) is more likely to have consented to the sexual activity that forms the subject-matter of the charge; or (b) is less worthy of belief (s. 276(1)). No evidence shall be adduced by or on behalf of the accused that the complainant has engaged in sexual activity other than the sexual activity that forms the subject-matter of the charge, whether

with the accused or with any other person, unless the judge, provincial court judge or justice determines, in accordance with the procedures set out in ss. 276.1 and 276.2, that the evidence (a) is of specific instances of sexual activity; (b) is relevant to an issue at trial;o and (c) has significant probative value that is not substantially outweighed by the danger of prejudice to the proper administration of justice (s. 276(2)).

In determining whether evidence is admissible under s. 276(2), the judge, provincial court judge or justice shall take into account (a) the interests of justice, including the right of the accused to make a full answer and defence; (b) society's interest in encouraging the reporting of sexual assault offences; (c) whether there is a reasonable prospect that the evidence will assist in arriving at a just determination in the case; (d) the need to remove from the fact-finding process any discriminatory belief or bias; (e) the risk that the evidence may unduly arouse sentiments of prejudice, sympathy or hostility in the jury; (f) the potential prejudice to the complainant's personal dignity and right of privacy; (g) the right of the complainant and of every individual to personal security and to the full protection and benefit of the law; and (h) any other factor that the judge, provincial court judge or justice considers relevant (s. 276(3)).

Application may be made to the judge, provincial court judge or justice by or on behalf of the accused for a hearing under s. 276.2 to determine whether evidence is admissible under s. 276(2) (s. 276.2(1)).

An application referred to in s. 276.1(1) must be made in writing and set out (a) detailed particulars of the evidence that the accused seeks to adduce, and (b) the relevance of that evidence to an issue at trial, and a copy of the application must be given to the prosecutor and to the clerk of the court l(s. 276.1(2)). The judge, provincial court judge or justice shall consider the application with the jury and the public excluded (s. 276.1(3)). Where the judge, provincial court judge or justice is satisfied (a) that the application was made in accordance with s. 276.1(2), (b) that a copy of the application was given to the prosecutor and to the clerk of the court at least 7 days previously, or such shorter interval as the judge, provincial court judge or justice may allow where the interests of justice so require, and (c) that the evidence sought to be adduced is capable of being admissible under s. 276(2), the judge, provincial court judge or justice shall grant the application and hold a hearing under s. 276.2 to determine whether the evidence is admissible under s. 276(2) (s. 276.1(4)).

At a hearing to determine whether evidence is admissible under s. 276(2), the jury and the public shall be excluded (s. 276.2(1)). The complainant is not a compellable witness at the hearing (s. 276.2(2)). At the conclusion of the hearing, the judge, provincial court judge or justice shall determine whether the evidence, or any part thereof, is admissible under s. 276(2) and shall provide reasons for that determination, and (a) where not all of the evidence is to be admitted, the reasons must state the part of the evidence that is to be admitted; (b) the reasons must state the factors referred to in s. 276(3) that affected the determination; and (c) where all or any part of the evidence is to be admitted, the reasons must state the manner in which that evidence is expected to be relevant to an issue at trial (s. 276.2(3)). The reasons provided under s. 276.2(3) shall be entered in the record of the proceedings or, where the proceedings are not recorded, shall be provided in writing (s. 276.2(4)).

No person shall publish in a newspaper, as defined in s. 297, or in a broadcast, any of the following: (a) the contents of an application made under s. 276.1; (b) any evidence taken, the information given and the representations made at an application under s. 276.1 or at a hearing under s. 276.2; (c) the decision of a judge, provincial court judge or justice under s. 276.1(4), unless the judge, provincial court judge or justice, after taking into account the complainant's right of privacy and the interests of justice, orders that the decision may be published; and (d) the determination made and the reasons provided under s. 276.2, unless (i) that determination is that evidence is admissible, or (ii) the judge, provincial court judge or justice, after taking into account the complainant's right of privacy and the interests of justice, orders that the determination and reasons may be published (s. 276.3(1)).

For definitions, see NEWSPAPER. Every person who contravenes s. 276.3(1) is guilty of an offence punishable on summary conviction (s. 276.3(2)).

Where evidence is admitted at trial pursuant to a determination made under s. 276.2, the judge shall instruct the jury as to the uses that the jury may and may not make of that evidence (s. 276.4).

For the purposes of ss. 675 and 676, a determination made under s. 276.2 shall be deemed to be a question of law (s. 276.5).

5. In proceedings in respect of this offence, evidence of sexual reputation, whether general or specific, is not admissible for the purpose of challenging or supporting the credibility of the complainant (s. 277).

6. The wife or husband of a person charged with this offence is a competent and compellable witness for the prosecution without the consent of the person charged (Canada Evidence Act, s. 4(2)).

Informations

A.B., on or about the —— day of ——, 19——, at the —— of ——, in the said (territorial division), wilfully did an indecent act in a public place in the presence of C.D., to wit: (specify the particulars of the offence), contrary to s. 173(1)(a) of the Criminal Code of Canada.

A.B., on or about the —— day of ——, 19——, at the —— of ——, in the said (territorial division), wilfully did an indecent act with intent thereby to insult or offend C.D., to wit: (specify the particulars of the offence), contrary to s. 173(1)(b) of the Criminal Code of Canada.

2. Exposure — Section 173(2)

Every person who — in any place — for a sexual purpose — exposes his or her genital organs — to a person who is under the age of 14 years — is guilty of an offence punishable on summary conviction.

Intent. For sexual purpose.

Exceptions. No person aged 12 or 13 years shall be tried for this offence unless the person is in a position of trust or authority towards the complainant or is a person with whom the complainant is in a relationship of dependency (s. 150.1(3)).

Limitation period. No proceedings in respect of offences that are declared to be punishable on summary conviction shall be instituted more than 6 months after the time when the subject matter of the proceedings arose (s. 786(2) and 785(1)).

Included offences. Attempts (s. 660 and s. 662(1)(b)).

Punishment. A fine not exceeding $2,000, or 6 months' imprisonment, or both (s. 173(2) and s. 787(1)).

Release. Initial decision to release made by peace officer (s. 497).

Election. No election, summary conviction offence.

Defences. 1. Where an accused is charged with this offence in respect of a complainant under the age of 14 years, it is not a defence that the complainant consented to the activity that forms the subject matter of the charge (s. 150.1(1)).

2. Where an accused is charged with this offence in respect of a complainant who is 12 years of age or more but under the age of 14 years, it is not a defence that the complainant consented to the activity that forms the subject matter of the charge unless the accused is (a) 12 years of age or more but under the age of 16 years; (b) is less than 2 years older than the complainant; and (c) is neither in a position of trust or authority towards the complainant nor is a person with whom the complainant is in a relationship of dependency (s. 150.1(2)).

3. It is not a defence to a charge under this offence that the accused believed that the complainant was 14 years of age or more at the time the offence is alleged to have been committed unless the accused took all reasonable steps to ascertain the age of the complainant (s. 150.1(4)).

Evidence. See Evidence under **1**, *above.*

3. Nudity — Section 174(1)

Every one who — without lawful excuse — either is nude in a public place — or is nude and exposed to public view while on private property (whether or not the property is his own) — is guilty of an offence punishable on summary conviction.

Limitation period. No proceedings in respect of offences that are declared to be punishable on summary conviction shall be instituted more than 6 months after the time when the subject matter of the proceedings arose (s. 786(2) and s. 785(1)).

Consent to prosecute. No proceedings shall be commenced under s. 174 without the consent of the Attorney General (s. 174(3)).

Included offences. Attempts (s. 660 and s. 662(1)(b)).

Punishment. A fine not exceeding $2,000, or 6 months' imprisonment, or both (s. 174(1) and s. 787(1)).

Release. Initial decision to release made by peace officer (s. 497).

Election. No election, summary conviction offence.

Evidence. For the purposes of this offence, a person is "nude" who is so clad as to offend against public decency or order (s. 174(2)).

Informations

A.B., on or about the —— day of ——, 19——, at the —— of ——, in the said (territorial division), without lawful excuse, was nude in a public place, to wit: (specify the particulars of the offence), contrary to s. 174(1)(a) of the Criminal Code of Canada.

A.B., on or about the —— day of ——, 19——, at the —— of ——, in the said (territorial division), without lawful excuse, was nude and exposed to public view while on private property, to wit: (specify the particulars of the offence), contrary to s. 174(1)(b) of the Criminal Code of Canada.

4. Causing a disturbance — Section 175(1)(a)

Every one who — not being in a dwelling-house — causes a disturbance in or near a public place — either by fighting or screaming or shouting or swearing or singing or using insulting or obscene language — or by being drunk — or by impeding or molesting other persons — is guilty of an offence punishable on summary conviction.

Limitation period. No proceedings in respect of offences that are declared to be punishable on summary conviction shall be instituted more than 6 months after the time when the subject matter of the proceedings arose (s. 786(2) and s. 785(1)).

Included offences. Attempts (s. 660 and s. 662(1)(b)).

Punishment. A fine not exceeding $2,000, or 6 months' imprisonment, or both (s. 175(1) and s. 787(1)).

Release. Initial decision to release made by peace officer (s. 497).

Election. No election, summary conviction offence.

Evidence. 1. The offence here is causing a disturbance and is not the same thing as disturbing the peace. To disturb someone is to annoy that person, but to cause a disturbance is to create a commotion or a quarrel or a fight.
2. Mere drunkenness is not enough if in fact no disturbance has been caused.
3. In the absence of other evidence, or by way of corroboration of other evidence, a summary conviction court may infer from the evidence of a peace officer relating to the conduct of a person or persons, whether ascertained or not, that such a disturbance was caused or occurred (s. 175(2)).

Informations

A.B., on or about the —— day of ——, 19——, at the —— of ——, in the said (territorial division), not being in a dwelling-house, did cause a disturbance in [OR near] a public place by fighting [OR screaming OR shouting OR swearing OR singing OR using insulting language OR using obscene language OR impeding C.D. OR molesting C.D. OR being drunk], to wit: (specify the particulars of the offence), contrary to s. 175(1)(a) of the Criminal Code of Canada.

5. Indecent exhibition — Section 175(1)(b)

Every one who — openly exposes or exhibits — an indecent exhibition — in a public place — is guilty of an offence punishable on summary conviction.

Limitation period. No proceedings in respect of offences that are declared to be punishable on summary conviction shall be instituted more than 6 months after the time when the subject matter of the proceedings arose (s. 786(2) and s. 785(1)).

Included offences. Attempts (s. 660 and s. 662(1)(b)).

Punishment. A fine not exceeding $2,000, or 6 months' imprisonment, or both (s. 175(1) and s. 787(1)).

Release. Initial decision to release made by peace officer (s. 497).

Election. No election, summary conviction offence.

Informations

A.B., on or about the —— day of ——, 19——, at the —— of ——, in the said (territorial division), did openly expose [OR exhibit] an indecent exhibition in a public place, to wit: (specify the particulars of the offence), contrary to s. 175(1)(b) of the Criminal Code of Canada.

6. Loitering and obstructing — Section 175(1)(c)

Every one who — loiters in a public place — and in any way obstructs persons who are in that place — is guilty of an offence punishable on summary conviction.

Limitation period. No proceedings in respect of offences that are declared to be punishable on summary conviction shall be instituted more than 6 months after the time when the subject matter of the proceedings arose (s. 786(2) and s. 785(1)).

Included offences. Attempts (s. 660 and s. 662(1)(b)).

Punishment. A fine not exceeding $2,000, or 6 months' imprisonment, or both (s. 175(1) and s. 787(1)).

Release. Initial decision to release made by peace officer (s. 497).

Election. No election, summary conviction offence.

Evidence. To be convicted of this offence, the accused must be both loitering in a public place and obstructing someone else who was in that place.

Informations

A.B., on or about the —— day of ——, 19——, at the —— of ——, in the said (territorial division), did loiter in a public place and did obstruct C.D., a person who was there, to wit: (specify the particulars of the offence), contrary to s. 175(1)(c) of the Criminal Code of Canada.

7. Disturbing the occupants of a dwelling-house — Section 175(1)(d)

Every one who — either disturbs the peace and quiet of the occupants of a dwelling-house — by discharging firearms or by other disorderly conduct — in a public place — is guilty of an offence punishable on summary conviction.

Every one who — not being an occupant of a dwelling-house comprised in a particular building or structure — disturbs the peace and quiet of the occupants of a dwelling-house comprised in the building or structure — by discharging firearms or by other disorderly conduct — in any part of a building or structure to which (at the time of such conduct) the occupants of two or more dwelling-houses comprised in the building or structure have access as of right or by invitation, express or implied — is guilty of an offence punishable on summary conviction.

Limitation period. No proceedings in respect of offences that are declared to be punishable on summary conviction shall be instituted more than 6 months after the time when the subject matter of the proceedings arose (s. 786(2) and s. 785(1)).

Included offences. Attempts (s. 660 and s. 662(1)(b)).

Punishment. A fine not exceeding $2,000, or 6 months' imprisonment, or both (s. 175(1) and s. 787(1)).

Release. Initial decision to release made by peace officer (s. 497).

Election. No election, summary conviction offence.

Evidence. See Evidence, item 3., under **4**, above.

Informations

A.B., on or about the —— day of ——, 19——, at the —— of ——, in the said (territorial division), did disturb the peace and quiet of C.D., the occupant of a dwelling-house, by discharging firearms [OR by disorderly conduct] in a public place, to wit: (specify the particulars of the offence), contrary to s. 175(1)(d) of the Criminal Code of Canada.

A.B., on or about the —— day of ——, 19——, at the —— of ——, in the said (territorial division), did disturb the peace and quiet of C.D., the occupant of a dwelling-house comprised in a particular building [OR structure] in which A.B. was not himself an occupant, by discharging a firearm [OR by disorderly conduct] in a part of the building [OR structure] to which other occupants of dwelling-houses in the building [OR structure] have access, to wit: (specify the particulars of the offence), contrary to s. 175(1)(d) of the Criminal Code of Canada.

8. Obstructing officiating clergyman

Section 176(1)(a)

Every one who — by threats or force — unlawfully obstructs or prevents or endeavours to obstruct or prevent — a clergyman or minister — from celebrating divine service or performing any other function in connection with his calling — is guilty of an indictable offence.

Section 176(1)(b)

Every one who — knowing that a clergyman or minister is about to perform or is on his way to perform or is returning from the performance of any duties or functions in connection with his calling — either assaults or offers any violence to him — or arrests him on a civil process or under the pretence of executing a civil process — is guilty of an indictable offence.

Intent. Knowledge of performance of duties (s. 176(1)(b)).

Included offences. Attempts (s. 660 and s. 662(1)(b)).

Punishment. Imprisonment for a term not exceeding 2 years (s. 176(1)).

Release. Initial decision to release made by officer in charge or justice (s. 498).

Election. Accused may elect trial by judge and jury, judge alone, or provincial court judge (s. 536).

Informations

A.B., on or about the —— day of ——, 19——, at the —— of ——, in the said (territorial division), by threats [OR force] unlawfully did obstruct [OR prevent OR endeavour to obstruct OR endeavour to prevent] C.D., a clergyman [OR minister] from celebrating divine service [OR from performing a function in connection with his calling], to wit: (specify the particulars of the offence), contrary to s. 176(1)(a) of the Criminal Code of Canada.

A.B., on or about the —— day of ——, 19——, at the —— of ——, in the said (territorial division), knowing that C.D., a clergyman [OR minister], was about to perform [OR was on his way to perform OR was returning from the performance of] divine service [OR from a function in connection with his calling], did assault [OR offer violence to OR arrest upon a civil process OR arrest under the pretence of executing a civil process] the said C.D., to wit: (specify the particulars of the offence), contrary to s. 176(1)(b) of the Criminal Code of Canada.

9. Disturbing religious worship

Section 176(2)

Every one who — wilfully — disturbs or interrupts — an assemblage of persons met for religious worship or for a moral or social or benevolent purpose — is guilty of an offence punishable on summary conviction.

Section 176(3)

Every one who — at or near such a meeting — wilfully — does anything that disturbs the order or solemnity of the meeting — is guilty of an offence punishable on summary conviction.

Intent. Wilfully.

Limitation period. No proceedings in respect of offences that are declared to be punishable on summary conviction shall be instituted more than 6 months after the time when the subject matter of the proceedings arose (s. 786(2) and s. 785(1)).

Included offences. Attempts (s. 660 and s. 662(1)(b)).

Punishment. A fine not exceeding $2,000, or 6 months' imprisonment, or both (s. 176(2) and (3) and s. 787(1)).

Release. Initial decision to release made by peace officer (s. 497).

Election. No election, summary conviction offence.

Informations

A.B., on or about the —— day of ——, 19——, at the —— of ——, in the said (territorial division), did wilfully disturb [OR interrupt] an assemblage of persons meeting for religious worship [OR for a moral purpose OR for a social purpose OR for a benevolent purpose], to wit: (specify the particulars of the offence), contrary to s. 176(2) of the Criminal Code of Canada.

A.B., on or about the —— day of ——, 19——, at the —— of——, in the said (territorial division), being at [OR near] a meeting for religious worship [OR for a moral purpose OR for a social purpose OR for a benevolent purpose], by (specify action), disturbed the order [OR solemnity] of the meeting, to wit: (specify the particulars of the offence), contrary to s. 176(3) of the Criminal Code of Canada.

10. Trespassing at night — Section 177

Every one who — without lawful excuse — loiters or prowls — at night — on the property of another person near a dwelling-house situated on that property — is guilty of an offence punishable on summary conviction.

Limitation period. No proceedings in respect of offences that are declared to be punishable on summary conviction shall be instituted more than 6 months after the time when the subject matter of the proceedings arose (s. 786(2) and s. 785(1)).

Included offences. Attempts (s. 660 and s. 662(1)(b)).

Punishment. A fine not exceeding $2,000, or 6 months' imprisonment, or both (s. 177 and s. 787(1)).

Release. Initial decision to release made by peace officer (s. 497).

Election. No election, summary conviction offence.

Evidence. 1. Prowling and loitering are separate offences. "Prowling" means hunting in a stealthy manner for an opportunity to commit a criminal offence. "Loitering" means the act of hanging around.
2. For the purposes of this offence, the proof of lawful excuse lies on the accused (s. 177).

Informations

A.B., on or about the —— day of ——, 19——, at the —— of ——, in the said (territorial division), without lawful excuse, did loiter [OR prowl] at night upon the property of C.D. near the dwelling-house situated on that property, to wit: (specify the particulars of the offence), contrary to s. 177 of the Criminal Code of Canada.

11. Stink or stench bombs — Section 178

Every one who — other than a peace officer engaged in the discharge of his duty — either has in his possession in a public place — or deposits or throws or injects or causes to be deposited or thrown or injected in or into or near any place — either an offensive volatile substance that is likely to harm or inconvenience or discommode or cause discomfort to any person or to cause damage to property — or a stink or stench bomb or device from which any such substance is or is capable of being liberated — is guilty of an offence punishable on summary conviction.

Limitation period. No proceedings in respect of offences that are declared to be punishable on summary conviction shall be instituted more than 6 months after the time when the subject matter of the proceedings arose (s. 786(2) and s. 785(1)).

Included offences. Attempts (s. 660 and s. 662(1)(b)).

Punishment. A fine not exceeding $2,000, or 6 months' imprisonment, or both (s. 178 and s. 787(1)).

Release. Initial decision to release made by peace officer (s. 497).

Election. No election, summary conviction offence.

DISORDERLY HOUSES

1. *Definitions*
2. *Keeping a gaming house*
3. *Keeping a betting house*
4. *Found in gaming house or betting house*
5. *Allowing premises to be used as gaming house or betting house*
6. *Betting, pool-selling and book-making*
7. *Placing bets on behalf of others*
8. *Pari-mutuel betting*
9. *Violation or non-compliance with race-track regulations*
10. *Lotteries and games of chance prohibited by law*
11. *Cheating at play*
12. *Keeping common bawdy-house*
13. *Being an inmate or being found in a common bawdy-house*
14. *Having charge or control of place used for common bawdy-house*

210 DISORDERLY HOUSES

15. Transporting person to bawdy-house
16. Search and seizure in disorderly houses. See SEARCH AND SEIZURE, 10.

See also PROCURING and PROSTITUTION.

1. Definitions

"Disorderly house". For the purposes of Part VII of the Criminal Code (Disorderly Houses, Gaming and Betting), "disorderly house" means a common bawdy-house, a common betting house or a common gaming house (s. 197(1)).

"Common bawdy-house". For the purposes of Part VII of the Criminal Code, "common bawdy-house" means a place that is (a) kept or occupied, or (b) resorted to by one or more persons for the purpose of prostitution or the practice of acts of indecency (s. 197(1)).

"Common betting house". For the purposes of Part VII of the Criminal Code, "common betting house" means a place that is opened, kept or used for the purpose of (a) enabling, encouraging or assisting persons who resort thereto to bet between themselves or with the keeper, or (b) enabling any person to receive, record, register, transmit or pay bets or to announce the results of betting (s. 197(1)).

"Common gaming house". For the purposes of Part VII of the Criminal Code, "common gaming house" means a place that is (a) kept for gain to which persons resort for the purpose of playing games, or (b) kept or used for the purpose of playing games in which a bank is kept by one or more but not all of the players, or in which all or any portion of the bets on or proceeds from a game is paid, directly or indirectly, to the keeper of the place, or in which, directly or indirectly, a fee is charged to or paid by the players for the privilege of playing or participating in a game or using gaming equipment, or in which the chances of winning are not equally favourable to all persons who play the game, including the person, if any, who conducts the game (s. 197(1)).

2. Keeping a gaming house — Section 201(1)

Every one who — keeps — a common gaming house — is guilty of an indictable offence.

Exceptions. This offence does not apply to the following:

DISORDERLY HOUSES 211

(a) any person or association by reason of his or their becoming the custodian or depository of any money, property or valuable thing staked, to be paid to the winner of a lawful race, sport, game or exercise, the owner of a horse engaged in a lawful race, or the winner of any bets between not more than ten individuals,

(b) a private bet between individuals not engaged in any way in the business of betting,

(c) bets made or records of bets made through the agency of a pari-mutuel system on running, trotting or pacing horse-races if the bets or records of bets are made on the race-course of an association in respect of races conducted at that race-course or another race-course, and the provisions of this section and the regulations are complied with (s. 204(1)).

Jurisdiction. The jurisdiction of a provincial court judge to try an accused is absolute and does not depend on the consent of the accused where the accused has been charged in an information with this offence (s. 553(c)(i)).

Included offences. Attempts (s. 660 and s. 662(1)(b)).

Punishment. Imprisonment for a term not exceeding 2 years (s. 201(1)).

Release. Initial decision to release made by peace officer (s. 497).

Election. No election, absolute jurisdiction of provincial court judge (s. 553).

Informations

A.B., on or about the —— day of ——, 19——, at the —— of ——, in the said (territorial division), did keep a common gaming house, to wit: (specify the particulars of the offence), contrary to s. 201(1) of the Criminal Code of Canada.

3. Keeping a betting house — Section 201(1)

Every one who — keeps — a common betting house — is guilty of an indictable offence.

Exceptions. See Exceptions under **2**, above.

Jurisdiction. See Jurisdiction under **2**, above.

Included offences. Attempts (s. 660 and s. 662(1)(b)).

Punishment. Imprisonment for a term not exceeding 2 years (s. 201(1)).

Release. Initial decision to release made by peace officer (s. 497).

Election. No election, absolute jurisdiction of provincial court judge (s. 553).

Informations

A.B., on or about the —— day of ——, 19——, at the —— of ——, in the said (territorial division), did keep a common betting house, to wit: (specify the particulars of the offence), contrary to s. 201(1) of the Criminal Code of Canada.

4. Found in gaming house or betting house — Section 201(2)(a)

Every one who — is found — without lawful excuse — in a common gaming house or common betting house — is guilty of an offence punishable on summary conviction.

Exceptions. See Exceptions under **2**, above.

Jurisdiction. See Jurisdiction under **2**, above.

Limitation period. No proceedings in respect of offences that are declared to be punishable on summary conviction shall be instituted more than 6 months after the time when the subject matter of the proceedings arose (s. 786(2) and s. 785(1)).

Included offences. Attempts (s. 660 and s. 662(1)(b)).

Punishment. A fine not exceeding $2,000, or 6 months' imprisonment, or both (s. 201(2)(a) and s. 787(1)).

Release. Initial decision to release made by peace officer (s. 497).

Election. No election, absolute jurisdiction of provincial court judge (s. 553).

Informations

A.B., on or about the —— day of ——, 19——, at the —— of ——, in the said (territorial division), was found, without lawful excuse, in a common gaming [OR betting] house, to wit: (specify the particulars of the offence), contrary to s. 201(2)(a) of the Criminal Code of Canada.

DISORDERLY HOUSES

5. Allowing premises to be used as gaming house or betting house — Section 201(2)(b)

Every one who — as owner or landlord or lessor or tenant or occupier or agent — knowingly — permits a place to be let or used — for the purposes of a common gaming house or common betting house — is guilty of an offence punishable on summary conviction.

Intent. Knowingly.

Exceptions. See Exceptions under 2, above.

Jurisdiction. See Jurisdiction under 2, above.

Limitation period. No proceedings in respect of offences that are declared to be punishable on summary conviction shall be instituted more than 6 months after the time when the subject matter of the proceedings arose (s. 786(2) and s. 785(1)).

Included offences. Attempts (s. 660 and s. 662(1)(b)).

Punishment. A fine not exceeding $2,000, or 6 months' imprisonment, or both (s. 201(2)(b) and s. 787(1)).

Release. Initial decision to release made by peace officer (s. 497).

Election. No election, absolute jurisdiction of provincial court judge (s. 553).

Informations

A.B., on or about the —— day of ——, 19——, at the —— of ——, in the said (territorial division), being the owner *[OR landlord OR lessor OR tenant OR occupier OR agent]* of (specify the place), did knowingly permit such place to be let *[OR used]* for the purposes of a common gaming *[OR betting]* house, to wit: (specify the particulars of the offence), contrary to s. 201(2)(b) of the Criminal Code of Canada.

6. Betting, pool-making and book-making — Section 202(1) and (2)

Section 202(1)(a)

Every one who — uses or knowingly allows to be used — a place under his control — for the purpose of recording or registering bets or selling a pool — is guilty of an indictable offence.

Section 202(1)(b)

Every one who — imports or makes or buys or sells or rents or leases or hires or keeps or exhibits or employs or knowingly allows to be kept or exhibited or employed — in any place under his control

— either any device or apparatus for the purpose of recording or registering bets or selling a pool — or any machine or device for gambling or betting — is guilty of an indictable offence.

Section 202(1)(c)

Every one who — has under his control — any money or other property relating to a transaction that is an offence under s. 202 — is guilty of an indictable offence.

Section 202(1)(d)

Every one who — either records bets or registers bets — or sells a pool — is guilty of an indictable offence.

Section 202(1)(e)

Every one who — either engages in pool-selling or book-making, or in the business or occupation of betting — or makes any agreement for the purchase or sale of betting or gaming privileges — or makes any agreement for the purchase or sale of information that is intended to assist in book-making or pool-selling or betting — is guilty of an indictable offence.

Section 202(1)(f)

Every one who — prints or provides or offers to print or provide — information intended for use in connection with book-making or pool-selling or betting on any horse-race or fight or game or sport — whether or not it takes place in or outside Canada or has or has not taken place — is guilty of an indictable offence.

Section 202(1)(g)

Every one who — imports or brings into Canada — any information or writing — that is intended or is likely to promote or be of use in gambling or book-making or pool-selling or betting on a horse-race or fight or game or sport — is guilty of an indictable offence.

Section 202(1)(h)

Every one who — advertises or prints or publishes or exhibits or posts up or otherwise gives notice of — any offer or invitation or inducement — to be on or to guess or to foretell the results of a contest or a result of or contingency relating to any contest — is guilty of an indictable offence.

Section 202(1)(i)

Every one who — wilfully and knowingly — sends or transmits or delivers or receives any message — by radio or telegraph or telephone or mail or express — that conveys any information — either relating to book-making or pool-selling or betting or wagering — or that is intended to assist in book-making or pool-selling or betting or wagering — is guilty of an indictable offence.

Section 202(1)(j)

Every one who — aids or assists in any manner — in anything that is an offence under s. 202 — is guilty of an indictable offence.

Intent. Knowingly allows (s. 202(1)(a) and (b)); wilfully and knowingly (s. 202(1)(i)).

Exceptions. 1. The offence set out in s. 202(1)(g) does not apply to a newspaper, magazine or other periodical published in good faith primarily for a purpose other than the publication of such information (s. 202(1)(g)).
2. *See also Exceptions under* **2**, *above.*

Jurisdiction. The jurisdiction of a provincial court judge to try an accused is absolute and does not depend upon the consent of the accused where the accused is charged in an information with one of these offences (s. 553(c)(ii)).

Included offences. Attempts (s. 660 and s. 662(1)(b)).

Punishment. For a first offence, imprisonment for not more than 2 years. For a second offence, imprisonment for not more than 2 years and not less than 14 days. For each subsequent offence, imprisonment for not more than 2 years and not less than 3 months (s. 202(2)).

Release. Initial decision to release made by peace officer (s. 497).

Election. No election, absolute jurisdiction of provincial court judge (s. 553).

Evidence. Where s. 202(1)(g) applies, it is immaterial whether the information is published before, during or after the race, fight, game or sport or whether the race, fight, game or sport takes place in Canada or elsewhere (s. 202(1)(g)).

Informations

A.B., on or about the —— day of ——, 19——, at the —— of ——, in the said (territorial division), did use [OR knowingly allow to be used], a place under his (OR her) control, for the purpose of recording bets [OR registering bets OR selling a pool], to wit: (specify the particulars of the offence), contrary to s. 202(1)(a) of the Criminal Code of Canada.

A.B., on or about the —— day of ——, 19——, at the —— of ——, in the said (territorial division), did import [OR made OR buy OR sell OR rent OR lease OR hire OR keep OR exhibit OR employ OR knowingly allow to be kept (OR exhibited OR employed)] a device [OR apparatus] for the purpose of recording bets [OR registering bets OR selling a pool], to wit: (specify the particulars of the offence), contrary to s. 202(1)(b) of the Criminal Code of Canada.

A.B., on or about the —— day of ——, 19——, at the —— of ——, in the said (territorial division), did import [OR make OR buy OR sell OR rent OR lease OR hire OR keep OR exhibit OR employ OR knowingly allow to be kept (OR exhibited OR employed)] a machine [OR device] for gambling [OR betting], to wit: (specify the particulars of the offence), contrary to s. 202(1)(b) of the Criminal Code of Canada.

A.B., on or about the —— day of ——, 19——, at the —— of ——, in the said (territorial division), did have under his [OR her] control money in the amount of -- [OR (specify other property)] relating to a transaction that is an offence under s. 202 of the Criminal Code, to wit: (specify the particulars of the offence), contrary to s. 202(1)(c) of the Criminal Code of Canada.

A.B., on or about the —— day of ——, 19——, at the —— of ——, in the said (territorial division), did record bets [OR register bets OR sell a pool], to wit: (specify the particulars of the offence), contrary to s. 202(1)(d) of the Criminal Code of Canada.

A.B., on or about the —— day of ——, 19——, at the —— of ——, in the said (territorial division), did engage in pool-selling [OR book-making OR in the business (OR occupation) of betting], to wit: (specify the particulars of the offence), contrary to s. 202(1)(e) of the Criminal Code of Canada.

A.B., on or about the —— day of ——, 19——, at the —— of ——, in the said (territorial division), did make an agreement for the purchase [OR sale] of betting [OR gaming] privileges, to wit: (specify the particulars of the offence), contrary to s. 202(1)(e) of the Criminal Code of Canada.

A.B., on or about the —— day of ——, 19——, at the —— of ——, in the said (territorial division), did make an agreement for the purchase [OR sale]

DISORDERLY HOUSES 217

of information that is intended to assist in book-making [OR pool-selling OR betting], to wit: (specify the particulars of the offence), contrary to s. 202(1)(e) of the Criminal Code of Canada.

A.B., on or about the —— day of ——, 19——, at the —— of ——, in the said (territorial division), did print [OR provide OR offer to print (OR provide)] information intended for use in connection with book-making [OR pool-selling OR betting] on a horse-race [OR fight OR game OR (specify a sport)] that has [OR has not yet] taken place in [OR outside] Canada, to wit: (specify the particulars of the offence), contrary to s. 202(1)(f) of the Criminal Code of Canada.

A.B., on or about the —— day of ——, 19——, at the —— of ——, in the said (territorial division), did import [OR bring] into Canada information [OR writing] that was intended [OR was likely] to promote [OR to be of use in] gambling [OR book-making OR pool-selling OR betting] upon a horse-race [OR fight OR game OR (specify a sport)], to wit: (specify the particulars of the offence), contrary to s. 202(1)(g) of the Criminal Code of Canada.

A.B., on or about the —— day of ——, 19——, at the —— of ——, in the said (territorial division), did advertise [OR print OR publish OR exhibit OR post up OR give notice of] an offer [OR invitation OR inducement] to be on [OR guess OR foretell] the results of a contest [OR a result of (OR contingency) relating to any contest], to wit: (specify the particulars of the offence), contrary to s. 202(1)(h) of the Criminal Code of Canada.

A.B., on or about the —— day of ——, 19——, at the —— of ——, in the said (territorial division), did wilfully and knowingly send [OR transmit OR deliver OR receive] a message by radio [OR telegraph OR telephone OR mail OR express] that conveyed information relating to book-making [OR pool-selling OR betting OR wagering], to wit: (specify the particulars of the offence), contrary to s. 202(1)(i) of the Criminal Code of Canada.

A.B., on or about the —— day of ——, 19——, at the —— of ——, in the said (territorial division), did wilfully and knowingly send [OR transmit OR deliver OR receive] a message by radio [OR telegraph OR telephone OR mail OR express] that conveyed information that was intended to assist in book-making [OR pool-selling OR betting OR wagering], to wit: (specify the particulars of the offence), contrary to s. 202(1)(i) of the Criminal Code of Canada.

A.B., on or about the —— day of ——, 19——, at the —— of ——, in the said (territorial division), did aid [OR assist] in the committing of an offence under s. 202 of the Criminal Code of Canada, to wit: (specify the particulars of the offence), contrary to s. 202(i)(j) of the Criminal Code of Canada.

7. Placing bets on behalf of others

Section 203(a)

Every one who — places or offers or agrees to place a bet on behalf of another person — for a consideration paid or to be paid by or on behalf of that other person — is guilty of an indictable offence.

Section 203(b)

Every one who — engages in the business or practice — of placing or agreeing to place bets on behalf of other persons — whether for a consideration or otherwise — is guilty of an indictable offence.

Section 203(c)

Every one who — holds himself out or allows himself to be held out — as engaging in the business of practice — of placing or agreeing to place bets on behalf of other persons — whether for a consideration or otherwise — is guilty of an indictable offence.

Jurisdiction. The jurisdiction of a provincial court judge to try an accused is absolute and does not depend on the consent of the accused where the accused has been charged in an information with this offence (s. 553(c)(iii)).

Included offences. Attempts (s. 660 and s. 662(1)(b)).

Punishment. For a first offence, imprisonment for not more than 2 years. For a second offence, imprisonment for not more than 2 years and not less than 14 days. For each subsequent offence, imprisonment for not more than 2 years and not less than 3 months (s. 203).

Release. Initial decision to release made by peace officer (s. 497).

Election. No election, absolute jurisdiction of provincial court judge (s. 553).

Informations

A.B., on or about the —— day of ——, 19——, at the —— of ——, in the said (territorial division), did place [OR offer to place OR agree to place] a bet on behalf of C.D. for a consideration paid [OR to be paid] by [OR on behalf of] C.D., to wit: (specify the particulars of the offence), contrary to s. 203(a) of the Criminal Code of Canada.

A.B., on or about the —— day of ——, 19——, at the —— of ——, in the said (territorial division), did engage in the business [OR practice] of placing [OR of agreeing to place] bets on behalf of C.D., to wit: (specify the particulars of the offence) contrary to s. 203(b) of the Criminal Code of Canada.

A.B., on or about the —— day of ——, 19——, at the —— of ——, in the said (territorial division), did hold himself out [OR allow himself to be held out] as engaging in the business [OR practice] of placing [OR of agreeing to place] bets on behalf of C.D., to wit: (specify the particulars of the offence), contrary to s. 203(c) of the Criminal Code of Canada.

8. Pari-mutuel betting

Prohibition — Section 204(3)

No person or association — shall use a pari-mutuel system of betting — in respect of a horse-race — unless the system has been approved by and its operation is carried on under the supervision of an officer appointed by the Minister of Agriculture.

S. 204(4) to (8) provides details as to how such a pari-mutuel system of betting may be conducted and authorizes the Minister of Agriculture to make regulations governing horse-racing and pari-mutuel betting (s. 204).

Statement of offence — Section 204(10)

Every person who — contravenes or fails to comply with — any of the provisions of s. 204 — is guilty of either an indictable offence or an offence punishable on summary conviction.

Limitation period. No proceedings in respect of offences that are declared to be punishable on summary conviction shall be instituted more than 6 months after the time when the subject matter of the proceedings arose (s. 786(2) and s. 785(1)).

Included offences. Attempts (s. 660 and s. 662(1)(b)).

Punishment. On indictment, imprisonment for a term not exceeding 2 years (s. 204(10)(a)). On summary conviction, a fine not exceeding $2,000, or 6 months' imprisonment, or both (s. 204(10)(b) and s. 787(1)).

Release. Initial decision to release made by peace officer (s. 497).

Election. On indictment, accused may elect trial by judge and jury, judge alone, or provincial court judge (s. 536). On summary conviction, no election.

9. Violation or non-compliance with race-track regulations

Regulations — Section 204(9)

The Minister of Agriculture may make regulations respecting — the supervision and operation of pari-mutuel systems related to race meetings and the fixing of the dates on which and the places at which an association may conduct such meetings — and the method of calculating the amount payable in respect of each dollar bet — and the conduct of race-meetings in relation to the supervision and operation of pari-mutuel systems — including photo-finishes and video patrol and the testing of bodily substances taken from the horses engages in a race at such meetings including, in the case of a horse that dies while engaged in racing or immediately before or after the race, the testing of any issue taken from its body — and the prohibition or restriction or regulation of — either the possession of drugs or medicaments or of equipment used in the administering of drugs or medicaments at or near race-courses — or the administering of drugs or medicaments to horses participating in races run at a race meeting during which a pari-mutuel system of betting is used — and the provision and equipment and maintenance of accommodation or services or other facilities for the proper supervision and operation of pari-mutuel systems related to race meetings, by association conducting the meetings or by other associations.

Statement of offence — Section 204(10)

Every person who — contravenes or fails to comply with — any regulations made under s. 204 — is guilty of either an indictable offence or an offence punishable on summary conviction.

Limitation period. No proceedings in respect of offences that are declared to be punishable on summary conviction shall be instituted more than 6 months after the time when the subject matter of the proceedings arose (s. 786(2) and s. 785(1)).

Included offences. Attempts (s. 660 and s. 662(1)(b)).

Punishment. On indictment, imprisonment for 2 years (s. 204(10)(a)). On summary conviction, a fine not exceeding $2,000, or 6 months' imprisonment, or both (s. 204(10)(b) and s. 787(1)).

Release. Initial decision to release made by peace officer (s. 497).

Election. On indictment, accused may elect trial by judge and jury, judge alone, or provincial court judge (s. 536). On summary conviction, no election.

10. Lotteries and games of chance prohibited by law

Section 206(1)(a)

Every one who — makes or prints or advertises or publishes — or causes or procures to be made or printed or advertised or published — any proposal or scheme or plan — for advancing or lending or giving or selling or in any way disposing of any property — by lots or cards or tickets or any mode of chance whatever — is guilty of an indictable offence.

Section 206(1)(b)

Every one who — either sells or barters or exchanges or otherwise disposes of — or causes or procures, or aids or assists in, the sale or barter or exchange or other disposal of — or offers for sale or barter or exchange — any lot or card or ticket or other means or device for advancing or lending or giving or selling or otherwise disposing of any property — by lots or tickets or any mode of chance whatever — is guilty of an indictable offence.

Section 206(1)(c)

Every one who — knowingly — either sends or transmits or mails or ships or delivers or allows to be sent or transmitted or mailed or shipped or delivered — or accepts for carriage or transport or conveys — any article that is used or intended for use in carrying out any device or proposal or scheme or plan for advancing or lending or giving or selling or otherwise disposing of any property — by any mode of chance whatever — is guilty of an indictable offence.

Section 206(1)(d)

Every one who — conducts or manages any scheme or contrivance or operation or any kind — for the purpose of determining who, or the holders of what lots, tickets or numbers or chances, are the winners of any property so proposed to be advanced or lent or given or sold or disposed of — is guilty of an indictable offence.

Section 206(1)(e)

Every one who — conducts or manages or is a party to any scheme or contrivance or operation of any kind — by which any person shall become entitled under the scheme or contrivance or operation — on payment of any sum of money, or the giving of any valuable security, or by obligating himself to pay any sum of money or give any valuable security — to receive from the person conducting or managing the scheme or contrivance or operation, or any other person a larger sum of money or amount of valuable security than the sum or amount paid or given, or to be paid or given — by reason of the fact that other persons have paid or given, or obligated themselves to pay or give any sum of money or valuable security under the scheme or contrivance or operation — is guilty of an indictable offence.

Section 206(1)(f)

Every one who — disposes of any goods or wares or merchandise — by any game of chance or any game of mixed chance and skill in which the contestant or competitor pays money or other valuable consideration — is guilty of an indictable offence.

Section 206(1)(g)

Every one who — induces any person — to stake or hazard any money or other valuable property or thing — on the result of any dice game or three-card monte, punch board or coin table or on the operation of a wheel of fortune — is guilty of an indictable offence.

Section 206(1)(h)

Every one who — for valuable consideration — either carries on or plays or offers to carry on or to play — or employs any person to carry on or play — in a public place or a place to which the public have access — the game of three-card monte — is guilty of an indictable offence.

Section 206(1)(i)

Every one who — receives bets of any kind — on the outcome of a game of three-card monte — is guilty of an indictable offence.

Section 206(1)(j)

Every one who — being the owner of a place — permits any person — to play the game of three-card monte therein — is guilty of an indictable offence.

Section 206(4)

Every one who — buys or takes or receives — a lot or ticket or other device mentioned in s. 206(1) — is guilty of an offence punishable on summary conviction.

Section 207(3)

Every one who — for the purposes of a lottery scheme — does anything that is not authorized by or pursuant to a provision of s. 207 — in the case of the conduct or management or operation of that lottery scheme — is guilty of either an indictable offence or an offence punishable on summary conviction.

Every one who — for the purposes of a lottery scheme — does anything that is not authorized by or pursuant to a provision of s. 207 — in the case of participating in that lottery scheme — is guilty of an offence punishable on summary conviction.

Intent. Knowingly (s. 206(1)(c)).

Exceptions. In so far as they do not relate to a dice game, three-card monte, punch board or coin table, s. 206(1)(f) and (g) do not apply to the board of an annual agricultural or fishing fair or exhibition, or to any operator of a concession leased by that board within its own grounds and operated during the fair or exhibition on those grounds (s. 206(3)).

For these purposes, "fair or exhibition" means an event where agricultural or fishing products are presented or where activities relating to agriculture or fishing take place (s. 206(3.1)).

Jurisdiction. The jurisdiction of a provincial court judge to try an accused is absolute and does not depend upon the consent of the accused where the accused is charged in an information with an offence under s. 206 (s. 553(c)(iv)).

Limitation period. No proceedings in respect of offences that are declared to be punishable on summary conviction shall be instituted more than 6 months after the time when the subject matter of the proceedings arose (s. 786(2) and s. 785(1)).

Included offences. Attempts (s. 660 and s. 662(1)(b)).

Punishment. On indictment, imprisonment for a term not exceeding 2 years (s. 206(1) and s. 207(3)(a)). On summary conviction, a fine not exceeding $2,000, or 6 months' imprisonment, or both (s. 206(4), s. 207(3)(a) and (b) and s. 787(1)).

Release. Initial decision to release made by peace officer (s. 497).

Election. No election, absolute jurisdiction of provincial court judge (s. 553).

11. Cheating at play — Section 209

Every one who — with intent to defraud any person — cheats — while playing a game — or in holding the stakes for a game — or in betting — is guilty of an indictable offence.

Intent. Intent to defraud.

Jurisdiction. The jurisdiction of a provincial court judge to try an accused is absolute and does not depend upon the consent of the accused where the accused is charged in an information with this offence (s. 553(c)(v)).

Included offences. Attempts (s. 660 and s. 662(1)(b)).

Punishment. Imprisonment for a term not exceeding 2 years (s. 209).

Release. Initial decision to release made by peace officer (s. 497).

Election. No election, absolute jurisdiction of provincial court judge (s. 553).

Evidence. In the case of cheating, if two or more persons are involved and there is doubt whether it comes under this section, consider the charge of conspiracy to effect an unlawful purpose.

Sufficiency of count. No count that alleges false pretences, fraud or any attempt or conspiracy by fraudulent means is insufficient by reason only that it does not set out in detail the nature of the false pretence, fraud or fraudulent means (s. 586).

Informations

A.B., on or about the —— day of ——, 19——, at the —— of ——, in the said (territorial division), with intent to defraud C.D., did cheat while playing a game [OR in holding the stakes for a game OR in betting], to wit: (specify the particulars of the offence), contrary to s. 209 of the Criminal Code of Canada.

12. Keeping common bawdy-house — Section 210(1)

Every one who — keeps — a common bawdy house — is guilty of an indictable offence.

Jurisdiction. The jurisdiction of a provincial court judge to try an accused is absolute and does not depend upon the consent of the accused where the accused is charged in an information with this offence (s. 553(c)(vi)).

Included offences. Attempts (s. 660 and s. 662(1)(b)).

Punishment. Imprisonment for a term not exceeding 2 years (s. 210(1)).

Release. Initial decision to release made by peace officer (s. 497).

Election. No election, absolute jurisdiction of provincial court judge (s. 553).

Informations

A.B., on or about the —— day of ——, 19——, at the —— of ——, in the said (territorial division), did keep a common bawdy-house, to wit: (specify the particulars of the offence), contrary to s. 210(1) of the Criminal Code of Canada.

13. Being an inmate or being found in a common bawdy-house

Section 210(2)(a)

Every one who — is an inmate — of a common bawdy-house — is guilty of an offence punishable on summary conviction.

Section 210(2)(b)

Every one who — is found — without lawful excuse — in a common bawdy-house — is guilty of an offence punishable on summary conviction.

Jurisdiction. *See Jurisdiction under* **12**, *above.*

Limitation period. No proceedings in respect of offences that are declared to be punishable on summary conviction shall be instituted more than 6 months after the time when the subject matter of the proceedings arose (s. 786(2) and s. 785(1)).

Included offences. Attempts (s. 660 and s. 662(1)(b)).

Punishment. A fine not exceeding $2,000, or 6 months' imprisonment, or both (s. 210(2) and s. 787(1)).

Release. Initial decision to release made by peace officer (s. 497).

Election. No election, absolute jurisdiction of provincial court judge (s. 553).

Informations

A.B., on or about the —— day of ——, 19——, at the —— of ——, in the said (territorial division), was an inmate of a common bawdy-house, to wit:

(specify the particulars of the offence), contrary to s. 210(2)(a) of the Criminal Code of Canada.

A.B., on or about the —— day of ——, 19——, at the —— of ——, in the said (territorial division), was found, without lawful excuse, in a common bawdy-house, to wit: (specify the particulars of the offence), contrary to s. 210(2)(b) of the Criminal Code of Canada.

14. Having charge or control of place used for common bawdy-house — Section 210(2)(c)

Every one who — as owner or landlord or lessor or tenant, or occupier or agent or otherwise having charge or control of any place — knowingly — permits the place or any part thereof — to be let or used for the purposes of a common bawdy-house — is guilty of an offence punishable on summary conviction.

Intent. Knowingly.

Jurisdiction. See Jurisdiction under **12***, above.*

Limitation period. No proceedings in respect of offences that are declared to be punishable on summary conviction shall be instituted more than 6 months after the time when the subject matter of the proceedings arose (s. 786(2) and s. 785(1)).

Included offences. Attempts (s. 660 and s. 662(1)(b)).

Punishment. A fine not exceeding $2,000, or 6 months' imprisonment, or both (s. 210(2) and s. 787(1)).

Release. Initial decision to release made by peace officer (s. 497).

Election. No election, absolute jurisdiction of provincial court judge (s. 553).

Informations

A.B., on or about the —— day of ——, 19——, at the —— of ——, in the said (territorial division), being the owner [OR landlord OR lessor OR tenant OR occupier OR agent OR having charge or control] of (specify the place) did knowingly permit the place [OR part of the place], to be let [OR used] for the purposes of a common bawdy-house, to wit: (specify the particulars of the offence), contrary to s. 210(2)(c) of the Criminal Code of Canada.

15. Transporting person to bawdy-house — Section 211

Every one who — knowingly — either takes or transports or directs — or offers to take or transport or direct — any other person — to a common bawdy-house — is guilty of an offence punishable on summary conviction.

Intent. Knowingly.

Limitation period. No proceedings in respect of offences that are declared to be punishable on summary conviction shall be instituted more than 6 months after the time when the subject matter of the proceedings arose (s. 786(2) and s. 785(1)).

Included offences. Attempts (s. 660 and s. 662(1)(b)).

Punishment. A fine not exceeding $2,000, or 6 months' imprisonment, or both (s. 211 and s. 787(1)).

Release. Initial decision to release made by peace officer (s. 497).

Election. No election, summary conviction offence.

Informations

A.B., on or about the —— day of ——, 19——, at the —— of ——, in the said (territorial division), did knowingly take [OR transport OR direct OR offer to take OR offer to transport OR offer to direct] C.D. to a common bawdy-house, to wit: (specify the particulars of the offence), contrary to s. 211 of the Criminal Code of Canada.

DISPOSITION PROCESS. In the case of young offenders appearing in Youth Court, the "sentencing process" is known as the "disposition process" (Mewett, Introduction to the Criminal Process).

Pre-disposition report. A report on the background of a young offender, his previous history and prognostication for the future, prepared for the Youth Court to enable it to select the most appropriate disposition for the young offender (Mewett, Introduction to the Criminal Process).

DISQUALIFICATION. For the purposes of s. 259, "disqualification" means (a) a prohibition from operating a motor vehicle, vessel, aircraft or railway equipment ordered pursuant to s. 259(1) or (2); or (b) a disqualification or any other form of legal restriction of the right or privilege to operate a motor vehicle, vessel or aircraft imposed (i) in the case of a motor vehicle, under the law of a province, or (ii) in the case of a vessel or an aircraft, under an Act of Parliament, in respect of a conviction or discharge under s. 736 of any offence referred to in s. 259(1) or (2) (s. 259(5)).

DISTINGUISHING MARK. For the purposes of s. 417, this expression means a distinguishing mark that is appropriated for use on public stores pursuant to s. 416 of the Code (s. 417(3)). S. 416 provides that the Governor in Council may, by notice to be published in the Canada Gazette, prescribe distinguishing marks that are appropriated for use on public stores to denote the property of Her Majesty therein, whether the stores belong to Her Majesty in right of Canada or to Her Majesty in any other right. *See also PUBLIC STORES, 1, 2, and TRADE-MARK OFFENCES, 1.*

DISTRESS. A summary remedy by which a person may, without legal process, take possession of the personal chattels of another and hold them to compel the performance of a duty or the satisfaction of a debt or demand. The most frequent case is distress for rent, whereby, at common law, a landlord may seize the goods or chattels found on the premises to secure the payment of rent. The remedy is now generally regulated by statute. *See also ASSAULTS, 9 and 10.*

DOCUMENT. For the purpose of Part IX of the Criminal Code (Offences Against Rights of Property), "document" means any paper, parchment or other material on which is recorded or marked anything that is capable of being read or understood by a person, computer system or other device, and includes a credit card, but does not include trade marks on articles of commerce or inscriptions on stone or metal or other like material (s. 321).

Document of title to goods. For the purposes of the Criminal Code, "document of title to goods" includes a bought and sold note, bill of lading, warrant, certificate or order for the delivery or transfer of goods or any other valuable thing, and any other document used in the ordinary course of business as evidence of the possession or control of goods, authorizing or purporting to authorize, by endorsement or by delivery, the person in possession of the document to transfer or receive any goods thereby represented or therein mentioned or referred to (s. 2).

Document of title to lands. For the purposes of the Criminal Code, "document of title to lands" includes any writing that is or contains evidence of the title, or any part of the title, to real property, or to any interest in real property, and any notarial or registrar's copy thereof and any duplicate instrument, memorial, certificate or document authorized or required by any law in force in any part of Canada with respect to registration of titles, that relates to title to real property or to any interest in real property (s. 2).

DOCUMENTARY EVIDENCE

1. *Hearsay evidence*
2. *Production of documents*
3. *Authentication*
4. *Public and judicial documents*
5. *Records kept in financial institutions*
6. *Business records*
7. *Ancient documents*
8. *Attested documents*

1. Hearsay evidence. All documents, if offered as proof of the truth of their contents, are hearsay and are only admissible pursuant to an exception to the hearsay rule. That rule provides that "It is settled law that evidence of a statement made to a witness by a person who is not himself called as a witness is hearsay and inadmissible when the object of the evidence is to establish the truth of what is contained in the statement; it is not hearsay and is admissible when it is proposed to establish by the evidence, not the truth of the statement, but the fact that it was made" (R. v. O'Brien, [1978] 1 S.C.R. 591 per Dickson J.).

However, documentary evidence may be offered for some other purpose, i.e., for the purpose of proving that an accused had knowledge of its contents, to establish complicity or intent, or to show the state of mind of a person.

2. Production of documents. To assure that documentary evidence produced to the court was free from error, the courts have held: (1) that the original document must be produced if it is available (the Best Evidence Rule); (2) that the proponent of the document prove that the document is what it purports to be (Authentication); and (3) that no extrinsic evidence be allowed for the purpose of adding to, varying or contradicting the terms of a document that the law requires to be kept or that embodies the terms of an agreement to the parties (the Parole Evidence Rule) (Report of the Federal/Provincial Task Force on Uniform Rules of Evidence).

3. Authentication. Before a document can be treated as evidence, its relationship to the cause must be established. It must be identified and associated with a person, thing, condition or event that is relevant to the litigation. This process of association is called "authentication". In the case of private documents it usually takes the form of proving that one of the parties to the litigation executed the document. The handwriting or signature may be proved: (1) by calling the writer; (2) by calling a witness who saw the document signed; (3) by calling a witness who has acquired a knowledge of writing; (4) by comparison of the document in dispute with another proved to the satisfaction of the judge to be genuine; (5) by experts, with or without comparison; (6) by the admissions of the party against whom the document is tendered (Report of the Federal/Provincial Task Force on Uniform Rules of Evidence).

4. Public and judicial documents. In the case of public and judicial documents, there are a number of statutory provisions setting out how they may be proved. In many instances proof is made easy by virtue of a doctrine of judicial notice, and in most other cases, statutory provisions expedite proof by making copies admissible and dispensing with the necessity of proving seals or signatures. Such documents are said to be self-authenticating (Report of the Federal/Provincial Task Force on Uniform Rules of Evidence.)

Statutes printed by Queen's Printer. Every copy of any Act of the Parliament of Canada, public or private, printed by the Queen's Printer, is evidence of such Act and of its contents; and every copy purporting to be printed by the Queen's Printer shall be deemed to be so printed, unless the contrary is shown (Canada Evidence Act, s. 19).

Documents made or issued by Governor General. Evidence of any proclamation, order, regulation or appointment, made or issued by the Governor General or by the Governor in Council, or by or under the authority of any minister or head of any department of the Government of Canada and evidence of a treaty to which Canada is a party, may be given in all or any of the modes following, that is to say: (a) by the production of a copy of the *Canada Gazette*, or a volume of the Acts of the Parliament of Canada purporting to contain a copy of such treaty, proclamation, order, regulation, or appointment or a notice thereof; (b) by the production of a copy of such proclamation, order, regulation, or appointment or a notice thereof; (c) by the production of a copy of such treaty purporting to be printed by the Queen's Printer; and (d) by the production, in the case of any proclamation, order, regulation or appointment made or issued by the Governor General or by the Governor in Council, of a copy or extract purporting to be certified to be true by the clerk, or assistant or acting clerk of the Queen's Privy Council for Canada; and in the case of any order, regulation or appointment made or issued by or under the authority of any such minister or head of a department, by the production of a copy or extract purporting to be certified to be true by the minister, or by his deputy or acting deputy, or by the secretary or acting secretary of the department over which he presides (Canada Evidence Act, s. 21).

Documents made or issued by Lieutenant Governor. Evidence of any proclamation, order, regulation, or appointment made or issued by a lieutenant governor or lieutenant governor in council of any province, or by or under the authority of any member of the executive council, being the head of any department of the government of the province, may be given in all or any of the modes following, that is to say: (a) by the production of a copy of the official gazette for the province, purporting to contain a copy of such proclamation, order, regulation or appointment, or a notice thereof; (b) by the production of a copy of such proclamation, order, regulation or appointment, purporting to be printed by the government or Queen's Printer for the province; and (c) by the production of a copy or extract of such proclamation, order, regulation or appointment, purporting to be certified to be true by the clerk or assistant or acting clerk of the executive council, or by the head of any department of the government of a province, or by his deputy or acting deputy as the case may be (Canada Evidence Act, s. 22(1)).

Evidence of any proclamation, order, regulation, or appointment made by the Lieutenant Governor or Lieutenant Governor in Council of the Northwest Territories, as constituted previously to the 1st day of September 1905, or of the Commissioner in Council of the Northwest Territories, or of the Commissioner in Council of the Yukon Territory, may also be given by the production of a copy of the *Canada Gazette* purporting to contain a copy of such proclamation, order, regulation or appointment, or a notice thereof (Canada Evidence Act, s. 22(2)).

Evidence of judicial proceedings. Evidence of any proceeding or record whatever of, in or before any court in Great Britain, the Supreme Court, Federal Court or Tax Court of Canada, any court in any province, any court in any British colony or possession or any court of record of the United States of any state of the United States or of any other foreign country, or before any justice of the peace or coroner in any province, may be given in any action or proceeding by an exemplification or certified copy of the proceeding or record, purporting to be under the seal of the court or under the hand or seal of the justice or coroner, as the case may be, without any proof of the authenticity of the seal or of the signature of the justice or coroner, or other proof whatever (Canada Evidence Act, s. 23(1)). Where any such court, justice or coroner, has no seal, or so certifies, such evidence may be made by a copy purporting to be certified under the signature of a judge or presiding magistrate of such court or of such justice or coroner, without any proof of the authenticity of the signature, or other proof whatever (Canada Evidence Act, s. 23(2)).

Certified copies. In every case in which the original record could be admitted in evidence, either a copy of any official or public document of Canada or of any province, purporting to be certified under the hand of the proper officer or person in whose custody such official or public document is placed, or a copy of a document, by-law, rule, regulation or proceeding, or a copy of any entry in any register or other book of any municipal or other corporation, created by charter or Act of Canada or of any province, purporting to be certified under the seal of the corporation, and the hand of the presiding officer, clerk or secretary thereof, is admissible in evidence without proof of the seal of the corporation, or of the signature or of the official character of the person or persons appearing to have signed the same, and without further proof thereof (Canada Evidence Act, s. 24).

Books or documents of a public nature. Where a book or other document is of so public a nature as to be admissible in evidence on its mere production from the proper custody, and no other Act exists that renders its contents provable by means of a copy, a copy thereof or extract therefrom is admissible in evidence in any court of justice, or before a person having, by law or by consent of parties, authority to hear, receive and examine evidence, if it is proved that it is a copy or extract purporting to be certified to be true by the officer to whose custody the original has been entrusted (Canada Evidence Act, s. 25).

Books kept in government offices. A copy of any entry in any book kept in any office or department of the Government of Canada, or in any commission, board or other branch of the public service of Canada, shall be received as evidence of such entry, and of the matters, transactions and accounts therein recorded, if it is proved by the oath or affidavit of an officer of such department, commission, board or other branch of the public service, that the books was, at the time of the making of the entry, one of the ordinary books kept in such office, department, commission, board or other branch of the public service, that the entry was made in the usual and ordinary course of business of such office, department, commission, board or other branch of the public service, and that such a copy is a true copy thereof (Canada Evidence Act, s. 26(1)).

Evidence of non-issue of licence or document. Where by any Act of Canada or regulation thereunder provision is made for the issue by a department, commission, board or other branch of the public service, of a licence requisite to the doing or having of any act or thing or for the issue of any other document, an affidavit of an officer of the department, commission, board or other branch of the public service, sworn before any commissioner or other person authorized to take affidavits, that he has charge of the appropriate records and that after careful examination and search of such records he has been unable to find in any given case that any such licence or other document has been issued, shall be received in evidence as proof, in the absence of evidence to the contrary, that in such case no licence or other document has been issued (Canada Evidence Act, s. 26(2)).

Evidence of mailing of government documents. Where by any Act of Canada or regulation thereunder provision is made for sending by mail any request for information, notice or demand by a department or other branch of the public service, an affidavit of an officer of the department or other branch of the public service sworn before any commissioner or other person authorized to take affidavits setting out that he has charge of the appropriate records, that he has a knowledge of the facts in the particular case, that such a request, notice or demand was sent by registered letter on a named date to the person or firm to whom it was addressed (indicating such address) and that he identifies as exhibits attached to such affidavit the post office certificate of registration of such letter and a true copy of such request, notice or demand, shall, upon production and proof of the post office receipt for the delivery of such registered letter to the addressee, be received in evidence as proof, in the absence of evidence to the contrary, of such sending and of such request, notice or demand (Canada Evidence Act, s. 26(3)).

Print from photographic film. A print, whether enlarged or not, from any photographic film of, an entry in any book or record kept by any government or corporation and destroyed, lost or delivered to a customer after such film was taken, any bill of exchange, promissory note, cheque, receipt, instrument or document held by any government or corporation and destroyed, lost, or delivered to a customer after such film was taken, or any record, document, plan, book or paper belonging to or deposited with any government or corporation, is admissible in evidence in all cases in which and for all purposes for which the object photographed would have been received upon proof that while such book, record, bill of exchange, promissory note, cheque, receipt, instrument or document, plan, book or paper was in the custody or control of the government or corporation, the photographic film was taken thereof in order to keep a permanent record thereof, and the object photographed was subsequently destroyed by or in the presence of one or more of the employees of the government or corporation, or was lost or was delivered to a customer (Canada Evidence Act, s. 31(2)).

Order signed by Secretary of State. An order in writing, signed by the Secretary of State of Canada, and purporting to be written by command of the Governor General shall be received in evidence as the order of the Governor General (Canada Evidence Act, s. 32(1)).

Copies of documents printed in Canada Gazette. All copies of official and other notices, advertisements and documents printed in the *Canada Gazette* are admissible in evidence as proof, in the absence of evidence to the contrary, of the originals, and of the contents thereof (Canada Evidence Act, s. 32(2)).

5. Records kept in financial institutions

Definitions

Financial institution. The Bank of Canada, the Federal Business Development Bank and any institution incorporated in Canada that accepts deposits of money from its members or the public, and includes a branch agency or office of any such Bank or institution.

Court. The court, judge, arbitrator or person before whom a legal proceeding is held or taken.

Legal proceedings. Any civil or criminal proceeding or inquiry in which evidence is or may be given, and includes an arbitration (Canada Evidence Act, s. 29(8)).

Copies of records of financial institutions. A copy of any entry in any book or record kept in any financial institution shall in all legal proceedings be received in evidence as proof, in the absence of evidence to the contrary, of such entry and of the matters, transactions and accounts therein recorded (Canada Evidence Act, s. 29(1)). However, a copy of an entry in such book or record shall not be received in evidence unless it is first proved that the book or record was, at the time of the making of the entry, one of the ordinary books or records of the financial institution, that the entry was made in the usual and ordinary course of business, that the book or record is in the custody or control of the financial institution and that such copy is a true copy thereof; and such proof may be given by the manager or accountant of the financial institution and may be given orally or by affidavit sworn before any commissioner or other person authorized to take affidavits (Canada Evidence Act, s. 29(2)).

Cheques. Where a cheque has been drawn on any financial institution or branch thereof by any person, an affidavit of the manager or accountant of the financial institution or branch, sworn before any commissioner or other person authorized to take affidavits, setting out that he is the manager or accountant, that he has made a careful examination and search of the books and records for the purpose of ascertaining whether or not such person has an account with the financial institution or branch, and that he has been unable to find such an account, shall be received in evidence as proof, in the absence of evidence to the contrary, that such person has no account in the financial institution or branch (Canada Evidence Act, s. 29(3)).

Compulsion of production or appearance. A financial institution or officer of a financial institution is not in any legal proceedings to which the financial institution is not a party compellable to produce any book or record, the contents of which can be proved under s. 29 of the Canada Evidence Act or to appear as a witness to prove the matters, transactions and accounts therein recorded unless by order of the court made for special cause (Canada Evidence Act, s. 29(5)).

Order to inspect and take copies. On the application of any party to a legal proceeding the court may order that such party be at liberty to inspect and take copies of any entries in the books or records of a financial institution for the purposes of the legal proceeding; and the person whose account is to be inspected shall be notified of the application at least two clear days before the hearing thereof, and if it is shown to the satisfaction of the court that he cannot be notified personally, the notice may be given by addressing it to the financial institution (Canada Evidence Act, s. 29(6)).

Warrants to search financial institutions. Nothing in s. 29 of the Canada Evidence Act shall be construed as prohibiting any search of the premises of a financial institution under the authority of a warrant to search issued under any other Act of the Parliament of Canada, but unless the warrant is expressly endorsed by the person under whose hand it is issued as not being limited by this section, the authority conferred by any such warrant to search the premises of a financial institution and to seize and take away anything therein shall, as regards the books or records of such institution, be construed as limited to the searching of such premises for the purpose of inspecting and taking copies of entries in such books or records (Canada Evidence Act, s. 29(7)).

6. Business records

Definitions

Business. Any business, profession, trade, calling, manufacture or undertaking of any kind carried on in Canada or elsewhere whether for profit or otherwise, including any activity or operation carried on or performed in Canada or elsewhere by any government, by any department, branch, board, commission or agency of any government, by any court or other tribunal or by any other body or authority performing a function of government.

Copy. In relation to any record, includes a print, whether enlarged or not, from a photographic film of the record.

Court. The court, judge, arbitrator or person before whom a legal proceeding is held or taken.

Legal proceeding. Any civil or criminal proceeding or inquiry in which evidence is or may be given, and includes an arbitration.

Photographic film. A photographic plate, microphotographic film or photostatic negative (Canada Evidence Act, s. 30(12)).

Records made in the usual and ordinary course of business. Where oral evidence in respect of a matter would be admissible in a legal proceeding, a record made in the usual and ordinary course of business that contains information in respect of that matter is admissible in evidence in the legal proceeding on production of the record (Canada Evidence Act, s. 30(1)).

Where a record made in the usual and ordinary course of business does not contain information in respect of a matter the occurrence or existence of which might reasonably be expected to be recorded in that record, the court may, on production of the record, admit the record for the purpose of establishing that fact and may draw the inference that such matter did not occur or exist (Canada Evidence Act, s. 30(2)).

Copies of business records. Where it is not possible or reasonably practicable to produce any record made in the usual and ordinary course of business, a copy of the record accompanied by an affidavit setting out the reasons why it is not possible or reasonably practicable to produce the record and an affidavit of the person who made the copy setting out the source from which the copy was made and attesting to its authenticity, each affidavit having been sworn before a commissioner or other person authorized to take affidavits, is admissible in evidence under this section in the same manner as if it were the original of such record (Canada Evidence Act, s. 30(3)).

Where explanation of business record required. Where production of any record or of a copy of any record made in the usual and ordinary course of business would not convey to the court the information contained in the record by reason of its having been kept in a form that requires explanation, a transcript of the explanation of the record or copy prepared by a person qualified to make the explanation, accompanied by an affidavit of that person setting forth his qualifications to make the explanation, attesting to the accuracy of the explanation and sworn before any commissioner or other person authorized to take affidavits, is admissible in evidence under this section in the same manner as if it were the original of such record (Canada Evidence Act, s. 30(4)). Subject to what has just been stated, any person who has or may reasonably be expected to have knowledge of the making or contents of any record produced or received in evidence under this section may, with leave of the court, be examined or cross-examined thereon by any party to the legal proceeding (Canada Evidence Act, s. 30(9))

Inadmissible business records. Nothing in s. 30 of the Canada Evidence Act regarding records made in the usual and ordinary course of business renders admissible in evidence in any legal proceeding such part of any record as is proved to be (i) a record made in the course of an investigation or inquiry, (ii) a record made in the course of obtaining or giving legal advice or in contemplation of a legal proceeding; (iii) a record in respect of the production of which any privilege exists and is claimed, or (iv) a record of or alluding to a statement made by a person who is not, or if he were living and of sound mind would not be, competent and compellable to disclose in the legal proceeding a matter disclosed in the record; (b) any record the production of which would be contrary to public policy; or (c) any transcript or recording of evidence taken in the course of another legal proceeding (Canada Evidence Act, s. 30(10)). Further, the provisions of s. 30 of the Canada Evidence Act shall be deemed to be in addition to and not in derogation of any other provision of this or any other Act of the Parliament of Canada respecting the admissibility in evidence of any record or the proof of any matter, or any existing rule of law under which any record is admissible in evidence or any matter may be proved (Canada Evidence Act, s. 30(11)).

7. Ancient documents. At common law, ancient documents produced from proper custody and otherwise free from suspicion prove themselves. The rule applies not only to wills and deeds, but to accounts, letters entries, receipts and settlement certificates. The period required to qualify as an ancient document has varied: originally 40 years, it was reduced by the courts to 30 years in the 19th century and has been reduced by statute to 20 years from its execution in some jurisdictions (Report of the Federal/Provincial Task Force on Uniform Rules of Evidence).

8. Attested documents. It is not necessary to prove by the attesting witness any instrument to the validity of which attestation is not requisite. Any such instrument may be proved by admission or otherwise as if there had been no attesting witness thereto (Canada Evidence Act, s. 34).

DOMINUS LITUS. The principal in a suit (Latin).

DONATIO. Gift (Latin). *Donatio mortis causa.* A gift in contemplation of death (Latin).

DOUBLE ACTION. As applied to handguns, "double action" refers to a mechanism whereby the hammer cocks itself when the trigger is pulled (Jaffe, A Guide to Pathological Evidence, 2nd ed.).

DROWNING. Death due to the immersion of the nose and the mouth in water or other fluid (Jaffe, A Guide to Pathological Evidence, 2nd ed.).

Dry drowning. Asphyxia caused by spasm of the larynx caused by the aspiration of small quantities of fluid (Jaffe, A Guide to Pathological Evidence, 2nd ed.).

Wet drowning. Drowning due to the aspiration of large quantities of fluid (Jaffe, A Guide to Pathological Evidence, 2nd ed.).

DRUG OFFENCES

1. *Definition of "drug"*
2. *Drug for causing abortion or miscarriage*
3. *Drug for restoring sexual virility or curing venereal diseases*
4. *Drug for obtaining illicit sexual intercourse*
5. *Causing death in commission of offences*
6. *Administering noxious thing*
7. *Drug for overcoming resistance to commission of offence*
8. *Narcotic drugs*
9. *Controlled drugs and restricted drugs*

1. Definition of "drug". A drug includes any substance and mixture of substances manufactured, sold or represented for use in:

(a) the diagnosis, treatment, mitigation or prevention of a disease, disorder or abnormal physical state, or its symptoms, in human beings or animals, or
(b) restoring, correcting or modifying organic functions in human beings or animals, or
(c) disinfection in premises in which food is manufactured, prepared or kept (Food and Drugs Act, s. 2).

The non-medical use and distribution of drugs in Canada is regulated by three federal statutes — the Narcotic Control Act, the Food and Drugs Act and the Criminal Code.

2. Drug for causing abortion or miscarriage. The Criminal Code provides that everyone commits an offence who knowingly, without lawful justification or excuse, offers to sell, advertises, or publishes an advertisement or, has for sale or disposal, any means, instructions, medicine, drug or article intended or represented as a method of causing abortion or miscarriage (s. 163(2)(c)). *See also ABORTION AND MISCARRIAGE.*

3. Drug for restoring sexual virility or curing venereal diseases. The Criminal Code provides that everyone commits an offence who knowingly, without lawful justification or excuse, advertises or publishes an advertisement of any means, instructions, medicine, drug or article intended or represented as a method for restoring sexual virility or curing venereal diseases or diseases of the degenerative organs (s. 163(2)(d)). *See also ADVERTISING OFFENCES.*

4. Drug for obtaining illicit sexual intercourse. The Criminal Code provides that every one commits an indictable offence who applies or administers to a person, or causes that person to take any drug, intoxicating liquor, matter or thing with intent to stupefy or overpower that person in order thereby to enable any person to have illicit sexual intercourse with that person (s. 212(1)(i)). *See also PROCURING.*

5. Causing death in commission of offences. The Criminal Code provides that a person commits murder where a person causes the death of a human being by administering a stupefying or overpowering thing while committing or attempting to commit certain offences (s. 230(b)). *See also HOMICIDE.*

6. Administering noxious thing. The Criminal Code provides that every one who administers or causes to be administered to any person or causes any person to take poison or any other destructive or noxious thing is guilty of an indictable offence (s. 245). *See also BODILY HARM AND ACTS AND OMISSIONS CAUSING DANGER TO THE PERSON.*

7. Drug for overcoming resistance to commission of offence. The Criminal Code provides that every one who, with intent to enable or assist himself or another person to commit an indictable offence, administers, or causes to be administered to any person, or attempts to administer to any person, or causes or attempts to cause any person to take a stupefying or overpowering drug, matter or thing (s. 246). *See also BODILY HARM AND ACTS AND OMISSIONS CAUSING DANGER TO THE PERSON.*

8. Narcotic drugs. The Narcotic Drug Act creates a number of offences regarding "narcotics" which are defined simply as being any substance included in the schedule to the Act, or anything that contains any substance included in the schedule of the Act. These substances include opium poppy, coca, cannabis sativa, phenylpiperidines, phenazepines, amidones, methadols, phenalkoxams, thiambutenes, moramides, morphinans, benzazocines, ampromides, benzimidazoles, phencyclidine, fentanyl, sulfentanil, tilidine, carfentanil and alfentanil. *See also NARCOTIC DRUGS.*

9. Controlled drugs and restricted drugs. The Food and Drug Act creates a series of offences regarding a number of drugs that are designated as being either "controlled drugs" or "restricted drugs" by the schedules to the Act. *See also CONTROLLED DRUGS and RESTRICTED DRUGS.*

DUELLING

1. *Definition of "duelling"*
2. *Killing or attempting to kill a person in a duel*
3. *Offences in connection with duelling*

1. Definition of "duelling"

The fighting of two persons, one against the other, at an appointed time and place, upon a precedent quarrel.

2. Killing or attempting to kill a person in a duel

Killing or attempting to kill a man in a duel is regarded by the law as differing in no way whatever from any other deliberate and unlawful homicide or attempted homicide, and the principals in a duel or such one of them as may survive, as well as the seconds and other persons who are present and encourage the combatants by advice or assistance, are punishable just as they would be in any ordinary case of murder or attempted murder.

3. Offences in connection with duelling — Section 71

Every one who — either challenges or attempts by any means to provoke another person to fight a duel — or attempts to provoke a person to challenge another person to fight a duel — or accepts a challenge to fight a duel — is guilty of an indictable offence.

Included offences. Attempts (s. 660 and s. 662(1)(b)).

Punishment. Imprisonment for a term not exceeding 2 years (s. 71).

Release. Initial decision to release made by officer in charge or justice (s. 498).

Election. Accused may elect trial by judge and jury, judge alone, or provincial court judge (s. 536).

DUM SE BENE GESSERINT. During good behaviour (Latin).

DUPLICITY. The technical fault of combining two offences in the same charge or count of an information or indictment (The Charge Document in Criminal Cases, Law Reform Commission of Canada, Working Paper 55).

DUTIES TENDING TO PRESERVATION OF LIFE

1. *Parent, foster parent, guardian or head of family*
2. *Married person*
3. *Person under the charge of another person*
4. *Duties of persons undertaking acts*
5. *Abandoning child*
6. *Definition*

1. Parent, foster parent, guardian or head of family

Duty — Section 215(1)(a)

Every one is under a legal duty — as a parent or foster parent or guardian or head of a family — to provide necessaries of life — for a child under the age of 16 years.

Statement of offence — Section 215(2)(a) and (3)

Every one who — being under such a legal duty — without lawful excuse — fails to perform that duty — either if the person to whom the duty is owed is in destitute or necessitous circumstances — or if the failure to perform the duty endangers the life of the person to whom the duty is owed, or causes or is likely to cause the health of that person to be endangered permanently — is guilty of either an indictable offence or an offence punishable on summary conviction.

Limitation period. No proceedings in respect of offences that are declared to be punishable on summary conviction shall be instituted more than 6 months after the time when the subject matter of the proceedings arose (s. 786(2) and s. 785(1)).

Included offences. Attempts (s. 660 and s. 662(1)(b)).

Punishment. On indictment, imprisonment for a term not exceeding 2 years (s. 215(3)(a)). On summary conviction, a fine not exceeding $2,000, or 6 months' imprisonment, or both (s. 215(3)(b) and s. 787(1)).

Release. Initial decision to release made by peace officer (s. 497).

Election. On indictment, accused may elect trial by judge and jury, judge alone, or provincial court judge (s. 536). On summary conviction, no election.

Defences. The fact that a spouse or child is receiving or has received necessaries of life from another person who is not under a legal duty to provide them is not a defence (s. 215(4)(d)).

Evidence. 1. For the purposes of this offence, the proof of lawful excuse lies on the accused (s. 215(2)).

2. Evidence that a person has in any way recognized a child as being his child is, in the absence of any evidence to the contrary, proof that the child is his child (s. 215(4)(b)).

3. Evidence that a person has left his spouse and has failed, for a period of any one month subsequent to the time of his so leaving, to make provision for the maintenance of his spouse or for the maintenance of any child of his under the age of 16 years is, in the absence of any evidence to the contrary, proof that he has failed without lawful excuse to provide necessaries of life for them (s. 215(4)(c)).

4. The wife or husband of a person charged with this offence is a competent and compellable witness for the prosecution without the consent of the person charged (Canada Evidence Act, s. 4(2)).

Informations

A.B., on or about the —— day of ——, 19——, at the —— of ——, in the said (territorial division), being the parent of C.D. [OR the foster parent of C.D. OR the guardian of C.D. OR the head of a family of which C.D. was a member] did fail without lawful excuse to provide the necessaries of life to C.D., a child under the age of 16 years, who was in destitute or necessitous circumstances, to wit: (specify the particulars of the offence), contrary to s. 215 of the Criminal Code of Canada.

2. Married person

Duty — Section 215(1)(b)

Every one is under a legal duty — as a married person — to provide necessaries of life — to his spouse.

Statement of offence — Section 215(2)(a) and (3)

Every one who — being under such a legal duty — without lawful excuse — fails to perform that duty — either if the person to whom the duty is owed is in destitute or necessitous circumstances — or if the failure to perform the duty endangers the life of the person to whom the duty is owed, or causes or is likely to cause the health of that person to be endangered permanently — is guilty of either an indictable offence or an offence punishable on summary conviction.

Limitation period. No proceedings in respect of offences that are declared to be punishable on summary conviction shall be instituted

more than 6 months after the time when the subject matter of the proceedings arose (s. 786(2) and s. 785(1)).

Included offences. Attempts (s. 660 and s. 662(1)(b)).

Punishment. On indictment, imprisonment for a term not exceeding 2 years (s. 215(3)(a)). On summary conviction, a fine not exceeding $2,000, or 6 months' imprisonment, or both (s. 215(3)(b) and s. 787(1)).

Release. Initial decision to release made by peace officer (s. 497).

Election. On indictment, accused may elect trial by judge and jury, judge alone, or provincial court judge (s. 536). On summary conviction, no election.

Defences. See Defences under **1**, above.

Evidence. 1. Evidence that a person has cohabited with a person of the opposite sex or has in any way recognized that person as being his spouse is, in the absence of any evidence to the contrary, proof that they are lawfully married (s. 215(4)(a)).
2. *See also Evidence, items 1., 3. and 4., under* **1**, *above.*

3. Person under the charge of another person

Duty — Section 215(1)(c)

Every one is under a legal duty — to provide necessaries of life — to a person under his charge — if that person — by reason of detention or age or illness or mental disorder or other cause, is unable to withdraw himself from that charge — and is unable to provide himself with necessaries of life.

Statement of offence — Section 215(2)(b) and (3)

Every one who — being under such a legal duty — without lawful excuse — fails to perform that duty — if the failure to perform the duty endangers the life of the person to whom the duty is owed or causes or is likely to cause the health of that person to be injured permanently — is guilty of either an indictable offence or an offence punishable on summary conviction.

Limitation period. No proceedings in respect of offences that are declared to be punishable on summary conviction shall be instituted more than 6 months after the time when the subject matter of the proceedings arose (s. 786(2) and s. 785(1)).

Included offences. Attempts (s. 660 and s. 662(1)(b)).

Punishment. On indictment, imprisonment for a term not exceeding 2 years (s. 215(3)(a)). On summary conviction, a fine not exceeding $2,000, or 6 months' imprisonment, or both (s. 215(3)(b) and s. 787(1)).

Release. Initial decision to release made by peace officer (s. 497).

Election. On indictment, accused may elect trial by judge and jury, judge alone, or provincial court judge (s. 536). On summary conviction, no election.

Evidence. *See Evidence, items 1. and 4., under* **1**, *above.*

4. Duties of persons undertaking acts

Duty — General — Section 217

Every one who — undertakes to do an act — is under a legal duty to do it — if an omission to do the act is or may be dangerous to life.

Duty — Surgical and medical treatment — Section 216

Every one who — undertakes to administer surgical or medical treatment to another person — or to do any other lawful act that may endanger the life of another person — except in cases of necessity — is under a legal duty — to have and to use reasonable knowledge and skill and care in so doing.

5. Abandoning child — Section 218

Every one who — unlawfully abandons or exposes — a child who is under the age of 10 years — so that its life is or is likely to be endangered or its health is or is likely to be permanently injured — is guilty of an indictable offence.

Included offences. Attempts (s. 660 and s. 662(1)(b)).

Punishment. Imprisonment for a term not exceeding 2 years (s. 218).

Release. Initial decision to release made by officer in charge or justice (s. 498).

Election. Accused may elect trial by judge and jury, judge alone, or provincial court judge (s. 536).

Evidence. *See Evidence, item 4., under* **1**, *above.*

Informations

A.B., on or about the —— day of ——, 19——, at the —— of ——, in the said (territorial division), did unlawfully abandon [OR expose] C.D., a child under the age of 10 years, so that the life of C.D. was endangered [OR was likely to be endangered] to wit: (specify the particulars of the offence), contrary to s. 218 of the Criminal Code of Canada.

A.B., on or about the —— day of ——, 19——, at the —— of ——, in the said (territorial division), did unlawfully abandon [OR expose] C.D., a child under the age of 10 years, so that the health of C.D. was permanently injured [OR was likely to be permanently injured], to wit: (specify the particulars of the offence), contrary to s. 218 of the Criminal Code of Canada.

6. Definition

Duty. For the purposs of s. 219, "duty" means a duty imposed by law (s. 219(2)).

DWELLING-HOUSE. For the purposes of the Criminal Code, "dwelling-house" means the whole or any part of a building or structure that is kept or occupied as a permanent or temporary residence, and includes (a) a building within the curtilage of a dwelling-house that is connected to it by a doorway or by a covered and enclosed passageway, and (b) a unit that is designed to be mobile and to be used as a permanent or temporary residence and that is being used as such a residence (s. 2). *See also DISORDERLY CONDUCT, 7.*

E

EI QUI AFFIRMAT, NON EI QUI NEGAT, INCUMBIT PROBATIO. "The burden of proof lies on him who affirms, not on him who denies a fact" (Latin).

EJECTOR. A mechanism which expels the empty cartridge from the firearm after it has been withdrawn from the firing chamber by the extractor (Jaffe, A Guide to Pathological Evidence, 2nd ed.). *See also EXTRACTOR.*

EJUSDEM GENERIS. "Of the same kind or nature" (Latin).

ELECTION DOCUMENT. For the purposes of s. 377, "election document" means any document of writing issued under the authority of an Act of Parliament or the legislature of a province with respect to an election held pursuant to the authority of that Act (s. 377(2)).

ELECTROCUTION. Death caused by the passage of an electric current through the body is known as "electrocution." The usual mechanism of death is irregular and ineffective contractions of the ventricles of the heart or paralysis of the respiratory centre of the brain. (Jaffe, A Guide to Pathological Evidence, 2nd ed.).

ELECTROMAGNETIC, ACOUSTIC, MECHANICAL OR OTHER DEVICE. For the purposes of Part VI of the Criminal Code, "electromagnetic, acoustic, mechanical or other device" means any device or apparatus that is used or is capable of being used to intercept a private communication, but does not include a hearing aid used to correct subnormal hearing of the user to not better than normal hearing (s. 183).

ELECTRONIC SURVEILLANCE. Any means whereby a third party clandestinely overhears, by means of any electromagnetic, acoustic, mechanical or other device, oral communications or telecommunications between two or more other persons.

Different methods of electronic surveillance include the following:

Wiretapping. The clandestine interception of telephonic communications.

Bugging. The clandestine recording of a speaker's oral communications by means of a miniature electronic device which overhears, broadcasts or records the relevant oral communications.

EMBALMING. A method of preserving the cadaver by preventing autolysis and putrefaction. It usually involves the perfusion of the blood vessels with a fixative and the introduction of such a fluid into the body cavities. Modern embalming also involves the application of chemicals to the body surface for cosmetic purposes (Jaffe, A Guide to Pathological Evidence, 2nd ed.).

EMBOLUS. A mass of undissolved matter brought by the blood stream and plugging a vessel which is too narrow to permit its passage (Jaffe, A Guide to Pathological Evidence, 2nd ed.).

Embolism. The plugging of a blood vessel by an embolus (Jaffe, A Guide to Pathological Evidence, 2nd ed.).

EMBRYO. The developing child in the uterus during the first trimester of pregnancy. Also "conceptus" (Jaffe, A Guide to Pathological Evidence, 2nd ed.).

EMPLOYERS OFFENCES

1. *Refusing to employ union members*	3. *Conspiring to refuse to employ*
2. *Intimidation of employees*	4. *Conspiring to intimidate*

1. Refusing to employ trade union members — Section 425(a)

Every one who — being an employer or the agent of an employer — wrongfully and without lawful authority — refuses to employ or dismisses from his employment any person — for the reason only that the person is a member of a lawful trade union or of a lawful association or combination of workmen or employees formed for the purpose of advancing, in a lawful manner, their interests and organized for their protection in the regulation of wages and conditions of work — is guilty of an offence punishable on summary conviction.

Limitation period. No proceedings in respect of offences that are declared to be punishable on summary conviction shall be instituted more than 6 months after the time when the subject matter of the proceedings arose (s. 786(2) and s. 785(1)).

Included offences. Attempts (s. 660 and s. 662(1)(b)).

Punishment. A fine not exceeding $2,000, or 6 months' imprisonment, or both (s. 425 and s. 787(1)).

Release. Initial decision to release made by peace officer (s. 497).

Election. No election, summary conviction offence.

Informations

A.B., on or about the —— day of ——, 19——, at the —— of ——, in the said (territorial division), being an employer [OR the agent of C.D., an employer] wrongfully and without lawful authority refused to employ E.F. [OR dismissed E.F. from his employment] for the reason only that the said E.F. was a member of a lawful trade union [OR a lawful association (OR combination) of workmen (OR employees)] formed for the purpose of advancing, in a lawful manner, their interests and organized for their protection in the regulation of wages and conditions of work, to wit: (specify the particulars of the offence), contrary to s. 425(a) of the Criminal Code of Canada.

2. Intimidation of employees — Section 425(b)

Every one who — being an employer or the agent of an employer — wrongfully and without lawful authority — either by intimidation — or threat of loss of position or employment — or by causing actual loss of position or employment — or by threatening or imposing any pecuniary penalty — seeks to compel workmen or employees to abstain from belonging to a trade union or association or combination to which they have a lawful right to belong — is guilty of an offence punishable on summary conviction.

Limitation period. No proceedings in respect of offences that are declared to be punishable on summary conviction shall be instituted more than 6 months after the time when the subject matter of the proceedings arose (s. 786(2) and s. 785(1)).

Included offences. Attempts (s. 660 and s. 662(1)(b)).

Punishment. A fine not exceeding $2,000, or 6 months' imprisonment, or both (s. 425 and s. 787(1)).

Release. Initial decision to release made by peace officer (s. 497).

Election. No election, summary conviction offence.

Informations

A.B., on or about the —— day of ——, 19——, at the —— of ——, in the said (territorial division), being an employer [OR the agent of C.D. an employer] wrongfully and without lawful authority did seek by intimidation [OR by threat of loss of position (OR employment) OR by causing actual loss of position (OR employment) OR by threatening (OR imposing) a pecuniary penalty] to compel E.F. and F.G., workmen [OR employees], in the employ of C.D., to abstain from belonging to a trade union [OR an association (OR combination) of workmen (OR employees)] to which they had a lawful right to belong, to wit: (specify the particulars of the offence), contrary to s. 425(b) of the Criminal Code of Canada.

3. Conspiring to refuse to employ — Section 425(a) and (c)

Every one who — being an employer or the agent of an employer — wrongfully and without lawful authority — conspires or combines or agrees or arranges with any other employer or his agent — to refuse to employ or to dismiss from his employment any person — for the reason only that the person is a member of a lawful trade union or of a lawful association or combination of workmen or employees formed for the purpose of advancing, in a lawful manner, their interests and organized for their protection in the regulation

of wages and conditions of work — is guilty of an offence punishable on summary conviction.

Limitation period. No proceedings in respect of offences that are declared to be punishable on summary conviction shall be instituted more than 6 months after the time when the subject matter of the proceedings arose (s. 786(2) and s. 785(1)).

Included offences. Attempts (s. 660 and s. 662(1)(b)).

Punishment. A fine not exceeding $2,000, or 6 months' imprisonment, or both (s. 425 and s. 787(1)).

Release. Initial decision to release made by peace officer (s. 497).

Election. No election, summary conviction offence.

4. Conspiring to intimidate — Section 425(b) and (c)

Every one who — being an employer or the agent of an employer — wrongfully and without lawful authority — conspires or combines or agrees or arranges with any other employer or his agent — either by intimidation or threat of loss of position or employment — or by causing actual loss of position or employment — or by threatening or imposing any pecuniary penalty — seeks to compel workmen or employees to abstain from belonging to a trade union or association or combination to which they have a lawful right to belong — is guilty of an offence punishable on summary conviction.

Limitation period. No proceedings in respect of offences that are declared to be punishable on summary conviction shall be instituted more than 6 months after the time when the subject matter of the proceedings arose (s. 786(2) and s. 785(1)).

Included offences. Attempts (s. 660 and s. 662(1)(b)).

Punishment. A fine not exceeding $2,000, or 6 months' imprisonment, or both (s. 425 and s. 787(1)).

Release. Initial decision to release made by peace officer (s. 497).

Election. No election, summary conviction offence.

ENACTMENT. An Act or regulation or any portion of an Act or regulation (Interpretation Act, s. 2(1)).

ENTRAPMENT. The conception and planning of an offence by a peace officer, and his procurement of its commission by one who would not have perpetrated it except for the trickery, persuasion, or fraud of the peace officer. Increasingly, it is believed that entrapment will be accepted as a defence in Canadian criminal courts, but for the time being, it is used for its mitigating effect on sentence (Stober, Entrapment in Canadian Criminal Law).

ENTRY. 1. For the purposes of ss. 348 and 349 a person enters as soon as any part of his body or any part of an instrument that he uses is within any thing that is being entered (s. 350(a)). 2. A person shall be deemed to have broken and entered if he obtained entrance by a threat or an artifice or by collusion with a person within, or if he entered without lawful justification or excuse, the proof of which lies upon him, by a permanent or temporary opening (s. 350(b)).

EO INSTANTI. At that instant (Latin).

ESCAPE. For the purposes of s. 149, "escape" means breaking prison, escaping from lawful custody or, without lawful excuse, being at large before the expiration of a term of imprisonment to which a person has been sentenced (s. 149(3)). *See also ESCAPES AND RESCUES.*

ESCAPES AND RESCUES

1. *Prison breach*
2. *Escaping lawful custody*
3. *Being at large without lawful excuse*
4. *Failure to attend at court when at large on undertaking or recognizance*
5. *Failure to attend at court after appearing before court, justice or judge*
6. *Failure to comply with condition of undertaking or recognizance*
7. *Failure to appear or to comply with summons*
8. *Failure to appear or to comply with appearance notice or promise to appear*
9. *Permitting or assisting escape*
10. *Rescue or permitting escape*
11. *Assisting prisoner of war to escape*

See also ACCESSORY AFTER THE FACT.

1. Prison breach

Section 144(a)

Every one who — by force or violence — breaks a prison — with intent to set at liberty himself or any other person confined therein — is guilty of an indictable offence.

ESCAPES AND RESCUES

Section 144(b)

Every one who — with intent to escape — forcibly — breaks out of, or makes any breach in — a cell or other place within a prison in which he is confined — is guilty of an indictable offence.

Intent. Intention to escape.

Included offences. Attempts (s. 660 and s. 662(1)(b)).

Punishment. Imprisonment for a term not exceeding 10 years (s. 144).

Release. Initial decision to release made by justice (s. 515(1)).

Election. Accused may elect trial by judge and jury, judge alone, or provincial court judge (s. 536).

Informations

A.B., on or about the —— day of ——, 19——, at the —— of ——, in the said (territorial division), by force [OR violence] did break a prison, with intent to set at liberty himself [OR C.D., a person confined therein], to wit: (specify the particulars of the offence), contrary to s. 144(a) of the Criminal Code of Canada.

A.B., on or about the —— day of ——, 19——, at the —— of ——, in the said (territorial division), with intent to escape did forcibly break out of [OR make a breach in] the cell [OR (specify what other place)] within the prison in which he was confined, to wit: (specify the particulars of the offence), contrary to s. 144(b) of the Criminal Code of Canada.

2. Escaping lawful custody — Section 145(1)(a)

Every one who — escapes from lawful custody — is guilty of either an indictable offence or an offence punishable on summary conviction.

Intent. Intention to escape.

Limitation period. No proceedings in respect of offences that are declared to be punishable on summary conviction shall be instituted more than 6 months after the time when the subject matter of the proceedings arose (s. 786(2) and s. 785(1)).

Included offences. Attempts (s. 660 and s. 662(1)(b)).

Punishment. On indictment, imprisonment for a term not exceeding 2 years (s. 145(1)). On summary conviction, a fine not exceeding $2,000, or 6 months' imprisonment, or both (s. 145(1) and s. 787(1)).

ESCAPES AND RESCUES 253

Release. Initial decision to release made by peace officer (s. 497).

Election. On indictment, accused may elect trial by judge and jury, judge alone, or provincial court judge (s. 536). On summary conviction, no election.

Informations

A.B., on or about the —— day of ——, 19——, at the —— of ——, in the said (territorial division), did escape from lawful custody, to wit: (specify the particulars of the offence), contrary to s. 145(1)(a) of the Criminal Code of Canada.

3. Being at large without lawful excuse — Section 145(1)(b)

Every one who — before the expiration of a term of imprisonment to which he was sentenced — is at large in or out of Canada — without lawful excuse — is guilty of either an indictable offence or an offence punishable on summary conviction.

Limitation period. No proceedings in respect of offences that are declared to be punishable on summary conviction shall be instituted more than 6 months after the time when the subject matter of the proceedings arose (s. 786(2) and s. 785(1)).

Included offences. Attempts (s. 660 and s. 662(1)(b)).

Punishment. On indictment, imprisonment for a term not exceeding 2 years (s. 145(1)). On summary conviction, a fine not exceeding $2,000, or 6 months' imprisonment, or both (s. 145(1) and s. 787(1)).

Release. Initial decision to release made by peace officer (s. 497).

Election. On indictment, accused may elect trial by judge and jury, judge alone, or provincial court judge (s. 536). On summary conviction, no election.

Evidence. For the purposes of this offence, the proof of lawful excuse lies on the accused (s. 145(1)(b)).

Informations

A.B., on or about the —— day of ——, 19——, at the —— of ——, in the said (territorial division), was at large within [OR outside] Canada without lawful excuse before the expiration of a term of imprisonment to which he was sentenced, to wit: (specify the particulars of the offence), contrary to s. 145(1)(b) of the Criminal Code of Canada.

4. Failure to attend at court when at large on undertaking or recognizance — Section 145(2)(a)

Every one who — being at large on his undertaking or recognizance given to or entered into before a justice or a judge — without lawful excuse — either fails to attend court in accordance with the undertaking or recognizance — or fails to surrender himself in accordance with an order of the court or justice or judge — is guilty of either an indictable offence or an offence punishable on summary conviction.

Limitation period. No proceedings in respect of offences that are declared to be punishable on summary conviction shall be instituted more than 6 months after the time when the subject matter of the proceedings arose (s. 786(2) and s. 785(1)).

Included offences. Attempts (s. 660 and s. 662(1)(b)).

Punishment. On indictment, imprisonment for a term not exceeding 2 years (s. 145(2)). On summary conviction, a fine not exceeding $2,000, or 6 months' imprisonment, or both (s. 145(2) and s. 787(1)).

Release. Initial decision to release made by peace officer (s. 497).

Election. On indictmet, accused may elect trial by judge and jury, judge alone, or provincial court judge (s. 536). On summary conviction, no election.

Evidence. For the purposes of this offence, the proof of lawful excuse lies on the accused (s. 145(2)(a)).

Informations

A.B., on or about the —— day of ——, 19——, at the —— of ——, in the said (territorial division), being at large on an undertaking [OR recognizance] given to [OR entered into before] C.D., a justice [OR judge], did fail without lawful excuse to attend court in accordance therewith [OR to surrender himself in accordance with the order of C.D.], to wit: (specify the particulars of the offence), contrary to s. 145(2)(a) of the Criminal Code of Canada.

5. Failure to attend at court after appearing before court, justice or judge — Section 145(2)(b)

Every one who — having appeared before a court or justice or judge — without lawful excuse — either fails to attend court as thereafter required by the court or justice or judge — or fails to surrender himself in accordance with an order of the court or justice

ESCAPES AND RESCUES

or judge — **is guilty of either an indictable offence or an offence punishable on summary conviction.**

Limitation period. No proceedings in respect of offences that are declared to be punishable on summary conviction shall be instituted more than 6 months after the time when the subject matter of the proceedings arose (s. 786(2) and s. 785(1)).

Included offences. Attempts (s. 660 and s. 662(1)(b)).

Punishment. On indictment, imprisonment for a term not exceeding 2 years (s. 145(2)). On summary conviction, a fine not exceeding $2,000, or 6 months' imprisonment, or both (s. 145(2) and s. 787(1)).

Release. Initial decision to release made by peace officer (s. 497).

Election. On indictment, accused may elect trial by judge and jury, judge alone, or provincial court judge (s. 536). On summary conviction, no election.

Evidence. For the purposes of this offence, the proof of lawful excuse lies on the accused (s. 145(2)(b)).

Informations

A.B., on or about the —— day of ——, 19——, at the —— of ——, in the said (territorial division), having appeared before a court [OR C.D., a justice OR C.D., a judge], did fail without lawful excuse to attend court as thereafter required by the court [OR C.D.] [OR to surrender himself in accordance with the order of the court (OR C.D.)], to wit: (specify the particulars of the offence), contrary to s. 145(2)(b) of the Criminal Code of Canada.

6. Failure to comply with condition of undertaking or recognizance — Section 145(3)

Every one who — being at large on his undertaking or recognizance given to or entered into before a justice or a judge — and being bound to comply with a condition of that undertaking or recognizance directed by a justice or a judge — without lawful excuse — fails to comply with that condition — is guilty of either an indictable offence or an offence punishable on summary conviction.

Limitation period. No proceedings in respect of offences that are declared to be punishable on summary conviction shall be instituted more than 6 months after the time when the subject matter of the proceedings arose (s. 786(2) and s. 785(1)).

Included offences. Attempts (s. 660 and s. 662(1)(b)).

Punishment. On indictment, imprisonment for a term not exceeding 2 years (s. 145(3)(a)). On summary conviction, a fine not exceeding $2,000, or 6 months' imprisonment, or both (s. 145(3)(b) and s. 787(1)).

Release. Initial decision to release made by peace officer (s. 497).

Election. On indictment, accused may elect trial by judge and jury, judge alone, or provincial court judge (s. 536). On summary conviction, no election.

Evidence. For the purposes of this offence, the proof of lawful excuse lies on the accused (s. 145(3)).

Informations

A.B., on or about the —— day of ——, 19——, at the —— of ——, in the said (territorial division), being at large on an undertaking [OR recognizance] given to [OR entered into before] C.D., a justice [OR judge], did fail without lawful excuse to comply with a condition of that undertaking [OR recognizance] directed by C.D., to wit: (specify the particulars of the offence), contrary to s. 145(3) of the Criminal Code of Canada.

7. Failure to appear or to comply with summons — Section 145(4)

Every one who — is served with a summons — and without lawful excuse — either fails to appear at a time and place stated therein (if any) for the purposes of the Identification of Criminals Act — or fails to attend court in accordance therewith — is guilty of either an indictable offence or an offence punishable on summary conviction.

Limitation period. No proceedings in respect of offences that are declared to be punishable on summary conviction shall be instituted more than 6 months after the time when the subject matter of the proceedings arose (s. 786(2) and s. 785(1)).

Included offences. Attempts (s. 660 and s. 662(1)(b)).

Punishment. On indictment, imprisonment for a term not exceeding 2 years (s. 145(4)(a)). On summary conviction, a fine not exceeding $2,000, or 6 months' imprisonment, or both (s. 145(4)(b) and s. 787(1)).

Release. Initial decision to release made by peace officer (s. 497).

Election. On indictment, accused may elect trial by judge and jury, judge alone, or provincial court judge (s. 536). On summary conviction, no election.

Evidence. For the purposes of this offence, the proof of lawful excuse lies on the accused (s. 145(4)).

Informations

A.B., on or about the —— day of ——, 19——, at the —— of ——, in the said (territorial division), having been served with a summons, did fail without lawful excuse to appear at the time and place stated therein for the purposes of the Identification of Criminals Act, to wit: (specify the particulars of the offence), contrary to s. 145(4) of the Criminal Code of Canada.

A.B., on or about the —— day of ——, 19——, at the —— of ——, in the said (territorial division), having been served with a summons, did fail without lawful excuse to attend at court in accordance therewith, to wit: (specify the particulars of the offence), contrary to s. 145(4) of the Criminal Code of Canada.

8. Failure to appear or to comply with appearance notice or promise to appear — Section 145(5)

Every one who — is named in an appearance notice or promise to appear or in a recognizance entered into before an officer in charge, that has been confirmed by a justice under s. 508 — and without lawful excuse — either fails to appear at a time and place stated therein (if any) for the purposes of the Identification of Criminals Act — or fails to attend court in accordance therewith — is guilty of either an indictable offence or an offence punishable on summary conviction.

Limitation period. No proceedings in respect of offences that are declared to be punishable on summary conviction shall be instituted more than 6 months after the time when the subject matter of the proceedings arose (s. 786(2) and s. 785(1)).

Included offences. Attempts (s. 660 and s. 662(1)(b)).

Punishment. On indictment, imprisonment for a term not exceeding 2 years (s. 145(5)(a)). On summary conviction, a fine not exceeding $2,000, or 6 months' imprisonment or both (s. 145(5)(b) and s. 787(1)).

Release. Initial decision to release made by peace officer (s. 497).

Election. On indictment, accused may elect trial by judge and jury, judge alone, or provincial court judge (s. 536). On summary conviction, no election.

Evidence. 1. It is not a lawful excuse that an appearance notice, promise to appear or recognizance states defectively the substance of the alleged offence (s. 145(6)).
2. For the purposes of this offence, the proof of lawful excuse lies on the accused (s. 145(5)).

Informations

A.B., on or about the —— day of ——, 19——, at the —— of ——, in the said (territorial division), having been named in an appearance notice [OR a promise to appear OR a recognizance entered into before C.D., an officer in charge], that was confirmed by E.F., a justice, under s. 508, did fail without lawful excuse to appear at the time and place stated therein for the purposes of the Identification of Criminals Act, to wit: (specify the particulars of the offence), contrary to s. 145(5) of the Criminal Code of Canada.

A.B., on or about the —— day of ——, 19——, at the —— of ——, in the said (territorial division), having been named in an appearance notice [OR a promise to appear OR a recognizance entered into before C.D., an officer in charge], that was confirmed by E.F., a justice, under s. 508, did fail without lawful excuse to attend court in accordance therewith, to wit: (specify the particulars of the offence), contrary to s. 145(5) of the Criminal Code of Canada.

9. Permitting or assisting escape

Section 146(a)

Every one who — permits a person whom he has in lawful custody to escape — by failing to perform a legal duty — is guilty of an indictable offence.

Section 146(b)

Every one who — conveys or causes to be conveyed into a prison anything — with intent to facilitate the escape of a person imprisoned therein — is guilty of an indictable offence.

Section 146(c)

Every one who — directs or procures — under colour of pretended authority — the discharge of a prisoner who is not entitled to be discharged — is guilty of an indictable offence.

Intent. Intention to facilitate escape (s. 146(b)).

Included offences. Attempts (s. 660 and s. 662(1)(b)).

Punishment. Imprisonment for a term not exceeding 2 years (s. 146).

Release. Initial decision to release made by officer in charge or justice (s. 498).

Election. Accused may elect trial by judge and jury, judge alone, or provincial court judge (s. 536).

Informations

A.B., on or about the —— day of ——, 19——, at the —— of ——, in the said (territorial division), did permit C.D., a person who A.B. had in lawful custody, to escape such custody by failing to perform a legal duty, to wit: (specify the particulars of the offence), contrary to s. 146(a) of the Criminal Code of Canada.

A.B., on or about the —— day of ——, 19——, at the —— of ——, in the said (territorial division), did convey [OR cause to be conveyed] into a prison a (specify the thing conveyed), with intent to facilitate the escape of C.D., a person imprisoned therein, to wit: (specify the particulars of the offence), contrary to s. 146(b) of the Criminal Code of Canada.

A.B., on or about the —— day of ——, 19——, at the —— of ——, in the said (territorial division), did direct [OR procure], under colour of pretended authority, the discharge of C.D., a prisoner who was not entitled to be discharged, to wit: (specify the particulars of the offence), contrary to s. 146(c) of the Criminal Code of Canada.

10. Rescue or permitting escape

Section 147(a)

Every one who — either rescues any person from lawful custody — or assists any person in escaping or attempting to escape from lawful custody — is guilty of an indictable offence.

Section 147(b)

Every one who — being a peace officer — wilfully — permits a person in his lawful custody to escape — is guilty of an indictable offence.

Section 147(c)

Every one who — being an officer of or an employee in a prison — wilfully — permits a person to escape from lawful custody therein — is guilty of an indictable offence.

Intent. Wilfully (s. 147(b) and (c)).

Included offences. Attempts (s. 660 and s. 662(1)(b)).

Punishment. Imprisonment for a term not exceeding 5 years (s. 147).

Release. Initial decision to release made by officer in charge or justice (s. 498).

Election. Accused may elect trial by judge and jury, judge alone, or provincial court judge (s. 536).

Informations

A.B., on or about the —— day of ——, 19——, at the —— of ——, in the said (territorial division), did rescue C.D. from lawful custody, to wit: (specify the particulars of the offence), contrary to s. 147(a) of the Criminal Code of Canada.

A.B., on or about the —— day of ——, 19——, at the —— of ——, in the said (territorial division), did assist C.D. in escaping [OR in attempting to escape] from lawful custody, to wit: (specify the particulars of the offence), contrary to s. 147(a) of the Criminal Code of Canada.

A.B., on or about the —— day of ——, 19——, at the —— of ——, in the said (territorial division), did wilfully permit C.D., a person in his lawful custody to escape, to wit: (specify the particulars of the offence), contrary to s. 147(b) of the Criminal Code of Canada.

A.B., on or about the —— day of ——, 19——, at the —— of ——, in the said (territorial division), being an officer of [OR an employee in] a prison, did lawfully permit C.D. to escape from lawful custody therein, to wit: (specify the particulars of the offence), contrary to s. 147(c) of the Criminal Code of Canada.

11. Assisting prisoner of war to escape

Section 148(a)

Every one who — knowingly and wilfully — assists a prisoner of war in Canada — to escape from a place where he is detained — is guilty of an indictable offence.

Section 148(b)

Every one who — knowingly and wilfully — assists a prisoner of war — who is permitted to be at large on parole in Canada — to escape from the place where he is at large on parole — is guilty of an indictable offence.

Intent. Knowingly and wilfully.

Included offences. Attempts (s. 660 and s. 662(1)(b)).

Punishment. Imprisonment for a term not exceeding 5 years (s. 148).

Release. Initial decision to release made by officer in charge or justice (s. 498).

Election. Accused may elect trial by judge and jury, judge alone, or provincial court judge (s. 536).

Informations

A.B., on or about the —— day of ——, 19——, at the —— of ——, in the said (territorial division), knowingly and wilfully did assist C.D., a prisoner of war in Canada, to escape from the place where he was detained, to wit: (specify the particulars of the offence), contrary to s. 148(a) of the Criminal Code of Canada.

A.B., on or about the —— day of ——, 19——, at the —— of ——, in the said (territorial division), knowingly and wilfully did assist C.D., a prisoner of war, who was permitted to be at large on parole in Canada, to escape from the place where he was at large on parole, to wit: (specify the particulars of the offence), contrary to s. 148(b) of the Criminal Code of Canada.

ESSENTIAL AVERMENTS. Those assertions of fact which are essential to successful prosecution and which must be proved at trial, such as the date, time and place of the offence (The Charge Document in Criminal Cases, Law Reform Commission of Canada Working Paper 55).

ET AL. An abbreviation for "et alia", which means "and others" (Latin).

ET SEQ. An abbreviation for "et sequentes", which means "and following" (Latin).

EVERY ONE. For the purposes of the Criminal Code, "every one," "person," "owner," and similar expressions include Her Majesty and public bodies, bodies corporate, societies, companies and inhabitants of counties, parishes, municipalities or other districts in relation to the acts and things that they are capable of doing and owning respectively (s. 2).

EVIDENCE

1. *Definition*
2. *Direct evidence*
3. *Circumstantial evidence*
4. *Character evidence*
5. *Expert evidence*
6. *Handwriting*
7. *Hearsay*
8. *Dying declarations*
9. *Self-incrimination*
10. *Admissions by the accused*
11. *Confessions*
12. *Evidence of accomplices*
13. *Corroboration*
14. *Husband and wife*
15. *Burden of proof*
16. *Application of provincial rules of evidence*

1. Definition. 1. In general, evidence consists of proof in accordance with legal principles of the various elements necessary to establish that the charge laid was in fact committed by the accused. 2. In Part IV of the Criminal Code ("Offences Against the Administration of Law and Justice"), "evidence" means an assertion of fact, opinion, belief or knowledge whether material or not and whether admissible or not (s. 118).

2. Direct evidence. If the evidence is the testimony of an eyewitness who perceived the material fact, the testimony is called direct evidence (Sheppard, Evidence).

3. Circumstantial evidence. Any item of evidence other than the testimony of an eyewitness to the material fact (Sheppard, Evidence).

4. Character evidence

The victim in non-sexual cases. The character of the victim in non-sexual cases is generally irrelevant. Neither the Crown nor the defence can lead such evidence. In the Crown's case, the victim's character is presumed to be good and therefore does not require support. As for the defence, the victim's character can be no justification for a crime against him. An exception has been permitted in homicide cases where the accused claims self-defence (Report of the Federal/Provincial Task Force on Uniform Rules of Evidence).

The victim in sexual cases. The Criminal Code restricts the introduction of evidence of the victim's sexual activities with persons other than the accused and of the victim's sexual reputation (ss 276 to 277).

The accused's character. It is the right of the accused to adduce evidence of his own good character. This evidence, offered on behalf of the defence, is admissible to support the conclusion that the accused did not act in the manner alleged by the Crown. The Crown is precluded from initiating evidence of the accused's bad character, except where the accused has adduced evidence of his good character (Report of the Federal/Provincial Task Force on Uniform Rules of Evidence).

Methods of proving character. There are four methods of proving character: by evidence of general reputation, opinion, specific instances of conduct, and prior convictions. To this list may be added an accused's testimony as to his own character or disposition (Report of the Federal/Provincial Task Force on Uniform Rules of Evidence).

5. Expert evidence

Expert evidence, because it is merely the opinion of someone specially trained and not direct proof of any fact, is only admitted where the witness, because of his study of facts already in evidence, can draw inferences from them which would be beyond the powers of the average juryman. Before such evidence is receivable, the qualifications of the expert to speak with authority on the matter in issue must be established. They are only to be regarded as assisting the jury who may disregard the views of every expert if they choose.

Experts may be called to prove the chemical contents of the stomach of one suspected to have been poisoned, or the pathological condition of organs in cases of wounds, abortions, drownings, etc., and in all such cases the greatest care must be taken if it is necessary to send any organ away to be examined. The questions of identification and custody being most important, every precaution to prevent doubt as to identity of the material and its safekeeping must be taken by the officer, as defence counsel will be only too happy to bring out evidence of carelessness in the handling, marking, identifying and safekeeping of such things.

Expert accountants may also be called to give evidence of what the books show. Men skilled in the science of ballistics are constantly used to identify the weapon used to fire missiles that have caused death.

Where, in any trial or other proceeding, criminal or civil, it is intended by the prosecution or the defence, or by any party, to examine as witnesses professional or other experts entitled according to the law or practice to give opinion evidence, not more than five such witnesses may be called upon either side without the leave of the court or judge or person presiding (Canada Evidence Act, s. 7).

6. Handwriting

Comparison of a disputed writing with any writing proved to the satisfaction of the court to be genuine shall be permitted to be made by witnesses; and such writings, and the evidence of witnesses respecting such writings, may be submitted to the court and jury as proof of the genuineness or otherwise of the writing in dispute (Canada Evidence Act, s. 8).

No proof shall be required of the handwriting or official position of any person certifying, in pursuance of this Act, to the truth of any copy of or extract from any proclamation, order, regulation, appointment, book or other document. Any such copy or extract may be in print or in writing, or partly in print and partly in writing (Canada Evidence Act, s. 33).

7. Hearsay

Hearsay evidence, the statement by one person of what another said, is excluded because the person making the original statement is not on oath and cannot be cross-examined. This rule does not apply to remarks by the accused, whose acts and words on the material points can only be proved by those who observed or heard them. He cannot be called by the Crown to give evidence.

Certain exceptions to this rule exist including dying declarations, admissions and confessions.

8. Dying declarations

Dying declarations or ante-mortem statements are received in homicide cases where the words of the deceased spoken when he was under a settled hopeless expectation of death, are accepted as having the adequacy of an oath. Such statements are not receivable in any other kind of case and must be confined to the cause of his present condition. Hence, in a case of manslaughter arising out of an abortion, the dying declaration of the girl as to the acts of the accused which brought on the abortion were receivable; other parts of the statement indicating her movements some weeks before, when she met the accused, were held not to be receivable. Again, to render the statement receivable, it must not contain anything which the deceased, if living, could not give in evidence, such as hearsay. Any hope of recovery will render the evidence inadmissible and the courts always insist upon the most careful proof of the circumstances under which the statement was made. That "there must be an unqualified belief, without any hope of recovery that the declarant is about to die," is the way one judge expressed it. Proof of this does not depend only on the words of the deceased, for inferences may be drawn as to his feelings from the evidence of the doctor and others of his condition and conduct. It is better, in case of doubt, to have a statement to that effect from the deceased, in writing or in words, either just before or after the principal declaration is made.

Such as statement may be as follows:

"I, A.B., being of the firm belief that my death is certain and imminent, with no hope of recovery, declare that —".

9. Self-incrimination

A witness who testifies in any proceedings has the right not to have any incriminating evidence so given used to incriminate that witness in any other proceedings, except in a prosecution for perjury or for the giving of contradictory evidence (Charter of Rights and Freedoms, s. 13).

10. Admissions by the accused

Admissions by the accused, as already explained, are evidence against him. This includes his conduct, such as silence when accused of a crime which an innocent person would at once deny, especially if the accused in any way appears to accept the truth of the charge.

The Criminal Code specifically provides that nothing in the Code prevents a prosecutor giving in evidence at a preliminary inquiry any admission, confession or statement made at any time by the accused that by law is admissible against him (s. 542(1)).

11. Confessions

Confessions to police or other persons in authority are always scrutinized by the courts with the greatest care before they are accepted. The circumstances under which the confession was made must be given in detail so that the court may determine whether the statement was made voluntarily — that is the test. If there is any suggestion that there was inducement, threat or coercion, the evidence will be rejected. In the words of the Supreme Court of Canada:

> "that burden (of proving the confession to have been given freely) can rarely, if every, be discharged merely by proof that the giving of the statement was preceded by the customary warning and an expression of opinion on oath by the police officer who obtained it, that it was made freely and voluntarily; what took place in the process by which the statement was ultimately obtained should be fully disclosed; and with all the facts before him, the judge should form his own opinion that the tendered statement was indeed free and voluntary, before admitting it in evidence."

As a matter of law, no caution or warning by the police officer to the accused is necessary, but the fact that the latter is in custody is an important factor and gives rise to a possibility of inducement that is best rebutted by the warning that he is not obliged to answer questions, and that if he does his statements may be used in evidence.

If he is willing to make a written statement, it is better to let him write it himself, prefaced by words to the effect that he is making it freely and voluntarily, notwithstanding that he has been warned that he need not write anything, and that what he writes may be used in evidence.

For safety's sake, each officer who talks to him should repeat the warning and there should be no resort to false statements to the accused in order to trick him into making an incriminating remark. The greatest care must be exercised by the officer that he does not offer any inducement to the accused. Even the slightest hint of inducement, such as "You had better tell me" or "It would be well to tell me" will in all probability render the statement inadmissible.

Too many officers present at the time might indicate a show of force which will detract from the voluntary nature of the statement.

It should be noted that the law in Canada requires all statements of an accused tendered by the Crown to be proven voluntary, even if the statement is one wherein the accused professes his innocence. It is therefore essential that care be taken in the obtaining of any statement from an accused and not merely those which indicate guilt. A statement proclaiming innocence may subsequently be proven a lie and important to the case for the Crown.

12. Evidence of accomplices

Accomplices' evidence as a rule of practice, should be corroborated by some other material evidence implicating the accused, and juries must be warned that although they may convict without such corroboration, it is dangerous to do so. The test as to whether a witness is an accomplice or not is whether he could be charged with the same crime for which the accused is standing trial, so that all who might be charged as parties to the same offence, not a similar one, are accomplices. This does not include accessories after the fact, nor police spies or spotters, though there are a few decisions to the contrary in the case of spotters.

13. Corroboration

When corroboration is necessary to prove an offence, the expression means that an accused person shall not be convicted upon the evidence of one witness, unless such witness is corroborated in some material particular by evidence, implicating the accused. It is indicated under each heading whether corroboration is required.

14. Husband and wife

Every person charged with an offence, and, except as otherwise provided, the wife or husband, as the case may be, of the person so charged, is a competent witness for the defence, whether the person so charged is charged solely or jointly with any other person (Canada Evidence Act, s. 4(1)).

No husband is compellable to disclose any communication made to him by his wife during their marriage, and no wife is compellable to disclose any communication made to her by her husband during their marriage (Canada Evidence Act, s. 4(3)).

The wife or husband of a person charged with an offence against s. 50(1) of the Young Offenders Act or any one of the following Criminal Code offences, or an attempt to commit any such offence, is a competent and compellable witness for the prosecution without the consent of the person charged.

s. 151	(sexual interference)
s. 152	(invitation to sexual touching)
s. 153	(sexual exploitation)
s. 155	(incest)
s. 159	(anal intercourse)
s. 160(2)	(compulsion to commit bestiality)

s. 160(3)	(bestiality in presence of or by child)
s. 170	(parent or guardian procuring sexual activity)
s. 171	(householder permitting sexual activity)
s. 172	(corrupting children)
s. 173(1)	(indecent acts)
s. 173(2)	(exposure)
s. 179	(vagrancy)
s. 212	(procuring)
s. 215	(breach of duty to provide necessaries)
s. 218	(abandoning child)
s. 271	(sexual assault)
s. 272	(sexual assault with a weapon, threats to a third party or causing bodily harm)
s. 273	(aggravated sexual assault)
ss. 280-283	(abduction and detention of young persons)
s. 291	(bigamy)
s. 292	(procuring feigned marriage)
s. 293	(polygamy)
s. 294	(pretending to solemnize marriage)
s. 329	(theft by spouse)

(Canada Evidence Act, s. 4(2)).

The wife or husband of a person charged with any of the following Criminal Code offences where the complainant or victim is under the age of 14 years is a competent and compellable witness for the prosecution without the consent of the person charged:

s. 220	(causing death by criminal negligence)
s. 221	(causing bodily harm by criminal negligence)
s. 235	(murder)
s. 236	(manslaughter)
s. 237	(infanticide)
s. 239	(attempt to commit murder)
s. 240	(accessory after fact to murder)
s. 266	(assault)
s. 267	(assault with a weapon or causing bodily harm)
s. 268	(aggravated assault)
s. 269	(unlawfully causing bodily harm)

(Canada Evidence Act, s. 4(4)).

The failure of the person charged, or of the wife or husband of such person, to testify, shall not be made the subject of comment by the judge, or by counsel for the prosecution (Canada Evidence Act, s. 4(6)).

15. Burden of Proof

Evidential burden. The burden of producing evidence is usually cast first on the party who has pleaded the existence of a disputed fact. If a party who is under this burden does not introduce sufficient evidence, the judge on a motion by defence counsel will dismiss the case (where the trial is by judge alone) or will instruct the jury to find against the party (a directed verdict) (Report of the Federal/Provincial Task Force on the Uniform Rules of Evidence).

Legal burden. When all of the evidence has been introduced and each party has discharged the burden or producing evidence, the jury must determine, on the evidence before it, whether the disputed issue is established and whether the burden of persuasion has been satisfied. The judge must instruct the jury that if it is not convinced by the evidence it must decide the issue against a particular party. The party who must lose in these circumstances bears the burden of persuasion. By winning on that issue, the party meets the burden (Report of the Federal/Provincial Task Force on the Uniform on Rules of Evidence).

16. Application of provincial rules of evidence. In criminal proceedings, the laws of evidence in force in the province in which such proceedings are taken, including the laws of proof of service of any warrant, summons, subpoena or other document, apply to such proceedings (Canada Evidence Act, s. 40).

EX. From; out of; since; on account of; according to; with respect to (Latin). ***Ex cathedra.*** With high authority (Latin). ***Ex curia.*** Out of court (Latin). ***Ex debito justitiae.*** By debt of justice (Latin). ***Ex delicto.*** Founded on tort (Latin). ***Ex gratia.*** Voluntary (Latin). ***Ex mero motu.*** Of one's own free will (Latin). ***Ex officio.*** By virtue of office; officially (Latin). ***Ex parte.*** 1. On behalf of (Latin). 2. In its primary sense, ex parte, as applied to an application in a judicial proceeding, means that it is made by a person who is not a party to a proceeding, but has an interest in the matter which entitles him to make the application. In its more usual sense, ex parte means that an application is made by one party to a proceeding in the absence of the other. ***Ex post facto.*** By a subsequent act; retrospective (Latin). ***Ex rel.*** An abbreviation for ex relatione, which means "on the information of" (Latin). ***Ex turpi causa (or Ex dolo malo) non oritur actio.*** "From an evil cause no action arises" (Latin).

EXCAVATION

Duty — Section 263(2)

Every one who — leaves an excavation — on land that he owns or on land of which he has charge or supervision — is under a legal duty — to guard it in a manner that is adequate to prevent persons from falling in by accident and is adequate to warn them that the excavation exists.

Statement of offence — Section 263(3)

Every one who fails to perform this duty — is guilty of — either the indictable offence of manslaughter if the death of any person results therefrom — or an indictable offence under s. 269 (unlawfully causing bodily harm) if bodily harm to any person results therefrom — or an offence punishable on summary conviction.

Limitation period. No proceedings in respect of offences that are declared to be punishable on summary conviction shall be instituted more than 6 months after the time when the subject matter of the proceedings arose (s. 786(2) and s. 785(1)).

Included offences. Attempts (s. 660 and s. 662(1)(b)).

Punishment. Every one who is guilty of manslaughter is liable to imprisonment for life (s. 263(3)(a) and s. 236). Every one who is guilty of unlawfully causing bodily harm is liable to imprisonment for a term not exceeding 10 years (s. 263(3)(b) and s. 269). Every one who is guilty of an offence punishable on summary conviction is liable to a fine not exceeding $2,000, or 6 months' imprisonment, or both (s. 263(3)(c) and s. 787(1)).

Release. Initial decision to release made by peace officer (s. 497).

Election. On indictment, accused may elect trial by judge and jury, judge alone, or provincial court judge (s. 536). On summary conviction, no election.

EXCEPTIO CONFIRMAT (or PROBAT) REGULUM. "The exception proves the rule" (Latin).

EXCHEQUER BILL. For the purposes of Part IX of the Criminal Code (Offences Against Rights of Property), "exchequer bill" means a bank note, bond, note, debenture or security that is issued or guaranteed by Her Majesty under the authority of Parliament or the legislature of a province (s. 321).

EXCHEQUER BILL PAPER. For the purposes of Part IX of the Criminal Code (Offences Against Rights of Property), "exchequer bill paper" means paper that is used to manufacture exchequer bills (s. 321). *See also FORGERY AND OFFENCES RESEMBLING FORGERY, 3.*

EXEAT. 1. "Let him go" (Latin). 2. Permission to leave.

EXECUTION OF PROCESS

1. *Execution of process*
2. *Assault with intent to rescue thing taken under lawful process. See ASSAULTS, 10.*
3. *Misconduct in the execution of a process. See PEACE OFFICER, 2.*

1. Execution of process — Section 129(c)

Every one who — resists or wilfully obstructs any person — either in the lawful execution of a process against lands or goods — or in making a lawful distress or seizure — is guilty of an indictable offence or an offence punishable on summary conviction.

Intent. Wilfully.

Limitation period. No proceedings in respect of offences that are declared to be punishable on summary conviction shall be instituted more than 6 months after the time when the subject matter of the proceedings arose (s. 786(2) and s. 785(1)).

Included offences. Attempts (s. 660 and s. 662(1)(b)).

Punishment. On indictment, imprisonment for a term not exceeding 2 years (s. 129(d)). On summary conviction, a fine not exceeding $2,000, or 6 months' imprisonment, or both (s. 129(e) and s. 787(1)).

Release. Initial decision to release made by peace officer (s. 497).

Election. On indictment, accused may elect trial by judge and jury, judge alone, or provincial court judge (s. 536). On summary conviction, no election.

Informations

A.B., on or about the —— day of ——, 19——, at the —— of ——, in the said (territorial division), did resist [OR wilfully obstruct] C.D. in the lawful execution of a process against land [OR goods], to wit: (specify the particulars of the offence), contrary to s. 129(c) of the Criminal Code of Canada.

A.B., on or about the —— day of ——, 19——, at the —— of ——, in the said (territorial division), did resist [OR wilfully obstruct] C.D. in making a lawful distress [OR seizure], to wit: (specify the particulars of the offence), contrary to s. 129(c) of the Criminal Code of Canada.

EXHIBIT. An object admitted in court as evidence (Jaffe, A Guide to Pathological Evidence, 2nd ed.).

EXHIBITIONISM. The exposure, usually by a male, of the genital organs to a person of the other sex as a means of obtaining sexual pleasure and not as a threat of or invitation to intercourse. It is usually treated as a breach of the peace or statutory nuisance (Walker, The Oxford Companion to Law).

EXHUMATION. The recovery of a body from the ground. It is usually applied to the removal of a body from a grave for the purpose of medical examination or transportation to another burial site. Also, "disinterment" (Jaffe, A Guide to Pathological Evidence, 2nd ed.).

EXPLOSIVE SUBSTANCES

1. *Definition of "explosive substances"*
2. *Breach of duty of care*
3. *Using explosives (causing injury with intent)*
4. *Possession without lawful excuse*
5. *Explosive substances on aircraft. See AIRCRAFT OFFENCES, 3.*

1. Definition of "explosive substances"

For the purposes of the Criminal Code, "explosive substance" includes

(a) anything intended to be used to make an explosive substance,

(b) anything, or any part thereof, used or intended to be used, or adapted to cause, or to aid in causing an explosion in or with an explosive substance, and

(c) an incendiary grenade, fire bomb, molotov cocktail or other similar incendiary substance or device and a delaying mechanism or other thing intended for use in connection with such a substance or device (s. 2).

2. Breach of duty of care

Duty — Section 79

Every one who — has in his possession or under his care or control — an explosive substance — is under a legal duty — to use reasonable care — to prevent bodily harm or death to persons or damage to property — by that explosive substance.

Statement of offence — Section 80

Every one who — being under such a legal duty — without lawful excuse — fails to perform that duty — is guilty of an indictable offence.

Included offences. Attempts (s. 660 and s. 662(1)(b)).

Punishment. Life imprisonment if death is caused or likely to be caused (s. 80(a)). A term not exceeding 14 years' imprisonment if bodily harm or damage to property is caused or likely to be caused (s. 80(b)).

Release. Initial decision to release made by justice (s. 515(1)).

Election. Accused may elect trial by judge and jury, judge alone, or provincial court judge (s. 536).

Informations

A.B., on or about the —— day of ——, 19——, at the —— of ——, in the said (territorial division), being a person who had an explosive substance in his possession [OR under his care and control], did fail without lawful excuse to perform his legal duty to use reasonable care to prevent bodily harm to C.D. [OR death to C.D. OR damage to property] by that explosive substance, to wit: (specify the particulars of the offence), contrary to s. 80 of the Criminal Code of Canada.

3. Using explosives (causing injury with intent) — Section 81(1) and (2)

Section 81(1)(a)

Every one who — does anything with intent to cause an explosion of an explosive substance that — either is likely to cause serious bodily harm or death to persons — or is likely to cause serious damage to property — is guilty of an indictable offence.

Section 81(1)(b)

Every one who — with intent to do bodily harm to any person — either causes an explosive substance to explode — or sends or delivers to a person or causes a person to take or receive an explosive substance or any other dangerous substance or thing — or places or throws anywhere or at or on a person a corrosive fluid or explosive substance or any other dangerous substance or thing — is guilty of an indictable offence.

Section 81(1)(c)

Every one who — with intent to destroy or damage property — without lawful excuse — places or throws an explosive substance anywhere — is guilty of an indictable offence.

Section 81(1)(d)

Every one who — makes or has in his possession or has under his care or control any explosive substance — with intent thereby — either to endanger life or cause serious damage to property — or to enable another person to endanger life or to cause serious damage to property — is guilty of an indictable offence.

Included offences. Attempts (s. 660 and s. 662(1)(b)).

Punishment. Imprisonment for life for an offence under s. 80(1)(a) or (b) (s. 80(2)(a)). Imprisonment for a term not exceeding 14 years for an offence under s. 80(1)(c) or (d) (s. 80(2)(b)).

Release. Initial decision to release made by justice (s. 515(1)).

Election. Accused may elect trial by judge and jury, judge alone, or provincial court judge (s. 536).

Informations

A.B., on or about the —— day of ——, 19——, at the —— of ——, in the said (territorial division), with intent to cause an explosion of (specify the type of explosive substance), an explosive substance that was likely to cause serious bodily harm to C.D. [OR death to C.D. OR damage to (specify the property)] did (specify the act), to wit: (specify the particulars of the offence), contrary to s. 81(1)(a) of the Criminal Code of Canada.

A.B., on or about the —— day of ——, 19——, at the —— of ——, in the said (territorial division), with intent to do bodily harm to C.D., did cause (specify the type of explosive substance), an explosive substance to explode, to

EXPLOSIVE SUBSTANCES 275

wit: (specify the particulars of the offence), contrary to s. 81(1)(b)(i) of the Criminal Code of Canada.

A.B., on or about the —— day of ——, 19——, at the —— of ——, in the said (territorial division), with intent to do bodily harm to C.D., did send [OR deliver] to C.D. [OR cause C.D. to take (OR receive)] (specify the type of explosive substance or other dangerous substance or thing), an explosive substance [OR a dangerous substance (OR thing)], to wit: (specify the particulars of the offence), contrary to s. 81(1)(b)(ii) of the Criminal Code of Canada.

A.B., on or about the —— day of ——, 19——, at the —— of ——, in the said (territorial division), with intent to do bodily harm to C.D., did place on C.D. [OR throw at C.D. or throw on C.D. OR throw (specify where thrown)] (specify the type of substance or thing thrown), a corrosive fluid [OR an explosive substance OR a dangerous substance OR a dangerous thing], to wit: (specify the particulars of the offence), contrary to s. 81(1)(b)(iii) of the Criminal Code of Canada.

A.B., on or about the —— day of ——, 19——, at the —— of ——, in the said (territorial division), with intent to destroy [OR damage] property without lawful excuse, did place [OR throw] (specify the type of explosive substance), an explosive substance (specify where), to wit: (specify the particulars of the offence), contrary to s. 81(1)(c) of the Criminal Code of Canada.

A.B., on or about the —— day of ——, 19——, at the —— of ——, in the said (territorial division), did make [OR have in his possession OR have under his care OR have under his control] (specify the type of explosive substance), an explosive substance, with intent thereby to endanger the life of C.D. [OR to cause serious damage to property OR to enable E.F. to endanger the life of C.D. OR to enable E.F. to cause serious damage to property], to wit: (specify the particulars of the offence), contrary to s. 81(1)(d) of the Criminal Code of Canada.

4. Possession without lawful excuse — Section 82

Every one who — without lawful excuse — either makes — or has in his possession or under his care or control — any explosive substance — is guilty of an indictable offence.

Included offences. Attempts (s. 660 and s. 662(1)(b)).

Punishment. Imprisonment for a term not exceeding 5 years (s. 82).

Release. Initial decision to release made by officer in charge or justice (s. 498).

Election. Accused may elect trial by judge and jury, judge alone, or provincial court judge (s. 536).

Evidence. For the purposes of this offence, the proof of lawful excuse lies on the accused (s. 82).

Informations

> A.B., on or about the —— day of ——, 19——, at the —— of ——, in the said (territorial division), did without lawful excuse make [OR have in his possession OR have under his care or control] an explosive substance, to wit: (specify the particulars of the offence), contrary to s. 82 of the Criminal Code of Canada.

EXPOSE. For the purposes of Part VIII of the Criminal Code, "expose" includes (a) a wilful omission to take charge of a child by a person who is under a legal duty to do so, and (b) dealing with a child in a manner that is likely to leave that child exposed to risk without protection (s. 214).

EXTRACTOR. A device for removing the fired cartridge from the firing chamber (Jaffe, A Guide to Pathological Evidence, 2nd ed.).

EXTRADITION

1. Definition
2. From Canada to other Commonwealth countries
3. From Canada to countries that are not members of the Commonwealth
4. To Canada from other Commonwealth countries
5. To Canada from countries that are not members of the Commonwealth

1. Definition

Extradition is the surrender by one state at the request of another state, of a person who is accused, or has been convicted, of a crime committed within the jurisdiction of the requesting state (LaForest, Extradition to and from Canada).

2. From Canada to Commonwealth countries

Fugitive Offenders Act. The procedure for the apprehending and returning fugitives to other parts of "Her Majesty's Realms and Territories" is set out in the Fugitive Offenders Act. By use of the term "Her Majesty's Realms and Territories" is meant Great Britain, the remaining British colonies, and the self-governing dominions that form part of the Commonwealth that still owe allegiance to the Crown.

Fugitive. The term "fugitive" means a person accused of having committed an offence to which the Fugitive Offenders Act applies in any part of Her Majesty's Realms and Territories, except Canada, and who is now in Canada (Fugitive Offenders Act, s. 2).

Offences to which the Fugitive Offender Act applies

This act applies to high treason, treason and piracy, and to every offence, whatever it may be called that is punishable by imprisonment with hard labour for a term of twelve months or more, or by any greater punishment. Rigorous imprisonment and any confinement in a prison combined with labour, by whatever name it is called, is deemed to be "imprisonment with hard labour" (Fugitive Offenders Act, s. 3).

A superior court, however, has the power to discharge a fugitive, or to delay the return of a fugitive, whenever it would be unjust or oppressive or too severe a punishment by reason of the trivial nature of the case, or by reason of the application for the return of a fugitive not being made in good faith in the interests of justice (Fugitive Offenders Act, s. 16).

Arrest. A "fugitive" found in Canada may be apprehended under either an endorsed warrant or a provisional warrant (Fugitive Offenders Act, s. 612). An "endorsed warrant" in this instance refers to a warrant issued in that part of Her Majesty's Realms and Territories for the apprehension of a fugitive who is or is suspected to be in or on the way to Canada and which has been endorsed by either the Governor General or a judge of superior court (Fugitive Offenders Act, s. 7). A "provisional warrant" is a warrant issued by a provincial court judge for the apprehension of a fugitive who is or is suspected of being in or on his way to Canada. The basis for a provisional warrant is information and circumstances that would justify the issue of a warrant if the offence of which the fugitive is accused had been committed within the provincial court judge's jurisdiction (Fugitive Offenders Act, s. 8). When apprehended, the fugitive is to be brought before a provincial court judge (Fugitive Offenders Act, s. 10).

Committal. The provincial court judge may order the committal of the fugitive in appropriate circumstances but the fugitive is not to be surrendered or returned until after the expiration of fifteen days. In that period, the fugitive has the right to apply for a writ of habeas corpus.

Return. The Governor General issued the warrant for the return of a fugitive (Fugitive Offenders Act, s. 14). Unless this is done within two months, the judge may order the fugitive to be discharged (Fugitive Offenders Act, s. 15).

3. From Canada to countries that are not members of the Commonwealth

Extradition Act. The procedure for apprehending and returning fugitives or fugitive criminals to foreign states are set out in treaties made for the purpose of surrendering fugitive criminals and in the Extradition Act. Both the Act and a treaty with a foreign state are to be read together in determining the correct procedure to be followed and when they conflict, the terms of the treaty prevail. "Foreign state" for this purpose includes every colony, dependency and constituent part of the foreign state" (Extradition Act, s. 2).

Fugitive or fugitive criminal. The Extradition Act uses the expression "fugitive criminal" as an alternative to "fugitive". The terms mean "a person being or suspected of being in Canada, who is accused or convicted of an extradition crime committed within the jurisdiction of a foreign state (Extradition Act, s. 2).

Offences to which the Extradition Act applies

The Extradition Act uses the expression "extradition crime" which it defines in two ways. The first definition states that an "extradition crime" means "any crime that, if committed in Canada, or within Canadian jurisdiction, would be one of the crimes described in Schedule 1". Schedule 1 crimes include the following:

1. Murder, or attempt or conspiracy to murder
2. Manslaughter
3. Counterfeiting or altering money, and uttering counterfeit or altered money
4. Forgery, counterfeiting or altering, or uttering what is forged, counterfeited or altered
5. Larceny or theft
6. Embezzlement
7. Obtaining money or goods, or valuable securities, by false pretences
8. Crimes against bankruptcy or insolvency law
9. Fraud committed by a bailee, banker, agent, factor, trustee, or by a director or member or officer of any company, which fraud is made criminal by any Act for the time being in force
10. Sexual assault, sexual assault with a weapon, threats to a third party or causing bodily harm or aggravated sexual assault

11. Abduction
12. Child stealing
13. Kidnapping
14. False imprisonment
15. Burglary, housebreaking or shop-breaking
16. Arson
17. Robbery
18. Threats, by letter or otherwise, with intent to extort
19. Perjury or subornation of perjury
20. Piracy by municipal law or law of nations committed on board of or against a vessel of a foreign state
21. Criminal scuttling or destruction of a vessel of a foreign state at sea, whether on the high seas or on the Great lakes of North America, or attempting or conspiring to do so
22. Assault on board, a vessel of a foreign state at sea, whether on the high seas or on the Great Lakes of North America, with intent to destroy life or to do grievous bodily harm
23. Revolt, or conspiracy to revolt, by two or more persons, on board a vessel of a foreign state at sea, whether on the high seas or on the Great Lakes of North America, against the authority of the master
24. Any offence under
    (a) sections 52, 57, 58, 79 to 81, 153, 154, 178, 280 to 283, 385 to 391, 393 to 396, subsection 397(1), sections 398, 400, 401, 405 and paragraph 465(1)(a) of the *Criminal Code*,
    (b) Part VIII of the *Criminal Code*, except sections 249, 250, 252, 253, 255 and 259 in relation to a vessel and sections 264.1 and 290 to 317;
    (c) Part IX of the *Criminal Code*, except subsection 339(2);
    (d) Part of XI of the *Criminal Code*, except sections 438, 440, 441, 446 and 447,
    (e) Part XII of the *Criminal Code*, except section 454,
    that is not included in any foregoing portion of this Schedule
25. Any offence that is, in the case of the principal offender, included in any foregoing portion of this Schedule, and for which the fugitive criminal, though not the principal, is liable to be tried or punished as if he were the principal.

(R.S., c. E-21, Sch. I; 1980-81-82-83, c. 125, s. 31; R.S.C. 1985, c. 27 (1st Supp), s. 187).

The second definition states that an extradition crime means any crime described in a treaty with a foreign state (Extradition Act, s. 2).

A judge (in this case any person authorized to act judicially in extradition matters) has the power to order a fugitive to be discharged if sufficient evidence is not produced to justify the extradition (Extradition Act, s. 18). Further, no fugitive is liable to surrender if it appears that the offence in respect of which proceedings are being taken is one of a political character or if it appears that the proceedings are being taken with a view to prosecute the fugitive for an offence of a political character (Extradition Act, s. 21).

Arrest. A judge may issue a warrant for the apprehension of a fugitive based on a foreign warrant of arrest, or on an information or complaint laid before the judge, and on such evidence or after such proceedings as in the opinion of the judge would justify the issue of the warrant if the crime of which the fugitive is accused or is alleged to have been convicted had been committed in Canada (Extradition Act, s. 10(1)). When apprehended, the fugitive is to be brought before a judge who is to hear the case, in the same manner, as nearly as may be, as if the fugitive were brought before a justice of the peace, charged with an indictable offence committed in Canada (Extradition Act, s. 13).

Committal. The judge may order the committal of the fugitive if there is sufficient evidence to justify doing so but the fugitive is not to be returned or surrendered until after the expiration of thirty days. In that period, the fugitive has the right to apply for a writ of habeas corpus.

Return. The Minister of Justice, on the requisition of a foreign state, has the authority to order the surrender of a fugitive after appropriate time periods have elapsed in which the fugitive may exercise certain rights to appeal his committal.

4. To Canada from other Commonwealth countries

In general, other Commonwealth countries have laws that are equivalent to the Canadian Fugitive Offenders Act. These laws set out the procedure that governs the return to Canada of fugitives from Canadian justice who have gone to some other part of Her Majesty's Realms and Territories. Under these laws, the Government of Canada makes the formal request for the return of an accused. Such requests must be accompanied by a Canadian warrant for the arrest of the fugitive and such other documentation as the circumstances may require.

5. To Canada from countries that are not members of the Commonwealth

Persons who are charged with an offence in Canada and have escaped to countries that are not members of the Commonwealth *may* be subject to extradition to Canada.

Police officers should not ask foreign police to arrest a fugitive unless the Attorney General of the province has consented to institute extradition proceedings. If the case is urgent the Attorney General will request the Canadian consul by telegraph to have a provisional warrant issued for the arrest of the fugitive. This will prevent his release on habeas corpus, which might happen if the arrest is made by the foreign police at the request of local police.

Questions to be considered are:

(i) Is there a treaty with the country where the fugitive has gone?

(ii) Is the offence included in the treaty?

(iii) Is the fugitive subject to extradition? (Some countries will not extradite their own subjects or persons who are liable to the death penalty.)

The depositions of the witnesses are taken before a justice of the peace or magistrate and should be sufficient to obtain a committal for trial where the accused is held. Therefore it is better to put in too much evidence than too little. A picture and finger prints of the fugitive should form part of the evidence or record and should be marked as an exhibit and identified by witnesses. The evidence so taken is sent to the Attorney General and certified by the provincial secretary or an officer of state; it is then authenticated by the Consul General of the country applied to who certifies that papers so prepared would be acceptable by tribunals in Canada in similar cases.

It is also necessary to obtain from all the other provinces an undertaking that they will not prosecute the accused for any offence other than the offence(s) for which he is being returned to Canada. This is usually done by telegram by the office of the Attorney General of the province.

The Minister of Justice is informed by the Attorney General of the application and he ensures an application being made through diplomatic channels to the executive government of the foreign country for the surrender of the fugitive. If surrender is granted, the warrant issued by the Secretary of State for Canada, called the Warrant of Recipias, names the police officers who are to act as escort, and the foreign government issues a warrant of surrender in duplicate. The officer who is to be the escort takes both copies of the warrant of surrender and the Canadian Warrant of Recipias with him, he produces both to the jailer and leaves with him one copy of the warrant of surrender endorsed with a receipt for the body of the prisoner.

The officer who is acting as escort should have sufficient personal identification on his person when he goes to make the pickup.

F

FACTUM. 1. Act or deed (Latin). 2. A statement of facts.

FALSE DOCUMENT. For the purposes of Part IX of the Criminal Code (Offences Against Rights of Property), "false document" means a document:

(a) the whole or a material part of which purports to be made by or on behalf of a person who did not make it or authorize it to be made, or who did not in fact exist;

(b) that is made by or on behalf of the person who purports to make it but is false in some material particular;

(c) that is made in the name of an existing person, by him or under his authority, with a fraudulent intention that it should pass as being made by a person, real or fictitious, other than the person who makes it or under whose authority it is made (s. 321).

See also FORGERY and OFFENCES RESEMBLING FORGERY.

FALSE IMPRISONMENT. There must be an actual detention and loss of freedom. If a constable acts on a warrant, that is complete justification for anything he does within its provisions. If a police officer arrests the accused without a warrant for an offence upon which he may be arrested without a warrant, he may justify his actions by pleading and proving that he had reasonable grounds for supposing that the accused had committed the crime. It has been held that the onus of proving the existing of reasonable and probable cause lies upon the defendant.

FALSE PRETENCES

1. *Definition of a "false pretence"*
2. *Obtaining anything that may be the object of theft*
3. *Obtaining credit*
4. *False statement in writing*
5. *Obtaining execution of valuable security by fraud*
6. *Fraudulently obtaining food and lodging*
7. *Witchcraft*
8. *Sufficiency of count*

1. Definition of a "false pretence"

A false pretence is a representation of a matter of fact either present or past, made by words or otherwise, that is known by the person who makes it to be false and that is made with a fraudulent intent to induce the person to whom it is made to act on it (s. 361(1)).

Exaggerated commendation or depreciation of the quality of anything is not a false pretence unless it is carried to such an extent that it amounts to a fraudulent misrepresentation of fact (s. 361(2)).

It is a question of fact whether commendation or depreciation amounts to a fraudulent misrepresentation of fact (s. 361(3)).

2. Obtaining anything that may be the object of theft — Section 362(1)(a) and (2)(a), (b)

Every one who — by a false pretence — whether directly or through the medium of a contract obtained by a false pretence — either obtains anything in respect of which the offence of theft may be committed — or causes it to be delivered to another person — is guilty of either an indictable offence or an offence punishable on summary conviction.

Where the property obtained is a testamentary instrument or where its value exceeds $1,000, the person is guilty of an indictable offence.

Where the value of what is obtained does not exceed $1,000, the person may be found guilty of either an indictable offence or an offence punishable on summary conviction.

Intent. False pretence.

Limitation period. No proceedings in respect of offences that are declared to be punishable on summary conviction shall be instituted more than 6 months after the time when the subject matter of the proceedings arose (s. 786(2) and s. 785(1)).

Included offences. Attempts (s. 660 and s. 662(1)(b)).

Punishment. On indictment, where the property obtained is a testamentary instrument or where the value of what is obtained exceeds $1,000, imprisonment for a term not exceeding 10 years (s. 362(2)(a)). Where the value of what is obtained does not exceed $1,000, imprisonment for a term not exceeding 2 years (s. 362(2)(b)(i)). On summary conviction, a fine not exceeding $2,000, or 6 months' imprisonment, or both (s. 362(2)(b)(ii) and s. 787(1)).

Release. Where the property obtained is a testamentary instrument or where its value exceeds $1,000, initial decision to release made by justice (s. 515(1)). Where the value of what is obtained does not exceed $1,000, initial decision to release made by peace officer (s. 497).

Election. On indictment, where the property obtained is a testamentary instrument or where its value exceeds $1,000, accused may elect trial by judge and jury, judge alone, or provincial court judge (s. 536). Where value of what is obtained does not exceed $1,000, no election, absolute jurisdiction of provincial court judge. On summary conviction, no election.

Evidence. *See* **8**, *below.*

Informations

A.B., on or about the —— day of ——, 19——, at the —— of ——, in the said (territorial division), by a false pretence did obtain [OR cause to be delivered to C.D.] (specify a thing in respect of which the offence of theft may be committed), to wit: (specify the particulars of the offence), contrary to s. 362(1)(a) of the Criminal Code of Canada.

3. Obtaining credit — Section 362(1)(b) and (3)

Every one who — obtains credit — by a false pretence or by fraud — is guilty of an indictable offence.

Intent. False pretence.

Included offences. Attempts (s. 660 and s. 662(1)(b)).

Punishment. Imprisonment for a term not exceeding 10 years (s. 362(3)).

Release. Initial decision to release made by justice (s. 515(1)).

Election. Accused may elect trial by judge and jury, judge alone, or provincial court judge (s. 536).

Evidence. *See* **8** *below.*

Informations

A.B., on or about the —— day of ——, 19——, at the —— of ——, in the said (territorial division), did obtain credit by a false pretence [OR fraud] to wit: (specify the particulars of the offence), contrary to s. 362(1)(b) of the Criminal Code of Canada.

4. False statement in writing — Section 362(1) and (3)

Section 362(1)(c)

Every one who — knowingly — makes or causes to be made, directly or indirectly — a false statement in writing — with intent that it should be relied on — with respect to the financial condition or means or ability to pay of himself or any person or firm or corporation that he is interested in or that he acts for — for the purpose of procuring, in any form whatever whether for his benefit or the benefit of that person or firm or corporation — either the delivery of personal property — or the payment of money — or the making of a loan — or the grant or extension of credit — or the discount of an account receivable — the making or accepting or discounting or endorsing of a bill of exchange or cheque or draft or promissory note — is guilty of an indictable offence.

Section 362(1)(d)

Every one who — knowing that a false statement in writing has been made — with respect to the financial condition or means or ability to pay of himself or another person or firm or corporation that he is interested in or that he acts for — on the faith of that statement — procures anything mentioned above whether for his benefit or for the benefit of that person or firm or corporation — is guilty of an indictable offence.

Intent. Knowingly.

Included offences. Attempts (s. 660 and s. 662(1)(b)).

Punishment. Imprisonment for a term not exceeding 10 years (s. 362(3)).

Release. Initial decision to release made by justice (s. 515(1)).

Election. Accused may elect trial by judge and jury, judge alone, or provincial court judge (s. 536).

Definitions. See CHEQUE.

Evidence. 1. Where it is shown that anything was obtained by the accused by means of a cheque that, when presented for payment within a reasonable time, was dishonoured on the ground that no funds or insufficient funds were on deposit to the credit of the accused in the bank or other institution on which the cheque was drawn, it shall be presumed to have been obtained by a false pretence, unless the court is satisfied by evidence that when the accused issued the cheque he

believed on reasonable grounds that it would be honoured if presented for payment within a reasonable time after it was issued (s. 362(4)).
2. *See also* **8**, *below.*

5. Obtaining execution of valuable security by fraud — Section 363

Every one who — with intent to defraud or injure another person — by a false pretence — causes or induces any person — either to execute or make or accept or endorse or destroy the whole or any part of a valuable security — or to write or impress or affix a name or seal on any paper or parchment in order that it may afterward be made or converted into or used or dealt with as a valuable security — is guilty of an indictable offence.

Intent. Intention to defraud or injure; false pretence.

Included offences. Attempts (s. 660 and s. 662(1)(b)).

Punishment. Imprisonment for a term not exceeding 5 years (s. 363).

Release. Initial decision to release made by officer in charge or justice (s. 498).

Election. Accused may elect trial by judge and jury, judge alone, or provincial court judge (s. 536).

Evidence. See **8**, *below.*

Informations

A.B., on or about the —— day of ——, 19——, at the —— of ——, in the said (territorial division), with intent to defraud [OR injure] C.D., by a false pretence did cause [OR induce] C.D. to execute [OR make OR accept OR endorse OR destroy] the whole of [OR a part of] a valuable security, to wit: (specify the particulars of the offence), contrary to s. 363(a) of the Criminal Code of Canada.

6. Fraudulently obtaining food and lodging — Section 364(1)

Every one who — fraudulently — obtains food or lodging or other accommodation — at a hotel or an inn or at a lodging or boarding or eating house — is guilty of an offence punishable on summary conviction.

Intent. Fraudulently.

Limitation period. No proceedings in respect of offences that are declared to be punishable on summary conviction shall be instituted

more than 6 months after the time when the subject matter of the proceedings arose (s. 786(2) and s. 785(1)).

Included offences. Attempts (s. 660 and s. 662(1)(b)).

Punishment. A fine not exceeding $2,000, or 6 months' imprisonment, or both (s. 364(1) and s. 787(1)).

Release. Initial decision to release made by peace officer (s. 497).

Election. No election, summary conviction offence.

Definitions. See CHEQUE.

Evidence. 1. In proceedings for this offence, evidence that an accused obtained food, lodging or other accommodation at a hotel or an inn or at a lodging, boarding or eating house, and did not pay for it and (a) made a false or fictitious show or pretence of having baggage, (b) had any false or pretended baggage, (c) surreptitiously removed or attempted to remove his baggage or any material part of it, (d) absconded or surreptitiously left the premises, (e) knowingly made a false statement to obtain credit or time for payment, or (f) offered a worthless cheque, draft or security in payment for his food, lodging or other accommodation, is, in the absence of any evidence to the contrary, proof of fraud (s. 364(2)).
2. *See also* **8**, *below.*

Informations

A.B., on or about the —— day of ——, 19——, at the —— of ——, in the said (territorial division), did fraudulently obtain food [OR lodging OR (specify other accommodation)] at a hotel [OR an inn OR a lodging house OR a boarding house OR an eating house], to wit: (specify the particulars of the offence), contrary to s. 364(1) of the Criminal Code of Canada.

7. Witchcraft

Section 365(a)

Every one who — fraudulently — pretends to exercise or to use — any kind of witchcraft or sorcery or enchantment or conjuration — is guilty of an offence punishable on summary conviction.

Section 365(b)

Every one who — fraudulently — for a consideration — undertakes to tell fortunes — is guilty of an offence punishable on summary conviction.

288 FALSE PRETENCES

Section 365(c)

Every one who — fraudulently — from his skill in or knowledge of an occult or crafty science — pretends to discover where or in what manner anything that is supposed to have been stolen or lost may be found — is guilty of an offence punishable on summary conviction.

Intent. Fraudulently.

Limitation period. No proceedings in respect of offences that are declared to be punishable on summary conviction shall be instituted more than 6 months after the time when the subject matter of the proceedings arose (s. 786(2) and s. 785(1)).

Included offences. Attempts (s. 660 and s. 662(1)(b)).

Punishment. A fine not exceeding $2,000, or 6 months' imprisonment, or both (s. 365 and s. 787(1)).

Release. Initial decision to release made by peace officer (s. 497).

Election. No election, summary conviction offence.

Evidence. 1. Any kind of fortune telling is covered, by cards, crystal gazing or anything else, unless it is stipulated or understood that the prediction of the future was made pursuant to certain rules and not because of the pretended occult powers of the accused. Deception is one of the elements. The fact that the accused himself believes he has the ability to commune with departed spirits is no defence.
2. *See also* **8**, *below*.

Informations

A.B., on or about the —— day of ——, 19——, at the —— of ——, in the said (territorial division), fraudulently did pretend to use [OR to exercise] witchcraft [OR sorcery OR an enchantment OR a conjuration], to wit: (specify the particulars of the offence), contrary to s. 365(a) of the Criminal Code of Canada.

A.B., on or about the —— day of ——, 19——, at the —— of ——, in the said (territorial division), fraudulently did undertake, for a consideration, to tell fortunes, to wit: (specify the particulars of the offence), contrary to s. 365(b) of the Criminal Code of Canada.

A.B., on or about the —— day of ——, 19——, at the —— of ——, in the said (territorial division), did pretend from his skill in [OR knowledge of] an occult [OR crafty] science to discover where [OR in what manner] (specify a thing), that was supposed to have been stolen [OR lost], may be found, to wit: (specify the particulars of the offence), contrary to s. 365(c) of the Criminal Code of Canada.

8. Sufficiency of count

No count that alleges false pretences, fraud or any attempt or conspiracy by fraudulent means is insufficient by reason only that it does not set out in detail the nature of the false pretence, fraud or fraudulent means (s. 586).

FALSIFICATION OF BOOKS AND DOCUMENTS

1. *Book, paper, writing, valuable security or document*
2. *Employment record*
3. *Statement or return of public officer*
4. *Prospectus*
5. *Obtaining carriage by false billing*
6. *Trader of businessman failing to keep accounts*
7. *Sufficiency of count*

1. Book, paper, writing, valuable security or document

Section 397(1)(a)

Every one who — with intent to defraud — destroys or mutilates or alters or falsifies, or makes a false entry in — a book or paper or writing or valuable security or document — is guilty of an indictable offence.

Section 397(1)(b)

Every one who — with intent to defraud — omits a material particular from, or alters a material particular in — a book or paper or writing or valuable security or document — is guilty of an indictable offence.

Section 397(2)

Every one who — with intent to defraud his creditors — is privy to the commission of such an offence — is guilty of an indictable offence.

Intent. Intention to defraud.

Included offences. Attempts (s. 660 and s. 662(1)(b)).

Punishment. Imprisonment for a term not exceeding 5 years (s. 397(1) and (2)).

Release. Initial decision to release made by officer in charge or justice (s. 498).

Election. Accused may elect trial by judge and jury, judge alone, or provincial court judge (s. 536).

Evidence. *See* **7**, *below.*

Informations

A.B., on or about the —— day of ——, 19——, at the —— of ——, in the said (territorial division), with intent to defraud, did destroy [OR mutilate OR alter OR falsify OR make a false entry in] a book [OR a paper OR a writing OR a valuable security OR a document], to wit: (specify the particulars of the offence), contrary to s. 397(1)(a) of the Criminal Code of Canada.

A.B., on or about the —— day of ——, 19——, at the —— of ——, in the said (territorial division), with intent to defraud, did omit a material particular from [OR alter a material particular in] a book [OR a paper OR a writing OR a valuable security OR a document], to wit: (specify the particulars of the offence), contrary to s. 397(1)(b) of the Criminal Code of Canada.

2. Employment record — Section 398

Every one who — with intent to deceive — falsifies an employment record — by any means, including the punching of a time clock — is guilty of an offence punishable on summary conviction.

Intent. Intention to deceive.

Limitation period. No proceedings in respect of offences that are declared to be punishable on summary conviction shall be instituted more than 6 months after the time when the subject matter of the proceedings arose (s. 786(2) and s. 785(1)).

Included offences. Attempts (s. 660 and s. 662(1)(b)).

Punishment. A fine not exceeding $2,000, or 6 months' imprisonment, or both (s. 398 and s. 787(1)).

Release. Initial decision to release made by peace officer (s. 497).

Election. No election, summary conviction offence.

Evidence. *See* **7**, *below.*

Informations

A.B., on or about the —— day of ——, 19——, at the —— of ——, in the said (territorial division), with intent to deceive, did falsify an employment record by (specify the means), to wit: (specify the particulars of the offence), contrary to s. 398 of the Criminal Code of Canada.

3. Statement or return of public officer — Section 399

Every one who — being entrusted with the receipt or custody or management of any part of the public revenues — knowingly — furnishes a false statement or return of — either any sum of money collected by him or entrusted to his care — or any balance of money in his hands or under his control — is guilty of an indictable offence.

Intent. Knowingly.

Included offences. Attempts (s. 660 and s. 662(1)(b)).

Punishment. Imprisonment for a term not exceeding 5 years (s. 399).

Release. Initial decision to release made by officer in charge or justice (s. 498).

Election. Accused may elect trial by judge and jury, judge alone, or provincial court judge (s. 536).

Evidence. See **7**, *below.*

4. Prospectus — Section 400(1)

Every one who — makes or circulates or publishes — a prospectus or statement or an account, whether written or oral — that he knows is false in a material particular — with intent — either to induce persons, whether ascertained or not, to become shareholders or partners in a company — or to deceive or defraud the members or shareholders or creditors, whether ascertained or not, of a company — or to induce any person to entrust or advance anything to a company — or to enter into any security for the benefit of a company — is guilty of an indictable offence.

Intent. Knowingly; intention to induce, deceive, defraud or enter into.

Included offences. Attempts (s. 660 and s. 662(1)(b)).

Punishment. Imprisonment for a term not exceeding 10 years (s. 400(1)).

Release. Initial decision to release made by justice (s. 515(1)).

Election. Accused may elect trial by judge and jury, judge alone, or provincial court judge (s. 536).

Definitions. See COMPANY.

Evidence. 1. The falsity may be found in a statement of purposes which the author never had any intention of carrying out.
2. A material omission may render a statement false.
3. *See also* **7**, *below.*

5. Obtaining carriage by false billing — Section 401(1)

Every one who — by means of a false or misleading representation — knowingly — obtains or attempts to obtain the carriage of anything by any person — into a country or province or district or other place, whether or not within Canada — where the importation or transportation of it is, in the circumstances of the case, unlawful — is guilty of an offence punishable on summary conviction.

Intent. Knowingly.

Limitation period. No proceedings in respect of offences that are declared to be punishable on summary conviction shall be instituted more than 6 months after the time when the subject matter of the proceedings arose (s. 786(2) and s. 785(1)).

Included offences. Attempts (s. 660 and s. 662(1)(b)).

Punishment. A fine not exceeding $2,000, or 6 months' imprisonment, or both (s. 401(1) and s. 787(1)).

Release. Initial decision to release made by peace officer (s. 497).

Election. No election, summary conviction offence.

Evidence. 1. Where a person is convicted of this offence, anything by means of or in relation to which the offence was committed, on such conviction, in addition to any punishment that is imposed, is forfeited to Her Majesty and shall be disposed of as the court may direct (s. 401(2)).
2. *See also* **7**, *below.*

6. Trader or businessman failing to keep accounts — Section 402(1)

Every one who — being a trader or in business — is indebted in an amount exceeding $1,000 — and is unable to pay his creditors in full — and has not kept books of account that, in the ordinary course of the trade or business in which he is engaged, are necessary

to exhibit or explain his transactions — is guilty of an indictable offence.

Exception. No person shall be convicted of this offence (a) where, to the satisfaction of the court or judge, he accounts for his losses and shows that his failure to keep books was not intended to defraud his creditors or (b) where his failure to keep books occurred at a time more than 5 years prior to the day on which he was unable to pay his creditors in full (s. 402(2)).

Included offences. Attempts (s. 660 and s. 662(1)(b)).

Punishment. Imprisonment for a term not exceeding 2 years (s. 402(1)).

Release. Initial decision to release made by officer in charge or justice (s. 498).

Election. Accused may elect trial by judge and jury, judge alone, or provincial court judge (s. 536).

7. Sufficiency of count

No count that alleges false pretences, fraud or any attempt or conspiracy by fraudulent means is insufficient by reason only that it does not set out in detail the nature of the false pretence, fraud or fraudulent means (s. 586).

FEDERAL COURT. "Federal Court" means the Federal Court of Canada.

"Federal Court — Appeal Division" or "Federal Court of Appeal" means that division of the Federal Court of Canada called the Federal Court — Appeal Division or referred to as the Federal Court of Appeal by the Federal Court Act.

"Federal Court — Trial Division" means that division of the Federal Court of Canada so named by the Federal Court Act (Interpretation Act, s. 35).

FEIGNED MARRIAGE

Section 292(1)

Every person who — procures or knowingly aids in procuring — a feigned marriage between himself and another person — is guilty of an indictable offence.

Included offences. Attempts (s. 660 and s. 662(1)(b)).

Punishment. Imprisonment for a term not exceeding 5 years (s. 292(1)).

Release. Initial decision to release made by officer in charge or justice (s. 498).

Election. Accused may elect trial by judge and jury, judge alone, or provincial court judge (s. 536).

Evidence. 1. No person shall be convicted of this offence on the evidence of only one witness unless the evidence of that witness is corroborated in a material particular by evidence that implicates the accused (s. 292(2)).
2. The wife or husband of a person charged with this offence is a competent and compellable witness for the prosecution without the consent of the accused (Canada Evidence Act, s. 4(2)).

Informations

A.B., on or about the —— day of ——, 19——, at the —— of ——, in the said (territorial division), did procure a feigned marriage to be performed between himself and C.D., [OR did assist E.F. in procuring a feigned marriage between E.F. and C.D.], to wit: (specify the particulars of the offence), contrary to s. 292(1) of the Criminal Code of Canada.

FELO DE SE. Suicide (Latin).

FELONY. The terms "felony" and "misdemeanour" are now abolished in our criminal procedure. Therefore it is unnecessary to consider their meaning, except possibly to say that the division of crimes into felony and misdemeanour was quite arbitrary and was not based on any scientific rule. It was supposed that the more serious crimes were called felonies, but some of the so called misdemeanours were as serious as some of the felonies. Our offences are now known as indictable or summary conviction offences.

FETUS. The developing child in the uterus during the 2nd and 3rd trimesters of pregnancy. Also "conceptus" (Jaffe, A Guide to Pathological Evidence, 2nd ed.).

FIAT. 1. "Let it be done" (Latin). 2. A command.

FIERI FACIAS (FI. FA.). A writ of fieri facias is an order issued in the name of the sovereign commanding him to levy of the goods and chattels, lands and tenements of the person and for the amount of money specified in the writ. In criminal law, this writ is the means whereby a judge orders the forfeiture of a recognizance that has been entered into on behalf of an accused to ensure his attendance at court or to ensure his compliance with any conditions that have been attached to his release (s. 771). Such a writ is to be issued in the prescribed form (Form 34).

FINANCIAL INSTITUTION. For the purposes of s. 29 of the Canada Evidence Act, "financial institution" means the Bank of Canada, the Federal Business Development Bank and any institution incorporated in Canada that accepts deposits of money from its members or the public, and includes a branch, agency or office of any such Bank or institution (Canada Evidence Act, s. 29(9)).

FINE. 1. A fine is a sum of money ordered to be paid to the Crown by an offender, as a punishment for his offence. 2. For the purposes of s. 718, "fine" includes a pecuniary penalty or other sum of money (s. 718(12)). *See also PUNISHMENT.*

FINGERPRINTS. Marks made on any firm surface by the ridges on the skin at the tip of the thumb and fingers. The marks can be made more visible and photographed and compared with the marks made by the fingers of known persons, forming a valuable means of identifying the maker of the marks. This identification proceeds on the basis of the discovery that no two persons in the world have exactly the same patterns of ridges and marks, and that the patterns can be classified and filed (David M. Walker, The Oxford Companion to Law).

Genetic fingerprinting. The first major break through in forensic detection since Edward Richard Henry figured how to use human fingerprints to identify criminals at the turn of the century. Virtually every human cell contains DNA (deoxyribonucleic acid) which carries the complete human genetic code. Researchers are now able to literally disassemble DNA and examine it for microscopic variations that make human beings (except for identical twins) verifiably unique to a statistical certainty. Almost any tissue sample is a potential candidate for testing: bone, blood, semen, skin and hair (if it contains the root). All of these items contain DNA and are recovered at the scenes of violent crimes more often than are fingerprints. Noncellular body fluids such as saliva, urine and sweat can also carry testable quantities of DNA. This means that a discarded cigarette butt, a wad of gum, or even the inner part of a hat or watchband could yield DNA evidence to solve a crime (Stephen G. Michaud, The New York Times Magazine, November 6, 1988).

Fingerprint examiner. For the purposes of s. 667 "fingerprint examiner" means a person designated as such for the purposes of s. 667 by the Solicitor General of Canada (s. 667(5)).

FIREARM. Any barrelled weapon from which any shot, bullet or other projectile can be discharged and that is capable of causing serious bodily injury or death to a person, and includes any frame or receiver of such a barrelled weapon and anything that can be adapted for use as a firearm (s. 84(1)).

Notwithstanding this definition of "firearm", for the purposes of the definitions "prohibited weapon" and "restricted weapon" and for the purpose of ss. 93, 97(1) and (3), and 102, 104, 105 and 116, the following weapons shall be deemed not to be firearms, namely:

(a) an antique firearm unless, but for s. 84(2), it would be a restricted weapon, and the person in possession thereof intends to discharge it;

(b) any device designed, and intended by the person in possession thereof, for use exclusively for signalling, notifying of distress or firing stud cartridges, explosive-driven rivets or similar industrial ammunition, or for firing blank cartridges;

(c) any shooting device designed, and intended by the person in possession thereof, for use exclusively for slaughtering of domestic animals, or for tranquilizing animals, or for discharging projectiles with lines attached thereto; and,

(d) any other barrelled weapon where it is proved that that weapon is not designed or adapted to discharge a shot, bullet or other projectile at a muzzle velocity exceeding 152.4 m per second or to discharge a shot, bullet or other projectile that is designed or adapted to attain a velocity exceeding 152.4 m per second (s. 84(2)).

Antique firearm. Any firearm manufactured before 1898 that was not designed to use rim-fire or centre-fire ammunition and that has not been redesigned to use such ammunition or, if so designed or redesigned, is capable only of using rim-fire or centre-fire ammunition that is not commonly available in Canada (s. 84(1)).

Firearms acquisition certificate. A certificate issued by a firearms officer under s. 106 or s. 107 (s. 84(1)).

Firearms officer. Any person who has been designated in writing as a firearms officer by the Commissioner or the Attorney General of a province or who is a member of a class of persons that has been so designated (s. 84(1)).

Genuine gun collector. An individual who possesses or seeks to acquire one or more restricted weapons that are related or distinguished by historical, technological or scientific characteristics, has knowledge of those characteristics, has consented to the periodic inspection, conducted in a reasonable manner and in accordance with the regulations, of the premises in which the restricted weapons are to be kept and has complied with such other requirements as are prescribed by regulation respecting knowledge, secure storage and the keeping of records in respect of the restricted weapons (s. 84(1)).

Large-capacity cartridge magazine. Any device or container from which ammunition may be fed into the firing chamber of a firearm (s. 84(1)).

FIREARMS AND WEAPONS OFFENCES

Firearms Offences

1. *Using firearm during commission of indictable offence*
2. *Pointing a firearm*
3. *Careless use of firearm*
4. *Storing, displaying, handling or transporting firearm contrary to regulation*
5. *Transfer of firearm to person under 16 years*
6. *Wrongful delivery of firearms, ammunition or explosive substances*
7. *Making automatic firearm*
8. *Acquisition of firearm without firearms acquisition certificate*
9. *Delivery of firearm to person without firearms acquisition certificate*
10. *Possession of firearm, ammunition, explosive substance or firearms acquisition certificate while prohibited*
11. *Finding firearm*
12. *Tampering with serial number*
13. *False statements to procure firearms acquisition certificate, registration certificate or permit*
14. *Tampering with firearms acquisition certificate, registration certificate or permit*
15. *Failure to comply with conditions or permit*
16. *Failure to deliver up revoked certificates or permits*
17. *Records of transactions in firearms*
18. *Business person reporting loss, destruction or theft*
19. *Carrying on business in firearms or ammunition without permit*
20. *Handling, storing, displaying, advertising or selling by mail order of firearms or ammunition*
21. *Handling, shipping, storage and transportation of firearms and ammunition*

Weapons Offences

22. *Possession for dangerous purpose*
23. *Possession at public meeting*

24. *Carrying concealed weapon*
25. *Possession of prohibited weapon*
26. *Prohibited weapon in motor vehicle*
27. *Possession of unregistered restricted weapon*
28. *Possession of restricted weapon elsewhere than at place authorized*
29. *Restricted weapon in motor vehicle*
30. *Wrongful delivery of offensive weapons, ammunition or explosive substances*
31. *Importing or delivering weapon or part of prohibited weapon*
32. *Delivery of restricted weapon to person without permit*
33. *Importation of restricted weapon by person without permit*
34. *Possession of offensive weapon, ammunition, explosive substance or firearms acquisition certificate while prohibited*
35. *Finding weapon*
36. *Losing or mislaying restricted weapon*
37. *Records of transactions in restricted or prohibited weapons*
38. *Carrying on business in restricted weapons or ammunition without permit*
39. *Business person reporting loss, destruction or theft*
40. *Handling, storing, displaying, advertising or selling by mail order of restricted weapon or ammunition*
41. *Handling or storing of prohibited weapon*
42. *Handling, shipping, storing and transportation of prohibited weapon*

---

1. Using firearm during commission of indictable offence

Section 85(1)(a)

Every one who — uses a firearm — while committing or attempting to commit an indictable offence — whether or not he causes or means to cause bodily harm to any person as a result thereof — is guilty of an indictable offence.

Section 85(1)(b)

Every one who — uses a firearm — during his flight after committing or attempting to commit an indictable offence — whether or not he causes or means to cause bodily harm to any person as a result thereof — is guilty of an indictable offence.

Included offences. Attempts (s. 660 and s. 662(1)(b)).

Punishment. Imprisonment in the case of a first offence, for not more than 14 years and not less than one year (s. 85(1)(c)). In the case of a second or subsequent offence, for not more than 14 years and not less than 3 years (s. 85(1)(d)).

A sentence imposed on a person for this offence shall be served consecutively to any other punishment imposed on him for an offence arising out of the same event or series of events and to any other sentence to which he is subject at the time the sentence is imposed on him for this offence (s. 85(2)).

Release. Initial decision to release made by justice (s. 515(1)).

Election. Accused may elect trial by judge and jury, judge alone, or provincial court judge (s. 536).

Evidence. 1. Where any question arises as to whether a person is or was the holder of a firearms acquisition certificate, registration certificate or permit, the onus is on the accused to prove that that person is or was the holder of the firearms acquisition certificate, registration certificate or permit (s. 115(1)).

In any proceedings, a document purporting to be a firearms acquisition certificate, registration certificate or permit is evidence of the statements contained therein (s. 115(2)).

2. Whatever is used as a firearm at the scene of the crime must be proven to be capable, either at the outset or through adaptation or assembly, of being loaded, fired and thereby of having the potential to cause serious bodily harm during the commission of the offence, or during the flight after the commission of the offence. (R. v. Covin (1983), 8 C.C.C. (3d) 240 (S.C.C.)).

3. The "use" of a firearm is an essential element of the offence. Being "armed" with an offensive weapon and "using" it are not the same thing. "Using" a firearm includes pulling out a firearm which the offender has on his person and holding it in his hand to intimidate another (R. v. Langevin (1979), 47 C.C.C. (2d) 138 (Ont. C.A.)).

Informations

A.B., on or about the —— day of ——, 19——, at the —— of ——, in the said (territorial division), did use a firearm while committing [OR while attempting to commit] an indictable offence, to wit: (specify the particulars of the offence), contrary to s. 85(1)(a) of the Criminal Code of Canada.

A.B., on or about the —— day of ——, 19——, at the —— of ——, in the said (territorial division), did use a firearm during his flight after committing [OR after attempting to commit] an indictable offence, to wit: (specify the particulars of the offence), contrary to s. 85(1)(b) of the Criminal Code of Canada.

2. Pointing a firearm — Section 86(1)

Every one who — without lawful excuse — points a firearm at another person — whether the firearm is loaded or unloaded — is

guilty of either an indictable offence or an offence punishable on summary conviction.

Limitation period. No proceedings in respect of offences that are declared to be punishable on summary conviction shall be instituted more than 6 months after the time when the subject matter of the proceedings arose (s. 786(2) and s. 785(1)).

Included offences. Attempts (s. 660 and s. 662(1)(b)).

Punishment. On indictment, imprisonment for a term not exceeding 5 years (s. 86(1)(a)). On summary conviction, a fine not exceeding $2,000, or 6 months' imprisonment, or both (s. 86(1)(b) and s. 787(1)).

Release. Initial decision to release made by peace officer (s. 497).

Election. On indictment, accused may elect trial by judge and jury, judge alone, or provincial court judge (s. 536). On summary conviction, no election.

Evidence. 1. The lack or absence of a "lawful excuse" for pointing the firearm at another person is an essential element of the offence (Allan v. R., [1972] 3 W.W.R. 79 (B.C. S.C.)).
2. *See also Evidence, item 1., under* **1**, *above.*

Informations

A.B., on or about the —— day of ——, 19——, at the —— of ——, in the said (territorial division), without lawful excuse, did point a firearm at C.D., to wit: (specify the particulars of the offence), contrary to s. 86(1) of the Criminal Code of Canada.

3. Careless use of firearm — Section 86(2)

Every one who — without lawful excuse — uses or carries or handles or ships or stores — any firearm or ammunition — in a careless manner or without reasonable precautions for the safety of other persons — is guilty of either an indictable offence or an offence punishable on summary conviction.

Limitation period. No proceedings in respect of offences that are declared to be punishable on summary conviction shall be instituted more than 6 months after the time when the subject matter of the proceedings arose (s. 786(2) and s. 785(1)).

Included offences. Attempts (s. 660 and s. 662(1)(b)).

Punishment. On indictment, imprisonment in the case of a first offence, for a term not exceeding 2 years, and in the case of a second or subsequent offence, for a term not exceeding 5 years (s. 86(2)(a)). On summary conviction, a fine not exceeding $2,000, or 6 months' imprisonment, or both (s. 86(2)(b) and s. 787(1)).

Release. Initial decision to release made by peace officer (s. 497).

Election. On indictment, accused may elect trial by judge and jury, judge alone, or provincial court judge (s. 536). On summary conviction, no election.

Evidence. 1. Inadvertent negligence provides the necessary mens rea for this offence. The proper standard in considering the evidence is what an ordinary prudent person would do in the circumstances (R. v. Wright, [1980] 4 W.W.R. 92 (Sask. Prov. Ct.)).
2. *See also Evidence, item 1., under* **1**, *above.*

Informations

A.B., on or about the —— day of ——, 19——, at the —— of ——, in the said (territorial division), without lawful excuse, did use [OR carry OR handle OR ship OR store] a firearm [OR ammunition] in a careless manner [OR without reasonable precautions for the safety of other persons], to wit: (specify the particulars of the offence), contrary to s. 86(2) of the Criminal Code of Canada.

4. Storing, displaying, handling or transporting firearm contrary to regulation — Section 86(3)

Every person who — stores or displays or handles or transports — any firearm — in a manner contrary to a regulation made under s. 116(1)(g) (regulation respecting the storage, display, handling and transportation of firearms) — is guilty of either an indictable offence or an offence punishable on summary conviction.

Limitation period. No proceedings in respect of offences that are declared to be punishable on summary conviction shall be instituted more than 6 months after the time when the subject matter of the proceedings arose (s. 786(2) and s. 785(1)).

Included offences. Attempts (s. 660 and s. 662(1)(b)).

Punishment. On indictment, imprisonment for a term not exceeding 2 years (s. 86(3)(a)). On summary conviction, a fine not exceeding $2,000, or 6 months' imprisonment, or both (s. 86(3)(b) and s. 787(1)).

Release. Initial decision to release made by peace officer (s. 497).

Election. On indictment, accused may elect trial by judge and jury, judge alone, or provincial court judge (s. 536). On summary conviction, no election.

Evidence. See Evidence, item 1, under **1**, *above.*

Informations

A.B., on or about the —— day of ——, 19——, at the —— of ——, in the said (territorial division), did store [OR display OR handle OR transport] a firearm in a manner contrary to a regulation made under s. 116(1)(g), to wit: (specify the particulars of the offence), contrary to s. 86(3) of the Criminal Code of Canada.

5. Transfer of firearm to person under 16 years — Section 93(1)

Every one who — gives or lends or transfers or delivers any firearm — to a person under the age of 16 years — who is not the holder of a permit under which he may lawfully possess the firearm — is guilty of either an indictable offence or an offence punishable on summary conviction.

Exceptions. This offence does not apply to a person lawfully in possession of a firearm who permits a person under the age of 16 years to use the firearm under his immediate supervision in the same manner in which he may lawfully use it (s. 93(2)).

Limitation period. No proceedings in respect of offences that are declared to be punishable on summary conviction shall be instituted more than 6 months after the time when the subject matter of the proceedings arose (s. 786(2) and s. 785(1)).

Included offences. Attempts (s. 660 and s. 662(1)(b)).

Punishment. On indictment, imprisonment for a term not exceeding 2 years (s. 93(1)(a)). On summary conviction, a fine not exceeding $2,000, or 6 months' imprisonment, or both (s. 93(1)(b) and s. 787(1)).

Release. Initial decision to release made by peace officer (s. 497).

Election. On indictment, accused may elect trial by judge and jury, judge alone, or provincial court judge (s. 536). On summary conviction, no election.

Evidence. See Evidence, item 1., under **1**, *above.*

Informations

A.B., on or about the —— day of ——, 19——, at the —— of ——, in the said (territorial division), did give [OR lend OR transfer OR deliver] a firearm to C.D., a person under the age of 16 years, who was not the holder of a permit under which he might lawfully possess the firearm, to wit: (specify the particulars of the offence), contrary to s. 93 of the Criminal Code of Canada.

6. Wrongful delivery of firearms, ammunition or explosive substances — Section 94

Every one who — sells or barters or gives or lends or transfers or delivers — any firearm or any ammunition or explosive substance — to a person who he knows or has good reason to believe — either is of unsound mind — or is impaired by alcohol or drugs — or is a person who is prohibited by an order or by a condition of a probation order from possessing the firearm or ammunition or explosive substance so sold or bartered or given or lent or transferred or delivered — is guilty of either an indictable offence or an offence punishable on summary conviction.

Intent. Knowingly or with reason to believe.

Limitation period. No proceedings in respect of offences that are declared to be punishable on summary conviction shall be instituted more than 6 months after the time when the subject matter of the proceedings arose (s. 786(2) and s. 785(1)).

Included offences. Attempts (s. 660 and s. 662(1)(b)).

Punishment. On indictment, imprisonment for a term not exceeding 5 years (s. 94(a)). On summary conviction, a fine not exceeding $2,000, or 6 months' imprisonment, or both (s. 94(b) and s. 787(1)).

Release. Initial decision to release made by peace officer (s. 497).

Election. On indictment, accused may elect trial by judge and jury, judge alone, or provincial court judge (s. 536). On summary conviction, no election.

Evidence. See Evidence, item 1., under **1**, *above.*

Informations

A.B., on or about the —— day of ——, 19——, at the —— of ——, in the said (territorial division), did sell [OR barter OR give OR lend OR transfer OR deliver] a firearm [OR ammunition OR an explosive substance] to C.D., a person who he knew [OR had good reason to believe] was of unsound mind

[OR was impaired by alcohol (OR drugs)], to wit: (specify the particulars of the offence), contrary to s. 94 of the Criminal Code of Canada.

A.B., on or about the —— day of ——, 19——, at the —— of ——, in the said (territorial division), did sell [OR barter OR give OR lend OR transfer OR deliver] a firearm [OR ammunition OR an explosive substance] to C.D., a person who he knew [OR had good reason to believe] was a person prohibited by an order made pursuant to s. 100 of the Criminal Code [OR prohibited by an order made pursuant to s. 103 of the Criminal Code OR prohibited by a condition of a probation order] from possessing the firearm [OR ammunition OR explosive substance] so sold [OR bartered OR given OR lent OR transferred OR delivered], to wit: (specify the particulars of the offence), contrary to s. 94 of the Criminal Code of Canada.

7. Making automatic firearm — Section 95.1

Every person who — without lawful justification or excuse — alters a firearm so that it is capable of — or manufactures or assembles any firearm with intent to produce a firearm that is capable of — firing projectiles in rapid succession during one pressure of the trigger — is guilty of either an indictable offence or an offence punishable on summary conviction.

Intent. Intention to produce a firearm that is capable of firing projectiles in rapid succession during one pressure of the trigger.

Limitation period. No proceedings in respect of offences that are declared to be punishable on summary conviction shall be instituted more than 6 months after the time when the subject matter of the proceedings arose (s. 786(2) and s. 785(1)).

Included offences. Attempts (s. 660 and s. 662(1)(b)).

Punishment. On indictment, imprisonment for a term not exceeding 5 years (s. 95.1(a)). On summary conviction, a fine not exceeding $2,000, or 6 months' imprisonment, or both (s. 95.1(b) and s. 787(1)).

Release. Initial decision to release made by peace officer (s. 497).

Election. On indictment, accused may elect trial by judge and jury, judge alone, or provincial court judge (s. 536). On summary conviction, no election.

Evidence. *See Evidence, item 1., under* **1**, *above.*

Informations

A.B., on or about the —— day of ——, 19——, at the —— of ——, in the said (territorial division), without lawful justification or excuse, did alter [OR manufacture OR assembe] a firearm [OR any firearm] so that it was capable of [Or with intent to produce a firearm that was capable of] firing projectiles in rapid succession during one pressure of the trigger, to wit: (specify the particulars of the offence), contrary to s. 95.1 of the Criminal Code of Canada.

8. Acquisition of firearm without firearms acquisition certificate — Section 97(3)

Every one who — imports or otherwise acquires possession of — a firearm — in any manner whatever — while he is not the holder of a firearms acquisition certificate — is guilty of either an indictable offence or an offence punishable on summary conviction.

Exceptions. This offence does not apply to a person who acquires a firearm from a person who is either (a) lawfully in possession of a firearm and lends the firearm to a person for use by that person in his company and under his guidance or supervision in the same manner in which he may lawfully use it, or requires the firearm to hunt or trap in order to sustain himself or his family, or is the holder of a permit issued under s. 110(1), (6) or (7) permitting the lawful possession of the firearm, or (b) who returns a firearm to a person who lent it to him in circumstances described above or (c) who comes into possession of a firearm in the ordinary course of a business described in s. 105(1)(a) and who returns the firearm to the person from whom it is received, or (d) who is a peace officer, local registrar of firearms or firearms officer who returns a firearm to a person who had lawfully possessed the firearm and subsequently lost it or from whom it had been stolen (s. 97(4)(a) and s. 97(2)).

In addition, this offence does not apply to a person who (e) reacquires a firearm from a person to whom he lent the firearm, or (f) imports a firearm at a time when he is not a resident of Canada, or (g) comes into possession of a firearm by operation of law and thereafter, with reasonable despatch, lawfully disposes thereof or obtains a firearms acquisition certificate under which he could have lawfully acquired the firearm, or (f) comes into possession of a firearm in the ordinary course of a business described in s. 105(1)(a) or (b) or s. 105(2)(a) or (b), or (i) has lawfully possessed a firearm and has subsequently lost it, or from whom it had been stolen, and who then requires it from a peace officer, local registrar of firearms or firearms officer or finds it and so reports to a peace officer, local registrar of firearms or firearms officer (s. 97(4)).

Limitation period. No proceedings in respect of offences that are declared to be punishable on summary conviction shall be instituted more than 6 months after the time when the subject matter of the proceedings arose (s. 786(2) and s. 785(1)).

Included offences. Attempts (s. 660 and s. 662(1)(b)).

Punishment. On indictment, imprisonment for a term not exceeding 2 years (s. 97(3)(a)). On summary conviction, a fine not exceeding $2,000, or 6 months' imprisonment, or both (s. 97(3)(b) and s. 787(1)).

Release. Initial decision to release made by peace officer (s. 497).

Election. On indictment, accused may elect trial by judge and jury, judge alone, or provincial court judge (s. 536). On summary conviction, no election.

Evidence. *See Evidence, item 1., under* **1***, above.*

9. Delivery of firearm to person without firearms acquisition certificate — Section 97(1)

Every one who — sells or barters or give or lends or transfers or delivers — any firearm — to a person who — at the time of the sale or barter or giving or lending or transfer or delivery or, in the case of a mail-order sale, within a reasonable time prior thereto — does not produce a firearms acquisition certificate for inspection by the person selling or bartering or giving or lending or transferring or delivering the firearm — that that person has no reason to believe is invalid or was issued to a person other than the person so producing it — is guilty of either an indictable offence or an offence punishable on summary conviction.

Exceptions. This offence does not apply to a person who acquires a firearm from a person who is (a) lawfully in possession of a firearm who lends the firearm to a person for use by that person in his company and under his guidance or supervision in the same manner in which he may lawfully use it, or to a person who requires the firearm to hunt or trap in order to sustain himself or his family, or to a person who is the holder of a permit issued under s. 110(1), (6) or (7) permitting the lawful possession of the firearm, or (b) who returns a firearm to a person who lent it to him in circumstances described above, or (c) who comes into possession of a firearm in the ordinary course of a business described in s. 105(1)(a) and who returns the firearm to the person from whom it is received, or (d) who is a peace officer, local registrar of firearms or firearms officer who returns a firearm to a person who had lawfully possessed the firearm and subsequently lost it or from whom it had been stolen (s. 97(2)).

Limitation period. No proceedings in respect of offences that are declared to be punishable on summary conviction shall be instituted more than 6 months after the time when the subject matter of the proceedings arose (s. 786(2) and s. 785(1)).

Included offences. Attempts (s. 660 and s. 662(1)(b)).

Punishment. On indictment, liable to imprisonment for a term not exceeding 2 years (s. 97(1)(a)). On summary conviction, liable to a fine not exceeding $2,000, or 6 months' imprisonment, or both (s. 97(1)(b) and s. 787(1)).

Release. Initial decision to release made by peace officer (s. 497).

Election. On indictment, accused may elect trial by judge and jury, judge alone, or provincial court judge (s. 536). On summary conviction, no election.

Evidence. See Evidence, item 1., under **1**, *above.*

10. Possession of firearm, ammunition, explosive substance or firearms acquisition certificate while prohibited

Section 100(12)

Every one who — has in his possession — any firearm or any ammunition or explosive substance — while he is prohibited from doing so by any order made pursuant to s. 100 (prohibition order) — is guilty of either an indictable offence or an offence punishable on summary conviction.

Section 103(10)

Every person who — possesses — any firearm or any ammunition, explosive substance or firearms acquisition certificate — while prohibited from doing so by any order made pursuant to s. 103(6)(b) (prohibition order) — is guilty of either an indictable offence or an offence punishable on summary conviction.

Limitation period. No proceedings in respect of offences that are declared to be punishable on summary conviction shall be instituted

more than 6 months after the time when the subject matter of the proceedings arose (s. 786(2) and s. 785(1)).

Included offences. Attempts (s. 660 and s. 662(1)(b)).

Punishment. On indictment, imprisonment for a term not exceeding 10 years (s. 100(12)(a) and s. 103(10)(a)). On summary conviction, a fine not exceeding $2,000, or 6 months' imprisonment, or both (s. 100(12)(b), s. 103(10)(b) and s. 787(1)).

Release. Initial decision to release made by peace officer (s. 497).

Election. On indictment, accused may elect trial by judge and jury, judge alone, or provincial court judge (s. 536). On summary conviction, no election.

Evidence. *See Evidence, item 1., under* **1***, above.*

Informations

A.B., on or about the —— day of ——, 19——, at the —— of ——, in the said (territorial division), did have in his possession a firearm *[OR ammunition OR an explosive substance]* while he was prohibited from doing so by an order made pursuant to s. 100 of the Criminal Code, to wit: (specify the particulars of the offence), contrary to s. 100(12) of the Criminal Code of Canada.

A.B., on or about the —— day of ——, 19——, at the —— of ——, in the said (territorial division), did possess a firearm *[OR ammunition OR explosive substance OR firearms acquisition certificate]* while prohibited from doing so by an order made pursuant to s. 103(6)(b) of the Criminal Code of Canada, to wit: (specify the particulars of the offence), contrary to s. 103(10) of the Criminal Code of Canada.

11. Finding firearm — Section 104(1) and (5)

Every one who — on finding a firearm that he has reasonable grounds to believe has been lost or abandoned — does not with reasonable despatch — either deliver it to a peace officer or a local registrar of firearms or a firearms officer — or report to a peace officer or a local registrar of firearms or a firearms officer that he has found it — is guilty of either an indictable offence or an offence punishable on summary conviction.

Limitation period. No proceedings in respect of offences that are declared to be punishable on summary conviction shall be instituted more than 6 months after the time when the subject matter of the proceedings arose (s. 786(2) and s. 785(1)).

Included offences. Attempts (s. 660 and s. 662(1)(b)).

Punishment. On indictment, imprisonment for a term not exceeding 5 years (s. 104(5)(a)). On summary conviction, a fine not exceeding $2,000, or 6 months' imprisonment, or both (s. 104(5)(b) and s. 787(1)).

Release. Initial decision to release made by peace officer (s. 497).

Election. On indictment, accused may elect trial by judge and jury, judge alone, or provincial court judge (s. 536). On summary conviction, no election.

Evidence. See Evidence, item 1., under **1**, *above.*

Informations

A.B., on or about the —— day of ——, 19——, at the —— of ——, in the said (territorial division), did find a firearm that he had reasonable grounds to believe was lost or abandoned, and did not with reasonable despatch deliver it [OR report that he had found it] to a peace officer [OR a local registrar of firearms OR a firearms officer], to wit: (specify the particulars of the offence), contrary to s. 104(1) of the Criminal Code of Canada.

12. Tampering with serial number

Section 104(3)(a) and (5)

Every one who — without lawful excuse — alters or defaces or removes — a serial number on a firearm — is guilty of either an indictable offence or an offence punishable on summary conviction.

Section 104(3)(b) and (5)

Every one who — without lawful excuse — possesses a firearm — knowing that the serial number thereon has been altered or defaced or removed — is guilty of either an indictable offence or an offence punishable on summary conviction.

Intent. Knowingly (s. 104(3)(b)).

Exceptions. No person is guilty of an offence under s. 104(3)(b) by reason only of possessing a restricted weapon the serial number on which has been altered, defaced or removed, where that serial number has been replaced and a registration certificate has been issued in respect of the restricted weapon that mentions the new serial number (s. 104(3.1)).

Limitation period. No proceedings in respect of offences that are declared to be punishable on summary conviction shall be instituted more than 6 months after the time when the subject matter of the proceedings arose (s. 786(2) and s. 785(1)).

Included offences. Attempts (s. 660 and s. 662(1)(b)).

Punishment. On indictment, imprisonment for a period not exceeding 5 years (s. 104(5)(a)). On summary conviction, a fine not exceeding $2,000, or 6 months' imprisonment, or both (s. 104(5)(b) and s. 787(1)).

Release. Initial decision to release made by peace officer (s. 497).

Election. On indictment, accused may elect trial by judge and jury, judge alone, or provincial court judge (s. 536). On summary conviction, no election.

Evidence. 1. Evidence that a person possess a firearm the serial number of which has been wholly or partially obliterated otherwise than through normal use over time is, in the absence of any evidence to the contrary, proof that the person possesses the firearm knowing that the serial number thereon has been altered, defaced or removed (s. 104(4)).
2. For the purposes of this offence, the proof of lawful excuse lies upon the accused (s. 104(3)).
3. *See Evidence, item 1., under* **1**, *above.*

Informations

A.B., on or about the —— day of ——, 19——, at the —— of ——, in the said (territorial division), without lawful excuse, did alter [OR deface OR remove] a serial number on a firearm, to wit: (specify the particulars of the offence), contrary to s. 104(3)(a) of the Criminal Code of Canada.

A.B., on or about the —— day of ——, 19——, at the —— of ——, in the said (territorial division), without lawful excuse, did possess a firearm knowing that the serial number thereon had been altered [OR defaced OR removed], to wit: (specify the particulars of the offence), contrary to s. 104(3)(b) of the Criminal Code of Canada.

13. False statements to procure firearms acquisition certificate, registration certificate or permit — Section 113(1)

Every one who — for the purpose of procuring a firearms acquisition certificate or registration certificate or permit for himself or any other person — knowingly — either makes a statement orally

FIREARMS AND WEAPONS OFFENCES

or in writing that is false or misleading — or fails to disclose any information that is relevant to the application for the firearms acquisition certificate or registration certificate or permit — is guilty of either an indictable offence or an offence punishable on summary conviction.

Intent. Knowingly for purpose of procuring.

Limitation period. No proceedings in respect of offences that are declared to be punishable on summary conviction shall be instituted more than 6 months after the time when the subject matter of the proceedings arose (s. 786(2) and s. 785(1)).

Included offences. Attempts (s. 660 and s. 662(1)(b)).

Punishment. On indictment, imprisonment for a term not exceeding 2 years (s. 113(1)(a)). On summary conviction, a fine not exceeding $2,000, or 6 months' imprisonment, or both (s. 113(1)(b) and s. 787(1)).

Release. Initial decision to release made by peace officer (s. 497).

Election. On indictment, accused may elect trial by judge and jury, judge alone, or provincial court judge (s. 536). On summary conviction, no election.

Evidence. See Evidence, item 1., under **1**, *above.*

Sufficiency of count. No count that alleges false pretences, fraud or any attempt or conspiracy by fraudulent means is insufficient by reason only that it does not set out in detail the nature of the false pretence, fraud or fraudulent means (s. 586).

14. Tampering with firearms acquisition certificate, registration certificate or permit — Section 113(2)

Every one who — without lawful excuse — alters or defaces or falsifies — a firearms acquisition certificate or registration certificate or permit — is guilty of either an indictable offence or an offence punishable on summary conviction.

Limitation period. No proceedings in respect of offences that are declared to be punishable on summary conviction shall be instituted more than 6 months after the time when the subject matter of the proceedings arose (s. 786(2) and s. 785(1)).

Included offences. Attempts (s. 660 and s. 662(1)(b)).

Punishment. On indictment, imprisonment for a term not exceeding 2 years (s. 113(2)(a)). On summary conviction, a fine not exceeding $2,000, or 6 months' imprisonment, or both (s. 113(2)(b) and s. 787(1)).

Release. Initial decision to release made by peace officer (s. 497).

Election. On indictment, accused may elect trial by judge and jury, judge alone, or provincial court judge (s. 536). On summary conviction, no election.

Evidence. 1. For the purposes of this offence, the proof of lawful excuse lies upon the accused (s. 113(2)).
2. *See also Evidence, item 1., under* **1**, *above.*

Informations

A.B., on or about the —— day of ——, 19——, at the —— of ——, in the said (territorial division), without lawful excuse, did alter [OR deface OR falsify] a firearms acquisition certificate [OR a registration certificate OR permit], to wit: (specify the particulars of the offence), contrary to s. 113(2) of the Criminal Code of Canada.

15. Failure to comply with conditions or permit — Section 113(3)

Every one who — without lawful excuse — fails to comply — with any condition of a permit held by him — is guilty of either an indictable offence or an offence punishable on summary conviction.

Limitation period. No proceedings in respect of offences that are declared to be punishable on summary conviction shall be instituted more than 6 months after the time when the subject matter of the proceedings arose (s. 786(2) and s. 785(1)).

Included offences. Attempts (s. 660 and s. 662(1)(b)).

Punishment. On indictment, imprisonment for a term not exceeding 2 years (s. 113(3)(a)). On summary conviction, a fine not exceeding $2,000, or 6 months' imprisonment, or both (s. 113(3)(b) and s. 787(1)).

Release. Initial decision to release made by peace officer (s. 497).

Election. On indictment, accused may elect trial by judge and jury, judge alone, or provincial court judge (s. 536). On summary conviction, no election.

Evidence. *See Evidence, item 1., under* **1**, *above.*

Informations

A.B., on or about the —— day of ——, 19——, at the —— of ——, in the said (territorial division), without lawful excuse, did fail to comply with a condition of a permit held by him, to wit: *(specify the particulars of the offence)*, contrary to s. 113(3) of the Criminal Code of Canada.

16. Failure to deliver up revoked certificates or permits — Section 113(4)

Every one who — either being a holder of a registration certificate or permit or firearms acquisition certificate that is revoked in accordance with Part III — or being a person against whom an order prohibiting possession of any firearm or ammunition is made under s. 100 or s. 103(6)(b), or being prohibited by a condition of a probation order from having a firearm in his possession — fails to deliver up — the registration certificate or permit or firearms acquisition certificate or registration certificate or permit held by him — to a peace officer or a local registrar of firearms or a firearms officer — forthwith after the revocation or the making of the order or probation order — is guilty of an offence punishable on summary conviction.

Limitation period. No proceedings in respect of offences that are declared to be punishable on summary conviction shall be instituted more than 6 months after the time when the subject matter of the proceedings arose (s. 786(2) and s. 785(1)).

Included offences. Attempts (s. 660 and s. 662(1)(b)).

Punishment. A fine not exceeding $2,000, or 6 months' imprisonment, or both (s. 113(4) and s. 787(1)).

Release. Initial decision to release made by peace officer (s. 497).

Election. No election, summary conviction offence.

Evidence. See Evidence, item 1., under **1**, above.

17. Records of transactions in firearms

Duties — Section 105(1) and (1.1)

Every person who — operates a museum approved for the purposes of Part III by the Commissioner or the Attorney General of the province in which it is situated — or who carries on a business that includes the manufacturing or buying or selling at wholesale

or retail or storing or importing or repairing or modifying or taking in pawn of — firearms — shall keep records of transactions entered into by that person with respect to the firearms in a form prescribed by the Commissioner and containing such information as is prescribed by the Commissioner — and shall keep an inventory of all the firearms on hand at the location of the museum or at that person's place of business — and shall produce the records and inventory for inspection at the request of any police officer or police constable or any other person authorized by regulations made by the Governor in Council pursuant to s. 116(1)(a) or (b), as the case may be, to enter any place where the museum is located or any place where the business is carried on — and shall mail a copy of the records and inventory to the Commissioner or to any person authorized by s. 110(5) to issue a permit to carry on the business in accordance with any request in writing made by the Commissioner or person so authorized.

Statement of offence — Section 105(8)

Every one who — contravenes s. 105(1) — is guilty of either an indictable offence or an offence punishable on summary conviction.

Limitation period. No proceedings in respect of offences that are declared to be punishable on summary conviction shall be instituted more than 6 months after the time when the subject matter of the proceedings arose (s. 786(2) and s. 785(1)).

Included offences. Attempts (s. 660 and s. 662(1)(b)).

Punishment. On indictment, imprisonment for a term not exceeding 5 years (s. 105(8)(a)). On summary conviction, a fine not exceeding $2,000, or 6 months' imprisonment, or both (s. 105(8)(b) and s. 787(1)).

Release. Initial decision to release made by peace officer (s. 497).

Election. On indictment, accused may elect trial by judge and jury, judge alone, or provincial court judge (s. 536). On summary conviction, no election.

Evidence. See Evidence, item 1., under **1***, above.*

18. Business person reporting loss, destruction or theft

Duties — Section 105(2)

A person who — operates a museum approved for the purposes of Part III by the Commissioner or the Attorney General of the province in which it is situated — or who carries on either a business that includes the manufacturing or buying or selling at wholesale or retail or storing or importing or repairing or modifying or taking in pawn of firearms (s. 105(1)) — or who carries on a business that includes either the manufacturing or buying or selling at wholesale or retail or importing of ammunition or the transportation or shipping of firearms or ammunition — shall immediately report to a local registrar of firearms or a peace officer — any loss or destruction or theft of any firearm or ammunition — that occurs in the operation of the museum or in the course of the business.

Statement of offence — Section 105(8)

Every one who — contravenes s. 105(2) — is guilty of either an indictable offence or an offence punishable on summary conviction.

Limitation period. No proceedings in respect of offences that are declared to be punishable on summary conviction shall be instituted more than 6 months after the time when the subject matter of the proceedings arose (s. 786(2) and s. 785(1)).

Included offences. Attempts (s. 660 and s. 662(1)(b)).

Punishment. On indictment, imprisonment for a term not exceeding 5 years (s. 105(8)(a)). On summary conviction, a fine not exceeding $2,000, or 6 months' imprisonment, or both (s. 105(8)(b) and s. 787(1)).

Release. Initial decision to release made by peace officer (s. 497).

Election. On indictment, accused may elect trial by judge and jury, judge alone, or provincial court judge (s. 536). On summary conviction, no election.

Evidence. See Evidence, item 1., under **1**, above.

19. Carrying on business in firearms or ammunition without permit

Prohibition — Section 105(4)

No person shall — carry on — either a business that includes the manufacturing or buying or selling at wholesale or retail or storing or importing or repairing or modifying or taking in pawn of firearms (s. 105(1)) — or a business that includes the manufacturing or buying or selling at wholesale or retail or importing of ammunition (s. 105(2)(b)(i)) — unless he is the holder of a permit to carry on that business.

Statement of offence — Section 105(8)

Every one who — contravenes s. 105(4) — is guilty of either an indictable offence or an offence punishable on summary conviction.

Limitation period. No proceedings in respect of offences that are declared to be punishable on summary conviction shall be instituted more than 6 months after the time when the subject matter of the proceedings arose (s. 786(2) and s. 785(1)).

Included offences. Attempts (s. 660 and s. 662(1)(b)).

Punishment. On indictment, imprisonment for a term not exceeding 5 years (s. 105(8)(a)). On summary conviction, a fine not exceeding $2,000, or 6 months' imprisonment, or both (s. 105(8)(b) and s. 787(1)).

Release. Initial decision to release made by peace officer (s. 497).

Election. On indictment, accused may elect trial by judge and jury, judge alone, or provincial court judge (s. 536). On summary conviction, no election.

Evidence. See Evidence, item 1., under **1**, *above.*

20. Handling, storing, displaying, advertising or selling by mail order of firearms or ammunition

Prohibition — Section 105(6)

No person shall — either handle or store or display or advertise — any firearm or ammunition — in a manner that contravenes any regulation made pursuant to s. 116(1)(a) — or sell by mail-order any firearm or ammunition in a manner that contravenes any regulation made pursuant to s. 116(1)(c) — in the course of either — operating a museum approved for the purposes of Part III by the Commissioner or the Attorney General of the province in which it is situated — or of carrying on a business that includes the manufacturing or buying or selling at wholesale or retail or storing or importing or repairing or modifying or taking in pawn of firearms (s. 105(1)(a)) — or a business that includes the manufacturing or buying or selling at wholesale or retail or importing of ammunition (s. 105(2)(b)(i)).

Statement of offence — Section 105(8)

Every one who — contravenes s. 105(6) — is guilty of either an indictable offence or an offence punishable on summary conviction.

Limitation period. No proceedings in respect of offences that are declared to be punishable on summary conviction shall be instituted more than 6 months after the time when the subject matter of the proceedings arose (s. 786(2) and s. 785(1)).

Included offences. Attempts (s. 660 and s. 662(1)(b)).

Punishment. On indictment, imprisonment for a term not exceeding 5 years (s. 105(8)(a)). On summary conviction, a fine not exceeding $2,000, or 6 months' imprisonment, or both (s. 105(8)(b) and s. 787(1)).

Release. Initial decision to release made by peace officer (s. 497).

Election. On indictment, accused may elect trial by judge and jury, judge alone, or provincial court judge (s. 536). On summary conviction, no election.

Evidence. *See Evidence, item 1., under* **1**, *above.*

21. Handling, shipping, storage and transportation of firearms and ammunition

Prohibition — Section 105(7)

No person shall — knowingly — handle or ship or store or transport — any firearm or ammunition — in a manner that contravenes any regulation made by the Governor in Council relating to the secure handling and shipping and storage and transportation of firearms and ammunition (s. 116(1)(d)) — in the course of — operating a museum approved for the purposes of Part III by the Commissioner or the Attorney General of the province in which it is situated — or carrying on either a business that includes the manufacturing or buying or selling at wholesale or retail or storing or importing or repairing or modifying or taking in pawn of firearms (s. 105(1)) — or a business that includes either the manufacturing or buying or selling at wholesale or retail or importing of ammunition or the transportation or shipping of firearms or ammunition (s. 105(2)).

Statement of offence — Section 105(8)

Every one who — contravenes s. 105(7) — is guilty of either an indictable offence or an offence punishable on summary conviction.

Intent. Knowingly.

Limitation period. No proceedings in respect of offences that are declared to be punishable on summary conviction shall be instituted more than 6 months after the time when the subject matter of the proceedings arose (s. 786(2) and s. 785(1)).

Included offences. Attempts (s. 660 and s. 662(1)(b)).

Punishment. On indictment, imprisonment for a term not exceeding 5 years (s. 105(8)(a)). On summary conviction, a fine not exceeding $2,000, or 6 months' imprisonment, or both (s. 105(8)(b) and s. 787(1)).

Release. Initial decision to release made by peace officer (s. 497).

Election. On indictment, accused may elect trial by judge and jury, judge alone, or provincial court judge (s. 536). On summary conviction, no election.

Evidence. See Evidence, item 1., under **1***, above.*

22. Possession of weapon or imitation for dangerous purpose — Section 87

Every one who — carries or has in his possession — a weapon or imitation thereof — for a purpose dangerous to the public peace or for the purpose of committing an offence — is guilty of an indictable offence.

Intent. For purpose dangerous to public peace or of committing offence.

Included offences. Attempts (s. 660 and s. 662(1)(b)).

Punishment. Imprisonment for a term not exceeding 10 years (s. 87).

Release. Initial decision to release made by justice (s. 515(1)).

Election. Accused may elect trial by judge and jury, judge alone, or provincial court judge (s. 536).

Evidence. Where any question arises as to whether a person is or was the holder of a firearms acquisition certificate, registration certificate or permit, the onus is on the accused to prove that that person is or was the holder of the firearms acquisition certificate, registration certificate or permit (s. 115(1)).

In any proceedings, a document purporting to be a firearms acquisition certificate, registration certificate or permit is evidence of the statements contained therein (s. 115(2)).

FIREARMS AND WEAPONS OFFENCES

Informations

A.B., on or about the —— day of ——, 19——, at the —— of ——, in the said (territorial division), did carry [OR have in his possession] a weapon [OR an imitation of a weapon], for a purpose dangerous to the public peace [OR for the purpose of committing an offence], to wit: (specify the particulars of the offence), contrary to s. 87 of the Criminal Code of Canada.

23. Possession of weapon at public meeting — Section 88

Every one who — without lawful excuse — has a weapon in his possession — while he is attending or is on his way to attend a public meeting — is guilty of an offence punishable on summary conviction.

Limitation period. No proceedings in respect of offences that are declared to be punishable on summary conviction shall be instituted more than 6 months after the time when the subject matter of the proceedings arose (s. 786(2) and s. 785(1)).

Included offences. Attempts (s. 660 and s. 662(1)(b)).

Punishment. A fine not exceeding $2,000, or 6 months' imprisonment, or both (s. 88 and s. 787(1)).

Release. Initial decision to release made by peace officer (s. 497).

Election. No election, summary conviction offence.

Evidence. See Evidence under **22**, *above.*

Informations

A.B., on or about the —— day of ——, 19——, at the —— of ——, in the said (territorial division), without lawful excuse, did have a weapon in his possession while he was attending [OR while he was on his way to attend] a public meeting, to wit: (specify the particulars of the offence), contrary to s. 88 of the Criminal Code of Canada.

24. Carrying concealed weapon — Section 89

Every one who — carries a weapon — that is concealed — unless he is the holder of a permit under which he may lawfully so carry it — is guilty of either an indictable offence or an offence punishable on summary conviction.

Limitation period. No proceedings in respect of offences that are declared to be punishable on summary conviction shall be instituted

more than 6 months after the time when the subject matter of the proceedings arose (s. 786(2) and s. 785(1)).

Included offences. Attempts (s. 660 and s. 662(1)(b)).

Punishment. On indictment, imprisonment for a term not exceeding 5 years (s. 89). On summary conviction, a fine not exceeding $2,000, or 6 months' imprisonment, or both (s. 89 and s. 787(1)).

Release. Initial decision to release made by peace officer (s. 497).

Election. On indictment, accused may elect trial by judge and jury, judge alone, or provincial court judge (s. 536). On summary conviction, no election.

Evidence. See Evidence under **22**, *above.*

Informations

A.B., on or about the —— day of ——, 19——, at the —— of ——, in the said (territorial division), did carry a weapon concealed, without being the holder of a permit under which he might lawfully so carry it, to wit: (specify the particulars of the offence), contrary to s. 89 of the Criminal Code of Canada.

25. Possession of prohibited weapon — Section 90(1)

Every one who — has in his possession — a prohibited weapon — is guilty of either an indictable offence or an offence punishable on summary conviction.

Exceptions. 1. This offence does not apply to a person who comes into possession of a prohibited weapon by operation of law and thereafter, with reasonable despatch, lawfully disposes thereof (s. 90(3)).
2. This offence does not apply in a province with respect to any person designated by the Attorney General of the province as a person who belongs to a class of persons who require a prohibited weapon described in paragraph (c), (e) or (f) of the definition "prohibited weapon" in s. 84(1) or component or part thereof for a purpose that the Governor in Council prescribes by regulation to be an industrial purpose, or to any person who is under the direct and immediate supervision of such a person (s. 90(3.1)).
3. Notwithstanding anything in the Criminal Code, no person is guilty of this offence by reason only that the person possesses a prohibited weapon described in paragraph (f) of the definition "prohibited weapon" in s. 84(1) where, (a) that person has been authorized in

writing by the local registrar of firearms to be a person who may possess such a weapon for use in conjunction with a firearm that is suitable for use in shooting competitions designated by the Attorney General and is lawfully possessed by the person and where that person has complied with all conditions for the possession of that weapon that are prescribed by regulations or that are required by the local registrar of firearms in the particular circumstances and in the interests of the safety of the person or of any other person, or (b) that person is a person designated for the purposes of s. 95(3)(b) (carrying on a business described in s. 105(1)(b) and exporting or importing a prohibited weapon for an industrial purpose) (s. 90(3.2)).

4. Notwithstanding anything in the Criminal Code, (a) a member of the Canadian Forces or of the armed forces of a state other than Canada who is authorized under s. 14(1) of the Visiting Forces Act or who is attached or seconded to any of the Canadian Forces or, (b) a peace officer or a person in the public service of Canada or employed by the government of a province or, (c) an officer under the Immigration Act, the Customs Act or the Excise Act, is not guilty of this offence by reason only that, in the case of a person just described, the person is required to possess and possesses a restricted or prohibited weapon for the purpose of the person's duties or employment (s. 92(1)(a)-(c)).

5. Notwithstanding anything in the Criminal Code, a person who, under the authority of the Canadian Forces or a police force that includes peace officers or public officers, imports, manufactures, repairs, alters, modifies or sells weapons for or on behalf of the Canadian Forces or that police force, is not guilty of this offence by reason only that, in the case of a person just described, the person possesses a restricted or prohibited weapon in the course of business on behalf of the Canadian Forces or a police force (s. 92(1)(d)).

6. Notwithstanding anything in the Criminal Code, no operator of or person employed in a museum established by the Chief of the Defence Staff or a museum approved for the purposes of Part III by the Commissioner or the Attorney General of the province in which it is situated is guilty of this offence by reason only that the person possesses a restricted or prohibited weapon for the purpose of exhibiting that weapon or of storing, repairing, restoring, maintaining or transporting that weapon for the purpose of exhibiting it (s. 92(2)).

Limitation period. No proceedings in respect of offences that are declared to be punishable on summary conviction shall be instituted more than 6 months after the time when the subject matter of the proceedings arose (s. 786(2) and s. 785(1)).

Included offences. Attempts (s. 660 and s. 662(1)(b)).

Punishment. On indictment, imprisonment for a term not exceeding 10 years (s. 90(1)(a)). On summary conviction, a fine not exceeding $2,000, or 6 months' imprisonment, or both (s. 90(1)(b) and s. 787(1)).

Release. Initial decision to release made by peace officer (s. 497).

Election. On indictment, accused may elect trial by judge and jury, judge alone, or provincial court judge (s. 536). On summary conviction, no election.

Evidence. See Evidence under **22**, *above.*

Informations

    A.B., on or about the —— day of ——, 19——, at the —— of ——, in the said (territorial division), did have in his possession a prohibited weapon, to wit: (specify the particulars of the offence), contrary to s. 90(1) of the Criminal Code of Canada.

26. Prohibited weapon in motor vehicle — Section 90(2)

Every one who — is an occupant of a motor vehicle — in which he knows there is a prohibited weapon — is guilty of either an indictable offence or an offence punishable on summary conviction.

Exceptions. 1. This offence does not apply to an occupant of a motor vehicle in which there is a prohibited weapon in the possession of a person who obtained the weapon by operation of law and who thereafter, with reasonable despatch, lawfully disposes thereof (s. 90(3) and (4)).
2. *See also Exceptions, items 4. to 6., under* **25**, *above.*

Limitation period. No proceedings in respect of offences that are declared to be punishable on summary conviction shall be instituted more than 6 months after the time when the subject matter of the proceedings arose (s. 786(2) and s. 785(1)).

Included offences. Attempts (s. 660 and s. 662(1)(b)).

Punishment. On indictment, imprisonment for a term not exceeding 5 years (s. 90(2)(a)). On summary conviction, a fine not exceeding $2,000, or 6 months' imprisonment, or both (s. 90(2)(b) and s. 787(1)).

Release. Initial decision to release made by peace officer (s. 497).

FIREARMS AND WEAPONS OFFENCES 323

Election. On indictment, accused may elect trial by judge and jury, judge alone, or provincial court judge (s. 536). On summary conviction, no election.

Evidence. *See Evidence under* **22**, *above.*

Informations

A.B., on or about the —— day of ——, 19——, at the —— of ——, in the said (territorial division), was the occupant of a motor vehicle in which he knew there was a prohibited weapon, to wit: (specify the particulars of the offence), contrary to s. 90(2) of the Criminal Code of Canada.

27. Possession of unregistered restricted weapon — Section 91(1)

Every one who — has in his possession — a restricted weapon — for which he does not have a registration certificate — is guilty of either an indictable offence or an offence punishable on summary conviction.

Exceptions. 1. This offence does not apply to the following:
 (a) a person in respect of a restricted weapon, where a permit relating to the restricted weapon has been issued under s. 110(1), (2.1) or (3.1) and the person is not the person mentioned in the registration certificate issued in respect of that restricted weapon;
 (b) a person to whom a permit relating to a restricted weapon has been issued under s. 110(3) or (4) and who possesses the weapon for the purpose for which that permit was issued;
 (c) a person who has a restricted weapon in his possession while he is under the immediate supervision of a person who may lawfully possess the weapon for the purpose of using the weapon in a manner in which the supervising person may lawfully use it; or
 (d) a person who comes into possession of a restricted weapon by operation of law and thereafter, with reasonable despatch, lawfully disposes of it or obtains a registration certificate or permit under which he may lawfully possess it (s. 91(4)).
2. *See also Exceptions, items 4. to 6., under* **25**, *above.*

Limitation period. No proceedings in respect of offences that are declared to be punishable on summary conviction shall be instituted more than 6 months after the time when the subject matter of the proceedings arose (s. 786(2) and s. 785(1)).

Included offences. Attempts (s. 660 and s. 662(1)(b)).

Punishment. On indictment, imprisonment for a term not exceeding 5 years (s. 91(1)(a)). On summary conviction, a fine not exceeding $2,000, or 6 months' imprisonment, or both (s. 91(1)(b) and s. 787(1)).

Release. Initial decision to release made by peace officer (s. 497).

Election. On indictment, accused may elect trial by judge and jury, judge alone, or provincial court judge (s. 536). On summary conviction, no election.

Evidence. See Evidence under **22**, *above.*

Informations

A.B., on or about the —— day of ——, 19——, at the —— of ——, in the said (territorial division), did have in his possession a restricted weapon for which he did not have a registration certificate, to wit: (specify the particulars of the offence), contrary to s. 91(1) of the Criminal Code of Canada.

28. Possession of restricted weapon elsewhere than at place authorized — Section 91(2)

Every one who — has in his possession — a restricted weapon — elsewhere than at the place at which he is entitled to possess it (as indicated on the registration certificate issued therefor) — unless he is the holder of a permit under which he may lawfully so possess it — is guilty of either an indictable offence or an offence punishable on summary conviction.

Exceptions. 1. This offence does not apply to a person to whom a permit to possess a particular restricted weapon has been issued under s. 110(1) where the person is not the person mentioned in the registration certificate issued in respect of the restricted weapon, when the person to whom the permit has been issued possesses the restricted weapon at the place authorized by the permit (s. 91(4.1)).
2. *See also Exceptions, items 4. to 6., under* **25**, *above.*

Limitation period. No proceedings in respect of offences that are declared to be punishable on summary conviction shall be instituted more than 6 months after the time when the subject matter of the proceedings arose (s. 786(2) and s. 785(1)).

Included offences. Attempts (s. 660 and s. 662(1)(b)).

Punishment. On indictment, imprisonment for a term not exceeding 5 years (s. 91(2)(a)). On summary conviction, a fine not exceeding $2,000, or 6 months' imprisonment, or both (s. 91(2)(b) and s. 787(1)).

Release. Initial decision to release made by peace officer (s. 497).

Election. On indictment, accused may elect trial by judge and jury, judge alone, or provincial court judge (s. 536). On summary conviction, no election.

Evidence. See Evidence under **22**, *above.*

29. Restricted weapon in motor vehicle — Section 91(3)

Every one who — is an occupant of a motor vehicle — in which he knows there is a restricted weapon — unless some occupant of the motor vehicle is the holder of a permit under which he may lawfully have that weapon in his possession in the vehicle — or unless he establishes that he had reason to believe that some occupant of the motor vehicle was the holder of such permit — is guilty of either an indictable offence or an offence punishable on summary conviction.

Intent. Knowledge of weapon.

Exceptions. 1. This offence does not apply to an occupant of a motor vehicle in which there is a restricted weapon in the possession of a person, (a) in respect of a restricted weapon, where a permit relating to the restricted weapon has been issued under s. 110(1), (2.1) or (3.1) and the person is not the person mentioned in the registration certificate issued in respect of that restricted weapon, (b) to whom a permit relating to a restricted weapon has been issued under s. 110(3) or (4) and who possesses the weapon for the purpose for which that permit was issued, (c) who has a restricted weapon in his possession while he is under the immediate supervision of a person who may lawfully possess the weapon for the purpose of using the weapon in a manner in which the supervising person may lawfully use it, (d) who comes into possession of a restricted weapon by operation of law and thereafter, with reasonable despatch, lawfully disposes of it or obtains a registration certificate or permit under which he may lawfully possess it (s. 91(4) and (5)).
2. *See also Exceptions, items 4. to 6., under* **25**, *above.*

Limitation period. No proceedings in respect of offences that are declared to be punishable on summary conviction shall be instituted more than 6 months after the time when the subject matter of the proceedings arose (s. 786(2) and s. 785(1)).

Included offences. Attempts (s. 660 and s. 662(1)(b)).

Punishment. On indictment, imprisonment for a term not exceeding 5 years (s. 91(3)(a)). On summary conviction, a fine not exceeding $2,000, or 6 months' imprisonment, or both (s. 91(3)(b) and s. 787(1)).

Release. Initial decision to release made by peace officer (s. 497).

Election. On indictment, accused may elect trial by judge and jury, judge alone, or provincial court judge (s. 536). On summary conviction, no election.

Evidence. *See Evidence under* **22**, *above.*

30. Wrongful delivery of offensive weapons, ammunition or explosive substances — Section 94

Every one who — sells or barters or gives or lends or transfers or delivers — any offensive weapon or any ammunition or explosive substance — to a person who he knows or has good reason to believe — either is of unsound mind — or is impaired by alcohol or drugs — or is a person who is prohibited by an order or by a condition of a probation order from possessing the offensive weapon or ammunition or explosive substance so sold or bartered or given or lent or transferred or delivered — is guilty of either an indictable offence or an offence punishable on summary conviction.

Limitation period. No proceedings in respect of offences that are declared to be punishable on summary conviction shall be instituted more than 6 months after the time when the subject matter of the proceedings arose (s. 786(2) and s. 785(1)).

Included offences. Attempts (s. 660 and s. 662(1)(b)).

Punishment. On indictment, imprisonment for a term not exceeding 5 years (s. 94(a)). On summary conviction, a fine not exceeding $2,000, or 6 months' imprisonment, or both (s. 94(b) and s. 787(1)).

Release. Initial decision to release made by peace officer (s. 497).

Election. On indictment, accused may elect trial by judge and jury, judge alone, or provincial court judge (s. 536). On summary conviction, no election.

Evidence. *See Evidence under* **22**, *above.*

Informations

A.B., on or about the —— day of ——, 19——, at the —— of ——, in the said (territorial division), did sell [OR barter OR give OR lend OR transfer

OR deliver] an offensive weapon [OR ammunition OR an explosive substance] to C.D., a person who he knew [OR had good reason to believe] was of unsound mind [OR was impaired by alcohol (OR drugs)], to wit: (specify the particulars of the offence), contrary to s. 94 of the Criminal Code of Canada.

A.B., on or about the —— day of ——, 19——, at the —— of ——, in the said (territorial division), did sell [OR barter OR give OR lend OR transfer OR deliver] an offensive weapon [OR ammunition OR an explosive substance] to C.D., a person who he knew [OR had good reason to believe] was a person prohibited by an order made pursuant to s. 100 of the Criminal Code [OR prohibited by an order made pursuant to s. 103 of the Criminal Code OR prohibited by a condition of a probation order] from possessing the offensive weapon [OR ammunition OR explosive substance] so sold [OR bartered OR given OR lent OR transferred OR delivered], to wit: (specify the particulars of the offence), contrary to s. 94 of the Criminal Code of Canada.

31. Importing or delivering prohibited weapon or part of prohibited weapon — Section 95

Every one who — imports or exports or buys or sells or barters or gives or lends or transfers or delivers — either a prohibited weapon — or any component or part designed exclusively for use in the manufacture or assembly into a prohibited weapon — is guilty of either an indictable offence or an offence punishable on summary conviction.

Exceptions. 1. Notwithstanding s. 95(1), a person who carries on a business described in s. 105(1)(b) may export or import for a purpose that the Governor in Council prescribes by regulation, for the purposes of s. 90(3.1), to be an industrial purpose a prohibited weapon described in paragraph (c), (e) or (f) of the definition "prohibited weapon" in s. 84(1) or components or parts thereof, if that person does so under and in accordance with an export permit or an import permit, as the case may be, issued under the Export and Import Permits Act s. 95(2)). 2. Section 95(1) does not apply to a person who, (a) carries on a business referred to in s. 105(1)(a) and who, on behalf of a person described in s. 90(3.2), imports, buys, sells, barters, gives, lends, transfers or delivers a prohibited weapon described in paragraph (f) of the definition of that expressionn in s. 84(1), or (b) manufactures a prohibited weapon described in paragraph (f) of the definition of that expression in s. 84(1) for the purpose of exporting the prohibited weapon or of selling it in Canada to a person who may lawfully possess such a prohibited weapon, where the person who manufactures the prohibited weapon is designated for the purposes of s. 95(3) by the

Attorney General of the province in which the prohibited weapon is manufactured (s. 95(3)).

3. Notwithstanding s. 95(1), a person who carries on a business described in s. 105(1)(b) may transfer to a person designated by the Attorney General of a province pursuant to s. 90(3.1) a prohibited weapon described in paragraph (c), (e) or (f) of the definition "prohibited weapon" in s. 84(1) or components or parts thereof (s. 95(4)).

4. Notwithstanding s. 95(1), a person who is authorized in writing by a local registrar of firearms under s. 90(3.2)(a) may import or export a prohibited weapon described in paragraph (f) of the definition "prohibited weapon" in s. 84(1), and to which the authorization applies, for personal use in shooting competitions designated under s. 90(3.2)(a) (s. 95(5)).

5. A member of the Canadian Forces, or of the armed forces of a state other than Canada who is authorized under s. 14(a) of the Visiting Forces Act or who is attached or seconded to any of the Canadian Forces, or a peace officer or a person in the public service of Canada or employed by the government of a province, or an operator of or a person employed in a museum established by the Chief of the Defence Staff or a museum approved for the purposes of Part III by the Commissioner or the Attorney General of the province in which it is situated, is not guilty of this offence by reason only that the person imports or otherwise acquires possession in any manner of any weapon or component or part of a weapon in the course of the duties or employment of that person (s. 98(1)).

6. A person who, under the authority of the Canadian Armed Forces or a police force that includes peace officers or public officers, imports, manufactures, repairs, alters, modifies or sells weapons or components or parts of weapons for or on behalf of the Canadian Armed Forces or such a police force, is not guilty of an offence under the Criminal Code by reason only that that person so imports or manufactures weapons, or components or parts of weapons, or sells, barters, gives, lends, transfers or delivers weapons, or components or parts of weapons, to the Canadian Armed Forces or such a police force (s. 98(2)).

7. A person who, under the supervision of an operator of or a person employed in a museum established by the Chief of the Defence Staff or a museum approved for the purposes of Part III by the Commissioner or the Attorney General of the province in which it is situated, imports, buys, repairs, restores or maintains weapons or components or parts of weapons for or on behalf of the museum, is not guilty of this offence

FIREARMS AND WEAPONS OFFENCES

by reason only that that person so imports, buys, repairs, restores or maintains weapons or components or parts thereof or sells, barters, gives, lends, transfers or delivers weapons or components or parts thereof to the museum (s. 98(3)).

Limitation period. No proceedings in respect of offences that are declared to be punishable on summary conviction shall be instituted more than 6 months after the time when the subject matter of the proceedings arose (s. 786(2) and s. 785(1)).

Included offences. Attempts (s. 660 and s. 662(1)(b)).

Punishment. On indictment, imprisonment for a term not exceeding 10 years (s. 95(1)(a)). On summary conviction, a fine not exceeding $2,000, or 6 months' imprisonment, or both (s. 95(1)(b) and s. 787(1)).

Release. Initial decision to release made by peace officer (s. 497).

Election. On indictment, accused may elect trial by judge and jury, judge alone, or provincial court judge (s. 536). On summary conviction, no election.

Evidence. *See Evidence under* **22**, *above.*

Informations

A.B., on or about the —— day of ——, 19——, at the —— of ——, in the said (territorial division), did import [OR export OR buy OR sell OR barter OR give OR lend OR transfer OR deliver] a prohibited weapon [OR a component (OR a part) designed exclusively for use in the manufacture (OR assembly) into a prohibited weapon], to wit: (specify the particulars of the offence), contrary to s. 95 of the Criminal Code of Canada.

32. Delivery of restricted weapon to person without permit — Section 96(1)

Every one who — sells or barters or gives or lends or transfers or delivers — any restricted weapon — to a person who is not the holder of a permit authorizing him to possess that weapon — is guilty of either an indictable offence or an offence punishable on summary conviction.

Exceptions. 1. This offence does not apply to a person lawfully in possession of a restricted weapon who permits a person who is not the holder of a permit authorizing him to possess that weapon to use the weapon under his immediate supervision in the same manner in which he may lawfully use it (s. 96(2)).

2. *See also Exceptions, items 4. to 6., under* **31**, *above*.

Limitation period. No proceedings in respect of offences that are declared to be punishable on summary conviction shall be instituted more than 6 months after the time when the subject matter of the proceedings arose (s. 786(2) and s. 785(1)).

Included offences. Attempts (s. 660 and s. 662(1)(b)).

Punishment. On indictment, imprisonment for a term not exceeding 5 years (s. 96(1)(a)). On summary conviction, a fine not exceeding $2,000, or 6 months' imprisonment, or both (s. 96(1)(b) and s. 787(1)).

Release. Initial decision to release made by peace officer (s. 497).

Election. On indictment, accused may elect trial by judge and jury, judge alone, or provincial court judge (s. 536). On summary conviction, no election.

Evidence. *See Evidence under* **22**, *above*.

Informations

   A.B., on or about the —— day of ——, 19——, at the —— of ——, in the said (territorial division), did sell [OR barter OR give OR lend OR transfer OR deliver] a restricted weapon to C.D., a person who was not the holder of a permit authorizing him to possess that weapon, to wit: (specify the particulars of the offence), contrary to s. 96(1) of the Criminal Code of Canada.

33. Importation of restricted weapon by person without permit — Section 96(3)

Every one who — imports — any restricted weapon — when he is not the holder of a permit authorizing him to possess that weapon — is guilty of either an indictable offence or an offence punishable on summary conviction.

Exceptions. *See Exceptions, items 4. to 6., under* **31**, *above*.

Limitation period. No proceedings in respect of offences that are declared to be punishable on summary conviction shall be instituted more than 6 months after the time when the subject matter of the proceedings arose (s. 786(2) and s. 785(1)).

Included offences. Attempts (s. 660 and s. 662(1)(b)).

Punishment. On indictment, imprisonment for a term not exceeding 5 years (s. 96(3)(a)). On summary conviction, a fine not exceeding $2,000, or 6 months' imprisonment, or both (s. 96(3)(b) and s. 787(1)).

Release. Initial decision to release made by peace officer (s. 497).

Election. On indictment, accused may elect trial by judge and jury, judge alone, or provincial court judge (s. 536). On summary conviction, no election.

Evidence. *See Evidence under* **22**, *above.*

Informations

A.B., on or about the —— day of ——, 19——, at the —— of ——, in the said (territorial division), did import a restricted weapon when he was not the holder of a permit authorizing him to possess that weapon, to wit: (specify the particulars of the offence), contrary to s. 96(3) of the Criminal Code of Canada.

34. Possession of offensive weapon, ammunition, explosive substance or firearms acquisition certificate while prohibited — Section 103(10)

Every person who — possesses — any offensive weapon or any ammunition or explosive substance or firearms acquisition certificate — while prohibited from doing so by an order made pursuant to s. 103(6)(b) (prohibition order) — is guilty of either an indictable offence or an offence punishable on summary conviction.

Exceptions. *See Exceptions, items 4. to 6., under* **25**, *above.*

Limitation period. No proceedings in respect of offences that are declared to be punishable on summary conviction shall be instituted more than 6 months after the time when the subject matter of the proceedings arose (s. 786(2) and s. 785(1)).

Included offences. Attempts (s. 660 and s. 662(1)(b)).

Punishment. On indictment, imprisonment for a term not exceeding 10 years (s. 103(10)(a)). On summary conviction, a fine not exceeding $2,000, or 6 months' imprisonment, or both (s. 103(10)(b) and s. 787(1)).

Release. Initial decision to release made by peace officer (s. 497).

Election. On indictment, accused may elect trial by judge and jury, judge alone, or provincial court judge (s. 536). On summary conviction, no election.

Evidence. *See Evidence under* **22**, *above.*

Informations

A.B., on or about the —— day of ——, 19——, at the —— of ——, in the said (territorial division), did possess an offensive weapon [OR ammunition OR an explosive substance OR a firearms acquisition certificate] while prohibited from doing so by an order made pursuant to s. 103(6)(b) of the Criminal Code, to wit: (specify the particulars of the offence), contrary to s. 103(10) of the Criminal Code of Canada.

35. Finding weapon — Section 104(1) and (5)

Every one who — on finding a prohibited weapon or restricted weapon that he has reasonable grounds to believe has been lost or abandoned — does not with reasonable despatch — either deliver it to a peace officer or a local registrar of firearms or a firearms officer — or report to a peace officer or a local registrar of firearms or a firearms officer that he has found it — is guilty of either an indictable offence or an offence punishable on summary conviction.

Limitation period. No proceedings in respect of offences that are declared to be punishable on summary conviction shall be instituted more than 6 months after the time when the subject matter of the proceedings arose (s. 786(2) and s. 785(1)).

Included offences. Attempts (s. 660 and s. 662(1)(b)).

Punishment. On indictment, imprisonment for a term not exceeding 5 years (s. 104(5)(a)). On summary conviction, a fine not exceeding $2,000, or 6 months' imprisonment, or both (s. 104(5)(b) and s. 787(1)).

Release. Initial decision to release made by peace officer (s. 497).

Election. On indictment, accused may elect trial by judge and jury, judge alone, or provincial court judge (s. 536). On summary conviction, no election.

Evidence. *See Evidence under* **22**, *above.*

Informations

A.B., on or about the —— day of ——, 19——, at the —— of ——, in the said (territorial division), did find a prohibited weapon [OR a restricted weapon

FIREARMS AND WEAPONS OFFENCES

that he had reasonable grounds to believe was lost or abandoned], and did not with reasonable despatch deliver it [OR report that he had found it] to a peace officer [OR a local registrar of firearms OR a firearms officer], to wit: (specify the particulars of the offence), contrary to s. 104(1) of the Criminal Code of Canada.

36. Losing or mislaying restricted weapon — Section 104(2) and (5)

Every one who — having lost or mislaid a restricted weapon for which he has a registration certificate or permit — does not report with reasonable despatch to a peace officer or a local registrar of firearms — that he has lost or mislaid the weapon — is guilty of either an indictable offence or an offence punishable on summary conviction.

Every one who — having had such a restricted weapon stolen from his possession — does not report with reasonable despatch to a peace officer or a local registrar of firearms — that the weapon has been stolen from him — is guilty of either an indictable offence or an offence punishable on summary conviction.

Limitation period. No proceedings in respect of offences that are declared to be punishable on summary conviction shall be instituted more than 6 months after the time when the subject matter of the proceedings arose (s. 786(2) and s. 785(1)).

Included offences. Attempts (s. 660 and s. 662(1)(b)).

Punishment. On indictment, imprisonment for a term not exceeding 5 years (s. 104(5)(a)). On summary conviction, a fine not exceeding $2,000, or 6 months' imprisonment, or both (s. 104(5)(b) and s. 787(1)).

Release. Initial decision to release made by peace officer (s. 497).

Election. On indictment, accused may elect trial by judge and jury, judge alone, or provincial court judge (s. 536). On summary conviction, no election.

Evidence. See Evidence under **22**, *above.*

Informations

A.B., on or about the —— day of ——, 19——, at the —— of ——, in the said (territorial division), having lost or mislaid a restricted weapon for which he had a registration certificate [OR permit], did not with reasonable despatch report to a peace officer [OR a local registrar of firearms] that he had lost or mislaid such weapon, to wit: (specify the particulars of the offence), contrary to s. 104(2) of the Criminal Code of Canada.

A.B., on or about the —— day of ——, 19——, at the —— of ——, in the said (territorial division), having had a restricted weapon for which he had a registration certificate [OR permit] stolen from his possession, did not with reasonable despatch report to a peace officer [OR a local registrar of firearms] that such a weapon had been stolen from him, to wit: (specify the particulars of the offence), contrary to s. 104(2) of the Criminal Code of Canada.

37. Records of transactions in restricted or prohibited weapons

Duties — Section 105(1) and (1.1)

Every person who — operates a museum approved for the purposes of Part III by the Commissioner or the Attorney General of the province in which it is situated — or who carries on a business that includes either — the manufacturing or buying or selling at wholesale or retail or storing or importing or repairing or modifying or taking in pawn of restricted weapons — or, in the case referred to in s. 95(2), the importing or buying or selling or transferring or delivering, at wholesale or retail, of prohibited weapons described in paragraph (f) of the definition "prohibited weapon" in s. 84(1) — or the manufactuing or importing or exporting, for a purpose that the Governor in Council prescribes by regulation, for the purposes of s. 90(3.1), to be an industrial purpose, of prohibited weapons described in paragraph (c), (e) or (f) of the definition "prohibited weapon" in s. 84(1) or components or parts thereof — shall keep records of transactions entered into by that person with respect to the restricted weapons or the prohibited weapons or the components or parts thereof, as the case may be, in a form prescribed by the Commissioner and containing such information as is prescribed by the Commissioner — and shall keep an inventory of all the restricted weapons or the prohibited weapons or the components or parts thereof, as the case may be, on hand at the location of the museum or at that person's place of business — and shall produce the records and inventory for inspection at the request of any police officer or police constable or any other person authorized by regulations made by the Governor in Council pursuant to s. 116(1)(a) or (b), as the case may be, to enter any place where the museum is located or any place where the business is carried on — and shall mail a copy of the records and inventory to the Commissioner or to any person authorized by s. 110(5) to issue a permit to carry on the business in accordance with any request in writing made by the Commissioner or person so authorized.

FIREARMS AND WEAPONS OFFENCES 335

Statement of offence — Section 105(8)

Every one who — contravenes s. 105(1) — is guilty of either an indictable offence or an offence punishable on summary conviction.

Limitation period. No proceedings in respect of offences that are declared to be punishable on summary conviction shall be instituted more than 6 months after the time when the subject matter of the proceedings arose (s. 786(2) and s. 785(1)).

Included offences. Attempts (s. 660 and s. 662(1)(b)).

Punishment. On indictment, imprisonment for a term not exceeding 5 years (s. 105(8)(a)). On summary conviction, a fine not exceeding $2,000, or 6 months' imprisonment, or both (s. 105(8)(b) and s. 787(1)).

Release. Initial decision to release made by peace officer (s. 497).

Election. On indictment, accused may elect trial by judge and jury, judge alone, or provincial court judge (s. 536). On summary conviction, no election.

Evidence. *See Evidence under* **22**, *above.*

38. Carrying on business in restricted weapons or ammunition without permit

Prohibition — Section 105(4)

No person shall — carry on — either a business that includes the manufacturing or buying or selling at wholesale or retail or storing or importing or repairing or modifying or taking in pawn of restricted weapons (s. 105(1)) — or a business that includes the manufacturing or buying or selling at wholesale or retail or importing of ammunition (s. 105(2)(b)(i)) — unless he is the holder of a permit to carry on that business.

Statement of offence — Section 105(8)

Every one who — contravenes s. 105(4) — is guilty of either an indictable offence or an offence punishable on summary conviction.

Limitation period. No proceedings in respect of offences that are declared to be punishable on summary conviction shall be instituted more than 6 months after the time when the subject matter of the proceedings arose (s. 786(2) and s. 785(1)).

Included offences. Attempts (s. 660 and s. 662(1)(b)).

Punishment. On indictment, imprisonment for a term not exceeding 5 years (s. 105(8)(a)). On summary conviction, a fine not exceeding $2,000, or 6 months' imprisonment, or both (s. 105(8)(b) and s. 787(1)).

Release. Initial decision to release made by peace officer (s. 497).

Election. On indictment, accused may elect trial by judge and jury, judge alone, or provincial court judge (s. 536). On summary conviction, no election.

Evidence. See Evidence under 22, above.

39. Business person reporting loss, destruction or theft

Duties — Section 105(2)

A person who — operates a museum approved for the purposes of Part III by the Commissioner or the Attorney General of the province in which it is situated — or who carries on a business that includes either — the manufacturing or buying or selling at wholesale or retail or storing or importing or repairing or modifying or taking in pawn of restricted weapons, or in the case of s. 95(2), the importing or buying or selling or transferring or delivering, at wholesale or retail, of prohibited weapons described in paragraph (f) of the definition "prohibited weapon" in s. 84(1) (s. 105(1)(a)) — or the manufacturing or importing or exporting, for a purpose that the Governor in Council prescribes by regulation, for the purposes of s. 90(3.1), to be an industrial purpose, of prohibited weapons described in paragraph (c), (e) or (f) of the definition "prohibited weapon" in s. 84(1) or components or parts thereof (s. 105(1)(b)) — or the manufacturing or buying or selling at wholesale or retail or importing of ammunition — or the transportation or shipping of prohibited or restricted weapons or ammunition — shall immediately report to a local registrar of firearms or a peace officer — any loss or destruction or theft of any restricted weapon or ammunition — or any loss or destruction or theft or transfer of any prohibited weapon or a component or part thereof — that occurs in the operation of the museum or in the course of the business.

Statement of offence — Section 105(8)

Every one who — contravenes s. 105(2) — is guilty of either an indictable offence or an offence punishable on summary conviction.

Limitation period. No proceedings in respect of offences that are declared to be punishable on summary conviction shall be instituted more than 6 months after the time when the subject matter of the proceedings arose (s. 786(2) and s. 785(1)).

Included offences. Attempts (s. 660 and s. 662(1)(b)).

Punishment. On indictment, imprisonment for a term not exceeding 5 years (s. 105(8)(a)). On summary conviction, a fine not exceeding $2,000, or 6 months' imprisonment, or both (s. 105(8)(b) and s. 787(1)).

Release. Initial decision to release made by peace officer (s. 497).

Election. On indictment, accused may elect trial by judge and jury, judge alone, or provincial court judge (s. 536). On summary conviction, no election.

Evidence. *See Evidence under* **22**, *above.*

40. Handling, storing, displaying, advertising or selling by mail order of restricted weapon or ammunition

Prohibition — Section 105(6)

No person shall — either handle or store or display or advertise — any restricted weapon or ammunition — in a manner that contravenes any regulation made pursuant to s. 116(1)(a) — or sell by mail-order any restricted weapon or ammunition in a manner that contravenes any regulation made pursuant to s. 116(1)(c) — in the course of operating a museum approved for the purposes of Part III by the Commissioner or the Attorney General of the province in which it is situated — or in the course of either — a business that includes the manufacturing or buying or selling at wholesale or retail or importing or repairing or modifying or taking in pawn of restricted weapons, or in the case referred to in s. 95(2), the importing or buying or selling or transferring or delivering, at wholesale or retail, of prohibited weapons described in paragraph (f) of the definition "prohibited weapon" in s. 84(1) (s. 105(1)(a)) — or a business that includes the manufacturing or importing or exporting, for a purpose that the Governor in Council prescribes by regulation, for the purpose of s. 90(3.1), to be an industrial purpose, of prohibited weapons described in paragraph (c), (e) or (f) of the definition "prohibited weapon" in s. 84(1) or components or parts thereof (s. 105(1)(b)) or a business that includes the manufacturing or buying or selling at wholesale or retail or importing of ammunition (s. 105(2)(b)(i)).

Statement of offence — Section 105(8)

Every one who — contravenes s. 105(6) — is guilty of either an indictable offence or an offence punishable on summary conviction.

Limitation period. No proceedings in respect of offences that are declared to be punishable on summary conviction shall be instituted more than 6 months after the time when the subject matter of the proceedings arose (s. 786(2) and s. 785(1)).

Included offences. Attempts (s. 660 and s. 662(1)(b)).

Punishment. On indictment, imprisonment for a term not exceeding 5 years (s. 105(8)(a)). On summary conviction, a fine not exceeding $2,000, or 6 months' imprisonment, or both (s. 105(8)(b) and s. 787(1)).

Release. Initial decision to release made by peace officer (s. 497).

Election. On indictment, accused may elect trial by judge and jury, judge alone, or provincial court judge (s. 536). On summary conviction, no election.

Evidence. See Evidence under **22**, above.

41. Handling or storing of prohibited weapon

Prohibition — Section 105(6.1)

No person shall — handle or store — any prohibited weapon or any component or part thereof — in a manner that contravenes any regulation made by the Governor in Council pursuant to s. 116(1)(a.1) — in the course of — a business that includes the manufacturing or importing or exporting, for a purpose that the Governor in Council prescribes by regulation, for the purposes of s. 90 (3.1), to be an industrial purpose, of prohibited weapons described in paragraph (c), (e) or (f) of the definition "prohibited weapon" in s. 84(1) or components or parts thereof (s. 105(1)(b)).

Statement of offence — Section 105(8)

Every one who — contravenes s. 105(6.1) — is guilty of either an indictable offence or an offence punishable on summary conviction.

Limitation period. No proceedings in respect of offences that are declared to be punishable on summary conviction shall be instituted

FIREARMS AND WEAPONS OFFENCES 339

more than 6 months after the time when the subject matter of the proceedings arose (s. 786(2) and s. 785(1)).

Included offences. Attempts (s. 660 and s. 662(1)(b)).

Punishment. On indictment, imprisonment for a term not exceeding 5 years (s. 105(8)(a)). On summary conviction, a fine not exceeding $2,000, or 6 months' imprisonment, or both (s. 105(8)(b) and s. 787(1)).

Release. Initial decision to release made by peace officer 9s. 497).

Election. On indictment, accused may elect trial by judge and jury, judge alone, or provincial court judge (s. 536). On summary conviction, no election.

Evidence. See Evidence under **22,** *above.*

42. Handling, shipping, storing and transportation of prohibited weapon

Prohibition — Section 105(7)

No person shall — knowingly — handle or ship or store or transport — any prohibited weapon referred to in s. 105(1)(b) or any component or part thereof — in a manner that contravenes any regulation made by the Governor in Council pursuant to s. 116(1)(d) — in the course of operating a museum approved for the purposes of Part III by the Commissioner or the Attorney General of the province in which it is situated (s. 105(1)) — or in the course of either — a business that includes, in the case referred to in s. 95(2), the importing or buying or selling or transferring or delivering, at wholesale or retail, of prohibited weapons described in paragraph (f) of the definition "prohibited weapon" in s. 84(1) (s. 105(1)(a)) — or a business that includes the manufacturing or importing or exporting, for a purpose that the Governor in Council prescribes by regulation, for the purposes of s. 90(3.1), to be an industrial purpose, of prohibited weapons described in paragraph (c), (e) or (f) of the definition "prohibited weapon" in s. 84(1) or components or parts thereof (s. 105(1)(b)).

Statement of offence — Section 105(8)   Every one who — contravenes s. 105(7) — is guilty of either an indictable offence or an offence punishable on summary conviction.

Intent. Knowingly.

Limitation period. No proceedings in respect of offences that are declared to be punishable on summary conviction shall be instituted more than 6 months after the time when the subject matter of the proceedings arose (s. 786(2) and s. 785(1)).

Included offences. Attempts (s. 660 and s. 662(1)(b)).

Punishment. On indictment, imprisonment for a term not exceeding 5 years (s. 105(8)(a)). On summary conviction, a fine not exceeding $2,000, or 6 months' imprisonment, or both (s. 105(8)(b) and s. 787(1)).

Release. Initial decision to release made by peace officer 9s. 497).

Election. On indictment, accused may elect trial by judge and jury, judge alone, or provincial court judge (s. 536). On summary conviction, no election.

Evidence. *See Evidence under* **22**, *above.*

FIXED PLATFORM. For the purposes of s. 78.1, "fixed platform" means an artificial island or a marine installation or structure that is permanently attached to the seabed for the purpose of exploration or exploitation of resources or for other economic purposes (s. 78.1(5)).

FLIGHT. For the purposes of ss. 2 "peace officer", 7, 76 and 77, "flight" means the act of flying or moving through the air. An aircraft shall be deemed to be in flight from the time when all external doors are closed following embarkation until the later of (a) the time at which any such door is opened for the purpose of disembarkation; and (b) where the aircraft makes a forced landing in circumstances in which the owner or operator thereof or a person acting on behalf of either of them is not in control of the aircraft, the time at which control of the aircraft is restored to the owner or operator thereof or a person acting on behalf of either of them (s. 7(8)).

FLOATER. A decomposing body recovered from water (Jaffe, A Guide to Pathological Evidence, 2nd ed.).

FONTANELLES. Soft spots between the skull bones of a fetus or infant. Normally the newborn infant has two fontanelles, an anterior which closes at the age of about 18 months, and a posterior which closes at 6 weeks (Jaffe, A Guide to Pathological Evidence, 2nd ed.).

FORCIBLE CONFINEMENT

Section 279(2)

Every one who — without lawful authority — confines or imprisons or forcibly seizes — another person — is guilty of an indictable offence.

Included offences. Attempts (s. 660 and s. 662(1)(b)).

Punishment. Imprisonment for a term not exceeding 10 years (s. 279(2)).

Release. Initial decision to release made by justice (s. 515(1)).

Election. Accused may elect trial by judge and jury, judge alone, or provincial court judge (s. 536).

Defences. The fact that the person in relation to whom the offence is alleged to have been committed did not resist is not a defence unless the accused proves that the failure to resist was not caused by threats, duress, force or exhibition of force (s. 279(3)).

Informations

A.B., on or about the —— day of ——, 19——, at the —— of ——, in the said (territorial division), did without lawful authority confine [OR imprison OR forcibly seize] C.D., to wit: (specify the particulars of the offence), contrary to s. 279(2) of the Criminal Code of Canada.

FORCIBLE ENTRY AND DETAINER

1. *Committing forcible entry*	2. *Committing forcible detainer*

1. Committing forcible entry

Definition of offence — Section 72(1)

Every one who — enters real property — that is in the actual and peaceable possession of another — in a manner that is likely to cause a breach of the peace or reasonable apprehension of a breach of the peace — commits forcible entry.

Statement of offence — Section 73

Every one who — commits forcible entry — is guilty of either an indictable offence or an offence punishable on summary conviction.

FORCIBLE ENTRY AND DETAINER

Limitation period. No proceedings in respect of offences that are declared to be punishable on summary conviction shall be instituted more than 6 months after the time when the subject matter of the proceedings arose (s. 786(2) and s. 785(1)).

Included offences. Attempts (s. 660 and s. 662(1)(b)).

Punishment. On indictment, imprisonment for a term not exceeding 2 years (s. 73(a)). On summary conviction, a fine not exceeding $2,000 or 6 months' imprisonment, or both (s. 73(b) and s. 787(1)).

Release. Initial decision to release made by peace officer (s. 497).

Election. On indictment, accused may elect trial by judge and jury, judge alone, or provincial court judge (s. 536). On summary conviction, no election.

Evidence. 1. For these purposes, it is immaterial whether or not a person is entitled to enter the real property or whether or not that person has any intention of taking possession of the real property (s. 72(1.1)).
2. The question whether a person is in actual and peaceable possession is a question of law (s. 72(3)).
3. To constitute the crime of forcible entry, actual violence is not necessary. Violence or threatened violence upon the occupant is sufficient.

Informations

A.B., on or about the —— day of ——, 19——, at the —— of ——, in the said (territorial division), did commit forcible entry, to wit: (specify the particulars of the offence), contrary to s. 73 of the Criminal Code of Canada.

2. Committing forcible detainer

Definition of offence — Section 72(2)

Every one who — being in actual possession of real property without colour of right — detains the property — in a manner that is likely to cause a breach of the peace or reasonable apprehension of a breach of the peace — against a person who is entitled by law to possession commits forcible detainer.

Statement of offence — Section 73

Every one who — commits forcible detainer — is guilty of either an indictable offence or an offence punishable on summary conviction.

Limitation period. No proceedings in respect of offences that are declared to be punishable on summary conviction shall be instituted more than 6 months after the time when the subject matter of the proceedings arose (s. 786(2) and s. 785(1)).

Included offences. Attempts (s. 660 and s. 662(1)(b)).

Punishment. On indictment, imprisonment for a term not exceeding 2 years (s. 73(a)). On summary conviction, a fine not exceeding $2,000, or 6 months' imprisonment, or both (s. 73(b) and s. 787(1)).

Release. Initial decision to release made by peace officer (s. 497).

Election. On indictment, accused may elect trial by judge and jury, judge alone, or provincial court judge (s. 536). On summary conviction, no election.

Evidence. See Evidence, item 2., under **1**, *above.*

Informations

A.B., on or about the —— day of ——, 19——, at the —— of ——, in the said (territorial division), did commit forcible detainer, to wit: (specify the particulars of the offence), contrary to s. 73 of the Criminal Code of Canada.

FORENSIC. "Applied to the law" (Jaffe, A Guide to Pathological Evidence, 2nd ed.).

Forensic medicine. Those parts of medical knowledge which are applied to legal problems (Jaffe, A Guide to Pathological Evidence, 2nd ed.).

FORGERY AND RELATED OFFENCES

1. *Forgery*
2. *Uttering forged document*
3. *Exchequer bill paper, revenue paper and bank note paper*
4. *Instrument, writing or material adapted and intended to be used in forgery*
5. *Seal of public body or authority*
6. *Counterfeit proclamation, order, regulation or appointment*
7. *Drawing or using documents without authority*
8. *Obtaining anything by instrument based on forged document*
9. *Counterfeiting stamp*
10. *Counterfeiting mark*

11. *Damaging documents*
12. *False certified copies*
13. *False certificate or declaration*
14. *Sufficiency of count*

See also CURRENCY OFFENCES and TELECOMMUNICATION OFFENCES.

1. Forgery

Definition of offence — Section 366(1)

Every one who — makes a false document, knowing it to be false — with intent — either that it should in any way be used or acted upon as genuine, to the prejudice of any one, whether within Canada or not — or that a person should be induced, by the belief that it is genuine, to do or to refrain from doing anything, whether within Canada or not — commits forgery.

Making a false document includes

(a) altering a genuine document in any material part, or
(b) making a material addition to a genuine document or adding to it a false date or attestation or seal or other thing that is material, or
(c) making a material alteration in a genuine document by erasure or obliteration or removal or in any other way (s. 366(2)).

Statement of offence — Section 367(1)

Every one who — commits forgery — is guilty of an indictable offence.

Included offences. Attempts (s. 660 and s. 662(1)(b)).

Punishment. Imprisonment for a term not exceeding 14 years (s. 367(1)).

Release. Initial decision to release made by justice (s. 515(1)).

Election. Accused may elect trial by judge and jury, judge alone, or provincial court judge (s. 536).

Evidence. 1. Forgery is complete as soon as a document is made with the knowledge and intent that it should in any way be used or acted upon as genuine, to the prejudice of any one whether within Canada or not, or that a person should be induced, by the belief that it is genuine, to do or to refrain from doing anything, whether within Canada or not, notwithstanding that the person who makes it does not intend that any particular person should use or act on it as genuine or be

induced, by the belief that it is genuine, to do or refrain from doing anything (s. 366(3)).
2. Forgery is complete notwithstanding that the false document is incomplete or does not purport to be a document that is binding in law, if it is such as to indicate that it was intended to be acted on as genuine (s. 366(4)).
3. No person shall be convicted of such an offence on the evidence of only one witness unless the evidence of that witness is corroborated in a material particular by evidence that implicates the accused (s. 367(2)).
4. *See also* **14**, *below.*

Informations

A.B., on or about the —— day of ——, 19——, at the —— of ——, in the said (territorial division), did make a false document, knowing it to be false, with intent that it should be acted upon [OR used] as genuine, to the prejudice of C.D., and did thereby commit forgery, to wit: (specify the particulars of the offence), contrary to s. 366(1)(a) of the Criminal Code of Canada.

2. Uttering forged document — Section 368(1)

Every one who — knowing that a document is forged — either uses or deals with or acts upon it — or causes or attempts to cause any person to use or deal with or act upon it — as if the document were genuine — is guilty of an indictable offence.

Included offences. Attempts (s. 660 and s. 662(1)(b)).

Punishment. Imprisonment for a term not exceeding 14 years (s. 368(1)).

Release. Initial decision to release made by justice (s. 515(1)).

Election. Accused may elect trial by judge and jury, judge alone, or provincial court judge (s. 536).

Definitions. See UTTER.

Evidence. 1. For these purposes, the place where a document was forged is not material (s. 368(2)).
2. The requirement of corroboration that applies to the offence of forgery does not apply to the offence of uttering.
3. It is not necessary to prove the intent with which the document was forged in order to sustain a charge of uttering.
4. *See also* **14**, *below.*

Informations

A.B., on or about the —— day of ——, 19——, at the —— of ——, in the said (territorial division), knowing that a document was forged, did use it [OR deal with it OR act upon it OR cause C.D. (OR attempt to cause C.D.) to use it (OR deal with it OR act upon it)] as if it were genuine, to wit: (specify the particulars of the offence including a description of the document), contrary to s. 368(1) of the Criminal Code of Canada.

3. Exchequer bill paper, revenue paper and bank note paper — Section 369(a)

Every one who — without lawful authority or excuse — makes or uses or knowingly has in his possession — either any exchequer bill paper or revenue paper or paper that is used to make bank notes — or any paper that is intended to resemble such paper — is guilty of an indictable offence.

Included offences. Attempts (s. 660 and s. 662(1)(b)).

Punishment. Imprisonment for a term not exceeding 14 years (s. 369).

Release. Initial decision to release made by justice (s. 515(1)).

Election. Accused may elect trial by judge and jury, judge alone, or provincial court judge (s. 536).

Evidence. For the purposes of this offence, the proof of lawful excuse lies on the accused (s. 369).

4. Instrument, writing or material adapted and intended to be used in forgery — Section 369(b)

Every one who — without lawful authority or excuse — makes or offers or disposes of or knowingly has in his possession — any plate or die or machinery or instrument or other writing or material — that is adapted and intended to be used to commit forgery — is guilty of an indictable offence.

Included offences. Attempts (s. 660 and s. 662(1)(b)).

Punishment. Imprisonment for a term not exceeding 14 years (s. 369).

Release. Initial decision to release made by justice (s. 515(1)).

Election. Accused may elect trial by judge and jury, judge alone, or provincial court judge (s. 536).

Evidence. For the purposes of this offence, the proof of lawful excuse lies on the accused (s. 369).

5. Seal of public body or authority — Section 369(c)

Every one who — without lawful authority or excuse — makes or reproduces or uses — a public seal of Canada or of a province — or the seal of a public body or authority in Canada, or of a court of law — is guilty of an indictable offence.

Included offences. Attempts (s. 660 and s. 662(1)(b)).

Punishment. Imprisonment for a term not exceeding 14 years (s. 369).

Release. Initial decision to release made by justice (s. 515(1)).

Election. Accused may elect trial by judge and jury, judge alone, or provincial court judge (s. 536).

Evidence. For the purposes of this offence, the proof of lawful excuse lies on the accused (s. 369).

6. Counterfeit proclamation, order, regulation or appointment — Section 370

Every one who — knowingly — prints a proclamation or order or regulation or appointment, or notice thereof — and causes it falsely to purport to have been printed by the Queen's Printer for Canada, or the Queen's Printer for a province — is guilty of an indictable offence.

Every one who — knowingly — tenders in evidence a copy of a proclamation or order or regulation or appointment — that falsely purports to have been printed by the Queen's Printer for Canada or the Queen's Printer for a province — is guilty of an indictable offence.

Intent. Knowingly.

Included offences. Attempts (s. 660 and s. 662(1)(b)).

Punishment. Imprisonment for a term not exceeding 5 years (s. 370).

Release. Initial decision to release made by officer in charge or justice (s. 498).

Election. Accused may elect trial by judge and jury, judge alone, or provincial court judge (s. 536).

Evidence. See **14**, *below*.

7. Drawing or using documents without authority

Section 374(a)

Every one who — with intent to defraud — and without lawful authority — makes or executes or draws or signs or accepts or endorses a document — in the name or on the account of another person — by procuration or otherwise — is guilty of an indictable offence.

Section 374(b)

Every one who — makes use of or utters a document — knowing that it has been made or executed or signed or accepted or endorsed — with intent to defraud — and without lawful authority — in the name or on the account of another person — by procuration or otherwise — is guilty of an indictable offence.

Intent. Intention to defraud.

Included offences. Attempts (s. 660 and s. 662(1)(b)).

Punishment. Imprisonment for a term not exceeding 14 years (s. 374).

Release. Initial decision to release made by justice (s. 515(1)).

Election. Accused may elect trial by judge and jury, judge alone, or provincial court judge (s. 536).

Evidence. See **14**, *below*.

8. Obtaining anything by instrument based on forged document — Section 375

Every one who — either demands or receives or obtains anything — or causes or procures anything to be delivered or paid to any person — under or on or by virtue of any instrument issued under the authority of law — knowing that it is based on a forged document — is guilty of an indictable offence.

Intent. Knowledge of forged document.

Included offences. Attempts (s. 660 and s. 662(1)(b)).

Punishment. Imprisonment for a term not exceeding 14 years (s. 375).

Release. Initial decision to release made by justice (s. 515(1)).

Election. Accused may elect trial by judge and jury, judge alone, or provincial court judge (s. 536).

Evidence. *See* **14**, *below.*

9. Counterfeiting stamp

Section 376(1)(a)

Every one who — fraudulently — uses or mutilates of affixes or removes or counterfeits — a stamp or part thereof — is guilty of an indictable offence.

Section 376(1)(b)

Every one who — knowingly — and without lawful excuse — has in his possession — either a counterfeit stamp or a stamp that has been fraudulently mutilated — or anything bearing a stamp of which a part has been fraudulently erased or removed or concealed — is guilty of an indictable offence.

Section 376(1)(c)

Every one who — without lawful excuse — makes or knowingly has in his possession — a die or instrument — that is capable of making the impression of a stamp or part thereof — is guilty of an indictable offence.

Intent. Fraudulently (s. 376(1)(a)); knowingly (s. 376(1)(b) and (c)).

Included offences. Attempts (s. 660 and s. 662(1)(b)).

Punishment. Imprisonment for a term not exceeding 14 years (s. 376(1)).

Release. Initial decision to release made by justice (s. 515(1)).

Election. Accused may elect trial by judge and jury, judge alone, or provincial court judge (s. 536).

Definitions. *See* STAMP.

Evidence. 1. For the purposes of this offence, the proof of lawful excuse lies on the accused (s. 376).
2. *See also* **14**, *below.*

10. Counterfeiting mark — Section 376(2)

Every one who — without lawful authority — either makes a mark — or sells or exposes for sale or has in his possession a

counterfeit mark — or affixes a mark to anything that is required by law to be marked or branded or sealed or wrapped other than the thing to which the mark was originally affixed or was intended to be affixed — or affixes a counterfeit mark to anything that is required by law to be marked or branded or sealed or wrapped — is guilty of an indictable offence.

Included offences. Attempts (s. 660 and s. 662(1)(b)).

Punishment. Imprisonment for a term not exceeding 14 years (s. 376(2)).

Release. Initial decision to release made by justice (s. 515(1)).

Election. Accused may elect trial by judge and jury, judge alone, or provincial court judge (s. 536).

Definitions. See MARK.

Evidence. See **14**, *below.*

11. Damaging documents

Section 377(1)(a)

Every one who — unlawfully — destroys or defaces or injures — a register or any part of a register of birth or baptism or marriages or deaths or burials — that is required or authorized by law to be kept in Canada — or a copy or any part of a copy of such a register — that is required by law to be transmitted to a registrar or other officer — is guilty of an indictable offence.

Section 377(1)(b)

Every one who — unlawfully — inserts or causes to be inserted in such a register or copy — an entry that he knows is false — of any matter relating to a birth or baptism or marriage or death or burial — or erases any material part from that register or copy — is guilty of an indictable offence.

Section 377(1)(c)

Every one who — unlawfully — destroys or damages or obliterates an election document — or causes an election document to be destroyed or damaged or obliterated — is guilty of an indictable offence.

Section 377(1)(d)

Every one who — unlawfully — makes or causes to be made — an erasure or alteration or interlineation — in or on an election document — is guilty of an indictable offence.

Intent. Knowledge of false entry (s. 377(1)(b)).

Included offences. Attempts (s. 660 and s. 662(1)(b)).

Punishment. Imprisonment for a term not exceeding 5 years (s. 377(1)).

Release. Initial decision to release made by officer in charge or justice (s. 498).

Election. Accused may elect trial by judge and jury, judge alone, or provincial court judge (s. 536).

Definitions. See ELECTION DOCUMENT.

12. False certified copies

Section 378(a)

Every one who — being authorized or required by law to make or issue a certified copy of or extract from or certificate in respect of a register or record or document — knowingly — makes or issues — a false certified copy or extract or certificate — is guilty of an indictable offence.

Section 378(b)

Every one who — not being authorized or required by law to make or issue a certified copy of or extract from or certificate in respect of a register or record or document — fraudulently — makes or issues a copy or extract or certificate — that purports to be certified as authorized or required by law — is guilty of an indictable offence.

Intent. Knowingly (s. 378(a)); fraudulently (s. 378(b)).

Included offences. Attempts (s. 660 and s. 662(1)(b)).

Punishment. Imprisonment for a term not exceeding 5 years (s. 378).

Release. Initial decision to release made by officer in charge or justice (s. 498).

Election. Accused may elect trial by judge and jury, judge alone, or provincial court judge (s. 536).

Evidence. See **14**, *below.*

13. False certificate or declaration — Section 378(c)

Every one who — being authorized or required by law to make a certificate or declaration concerning any particular required for the purpose of making entries in a register or record or document — knowingly and falsely — makes the certificate or declaration — is guilty of an indictable offence.

Intent. Knowingly and falsely.

Included offences. Attempts (s. 660 and s. 662(1)(b)).

Punishment. Imprisonment for a term not exceeding 5 years (s. 378).

Release. Initial decision to release made by officer in charge or justice (s. 498).

Election. Accused may elect trial by judge and jury, judge alone, or provincial court judge (s. 536).

Evidence. See **14**, *below.*

14. Sufficiency of count

No count that alleges false pretences, fraud or any attempt or conspiracy by fraudulent means is insufficient by reason only that it does not set out in detail the nature of the false pretence, fraud or fraudulent means (s. 586).

FORM OF MARRIAGE. For the purposes of Part VIII of the Criminal Code (Offences Against the Person and Reputation), "form of marriage" includes a ceremony of marriage that is recognized as valid either (a) by the law of the place where it was celebrated, or (b) by the law of the place where an accused is tried, notwithstanding that it is not recognized as valid by the law of the place where it was celebrated (s. 214).

FORTHWITH. Not instantly, but as soon as is reasonably possible or practicable under all the circumstances (R. v. Cunningham (1979), 49 C.C.C. (2d) 390 (Man. Co. Ct.)).

FORUM. Court (Latin). *Forum (non) conveniens.* (In)convenient forum (Latin).

FRAUD

1. *Fraud*
2. *Frauds affecting public market price*
3. *Using mails to defraud*
4. *Fraudulent manipulation of stock exchange transactions*
5. *Gaming in stocks or merchandise*
6. *Broker reducing stock by selling for his own account*
7. *Fraudulent concealment of title documents*
8. *Fraudulent registration of title*
9. *Fraudulent sale of real property*
10. *Misleading receipt*
11. *Fraudulent disposal of goods on which money advanced*
12. *Fraudulent receipts under Bank Act*
13. *Disposal of property to defraud creditors*
14. *Fraud in relation to fares*
15. *Fraudulently obtaining transportation*
16. *Fraud in relation to minerals*
17. *Fraud in relation to mines*
18. *Sufficiency of count*

1. Fraud — Section 380(1)

Every one who — by deceit or falsehood or other fraudulent means — whether or not it is a false pretence within the meaning of the Criminal Code — defrauds the public or any person — whether ascertained or not — of any property or money or valuable security — is guilty of either an indictable offence or an offence punishable on summary conviction.

Where the subject matter of the fraud is a testamentary instrument or where the value thereof exceeds $1,000, the person is guilty of an indictable offence.

Where the value of the subject matter of the offence does not exceed $1,000, the person is guilty of either an indictable offence or an offence punishable on summary conviction.

Limitation period. No proceedings in respect of offences that are declared to be punishable on summary conviction shall be instituted more than 6 months after the time when the subject matter of the proceedings arose (s. 786(2) and s. 785(1)).

Included offences. Attempts (s. 660 and s. 662(1)(b)).

Punishment. On indictment, where the subject matter of the fraud is a testamentary instrument or where the value thereof exceeds $1,000, imprisonment for a term not exceeding 10 years (s. 380(1)(a)).

Where the value of the property of which the public or any person is defrauded does not exceed $1,000, liable on indictment to imprisonment for a term not exceeding 2 years, and on summary conviction, to a fine not exceeding $2,000, or 6 months' imprisonment, or both (s. 380(1)(b) and s. 787(1)).

Release. Where the subject matter of the fraud is a testamentary instrument or where the value thereof exceeds $1,000, initial decision to release made by justice (s. 515(1)). Where the value of the subject matter of the offence does not exceed $1,000, the initial decision to release made by peace officer (s. 497).

Election. On indictment, where the subject matter of the fraud is a testamentary instrument or where the value thereof exceeds $1,000, accused may elect trial by judge and jury, judge alone, or provincial court judge (s. 536). Where the value of the subject matter of the offence does not exced $1,000, no election, absolute jurisdiction of provincial court judge (s. 553). On summary conviction, no election.

Evidence. 1. To defraud is to deprive by deceit: it is by deceit to induce a man to act to his injury. More tersely it may be put, that to deceive is by falsehood to induce a state of mind; to defraud is by deceit to induce a course of action.
2. Economic loss does not have to be proven.
3. The fraudulent means need not amount to a false pretence. By its very terms, this offence is broader than the offence of obtaining by false pretences.
4. *See also* **18**, *below.*

Informations

A.B., on or about the —— day of ——, 19——, at the —— of ——, in the said (territorial division), by deceit [OR by falsehood OR by fraudulent means], did defraud the public [OR C.D.] of property [OR of money OR of a valuable security], to wit: (specify the particulars of the offence), contrary to s. 380(1) of the Criminal Code of Canada.

2. Frauds affecting public market price — Section 380(2)

Every one who — by deceit or falsehood or other fraudulent means — whether or not it is a false pretence within the meaning of the Criminal Code — with intent to defraud — affects the public market price — of stocks or shares or merchandise or anything that is offered for sale to the public — is guilty of an indictable offence.

Intent. Intention to defraud.

Included offences. Attempts (s. 660 and s. 662(1)(b)).

FRAUD

Punishment. Imprisonment for a term not exceeding 10 years (s. 380(2)).

Release. Initial decision to release made by justice (s. 515(1)).

Election. Accused may elect trial by judge and jury, judge alone, or provincial court judge (s. 536).

Evidence. See **18**, below.

Informations

A.B., on or about the —— day of ——, 19——, at the —— of ——, in the said (territorial division), by deceit [OR by falsehood OR by fraudulent means], with intent to defraud, did affect the public market price of stocks [OR shares OR merchandise OR (specify a thing that was offered for sale to the public)], to wit: (specify the particulars of the offence), contrary to s. 380(2) of the Criminal Code of Canada.

3. Using mails to defraud — Section 381

Every one who — makes use of the mails — either for the purpose of transmitting or delivering letters or circulars concerning schemes devised or intended to deceive or defraud the public — or for the purpose of obtaining money under false pretences — is guilty of an indictable offence.

Included offences. Attempts (s. 660 and s. 662(1)(b)).

Punishment. Imprisonment for a term not exceeding 2 years (s. 381).

Release. Initial decision to release made by officer in charge or justice (s. 498).

Election. Accused may elect trial by judge and jury, judge alone, or provincial court judge (s. 536).

Evidence. 1. Schemes often originate in Canada with letters being mailed to other countries. It has been held by the courts that this section regulates the use of Canadian postal facilities regardless of the location of the addressees.
2. *See also* **18**, below.

Informations

A.B., on or about the —— day of ——, 19——, at the —— of ——, in the said (territorial division), did make use of the mails for the purpose of transmitting [OR delivering] letters [OR circulars] concerning schemes devised [OR *intended] to deceive the public [OR to defraud the public OR for the purpose of obtaining money under false pretences], to wit: (specify the particulars of the offence), contrary to s. 381 of the Criminal Code of Canada.*

4. Fraudulent manipulation of stock exchange transactions — Section 382

Every one who — through the facility of a stock exchange or curb market or other market — with intent to create a false or misleading appearance of active public trading in a security — or with intent to create a false or misleading appearance with respect to the market price of a security — either effects a transaction in the security that involves no change in the beneficial ownership thereof — or enters an order for the purchase of the security knowing that an order of substantially the same size at substantially the same time and at substantially the same price for the sale of the security has been or will be entered by or for the same or different persons — or enters an order for the sale of the security knowing that an order of substantially the same size at substantially the same time and at substantially the same price for the purchase of the security has been or will be entered by or for the same or different persons — is guilty of an indictable offence.

Intent. Intention to create false or misleading appearance.

Included offences. Attempts (s. 660 and s. 662(1)(b)).

Punishment. Imprisonment for a term not exceeding 5 years (s. 382).

Release. Initial decision to release made by officer in charge or justice (s. 498).

Election. Accused may elect trial by judge and jury, judge alone, or provincial court judge (s. 536).

Evidence. See **18**, *below.*

5. Gaming in stocks or merchandise — Section 383(1)

Every one who — with intent to make gain or profit by the rise or fall in price of the stock of an incorporated or unincorporated company or undertaking, whether in or outside Canada, or of any goods or wares or merchandise — either makes or signs, or authorizes to be made or signed — any contract or agreement, oral or written — purporting to be for the purchase or sale of shares of stock or goods or wares or merchandise — without the bona fide intention of acquiring the shares or goods or wares or merchandise or of selling them, as the case may be — or makes or signs, or authorizes to be made or signed — any contract or agreement, oral or written — purporting to be for the sale or purchase of shares of stock or goods or wares or merchandise — in respect of which no delivery of the thing sold or purchased is made or received — and without the bona fide intention of making or receiving delivery thereof, as the case may be — is guilty of an indictable offence.

Intent. Intention to make gain or profit; intention to enter into agreement without bona fide intent of acquisition or disposal.

Exceptions. This offence does not apply where a broker, on behalf of a purchaser, receives delivery, notwithstanding that the broker retains or pledges what is delivered as security for the advance of the purchase money or any part thereof (s. 383(1)).

Included offences. Attempts (s. 660 and s. 662(1)(b)).

Punishment. Imprisonment for a term not exceeding 5 years (s. 383(1)).

Release. Initial decision to release made by officer in charge or justice (s. 498).

Election. Accused may elect trial by judge and jury, judge alone, or provincial court judge (s. 536).

Evidence. 1. Where it is established that the accused made or signed a contract or an agreement for the sale or purchase of shares of stock or goods, wares or merchandise, or acted, aided or abetted in the making or signing thereof, the burden of proof of a bona fide intention to acquire or to sell the shares, goods, wares or merchandise or to deliver or to receive delivery thereof, as the case may be, lies on the accused (s. 383(2)).
2. *See also* **18**, *below.*

6. Broker reducing stock by selling for his own account — Section 384

Every one who — being an individual or a member or an employee of a partnership, or a director or officer or an employee of a corporation — where he or the partnership or corporation is employed as a broker by any customer to buy and carry on margin any shares of an incorporated or unincorporated company or undertaking, whether in or out of Canada — thereafter sells or causes to be sold — shares of the company or undertaking — for any account in which — either he or his firm or a partner thereof — or the corporation or a director thereof — has a direct or indirect interest — if the effect of the sale is, otherwise than unintentionally, to reduce the amount of those shares in the hands of the broker or under his control in the ordinary course of business below the amount of those shares that the broker should be carrying for all customers — is guilty of an indictable offence.

Intent. Intention to reduce amount of shares below necessary minimum.

Included offences. Attempts (s. 660 and s. 662(1)(b)).

Punishment. Imprisonment for a term not exceeding 5 years (s. 384).

Release. Initial decision to release made by officer in charge or justice (s. 498).

Election. Accused may elect trial by judge and jury, judge alone, or provincial court judge (s. 536).

Evidence. See **18**, *below.*

7. Fraudulent concealment of title documents — Section 385(1)

Every one who — being a vendor or mortgagor of property or of a chose in action — or being a solicitor for or agent of a vendor or mortgagor of property or a chose in action — is served with a written demand for an abstract of title — by or on behalf of the purchaser or mortgagee — before the completion of the purchase or mortgage — and either with intent to defraud — and for the purpose of inducing the purchaser or mortgagee to accept the title offered or produced to him — conceals from him — any settlement or deed or will or other instrument material to the title or any encumbrance on the title — or falsifies — any pedigree on which the title depends — is guilty of an indictable offence.

Intent. Intent to defraud; inducing for prohibited purpose.

Consent to prosecute. No proceedings shall be instituted for this offence without the consent of the Attorney General (s. 385(2)).

Included offences. Attempts (s. 660 and s. 662(1)(b)).

Punishment. Imprisonment for a term not exceeding 2 years (s. 385(1)).

Release. Initial decision to release made by officer in charge or justice (s. 498).

Election. Accused may elect trial by judge and jury, judge alone, or provincial court judge (s. 536).

Evidence. See **18**, *below.*

8. Fraudulent registration of title — Section 386

Every one who — as principal or agent — in a proceeding to register title to real property — or in a transaction relating to real property that is or is proposed to be registered — knowingly and with intent to deceive — either makes a material false statement or representation — or suppresses or conceals from a judge or registrar, or any person employed by or assisting the registrar — any material document or fact or matter or information — or is privy to anything just mentioned — is guilty of an indictable offence.

Intent. Knowingly and with intent to deceive.

Included offences. Attempts (s. 660 and s. 662(1)(b)).

Punishment. Imprisonment for a term not exceeding 5 years (s. 386).

Release. Initial decision to release made by officer in charge or justice (s. 498).

Election. Accused may elect trial by judge and jury, judge alone, or provincial court judge (s. 536).

Evidence. See **18**, *below.*

9. Fraudulent sale of real property — Section 387

Every one who — knowing of an unregistered prior sale or of an existing unregistered grant or mortgage or hypothec or privilege or encumbrance of or on real property — fraudulently — sells the property or any part thereof — is guilty of an indictable offence.

Intent. Knowledge of fraudulent nature.

Included offences. Attempts (s. 660 and s. 662(1)(b)).

Punishment. Imprisonment for a term not exceeding 2 years (s. 387).

Release. Initial decision to release made by officer in charge or justice (s. 498).

Election. Accused may elect trial by judge and jury, judge alone, or provincial court judge (s. 536).

Evidence. *See* **18**, *below.*

10. Misleading receipt

Section 388(a)

Every one who — wilfully — with intent to mislead or injure or defraud any person — whether or not that person is known to him — gives to a person — anything in writing that purports to be a receipt for or an acknowledgment of property that has been delivered to or received by him — before the property referred to in the purported receipt or acknowledgment has been delivered to or received by him — is guilty of an indictable offence.

Section 388(b)

Every one who — wilfully — accepts or transmits or uses — such purported receipt or acknowledgment — is guilty of an indictable offence.

Intent. Wilfully; intention to mislead, injure or defraud.

Included offences. Attempts (s. 660 and s. 662(1)(b)).

Punishment. Imprisonment for a term not exceeding 2 years (s. 388).

Release. Initial decision to release made by officer in charge or justice (s. 498).

Election. Accused may elect trial by judge and jury, judge alone, or provincial court judge (s. 536).

Evidence. 1. Where this offence is committed by a person who acts in the name of a corporation, firm or partnership, no person other than the person who does the act by means of which the offence is committed or who is secretly privy to the doing of that act is guilty of the offence (s. 391).
2. *See also* **18**, *below.*

11. Fraudulent disposal of goods on which money advanced

Section 389(1)(a)

Every one who — having shipped or delivered to the keeper of a warehouse or to a factor or agent or carrier — anything on which the consignee thereof has advanced money or has given valuable

security — with intent to deceive or defraud or injure the consignee — thereafter disposes of it — in a manner that is different from and inconsistent with any agreement that has been made in that behalf between him and the consignee — is guilty of an indictable offence.

Section 389(1)(b)

Every one who — knowingly and wilfully — aids or assists any person to make a disposition of any such thing — for the purpose of deceiving or defrauding or injuring the consignee — is guilty of an indictable offence.

Intent. Intention to deceive, defraud or injure (s. 389(1)(a)); knowingly and wilfully for purpose of deceiving, defrauding or injuring (s. 389(1)(b)).

Included offences. Attempts (s. 660 and s. 662(1)(b)).

Punishment. Imprisonment for a term not exceeding 2 years (s. 389(1)).

Release. Initial decision to release made by officer in charge or justice (s. 498).

Election. Accused may elect trial by judge and jury, judge alone, or provincial court judge (s. 536).

Evidence. 1. No person is guilty of this offence where, before disposing of anything in a manner that is different from and inconsistent with any agreement that has been made in that behalf between him and the consignee, he pays or tenders to the consignee the full amount of money or valuable security that the consignee has advanced (s. 389(2)).
2. *See also Evidence, under* **10**, *above.*
3. *See also* **18**, *below.*

12. Fraudulent receipts under Bank Act

Section 390(a)

Every one who — wilfully — makes a false statement — in a receipt or certificate or acknowledgment — for anything that may be used for a purpose mentioned in the Bank Act — is guilty of an indictable offence.

Section 390(b)

Every one who — wilfully — either after giving to another person — or after a person employed by him to his knowledge has given to another person — or after obtaining and endorsing or assigning to another person — a receipt or certificate or acknowledgment for anything that may be used for a purpose mentioned in the Bank Act — without the consent in writing of the holder or endorsee — or without the production and delivery of the receipt or certificate or acknowledgment — alienates or parts with, or does not deliver to the holder or owner — the property mentioned in the receipt or certificate or acknowledgment — is guilty of an indictable offence.

Intent. Wilfully.

Included offences. Attempts (s. 660 and s. 662(1)(b)).

Punishment. Imprisonment for a term not exceeding 2 years (s. 390).

Release. Initial decision to release made by officer in charge or justice (s. 498).

Election. Accused may elect trial by judge and jury, judge alone, or provincial court judge (s. 536).

Evidence. 1. *See Evidence under* **10**, *above.*
2. *See also* **18**, *below.*

13. Disposal of property to defraud creditors

Section 392(a)

Every one who — with intent to defraud his creditors — either makes or causes to be made any gift or conveyance or assignment or sale or transfer or delivery of his property — or removes or conceals or disposes of any of his property — is guilty of an indictable offence.

Section 392(b)

Every one who — with intent that any one should defraud his creditors — receives any property — by means of or in relation to which such an offence has been committed — is guilty of an indictable offence.

Intent. Intention to defraud.

Included offences. Attempts (s. 660 and s. 662(1)(b)).

Punishment. Imprisonment for a term not exceeding 2 years (s. 392).

Release. Initial decision to release made by officer in charge or justice (s. 498).

Election. Accused may elect trial by judge and jury, judge alone, or provincial court judge (s. 536).

Evidence. See **18**, *below.*

14. Fraud in relation to fares

Section 393(1)

Every one who — whose duty it is to collect a fare or toll or ticket or admission — wilfully — either fails to collect it — or collects less than the proper amount payable in respect thereof — or accepts any valuable consideration for failing to collect it or for collecting less than the proper amount payable in respect thereof — is guilty of an indictable offence.

Section 393(2)

Every one who — gives or offers any valuable consideration — to a person whose duty it is to collect a fare or toll or ticket or admission fee — either for failing to collect it — or for collecting an amount less than the amount payable in respect thereof — is guilty of an indictable offence.

Intent. Wilfully (s. 393(1)).

Included offences. Attempts (s. 660 and s. 662(1)(b)).

Punishment. Imprisonment for a term not exceeding 2 years (s. 393(1) and (2)).

Release. Initial decision to release made by peace officer (s. 497).

Election. No election, absolute jurisdiction of provincial court judge (s. 553).

Evidence. See **18**, *below.*

15. Fraudulently obtaining transportation — Section 393(3)

Every one who — by any false pretence or fraud — unlawfully obtains transportation by land or water or air — is guilty of an offence punishable on summary conviction.

Limitation period. No proceedings in respect of offences that are declared to be punishable on summary conviction shall be instituted

more than 6 months after the time when the subject matter of the proceedings arose (s. 786(2) and s. 785(1)).

Included offences. Attempts (s. 660 and s. 662(1)(b)).

Punishment. A fine not exceeding $2,000, or 6 months' imprisonment, or both (s. 393(3) and s. 787(1)).

Release. Initial decision to release made by peace officer (s. 497).

Election. No election, summary conviction offence.

Evidence. See **18**, *below.*

16. Fraud in relation to minerals

Section 394(1)(a)

Every one who — being the holder of a lease or licence issued — either under an Act relating to the mining of precious metals — or by the owner of land that is supposed to contain precious metals by a fraudulent device or contrivance — either defrauds or attempts to defraud any person of any precious metals or money payable or reserved by the lease or licence — or fraudulently conceals or makes a false statement with respect to the amount of precious metals procured by him — is guilty of an indictable offence.

Section 394(1)(b)

Every one who — sells or purchases — any rock or mineral or other substance that contains precious metals or unsmelted or untreated or unmanufactured or partly smelted or partly treated or partly manufactured precious metals — unless he establishes that he is the owner or agent of the owner or is acting under lawful authority — is guilty of an indictable offence.

Section 394(1)(c)

Every one who — either has in his possession — or knowingly has upon his premises — either any rock or mineral of a value of 55¢ per kilogram or more — or any mica of a value of 15¢ per kilogram or more — or any precious metals — that there are reasonable grounds to believe have been stolen or have been dealt with contrary to this section — unless he establishes that he is lawfully in possession thereof — is guilty of an indictable offence.

Included offences. Attempts (s. 660 and s. 662(1)(b)).

Punishment. Imprisonment for a term not exceeding 5 years (s. 394(1)).

Release. Initial decision to release made by officer in charge or justice (s. 498).

Election. Accused may elect trial by judge and jury, judge alone, or provincial court judge (s. 536).

Evidence. See **18**, *below.*

17. Fraud in relation to mines

Section 396(1)(a)

Every one who — adds anything to or removes anything from — any existing or prospective mine or mining claim or oil well — with a fraudulent intent to affect the result of an assay or a test or a valuation that has been made or is to be made with respect to the mine or mining claim or oil well — is guilty of an indictable offence.

Section 396(1)(b)

Every one who — adds anything to or removes anything from or tampers with — a sample or material — that has been taken or is being or is about to be taken from any existing or prospective mine or mining claim or oil well for the purpose of being assayed or tested or otherwise valued — with a fraudulent intent to affect the result of the assay or test or valuation — is guilty of an indictable offence.

Intent. Fraudulent intent.

Included offences. Attempts (s. 660 and s. 662(1)(b)).

Punishment. Imprisonment for a term not exceeding 10 years (s. 396(1)).

Release. Initial decision to release made by justice (s. 515(1)).

Election. Accused may elect trial by judge and jury, judge alone, or provincial court judge (s. 536).

Evidence. 1. Evidence that (a) something has been added to or removed from anything to which this offence applies, or (b) anything to which this offence applies has been tampered with, is, in the absence of any evidence to the contrary, proof of a fraudulent intent to affect the result of an assay, test or valuation (s. 396(2)).
2. *See also* **18**, *below.*

18. Sufficiency of count

No count that alleges false pretences, fraud or any attempt or conspiracy by fraudulent means is insufficient by reason only that it does not set out in detail the nature of the false pretence, fraud or fraudulent means (s. 586).

FRAUDULENT CONVERSION. A taking or conversion of anything may be fraudulent notwithstanding that it is effected without secrecy or attempt at concealment (s. 322(3)).

For the purposes of the Criminal Code, the question whether anything that is converted is taken for the purpose of conversion or whether it is, at the time it is converted, in the lawful possession of the person who converts it is not material (s. 322(4)).

FUGITIVE OFFENDER. A person charged with an offence in Canada who has escaped to any part of the British Commonwealth, or a person charged in any part of the Commonwealth who has escaped to Canada. The return of such person is obtained under the Fugitive Offenders Act. An application for return may be made in the case of any offence punishable with imprisonment for 12 months or more, or any greater punishment. *See also EXTRADITION.*

FUNCTUS OFFICIO. Having discharged one's office or duty (Latin).

G

GAMES. For the purposes of Part VII of the Criminal Code, "game" means a game of chance or mixed chance and skill (s. 197(1)). *See also DISORDERLY HOUSES, 10.*

Gaming equipment. For the purposes of Part VII of the Criminal Code, "gaming equipment" means anything that is or may be used for the purpose of playing games or for betting (s. 197(1)).

GANGRENE. The death of a limb or portion of an organ in the living body (Jaffe, A Guide to Pathological Evidence, 2nd ed.).

GARROTTING. Asphyxia caused by the twisting of a ligature around the neck (Jaffe, A Guide to Pathological Evidence, 2nd ed.).

GAUGE. The unit of measurement for shotgun bore diameters, disregarding any choke. The gauge is equal to the number of solid lead balls of the bore diameter which weigh one pound (Jaffe, A Guide to Pathological Evidence, 2nd ed.).

GENETIC MARKERS. Inherited characteristics, such as blood groups, which are used in forensic investigations and paternity studies (Jaffe, A Guide to Pathological Evidence, 2nd ed.).

GESTATION. The period of intra-uterine development (Jaffe, A Guide to Pathological Evidence, 2nd ed.).

GOODS. For the purposes of Part X of the Criminal Code (Fraudulent Transactions Relating to Contracts and Trade), "goods" means anything that is the subject of trade or commerce (s. 379). *See also FRAUD, 11.*

GOVERNMENT. 1. For the purposes of Part IV of the Criminal Code (Offences Against the Administration of Law and Justice), "government" means (a) the Government of Canada, (b) the government of a province, or (c) Her Majesty in right of Canada or a province (s. 118). 2. For the purposes of s. 31 of the Canada Evidence Act, "government" means the government of Canada or of any province of Canada and includes any department, commission, board or branch of any such government (Canada Evidence Act, s. 31(1)).

GOVERNOR GENERAL. "Governor", "Governor of Canada" or "Governor General" means the Governor General of Canada or other chief executive officer or administrator carrying on the Government of Canada on behalf and in the name of the Sovereign, by whatever title that officer is designated (Interpretation Act, s. 35).

Governor General in Council. "Governor in Council" or "Governor General in Council" means the Governor General of Canada, acting by and with the advice of, or by and with the advice and consent of, or in conjunction with the Queen's Privy Council for Canada (Interpretation Act, s. 35).

GRAVAMEN. The serious aspect or matter of something (Latin).

GREY RING. A grey discolouration of the margins of an entrance wound caused by the metal of the bullet or by bullet lubricant. Also, "contact ring" (Jaffe, A Guide to Pathological Evidence, 2nd ed.).

GUARDIAN. For the purposes of Part V and Part VIII of the Criminal Code, "guardian" includes any person who has in law or in fact the custody or control of another person (s. 150 and s. 214). *See also DUTIES TENDING TO THE PRESERVATION OF LIFE.*

H

HABEAS CORPUS. A writ of habeas corpus is an order issued by a court calling upon the detainer of anyone to bring the body of the prisoner before the court in order to give the court an opportunity to determine whether the prisoner is being held according to the law. It is the remedy by which one can have the legality of any detention determined by the court and is guaranteed by the Canadian Bill of Rights. *See also BILL OF RIGHTS.*

HABENDUM ET TENENDUM. To have and to hold (Latin).

HALLUCINATION. A false perception by ear, smell or sight which has no basis in reality (Jaffe, A Guide to Pathological Evidence, 2nd ed.).

Hallucinogenic drug. A drug producing hallucinations, such as LSD or mescaline (Jaffe, A Guide to Pathological Evidence, 2nd ed.).

HANGING. A type of ligature strangulation in which the constricting force is due to gravity (Jaffe, A Guide to Pathological Evidence, 2nd ed.).

HARD LABOUR. A sentence of imprisonment is to be served in accordance with the enactments and rules that govern the institution to which the prisoner is sentenced. Any reference to hard labour in a conviction or a sentence is deemed to be a reference to the employment of prisoners in the manner provided for in the rules of the institution to which the person is sentenced (s. 732(1)).

Where hard labour is imposed improperly (i.e., where the enactment that creates the offence does not authorize the imposition of hard labour), the conviction or sentence is to be amended accordingly. The error is not a ground for quashing or setting aside the conviction or sentence (s. 732(2)).

HASHISH. The resinous juice of the flowering tops and the upper leaves of the hemp plant Cannabis sativa, sold in the form of cakes or blocks. It is usually smoked in a pipe. Due to its high content of cannabinols it is more potent that marihuana (Jaffe, A Guide to Pathological Evidence, 2nd ed.).

HATE PROPAGANDA

1. *Definitions*
2. *Advocating genocide*
3. *Public incitement of hatred*
4. *Wilful promotion of hatred*
5. *Seizure of material*

1. Definitions

"Genocide". For the purposes of s. 318 and s. 320, "genocide" means any of the following acts committed with intent to destroy in whole or in part any identifiable group, namely:

   (a) killing members of the group, or

   (b) deliberately inflicting on the group conditions of life calculated to bring about its physical destruction (s. 318(2) and s. 320(8)).

"Hate propaganda". For the purpose of s. 320, "hate propaganda" means any writing, sign or visible representation that advocates or promotes genocide or the communication of which by any person would constitute an offence under s. 319 of the Code (s. 320(8)).

"Identifiable group". For the purposes of s. 318 and s. 319, "identifiable group" means any section of the public distinguished by colour, race, religion or ethnic origin (s. 318(4) and s. 319(7)).

2. Advocating genocide — Section 318(1)

Every one who — advocates genocide — or promotes genocide — is guilty of an indictable offence.

Consent to prosecute. No proceedings shall be instituted for this offence without the consent of the Attorney General (s. 318(3)).

Included offences. Attempts (s. 660 and s. 662(1)(b)).

Punishment. 1. Imprisonment for a term not exceeding 5 years (s. 318(1)).

2. Where a person is convicted of this offence, anything by means of or in relation to which the offence was committed, on such conviction, may, in addition to any other punishment imposed, be ordered by the presiding provincial court judge or judge to be forfeited

to Her Majesty in right of the province in which that person is convicted, for disposal as the Attorney General may direct (s. 319(4)).

Release. Initial decision to release made by officer in charge or justice (s. 498).

Election. Accused may elect trial by judge and jury, judge alone, or provincial court judge (s. 536).

Informations

A.B., on or about the —— day of ——, 19——, at the —— of ——, in the said (territorial division), did advocate [OR promote] genocide, to wit: (specify the particulars of the offence), contrary to s. 318(1) of the Criminal Code of Canada.

3. Public incitement of hatred — Section 319(1)

Every one who — by communicating statements in any public place — incites hatred against any identifiable group — where such incitement is likely to lead to a breach of the peace — is guilty of either an indictable offence or an offence punishable on summary conviction.

Limitation period. No proceedings in respect of offences that are declared to be punishable on summary conviction shall be instituted more than 6 months after the time when the subject matter of the proceedings arose (s. 786(2) and s. 785(1)).

Included offences. Attempts (s. 660 and s. 662(1)(b)).

Punishment. 1. On indictment, imprisonment for a term not exceeding 2 years (s. 319(1)(a)). On summary conviction, a fine not exceeding $2,000, or 6 months' imprisonment, or both (s. 319(1)(b) and s. 787(1)). 2. *See also Punishment, item* **2.**, *under* **2**, above.

Release. Initial decision to release made by peace officer (s. 497).

Election. On indictment, accused may elect trial by judge and jury, judge alone, or provincial court judge (s. 536). On summary conviction, no election.

Definitions. For these purposes, "communicating" includes communicating by telephone, broadcasting or other audible or visible means (s. 319(7)).

Informations

A.B., on or about the —— day of ——, 19——, at the —— of ——, in the said (territorial division), in a public place, did by communicating statements incite hatred against an identifiable group where such incitement was likely to lead to a breach of the peace, to wit: (specify the particulars of the offence), contrary to s. 319(1) of the Criminal Code of Canada.

4. Wilful promotion of hatred — Section 319(2)

Every one who — by communicating statements, other than in private conversation — wilfully — promotes hatred against any identifiable group — is guilty of either an indictable offence or an offence punishable on summary conviction.

Intent. Wilfully.

Consent to prosecute. No proceedings shall be instituted for this offence without the consent of the Attorney General (s. 319(6)).

Limitation period. No proceedings in respect of offences that are declared to be punishable on summary conviction shall be instituted more than 6 months after the time when the subject matter of the proceedings arose (s. 786(2) and s. 785(1)).

Included offences. Attempts (s. 660 and s. 662(1)(b)).

Punishment. 1. On indictment, imprisonment for a term not exceeding 2 years (s. 319(2)(a)). On summary conviction, a fine not exceeding $2,000, or 6 months' imprisonment, or both (s. 319(2)(b) and s. 787(1)). 2. *See also Punishment, item 2., under* **2**, *above.*

Release. Initial decision to release made by peace officer (s. 497).

Election. On indictment, accused may elect trial by judge and jury, judge alone, or provincial court judge (s. 536). On summary conviction, no election.

Definitions. See Definitions under **3**, *above.*

Defences. No person shall be convicted of this offence:

(a) if he establishes that the statements communicated were true;

(b) if, in good faith, he expressed or attempted to establish by argument an opinion upon a religious subject;

(c) if the statements were relevant to any subject of public interest, the discussion of which was for the public benefit, and if on reasonable grounds he believed them to be true; or

(d) if, in good faith, he intended to point out, for the purpose of removal, matters producing or tending to produce feelings of hatred towards an identifiable group in Canada (s. 319(3)).

Informations

A.B., on or about the —— day of ——, 19——, at the —— of ——, in the said (territorial division), did by communicating statements wilfully promote hatred against an identifiable group, to wit: (specify the particulars of the offence), contrary to s. 319(2) of the Criminal Code of Canada.

5. Seizure of material

A judge who is satisfied by information on oath that there are reasonable grounds for believing that any publication, copies of which are kept for sale or distribution in premises within the jurisdiction of the court, is hate propaganda shall issue a warrant under his hand authorizing seizure of the copies (s. 320(1)).

Within 7 days of the issue of the warrant, the judge shall issue a summons to the occupier of the premises requiring him to appear before the court and show cause why the matter seized should not be forfeited to Her Majesty (s. 320(2)).

The owner and the author of the matter seized and alleged to be hate propaganda may appear and be represented in the proceedings in order to oppose the making of an order for the forfeiture of the said matter (s. 320(3)).

If the court is satisfied that the publication is hate propaganda, it shall make an order declaring the matter forfeited to Her Majesty in right of the province in which the proceedings take place, for disposal as the Attorney General may direct (s. 320(4)).

If the court is not satisfied that the publication is hate propaganda, it shall order that the matter be restored to the person from whom it was seized forthwith after the time for final appeal has expired (s. 320(5)).

An appeal lies from such an order made by any person who appeared in the proceedings (a) on any ground of appeal that involves a question of law alone, (b) on any ground of appeal that involves a question of fact alone, or (c) on any ground of appeal that involves a question of mixed law and fact, as if it were an appeal against conviction or against a judgment or verdict of acquittal, as the case may be, on a question of law alone under Part XXI, and ss. 673 to 696 apply with such modifications as the circumstances require (s. 320(6)).

No proceeding under this section shall be instituted without the consent of the Attorney General (s. 320(7)).

HEARSAY

1. *General*	4. *Declaration against interest*
2. *Hearsay exceptions*	5. *Declarations in the course of duty*
3. *Dying declarations*	6. *Former testimony*

1. General. Evidence of a statement made to a witness by a person who is not himself called as a witness is hearsay and inadmissible when the object of the evidence is to establish the truth of what is contained in the statement. It is not hearsay and is admissible when it is proposed to establish by the evidence, not the truth of the statement, but the fact that it was made (R. v. O'Brien, [1987] 1 S.C.R. 591).

2. Hearsay exceptions. Much relevant, though secondhand, evidence would be excluded if all hearsay evidence was inadmissible. Fortunately, a number of exceptions were devised to render certain forms of hearsay evidence admissible. These exceptions are based on principles of necessity and trustworthiness.

3. Dying declarations. The oral or written declaration of a deceased person is admissible evidence of the cause of his death at a trial for his murder or manslaughter, provided he was under a settled or hopeless expectation of death when the statement was made and provided that he would have been a competent witness if called to give evidence at that time (Cross, Evidence). The expectation of death must be "almost immediately". The trial may be for all forms of homicide including criminal negligence causing death, and evidence of the circumstances of the death is allowed to the extent that the declarant would have been allowed to testify to them if he had been called as a witness (Report of the Federal/Provincial Task Force on the Uniform Rules of Evidence, Chapdelaine v. R. (1935), 63 C.C.C. 5 (S.C.C.), R. v. Jurtyn (1958), 28 C.R. 295 (Ont. C.A.)).

4. Declaration against interest. A statement made by a deceased person asserting a fact against his pecuniary or proprietary interest is admissible as proof of the matters stated provided the following conditions are met: (1) that the deceased made a statement of some fact the truth of which he had peculiar knowledge; (2) that such fact was to his immediate prejudice at the time he stated it; (3) that the deceased knew the fact to be against his interest when he made it; and (4) that the interest to which the statement was adverse was a pecuniary, proprietary or penal one (Demeter v. R. (1978), 38 C.R.N.S. (317) (S.C.C.)). The courts have also held that an admission against penal interest could be adduced if the declarant was unavailable by reason of death, insanity, grave illness which prevents the giving of testimony even from a bed, or absence in a jurisdiction to which none of the processes of the Court extends (R. v. Demeter (1975), 25 C.C.C. (2d) 417) (Report of the Federal/Provincial Task Force on the Uniform Rules of Evidence).

5. Declarations in the course of duty. The oral or written statement of a deceased person made in pursuance of a duty to record or report his acts is admissible evidence of the truth of such contents of the statement as it was his duty to record or report, provided that the record or report was made roughly contemporaneously with the doing of the act, and provided the declarant had no motive to misrepresent the facts (Cross, Evidence).

6. Former testimony. Where, at the trial of an accused, a person whose evidence was given at a previous trial on the same charge, or whose evidence was taken in the investigation of the charge against the accused or on the preliminary inquiry into the charge, refuses to be sworn or to give evidence, or if facts are proved on oath from which it can be inferred reasonably that the person

(a) is dead,
(b) has since become and is insane,
(c) is so ill that he is unable to travel or testify, or
(d) is absent from Canada,

and where it is proved that his evidence was taken in the presence of the accused, it may be read as evidence in the proceedings without further proof, if the evidence purports to be signed by the judge or justice before whom it purports to have been taken, unless the accused proves that it was not in fact signed by that judge or justice or that he did not have full opportunity to cross-examine the witness (s. 715(1)).

Evidence that has been taken on the preliminary inquiry or other investigation of a charge against an accused may be read as evidence in the prosecution of the accused for any other offence on the same proof and in the same manner in all respects, as it might, according to law, be read in the prosecution of the offence with which the accused was charged when the evidence was taken (s. 715(2)).

For the purposes of this section, where evidence was taken at a previous trial of an accused in the absence of the accused, who was absent by reason of having absconded, he shall be deemed to have been present during the taking of the evidence and to have had full opportunity to cross-examine the witness (s. 715(3)).

HEMORRHAGE. The escape of blood from a blood vessel (Jaffe, A Guide to Pathological Evidence, 2nd ed.).

Subarachnoid hemorrhage. A hemorrhage between the arachnoid mater and the pia mater. It may be caused by injury or by rupture of a berry aneurysm (Jaffe, A Guide to Pathological Evidence, 2nd ed.).

Subdural hemorrhage. A hemorrhage between the dura mater and the arachnoid mater, usually of traumatic origin (Jaffe, A Guide to Pathological Evidence, 2nd ed.).

HER MAJESTY. "Her Majesty", "His Majesty", "the Queen", "the King", or "the Crown" mean the Sovereign of the United Kingdom, Canada and Her or His other Realms and Territories, and Head of the Commonwealth (Interpretation Act, s. 35).

Her Majesty's Realm and Territories. All realms and territories under the sovereignty of Her Majesty (Interpretation Act, s. 35).

Her Majesty's Forces. The naval, army and air forces of Her Majesty wherever raised, including the Canadian Forces (s. 2).

HEREIN. This expression used in any section of an Act shall be understood to relate to the whole enactment, and not to that section only (Interpretation Act, s. 35).

HEROIN. Diacetyl morphine, a semi-synthetic narcotic made by the acetylation of morphine. It is sold illicitly as a white powder, usually heavily adulterated with milk sugar or quinine. It is usually injected subcutaneously or intravenously but may be smoked or snuffed (Jaffe, A Guide to Pathological Evidence, 2nd ed.).

HIGH SEAS, OFFENCE ON. Where an offence is committed by a person, whether or not he is a Canadian citizen, on the sea adjacent to the coast of Canada and within 3 nautical miles of low water mark, whether or not it was committed on board or by means of a Canadian ship, the courts nearest to the place where the offence was committed have power to try him (s. 477(1)).

No proceedings for an offence so committed shall, where the accused is not a Canadian citizen, be instituted without the consent of the Attorney General of Canada (s. 477(2)). It has been held that under the provisions in the old Code respecting admiralty offences, which are replaced by the above, the prosecution may be commenced and the accused remanded to obtain the necessary consent.

HIGHWAY. For the purposes of the Criminal Code, "highway" means a road to which the public has the right of access, including bridges over which or tunnels through which a road passes (s. 2).

HOMICIDE

1. *Definitions*	5. *Killing unborn child in act of birth*
2. *Murder*	6. *Attempt to commit murder*
3. *Manslaughter*	7. *Accessory after fact to murder*
4. *Infanticide*	

1. Definitions

"Homicide". 1. A person commits homicide when, directly or indirectly, by any means, he causes the death of a human being (s. 222(1)). Homicide is culpable or not culpable (s. 222(2)). Homicide that is not culpable is not an offence (s. 222(3)).

2. A person does not commit homicide within the meaning of the Criminal Code by reason only that he causes the death of a human being by procuring, by false evidence, the conviction and death of that human being by sentence of the law (s. 222(6)).

3. A person commits homicide when he causes injury to a child before or during its birth as a result of which the child dies after becoming a human being (s. 223(2)). A child becomes a human being within the meaning of the Criminal Code when it has completely proceeded, in a living state, from the body of its mother whether or not (a) it has breathed, or (b) has an independent circulation, or (c) the navel string is severed (s. 223(1)).

"Culpable homicide". 1. Culpable homicide is murder or manslaughter or infanticide (s. 222(4)). A person commits culpable homicide when he causes the death of a human being (a) by means of an unlawful act (b) by criminal negligence (c) by causing that human being, by threats or fear of violence or by deception, to do anything that causes his death, or (d) by wilfully frightening that human being, in the case of a child or sick person (s. 222(5)).

2. No person commits culpable homicide unless the death occurs within one year and one day from the time of the occurrence of the last

event by means of which he caused or contributed to the cause of death (s. 227).
3. No person commits culpable homicide where he causes the death of a human being (a) by any influence on the mind alone, or (b) by any disorder or disease resulting from influence on the mind alone, but this section does not apply where a person causes the death of a child or sick person by wilfully frightening him (s. 228).

"Causing the death of a human being". 1. Where a person, by an act or omission, does any thing that results in the death of a human being, he causes the death of that human being, notwithstanding that death from that cause might have been prevented by resorting to proper means (s. 224).
2. Where a person causes to a human being bodily injury that is of itself of a dangerous nature and from which death results, he causes the death of that human being notwithstanding that the immediate cause of death is proper or improper treatment that is applied in good faith (s. 225).
3. Where a person causes to a human being bodily injury that results in death, he causes the death of that human being notwithstanding that the effect of the bodily injury is only to accelerate his death from a disease or disorder arising from some other cause (s. 226).
4. No person commits the offence of causing the death of a person by criminal negligence unless the death occurs within one year and one day from the time of the occurrence of the last event by means of which he caused or contributed to the cause of death (s. 227).

2. Murder

Definition of "murder". Culpable homicide is murder in the following circumstances:

(a) where the person who causes the death of a human being means to cause his death, or means to cause him bodily harm that he knows is likely to cause his death, and is reckless whether death ensues or not;

(b) where a person, meaning to cause death to a human being or meaning to cause him bodily harm that he knows is likely to cause his death, and being reckless whether death ensues or not, by accident or mistake causes death to another human being, notwithstanding that he does not mean to cause death or bodily harm to that human being; or

(c) where a person, for an unlawful object, does anything that he knows or ought to know is likely to cause death, and thereby causes death to a human being, notwithstanding that he desires to effect his object without causing death or bodily harm to any human being (s. 229).

Murder in the commission of offences. Culpable homicide is also murder where a person causes the death of a human being while committing or attempting to commit high treason or treason or an offence mentioned in any of the following sections:

s. 52 (sabotage)
s. 75 (piratical acts)
s. 76 (hijacking an aircraft)
s. 144 or s. 145(1) or ss. 146 to 148 (escape or rescue from prison or lawful custody)
s. 270 (assaulting a peace officer)
s. 271 (sexual assault)
s. 272 (sexual assault with a weapon, threats to a third party or causing bodily harm)
s. 273 (aggravated sexual assault)
s. 279 (kidnapping and forcible confinement)
s. 279.1 (hostage taking)
s. 343 (robbery)
s. 348 (breaking and entering) or
s. 433 or s. 434 (arson)

In such circumstances, it makes no difference whether or not the person means to cause death to any human being and whether or not he knows that death is likely to be caused to any human being, if:

(a) he means to cause bodily harm for the purpose of facilitating the commission of the offence, or for the purpose of facilitating his flight after committing or attempting to commit the offence, and the death ensues from the bodily harm;

(b) he administers a stupefying or overpowering thing for such a purpose, and the death ensues therefrom (s. 230).

Classification of different types of murder. Murder is classified as either first degree murder or as second degree murder (s. 231(1)).

Definition of "first degree murder". 1. Murder is first degree murder when it is planned and deliberate (s. 231(2)). Murder is planned and deliberate when it is committed pursuant to an arrangement under which money or anything of value passes or is intended to pass from one person to another, or is promised by one person to another, as consideration for that other's causing or assisting in causing the death of anyone or counselling another person to do any act causing or assisting in causing that death (s. 231(3)).

2. Irrespective of whether a murder is planned and deliberate on the part of any person, murder is first degree murder when the victim is either (a) a police officer, police constable, constable, sheriff, deputy sheriff, sheriff's officer or other person employed for the preservation and maintenance of the public peace, acting in the course of his duties; (b) a warden, deputy warden, instructor, keeper, jailer, guard or other officer or a permanent employee of a prison, acting in the course of his duties; or (c) a person working in a prison with the permission of the prison authorities and acting in the course of his work therein (s. 231(4)).

3. Irrespective of whether a murder is planned and deliberate on the part of any person, murder is first degree murder in respect of a person when the death is caused by that person while committing or attempting to commit an offence under any of the following sections (s. 231(5)):

s. 76 (hijacking aircraft)
s. 271 (sexual assault)
s. 272 (sexual assault with a weapon, threats to a third party or causing bodily harm)
s. 273 (aggravated sexual assault)
s. 279 (kidnapping and forcible confinement) or
s. 279.1 (hostage taking)

Definition of "second degree murder". All murder that is not first degree murder is second degree murder (s. 231(7)).

Statement of offence — Section 235(1)

Every one who — commits first degree murder — or commits second degree murder — is guilty of an indictable offence.

Jurisdiction. Triable only in a superior court of criminal jurisdiction (s. 468 and s. 469(a)(viii)).

Included offences. Manslaughter; infanticide; concealing child's body; attempts (s. 660 and s. 662(1)(b)).

Punishment. Imprisonment for life (s. 235(1)). The sentence of imprisonment for life is a minimum punishment (s. 235(2)).

A person convicted of first degree murder shall be sentenced to imprisonment for life without eligibility for parole until he has served 25 years of his sentence (s. 742(a)).

A person convicted of second degree murder, who has previously been convicted of culpable homicide that is murder, shall be sentenced to imprisonment for life without eligibility for parole until he has served 25 years of his sentence (s. 742(a.1)).

A person convicted of second degree murder, who has not previously been convicted of culpable homicide that is murder, shall be sentenced to imprisonment for life without eligibility for parole until he has served at least 10 years of his sentence or such greater number of years, not exceeding 25 years, as has been substituted therefor pursuant to s. 744 of the Criminal Code (s. 742(b)). That section provides that at the time of sentencing under s. 742(b) of an offender who is convicted of second degree murder, the court may, having regard to the character of the offender, the nature of the offence and the circumstances of its commission, and to any recommendation by the jury made pursuant to s. 743, by order, substitute for 10 years a number of years of imprisonment (being more than 10 but not more than 25), without eligibility for parole, as the court deems fit in the circumstances (s. 744).

A person, who was under the age of 18 at the time of the commission of the offence, convicted of first degree or second degree murder and sentenced to imprisonment for life, shall be sentenced to imprisonment for life without eligibility for parole until the person has served between 5 and 10 years of the sentence as is specified by the judge presiding at the trial (s. 742.1). At the time of the sentencing under s. 742.1 of an offender who is convicted of first degree or second degree murder and who was under the age of 18 at the time of the commission of the offence, the court may, having regard to the age and character of the offender, the nature of the offence and the circumstances surrounding its commission, and to any recommendation by the jury made pursuant to s. 743.1, by order, decide the period of imprisonment the offender is to serve that is between 5 and 10 years without eligibility for parole, as the court deems fit in the circumstances (s. 744.1).

Release. Initial decision to release may only be made by superior court judge (s. 522).

Election. Superior court (with jury) exclusive, except where accused elects superior court trial without jury with consent of Attorney General (s. 473) (s. 469).

Evidence. The wife or husband of a person charged with this offence where the complainant or victim is under the age of 14 years is a competent and compellable witness for the prosecution without the consent of the person charged (Canada Evidence Act, s. 4(4)).

Informations

A.B., on or about the —— day of ——, 19——, at the —— of ——, in the said (territorial division), did murder C.D., to wit: (specify the particulars of the offence), contrary to s. 235(1) of the Criminal Code of Canada.

3. Manslaughter

Definition of "manslaughter". 1. Culpable homicide that is not murder or infanticide is manslaughter (s. 234).
2. Culpable homicide that otherwise would be murder may be reduced to manslaughter if the person who committed it did so in the heat of passion caused by sudden provocation (s. 232(1)).

A wrongful act or insult that is of such a nature as to be sufficient to deprive an ordinary person of the power of self-control is provocation enough for the purposes of this section if the accused acted upon it on the sudden and before there was time for his passion to cool (s. 232(2)).

For these purposes, the questions (a) whether a particular wrongful act or insult amounted to provocation, and (b) whether the accused was deprived of the power of self-control by the provocation that he alleges he received, are questions of fact, but no one shall be deemed to have given provocation to another by doing anything that he had a legal right to do, or by doing anything that the accused incited him to do in order to provide the accused with an excuse for causing death or bodily harm to any human being (s. 232(3)).
3. Culpable homicide that otherwise would be murder is not necessarily manslaughter by reason only that it was committed by a person who was being arrested illegally, but the fact that the illegality of the arrest was known to the accused may be evidence of provocation for the purpose of this offence (s. 232(4)).

Statement of offence — Section 236

Every one who — commits manslaughter — is guilty of an indictable offence.

Included offences. Manslaughter: assault causing bodily harm; assault; attempts (s. 660 and s. 662(1)(b)); manslaughter by motor vehicle or vessel; dangerous driving or dangerous operation of motor vehicle.

Punishment. 1. Imprisonment for life (s. 236).
2. The sentence to be pronounced against a person who is to be sentenced to imprisonment for life in respect of a person who has

382 HOMICIDE

been convicted of this offence, shall be that he be sentenced to imprisonment for life with normal eligibility for parole (s. 742(c)).

Release. Initial decision to release made by justice (s. 515(1)).

Election. Accused may elect trial by judge and jury, judge alone, or provincial court judge (s. 536).

Evidence. *See Evidence under* **2,** *above.*

Informations

A.B., on or about the —— day of ——, 19——, at the —— of ——, in the said (territorial division), did cause the death of C.D. and thereby commit manslaughter, to wit: (specify the particulars of the offence), contrary to s. 236 of the Criminal Code of Canada.

4. Infanticide

Definition of offence. A female person commits infanticide when by a wilful act or omission she causes the death of her newly-born child, if at the time of the act or omission she is not fully recovered from the effects of giving birth to the child and by reason thereof or of the effect of lactation consequent on the birth of the child her mind is then disturbed (s. 233).

Statement of offence — Section 237

Every female person who — commits infanticide — is guilty of an indictable offence.

Included offences. Concealing child's body (s. 662(3)); attempts (s. 660 and s. 662(1)(b)).

Punishment. Imprisonment for a term not exceeding 5 years (s. 237).

Release. Initial decision to release made by officer in charge or justice (s. 498).

Election. Accused may elect trial by judge and jury, judge alone, or provincial court judge (s. 536).

Evidence. *See Evidence under* **2,** *above.*

Informations

A.B., on or about the —— day of ——, 19——, at the —— of ——, in the said (territorial division), being a female person, did commit infanticide, to wit: (specify the particulars of the offence), contrary to s. 237 of the Criminal Code of Canada.

5. Killing unborn child in act of birth — Section 238(1)

Every one who — causes the death — in the act of birth — of any child that has not become a human being — in such a manner that, if the child were a human being, he would be guilty of murder — is guilty of an indictable offence.

Exception. This offence does not apply to a person who, by means that, in good faith, he considers necessary to preserve the life of the mother of a child, causes the death of that child (s. 238(2)).

Included offences. Attempts (s. 660 and s. 662(1)(b)).

Punishment. 1. Imprisonment for life (s. 238(1)).
2. *See also Punishment, item 2., under* **3**, *above.*

Release. Initial decision to release made by justice (s. 515(1)).

Election. Accused may elect trial by judge and jury, judge alone, or provincial court judge (s. 536).

6. Attempt to commit murder — Section 239

Every one who — attempts by any means — to commit murder — is guilty of an indictable offence.

Included offences. Causing bodily harm with intent to endanger life (R. v. Wigman (1987), 56 C.R. (3d) 289 (S.C.C.)); attempting to unlawfully cause bodily harm (R. v. Colburne (1991), 66 C.C.C. (3d) 235 (Que. C.A.)).

Punishment. 1. Imprisonment for life (s. 239).
2. *See also Punishment, item 2., under* **3**, *above.*

Release. Initial decision to release made by justice (s. 515(1)).

Election. Accused may elect trial by judge and jury, judge alone, or provincial court judge (s. 536).

Evidence. See Evidence under **2**, *above.*

7. Accessory after fact to murder

Definition. An accessory after the fact to an offence is one who, knowing that a person has been a party to the offence, receives, comforts or assists that person for the purpose of enabling him to escape (s. 23(1)).

Statement of offence — Section 240

Every one who — is an accessory after the fact to murder — is guilty of an indictable offence.

Included offences. Attempts (s. 660 and s. 662(1)(b)).

Punishment. 1. Imprisonment for life (s. 240).
2. *See also Punishment, item 2., under* **3**, *above.*

Release. Initial decision to release made by justice (s. 515(1)).

Election. Accused may elect trial by judge and jury, judge alone, or provincial court judge (s. 536).

Evidence. 1. No married person whose spouse has been a party to an offence is accessory after the fact to that offence by receiving, comforting or assisting spouse for the purpose of enabling the spouse to escape (s. 23(2)).
2. *See also Evidence under* **2**, *above.*

HOSTAGE TAKING

1. *Offence of hostage taking*	2. *Offence deemed to be committed in Canada*

1. Offence of hostage taking

Definition of offence — Section 279.1(1)

Every one who — confines or imprisons or forcibly seizes or detains a person — and in any manner utters or conveys or causes any person to receive a threat — that the death of, or bodily harm to, the hostage will be caused — or that the confinement or imprisonment or detention of the hostage will be continued — with intent to induce any person, other than the hostage, or any group of persons or any state or international or intergovernmental organization to commit or cause to be committed any act or omission as a condition (whether express or implied) of the release of the hostage — takes that person hostage.

Statement of offence — Section 279.1(2)

Every one who — takes a person hostage — is guilty of an indictable offence.

Intent. Intention to induce third party to take course of action.

Included offences. Attempts (s. 660 and s. 662(1)(b)); forcible confinement (s. 279(2)).

Punishment. A maximum term of imprisonment for life (s. 279.1(2)).

The sentence to be pronounced against a person who is to be sentenced to imprisonment for life in respect of a person who has been convicted of this offence shall be that he be sentenced to imprisonment for life with normal eligibility for parole (s. 742(c)).

Release. Initial decision to release made by justice (s. 515(1)).

Election. Accused may elect trial by judge and jury, judge alone, or provincial court judge (s. 536).

Defences. The fact that the person in relation to whom the offence is alleged to have been committed did not resist is not a defence unless the accused proves that the failure to resist was not caused by threats, duress, force or exhibition of force (s. 279(3) and s. 279.1(3)).

Informations

A.B., on or about the —— day of ——, 19——, at the —— of ——, in the said (territorial division), did confine [OR imprison OR forcibly seize OR detain] C.D. and did utter [OR convey OR cause a person to receive] a threat that the death of [OR bodily harm to] C.D. would be caused, with intent to induce any act or omission as a condition of the release of C.D., to wit: (specify the particulars of the offence), contrary to s. 279.1(2) of the Criminal Code of Canada.

A.B., on or about the —— day of ——, 19——, at the —— of ——, in the said (territorial division), did confine [OR imprison OR forcibly seize OR detain] C.D. and did utter [OR convey OR cause a person to receive] a threat that the confinement [OR imprisonment OR detention] of C.D. [would] be continued, with intent to induce any act or omission as a condition of the release of C.D., to wit: (specify the particulars of the offence), contrary to s. 279.1(2) of the Criminal Code of Canada.

2. Offence deemed to be committed in Canada

Notwithstanding anything in the Criminal Code or any other Act, every one who, outside Canada, commits an act or omission that if committed in Canada would be an offence against s. 279.1 (hostage taking) shall be deemed to commit that act or omission in Canada in the following circumstances:

(a) if the act or omission is committed on a ship that is registered or licensed, or for which an identification number has been issued, pursuant to any Act of Parliament;

(b) if the act or omission is committed on an aircraft registered in Canada under regulations made under the Aeronautics Act, or leased without crew and operated by a person who is qualified under regulations made under the Aeronautics Act to be registered as owner of an aircraft in Canada under such regulations;

(c) if the person who commits the act or omission is a Canadian citizen, or is not a citizen of any state and ordinarily resides in Canada;

(d) if the act or omission is committed with intent to induce Her Majesty in right of Canada or of a province (i.e., the government of Canada or of a province) to commit or cause to be committed any act or omission;

(e) if a person taken hostage by the act or omission is a Canadian citizen; or

(f) if the person who commits the act or omission is, after the commission thereof, present in Canada (s. 7(3.1)).

HYPOSTASIS. The settling of blood after death into the dependent parts of the body. In the skin it is manifested as lividity (Jaffe, A Guide to Pathological Evidence, 2nd ed.).

I

IBID. An abbreviation for "ibidem", which means "in the same place" (Latin).

IDEM. The same (Latin).

IDENTIFICATION OF CRIMINALS

1. *Bertillon Signaletic System*
2. *Use of force*
3. *Publication of results*
4. *Liability under the Identification of Criminals Act*

1. Bertillon Signaletic System

The Identification of Criminals Act, provides that any person in lawful custody, charged with, or under conviction of, an indictable offence, or who has been apprehended under the Extradition Act or the Fugitive Offenders Act, may be subjected, by or under the direction of those in whose custody he is, to the measurements, processes and operations practised under the system for the identification of criminals commonly known as the Bertillon Signaletic System, or to any measurements, processes or operations sanctioned by the Governor in Council having the like object in view (Identification of Criminals Act, s. 2(1)).

The "Bertillon System" is a method of measuring the dimensions of the human body (anthropometry) used chiefly for the measurement of criminals, consisting of the taking and recording of a system of numerous, minute, and uniform measurements of various parts of the human body, absolutely and in relation to each other, the facial, cranial and other angles, and of any eccentricities or abnormalities noticed in the individual (Black's Law Dictionary).

2. Use of force

Such force may be used as is necessary to the effectual carrying out and application of such measurements, processes and operations as are permitted by the Identification of Criminals Act (Identification of Criminals Act, s. 2(2)).

3. Publication of results

The signaletic cards and other results of the Bertillon Signaletic System may be published for the purpose of affording information to officers and others engaged in the execution or administration of the law (Identification of Criminals Act, s. 2(3)).

4. Liability under the Identification of Criminals Act

No one having the custody of any such person, and no one acting in his aid or under his direction, and no one concerned in such publication, incurs any liability, civil or criminal, for anything lawfully done under the Identification of Criminals Act (Identification of Criminals Act, s. 3).

IGNORAMUS. "We do not know"; a word formally used to reject a bill of indictment (Latin).

IGNORANTIA JURIS NON (HAUD, NEMINEM) EXCUSAT. Ignorance of the law is no excuse" (Latin).

IMPEDING ATTEMPT TO SAVE LIFE

Section 262(a)

Every one who — prevents or impedes or attempts to prevent or impede — any person who is attempting to save — his own life — is guilty of an indictable offence.

Section 262(b)

Every one who — without reasonable cause — prevents or impedes or attempts to prevent or impede — any person who is attempting to save — the life of another person — is guilty of an indictable offence.

Included offences. Attempts (s. 660 and s. 662(1)(b)).

Punishment. Imprisonment for a term not exceeding 10 years (s. 262).

Release. Initial decision to release made by justice (s. 515(1)).

Election. Accused may elect trial by judge and jury, judge alone, or provincial court judge (s. 536).

Informations

A.B., on or about the —— day of ——, 19——, at the —— of ——, in the said (territorial division), did prevent [OR impede OR attempt to prevent OR attempt to impede] C.D., who was attempting to save his own life, to wit: (specify the particulars of the offence), contrary to s. 262(a) of the Criminal Code of Canada.

A.B., on or about the —— day of ——, 19——, at the —— of ——, in the said (territorial division), without reasonable cause, did prevent [OR impede OR attempt to prevent OR attempt to impede] C.D., who was attempting to save the life of E.F., to wit: (specify the particulars of the offence), contrary to s. 262(b) of the Criminal Code of Canada.

IN. In; into; at; on; to; for (Latin). *In banco.* 1. In bank. 2. The whole court sitting together. *In camera.* In secret. *In curia.* In court. *In extremis.* At the point of death. *In flagrante delicto.* 1. In the very act of committing a crime. 2. Red-handed. *In loco parentis.* In the place of a parent. *In mortuo.* In the dead body. *In pari delicto potior est conditio defendentis (or possidentis).* "In equal fault the defendant's (or possessor's) position is the stronger". ***In personam.*** Personal. ***In re.*** In the matter of. ***In rem.*** Directed to an actual piece of property. ***In situ.*** In its original place. ***In statu quo.*** In the former position or in the same state as formerly. ***In toto.*** Completely. ***In vitro.*** 1. In the glass. 2. In the test tube, under experimental conditions. ***In vivo.*** In the living body.

IN ABSENTIA. Not present (Latin). The term is used in the marginal note for s. 607(6) which provides that a person may not plead autrefois convict for a specified act or omission committed outside Canada that is an offence in Canada if the accused was not present at the trial outside Canada and was not represented by counsel acting under the accused's instructions, and if the person was not punished in accordance with the sentence imposed on conviction in respect of that act or omission. The acts or omissions specified are found in s. 7(2) to 7(3.4), s. 7(3.7), and s. 7 (3.71).

INCAPABLE. A person is incapable when there is a complete loss of ability to appreciate the nature and quality of the act or of knowing the act or omission is wrong. It is not merely an inability to calmly consider the act (Knoll, Criminal Law Defences) (Schwartz v. R., [1977] 1 S.C.R. 673).

INCITING TO MUTINY

Section 53(a)

Every one who — attempts to seduce — for a traitorous or mutinous purpose — a member of the Canadian Forces — from his duty and allegiance to Her Majesty — is guilty of an indictable offence.

Section 53(b)

Every one who — attempts to incite or to induce — a member of the Canadian Forces — to commit a traitorous or mutinous act — is guilty of an indictable offence.

Intent. For traitorous or mutinous purpose.

Jurisdiction. Triable only in a superior court of criminal jurisdiction (s. 468 and s. 469(a)(iv)).

Included offences. Attempts (s. 660 and s. 662(1)(b)).

Punishment. Imprisonment for a term not exceeding 14 years (s. 53).

Release. Initial decision to release may only be made by superior court judge (s. 522).

Election. Superior court (with jury) exclusive, except where accused elects superior court trial without jury with consent of Attorney General (s. 473) (s. 469).

Evidence. In proceedings for this offence, no evidence is admissible of an overt act unless that overt act is set out in the indictment or unless the evidence is otherwise relevant as tending to prove an overt act that is set out therein (s. 55).

INCLUDED OFFENCES. An included offence is a part of an offence that has been charged in an indictment. The Criminal Code provides that where the commission of the offence charged includes the commission of another offence, the accused may be convicted of an offence so included that is proved, notwithstanding that the whole offence that is charged is not proved (s. 662(1)(a)) or an attempt to commit an offence so included that is proved (s. 662(1)(b)).

In order to permit a jury or court to convict an accused of an included offence, two conditions must be present:

(i) the offence charged in the indictment must contain all the essential elements of the included offence and

(ii) the offence charged in the indictment and the included offence must both refer to the same transaction.

INDICIA. Indications or signs (Latin).

INDICTABLE OFFENCES. Offences are divided into indictable offences and summary conviction offences. The division is quite arbitrary. The section defining the crime declares whether an offence is one or the other. The fact that an offence is tried before a provincial court judge summarily, whether it is with the consent of the accused or under the provincial court judge's absolute jurisdiction to try certain indictable offences without the consent of the accused, does not make that offence a summary conviction offence if it is described in the section as an indictable offence or an offence punishable on indictment.

When the offence is described as punishable either upon indictment or upon summary conviction, the Crown should indicate at the opening of the case how he is proceeding. It is the right of the Crown to say whether the proceedings are by way of summary conviction or indictment, not the right of the accused. If the Crown elects to proceed by way of indictment and the provincial court judge is one of those described in s. 554 who has power to try the accused with the accused's consent, the provincial court judge should ask the accused to elect in the same manner as for other indictable offences. If the accused elects trial before the provincial court judge, the trial proceeds for the indictable offence.

INDICTMENT. One of two forms of charge documents (the other being the information) presently authorized under the Criminal Code. It is an accusation in writing of a serious (that is, indictable) offence and is brought in the name of Her Majesty the Queen. Typically, it is a document used only after an accused has been admitted to stand trial following a preliminary inquiry, but it may also be employed in the absence of a preliminary inquiry or where the accused has been discharged at a preliminary inquiry (The Charge Document in Criminal Cases, Law Reform Commission of Canada, Working Paper 55). By definition, an "indictment" includes: (a) an information or count therein; (b) a plea, replication or other pleading; and (c) any record (s. 2). *See also INFORMATIONS AND INDICTMENTS.*

INFORMANT. For the purposes of Part XXVII of the Criminal Code (Summary Convictions), "informant" means a person who lays an information (s. 785(1)).

INFORMATIONS AND INDICTMENTS

1. *Informations and indictments*
2. *Information to launch criminal proceedings*
3. *Contents of an information or indictment*
4. *Information to obtain a search warrant*

1. Informations and indictments

There are two types of charge documents: the information and the indictment. An information is sworn under oath by an informant; an indictment is not, but is signed by Crown counsel. Otherwise, there are no significant differences between their contents. In practice, there is one further contrasting feature: the information is usually drafted by a police officer; indictments by a Crown attorney, except in Québec where all charging documents are authorized and drafted by the Crown attorney, save those dealt with in municipal court. The same requirements of sufficiency are applied to both (The Charge Document in Criminal Cases, Law Reform Commission of Canada, Working Paper

55). An information is also used for the purpose of obtaining a search warrant.

2. Information to launch criminal proceedings

An accusation made in writing and under oath before a justice in which the informant states that he has personal knowledge or that he believes on reasonable grounds that the accused person has committed an offence (ss. 504, 788, 789 and Form 2). An information by definition includes (a) a count in an information, and (b) a complaint in respect of which a justice is authorized by an Act of Parliament or an enactment thereunder to make an order (s. 785(1)). All proceedings, both summary and indictable, are commenced by an information, except where an accused is directly indicted at the instance of the Attorney General.

3. Contents of an information or indictment

1. Any person charged with an offence has the right to be informed of the specific offence without unreasonable delay (Canadian Charter of Rights and Freedoms, s. 11(a)). Further, the accused must be reasonably informed of the transaction alleged against him, thus giving him the possibility of a full defence and a fair trial (R. v. Côté, [1978] 1 S.C.R. 8).

2. Each count in an information or indictment must be set out in a separate paragraph and shall, in general, refer to a single transaction (s. 581(1)).

A single transaction may involve multiple victims or multiple incidents if they are closely connected in time and place. Examples of validly charged single transactions of this type include the theft of several articles by one or more accused persons and sexual attacks perpetrated by one offender against the same victim (The Charge Document in Criminal Cases, Law Reform Commission of Canada, Working Paper 55).

3. The charge should contain a reference to the provision of the Criminal Code or other act that creates the offence (The Charge Document in Criminal Cases, Law Reform Commission of Canada, Working Paper 55).

4. The charge should include no surplusage, i.e. assertions of facts which are not essential to a successful prosecution and which need not be proved at trial (The Charge Document in Criminal Cases, Law Reform Commission of Canada, Working Paper 55).

5. A count in an information or indictment should contain no prejudicial matter, such as an alias, unless necessary to comply with the requirements of law. An alias is prejudicial since its existence may lead the trier of fact to conclude that the accused has a prior criminal record or is of unsavory character, in view of his alleged efforts to shield his identity (The Charge Document in Criminal Cases, Law Reform Commission of Canada, Working Paper 55).

4. Information to obtain a search warrant

An allegation made on oath in Form 1 for presentation to a justice in order to obtain a search warrant, in which the informant says that there are reasonable grounds to believe that there is in a building, receptacle or place:
1. anything on or in respect of which any offence against the Criminal Code or any other federal Act has been or is suspected to have been committed;
2. anything that there is reasonable ground to believe will afford evidence with respect to the commission of an offence against the Criminal Code or any other federal Act, or
3. anything that there are reasonable grounds to believe is intended to be used for the purpose of committing any offence against the person for which a person may be arrested without warrant (s. 487).

INFRA. "Below" (Latin).

INJURIA ABSQUE (or SINE) DAMNO. Legal injury without actual loss (Latin).

INJURIA NON EXCUSAT INJURIUM. "One wrong does not justify another" (Latin).

INJURY. 1. The disruption of a tissue by violence (Jaffe, A Guide to Pathological Evidence, 2nd ed.). 2. Any infringement of the rights of another, in his person, reputation or property, for which an action lies at law (Jowitt's Dictionary of English law).

Compression injury. An injury caused by a force acting perpendicularly to the surface of an organ or tissue compressing its substance (Jaffe, A Guide to Pathological Evidence, 2nd ed.).

Epiphyseal injury. Dislocation of the epiphysis of a bone often caused by forceful pulling of an extremity. It is a common type of injury in the battered child syndrome.

The "epiphysis" is a part of a bone which is separated from the main part during the period of active growth by a layer of cartilage and which unites with the main part during adolescence and early adult life (Jaffe, A Guide to Pathological Evidence, 2nd ed.).

Seat belt injury. Injuries sustained by flexion over a seat belt during sudden deceleration. Seat belt injuries include compression fractures of the spine and tears of the bowel and mesentery (Jaffe, A Guide to Pathological Evidence, 2nd ed.).

Shearing injury. An injury caused by a force acting parallel to the surface of an organ or tissue distorting its shape (Jaffe, A Guide to Pathological Evidence, 2nd ed.).

INQUEST. An inquest may be held in cases where the death of the deceased may have been caused by violence, misadventure or unfair means or by negligence, malpractice or misconduct of others. If death is caused by suicide it may be necessary to hold an inquest to determine what caused the deceased to take his own life; it may have been caused by ill-treatment or by some outside influence working on his mind. The coroner after investigating may in his discretion hold an inquest and in most provinces the attorney general may order one to be held. If a coroner issues his warrant to hold an inquest, he gives to the constable a warrant to take possession of the body and the warrant to hold an inquest. He will instruct the constable to summon a jury. The number in the different provinces varies.

INTER. Between; among; during (Latin). ***Inter alia.*** Among other things. ***Inter alios.*** Among other persons. ***Inter se.*** Between themselves. ***Inter vivos.*** Between living persons.

INTERCEPT. For the purposes of Part VI of the Criminal Code (Invasion of Privacy), "intercept" includes listen to, record or acquire a communication or acquire the substance, meaning or purport thereof (s. 183).

INTERCEPTION OF COMMUNICATIONS. *See WIRETAPPING OFFENCES.*

INTERNATIONALLY PROTECTED PERSON

1. *Definition of "internationally protected person"*
2. *Threatening to commit offence against internationally protected person*
3. *Attack on premises, residence or transport of internationally protected person*
4. *Offence deemed to be committed in Canada*

1. Definition of "internationally protected person"

This expression refers to the following persons:

(a) a head of state, including any member of a collegial body that performs the functions of a head of state under the constitution of the state concerned, a head of a government or a minister of foreign affairs, whenever that person is in a state other than the state in which he holds that position or office;

(b) a member of the family of a head of state, who accompanies that person in a state other than the state in which that person holds such position or office;

(c) a representative or an official of a state or an official or agent of an international organization of an intergovernmental character who, at the time when and at the place where an offence referred to in s. 7(3) (offence deemed to be committed in Canada) is committed against his person or any property referred to in s. 431 (attack on premises, residence or transport of internationally protected person) that is used by him, is entitled, pursuant to international law, to special protection from any attack on his person, freedom or dignity; or

(d) a member of the family of a representative, official or agent described above who forms part of his household, if the representative, official or agent, at the time when and at the place where any offence referred to in s. 7(3) (offence deemed to be committed in Canada) is committed against the member of his family or any property referred to in s. 431 (attack on premises, residence or transport of internationally protected person) that is used by that member, is entitled, pursuant to international law, to special protection from any attack on his person, freedom or dignity (s. 2).

2. Threatening to commit offence against internationally protected person — Section 424

Every one who — either threatens to commit an offence under s. 235 (murder) or s. 266 (assault) or s. 279 (kidnapping) or s. 279.1 (hostage taking) against an internationally protected person — or threatens to commit an offence under s. 431 (attack on premises, residence or transport of internationally protected person) — is guilty of an indictable offence.

Included offences. Attempts (s. 660 and s. 662(1)(b)).

Punishment. Imprisonment for a term not exceeding 5 years (s. 424).

Release. Initial decision to release made by officer in charge or justice (s. 498).

Election. Accused may elect trial by judge and jury, judge alone, or provincial court judge (s. 536).

Informations

A.B., on or about the —— day of ——, 19——, at the —— of ——, in the said (territorial division), did threaten to commit an offence under s. 235 [OR s. 266 OR s. 279 OR s. 279.1] of the Criminal Code against C.D., an internationally protected person, to wit: (specify the particulars of the offence), contrary to s. 424 of the Criminal Code of Canada.

A.B., on or about the —— day of ——, 19——, at the —— of ——, in the said (territorial division), did threaten to commit an offence under s. 431 of the Criminal Code, to wit: (specify the particulars of the offence), contrary to s. 424 of the Criminal Code of Canada.

3. Attack on premises, residence or transport of internationally protected person — Section 431

Every one who — commits an attack — on the official premises or private accommodation or means of transport — of an internationally protected person — that is likely to endanger the life or liberty of such person — is guilty of an indictable offence.

Included offences. Attempts (s. 660 and s. 662(1)(b)).

Punishment. Imprisonment for a term not exceeding 14 years (s. 431).

Release. Initial decision to release made by justice (s. 515(1)).

Election. Accused may elect trial by judge and jury, judge alone, or provincial court judge (s. 536).

4. Offence deemed to be committed in Canada

Notwithstanding anything in the Criminal Code or any other Act, every one who, outside Canada, commits an act or omission against the person of an internationally protected person or against any property referred to in s. 431 (attack on premises, residence or transport of internationally protected person) used by that person that if committed in Canada would be an offence against that section or any of the following sections:

s. 235	(murder)
s. 236	(manslaughter)
s. 266	(assault)
s. 267	(assault with a weapon or causing bodily harm
s. 268	(aggravated assault)
s. 269	(unlawfully causing bodily harm)
s. 271	(sexual assault)
s. 272	(sexual assault with a weapon, threats to a third party or causing bodily harm)
s. 273	(aggravated sexual assault)
s. 279	(kidnapping)
s. 279.1	(hostage taking)
ss. 280 to 283	(abduction and detention of young persons)
s. 424	(threats against internationally protected persons)

shall be deemed to commit that act or omission in Canada in the following circumstances:

(a) if the act or omission is committed on a ship that is registered or licensed, or for which an identification number has been issued, pursuant to any Act of Parliament;

(b) if the act or omission is committed on an aircraft registered in Canada under regulations made under the Aeronautics Act, or leased without crew and operated by a person who is qualified under regulations made under the Aeronautics Act to be registered as owner of an aircraft in Canada under those regulations;

(c) if the person who commits the act or omission is a Canadian citizen or is, after the act or omission has been committed, present in Canada; or

(d) if the act or omission is against either a person who enjoys the status of an internationally protected person by virtue of the functions that person performs on behalf of Canada, or a member of the family of a person just described who qualifies under the definition "internationally protected person" (s. 7(3)).

INTIMIDATION

1. *Intimidation of a person*
2. *Intimidation of Parliament or legislature*

1. Intimidation of a person — Section 423(1)

Every one who — wrongfully and without lawful authority — for the purpose of compelling another person to abstain from doing anything that he has a lawful right to do — or for the purpose of compelling another person to do anything that he has a lawful right to abstain from doing — either uses violence or threats of violence to that person or his spouse or children — or injures his property — or intimidates or attempts to intimidate that person or a relative of that person by threats that (in Canada or elsewhere) violence or other injury will be done to or punishment inflicted upon him or a relative of his or that the property of any of them will be damaged — or persistently follows that person about from place to place — or hides any tools or clothes or other property owned or used by that person or deprives him of them or hinders him in the use of them — or with one or more other persons follows that person in a disorderly manner on a highway — or besets or watches the dwelling-house or place where that person resides or works or carries on business or happens to be — or blocks or obstructs a highway — is guilty of an offence punishable on summary conviction.

Limitation period. No proceedings in respect of offences that are declared to be punishable on summary conviction shall be instituted more than 6 months after the time when the subject matter of the proceedings arose (s. 786(2) and s. 785(1)).

Included offences. Attempts (s. 660 and s. 662(1)(b)).

Punishment. A fine not exceeding $2,000, or 6 months' imprisonment, or both (s. 423(1) and s. 787(1)).

Release. Initial decision to release made by peace officer (s. 497).

Election. No election, summary conviction offence.

Evidence. 1. A person who attends at or near or approaches a dwelling-house or place, for the purpose only of obtaining or communicating information does not watch or beset within the meaning of s. 423(1) (s. 423(2)).
2. The courts have held that this offence is not confined to industrial disputes (Re R. and Baser aba (1975), 24 C.C.C. (2d) 296 (Man. C.A.)).

3. The onus is on the Crown to prove an accused's improper purpose in watching or besetting a place.

Informations

A.B., on or about the —— day of ——, 19——, at the —— of ——, in the said (territorial division), wrongfully and without lawful authority, for the purpose of compelling C.D. to abstain from (specify a thing that C.D. had a lawful right to do), did use violence [OR threats of violence] to C.D. [OR to the wife of C.D. OR to the children of C.D.], to wit: (specify the particulars of the offence), contrary to s. 423(1)(a) of the Criminal Code of Canada.

2. Intimidation of Parliament or legislature — Section 51

Every one who — does an act of violence — in order to intimidate Parliament or the legislature of a province — is guilty of an indictable offence.

Jurisdiction. Triable only in a superior court of criminal jurisdiction (s. 468 and s. 469(a)(iii)).

Included offences. Attempts (s. 660 and s. 662(1)(b)).

Punishment. Imprisonment for a term not exceeding 14 years (s. 51).

Release. Initial decision to release may only be made by superior court judge (s. 522).

Election. Superior court (with jury) exclusive, except where accused elects superior court trial without jury with consent of Attorney General (s. 473) (s. 469).

Evidence. In proceedings for this offence, no evidence is admissible of an overt act unless that overt act is set out in the indictment or unless the evidence is otherwise relevant as tending to prove an overt act that is set out therein (s. 55).

Informations

A.B., on or about the —— day of ——, 19——, at the —— of ——, in the said (territorial division), did an act of violence in order to intimidate Parliament [OR in order to intimidate the legislature of the Province of ——], to wit: (specify the particulars of the offence), contrary to s. 51 of the Criminal Code of Canada.

INTRA VIRES. Within the power of (Latin).

IPSE DIXIT. 1. "He himself said" (Latin). 2. A bare assertion.

IPSO FACTO. By that very fact (Latin).

ISSUANCE OF PROCESS. A writ, subpoena, warrant or similar document is said to be **issued** when it is presented to the proper officer of the court by the party seeking to have it issued, and has been authenticated by such officer and returned to the party. **Process** refers to the compelling nature of the document (Compelling Appearance, Interim Release and Pre-trial Detention, Law Reform Commission of Canada, Working Paper 57).

ITEM. Also (Latin).

J

JUDGE'S NOTES. Notes made by a judge as the trial proceeds. These notes record the evidence of each witness, any ruling made during the trial and the argument and authorities cited. Not a verbatim record, but the epitomizations of what has been said, recorded in a manner intelligible to the judge, if not to others.

In making notes, the judge must have in mind two factors: the necessity, in a jury trial, of a compendious review of the evidence in his charge to the jury, and the requirement in non-jury trials, of the delivery of oral or written reasons for judgment.

Judge's notes are to be distinguished from those made manually in shorthand notes by expert reporters or mechanically by tape machines in case transcripts of the evidence are required on appeal (Wilson, J., A Book for Judges).

JUDICIAL NOTICE

1. *Definition*
2. *Statutes*
3. *Regulations*

1. Definition. The act by which a court, in conducting a trial, or framing its decision, will, of its own motion and without the production of evidence, recognize the existence and truth of certain facts, having a bearing on the controversy at bar, which, from their nature, are not properly the subject of testimony, or which are universally regarded as established by common notoriety (Black's Law Dictionary).

2. Statutes. Judicial notice shall be taken of all Acts of the Imperial Parliament, of all ordinances made by the Governor in Council, or the lieutenant governor in council of any province or colony which, or some portion of which, now forms or hereafter may form part of Canada, and of all the Acts of the legislature of any such province or colony, whether enacted before or after the passing of the Constitution Act, 1867 (Canada Evidence Act, s. 17). Judicial notice shall be taken of all Acts of Parliament, public or private, without being specially pleaded (Canada Evidence Act, s. 18).

3. Regulations. The courts have held that judicial notice must be taken of all subordinate or delegated legislation that has been published in the Canada Gazette. (Statutory Instruments Act, s. 23(2)). There is no need to prove the fact of publication, but as a matter of courtesy, copies of regulations printed by the Queen's Printer that are being relied upon in the case should be supplied to the Judge and to the other parties (R. v. Eugenia Chandri (1976), 27 C.C.C. (2d) 241 (S.C.C.)).

JUDICIAL PROCEEDING. For the purposes of Part IV of the Criminal Code (Offences Against the Administration of Law and Justice), "judicial proceeding" means a proceeding

(a) in or under the authority of a court of justice,

(b) before the Senate or House of Commons of Canada or a committee of the Senate or House of Commons, or before a legislative council, legislative assembly or house of assembly or a committee thereof that is authorized by law to administer an oath,

(c) before a court, judge, justice, provincial court judge or coroner,

(d) before an arbitrator or umpire, or a person or body of persons authorized by law to make an inquiry and take evidence therein under oath, or

(e) before a tribunal by which a legal right or legal liability may be established,

whether or not the proceeding is invalid for want of jurisdiction or for any other reason (s. 118).

JURAT. 1. "He swears" (Latin). 2. Statement at end of affidavit showing when and before whom it was sworn.

JURIES

1. *General* 2. *Coroner's Jury*

1. General

The Criminal Code adopts the laws of the various provinces regarding the selection and qualifications of jurors (s. 626(1)). However, notwithstanding the law of any province, no person may be disqualified, exempted or excused from serving as a juror in criminal proceedings on the grounds of his or her sex (s. 626(2)).

This jury consists of 12 persons who are the judges of fact in all trials by jury. Either the accused or the prosecutor may challenge the jury panel on the ground of partiality, fraud or wilful misconduct on the part of the officer by whom the panel was returned (s. 629(1)). The panel is the whole list of jurors summoned by the sheriff. The judge shall determine whether the alleged ground of challenge is true or ot; if true, a new panel is returned (s. 630).

The prosecutor and the accused are each entitled to peremptory challenges, *i.e.*, without giving a cause. The number of challenges vary according to the charge against the accused. Where the charge is high treason or first degree murder, each is entitled to 20 such challenges. Where the charge is for an offence which carries a sentence of imprisonment for 5 years or more, each is entitled to 12 such challenges. For any other charge, each is entitled to 4 such challenges (s. 634(2)).

The prosecutor or the accused may also challenge for cause:

(a) that the name is not on its panel;

(b) that the juror is biased;

(c) that the juror has been convicted and sentenced to 12 months' imprisonment;

(d) that the juror is an alien;

(e) that the juror is unable to perform his duties; and

(f) that the juror cannot speak the official language of Canada in which testimony would be given (in force in Manitoba, New Brunswick, Ontario, Yukon Territory and Northwest Territories) (s. 638).

The jury must be unanimous in its verdict. If there is a disagreement the case is tried again. Usually after two disagreements the Attorney General considers whether he should order a stay of proceedings, called a Nolle Prosequi.

2. Coroner's Jury

This jury is differently constituted in each province, both as to number and the quorum which may find a verdict.

JURISDICTION

1. *Definition*
2. *Absolute jurisdiction*
3. *Original and appellate jurisdiction*
4. *Territorial jurisdiction*

1. Definition

Jurisdiction is the power of a court or judge to entertain a proceeding.

2. Absolute jurisdiction

When a proceeding in respect of a certain subject matter can only be brought in one court, that court is said to have absolute jurisdiction.

For example, the jurisdiction of a provincial court judge to try an accused is absolute where the accused is charged in an information with any one of the following offences:

(i) where the subject-matter of the offence is not a testamentary instrument and the alleged value thereof does not exceed $1,000, and the accused is charged with either:

theft, other than theft of cattle (s. 334),

obtaining money or property by false pretences (s. 362),

unlawfully having in his possession any property or thing or any proceeds of any property or thing knowing that all or a part of the property or thing or of the proceeds was obtained by or derived directly or indirectly from the commission in Canada of an offence punishable by indictment or an act or omission anywhere that, if it had occurred in Canada, would have constituted an offence punishable by indictment (ss. 354, 355), or

having, by deceit, falsehood or other fraudulent means, defrauded the public or any person, whether ascertained or not, of any property, money or valuable security (s. 380), or

mischief under s. 430(4) (mischief in relation to property)

(ii) where the accused is charged with counselling or with an attempt to commit or with being an accessory after the fact to the commission of any offence referred to in (i) or (iii); and

(iii) where the accused is charged with an offence under:

s. 201 (keeping gaming or betting house)
s. 202 (betting, pool-selling, book-making, etc.)
s. 203 (placing bets)
s. 206 (lotteries and games of chance)
s. 209 (cheating at play)
s. 210 (keeping common bawdy-house)
s. 259(4) (driving while disqualified) or
s. 393 (fraud in relation to fares).

3. Original and appellate jurisdiction

A court is said to have original jurisdiction in a particular matter when that matter can be initiated before it, while a court is said to have appellate jurisdiction when it can only go into the matter on appeal after it has been adjudicated on by a court of original jurisdiction.

4. Territorial jurisdiction

Jurisdiction also signifies the district or geographical limits within which the judgments and orders of a court can be executed. This is sometimes called territorial jurisdiction.

JUS. Right, law (Latin). ***Jus accrescendi.*** The right of accretion (e.g., succession to property by joint tenant). ***Jus civile.*** Civil law. ***Jus gentium.*** The law of nations. ***Jus naturale.*** Natural law. ***Jus quaesitum tertio.*** The right asserted by a third person. ***Jus spatiendi.*** The right of walking about. ***Jus tertii.*** The right of a third person. ***Jus venandi et piscandi.*** The right of hunting and fishing.

JUSTIFICATION OR EXCUSE. A form of common law defence. A justification challenges the wrongfulness of an action which technically constitutes a crime. An excuse concedes the wrongfulness of the action but asserts that the circumstances under which it was done are such that it ought not to be attributed to the actor (Colvin, Principles of Criminal Law).

JUVENILE DELINQUENT. For the purposes of the former Juvenile Delinquents Act, "juvenile delinquent" meant any child who violated any provision of the Criminal Code or of any federal or provincial statute, or of any by-law or ordinance of any municipality, or who was guilty of sexual immorality or any similar form of vice, or who was liable by reason of any other act to be committed to an industrial school or juvenile reformatory under any federal or provincial statute.

The Juvenile Delinquents Act was repealed and matters formerly governed by it are now subject to the Young Offenders Act, which was proclaimed in force on September 1, 1984. The term "juvenile delinquent" no longer has official status and is expected to fall into disuse.

K

KEEPER. For the purposes of Part VII of the Criminal Code, "keeper" includes a person who (a) is an owner or occupier of a place, (b) assists or acts on behalf of an owner or occupier of a place, (c) appears to be, or to assist or act on behalf of an owner or occupier of a place, (d) has the care or management of a place, or (e) uses a place permanently or temporarily, with or without the consent of the owner or occupier (s. 197(1)).

KIDNAPPING

Section 279(1)(a)

Every one who — kidnaps a person — with intent to cause him to be confined or imprisoned against his will — is guilty of an indictable offence.

Section 279(1)(b)

Every one who — kidnaps a person — with intent to cause him to be unlawfully sent or transported out of Canada against his will — is guilty of an indictable offence.

Section 279(1)(c)

Every one who — kidnaps a person — with intent to hold him for ransom or to service against his will — is guilty of an indictable offence.

Intent. Intention to cause confinement or imprisonment (s. 279(1)(a)), to send or transport (s. 279(1)(b)), or to hold for ransom or service (s. 279(1)(c)).

Included offences. Attempts (s. 660 and s. 662(1)(b)).

Punishment. Imprisonment for life (s. 279(1)).

Release. Initial decision to release made by justice (s. 515(1)).

Election. Accused may elect trial by judge and jury, judge alone, or provincial court judge (s. 536).

Defences. The fact that the person in relation to whom the offence is alleged to have been committed did not resist is not a defence unless the accused proves that the failure to resist was not caused by threats, duress, force or exhibition of force (s. 279(3)).

Informations

    A.B., on or about the —— day of ——, 19——, at the —— of ——, in the said (territorial division), did kidnap C.D. with intent to cause him to be confined [OR imprisoned] against his will, to wit: (specify the particulars of the offence), contrary to s. 279(1)(a) of the Criminal Code of Canada.

    A.B., on or about the —— day of ——, 19——, at the —— of ——, in the said (territorial division), did kidnap C.D. with intent to hold him to ransom [OR to service] against his will, to wit: (specify the particulars of the offence), contrary to s. 279(1)(c) of the Criminal Code of Canada.

See also ABDUCTION; SEXUAL ASSAULT, 7.

KNOWING. To know is to merely be aware of the physical character of the act without necessarily having the perception and ability to perceive the consequences, impact and results of the physical act (Knoll, Criminal Law Defences) (R. v. Barnier, [1980] 1 S.C.R. 1124).

Appreciate. Knowing and appreciating are not synonymous. A person appreciates the nature and quality of an act when there is an understanding of the physical nature, character and physical consequences of the act. A person may appreciate an act even though lacking appropriate feelings of remorse or guilt for what was done (Knoll, Criminal Law Defences) (R. v. Swain (1986), 50 C.R. (3d) 97).

L

LACERATION. A wound caused by crushing or tearing of the tissues and showing a break in the surface. Also rupture and tear (Jaffe, A Guide to Pathological Evidence, 2nd ed.).

LANDS. The areas on the inner surface of a firearm barrel which are located between rifling grooves (Jaffe, A Guide to Pathological Evidence, 2nd ed.). *See also RIFLING.*

LAW OF CANADA. For the purposes of Part I of the Canadian Bill of Rights, "law of Canada" means an Act of Parliament enacted before or after the coming into force of this Act, any order, rule or regulation thereunder, and any law in force in Canada or in any part of Canada at the commencement of this Act that is subject to be repealed, abolished or altered by Parliament (Canadian Bill of Rights, s. 5(2)).

LAW OF NATIONS. The former name given to public international law. *See also PIRACY, 2.*

LAWFUL PROCESS. 1. A summons, writ, warrant or other process issued by a court. 2. A process that is in fact valid.

LEGAL PROCEEDING. For the purposes of s. 29 of the Canada Evidence Act, "legal proceeding" means any civil or criminal proceeding or inquiry in which evidence is or may be given, and includes an arbitration (Canada Evidence Act, s. 29(9) and s. 30(12)).

LEX. Law (Latin).

LIBEL

1. *Publishing a blasphemous libel*
2. *Publishing a defamatory libel*
3. *Extortion by libel*
4. *Definition of "seditious libel". See SEDITION, 1.*

1. Publishing a blasphemous libel

Definition of "blasphemous libel". Blasphemous libel consists of attacking Christianity in a vulgar, profane or indecent manner; in such a way that it offends against public decency; in vilifying God, Jesus Christ, the Holy Ghost, the Bible. It may be spoken or written. It is not blasphemous libel to attack Christianity by means of sane argument in an attempt to prove its falsity.

Statement of offence — Section 296(1)

Every one who — publishes — a blasphemous libel — is guilty of an indictable offence.

Exceptions. No person shall be convicted of this offence for expressing in good faith and in decent language, or attempting to establish by argument used in good faith and conveyed in decent language, an opinion on a religious subject (s. 296(3)).

Included offences. Attempts (s. 660 and s. 662(1)(b)).

Punishment. Imprisonment for a term not exceeding 2 years (s. 296(1)).

Release. Initial decision to release made by officer in charge or justice (s. 498).

Election. Accused may elect trial by judge and jury, judge alone, or provincial court judge (s. 536).

Evidence. 1. A person publishes a libel when he (a) exhibits it in public, (b) causes it to be read or seen or (c) shows or delivers it, or causes it to be shown or delivered, with intent that it should be read or seen by the person whom it defames or by any other person (s. 299).
2. It is a question of fact whether or not any matter that is published is a blasphemous libel (s. 296(2)).

Sufficiency of count. 1. No count for publishing a blasphemous libel is insufficient by reason only that it does not set out the words that are alleged to be libellous (s. 584(1)).
2. A count for publishing a libel may charge that the published matter was written in a sense that by innuendo made the publication thereof criminal, and may specify that sense without any introductory assertion to show how the matter was written in that sense (s. 584(2)).
3. It is sufficient, on the trial of a count for publishing a libel, to prove that the matter published was libellous, with or without innuendo (s. 584(3)).

Informations

A.B., on or about the —— day of ——, 19——, at the —— of ——, in the said (territorial division), did publish a blasphemous libel, to wit: (specify the particulars of the offence), contrary to s. 296(1) of the Criminal Code of Canada.

2. Publishing a defamatory libel

Definition of "defamatory libel". A defamatory libel is matter published, without lawful justification or excuse, that is likely to injure the reputation of any person by exposing him to hatred, contempt or ridicule, or that is designed to insult the person of or concerning whom it is published (s. 298(1)).

A defamatory libel may be expressed directly or by insinuation or irony (a) in words legibly marked upon any substance, or (b) by any object signifying a defamatory libel otherwise than by words (s. 298(2)).

Statements of offences

Libel known to be false — Section 300

Every one who — publishes — a defamatory libel — that he knows is false — is guilty of an indictable offence.

Defamatory libel — Section 301

Every one who — publishes — a defamatory libel — is guilty of an indictable offence.

Intent. Knowledge of falsity (s. 300).

Included offences. Attempts (s. 660 and s. 662(1)(b)).

Punishment. Imprisonment for a term not exceeding 5 years where he knows the defamatory libel is false (s. 300). Imprisonment for a term not exceeding 2 years where he does not know the defamatory libel to be false (s. 301).

Release. Initial decision to release made by officer in charge or justice (s. 498).

Election. Accused may elect trial by judge and jury, judge alone, or provincial court judge (s. 536).

Definitions. See NEWSPAPER.

Defences. 1. The proprietor of a newspaper shall be deemed to publish defamatory matter that is inserted and published therein, unless he proves that the defamatory matter was inserted in the newspaper without his knowledge and without negligence on his part (s. 303(1)). 2. Where the proprietor of a newspaper gives to a person general authority to manage or conduct the newspaper as editor or otherwise, the insertion by that person of defamatory matter in the newspaper shall be deemed not to be negligence on the part of the proprietor unless it is proved that (a) he intended the general authority to include authority to insert defamatory matter in the newspaper, or (b) he continued to confer general authority after he knew that it had been exercised by the insertion of defamatory matter in the newspaper (s. 303(2)).

3. No person shall be deemed to publish a defamatory libel by reason only that he sells a number or part of a newspaper that contains a defamatory libel, unless he knows that the number or part contains defamatory matter or that defamatory matter is habitually contained in the newspaper (s. 303(3)).

4. No person shall be deemed to publish a defamatory libel by reason only that he sells a book, magazine, pamphlet or other thing, other than a newspaper that contains defamatory matter if, at the time of the sale, he does not know that it contains the defamatory matter (s. 304(1)).

5. Where a servant, in the course of his employment, sells a book, magazine, pamphlet or other thing, other than a newspaper, the employer shall be deemed not to publish any defamatory matter contained therein unless it is proved that the employer authorized the sale knowing that (a) defamatory matter was contained therein, or (b) defamatory matter was habitually contained therein, in the case of a periodical (s. 304(2)).

6. No person shall be deemed to publish a defamatory libel by reason only that he publishes defamatory matter (a) in a proceeding held before or under the authority of a court exercising judicial authority, or (b) in an inquiry made under the authority of an Act or by order of Her Majesty, or under the authority of a public department or a department of the government of a province (s. 305).

7. No person shall be deemed to publish a defamatory libel by reason only that he (a) publishes to the Senate or House of Commons or to a legislature, defamatory matter contained in a petition to the Senate or House of Commons or to the legislature of a province, as the case may be, (b) publishes by order or under the authority of the Senate or House of Commons or of the legislature of a province, a paper containing defamatory matter, or (c) publishes, in good faith and without ill-will to the person defamed, an extract from or abstract of a petition or paper just mentioned (s. 306).

8. No person shall be deemed to publish a defamatory libel by reason only that he publishes in good faith, for the information of the public, a fair report of the proceedings of the Senate or House of Commons or the legislature of a province, or a committee thereof, or of the public proceedings before a court exercising judicial authority, or publishes, in good faith, any fair comment on any such proceedings (s. 307(1)).

S. 307 does not apply to a person who publishes a report of evidence taken or offered in any proceeding before the Senate or House of Commons or any committee thereof, on a petition or bill relating to any matter of marriage or divorce, if the report is published without authority from or leave of the House in which the proceeding is held or is contrary to any rule, order or practice of that House (s. 307(2)).

9. No person shall be deemed to publish a defamatory libel by reason only that he publishes in good faith, in a newspaper, a fair report of the proceedings of any public meeting if (a) the meeting is lawfully convened for a lawful purpose and is open to the public, (b) the report is fair and accurate, (c) the publication of the matter complained of is for the public benefit, and (d) he does not refuse to publish in a conspicuous place in the newspaper a reasonable explanation or contradiction by the person defamed in respect of the defamatory matter (s. 303).

10. No person shall be deemed to publish a defamatory libel by reason only that he publishes defamatory matter that, on reasonable grounds, he believes is true, and that is relevant to any subject of public interest, the public discussion of which is for the public benefit (s. 309).

11. No person shall be deemed to publish a defamatory libel by reason only that he publishes fair comments: (a) upon the public conduct of a person who takes part in public affairs, or (b) upon a published book or other literary production, or on any composition or work of art or performance publicly exhibited, or on any other communication made to the public on any subject, if the comments are confined to criticism thereof (s. 310).

12. No person shall be deemed to publish a defamatory libel where he proves that the publication of the defamatory matter in the manner in which it was published was for the public benefit at the time when it was published and that the matter itself was true (s. 311).

13. No person shall be deemed to publish a defamatory libel by reason only that he publishes defamatory matter (a) on the invitation or challenge of the person in respect of whom it is published, or (b) that it is necessary to publish in order to refute defamatory matter published in respect of him by another person, if he believes that the defamatory matter is true and it is relevant to the invitation, challenge or necessary refutation, as the case may be, and does not in any respect exceed what is reasonably sufficient in the circumstances (s. 312).

14. No person shall be deemed to publish a defamatory libel by reason only that he publishes, in answer to inquiries made to him, defamatory matter relating to a subject matter in respect of which the person by whom or on whose behalf the inquiries are made has an interest in knowing the truth or who, on reasonable grounds, the person who publishes the defamatory matter believes has such an interest, if (a)

the matter is published, in good faith, for the purpose of giving information in answer to the inquiries, (b) the person who publishes the defamatory matter believes that it is true, (c) the defamatory matter is relevant to the inquiries, and (d) the defamatory matter does not in any respect exceed what is reasonably sufficient in the circumstances (s. 313).

15. No person shall be deemed to publish a defamatory libel by reason only that he publishes to another person defamatory matter for the purpose of giving information to that person with respect to a subject matter in which the person to whom the information is given has, or is believed on reasonable grounds by the person who gives it to have, an interest in knowing the truth with respect to that subject matter if (a) the conduct of the person who gives the information is reasonable in the circumstances, (b) the defamatory matter is relevant to the subject matter, (c) and the defamatory matter is true, or if it is not true, is made without ill-will toward the person who is defamed and is made in the belief, on reasonable grounds, that it is true (s. 314).

16. No person shall be deemed to publish a defamatory libel by reason only that he publishes defamatory matter in good faith for the purpose of seeking remedy or redress for a private or public wrong or grievance from a person who has, or who on reasonable grounds he believes has, the right or is under an obligation to remedy or redress the wrong or grievance, if (a) he believes that the defamatory matter is true, (b) the defamatory matter is relevant to the remedy or redress that is sought, and (c) the defamatory matter does not in any respect exceed what is reasonably sufficient in the circumstances (s. 315).

Evidence. 1. A person publishes a libel when he (a) exhibits it in public (b) causes it to be read or seen or (c) shows or delivers it, or causes it to be shown or delivered, with intent that it should be read or seen by the person whom it defames or by any other person (s. 299).

2. An accused who is alleged to have published a defamatory libel may, at any stage of the proceedings, adduce evidence to prove that the matter that is alleged to be defamatory was contained in a paper published by order or under the authority of the Senate or House of Commons or a legislature of a province (s. 316(1)).

3. For these purposes, a certificate under the hand of the Speaker or clerk of the Senate or House of Commons or the legislature of a province to the effect that the matter that is alleged to be defamatory was contained in a paper published by order or under the authority of the Senate, House of Commons or the legislature of a province, as the case may be, is conclusive evidence thereof (s. 316(3)).

Sufficiency of count. 1. No count for publishing a defamatory libel is insufficient by reason only that it does not set out the words that are alleged to be libellous (s. 584(1)).

2. A count for publishing a libel may charge that the published matter was written in a sense that by innuendo made the publication thereof criminal, and may specify that sense without any introductory assertion to show how the matter was written in that sense (s. 584(2)).

3. It is sufficient, on the trial of a count for publishing a libel, to prove that the matter published was libellous, with or without innuendo (s. 584(3)).

3. Extortion by libel

Section 302(1) and (3)

Every one who — with intent — either to extort money from any person — or to induce a person to confer on or procure for another person an appointment or office of profit or trust — publishes or threatens to publish or offers to abstain from publishing or to prevent the publication of — a defamatory libel — is guilty of an indictable offence.

Section 302(2) and (3)

Every one who — as the result of the refusal of any person to permit money to be extorted or to confer or procure an appointment or office of profit or trust — publishes or threatens to publish — a defamatory libel — is guilty of an indictable offence.

Intent. Intention to extort or induce (s. 302(1)).

Included offences. Attempts (s. 660 and s. 662(1)(b)).

Punishment. Imprisonment for a term not exceeding 5 years (s. 302(3)).

Release. Initial decision to release made by officer in charge or justice (s. 498).

Election. Accused may elect trial by judge and jury, judge alone, or provincial court judge (s. 536).

LIEUTENANT GOVERNOR IN COUNCIL. In Ontario, this expression means the Lieutenant Governor of Ontario or the person administering the government of Ontario for the time being acting by and with the advice of the Executive Council (or Cabinet) of Ontario

(Interpretation Act, R.S.O. 1990, c. I.11, s. 29(1)). In the other provinces of Canada, the expression has a similar meaning.

LIMITATION PERIODS. There is no limit within which proceedings must be taken for most criminal offences. Except in summary conviction cases where the limitation is 6 months (s. 786(2)), any limitation will be noted in the section. If a warrant is issued, it remains in force until executed. Under provincial statutes the limit is usually 6 months, but the statute creating the offence often fixes a limit. Where the offence is providing false information in an application for a licence, the statute may provide for a limitation period that runs from the time the offence is first discovered.

LIS PENDENS. A pending lawsuit (Latin).

LIVIDITY. A dark red or bluish red discolouration of the surface of the dependent portions of the body due to post mortem stasis of blood. Also "livor mortis" (Jaffe, A Guide to Pathological Evidence, 2nd ed.).

Congestion lividity. Lividity caused by the distension of the skin capillaries by blood (Jaffe, A Guide to Pathological Evidence, 2nd ed.).

Diffusion lividity. Lividity due to hemoglobin staining of the dependent portions of the skin. Diffusion lividity tends to be "fixed" in contrast to congestion lividity (Jaffe, A Guide to Pathological Evidence, 2nd ed.).

LOCAL REGISTRAR OF FIREARMS. This expression means any person who has been designated in writing as a local registrar of firearms by the Commissioner or the Attorney General of a province or who is a member of a class of police officers or police constables that has been so designated (s. 84(1)).

A police officer or police constable designated in writing by the Commissioner or the Attorney General of a province for these purposes or who is a member of a class of police officers or police constables that has been so designated may perform the functions and duties of a local registrar of firearms (s. 84(3)).

LOCO CITATO (LOC. CIT.). In the place cited (Latin).

LUMBER. For the purposes of s. 339, "lumber" means timber, mast, spar, shingle bolt, sawlog or lumber of any description (s. 339(6)). *See also THEFT AND OFFENCES RESEMBLING THEFT, 15.*

LUMBERING EQUIPMENT. For the purposes of s. 339, "lumbering equipment" includes a boom chain, chain, line and shackle (s. 339(6)). *See also THEFT AND OFFENCES RESEMBLING THEFT, 15 and 16.*

M

MALA FIDE. In bad faith (Latin).

MALICIOUS PROSECUTION. This action lies at the instance of a prosecuted person against the person who institutes criminal proceedings maliciously and without reasonable and probable cause. The following conditions must be fulfilled:

(a) the proceedings must have been instituted by the defendant in the action;

(b) he must have acted without reasonable and probable cause, i.e., no matter how malicious the prosecution was, the action will not lie unless the defendant did not have a genuine belief based on reasonable grounds that the prosecution was justified and the burden of proving the absence of reasonable and probable cause lies upon the plaintiff;

(c) he must have acted maliciously, i.e., even if there is no reasonable and probable cause, the action will not lie unless there is present some improper and wrongful motive, i.e., an intent to use the prosecution for some other purpose than the punishment of the offender, such as the collection of money, and the burden of proving malice lies on the plaintiff;

(d) the prosecution must have terminated in favour of the plaintiff. It is not enough that the plaintiff, if convicted, proves that he was in fact innocent. It is not necessary for the plaintiff to prove arrest and detention.

It will be seen therefore, that the laying of an information upon mere suspicion may subject the informant to an action for damages for malicious prosecution. Suspicion against the accused should be accompanied by reasonable and probable cause to believe that he committed the offence, before the information is laid. Reasonable suspicion of guilt might come from hearsay, but the hearsay should be from a credible and known source. It has been held that where the informant has acted on the advice of Crown counsel, he cannot be held responsible for the mistakes made by that officer, such a course disproving malice. Where a constable has been asked to swear to an information by a private party, and is not satisfied that there are good grounds to believe the accused to be guilty, he should advise the private party to lay the charge himself, unless the Crown prosecutor advises him differently.

MALUM (MALA) IN SE. Evil in itself (Latin).

MANDAMUS. A high prerogative writ issued by a superior court to compel the performance of a public duty in the absence of other means of redress.

MARIHUANA. 1. The flowering tops and upper leaves of the hemp plant (Cannabis sativa), usually sold as a coarse powder and smoked in the form of hand rolled cigarettes (Jaffe, A Guide to Pathological Evidence, 2nd ed.). 2. For the purposes of the Narcotic Control Act, "marihuana" means Cannabis sativa L. (Narcotic Control Act, s. 2).

MARK. For the purposes of s. 376, "mark" means a mark, brand, seal, wrapper or design used by or on behalf of either (a) the Government of Canada or a province, (b) the government of a state other than Canada, or (c) any department, board, commission or agent established by a government mentioned above in connection with the service or business of that government (s. 376(3)).

MAY. The Interpretation Act provides that "may" is to be construed as permissive (Interpretation Act, s. 11).

MENS REA. A guilty mind. It is a general rule that mens rea is an essential ingredient of criminal offences. There are exceptional cases in which the Code is so worded that mens rea is not essential to the commission of an offence (i.e., s. 125).

MENTAL DISORDER. For the purposes of the Criminal Code, "mental disorder" means a disease of the mind (s. 2).

MESCALINE. A hallucinogenic drug derived from the peyote cactus (Jaffe, A Guide to Pathological Evidence, 2nd ed.).

MILITARY. For the purposes of the Criminal Code, "military" shall be construed as relating to all or any part of the Canadian Forces (s. 2).

Military law. For the purposes of the Criminal Code, "military law" includes all law, regulations or orders relating to the Canadian Forces (s. 2).

MISCARRIAGE. The expulsion of the fetus, usually in the 3rd trimester of pregnancy (Jaffe, A Guide to Pathological Evidence, 2nd ed.).

MISCHIEF

1. *Mischief in relation to property*
2. *Mischief causing danger to life*
3. *Mischief in relation to testamentary instruments*
4. *Mischief in relation to property worth more than $1,000*
5. *Mischief in relation to other property*
6. *Mischief in relation to data*
7. *Acts or omissions likely to cause mischief*
8. *Public mischief.* See MISLEADING JUSTICE, 7.

1. Mischief in relation to property

Definition of offence — Section 430(1)

Every one who — wilfully — either destroys or damages property — or renders property dangerous or useless or inoperative or ineffective — or obstructs or interrupts or interferes with the lawful use or enjoyment or operation of property — or obstructs or interrupts or interferes with any person in the lawful use or enjoyment or operation of property — commits mischief.

2. Mischief causing danger to life — Section 430(2)

Every one who — commits mischief — that causes actual danger to life — is guilty of an indictable offence.

Intent. Wilfully (s. 430(1)).

Exceptions. 1. No person commits mischief by reason only that

(a) he stops work as a result of the failure of his employer and himself to agree upon any matter relating to his employment;

(b) he stops work as a result of the failure of his employer and a bargaining agent acting on his behalf to agree on any matter relating to his employment; or

(c) he stops work as a result of his taking part in a combination of workmen or employees for their own reasonable protection as workmen or employees (s. 430(6)).

2. No person commits mischief by reason only that he attends at or near or approaches a dwelling-house or place for the purpose only of obtaining or communicating information (s. 430(7)).

Included offences. Attempts (s. 660 and s. 662(1)(b)).

Punishment. Imprisonment for life (s. 430(2)).

Release. Initial decision to release made by justice (s. 515(1)).

Election. Accused may elect trial by judge and jury, judge alone, or provincial court judge (s. 536).

Evidence. No person shall be convicted of this offence where he proves that he acted with either legal justification or excuse and/or with colour of right (s. 429(2) and R. v. Creaghan (1982), 31 C.R. (3d) 277 (Ont. C.A.)).

Informations

A.B., on or about the —— day of ——, 19——, at the —— of ——, in the said (territorial division), wilfully did destroy [OR damage] property [OR render property dangerous (OR useless OR inoperative OR ineffective) OR obstruct (OR interrupt OR interfere with) the lawful use (OR enjoyment OR operation) of property OR obstruct (OR interfere with or interrupt) C.D. in the lawful use (OR enjoyment OR operation) of property], and thereby commit mischief that caused actual danger to life, to wit: (specify the particulars of the offence), contrary to s. 430(2) of the Criminal Code of Canada.

A.B., on or about the —— day of ——, 19——, at the —— of ——, in the said (territorial division), did commit mischief that caused actual danger to life, to wit: (specify the particulars of the offence), contrary to s. 430(2) of the Criminal Code of Canada.

3. Mischief in relation to testamentary instruments — Section 430(3)

Every one who — commits mischief — in relation to property — that is a testamentary instrument — is guilty of either an indictable offence or an offence punishable on summary conviction.

Exceptions. *See Exceptions under* **2**, *above.*

Limitation period. No proceedings in respect of offences that are declared to be punishable on summary conviction shall be instituted more than 6 months after the time when the subject matter of the proceedings arose (s. 786(2) and s. 785(1)).

Included offences. Attempts (s. 660 and s. 662(1)(b)).

Punishment. On indictment, imprisonment for a term not exceeding 10 years (s. 430(3)(a)). On summary conviction, a fine not exceeding $2,000, or 6 months' imprisonment, or both (s. 430(3)(b) and s. 787(1)).

Release. Initial decision to release made by peace officer (s. 497).

Election. On indictment, accused may elect trial by judge and jury, judge alone, or provincial court judge (s. 536). On summary conviction, no election.

Evidence. 1. A paper, instrument, document, gift or appointment is said to be testamentary when it is written or so made as not to take effect until after the death of the person making it and to be revocable during his life, although he may have believed that it would operate as an instrument of a different character. The term of course includes wills and codicils, which are in form as well as effect testamentary (Jowitt's Dictionary of English Law).
2. *See also Evidence under* **2**, *above.*

4. Mischief in relation to property worth more than $1,000 — Section 430(3)

Every one who — commits mischief — in relation to property — the value of which exceeds $1,000 — is guilty of either an indictable offence or an offence punishable on summary conviction.

Exceptions. See Exceptions under **2**, *above.*

Limitation period. No proceedings in respect of offences that are declared to be punishable on summary conviction shall be instituted more than 6 months after the time when the subject matter of the proceedings arose (s. 786(2) and s. 785(1)).

Included offences. Attempts (s. 660 and s. 662(1)(b)).

Punishment. On indictment, imprisonment for a term not exceeding 10 years (s. 430(3)(a)). On summary conviction, a fine not exceeding $2000, or 6 months' imprisonment, or both (s. 430(3)(b) and s. 787(1)).

Release. Initial decision to release made by peace officer (s. 497).

Election. On indictment, accused may elect trial by judge and jury, judge alone, or provincial court judge (s. 536). On summary conviction, no election.

Evidence. See Evidence under **2**, above.

5. Mischief in relation to other property — Section 430(4)

Every one who — commits mischief — in relation to property — other than property that is a testamentary instrument or the value of which exceeds $1,000 — is guilty of either an indictable offence or an offence punishable on summary conviction.

Exceptions. See Exceptions under **2**, above.

Limitation period. No proceedings in respect of offences that are declared to be punishable on summary conviction shall be instituted more than 6 months after the time when the subject matter of the proceedings arose (s. 786(2) and s. 785(1)).

Included offences. Attempts (s. 660 and s. 662(1)(b)).

Punishment. On indictment, imprisonment for a term not exceeding 2 years (s. 430(4)(a)). On summary conviction, a fine not exceeding $2,000, or 6 months' imprisonment, or both (s. 430(4)(b) and s. 787(1)).

Release. Initial decision to release made by peace officer (s. 497).

Election. On indictment, accused may elect trial by judge and jury, judge alone, or provincial court judge (s. 536). On summary conviction, no election.

Evidence. See Evidence under **2**, above.

6. Mischief in relation to data

Definition of offence — Section 430(1.1)

Every one who — wilfully — either destroys or alters data — or renders data meaningless or useless or ineffective — or obstructs or interrupts or interferes with the lawful use of data — or obstructs or interrupts or interferes with any person in the lawful use of data or denies access to data to any person who is entitled to access thereto — commits mischief.

Statement of offence — Section 430(5)

Every one who — commits mischief — in relation to data — is guilty of either an indictable offence or an offence punishable on summary conviction.

Intent. Wilfully.

Exceptions. See Exceptions under 2, above.

Limitation period. No proceedings in respect of offences that are declared to be punishable on summary conviction shall be instituted more than 6 months after the time when the subject matter of the proceedings arose (s. 786(2) and s. 785(1)).

Included offences. Attempts (s. 660 and s. 662(1)(b)).

Punishment. On indictment, imprisonment for a term not exceeding 10 years (s. 430(5)(a)). On summary conviction, a fine not exceeding $2,000, or 6 months' imprisonment, or both (s. 430(5)(b) and s. 787(1)).

Release. Initial decision to release made by peace officer (s. 497).

Election. On indictment, accused may elect trial by judge and jury, judge alone, or provincial court judge (s. 536). On summary conviction, no election.

Definitions. For these purposes, "data" means representations of information or of concepts that are being prepared or have been prepared in a form suitable for use in a computer system (s. 342.1(2) and s. 430(8)).

Evidence. See Evidence under 2, above.

7. Acts or omissions likely to cause mischief — Section 430(5.1)

Every one who — either wilfully does an act — or wilfully omits to do an act — that it is his duty to do — if that act or omission — is likely to constitute mischief causing actual danger to life — or is likely to constitute mischief in relation to property or data — is guilty of either an indictable offence or an offence punishable on summary conviction.

Intent. Wilfully.

Exceptions. See Exceptions under 2, above.

Limitation period. No proceedings in respect of offences that are declared to be punishable on summary conviction shall be instituted

more than 6 months after the time when the subject matter of the proceedings arose (s. 786(2) and s. 785(1)).

Included offences. Attempts (s. 660 and s. 662(1)(b)).

Punishment. On indictment, imprisonment for a term not exceeding 5 years (s. 430(5.1)(a)). On summary conviction, a fine not exceeding $2,000, or 6 months' imprisonment, or both (s. 430(5.1)(b) and s. 787(1)).

Release. Initial decision to release made by peace officer (s. 497).

Election. On indictment, accused may elect trial by judge and jury, judge alone, or provincial court judge (s. 536). On summary conviction, no election.

Evidence. See Evidence under **2**, above.

MISLEADING JUSTICE

1. *Perjury*
2. *False statements*
3. *Witness giving contradictory evidence*
4. *Fabricating evidence*
5. *Offences relating to affidavits*
6. *Obstructing justice*
7. *Public mischief*
8. *Compounding indictable offence*
9. *Corruptly taking reward for recovery of goods*
10. *Advertising reward and immunity*

1. Perjury

Definition of offence — Section 131(1) and (2)

Every one who — with intent to mislead — makes before a person who is authorized by law to permit it to be made before him — a false statement under oath or solemn affirmation — by affidavit or solemn declaration or deposition or orally — knowing that the statement is false — whether or not the statement is made in a judicial proceeding — commits perjury.

Statement of offence — Section 132

Every one who — commits perjury — is guilty of an indictable offence.

Intent. Intention to mislead; knowledge of falsity.

Exceptions. This offence does not include a statement that is made by a person who is not specially permitted, authorized or required by law to make that statement (s. 131(3)).

Included offences. Attempts (s. 660 and s. 662(1)(b)).

Punishment. Imprisonment for a term not exceeding 14 years (s. 132).

However, liable to a maximum term of imprisonment for life where a person commits perjury to procure the conviction of another person for an offence punishable by death (s. 132).

Release. Initial decision to release made by justice (s. 515(1)).

Election. Accused may elect trial by judge and jury, judge alone, or provincial court judge (s. 536).

Evidence. No person shall be convicted of perjury upon the evidence of only one witness unless the evidence of that witness is corroborated in a material particular by evidence that implicates the accused (s. 133).

Sufficiency of count. No count that charges perjury is insufficient by reason only that it does not state the nature of the authority of the tribunal before which the oath or statement was taken or made, or the subject of the inquiry, or the words used or the evidence fabricated, or that it does not expressly negative the truth of the words used (s. 585(a)).

Informations

A.B., on or about the —— day of ——, 19——, at the —— of ——, in the said (territorial division), did commit perjury, to wit: (specify the particulars of the offence), contrary to s. 132 of the Criminal Code of Canada.

2. False statements — Section 134

Every one who — not being specially permitted or authorized or required by law to make a statement under oath or solemn affirmation — makes such a statement — by affidavit or solemn declaration or deposition or orally — before a person who is authorized by law to permit it to be made before him — knowing that the statement is false — is guilty of an offence punishable on summary conviction.

Intent. Knowledge of falsity.

Exception. This offence does not apply to a statement that is made in the course of a criminal investigation (s. 134(2)).

Limitation period. No proceedings in respect of offences that are declared to be punishable on summary conviction shall be instituted

more than 6 months after the time when the subject matter of the proceedings arose (s. 786(2) and s. 785(1)).

Included offences. Attempts (s. 660 and s. 662(1)(b)).

Punishment. A fine not exceeding $2,000 or 6 months' imprisonment, or both (s. 134(1) and s. 787(1)).

Release. Initial decision to release made by peace officer (s. 497).

Election. No election, summary conviction offence.

Sufficiency of count. No count that charges the making of a false statement is insufficient by reason only that it does not state the nature of the authority of the tribunal before which the oath or statement was taken or made, or the subject of the inquiry, or the words used or the evidence fabricated, or that it does not expressly negative the truth of the words used (s. 585(b)).

Informations

A.B., on or about the —— day of ——, 19——, at the —— of ——, in the said (territorial division), not being specially required, authorized or required by law to make a statement under oath or solemn affirmation, did make a statement by affidavit [OR solemn declaration OR (as the case may be)] before C.D., a person authorized by law to permit it to be made before him, knowing that the statement was false, to wit: (specify the particulars of the offence), contrary to s. 134(1) of the Criminal Code of Canada.

3. Witness giving contradictory evidence — Section 136(1)

Every one who — being a witness in a judicial proceeding — gives evidence with respect to any matter of fact or knowledge — and subsequently in a judicial proceeding — gives evidence that is contrary to his previous evidence — whether or not the prior or later evidence or either of them is true — is guilty of an indictable offence.

Intent. Intention to mislead.

Consent to prosecute. No proceedings shall be instituted under this section without the consent of the Attorney General (s. 136(3)).

Included offences. Attempts (s. 660 and s. 662(1)(b)).

Punishment. Imprisonment for a term not exceeding 14 years (s. 136(1)).

Release. Initial decision to release made by justice (s. 515(1)).

Election. Accused may elect trial by judge and jury, judge alone, or provincial court judge (s. 536).

Evidence. 1. No person shall be convicted of this offence unless the court, judge or provincial court judge, as the case may be, is satisfied beyond a reasonable doubt that the accused, in giving evidence in either of the judicial proceedings, intended to mislead (s. 136(1)).

2. "Evidence", for these purposes, does not include evidence that is not material (s. 136(2)).

3. Where a person is charged with this offence, a certificate specifying with reasonable particularity the proceeding in which that person is alleged to have given the evidence in respect of which the offence is charged, is evidence that it was given in a judicial proceeding, without proof of the signature or official character of the person by whom the certificate purports to be signed if it purports to be signed by the clerk of the court or other official having the custody of the record of that proceeding or by his lawful deputy (s. 136(2.1)).

Informations

A.B., on or about the —— day of ——, 19——, at the —— of ——, in the said (territorial division), being a witness in a judicial proceeding, gave evidence with respect to a matter of fact [OR knowledge] and subsequently, in a judicial proceeding, gave evidence that was contrary to his previous evidence, to wit: (specify the particulars of the offence), contrary to s. 136(1) of the Criminal Code of Canada.

4. Fabricating evidence — Section 137

Every one who — with intent to mislead — fabricates anything — with intent that it shall be used as evidence in a judicial proceeding (existing or proposed) — by any means other than perjury or incitement to perjury — is guilty of an indictable offence.

Intent. Intention to mislead; intention of fabrication to be used as evidence.

Included offences. Attempts (s. 660 and s. 662(1)(b)).

Punishment. Imprisonment for a term not exceeding 14 years (s. 137).

Release. Initial decision to release made by justice (s. 515(1)).

Election. Accused may elect trial by judge and jury, judge alone, or provincial court judge (s. 536).

Sufficiency of count. No count that charges fabricating evidence is insufficient by reason only that it does not state the nature of the authority of the tribunal before which the oath or statement was taken or made, or the subject of the inquiry, or the words used or the evidence fabricated, or that it does not expressly negative the truth of the words used (s. 585(c)).

Informations

A.B., on or about the —— day of ——, 19——, at the —— of ——, in the said (territorial division), with intent to mislead, did fabricate (specify the thing fabricated) with intent that it should be used as evidence in a judicial proceeding, by a means other than perjury or incitement to perjury, to wit: (specify the particulars of the offence), contrary to s. 137 of the Criminal Code of Canada.

5. Offences relating to affidavits

Section 138(a)

Every one who — signs — a writing that purports to be an affidavit or statutory declaration and to have been sworn or declared before him — when the writing was not so sworn or declared — or when he knows that he has no authority to administer the oath or declaration — is guilty of an indictable offence.

Section 138(b)

Every one who — uses or offers for use — any writing purporting to be an affidavit or statutory declaration — that he knows was not sworn or declared (as the case may be) by the affiant or declarant or before a person authorized in that behalf — is guilty of an indictable offence.

Section 138(c)

Every one who — signs as affiant or declarant — a writing that purports to be an affidavit or statutory declaration and to have been sworn or declared by him (as the case may be) — when the writing was not so sworn or declared — is guilty of an indictable offence.

Intent. Knowledge of lack of authority (s. 138(a)); knowledge of spurious character (s. 138(b)).

Included offences. Attempts (s. 660 and s. 662(1)(b)).

Punishment. Imprisonment for a term not exceeding 2 years (s. 138).

Release. Initial decision to release made by officer in charge or justice (s. 498).

Election. Accused may elect trial by judge and jury, judge alone, or provincial court judge (s. 536).

Informations

A.B., on or about the —— day of ——, 19——, at the —— of ——, in the said (territorial division), did sign a writing that purported to be an affidavit [OR statutory declaration] and to have been sworn [OR declared] before him when the writing was not so sworn [OR when the writing was not so declared OR when he knew that he had no authority to administer the oath (OR declaration)], to wit: (specify the particulars of the offence), contrary to s. 138(a) of the Criminal Code of Canada.

6. Obstructing justice

Section 139(1)

Every one who — wilfully — attempts in any manner — to obstruct or pervert or defeat the course of justice — in a judicial proceeding — either by indemnifying or agreeing to indemnify a surety — in any way and either in whole or in part — or where he is a surety, by accepting or agreeing to accept a fee or any form of indemnity — whether in whole or in part from or in respect of a person who is released or is to be released from custody — is guilty of either an indictable offence or an offence punishable on summary conviction.

Section 139(2)

Every one who — wilfully — attempts in any manner other than a manner described above — to obstruct or pervert or defeat the course of justice — is guilty of an indictable offence.

Intent. Wilfully.

Limitation period. No proceedings in respect of offences that are declared to be punishable on summary conviction shall be instituted more than 6 months after the time when the subject matter of the proceedings arose (s. 786(2) and s. 785(1)).

Included offences. Attempts (s. 660 and s. 662(1)(b)).

Punishment. For an offence contrary to s. 139(1): on indictment, imprisonment for a term not exceeding 2 years (s. 139(1)(c)). On summary conviction, a fine not exceeding $2,000, or 6 months' imprisonment, or both (s. 139(1)(d) and s. 787(1)).

For an offence contrary to s. 139(2), imprisonment for a term not exceeding 10 years (s. 139(2)).

Release. For an offence contrary to s. 139(1), initial decision to release made by peace officer (s. 497). For an offence contrary to s. 139(2), initial decision to release made by justice (s. 515(1)).

Election. On indictment, accused may elect trial by judge and jury, judge alone, or provincial court judge (s. 536). On summary conviction, no election.

Evidence. Every one shall be deemed wilfully to attempt to obstruct, pervert or defeat the course of justice who in a judicial proceeding, existing or proposed, (a) dissuades or attempts to dissuade a person by threats, bribes or other corrupt means from giving evidence; (b) influences or attempts to influence by threats, bribes or other corrupt means a person in his conduct as a juror; or (c) accepts or obtains, agrees to accept or attempts to obtain a bribe or other corrupt consideration to abstain from giving evidence, or to do or to refrain from doing anything as a juror (s. 139(3)).

Informations

A.B., on or about the —— day of ——, 19——, at the —— of ——, in the said (territorial division), did wilfully attempt to obstruct [OR pervert OR defeat] the course of justice in a judicial proceeding, by indemnifying [OR by agreeing to indemnify] a surety, to wit: (specify the particulars of the offence), contrary to s. 139(1)(a) of the Criminal Code of Canada.

A.B., on or about the —— day of ——, 19——, at the —— of ——, in the said (territorial division), being a surety, did wilfully attempt to obstruct [OR pervert OR defeat] the course of justice in a judicial proceeding, by accepting [OR by agreeing to accept] a fee [OR an indemnity] from [OR in respect of] C.D., a person who was released [OR who was to be released] from custody, to wit: (specify the particulars of the offence), contrary to s. 139(1)(b) of the Criminal Code of Canada.

7. Public mischief

Definition of offence — Section 140(1)

Every one who — with intent to mislead — causes a peace officer to enter on or continue an investigation — by either making a false statement that accuses some other person of having committed an

offence — or by doing anything that is intended to cause some other person to be suspected of having committed an offence that the other person has not committed or to divert suspicion from himself — or by reporting that an offence has been committed — when it has not been committed — or by reporting or in any other way making it known or causing it to be made known that he or some other person has died — when he or that other person has not died — commits public mischief.

Statement of offence — Section 140(2)

Every one who — commits public mischief — is guilty of either an indictable offence or an offence punishable on summary conviction.

Intent. Intention to mislead.

Limitation period. No proceedings in respect of offences that are declared to be punishable on summary conviction shall be instituted more than 6 months after the time when the subject matter of the proceedings arose (s. 786(2) and s. 785(1)).

Included offences. Attempts (s. 660 and s. 662(1)(b)).

Punishment. On indictment, imprisonment for a term not exceeding 5 years (s. 140(2)(a)). On summary conviction, a fine not exceeding $2,000, or 6 months' imprisonment, or both (s. 140(2)(b) and s. 787(1)).

Release. Initial decision to release made by peace officer (s. 497).

Election. On indictment, accused may elect trial by judge and jury, judge alone, or provincial court judge (s. 536). On summary conviction, no election.

Definitions. For these purposes, "offence" is not restricted to a Criminal Code offence, but refers also to any breach of the law whether federal, provincial or otherwise that involves a penal sanction.

Informations

A.B., on or about the —— day of ——, 19——, at the —— of ——, in the said (territorial division), with intent to mislead, did cause C.D., a peace officer, to enter on [OR continue] an investigation by making a false statement that accused E.F. of having committed an offence, to wit: (specify the particulars of the offence), contrary to s. 140(1)(a) of the Criminal Code of Canada.

8. Compounding indictable offence — Section 141(1)

Every one who — asks for or obtains or agrees to receive or obtain — any valuable consideration — for himself or any other person — by agreeing to compound or conceal an indictable offence — is guilty of an indictable offence.

Exception. This offence does not apply to valuable consideration which is received or obtained or is to be received or obtained under an agreement for compensation or restitution or personal services that is (a) entered into with the consent of the Attorney General; or (b) made as part of a program, approved by the Attorney General, to direct persons charged with indictable offences from criminal proceedings (s. 141(2)).

Included offences. Attempts (s. 660 and s. 662(1)(b)).

Punishment. Imprisonment for a term not exceeding 2 years (s. 141(1)).

Release. Initial decision to release made by officer in charge or justice (s. 498).

Election. Accused may elect trial by judge and jury, judge alone, or provincial court judge (s. 536).

Informations

A.B., on or about the —— day of ——, 19——, at the —— of ——, in the said (territorial division), did ask for [OR obtain OR agree to receive OR agree to obtain] valuable consideration for himself [OR for C.D.] by agreeing to compound [OR conceal] an indictable offence, to wit: (specify the particulars of the offence), contrary to s. 141(1) of the Criminal Code of Canada.

9. Corruptly taking reward for recovery of goods — Section 142

Every one who — corruptly — accepts any valuable consideration — directly or indirectly — under pretence or on account of helping any person to recover anything obtained by the commission of an indictable offence — is guilty of an indictable offence.

Intent. Corruptly.

Included offences. Attempts (s. 660 and s. 662(1)(b)).

Punishment. Imprisonment for a term not exceeding 5 years (s. 142).

Release. Initial decision to release made by officer in charge or justice (s. 498).

Election. Accused may elect trial by judge and jury, judge alone, or provincial court judge (s. 536).

Informations

A.B., on or about the —— day of ——, 19——, at the —— of ——, in the said (territorial division), corruptly did accept valuable consideration under pretence [OR upon account] of helping C.D. to recover (specify the thing recovered) obtained by the commission of an indictable offence, to wit: (specify the particulars of the offence), contrary to s. 142 of the Criminal Code of Canada.

10. Advertising reward and immunity

Advertising

Section 143(a)

Every one who — publicly — advertises a reward — for the return of anything that has been stolen or lost — and in the advertisement — uses words to indicate that no questions will be asked if it is returned — is guilty of an offence punishable on summary conviction.

Section 143(b)

Every one who — in a public advertisement — uses words to indicate that a reward will be given or paid — for anything that has been stolen or lost — without interference with or inquiry about the person who produces it — is guilty of an offence punishable on summary conviction.

Section 143(c)

Every one who — in a public advertisement — promises or offers to return — to a person who had advanced money by way of loan on, or has bought, anything that has been stolen or lost — the money so advanced or paid, or any other sum of money for the return of that thing — is guilty of an offence punishable on summary conviction.

Printing or publishing advertisement — Section 143(d)

Every one who — prints or publishes — such an advertisement — is guilty of an offence punishable on summary conviction.

Limitation period. No proceedings in respect of offences that are declared to be punishable on summary conviction shall be instituted more than 6 months after the time when the subject matter of the proceedings arose (s. 786(2) and s. 785(1)).

Included offences. Attempts (s. 660 and s. 662(1)(b)).

Punishment. A fine not exceeding $2,000, or 6 months' imprisonment, or both (s. 143 and s. 787(1)).

Release. Initial decision to release made by peace officer (s. 497).

Election. No election, summary conviction offence.

MODUS OPERANDI. Manner of operating or working (Latin).

MOOT CASE or MOOT POINT. A case or point which is doubtful or arguable.

MORA. Delay (Latin).

MOTO PROPRIO. Of his own accord (Latin).

MOTOR VEHICLES AND VEHICLES GENERALLY

1. *Definition of "motor vehicle"*
2. *Dangerous operation of motor vehicle*
3. *Dangerous driving causing bodily harm*
4. *Dangerous driving causing death*
5. *Failing to stop at scene of accident*
6. *Operation of motor vehicle while impaired or with more than 80 mgs. of alcohol in blood*
7. *Impaired driving causing bodily harm*
8. *Impaired driving causing death*
9. *Failure or refusal to provide sample*
10. *Operation of motor vehicle while disqualified*
11. *Taking motor vehicle without consent. See THEFT AND OFFENCES RESEMBLING THEFT, 10.*

1. Definition of "motor vehicle"

For the purposes of the Criminal Code, "motor vehicle" means a vehicle that is drawn, propelled or driven by any means other than by muscular power, but does not include a vehicle of a railway that operates on rails (s. 2).

2. Dangerous operation of motor vehicle — Section 249(1)(a) and (2)

Every one who — operates a motor vehicle — on a street or road or highway or other public place — in a manner that is dangerous to the public — having regard to all the circumstances — including the nature and condition and use of that place — and including the

amount of traffic that at the time is or might reasonably be expected to be on that place — is guilty of either an indictable offence or an offence punishable on summary conviction.

Limitation period. No proceedings in respect of offences that are declared to be punishable on summary conviction shall be instituted more than 6 months after the time when the subject matter of the proceedings arose (s. 786(2) and s. 785(1)).

Included offences. Attempts (s. 660 and s. 662(1)(b)).

Punishment. On indictment, imprisonment for a term not exceeding 5 years (s. 249(2)(a)). On summary conviction, a fine not exceeding $2,000, or 6 months' imprisonment, or both (s. 249(2)(b) and s. 787(1)).

In addition to any other punishment that may be imposed, the court may make an order prohibiting the offender from operating a motor vehicle during any period not exceeding 3 years (s. 259(2)(c)).

Release. Initial decision to release made by peace officer (s. 497).

Election. On indictment, accused may elect trial by judge and jury, judge alone, or provincial court judge (s. 536). On summary conviction, no election.

Evidence. The degree of negligence required to support a charge of dangerous operation of a motor vehicle is something less than criminal negligence as defined by s. 219. It need not be wanton or reckless but must be more than inadvertence or momentary lapse. It must be such that it creates a situation dangerous to persons but it is not necessary that anyone be injured or killed.

Informations

A.B., on or about the —— day of ——, 19——, at the —— of ——, in the said (territorial division), did drive [OR operate] a motor vehicle on a street [OR road OR highway OR public place] in a manner dangerous to the public, to wit: (specify the particulars of the offence), contrary to s. 249(1)(a) of the Criminal Code of Canada.

3. Dangerous driving causing bodily harm — Section 249(3)

Every one who — commits an offence under s. 249(1)(a) (dangerous operation of motor vehicle) — and thereby causes bodily harm to any other person — is guilty of an indictable offence.

Included offences. Attempts (s. 660 and s. 662(1)(b)); dangerous operation of motor vehicle.

Punishment. Imprisonment for a term not exceeding 10 years (s. 249(3)).

In addition to any other punishment that may be imposed, the court may make an order prohibiting the offender from operating a motor vehicle during any period not exceeding 10 years (s. 259(2)(b)).

Release. Initial decision to release made by justice (s. 515(1)).

Election. Accused may elect trial by judge and jury, judge alone, or provincial court judge (s. 536).

Informations

A.B., on or about the —— day of ——, 19——, at the —— of ——, in the said (territorial division), did drive [OR operate] a motor vehicle on a street [OR road OR highway OR public place] in a manner dangerous to the public, thereby causing bodily harm to C.D., to wit: (specify the particulars of the offence), contrary to s. 249(3) of the Criminal Code of Canada.

4. Dangerous driving causing death — Section 249(4)

Every one who — commits an offence under s. 249(1)(a) (dangerous operation of motor vehicle) — and thereby causes the death of any other person — is guilty of an indictable offence.

Included offences. Attempts (s. 660 and s. 662(1)(b)); dangerous operation of motor vehicle.

Punishment. Imprisonment for a term not exceeding 14 years (s. 249(4)).

In addition to any other punishment that may be imposed, the court may make an order prohibiting the offender from operating a motor vehicle during any period not exceeding 10 years (s. 259(2)(b)).

Release. Initial decision to release made by justice (s. 515(1)).

Election. Accused may elect trial by judge and jury, judge alone, or provincial court judge (s. 536).

Informations

A.B., on or about the —— day of ——, 19——, at the —— of ——, in the said (territorial division), did drive [OR operate] a motor vehicle on a street [OR road OR highway OR public place] in a manner dangerous to the public, thereby causing the death of C.D., to wit: (specify the particulars of the offence), contrary to s. 249(4) of the Criminal Code of Canada.

5. Failing to stop at scene of accident — Section 252(1)

Every one who — has the care or charge of control of a vehicle — that is involved in an accident with — either another person — or another vehicle or a vessel or an aircraft — or cattle in the charge of a person — and with intent to escape civil or criminal liability — fails to stop his vehicle — and fails to give his name and address — and, where any person has been injured or appears to require assistance, fails to offer assistance — is guilty of either an indictable offence or an offence punishable on summary conviction.

Intent. Intention to escape civil or criminal liability.

Limitation period. No proceedings in respect of offences that are declared to be punishable on summary conviction shall be instituted more than 6 months after the time when the subject matter of the proceedings arose (s. 786(2) and s. 785(1)).

Included offences. Attempts (s. 660 and s. 662(1)(b)).

Punishment. On indictment, imprisonment for a term not exceeding 2 years (s. 252(1)). On summary conviction, a fine not exceeding $2,000, or 6 months' imprisonment, or both (s. 252(1) and s. 787(1)).

In addition to any other punishment that may be imposed, the court may make an order prohibiting the offender from operating a motor vehicle during any period not exceeding 3 years (s. 259(2)(c)).

Release. Initial decision to release made by peace officer (s. 497).

Election. On indictment, accused may elect trial by judge and jury, judge alone, or provincial court judge (s. 536). On summary conviction, no election.

Evidence. 1. Evidence that an accused failed to stop his vehicle, offer assistance where any person has been injured or appears to require assistance and give his name and address is, in the absence of evidence to the contrary, proof of an intent to escape civil or criminal liability (s. 252(2)).
2. The accused must be proved to have been driving the car (not merely the owner of it) or to have the care, charge or control; proof of the accident is necessary and that accused drove off without giving his name and address or without offering assistance where someone has been injured.
3. Provincial traffic laws have created offences of failure to remain at the scene of an accident. In some cases it is an offence to leave the scene of any accident, whether to persons or property. Insofar as

those offences are different from the above section, prosecution may be undertaken under the provincial statute, but where the same ground is covered the provincial enactment must give way to the Criminal Code, and the provincial enactment is inoperative to that extent and no prosecution should be instituted under it.

Informations

A.B., on or about the —— day of ——, 19——, at the —— of ——, in the said (territorial division), having the care [OR charge OR control] of a vehicle that was involved in an accident with C.D. [OR a vehicle in the charge of C.D. OR cattle in the charge of C.D.], did, with intent to escape civil or criminal liability, fail to stop his vehicle and give his name and address [and offer assistance to C.D. (OR E.F.), a person who was injured in the accident], to wit: (specify the particulars of the offence), contrary to s. 252(1) of the Criminal Code of Canada.

6. Operation of motor vehicle while impaired or with more than 80 mg of alcohol in blood — Section 253 and section 255(1)

Every one who — either operates a motor vehicle — or has the care or control of a motor vehicle — whether it is in motion or not — either while his ability to operate the motor vehicle is impaired by alcohol or a drug — or having consumed alcohol in such a quantity that the concentration thereof in his blood exceeds 80 mg of alcohol in 100 ml of blood — is guilty of either an indictable offence or an offence punishable on summary conviction.

Limitation period. No proceedings in respect of offences that are declared to be punishable on summary conviction shall be instituted more than 6 months after the time when the subject matter of the proceedings arose (s. 786(2) and s. 785(1)).

Included offences. Attempts (s. 660 and s. 662(1)(b)).

Punishment. On indictment, imprisonment for a term not exceeding 5 years (s. 255(1)(b)). On summary conviction, imprisonment for a term not exceeding 6 months (s. 255(1)(c)).

Whether on indictment or on summary conviction, liable to the following minimum punishment: namely, (i) for a first offence, to a fine of not less than $300; (ii) for a second offence, to imprisonment for not less than 14 days; and (iii) for each subsequent offence, to imprisonment for not less than 90 days (s. 255(1)(a)).

In addition to any other punishment that may be imposed, the court shall make an order prohibiting the offender from operating a motor vehicle (a) for a first offence, during a period of not more than

MOTOR VEHICLES AND VEHICLES GENERALLY 437

3 years and not less than 3 months; (b) for a second offence, during a period of not more than 3 years and not less than 6 months; and (c) for each subsequent offence, during a period of not more than 3 years and not less than one year (s. 259(1)).

Release. Initial decision to release made by peace officer (s. 497).

Election. On indictment, accused may elect trial by judge and jury, judge alone, or provincial court judge (s. 536). On summary conviction, no election.

Breath samples. Where a peace officer believes on reasonable and probable grounds that a person is committing, or at any time within the preceding 2 hours has committed, as a result of the consumption of alcohol, an offence under s. 253 (operation of motor vehicle while impaired or with more than 80 mg of alcohol in blood), the peace officer may, by demand made to that person forthwith or as soon as practicable, require that person to provide then or as soon thereafter as is practicable such samples of the person's breath as in the opinion of a qualified technician are necessary to enable proper analysis to be made in order to determine the concentration, if any, of alcohol in the person's blood, and to accompany the peace officer for the purpose of enabling such samples to be taken (s. 254(3)(a)).

Where samples of the breath of the accused have been taken pursuant to a demand made under s. 254(3), evidence of the results of the analyses so made is (in the absence of evidence to the contrary) proof of the concentration of alcohol in the blood of the accused at the time of the alleged offence, if the following conditions are met: (i) at the time each sample was taken, the person taking the sample offered to provide to the accused a specimen of the breath of the accused in an approved container for his own use, and, at the request of the accused made at that time, such a specimen was thereupon provided to the accused; (ii) each sample was taken as soon as practicable after the time of the alleged offence and, in the case of the first sample, not later than 2 hours after that time, with an interval of at least 15 minutes between the times when the samples were taken; (iii) each sample was received from the accused directly into an approved container or approved instrument operated by a qualified technician; and (iv) an analysis of each sample was made by means of an approved instrument operated by a qualified technician (s. 258(1)(c)).

However, the result of an analysis of a sample of the breath of the accused (other than a sample taken pursuant to a s. 254(3) demand) may be admitted in evidence notwithstanding that, before the accused gave the sample, he was not warned that he need not give the sample or that the result of the analysis of the sample might be used in evidence (s. 258(1)(b)).

Blood samples. Where a peace officer believes on reasonable and probable grounds that a person is committing, or at any time within the preceding 2 hours has committed, as a result of the consumption of alcohol, an offence under s. 253 (operation of motor vehicle while impaired or with more than 80 mg of alcohol in blood), the peace officer may, by demand made to that person forthwith or as soon as practicable, require that person to provide then or as soon thereafter as is practicable, where the peace officer has reasonable and probable grounds to believe that, by reason of any physical condition of the person, (i) the person may be incapable of providing a sample of his breath, or (ii) it would be impracticable to obtain a sample of his breath, such samples of the person's blood as in the opinion of a qualified medical practitioner or qualified technician taking the samples are necessary to enable power analysis to be made in order to determine the concentration, if any, of alcohol in the person's blood, and to accompany the peace officer for the purpose of enabling such samples to be taken (s. 254(3)(b)).

Samples of blood may be taken pursuant to a s. 254(3) demand only if the samples are taken by or under the direction of a qualified medical practitioner who is satisfied that the taking of such samples would not endanger the life or health of the person from whom those samples are taken (s. 254(4)).

Where justice is satisfied, on an information on oath in Form 1 or on an information on oath submitted to the justice pursuant to s. 487.1 by telephone or other means of telecommunications, that there are reasonable grounds to believe that (a) a person has, within the preceding 2 hours, committed, as a result of the consumption of alcohol, an offence under s. 253 (operation of motor vehicle while impaired or with more than 80 mg alcohol in blood) and that person was involved in an accident resulting in the death of another person or in bodily harm to himself or herself or to any other person, and (b) a qualified medical practitioner is of the opinion that (i) by reason of any physical or mental condition of the person that resulted from the consumption of alcohol, the accident or any other occurrence related to or resulting from the accident, the person is unable to consent to the taking of samples of his blood (ii) and the taking of samples of blood from the person would not endanger the life or health of the person, the justice may issue a warrant authorizing a peace officer to require a qualified medical practitioner to take, or to cause to be taken by a qualified technician under the direction of the qualified medical practitioner, such samples of the blood of the person as in the opinion of the person taking the samples are necessary to enable a proper analysis to be made in order to determine the concentration, if any, of alcohol in his blood (s. 256(1)). For the purposes of s. 256, an information on oath submitted by telephone or other means of telecommunication shall include a statement of the circumstances that make it impracticable for the peace officer to appear personally before a justice (s. 487.1(4)(a)), a statement setting out the offence alleged to have been committed and identifying the person from whom blood samples are to be taken (s. 256(3)) and a statement as to any prior application for a warrant in respect of the same matter, of which the peace officer has knowledge (s. 487.1(4)(d)). Where a warrant issued pursuant to s. 256(1) is executed, the peace officer shall, as soon as practicable thereafter, give a copy or, in the case of a warrant issued by telephone or other means of telecommunication, a facsimile of the warrant to the person from whom the samples were taken (s. 256(5)).

No qualified medical practitioner or qualified technician is guilty of an offence only by reason of his refusal to take a sample of blood from a person for the purposes of s. 254 or s. 256 and no qualified medical practitioner is guilty of an offence only by reason of his refusal to cause to be taken by a qualified technician under his direction a sample of blood from a person for such purposes (s. 257(1)).

No qualified medical practitioner by whom or under whose direction a sample of blood is taken from a person pursuant to a demand made under s. 254(3) or a warrant issued under s. 256 and no qualified technician acting under the direction of a qualified medical practitioner incurs any criminal or civil liability for anything necessarily done with reasonable care and skill in the taking of such a sample of blood (s. 257(2)).

Where a sample of the blood of the accused has been taken pursuant to a demand made under s. 254(3) or otherwise with the consent of the accused or pursuant to a warrant issued under s. 256, evidence of the result of the analysis is (in the absence of evidence to the contrary) proof of the concentration of alcohol in the blood of the accused at the time of the alleged offence if the following conditions are met: (i) at the time the sample was taken, the person taking the sample took an additional sample of the blood of the accused and one of the samples was retained, to permit an analysis thereof to be made by or on behalf of the accused and, at the request of the accused made within 3 months from the taking of the samples, one of the samples was ordered to be released; (ii) both such samples were taken as soon as practicable after the time of the alleged offence and in any event not later than 2 hours after that time; (iii) both such samples were taken by a qualified medical practitioner or a qualified technician under the direction of a qualified medical practitioner; (iv) both samples were received from the accused directly into, or placed directly into, approved containers that were subsequently sealed; and (v) an analysis was made by an analyst of at least one of the samples that was contained in a sealed approved container (s. 258(1)(d)). However, the result of an analysis of a sample of blood of the accused (other than a sample taken pursuant to s. 254(3) demand) may be admitted in evidence notwithstanding that, before the accused gave the sample, he was not warned that he need not give the sample or that the result of the analysis of the sample might be used in evidence (s. 258(1)(b)).

Other evidence. Physical evidence of impaired driving or impaired care or control should be obtained from the investigating officer and, if possible, one or more civilian witnesses, i.e., that (i) he staggered or was unsteady on his feet, (ii) his breath smelled of an alcoholic beverage, (iii) his speech was slurred, (iv) his eyes were bloodshot, and (v) his driving was erratic.

An accused shall be deemed to have had the care or control of a motor vehicle where it is proved that the accused occupied the seat or position ordinarily occupied by a person who operates a motor vehicle, unless the accused establishes that he did not occupy that seat or position for the purpose of setting the vehicle in motion (s. 258(1)(a)).

The result of an analysis of the urine or other bodily substance of the accused (other than a sample of breath or blood taken pursuant to s. 254(3) demand) may be admitted in evidence notwithstanding that, before the accused gave the sample, he was not warned that he need not give the sample or that the result of the analysis of the sample might be used in evidence (s. 258(1)(b)).

Evidence that the accused, without reasonable excuse, failed or refused to comply with a demand for samples made to him by a peace officer under s. 254 is admissible and the court may draw an inference therefrom adverse to the accused (s. 258(3)).

Informations

A.B., on or about the —— day of ——, 19——, at the —— of ——, in the said (territorial division), while his ability to operate a motor vehicle was impaired by alcohol [OR a drug], did operate [OR have the care or control of] a motor vehicle, to wit: (specify the particulars of the offence), contrary to s. 253 of the Criminal Code of Canada.

A.B., on or about the —— day of ——, 19——, at the —— of ——, in the said (territorial division), did operate [OR have the care or control of] a motor vehicle, having consumed alcohol in such a quantity that the concentration thereof in the blood of A.B. exceeded 80 mgs. of alcohol in 100 ml. of blood, to wit: (specify the particulars of the offence), contrary to s. 253 of the Criminal Code of Canada.

7. Impaired driving causing bodily harm — Section 255(2)

Every one who — commits an offence under s. 253(a) (operation of a motor vehicle while impaired) — and thereby causes bodily harm to any other person — is guilty of an indictable offence.

Included offences. Attempts (s. 660 and s. 662(1)(b)); operation of motor vehicle while impaired.

Punishment. Imprisonment for a term not exceeding 10 years (s. 255(2)).

In addition to any other punishment that may be imposed, the court may make an order prohibiting the offender from operating a motor vehicle during any period not exceeding 10 years (s. 259(2)(b)).

Release. Initial decision to release made by justice (s. 515(1)).

Election. Accused may elect trial by judge and jury, judge alone, or provincial court judge (s. 536).

Informations

A.B., on or about the —— day of ——, 19——, at the —— of ——, in the said (territorial division), while his ability to operate a motor vehicle was impaired by alcohol [OR a drug], did operate [OR have the care or control of] a motor vehicle, thereby causing bodily harm to C.D., to wit: (specify the particulars of the offence), contrary to s. 255(2) of the Criminal Code of Canada.

8. Impaired driving causing death — Section 255(3)

Every one who — commits an offence under s. 253(a) (operation of a motor vehicle while impaired) — and thereby causes the death of any other person — is guilty of an indictable offence.

Included offences. Attempts (s. 660 and s. 662(1)(b)); operation of a motor vehicle while impaired.

Punishment. Imprisonment for a term not exceeding 14 years (s. 255(3)).

In addition to any other punishment that may be imposed, the court may make an order prohibiting the offender from operating a motor vehicle during any period not exceeding 10 years (s. 259(2)(b)).

Release. Initial decision to release made by justice (s. 515(1)).

Election. Accused may elect trial by judge and jury, judge alone, or provincial court judge (s. 536).

Informations

A.B., on or about the —— day of ——, 19——, at the —— of ——, in the said (territorial division), while his ability to operate a motor vehicle was impaired by alcohol [OR a drug], did operate [OR have the care or control of] a motor vehicle, thereby causing the death of C.D., to wit: (specify the particulars of the offence), contrary to s. 255(3) of the Criminal Code of Canada.

9. Failure or refusal to provide sample — Section 254(5) and section 255(1)

Every one who — without reasonable excuse — fails or refuses to comply with a demand — made to him by a peace officer under s. 254 — is guilty of either an indictable offence or an offence punishable on summary conviction.

Intent. Intentional non-compliance.

Authority to test. Where a peace officer reasonably suspects that a person who is operating a motor vehicle or who has the care or control of a motor vehicle, whether it is in motion or not, has alcohol in his body, the peace officer may, by demand made to that person, require that person to provide forthwith such a sample of his breath as in the opinion of the peace officer is necessary to enable a proper analysis of his breath to be made by means of an approved screening device and, where necessary, to accompany the peace officer for the purpose of enabling such a sample of his breath to be taken (s. 254(2)). Where a peace officer believes on reasonable and probable grounds that a person is committing, or at any time within the preceding 2 hours has committed, as a result of the consumption of alcohol, an offence under s. 253 (operation of motor vehicle while impaired or with more than 80 mg of alcohol in blood), the peace officer may, by demand made to that person forthwith or as soon as practicable, require that person to provide then or as soon thereafter as practicable (a) such samples of the person's breath as in the opinion of a qualified technician (or (b) where the peace officer has reasonable and probable grounds to believe that, by reason of any physical condition of the person, (i) the person may be incapable of providing a sample of his breath, or (ii) it would be impracticable to obtain a sample of his breath, such samples of the person's blood, as in the opinion of a qualified medical practitioner or qualified technician taking the samples) are necessary to enable proper analysis to be made in order to determine the concentration, if any, of alcohol in the person's blood, and to accompany the peace officer for the purpose of enabling such samples to be taken (s. 254(3)).

Limitation period. No proceedings in respect of offences that are declared to be punishable on summary conviction shall be instituted more than 6 months after the time when the subject matter of the proceedings arose (s. 786(2) and s. 785(1)).

Included offences. Attempts (s. 660 and s. 662(1)(b)).

Punishment. On indictment, imprisonment for a term not exceeding 5 years (s. 255(1)(b)). On summary conviction, imprisonment for a term not exceeding 6 months (s. 255(1)(c)).

Whether on indictment or on summary conviction, the following minimum punishment: namely (i) for a first offence, to a fine not less than $300; (ii) for a second offence, to imprisonment for not less than 14 days; and (iii) for each subsequent offence, to imprisonment for not less than 90 days (s. 255(1)(a)).

In addition to any other punishment that may be imposed, the court shall make an order prohibiting the offender from operating a motor vehicle (a) for a first offence, during a period of not more than 3 years and not less than 3 months; (b) for a second offence, during a period of not more than 3 years and not less than 6 months; (c) for each subsequent offence, during a period of not more than 3 years and not less than one year (s. 259(1)).

Release. Initial decision to release made by peace officer (s. 497).

Election. On indictment, accused may elect trial by judge and jury, judge alone, or provincial court judge (s. 536). On summary conviction, no election.

Evidence. With respect to a s. 254(2) demand, proof is necessary that (i) there was in fact a demand, (ii) the accused was either driving a motor vehicle, or had the care or control of a motor vehicle, (iii) a peace officer formed a suspicion that the accused had alcohol in his body, and (iv) the suspicion was a reasonable one. A demand, not a request, must be made to the accused and it is usually made in the words of the section itself; for example, "I demand that you provide such a sample of your breath as is necessary to enable a proper analysis of your breath to be made by means of an approved screening device", or "I demand that you accompany me to [specify where] for the purpose of enabling you to provide such a sample of your breath as is necessary to enable a proper analysis of your breath to be made by means of an approved screening device". An "approved screening device" is a device of a kind that is designed to ascertain the presence of alcohol in the blood of a person and that is approved for the purposes of s. 254 by order of the Attorney General of Canada (s. 254(1)).

With respect to a s. 254(3) demand, proof is necessary that (i) there was in fact a demand, (ii) a peace officer formed a belief that the accused was committing or had committed within the 2 preceding hours an offence under s. 253 (operation of motor vehicle while impaired or with more than 80 mg of alcohol in blood), and (iii) the officer had reasonable and probable grounds for his belief. The belief must be formulated within 2 hours after the time of the operation or the care or control. A demand, not a request, must be made to the accused and is usually made in the words of the section itself; for example, "I demand that you accompany me to [specify where] to enable you to provide such samples of your breath as are necessary to enable proper analysis to be made in order to determine the concentration, if any, of alcohol in your blood". That demand must be made forthwith or as soon as practicable after the peace officer has formed the belief referred to above. The words "as soon as practicable" mean that as long as there is reasonable justification for any delay after the belief is formed, the demand will be a proper one.

Before making either a s. 254(2) demand or a s. 254(3) demand, the officer must inform the accused of his right to retain and instruct counsel without delay (Canadian Charter of Rights and Freedoms, s. 10(b)).

Proof is necessary that there was in fact a failure or refusal. There is no significant difference between the words failure and refusal. The qualified technician is entitled to determine what a suitable sample of breath is and anything less than that offered by the accused, such as short puffs or air, can constitute a refusal. The failure or refusal can be to fail or refuse to accompany the officer or to provide a sample or to do both.

What is a reasonable excuse? The burden is on the accused at trial to show that there was a reasonable excuse. A refusal by an officer to give the accused a reasonable opportunity to attempt to communicate with a solicitor in private before complying with the demand may be a reasonable excuse.

Informations

A.B., on or about the —— day of ——, 19——, at the —— of ——, in the said (territorial division), without reasonable excuse, did fail [OR refuse] to comply with a demand made to A.B. by C.D., a peace officer, under s. 254(2) [OR s. 254(3)] of the Criminal Code, to wit: (specify the particulars of the offence), contrary to s. 254(5) of the Criminal Code of Canada.

10. Operation of motor vehicle while disqualified — Section 259(4)

Every one who — operates a motor vehicle in Canada — while he is disqualified from doing so — is guilty of either an indictable offence or an offence punishable on summary conviction.

Limitation period. No proceedings in respect of offences that are declared to be punishable on summary conviction shall be instituted more than 6 months after the time when the subject matter of the proceedings arose (s. 786(2) and s. 785(1)).

Included offences. Attempts (s. 660 and s. 662(1)(b)).

Punishment. On indictment, imprisonment for a term not exceeding 2 years (s. 259(4)(a)). On summary conviction, a fine not exceeding $2,000, or 6 months' imprisonment, or both (s. 259(4)(b) and s. 787(1)).

In addition to any other punishment that may be imposed, the court may make an order prohibiting the offender from operating a motor vehicle during any period not exceeding 3 years (s. 259(2)(c)).

Release. Initial decision to release made by peace officer (s. 497).

Election. On indictment, no election, absolute jurisdiction of provincial court judge (s. 553). On summary conviction, no election.

Definitions. See DISQUALIFICATION.

Informations

A.B., on or about the —— day of ——, 19——, at the —— of ——, in the said (territorial division), did operate a motor vehicle in Canada while he was disqualified from doing so, to wit: (specify the particulars of the offence), contrary to s. 259(4) of the Criminal Code of Canada.

MULTIFARIOUS OR MULTIPLICITOUS. The combining of more than two offence in the same charge of count of an information or indictment is said to be either "multifarious" or "multiplicitous" (The Charge Document in Criminal Cases, Law Reform Commission of Canada, Working Paper 55).

MUNICIPAL OFFICIAL. For the purposes of s. 123, "municipal official" means a member of a municipal council or a person who holds an office under a municipal government (s. 123(3)).

MUNICIPALITY. For the purposes of the Criminal Code, "municipality" includes the corporation of a city, town, village, county, township, parish or other territorial or local division of a province, the inhabitants of which are incorporated or are entitled to hold property collectively for a public purpose (s. 2).

MUTATIS MUTANDIS. With the necessary changes (Latin).

MUTILATION. 1. In the case of a person, the depriving of the use of a limb or any essential part. 2. In the case of a document, the cutting, tearing, burning, erasure or alteration of it, but without totally destroying the document.

MUTINY. Any overt act of insubordination or defence of or attack on the established authority by members of the Armed Forces.

N

N.A. 1. The abbreviation for "non allocatur", which means "It is not allowed" (Latin). 2. The abbreviation for "not available" and "not applicable".

NARCOTIC ADDICT. "Narcotic addict" means a person who through the use of narcotics, (a) has developed a desire or need to continue to take a narcotic, or (b) has developed a psychological or physical dependence upon the effect of a narcotic (Narcotic Control Act, s. 2).

NARCOTICS

1. *Definitions*
2. *Possession of narcotic*
3. *Trafficking*
4. *Possession for purpose of trafficking*
5. *Importing and exporting*
6. *Cultivation of opium poppy or marihuana*
7. *Failure to disclose previous prescriptions*
8. *Prosecutions for narcotic offences*
9. *Search and seizure of narcotics. See SEARCH AND SEIZURE, 14.*

1. Definitions

"Narcotic". 1. A "narcotic" is any substance included in the Schedule to the Narcotic Control Act, or anything that contains any substance included in the Schedule (Narcotic Control Act, s. 2). The Schedule presently lists the following substances:

Opium poppy	Coca
Cannabis sativa	Phenylpiperidines
Phenazepines	Amidones
Methadols	Phenalkoxams
Thiambutenes	Moramides
Benzazocines	Benzimidazoles
Morphinans	Fentanyl
Ampromides	Phencyclidine
Sulfentanil	Tilidine
Carfentanil	Alfentanil

Their preparations, derivatives and salts.

2. A "narcotic" is a drug producing stupor, sleep and relief of pain. (Jaffe, A Guide to Pathological Evidence, 2nd ed.).

See also POSSESSION; TRAFFICKING.

2. Possession of narcotic — Narcotic Control Act, section 3(1) and (2)

Every one who — except as authorized by the Narcotic Control Act or the regulations — has in his possession — a narcotic — is guilty of an indictable offence or an offence punishable on summary conviction.

Punishment. On indictment, imprisonment for a term not exceeding 7 years (Narcotic Control Act, s. 3(2)(b)). On summary conviction (a) for a first offence, a fine not exceeding $1,000 or to imprisonment for a term not exceeding 6 months, or to both, and (b) for a subsequent offence, a fine not exceeding $2,000 or to imprisonment for a term not exceeding one year, or to both (Narcotic Control Act, s. 3(2)(a)).

Release. Initial decision to release made by peace officer (s. 497).

Election. On indictment, accused may elect trial by judge and jury, judge alone, or provincial court judge (s. 536). On summary conviction, no election.

3. Trafficking — Narcotic Control Act, section 4(1) and (3)

Every one who — traffics — in a narcotic or — in any substance represented or held out by him — to be a narcotic — is guilty of an indictable offence.

Punishment. Imprisonment for life (Narcotic Control Act, s. 4(3)).

Release. Initial decision to release made by justice (s. 515(1)).

Election. Accused may elect trial by judge and jury, judge alone, or provincial court judge (s. 536).

4. Possession for purpose of trafficking — Narcotic Control Act, section 4(2) and (3)

Every one who — has in his possession — any narcotic — for the purpose of trafficking — is guilty of an indictable offence.

Punishment. Imprisonment for life (Narcotic Control Act, s. 4(3)).

Release. Initial decision to release made by justice (s. 515(1)).

Election. Accused may elect trial by judge and jury, judge alone, or provincial court judge (s. 536).

Evidence. In any prosecution for this offence, if the accused does not plead guilty, the trial shall proceed as if it were a prosecution for possession, and after the close of the case for the prosecution and after the accused has had an opportunity to make full answer and defence, the court shall make a finding as to whether or not the accused was in possession of the narcotic; if the court finds that the accused was not in possession of the narcotic, he shall be acquitted but if the court finds that the accused was in possession of the narcotic, he shall be given an opportunity of establishing that he was not in possession of the narcotic for the purpose of trafficking, and thereafter the prosecutor shall be given an opportunity of adducing evidence to establish that the accused was in possession of the narcotic for the purpose of trafficking; if the accused establishes that he was not in possession of the narcotic for the purpose of trafficking, he shall be acquitted of the offence as charged but he shall be convicted of possession and sentenced accordingly; and if the accused fails to establish that he was not in possession of the narcotic for the purpose of trafficking, he shall be convicted of the offence as charged and sentenced accordingly (Narcotic Control Act, s. 8).

5. Importing and exporting — Narcotic Control Act, section 5(1)

Every one who — except as authorized by the Narcotic Control Act or the regulations — either imports into Canada — or exports from Canada — any narcotic — is guilty of an indictable offence.

Punishment. Imprisonment for life but not less than 7 years (Narcotic Control Act, s. 5(2)).

Release. Initial decision to release made by justice (s. 515(1)).

Election. Accused may elect trial by judge and jury, judge alone, or provincial court judge (s. 536).

6. Cultivation of opium poppy or marihuana — Narcotic Control Act, section 6(1) and (2)

Every one who — cultivates — either opium poppy or marihuana — except under authority of and in accordance with a licence issued to him under the regulations of the Narcotic Control Act — is guilty of an indictable offence.

Punishment. Imprisonment for a term not exceeding 7 years (Narcotic Control Act, s. 6(2)).

Further, the Minister of National Health and Welfare may cause to be destroyed any growing plant of opium poppy or marihuana cultivated otherwise than under authority of and in accordance with a licence issued under the regulations (Narcotic Control Act, s. 6(3)).

Release. Initial decision to release made by justice (s. 515(1)).

Election. Accused may elect trial by judge and jury, judge alone, or provincial court judge (s. 536).

Definitions. See OPIUM; MARIHUANA.

7. Failure to disclose previous prescriptions — Narcotic Control Act, section 3.1(1) and (2)

Every one who — at any time — seeks or obtains from a practitioner — a narcotic or a prescription for a narcotic — unless he discloses to that practitioner particulars of every narcotic or prescription for a narcotic issued to him by a different practitioner within the preceding 30 days — is guilty of an indictable offence or an offence punishable on summary conviction.

Limitation period. No summary conviction proceedings in respect of this offence shall be instituted after the expiration of one year from the time when the subject matter of the proceedings arose (Narcotic Control Act, s. 3.1(3)).

Punishment. On indictment, imprisonment for a term not exceeding 7 years (Narcotic Control Act, s. 3.1(2)(a)). On summary conviction (a) for a first offence, a fine not exceeding $1,000 or to imprisonment for a term not exceeding 6 months, and (b) for a subsequent offence, a fine not exceeding $2,000 or to imprisonment for a term not exceeding one year (Narcotic Control Act, s. 3.1(2)(b)).

Release. Initial decision to release made by peace officer (s. 497).

Election. On indictment, accused may elect trial by judge and jury, judge alone, or provincial court judge (s. 536). On summary conviction, no election.

Definitions. See PRACTITIONER; PRESCRIPTION.

8. Prosecutions for narcotic offences

No exception, exemption, excuse or qualification prescribed by law is required to be set out or negatived, as the case may be, in an information or indictment for this offence (Narcotic Control Act, s. 7(1)).

In any prosecution under the Narcotic Control Act the burden of proving that an exception, exemption, excuse or qualification prescribed by law operates in favour of the accused is on the accused, and the prosecutor is not required, except by way of rebuttal, to prove that the exception, exemption, excuse or qualification does not operate in favour of the accused, whether or not it is set out in the information or indictment (Narcotic Control Act, s. 7(2)).

A certificate purporting to be signed by an analyst stating that he has analyzed or examined a substance and stating the result of his analysis or examination is admissible in evidence in any prosecution for this offence and, in the absence of evidence to the contrary, is proof of the statements contained in the certificate without proof of the signature or the official character of the person appearing to have signed the certificate (Narcotic Control Act, s. 9(1)).

NE EXEAT REGNO. 1. "Let him not depart from the realm" (Latin). 2. The opening words of a writ to prevent a defendant from leaving the jurisdiction.

NEAT CATTLE. Oxen or heifers.

NEGLECT IN CHILDBIRTH

Section 242

A female person who — being pregnant and about to be delivered — either with intent that the child shall not live — or with intent to conceal the birth of the child — fails to make provision for reasonable assistance in respect of her delivery — if the child is permanently injured as a result thereof or dies immediately before or during or in a short time after birth, as a result thereof — is guilty of an indictable offence.

Intent. Intention that child shall not live or to conceal birth.

Included offences. Attempts (s. 660 and s. 662(1)(b)).

Punishment. Imprisonment for a term not exceeding 5 years (s. 242).

Release. Initial decision to release made by officer in charge or justice (s. 498).

Election. Accused may elect trial by judge and jury, judge alone, or provincial court judge (s. 536).

Evidence. 1. If the child is dead, death must be proved to have taken place just before or during or shortly after birth. This offence covers neglect only, not active steps to kill the child.
2. There must be a deliberate failure to obtain reasonable assistance at birth (R. v. Bryan (1959), 12 C.C.C. 160 (Ont. C.A.)).

Informations

A.B., on or about the —— day of ——, 19——, at the —— of ——, in the said (territorial division), being a pregnant female person about to be delivered, did fail to make provision for reasonable assistance in respect of her delivery, with intent that her child should not live [OR with intent to conceal the birth of the child], resulting in permanent injury to her child [OR resulting in the death of her child] before [OR during OR a short time after] birth, to wit: (specify the particulars of the offence), contrary to s. 242 of the Criminal Code of Canada.

NEMBUTAL. A brand of pentobarbital (Abbott Laboratories) (Jaffe, A Guide to Pathological Evidence, 2nd ed.).

NEMO. No one; no man (Latin). *Nemo dat quod non habet.* "No one gives what he does not have". *Nemo debet bis puniri pro uno delicto.* 1. "No one should be punished twice for one fault". 2. A decision of a competent court upon any given set of facts acts as a bar to a subsequent prosecution. *Nemo debet bis vexari pro eadem causa.* 1. "No one should be twice troubled by the same cause". 2. "No one should be twice sued or twice prosecuted upon one and the same set of facts, if there has been a final decision of a competent court." *Nemo debet esse judex in sua causa.* "No one should be judged in his own cause". *Nemo praesumitur malus.* "No one is presumed to be bad". *Nemo tenetur prodere seipsum.* "No one is bound to betray himself". *Nemo tenetur seipsum accusare.* "No one is bound to accuse himself".

NEWLY-BORN CHILD. For the purposes of the Criminal Code, "newly born child" means a person under the age of one year (s. 2).

NEWSPAPER. For the purposes of the Criminal Code, s. 276 (evidence of sexual activity) and ss. 303, 304 and 308 (defamatory libel), "newspaper" means any paper, magazine or periodical containing public news, intelligence or reports of events, or any remarks or observations thereon, printed for sale and published periodically or in parts or numbers, at intervals not exceeding 31 days between the publication of any two such papers, parts or numbers, and any paper, magazine or periodical printed in order to be dispersed and made public, weekly or more often, or at intervals not exceeding 31 days, that contains advertisements, exclusively or principally (s. 297 and s. 276.3(1)).

NIGHT. For the purposes of the Criminal Code, "night" means the period between 9 o'clock in the afternoon and 6 o'clock in the forenoon of the following day (s. 2).

NIHIL (NIL). Nothing (Latin).

NISI. 1. Unless; valid unless cause shown for rescinding (Latin). 2. A decree, order, rule, declaration or other adjudication of a court is said to be made nisi when it is not to take effect unless the person affected by it fails to show cause against it within a certain time, that is, unless he appears before the court, and gives some reason why it should not take effect (Jowitt's Dictionary of English Law). *Nisi prius.* 1. "Unless before". 2. The name of the civil assize court, originally directed to be tried in London unless before the trial an assize judge should try it on circuit.

NOLENS VOLENS. Whether willing or unwilling (Latin).

NOLLE PROSEQUI. 1. Unwillingness to prosecute (Latin). 2. A formal undertaking to discontinue criminal proceedings.

NOLO CONTENDERE. 1. "I do not wish to dispute" (Latin). 2. An admission of guilt.

NON. Not (Latin). *Non compos mentis.* Of unsound mind. *Non est factum.* "It is not [his] deed". *Non obstante.* Notwithstanding. *Non obstante veredicto (n.o.v.).* Notwithstanding the verdict. *Non sequitur.* 1. It does not follow. 2. Illogical inference.

NONFEASANCE. The neglect or failure of a person to do some act which he ought to do.

NOSCITUR A SOCIIS. "It is known by its associates" (Latin).

NOTA BENE (N.B.). "Note well" (Latin).

NOVUS ACTUS INTERVENIENS. 1. New act intervening (Latin). 2. To break a chain of causation.

NUCLEAR MATERIAL

1. *Definition of "nuclear material"*
2. *Offences deemed to be committed in Canada*

1. Definition of "nuclear material"

For these purposes, "nuclear material" means

(a) plutonium, except plutonium with an isotopic concentration of plutonium-238 exceeding 80%,

(b) uranium-233,

(c) uranium containing uranium-233 or uranium-235 or both in such an amount that the abundance ratio of the sum of those isotopes to the isotope uranium-238 is greater than 0.72%,

(d) uranium with an isotopic concentration equal to that occurring in nature, and

(e) any substance containing anything described above

but does not include uranium in the form of ore or ore-residue (s. 7(3.6)).

2. Offences deemed to be committed in Canada

Section 7(3.2) and (3.5)

Notwithstanding anything in the Criminal Code or any other Act — every one who — outside Canada — receives or has in his possession or uses or transfers the possession of, or sends or delivers to any person or transports or alters or disposes of or disperses or abandons nuclear material — and thereby either — causes or is likely to cause the death of, or serious bodily harm to, any person — or causes or is likely to cause serious damage to, or destruction of, property — and where the act or omission described above would, if committed in Canada, be an offence against the Criminal Code — shall be deemed to commit that act or omission in Canada — either if the act or omission is committed on a ship that is registered or licensed, or for which an identification number has been issued, pursuant to any Act of Parliament — or if the act or omission is committed on an aircraft — either registered in Canada under regulations made under the Aeronautics Act — or leased without crew and operated by a person who is qualified under regulations made under the Aeronautics Act to be registered as owner of an aircraft in Canada under such regulations — or if the person who commits the act or omission is a Canadian citizen or is, after the act or omission has been committed, present in Canada.

Section 7(3.3) and (3.5)

Notwithstanding anything in the Criminal Code or any other Act — every one who — outside Canada — commits an act or omission that if committed in Canada would constitute — either a conspiracy or an attempt to commit — or being an accessory after the fact in relation to — or counselling in relation to — an act or omission that

is an offence involving nuclear material — shall be deemed to commit that act or omission in Canada — either if the act or omission is committed on a ship that is registered or licensed, or for which an identification number has been issued, pursuant to any Act of Parliament — or if the act or omission is committed on an aircraft — either registered in Canada under regulations made under the Aeronautics Act — or leased without crew and operated by a person who is qualified under regulations made under the Aeronautics Act to be registered as owner of an aircraft in Canada under such regulations — or if the person who commits the act or omission is a Canadian citizen or is, after the act or omission has been committed, present in Canada.

Section 7(3.4) and (3.5)

Notwithstanding anything in the Criminal Code or any other Act — every one who — outside Canada — commits an act or omission that if committed in Canada would constitute — either an offence against — or a conspiracy or an attempt to commit or being an accessory after the fact in relation to an offence against — or any counselling in relation to an offence against — either s. 334 (theft) or s. 341 (fraudulent concealment) or s. 344 (robbery) or s. 362(1)(a) (false pretence) or s. 380 (fraud) in relation to nuclear material — or s. 346 (extortion) in respect of a threat to commit an offence against s. 334 (theft) or s. 344 (robbery) in relation to nuclear material — or s. 423 (intimidation) in relation to a demand for nuclear material — or s. 264.1(1)(a) or (b) (uttering threats) in respect of a threat to use nuclear material — shall be deemed to commit that act or omission in Canada — either if the act or omission is committed on a ship that is registered or licensed, or for which an identification number has been issued, pursuant to any Act of Parliament — or if the act or omission is committed on an aircraft — either registered in Canada under regulations made under the Aeronautics Act — or leased without crew and operated by a person who is qualified under regulations made under the Aeronautics Act to be registered as owner of an aircraft in Canada under such regulations — or if the person who commits the act or omission is a Canadian citizen or is, after the act or omission has been committed, present in Canada.

Consent to prosecute. No proceedings shall be instituted under this section without the consent of the Attorney General of Canada if the accused is not a Canadian citizen (s. 7.7).

NUDE. For the purposes of s. 174, a person is nude who is so clad as to offend against public decency or order (s. 174(2)).

NUISANCES

1. *Common nuisance*
2. *Spreading false news*
3. *Neglect of or indignity to dead human body*

1. Common nuisance

Definition of offence — Section 180(2)

Every one who — does an unlawful act — or fails to discharge a legal duty — and thereby — either endangers the lives or safety or health or property or comfort of the public — or obstructs the public in the exercise or enjoyment of any right that is common to all the subjects of Her Majesty in Canada — commits a common nuisance.

Statement of offence — Section 180(1)

Every one who — commits a common nuisance — and thereby — either endangers the lives or safety or health of the public — or causes physical injury to any person — is guilty of an indictable offence.

Included offences. Attempts (s. 660 and s. 662(1)(b)).

Punishment. Imprisonment for a term not exceeding 2 years (s. 180(1)).

Release. Initial decision to release made by officer in charge or justice (s. 498).

Election. Accused may elect trial by judge and jury, judge alone, or provincial court judge (s. 536).

Evidence. A common nuisance must be directed to the public generally and not to specific individuals.

Informations

A.B., on or about the —— day of ——, 19——, at the —— of ——, in the said (territorial division), did commit a common nuisance and did thereby endanger the lives, safety, or health of the public, to wit: (specify the particulars of the offence), contrary to s. 180 of the Criminal Code of Canada.

A.B., on or about the —— day of ——, 19——, at the —— of ——, in the said (territorial division), did commit a common nuisance and did thereby cause physical injury to C.D., to wit: (specify the particulars of the offence), contrary to s. 180 of the Criminal Code of Canada.

2. Spreading false news — Section 181

Every one who — wilfully — publishes a statement or tale or news — that he knows is false — and that causes or is likely to cause injury or mischief to a public interest — is guilty of an indictable offence.

Intent. Wilfully.

Included offences. Attempts (s. 660 and s. 662(1)(b)).

Punishment. Imprisonment for a term not exceeding 2 years (s. 181).

Release. Initial decision to release made by officer in charge or justice (s. 498).

Election. Accused may elect trial by judge and jury, judge alone, or provincial court judge (s. 536).

Informations

A.B., on or about the —— day of ——, 19——, at the —— of ——, in the said (territorial division), wilfully did publish a statement [OR tale OR news] that he knew was false and that did cause [OR was likely to cause] injury [OR mischief] to a public interest, to wit: (specify the particulars of the offence), contrary to s. 181 of the Criminal Code of Canada.

3. Neglect of or indignity to dead human body — Section 182

Every one who — either without lawful excuse — neglects to perform any duty — that is imposed on him by law or that he undertakes — with reference to the burial of a dead human — body or human remains — or improperly or indecently interferes with or offers any indignity to — a dead human body or human remains (whether buried or not) — is guilty of an indictable offence.

Included offences. Attempts (s. 660 and s. 662(1)(b)).

Punishment. Imprisonment for a term not exceeding 5 years (s. 182).

Release. Initial decision to release made by officer in charge or justice (s. 498).

Election. Accused may elect trial by judge and jury, judge alone, or provincial court judge (s. 536).

Informations

A.B., on or about the —— day of ——, 19——, at the —— of ——, in the said (territorial division), did without lawful excuse, neglect to perform a duty imposed upon him by law [OR undertaken by him] with reference to a dead human body [OR human remains], to wit: (specify the particulars of the offence), contrary to s. 182(a) of the Criminal Code of Canada.

A.B., on or about the —— day of ——, 19——, at the —— of ——, in the said (territorial division), did improperly [OR indecently] interfere with [OR offer an indignity to] a dead human body [OR human remains], to wit: (specify the particulars of the offence), contrary to s. 182(b) of the Criminal Code of Canada.

NULLA BONA. 1. No goods (Latin). 2. The name given to the return made by a sheriff or other officer to a writ or warrant authorizing him to seize the chattels of a person, when he has been unable to find anything to seize.

NULLA POENA SINE LEGE. No punishment without a law (Latin).

NULLITY. 1. Literally, a "nothing"; no proceeding; an act or proceeding which is taken as having absolutely no force or effect, as though it had never taken place (The Charge Document in Criminal Cases, Law Reform Commission of Canada, Working Paper 55). 2. An information which does not charge an offence known to law is a nullity and no magistrate or judge can act upon it (R. v. Vallée [1969] 3 C.C.C. 293 (B.C.C.A.)). *See also AMENDMENT.*

NUNC PRO TUNC. 1. "Now for then" (Latin). 2. Retroactively.

O

OATHS

Definition. 1. "Oath" includes a solemn affirmation or declaration, whenever the context applies to any person by whom and to any case in which a solemn affirmation or declaration may be made instead

of an oath; in like cases "sworn" includes "affirmed" or "declared" (Interpretation Act, s. 35).
2. "Oath" includes a solemn affirmation in cases in which, by the law of Canada, or of a province, as the case may be, an affirmation is allowed instead of an oath (Canada Evidence Act, s. 44).

General. Every court and judge, and every person having, by law or consent of parties, authority to hear and receive evidence, has power to administer an oath to every witness who is legally called to give evidence before that court, judge or person (Canada Evidence Act, s. 13). *See also AFFIRMATION.*

Where, by an enactment or by a rule of the Senate or House of Commons, evidence under oath is authorized or required to be taken, or an oath is authorized or directed to be made, taken or administered, the oath may be administered, and a certificate of its having been made, taken or administered may be given by any one authorized by the enactment or rule to take the evidence, or by a judge of any court, a notary public, a justice of the peace, or a commissioner for taking affidavits, having authority or jurisdiction within the place where the oath is administered (Interpretation Act, s. 19(1)).

Where power is conferred upon a justice of the peace to administer an oath or affirmation or to take an affidavit or declaration, the power may be exercised by a notary public or a commissioner for taking oaths (Interpretation Act, s. 19(2)).

OBITER. By the way (Latin). ***Obiter dictum.*** 1. A thing said by way. 2. A judicial observation not binding as a precedent.

OBSERVING PEOPLE

1. *Observation*
2. *General characteristics*
3. *Specific characteristics*
4. *Changeable characteristics*

1. Observation

In police work, observation means perception of details pertaining to persons, objects, places, and events through the use of the five senses.

The ability to observe accurately is developed through practice and experience.

Deliberate observation should proceed methodically. One way of proceeding is as follows:

(i) Observe general characteristics, such as sex, race, color of skin, height, build, weight and age.

(ii) Observe specific characteristics, such as color of hair and eyes, shape of head and face, distinguishing marks and scars, mannerisms and habits.

(iii) Observe changeable characteristics, such as clothing worn, use of cosmetics, hair styling, etc., at time of observation.

2. General characteristics

The following commonly accepted and understood terms are used in describing general characteristics of a person.

Sex. Male or female.

Race. Caucasian, Negroid, Native American, etc.

Height. Exact or estimated. Estimated height may be stated in 2-inch blocks, such as 5 feet 8 inches to 5 feet 10 inches, 5 feet 10 inches to 6 feet.

Build. Large, average, small, slight; obese, very stout, stout, stocky, medium, slim, or slender.
 Bust: Flat, medium or heavy.
 Posture: Straight, erect, medium or stooped.

Weight. Exact or estimated. Estimates may be stated in 10-pound increments, such as 160 to 170 pounds, 170 to 180 pounds.

Age. Actual or estimated. Age may be estimated in multiples of 5 years. Indicate not only the actual age but also the general age indicated by appearance.

Complexion. Pale, fair, dark, ruddy, sallow (sickly-pale) or florid (flushed). Clear, pimpled, blotched, freckled, pockmarked, etc.

3. Specific characteristics

The following terms are used in describing specific personal characteristics.

Head

Size and shape: Large, medium, or small; long or short; broad or narrow; round, flat in back, flat on top, egg-shaped, high in crown, bulging in back, etc.

Profile: Divide mentally into three parts or sections. Each third is then described in its relationship to the whole and in separate detail.

Except in the case of peculiarities, the description of the profile is not normally as important for identification purposes as is the description of the frontal view of the face.

Face: Round, square, oval, broad, or long (as seen from the front).

Hair: Color as blond (light or dark), brown (light or dark), red (light or dark), auburn, black, gray, streaked with gray, or white. In the case of bleached, tinted, or dyed hair, both the artificial and the natural color should be indicated when possible. Density as thick, medium, thin or sparse. Hairline as low, medium, receding, receding over temples, etc. Baldness should be described as complete, whole top of head, occipital, frontal, receding or the appropriate combination of types. Hair type as straight, wavy, curly or kinky. Hair texture as fine, medium or coarse. Appearance as neat, bushy, unkempt, oily or dry. Hair style as long, medium or short; parted on left, parted on right, parted in center or not parted. Current descriptive terms of hairstyles which are readily and widely understood should be used as appropriate. Wigs, toupees, and hairpieces should be observed carefully and in detail. The careful observer can often determine whether a person is wearing a toupee or other hairpiece from such indications as difference in hair texture, color, density, type or appearance. Furthermore, the arrangement of false hair will often be too nearly perfect, and the edges of the hairpiece will often be evident upon close scrutiny.

Forehead: High, medium or low. Slope as receding, medium, vertical, prominent or bulging. Width as wide, medium or narrow. Wrinkles or age lines as none, light, deep, horizontal, curved (up or down) or vertical.

Cheeks: Full, bony, angular, fleshy, sunken or flat. Cheekbones as high (prominent), medium or receding.

Eyes: Deep-set (sunken), medium or bulging. Separation as wide, medium or narrow. Crossed, watery, red or other noticeable peculiarity. Color of iris. Eyelids as normal, drooping, puffy, red, etc. Eyelashes as to color; long, medium, or short; straight, curled or drooping.

Eyebrows: Color, including any difference from hair color. Slant from center (horizontal, slanted up, slanted down). Line as straight or arched, separated or connected. Texture as heavy, medium, or thin, Hair as short, medium, or long; plucked; penciled.

Eyeglasses: Eyeglasses should be described in detail to include style and color of frames, type and color of lenses, and method of attachment to face. Contact lenses may prove difficult to observe. However, the careful observer will note such indications of the presence of contact lenses as watery eyes and excessive blinking. Special types of eyeglasses, such as monocles, pince-nez, and bifocal should be carefully noted.

Nose: Length as short, medium or long. Width as thin, medium or thick. Projection as long, medium or short. Base of the nose as turned up, horizontal or turned downward. The root of the nose (juncture with the forehead) should be described as flat, small, medium or large. And the line of the nose should be described as concave, straight, convex (hooked), roman or aquiline. Nostrils should be indicated as medium, wide, or narrow; large or small; high or low; round, elongated or flaring. Peculiarities, such as broken, twisted to right or left, turned up, pendulous, hairy, deep-pored, etc., should be carefully noted.

Mouth: Size (as viewed from front), small, medium or large. Expression as stern, sad (corners drooping), pleasant or smiling. Peculiarities, such as prominent changes made when speaking or laughing, twitching, habitually open, etc., should be indicated.

Teeth: Color; receding, normal, or protruding; large, medium, or small; stained, decayed, very white, broken, false, gold flared, uneven, missing or gaps between teeth.

Chin: Normal, receding, or jutting (as viewed in profile); short, medium, or long (as viewed from the front); small, large, pointed, square, dimpled, cleft or double.

Lips: Thin, medium or thick (as viewed from front); long, medium or short (as viewed in profile). Position as normal, lower protruding, upper protruding or both protruding. Color. Appearance as smooth, chapped, puffy, loose, compressed, tight (retracted over teeth), moist, dry, etc. Harelip and other peculiarities should be carefully noted.

Mustache and beard: Color, including any difference from hair color. Style and configuration, and state of grooming (unshaven).

Ears: Small, medium or large. Shape as oval, round, triangular, rectangular or other appropriate term. Lobe as descending, square, medium or gulfed. Separation from the head should be described as close, normal, or protruding; and setting (based on a line extended horizontally back from the outside corner of the eye, which crosses the normally-set ear at the upper third) should be indicated as low, normal or high.

Hearing aids: Hearing aids should be described in detail as to type (such as inside the ear, behind the ear, with cord, cordless, etc.), color and ear in which worn.

Trunk

Overall: Long, medium or short (in relation to rest of body).

Chest: Deep, medium, or flat, as seen in profile; broad, medium, or narrow, as seen from the front.

Back: Straight, curved, humped, bowed, etc., as viewed in profile; straight or curved, as viewed from the rear.

Waist: Small, medium or large.

Abdomen: Flat, medium or protruding.

Hips: Broad, medium, or narrow, as seen from the front; small, medium, or large, as seen in profile.

Neck: Short or long; straight or curved; thin or thick. Adam's apple as large (prominent), medium or small.

Shoulders. Small, medium, or heavy; narrow, medium, or broad; square or round, level or one side lower. As seen in profile, straight, stooped, slumped or humped.

Arms: Long, medium, or short in comparison to rest of the body (average or medium arms terminate with the heel of the hand about halfway between the hips and the knee when the arms are hanging naturally). Musculature as slight, medium or heavy.

Legs: Long, medium, or short in comparison to rest of the body (average or medium legs combined with the hips constitute about half the body length); straight, bowed (bandy), or knock-kneed; musculature as slight, medium or heavy.

Feet: Small, medium or large in relation to body size. Deformities and peculiarities, such as pigeon-toed, flat-footed, clubfooted, etc., should be carefully recorded.

Marks and scars: Such identifying marks as birthmarks, moles, warts, tattoos, and scars should be clearly described as to size, color, location on the body and shape.

Hands and fingers

Hands: Small, medium or large in relation to the size of the individual. Peculiarities should be noted in detail.

Fingers: Long, medium, or short; thin, medium, or thick (stubby). Deformities, such as missing fingers, disfigured nails, crooked fingers, etc., should be carefully indicated.

Speech. The tone and manner of a person's speech may often be very important aspects of his complete description. His habitual tone should be indicated as low, medium, or loud; soft or gruff; or by other descriptive qualities. His manner of speaking should be indicated as cultured, vulgar, clipped, fluent, broken English, with accent (identified whenever possible), or non-English speaking (language specified when possible). Such peculiarities as stuttering, nasal twang, pronounced drawl, or a mute condition should be clearly indicated and explained.

4. Changeable characteristics

Dress. Since a person may change the clothing he was wearing, its value for descriptive purposes is limited. Noticeable habits in manner of dress, such as neatness, carelessness and preferences of style should be indicated. Clothing worn by a person at the time of an offence or when last seen should be described in detail, such as military (service or fatigue), civilian, mixed military and civilian, color(s), and condition (clean, soiled, torn, ragged, greasy, or bloodstained).

Personal appearance. Neat or untidy; well-groomed or unkempt; refined or rough.

Mannerisms and habits. Often the peculiar mannerisms or traits of a person will constitute the major or key parts of his description. The investigator must be alert to record in description such characteristics as:

Peculiarities in walking, moving, or talking.

Outward emotional instability, nervousness or indecision.

Subconscious mannerisms, such as scratching the nose, running the hand through the hair, pulling on an ear, hitching up the pants, jingling keys or flipping coins.

Facial tics, muscular twitches and excessive talking with the hands.

Jewelry worn and types of jewelry preferred.

OBSTRUCTING

Loitering and obstructing. See DISORDERLY CONDUCT, 6.

Obstructing officiating clergyman. See DISORDERLY CONDUCT, 8.

Obstructing justice. See MISLEADING JUSTICE, 6.

Obstructing peace officer. See PEACE OFFICER, 3.

Obstructing public officer. See PUBLIC OFFICER, 2.

OBTURATION. The sealing of powder gases between the cartridge case and the walls of the firing chamber and the bullet and the barrel (Jaffe, A Guide to Pathological Evidence, 2nd ed.).

OFFENCES

Definition of "offence". 1. Any public wrong, including indictable offences and offences punishable on summary conviction offences. 2. For the purposes of the Young Offenders Act, "offence" means an offence created by an Act of Parliament or by any regulation, rule, order, by-law or ordinance made thereunder, other than an ordinance of the Yukon Territory or the Northwest Territories (Young Offenders Act, s. 2(1)).

Categories of offences. In R. v. Sault Ste Marie (1978), 40 C.C.C. (2d) 353 (S.C.C.), Dickson J. described the following three categories of offences:

1. "Offences in which mens rea, consisting of some positive state of mind such as intent, knowledge, or recklessness, must be proved by the prosecution either as an inference from the nature of the act committed, or by additional evidence.
2. Offences in which there is no necessity for the prosecution to prove the existence of mens rea; the doing of the prohibited act prima facie imports the offence, leaving it open to the accused to avoid liability by proving that he took all reasonable care. This involves consideration of what a reasonable man would have done in the circumstances. The defence will be available if the accused reasonably believed in a mistaken set of facts which, if true, would render the act or omission innocent, or if he took all reasonable steps to avoid the particular event. These offences may properly be called offences of strict liability.
3. Offences of absolute liability where it is not open to the accused to exculpate himself by showing that he was free of fault.

Offences which are criminal in the true sense fall in the first category. Public welfare offences would, prima facie, be in the second category. They are not subject to the presumption of full mens rea. An offence of this type would fall in the first category only if such words as 'wilfully', 'with intent', 'knowingly', or 'intentionally' are contained in the statutory provision creating the offence. On the other hand, the principle that punishment should in general not be inflicted on those without fault applies. Offences of absolute liability would be those in respect of which the Legislature had made it clear that guilt would follow proof merely of the proscribed act. The over-all regulatory pattern adopted by the Legislature, the subject-matter of the legislation, the importance of the penalty, and the precision of the language used will be primary considerations in determining whether the offence falls into the third category."

OFFENDER. For the purposes of the Criminal Code, "offender" means a person who has been determined by a court to be guilty of

OFFENSIVE WEAPON. For the purposes of the Criminal Code, "offensive weapon" means (a) anything used or intended for use in causing death or injury to persons whether designed for such purpose or not, or (b) anything used or intended for use for the purpose of threatening or intimidating any person, and, without restricting the generality of the foregoing, includes any firearm as defined in s. 84 (s. 2).

OFFICE. For the purposes of Part IV of the Criminal Code (Offences Against the Administration of Law and Justice), "office" includes (a) an office or appointment under the government, (b) a civil or military commission, and (c) a position or employment in a public department (s. 118).

OFFICER IN CHARGE. For the purposes of the Criminal Code, "officer in charge" means the officer for the time being in command of the police force responsible for the lock-up or other place to which an accused is taken after arrest or a peace officer designated by him for the purposes of Part XVI of the Code who is in charge of such place at the time an accused is taken to that place to be detained in custody (s. 493).

OFFICIAL. For the purposes of Part IV of the Criminal Code (Offences Against the Administration of Law and Justice), "official" means a person who (a) holds an office, or (b) is appointed to discharge a public duty (s. 118).

OMISSION. The failure to do an act, or the non-doing of an act, that the law requires.

Omissions causing danger to the person. See BODILY HARM AND ACTS AND OMISSIONS CAUSING DANGER TO THE PERSON.

Omitting to assist peace officer. See PEACE OFFICER, 4.

Omitting to prevent treason. See TREASON AND OTHER OFFENCES AGAINST THE QUEEN'S AUTHORITY AND PERSON, 6.

OMNIA PRAESUMUNTUR CONTRA SPOLIATOREM. "All is presumed against a wrongdoer" (Latin).

OMNIA PRAESUMUNTUR RITE ESSE ACTA. "Everything is presumed to have been properly done" (Latin).

ONUS. Burden (Latin). ***Onus probandi.*** Burden of proof.

OP. CIT. An abbreviation for "opere citare", which means "in the work or works just referred to" (Latin).

OPEN COURT. Every court of justice is in principle open to every subject of the Crown, except where the contrary is expressly provided for by law.

OPENING IN ICE

Duty — Section 263(1)

Every one who — makes or causes to be made — an opening in ice — that is open to or frequented by the public — is under a legal duty — to guard it — in a manner that is adequate to prevent persons from falling in by accident — and in a manner that is adequate to warn them that the opening exists.

Statement of offence — Section 263(3)

Every one who — fails to perform this duty — if the death of any person results therefrom — is guilty of the indictable offence of manslaughter.

Every one who — fails to perform this duty — if bodily harm to any person results therefrom — is guilty of the indictable offence of causing bodily harm.

Every one who — fails to perform this duty and no death or bodily harm results therefrom — is guilty of a summary conviction offence.

Limitation period. No proceedings in respect of offences that are declared to be punishable on summary conviction shall be instituted more than 6 months after the time when the subject matter of the proceedings arose (s. 786(2) and s. 785(1)).

Included offences. Attempts (s. 660 and s. 662(1)(b)).

Punishment. On indictment for manslaughter, imprisonment for life (s. 263(3)(a) and s. 236). On indictment for unlawfully causing bodily harm, imprisonment for a term not exceeding 10 years (s. 263(3)(b) and s. 269). On summary conviction, a fine not exceeding $2,000, or 6 months' imprisonment, or both (s. 263(3)(c) and s. 787(1)).

The sentence to be pronounced against a person who is to be sentenced to imprisonment for life in respect of a person who has been convicted of this offence, shall be that he be sentenced to imprisonment for life with normal eligibility for parole (s. 742(c)).

Release. Initial decision to release made by peace officer (s. 497).

Election. On indictment, accused may elect trial by judge and jury, judge alone, or provincial court judge (s. 536). On summary conviction, no election.

Informations

A.B., on or about the —— day of ——, 19——, at the —— of ——, in the said (territorial division), did make [OR cause to be made] an opening in ice frequented by [OR open to] the public and did fail to guard it in a manner adequate to prevent persons from falling in by accident and did fail to warn persons that the opening existed, to wit: (specify the particulars of the offence), contrary to s. 263(1) of the Criminal Code of Canada.

OPERATE. For the purposes of Part VIII of the Criminal Code (Offences Against the Person and Reputation), "operate" means (a) in respect of a motor vehicle, to drive the vehicle; and (b) in respect of a vessel or an aircraft, to navigate the vessel or aircraft (s. 214).

OPIUM. The juice of the unripe seed capsules of the poppy plant (Papaver somniferum). The milky juice is dried and the crude opium is sold as a dark brown, gummy substance. Its pharmacological activity is due to a number of alkaloids including morphine and codeine. Crude opium is usually smoked in pipes (Jaffe, A Guide to Pathological Evidence, 2nd ed.).

Opium poppy. For the purposes of the Narcotic Control Act, Papaver somniferum L. (Narcotic Control Act, s. 2). *See NARCOTICS, 1.*

ORDINARY COURT. For the purposes of the Young Offenders Act, "ordinary court" means the court that would, in the absence of the Act, have jurisdiction in respect of an offence alleged to have been committed (Young Offenders Act, s. 2(1)).

P

PCP. A hallucinogenic drug, which appears in powder, tablet or capsule form.

PARAFFIN TEST. A test for the nitrates and nitrites of gunpowder residues on the skin. Paraffin casts of the skin are treated with a solution of diphenylamine and diphenylbenzidine. The test is no longer regarded as sufficiently specific. Also, the dermal nitrate test, the diphenylamine test and the Gonzales test (Jaffe, A Guide to Pathological Evidence, 2nd ed.).

PARDON. 1. An act of the Crown which has the effect of releasing a person from the punishment he has incurred for some offence. A pardon may be granted before, during or after a prosecution. 2. For the purposes of the Criminal Records Act, "pardon" means a pardon granted or issued by the National Parole Board under s. 4.1 (Criminal Records Act, s. 2(1)). *See also CRIMINAL RECORDS.*

PARENT. For the purposes of the Young Offenders Act, "parent" includes any person who is under a legal duty to provide for another person or any person who has, in law or in fact, the custody or control of that other person (Young Offenders Act, s. 2(1)). *For offences respecting parents, see DUTIES TENDING TO PRESERVATION OF LIFE, 1, AND CORRUPTING MORALS, 15.*

PARI PASSU. Equally; without preference (Latin).

PARTICEPS CRIMINIS. Accessory to a crime (Latin).

PARTICULARS. 1. In an information or indictment, a reference to "particulars of offence" refers to the details of the alleged crime. 2. Where satisfied that it is necessary for a fair trial, a court may, in proceedings on indictment, order the prosecutor to furnish details or particulars of the act or omission and transaction referred to in the charge. Similarly, in summary conviction proceedings the court may order further particulars describing any matter relevant to the proceedings. The purpose of particulars is to supplement a charge which, although otherwise sufficient, is inadequate for the accused properly to prepare his defence or to ensure him a fair trial. Particulars also serve to define the issues in the case and thus assist the trial judge in ruling on the admissibility of evidence (The Charge Document in Criminal Cases, Law Reform Commission of Canada, Working Paper 55).

PARTIES TO OFFENCES. Everyone is a party to and guilty of an offence who
 (a) actually commits it,
 (b) does or omits to do anything for the purpose of aiding any person to commit the offence, or
 (c) abets any person in committing the offence (s. 21(1)).

If two or more persons form a common intention to carry out any unlawful purpose and to assist each other therein, each one is guilty of every offence committed by any one of them in carrying out such common purpose, the commission of which offence was or ought to have been known to be a probable consequence of the carrying out of such common purpose (s. 21(2)).

Everyone who counsels another person to be a party to an offence of which that person is afterwards guilty, is a party to that offence, although the offence was committed in a different way from that counselled or suggested (s. 22(1)).

Anyone who counsels another to be a party to an offence is a party to every offence that the other commits in consequence of such counselling, which he knew or ought to have known was likely to be committed in consequence of such counselling (s. 22(2)).

The charge or indictment may be worded in the same way as for the principal offender.

PASSIM. In various places (Latin).

PASSPORT OFFENCES

1. *Definition of "passport"*
2. *Forgery of passport*
3. *Uttering forged passport*
4. *False statement to procure passport*
5. *Possession of forged passport*
6. *Possession of passport obtained by false statement*
7. *Sufficiency of count*

1. Definition of "passport"

For the purposes of s. 57, "passport" means a document issued by or under the authority of the Secretary of State for External Affairs for the purpose of identifying the holder thereof (s. 57(5)).

2. Forgery of passport — Section 57(1)(a)

Every one who — while in or out of Canada — forges a passport — is guilty of an indictable offence.

Jurisdiction. Where a person is alleged to have committed this offence while out of Canada, proceedings in respect of the offence may, whether or not that person is in Canada, be commenced in any territorial division in Canada and the person may be tried and punished in respect of the offence in same manner as if the offence had been committed in that territorial division (s. 57(6)).

Included offences. Attempts (s. 660 and s. 662(1)(b)).

Punishment. Imprisonment for a term not exceeding 14 years (s. 57(1)).

Release. Initial decision to release made by justice (s. 515(1)).

Election. Accused may elect trial by judge and jury, judge alone, or provincial court judge (s. 536).

Evidence. 1. The place where a passport was forged is not material (s. 57(4)(a)).
2. The definitions of "false document" in s. 321, s. 366 and s. 367(2) are applicable with such modifications as circumstances require (s. 57(4)(b)).

Informations

A.B., on or about the —— day of ——, 19——, at the —— of ——, in the said (territorial division), did forge a passport, to wit: (specify the particulars of the offence), contrary to s. 57(1)(a) of the Criminal Code of Canada.

3. Uttering forged passport — Section 57(1)(b)

Every one who — while in or out of Canada — knowing that a passport is forged — either uses or deals with or acts on it — or causes or attempts to cause any person to use or deal with or act on it — as if the passport were genuine — is guilty of an indictable offence.

Intent. Knowledge of forgery.

Jurisdiction. See Jurisdiction under **2,** *above.*

Included offences. Attempts (s. 660 and s. 662(1)(b)).

Punishment. Imprisonment for a term not exceeding 14 years (s. 57(1)).

Release. Initial decision to release made by justice (s. 515(1)).

Election. Accused may elect trial by judge and jury, judge alone, or provincial court judge (s. 536).

Evidence. See Evidence under **2**, *above.*

Informations

A.B., on or about the —— day of ——, 19——, at the —— of ——, in the said (territorial division), knowing that a passport was forged, did use [OR deal with OR act on] it as if the passport were genuine, to wit: (specify the particulars of the offence), contrary to s. 57(1)(b)(i) of the Criminal Code of Canada.

A.B., on or about the —— day of ——, 19——, at the —— of ——, in the said (territorial division), knowing that a passport was forged, did cause [OR attempt to cause] C.D. to use [OR deal with OR act on] it as if the passport were genuine, to wit: (specify the particulars of the offence), contrary to s. 57(1)(b)(ii) of the Criminal Code of Canada.

4. False statement to procure passport — Section 57(2)

Every one who — while in or out of Canada — for the purpose of procuring a passport for himself or any other person — or for the purpose of procuring any material alteration or addition to any such passport — makes a written or oral statement — that he knows is false or misleading — is guilty of either an indictable offence or an offence punishable on summary conviction.

Intent. Knowledge of false or misleading nature.

Jurisdiction. See Jurisdiction under **2**, *above.*

Limitation period. No proceedings in respect of offences that are declared to be punishable on summary conviction shall be instituted more than 6 months after the time when the subject matter of the proceedings arose (s. 786(2) and s. 785(1)).

Included offences. Attempts (s. 660 and s. 662(1)(b)).

Punishment. On indictment, imprisonment for a term not exceeding 2 years (s. 57(2)(a)). On summary conviction, a fine not exceeding $2,000, or 6 months' imprisonment, or both (s. 57(2)(b) and s. 787(1)).

Release. Initial decision to release made by peace officer (s. 497).

Election. On indictment, accused may elect trial by judge and jury, judge alone, or provincial court judge (s. 536). On summary conviction, no election.

Evidence. See Evidence under **2**, above.

Informations

A.B., on or about the —— day of ——, 19——, at the —— of ——, in the said (territorial division), did make a written [OR oral] statement that he knew was false [OR misleading], for the purpose of procuring a passport for himself [OR C.D.], to wit: (specify the particulars of the offence), contrary to s. 57(2) of the Criminal Code of Canada.

A.B., on or about the —— day of ——, 19——, at the —— of ——, in the said (territorial division), did make a written [OR oral] statement that he knew was false [OR misleading], for the purpose of procuring a material alteration [OR addition] to a passport for himself [OR C.D.], to wit: (specify the particulars of the offence), contrary to s. 57(2) of the Criminal Code of Canada.

5. Possession of forged passport — Section 57(3)

Every one who — without lawful excuse — has in his possession — a forged passport — is guilty of an indictable offence.

Jurisdiction. See Jurisdiction under **2**, above.

Included offences. Attempts (s. 660 and s. 662(1)(b)).

Punishment. Imprisonment for a term not exceeding 5 years (s. 57(3)).

Release. Initial decision to release made by officer in charge or justice (s. 498).

Election. Accused may elect trial by judge and jury, judge alone, or provincial court judge (s. 536).

Evidence. 1. For the purposes of this offence, the proof of lawful excuse lies on the accused (s. 57(3)).
2. *See also Evidence under **2**, above.*

Informations

A.B., on or about the —— day of ——, 19——, at the —— of ——, in the said (territorial division), without lawful excuse, did have in his possession a forged passport, to wit: (specify the particulars of the offence), contrary to s. 57(3) of the Criminal Code of Canada.

6. Possession of passport obtained by false statement — Section 57(3)

Every one who — without lawful excuse — has in his possession — a passport in respect of which an offence under s. 57(2) (false statement in relation to passport) has been committed — is guilty of an indictable offence.

Jurisdiction. See Jurisdiction under **2**, above.

Included offences. Attempts (s. 660 and s. 662(1)(b)).

Punishment. Imprisonment for a term not exceeding 5 years (s. 57(3)).

Release. Initial decision to release made by officer in charge or justice (s. 498).

Election. Accused may elect trial by judge and jury, judge alone, or provincial court judge (s. 536).

Evidence. 1. For the purposes of this offence, the proof of lawful excuse lies on the accused (s. 57(3)).
2. *See also Evidence under **2**, above.*

Informations

A.B., on or about the —— day of ——, 19——, at the —— of ——, in the said (territorial division), without lawful excuse, did have in his possession a passport in respect of which an offence under s. 57(2) had been committed, to wit: (specify the particulars of the offence), contrary to s. 57(3) of the Criminal Code of Canada.

7. Sufficiency of count

No count that alleges false pretences, fraud or any attempt or conspiracy by fraudulent means is insufficient by reason only that it does not set out in detail the nature of the false pretence, fraud or fraudulent means (s. 586).

PATHOLOGY. That branch of medicine concerned with the alterations in the structure of tissues caused by disease, aging or violence. The practice of pathology includes the performance of autopsies (Jaffe, A Guide to Pathological Evidence, 2nd ed.).

PEACE OFFICER

1. *Definition of "peace officer"*
2. *Misconduct in the execution of a process*
3. *Resisting or obstructing peace officer*
4. *Omitting to assist peace officer*
5. *Personating a peace officer*
6. *Assaulting a peace officer. See ASSAULT, 7.*
7. *Neglect by a peace officer. See UNLAWFUL ASSEMBLIES AND RIOTS, 5.*

1. Definition of "peace officer"

For the purposes of the Criminal Code, "peace officer" includes:

(a) a mayor, warden, reeve, sheriff, deputy sheriff, sheriff's officer and justice of the peace,

(b) a member of the Correctional Service of Canada who is designated as a peace officer pursuant to Part I of the Corrections and Conditional Release Act, and a warden, deputy warden, instructor, keeper, jailer, guard and any other officer or permanent employee of a prison,

(c) a police officer, police constable, bailiff, constable, or other person employed for the preservation and maintenance of the public peace or for the service or execution of civil process,

(d) an officer or a person having the powers of a customs or excise officer when performing any duty in the administration of the Customs Act or the Excise Act,

(e) a person designated as a fishery guardian under the Fisheries Act when performing any duties or functions under that Act and a person designated as a fishery officer under the Fisheries Act when performing any duties or functions under that Act, the Coastal Fisheries Protection Act, the North Pacific Fisheries Convention Act, the Northern Pacific Halibut Fisheries Convention Act, or the Pacific Fur Seals Convention Act,

(f) the pilot in command of an aircraft registered in Canada under regulations made under the Aeronautics Act, or leased without crew and operated by a person who is qualified under regulations made under the Aeronautics Act to be registered as owner of an aircraft registered in Canada under those regulations, while the aircraft is in flight, and

(g) officers and non-commissioned members of the Canadian Forces who are either appointed for the purposes of s. 156 of the National Defence Act, or employed on duties that the Governor in Council, in regulations made under the National Defence Act for these purposes, has prescribed to be of such a kind as to necessitate that the officers and non-commissioned members performing them have the powers of peace officers (s. 2).

2. Misconduct in the execution of a process — Section 128

Every peace officer or coroner who — being entrusted with the execution of a process — wilfully — either misconducts himself in the execution of the process — or makes a false return to the process — is guilty of an indictable offence.

Intent. Wilfully.

Included offences. Attempts (s. 660 and s. 662(1)(b)).

Punishment. Imprisonment for a term not exceeding 2 years (s. 128).

Release. Initial decision to release made by officer in charge or justice (s. 498).

Election. Accused may elect trial by judge and jury, judge alone, or provincial court judge (s. 536).

3. Resisting or obstructing peace officer — Section 129(a)

Every one who — resists or wilfully obstructs — either a peace officer in the execution of his duty — or any person lawfully acting in aid of such an officer — is guilty of either an indictable offence or an offence punishable on summary conviction.

Intent. Wilfully.

Limitation period. No proceedings in respect of offences that are declared to be punishable on summary conviction shall be instituted more than 6 months after the time when the subject matter of the proceedings arose (s. 786(2) and s. 785(1)).

Included offences. Attempts (s. 660 and s. 662(1)(b)).

Punishment. On indictment, imprisonment for a term not exceeding 2 years (s. 129(d)). On summary conviction, a fine not exceeding $2,000, or 6 months' imprisonment, or both (s. 129(e) and s. 787(1)).

Release. Initial decision to release made by peace officer (s. 497).

Election. On indictment, accused may elect trial by judge and jury, judge alone, or provincial court judge (s. 536). On summary conviction, no election.

Informations

A.B., on or about the —— day of ——, 19——, at the —— of ——, in the said (territorial division), did resist [OR wilfully obstruct] C.D., a peace officer in the execution of his duty, to wit: (specify the particulars of the offence), contrary to s. 129(a) of the Criminal Code of Canada.

4. Omitting to assist peace officer — Section 129(b)

Every one who — without reasonable excuse — omits to assist a peace officer — in the execution of his duty in arresting a person or in preserving the peace — after having reasonable notice that he is required to do so — is guilty of either an indictable offence or an offence punishable on summary conviction.

Limitation period. No proceedings in respect of offences that are declared to be punishable on summary conviction shall be instituted more than 6 months after the time when the subject matter of the proceedings arose (s. 786(2) and s. 785(1)).

Included offences. Attempts (s. 660 and s. 662(1)(b)).

Punishment. On indictment, imprisonment for a term not exceeding 2 years (s. 129(d)). On summary conviction, a fine not exceeding $2,000, or 6 months' imprisonment, or both (s. 129(e) and s. 787(1)).

Release. Initial decision to release made by peace officer (s. 497).

Election. On indictment, accused may elect trial by judge and jury, judge alone, or provincial court judge (s. 536). On summary conviction, no election.

5. Personating a peace officer

Section 130(a)

Every one who — falsely represents himself — to be a peace officer — is guilty of an offence punishable on summary conviction.

Section 130(b)

Every one who — not being a peace officer — uses a badge or article of uniform or equipment — in a manner that is likely to cause persons to believe that he is a peace officer — is guilty of an offence punishable on summary conviction.

Limitation period. No proceedings in respect of offences that are declared to be punishable on summary conviction shall be instituted

more than 6 months after the time when the subject matter of the proceedings arose (s. 786(2) and s. 785(1)).

Included offences. Attempts (s. 660 and s. 662(1)(b)).

Punishment. A fine not exceeding $2,000, or 6 months' imprisonment, or both (s. 130 and s. 787(1)).

Release. Initial decision to release made by peace officer (s. 497).

Election. No election, summary conviction offence.

Sufficiency of count. No count that alleges false pretences, fraud or any attempt or conspiracy by fraudulent means is insufficient by reason only that it does not set out in detail the nature of the false pretence, fraud or fraudulent means (s. 586).

Informations

A.B., on or about the —— day of ——, 19——, at the —— of ——, in the said (territorial division), did falsely represent himself to be a peace officer, to wit: (specify the particulars of the offence), contrary to s. 130(a) of the Criminal Code of Canada.

A.B., on or about the —— day of ——, 19——, at the —— of ——, in the said (territorial division), not being a peace officer, did use a badge [OR article of uniform OR equipment] in a manner that was likely to cause persons to believe that he was a peace officer, to wit: (specify the particulars of the offence), contrary to s. 130(b) of the Criminal Code of Canada.

PEDOPHILIA. Sexual interest in children (Jaffe, A Guide to Pathological Evidence, 2nd ed.).

PENDENTE LITE. "The lawsuit pending" (Latin).

PER. By; through; during; because of (Latin). *Per annum.* Yearly; by the year. *Per capita.* 1. By heads. 2. Distribution of the property of an intestate is per capita if the property is equally divided among the descendants. *Per curiam.* 1. By the court. 2. A phrase used to distinguish the opinion of the whole court from that of any one judge. *Per incuriam.* 1. By carelessness. 2. A decision or dictum of a judge which clearly resulted from an oversight of a relevant statute or precedent is said to be per incuriam. *Per se.* By itself; taken alone. *Per stirpes.* 1. By stock or branches. 2. Distribution of the property of an intestate is per stirpes if it is divided amongst those entitled to it according to the number of stocks of descent; that is, if it is divided equally amongst the surviving children of an intestate individually, and the descendants of deceased children collectively, so that the descendants of a deceased child take that child's share between them.

PERIOD OF PROBATION. For the purposes of the Criminal Records Act, "period of probation" means a period during which a person convicted of an offence was directed by the court that convicted him (a) to be released upon his own recognizance to keep the peace and be of good behaviour, or (b) to be released upon or comply with the conditions prescribed in a probation order, which period shall be deemed to have terminated at the time the recognizance or the probation order, as the case may be, ceased to be in force (Criminal Records Act, s. 2(1)), (2)).

PERMANENT CAVITY. The track left in the tissue by the passage of a projectile. The diameter of the permanent cavity is usually greater than that of the projectile because of the tissue disruption caused by the temporary cavity (Jaffe, A Guide to Pathological Evidence, 2nd ed.).

PERSON. "Person", or any word or expression descriptive of a person, includes a corporation (Interpretation Act, s. 35(1)).

PERSONA DESIGNATA. A person designated or appointed for a special function (Latin).

PERSONA (NON) GRATA. (Un)welcome person (Latin).

PERSONAL PROPERTY. Movable property, or goods and chattels. Leasehold interests in land are personal property (Osborn's Concise Law Dictionary).

PERSONATION

1. *Definition of "personation"*
2. *With intent to gain property or advantage*
3. *With intent to cause disadvantage*
4. *At an examination*
5. *Acknowledging instrument in false name*
6. *Sufficiency of count*
7. *Personating a peace officer. See PEACE OFFICER, 5.*
8. *Personating a public officer. See PUBLIC OFFICER, 4.*
9. *Unlawful use of military uniforms or certificates. See PUBLIC STORES, 6.*

1. Definition of "personation"

The act of representing oneself to be someone else, whether living or dead, real or fictitious (Jowitt's Dictionary of English Law).

2. With intent to gain property or advantage

Section 403(a)

Every one who — fraudulently — personates any person, living or dead — with intent to gain advantage for himself or another person — is guilty of an indictable offence.

Section 403(b)

Every one who — fraudulently — personates any person, living or dead — with intent to obtain any property or an interest in any property — is guilty of an indictable offence.

Intent. Fraudulently with intent to gain advantage (s. 403(a)) or obtain property (s. 403(b)).

Included offences. Attempts (s. 660 and s. 662(1)(b)).

Punishment. Imprisonment for a term not exceeding 14 years (s. 403).

Release. Initial decision to release made by justice (s. 515(1)).

Election. Accused may elect trial by judge and jury, judge alone, or provincial court judge (s. 536).

Evidence. See **6**, below.

Informations

A.B., on or about the —— day of ——, 19——, at the —— of ——, in the said (territorial division), did fraudulently personate C.D., with intent to gain advantage for himself [OR for E.F.], to wit: (specify the particulars of the offence), contrary to s. 403(a) of the Criminal Code of Canada.

A.B., on or about the —— day of ——, 19——, at the —— of ——, in the said (territorial division), did fraudulently personate C.D., with intent to obtain property [OR an interest in property], to wit: (specify the particulars of the offence), contrary to s. 403(b) of the Criminal Code of Canada.

3. With intent to cause disadvantage — Section 403(c)

Every one who — fraudulently — personates any person, living or dead — with intent to cause disadvantage to the person whom he personates or another person — is guilty of an indictable offence.

Intent. Fraudulently with intent to cause disadvantage.

Included offences. Attempts (s. 660 and s. 662(1)(b)).

Punishment. Imprisonment for a term not exceeding 14 years (s. 403).

Release. Initial decision to release made by justice (s. 515(1)).

Election. Accused may elect trial by judge and jury, judge alone, or provincial court judge (s. 536).

Evidence. See **6***, below.*

Informations

A.B., on or about the —— day of ——, 19——, at the —— of ——, in the said (territorial division), did fraudulently personate C.D., with intent to cause disadvantage to C.D. [OR to E.F.] to wit: (specify the particulars of the offence), contrary to s. 403(c) of the Criminal Code of Canada.

4. At an examination — Section 404

Every one who — with intent to gain advantage for himself or some other person — falsely personates a candidate — at a competitive or qualifying examination held under the authority of law or in connection with a university or college or school — is guilty of an offence punishable on summary conviction.

Every one who — knowingly avails himself of the results of such personation — is guilty of an offence punishable on summary conviction.

Intent. Intention to gain advantage; knowingly.

Limitation period. No proceedings in respect of offences that are declared to be punishable on summary conviction shall be instituted more than 6 months after the time when the subject matter of the proceedings arose (s. 786(2) and s. 785(1)).

Included offences. Attempts (s. 660 and s. 662(1)(b)).

Punishment. A fine not exceeding $2,000, or 6 months' imprisonment, or both (s. 404 and s. 787(1)).

Release. Initial decision to release made by peace officer (s. 497).

Election. No election, summary conviction offence.

Evidence. See **6**, *below.*

Informations

A.B., on or about the —— day of ——, 19——, at the —— of ——, in the said (territorial division), falsely, with intent to gain advantage for himself [OR for C.D.], did personate C.D., a candidate at a competitive [OR a qualifying] examination held under the authority of law [OR in connection with a university (OR a college OR a school)], to wit: (specify the particulars of the offence), contrary to s. 404 of the Criminal Code of Canada.

A.B., on or about the —— day of ——, 19——, at the —— of ——, in the said (territorial division), did knowingly avail himself of the results of the personation of himself [OR of C.D.], a candidate at a competitive [OR a qualifying] examination held under the authority of law [OR in connection with a university (OR a college OR a school)], to wit: (specify the particulars of the offence), contrary to s. 404 of the Criminal Code of Canada.

5. Acknowledging instrument in false name — Section 405

Every one who — without lawful authority or excuse — acknowledges — in the name of another person — before a court or a judge or other person authorized to receive the acknowledgment — a recognizance of bail or a confession of judgment or a consent to judgment or a judgment or deed or other instrument — is guilty of an indictable offence.

Included offences. Attempts (s. 660 and s. 662(1)(b)).

Punishment. Imprisonment for a term not exceeding 5 years (s. 405).

Release. Initial decision to release made by officer in charge or justice (s. 498).

Election. Accused may elect trial by judge and jury, judge alone, or provincial court judge (s. 536).

Evidence. For the purposes of this offence, the proof of lawful excuse lies on the accused (s. 405).

Informations

A.B., on or about the —— day of ——, 19——, at the —— of ——, in the said (territorial division), without lawful authority or excuse, did acknowledge, *in the name of C.D., before a court [OR a judge OR (specify another person authorized to receive the acknowledgment)] a recognizance of bail [OR a confession of judgment OR a consent to judgment OR a judgment OR a deed OR (specify other instrument)], to wit: (specify the particulars of the offence), contrary to s. 405 of the Criminal Code of Canada.*

6. Sufficiency of count

No count that alleges false pretences, fraud or any attempt or conspiracy by fraudulent means is insufficient by reason only that it does not set out in detail the nature of the false pretence, fraud or fraudulent means (s. 586).

PHOTOGRAPHIC FILM. For the purposes of the Canada Evidence Act, "photographic film" includes any photographic plate, microphotographic film and photostatic negative (Canada Evidence Act, s. 31(1)).

PHOTOGRAPHY. For the purposes of the Identification of Criminals Act, the measurements, processes and operations fingerprinting, palmprinting and photography are sanctioned (SI/92-131 (Gaz. 29/7/92, p. 3287)).

PIRACY

1. *Definition of "piracy"*
2. *Piracy by law of nations*
3. *Offences in connection with Canadian ships*

See also VESSELS AND RELATED OFFENCES.

1. Definition of "piracy"

"Piracy" means the commission of those acts of robbery and violence upon the sea that would amount to felony.

2. Piracy by law of nations

Definition of offence — Section 74(1)

Every one who — does any act — that is piracy by the law of nations — commits piracy.

Statement of offence — Section 74(2)

Every one who — commits piracy — while in or out of Canada — is guilty of an indictable offence.

Jurisdiction. Triable only in a superior court of criminal jurisdiction (s. 468 and s. 469(a)(vi)).

Included offences. Attempts (s. 660 and s. 662(1)(b)).

Punishment. Imprisonment for life (s. 74(2)).

The sentence to be pronounced against a person who is to be sentenced to imprisonment for life in respect of a person who has been convicted of this offence shall be that he be sentenced to imprisonment for life with normal eligibility for parole (s. 742(c)).

Release. Initial decision to release made by superior court judge (s. 522).

Election. Superior court (with jury) exclusive, except where accused elects superior court trial without jury with consent of Attorney General (s. 473) (s. 469).

Informations

A.B., on or about the —— day of ——, 19——, at the —— of ——, in the said (territorial division), did commit piracy, to wit: (specify the particulars of the offence), contrary to s. 74 of the Criminal Code of Canada.

3. Offences in connection with Canadian ships

Section 75(a)

Every one who — while in or out of Canada — steals a Canadian ship — is guilty of an indictable offence.

Section 75(b)

Every one who — while in or out of Canada — steals or without lawful authority throws overboard or damages or destroys — anything that is part of the cargo or supplies or fittings in a Canadian ship — is guilty of an indictable offence.

Section 75(c)

Every one who — while in or out of Canada — does or attempts to do a mutinous act on a Canadian ship — is guilty of an indictable offence.

Section 75(d)

Every one who — while in or out of Canada — counsels a person to do anything mentioned above — is guilty of an indictable offence.

PLACE 485

Jurisdiction. Triable only in a superior court of criminal jurisdiction (s. 468 and s. 469(a)(vii)).

Included offences. Attempts (s. 660 and s. 662(1)(b)).

Punishment. Imprisonment for a term not exceeding 14 years (s. 75).

Release. Initial decision to release may only be made by superior court judge (s. 522).

Election. Superior court (with jury) exclusive, except where accused elects superior court trial without jury with consent of Attorney General (s. 473) (s. 469).

Informations

A.B., on or about the —— day of ——, 19——, at the —— of ——, in the said (territorial division), did steal [OR did counsel C.D. to steal] a Canadian ship [OR part of the cargo (OR part of the supplies OR part of the fittings) in a Canadian ship], to wit: (specify the particulars of the offence), contrary to s. 75 of the Criminal Code of Canada.

A.B., on or about the —— day of ——, 19——, at the —— of ——, in the said (territorial division), without lawful authority, did throw overboard [OR damage OR destroy] part of the cargo [OR part of the supplies OR part of the fittings] in a Canadian ship, to wit: (specify the particulars of the offence), contrary to s. 75 of the Criminal Code of Canada.

A.B., on or about the —— day of ——, 19——, at the —— of ——, in the said (territorial division), without lawful authority did counsel C.D. to throw overboard [OR damage OR destroy] part of the cargo [OR part of the supplies OR part of the fittings] in a Canadian ship, to wit: (specify the particulars of the offence), contrary to s. 75 of the Criminal Code of Canada.

A.B., on or about the —— day of ——, 19——, at the —— of ——, in the said (territorial division), did [OR attempted to do OR counselled C.D. to do OR counselled C.D. to attempt to do] a mutinous act on a Canadian ship, to wit: (specify the particulars of the offence), contrary to s. 75 of the Criminal Code of Canada.

PLACE. 1. For the purposes of Part VII of the Criminal Code (Disorderly Houses, Gaming and Betting), "place" includes any place, whether or not (a) it is covered or enclosed, (b) it is used permanently or temporarily, or (c) any person has an exclusive right of user with respect to it (s. 197(1)). 2. For the purposes of s. 348 (breaking and entering) and s. 351 (possession of break-in instrument) of the

Criminal Code, "place" means (a) a dwelling-house; (b) a building or structure or any part thereof, other than a dwelling-house, (c) a railway vehicle, a vessel, an aircraft or a trailer; or (d) a pen or an enclosure in which fur-bearing animals are kept in captivity for breeding or commercial purposes (s. 348(3)). *See also PUBLIC PLACE.*

PLEA BARGAINING. Plea bargaining in criminal cases appears to be an attempt to adapt to criminal proceedings the sort of procedure that may lead to settlement in a civil case. Crown counsel and defence counsel negotiate out of court and reach an agreement. Usually such agreements are:
(1) that Crown counsel will, if the accused pleads guilty to a lesser charge, withdraw a major charge. A common instance is the acceptance of a plea of guilty of manslaughter made on condition that a charge of murder be withdrawn;
(2) that Crown counsel, in return for a plea of guilty by the accused to a charge, will recommend to the court the imposition of some lenient form of sentence, e.g., probation; or
(3) there may be a bargain which embraces both the above factors (Wilson, J., A Book for Judges).

PLEADINGS. In criminal and civil cases, statements in writing served by each party on the other, and filed with the court, stating the facts relied on to support their case and including all essential averments or assertion of fact. The primary pleading in a criminal case is the charge document, either the "information" or the "indictment" (The Charge Document in Criminal Cases, Law Reform Commission of Canada, Working Paper 55).

POLYGAMY

Section 293(1)(a)

Every one who — practises or enters into or in any manner agrees or consents to practise or enter into — either any form of polygamy — or any kind of conjugal union with more than one person at the same time — whether or not it is by law recognized as a binding form of marriage — is guilty of an indictable offence.

Section 293(1)(b)

Every one who — celebrates or assists or is a party to — a rite or ceremony or contract or consent — that purports to sanction a relationship mentioned above — is guilty of an indictable offence.

Included offences. Attempts (s. 660 and s. 662(1)(b)).

Punishment. Imprisonment for a term not exceeding 5 years (s. 293(1)).

Release. Initial decision to release made by officer in charge or justice (s. 498).

Election. Accused may elect trial by judge and jury, judge alone, or provincial court judge (s. 536).

Evidence. 1. The wife or husband of a person charged with this offence is a competent and compellable witness for the prosecution without the consent of the accused (Canada Evidence Act, s. 4(2)).
2. Where an accused is charged with this offence, no averment or proof of the method by which the alleged relationship was entered into, agreed to or consented to is necessary in the indictment or on the trial of the accused, nor is it necessary on the trial to prove that the persons who are alleged to have entered into the relationship had or intended to have sexual intercourse (s. 293(2)).

Informations

A.B., a male person, and C.D. and E.F., females, on or about the —— day of ——, 19——, at the —— of ——, in the said (territorial division), did practise polygamy together, to wit: (specify the particulars of the offence), contrary to s. 293 of the Criminal Code of Canada.

POSSESSION

1. *Definition of "possession"*
2. *Attributed possession*
3. *Property obtained by crime — Having in possession*
4. *Property obtained by crime — Bringing into Canada*
5. *Mail*

For specific offences of possession, see BREAKING AND ENTERING, CONTROLLED DRUGS, CURRENCY OFFENCES, EXPLOSIVE SUBSTANCES, FIREARMS AND WEAPONS OFFENCES, NARCOTICS, PASSPORT OFFENCES, PROCEEDS OF CRIME, RESTRICTED DRUGS, AND TRADEMARK OFFENCES.

1. Definition of "possession"

A person has anything in possession when he has it in his personal possession, or when he knowingly has it in the actual possession or custody of another person, or when he knowingly has it in any place, whether or not the place belongs to or is occupied by him, for the use or benefit of himself or of another person (s. 4(3)(a)).

There can be no possession of a thing without knowledge of what that thing is. Mere manual handling, even if coupled with control, is insufficient, if the accused is unaware that what he is handling is something of which possession is illegal. For manual handling of a thing to constitute possession, the handling must be co-existent with knowledge of what the thing is, and both these elements must be co-existent with some sort of control. The possession may be momentary.

For the purposes of the Narcotic Control Act and Parts III and IV of the Food and Drugs Act, "possession" means possession as defined in the Criminal Code (Narcotic Control Act, s. 2; Food and Drugs Act, s. 38 and s. 46).

2. Attributed possession

Where one of two or more persons, with the knowledge and consent of the rest, has anything in his custody or possession, it shall be deemed to be in the custody and possession of each and all of them (s. 4(3)(b)).

Mere knowledge of the other person's possession is insufficient. There must be knowledge and consent as well as some measure of control over the subject matter.

3. Property obtained by crime — Having in possession — Section 354(1) and section 355

Every one who — has in his possession — any property or thing or any proceeds of any property or thing — knowing that all or part of the property or thing or of the proceeds was obtained by or derived directly or indirectly from — either the commission in Canada of an offence punishable by indictment — or an act or omission anywhere that, if it had occurred in Canada, would have constituted an offence punishable by indictment — is guilty of an indictable offence — where the subject matter of the offence is a testamentary instrument or the value exceeds $1,000 — or is guilty of either an indictable offence or of an offence punishable on summary conviction — where the value of what is in his possession does not exceed $1,000.

Intent. Knowledge of how obtained.

Jurisdiction. The jurisdiction of a provincial court judge to try an accused is absolute and does not depend upon the consent of the accused where the subject matter of the offence is not a testamentary instrument and where the alleged value thereof does not exceed $1,000 (s. 553(a)(iii)).

Limitation period. No proceedings in respect of offences that are declared to be punishable on summary conviction shall be instituted more than 6 months after the time when the subject matter of the proceedings arose (s. 786(2) and s. 785(1)).

Included offences. Attempts (s. 660 and s. 662(1)(b)).

Punishment. On indictment, where the subject matter of the offence is a testamentary instrument or the value thereof exceeds $1,000, imprisonment for a term not exceeding 10 years (s. 355(a)). Where the value of what is in his possession does not exceed $1,000, imprisonment for a term not exceeding 2 years (s. 355(b)(i)). On summary conviction, a fine not exceeding $2,000, or 6 months' imprisonment, or both (s. 355(b)(ii) and s. 787(1)).

Release. Where the subject matter of the offence is a testamentary instrument or the value thereof exceeds $1,000, initial decision to release made by justice (s. 515(1)). Where the value of what is in his possession does not exceed $1,000, initial decision to release made by peace officer (s. 497).

Election. On indictment, where the subject matter of the offence is a testamentary instrument or the value thereof exceeds $1,000, accused may elect trial by judge and jury, judge alone, or provincial court judge (s. 536). Where the value of what is in his possession does not exceed $1,000, no election, absolute jurisdiction of provincial court judge (s. 553). On summary conviction, no election.

Evidence. 1. For these purposes, the offence of having in possession is complete when a person has, alone or jointly with another person, possession of or control over anything mentioned in s. 354 or when he aids in concealing or disposing of it, as the case may be (s. 358).

2. In proceedings in respect of this offence, evidence that a person has in his possession a motor vehicle the vehicle identification number of which has been wholly or partially removed or obliterated (or a part of a motor vehicle being a part bearing a vehicle identification number that has been wholly or partially removed or obliterated) is, in the absence of any evidence to the contrary, proof that the motor vehicle (or part) was obtained, and that such person had the motor vehicle (or part) in his possession knowing that it was obtained, either (a) by the commission in Canada of an offence punishable by indictment, or (b) by an act or omission anywhere that, if it had occurred

in Canada, would have constituted an offence punishable by indictment (s. 354(2)).

A "vehicle identification number" means any number or other mark placed on a motor vehicle for the purpose of distinguishing the motor vehicle from other similar motor vehicles (s. 354(3)).

Informations

A.B., on or about the —— day of ——, 19——, at the —— of ——, in the said (territorial division), did have in his possession (specify the property or thing or proceeds of any property or thing) of a value of more than [OR less than]$1,000, knowing that it was [OR they were] obtained by [OR derived directly from or indirectly derived from] the commission in Canada of an offence punishable by indictment [OR an act (OR omission) that, if it had occurred in Canada, would have constituted an offence punishable by indictment] to wit: (specify the particulars of the offence), contrary to s. 354(1) of the Criminal Code of Canada.

4. Property obtained by crime — Bringing into Canada — Section 357

Every one who — brings into or has in Canada — anything that he has obtained outside Canada — by an act that, if it had been committed in Canada, would have been the offence of theft or an offence under s. 342 (theft, forgery, etc. of credit card) or s. 354 (property obtained by crime — having in possession) — is guilty of an indictable offence.

Included offences. Attempts (s. 660 and s. 662(1)(b)).

Punishment. Imprisonment for a term not exceeding 10 years (s. 357).

Release. Initial decision to release made by justice (s. 515(1)).

Election. Accused may elect trial by judge and jury, judge alone, or provincial court judge (s. 536).

Informations

A.B., on or about the —— day of ——, 19——, at the —— of ——, in the said (territorial division), did bring into [OR have in] Canada (specify the thing] that he had obtained outside Canada by an act that, if it had been committed in Canada, would have been an offence under s. 354 of the Criminal Code [OR an offence under s. 342 of the Criminal Code OR the offence of theft] to wit: (specify the particulars of the offence), contrary to s. 357 of the Criminal Code of Canada.

5. Mail — Section 356(1)(b)

Every one who — has in his possession — anything in respect of which he knows that an offence has been committed under s. 356(1)(a) (theft from mail) — is guilty of an indictable offence.

S. 356(1)(a) provides that every one who, steals anything sent by post after it is deposited at a post office and before it is delivered, or a bag or sack or other container or covering in which mail is conveyed, whether or not it contains mail, or a key suited to a lock adapted for use by the Canada Post Office is guilty of an indictable offence.

Intent. Knowledge of spurious character.

Included offences. Attempts (s. 660 and s. 662(1)(b)).

Punishment. Imprisonment for a term not exceeding 10 years (s. 356(1)).

Release. Initial decision to release made by justice (s. 515(1)).

Election. Accused may elect trial by judge and jury, judge alone, or provincial court judge (s. 536).

Evidence. 1. In proceedings for this offence, it is not necessary to allege in the indictment or to prove on the trial that anything in respect of which the offence was committed had any value (s. 356(2)).
2. The offence of having in possession is complete when a person has, alone or jointly with another person, possession of or control over anything mentioned in s. 356 or when he aids in concealing or disposing of it, as the case may be (s. 358).

Informations

A.B., on or about the —— day of ——, 19——, at the —— of ——, in the said (territorial division), did have in his possession (specify the thing in possession), a thing in respect of which he knew that an offence had been committed under s. 356(1)(a) of the Criminal Code, to wit: (specify the particulars of the offence), contrary to s. 356(1)(b) of the Criminal Code of Canada.

POST MORTEM. Present or occurring after death. Also autopsy (Jaffe, A Guide to Pathological Evidence, 2nd ed.).

Post mortem changes. Physical and chemical processes which commence immediately after death and eventually lead to the complete disintegration of the body (Jaffe, A Guide to Pathological Evidence, 2nd ed.).

Post mortem clot. A clot forming in the blood vessels, chambers of the heart or sites of hemorrhage after death (Jaffe, A Guide to Pathological Evidence, 2nd ed.).

Post mortem interval. The time between death and the examination of the body (Jaffe, A Guide to Pathological Evidence, 2nd ed.).

POWER OF ATTORNEY. A formal instrument by which one person empowers another person to represent him, or act in his stead for certain purposes.

PRACTITIONER. For the purposes of the Narcotic Control Act and Part III of the Food and Drugs Act (Controlled Drugs), "practitioner" means a person who is registered and entitled under the laws of a province to practise in that province the profession of medicine, dentistry or veterinary medicine (Narcotic Control Act, s. 2; Food and Drugs Act, s. 38).

PRE-HEARING CONFERENCE. A conference between the prosecutor and the accused or counsel for the accused to consider such matters as will promote a fair and expeditious hearing or trial. **Mandatory pre-hearing conference.** In any case to be tried by a judge and a jury, a judge of the court before which the accused is to be tried shall, prior to the trial, order that such a conference be held. The conference is to be presided over by a judge of that court and held in accordance with the rules of court (s. 625.1(2)). **Pre-hearing conference held with consent of the prosecutor and the accused.** A conference may also be held in respect of any other proceedings on application by the prosecutor or the accused or on the court's own motion with the consent of the prosecutor and the accused. The pre-trial conference is to be presided over by the court, judge, provincial court judge or justice and is to be held prior to the proceedings (s. 625.1(1)).

PRELIMINARY INQUIRY. This is a proceeding under Part XVIII of the Criminal Code (Procedure on Preliminary Inquiry) before a justice of the peace or provincial court judge for an indictable offence for the purpose of determining whether there is sufficient evidence to put the accused upon his trial.

If the offence is one of those mentioned in s. 469, the justice of the peace or provincial court judge has power only to hold a preliminary inquiry.

A provincial court judge may try, in some cases with the consent of the accused and in some cases without such consent, indictable offences except those mentioned in s. 469.

If, in the cases in which the jurisdiction of the provincial court judge depends upon the consent of the accused and upon putting the accused to his election, he elects trial by a judge without jury or before a jury, such provincial court judge then holds a preliminary hearing.

Upon a preliminary hearing, a prima facie case should be made out before the provincial court judge or justice of the peace orders the accused to stand trial. The hearing may be in private (s. 537(1)(h)).

See also CONTEMPT OF COURT, PUBLISHING OFFENCES, 2, and TRIAL PROCEDURE.

PRESCRIPTION. 1. For the purposes of Part III of the Food and Drugs Act (Controlled Drugs), "prescription" means in respect of a controlled drug, an authorization given by a practitioner that a stated amount of the controlled drug be dispensed for the person named therein (Food and Drugs Act, s. 38). 2. For the purposes of the Narcotic Control Act, "prescription" means in respect of a narcotic, an authorization given by a practitioner that a stated amount of the narcotic be dispensed for the person named therein (Narcotic Control Act, s. 2).

PRIMA FACIE. 1. At first sight (Latin). 2. The evidence discloses a prima facie case when it is such that, if uncontradicted and if believed, it will be sufficient to prove the case against the accused.

PRIMER. An explosive substance in firearm ammunition which is ignited by the percussion of the firing pin and which in turn ignites the propellant (Jaffe, A Guide to Pathological Evidence, 2nd ed.).

PRINTING OR PUBLISHING. For offences respecting printing or publishing, *see CORRUPTING MORALS, CURRENCY OFFENCES, and PUBLISHING OFFENCES.*

PRISON. For the purposes of the Criminal Code, "prison" includes a penitentiary, common jail, public or reformatory prison, lock-up, guard-room or other place in which persons who are charged with or convicted of offences are usually kept in custody (s. 2).

PRIVATE COMMUNICATION. For the purposes of Part VI of the Criminal Code (Invasion of Privacy), "private communication" means any oral communication, or any telecommunication, that is made by an originator who is in Canada or is intended by the originator to be received by a person who is in Canada and that is made under circumstances in which it is reasonable for the originator to expect that it will not be intercepted by any person other than the person intended by the originator to receive it, and includes any radio-based telephone communication that is treated electronically or otherwise for the purpose of preventing intelligible reception by any person other than the person intended by the originator to receive it (s. 183).

PRIZE FIGHTS

Definition. For the purposes of s. 83, "prize fight" means an encounter or fight with fists or hands between two persons who have met for that purpose by previous arrangement made by or for them, but a boxing contest between amateur sportsmen, where the contestants wear boxing gloves of not less than 140 grams each in mass, or any boxing contest held with the permission or under the authority of an athletic board or commission or similar body established by or under the authority of the legislature of a province for the control of sport within the province, shall be deemed not to be a prize fight (s. 83(2)).

Statements of offences — Section 83(1)(a)

Every one who — engages as a principal — in a prize fight — is guilty of an offence punishable on summary conviction.

Section 83(1)(b)

Every one who — advises or encourages or promotes — a prize fight — is guilty of an offence punishable on summary conviction.

Section 83(1)(c)

Every one who — is present at a prize fight — as an aid or second or surgeon or umpire or backer or reporter — is guilty of an offence punishable on summary conviction.

Limitation period. No proceedings in respect of offences that are declared to be punishable on summary conviction shall be instituted more than 6 months after the time when the subject matter of the proceedings arose (s. 786(2) and s. 785(1)).

Included offences. Attempts (s. 660 and s. 662(1)(b)).

Punishment. A fine not exceeding $2,000, or 6 months' imprisonment, or both (s. 83(1) and s. 787(1)).

Release. Initial decision to release made by peace officer (s. 497).

Election. No election, summary conviction offence.

Informations

A.B., on or about the —— day of ——, 19——, at the —— of ——, in the said (territorial division), did engage as a principal in a prize fight, to wit: (specify the particulars of the offence), contrary to s. 83(1)(a) of the Criminal Code of Canada.

A.B., on or about the —— day of ——, 19——, at the —— of ——, in the said (territorial division), did advise [OR encourage OR promote] a prize fight, to wit: (specify the particulars of the offence), contrary to s. 83(1)(b) of the Criminal Code of Canada.

A.B., on or about the —— day of ——, 19——, at the —— of ——, in the said (territorial division), was present at a prize fight as an aid [OR as a second OR as a surgeon OR as an umpire OR as a backer OR as a reporter] to wit, (specify the particulars of the offence), contrary to s. 83(1)(c) of the Criminal Code of Canada.

PRO. For; in respect of; on behalf of (Latin). ***Pro bono publico.*** For the public good. ***Pro forma.*** 1. As a matter of form. 2. For illustrative purposes. ***Pro rata.*** Proportionally; in proportion. "Pro rate" is the English derivation of "pro rata". ***Pro tanto.*** For so much; to that extent. ***Pro tem.*** An abbreviation for "pro tempore", which means "for the time being" or "temporarily".

PROCEEDINGS. 1. A general term which may be used to refer a procedural step that is part of a larger action, as well as to the entire course of an action. Also action; matter; suit. 2. For the purposes of Part XXVII of the Criminal Code (Summary Convictions), "proceedings" means (a) proceedings in respect of offences that are declared by an Act of Parliament or an enactment made thereunder to be punishable on summary conviction, and (b) proceedings where a justice is authorized by an Act of Parliament or an enactment made thereunder to make an order (s. 785(1)).

PROCEEDS OF CRIME

1. *Definitions*
2. *Laundering proceeds of crime*

1. Definitions

"Proceeds of crime". For the purposes of Part XII.2 of the Criminal Code (Proceeds of Crime), "proceeds of crime" means a property, benefit or advantage, within or outside Canada, obtained or derived directly or indirectly as a result of (a) the commission in Canada of an enterprise crime offence or a designated drug offence, (b) an act or omission anywhere that, if it had occurred in Canada, would have constituted an enterprise crime offence or a designated drug offence, or (c) the commissoin of an offence contrary to ss. 126.1 or 126.2 or 223(1) or 240(1) of the Excise Act or ss. 153, 159, 163.1 or 163.2 of the Customs Act (s. 462.3).

"Designated drug offence". For the purposes of Part X11.2 of the Criminal Code, "designated drug offence" means (a) an offence against ss. 39, 44.2, 44.3, 48, 50.2 or 50.3 of the Food and Drugs Act, (b) an offence against ss. 4, 5, 6, 19.1 or 19.2 of the Narcotic Control Act, or (c) a conspiracy or an attempt to commit, being an accessory after the fact in relation to or any counselling in relation to, an offence referred to in paragraph (a) or (b) (s. 462.3).

"Enterprise crime offence". For the purposes of Part XII.2 of the Criminal Code, "enterprise crime offence" means
(a) an offence against any of the following provisions, namely, (i) s. 119 (bribery of judicial officers, etc.), (ii) s. 120 (bribery of officers), (iii) s. 121 (frauds upon the government), (iv) s. 122 (breach of trust by public officer), (v) s. 163 (corrupting morals), (v.1) s. 163.1 (child pornography), (vi) s. 201(1) (keeping gaming or betting house), (vii) s. 202 (betting, pool-selling, book-making, etc.), (viii) s. 210 (keeping common bawdy-house), (ix) s. 212 (procuring), (x) s. 235 (punishment for murder), (xi) s. 334 (punishment for theft), (xii), s. 344 (punishment for robbery), (xiii) s. 346 (extortion), (xiv) s. 367 (punishment for forgery), (xv) s. 368 (uttering forged document), (xvi) s. 380 (fraud), (xvii) s. 382 (fraudulent manipulation of stock exchange transactions), (xviii) s. 426 (secret commissions), (xix) s. 433 (arson), (xx) s. 449 (making counterfeit money), (xxi) s. 450 (possession, etc., of coun-

terfeit money), (xxii) s. 452 (uttering, etc., counterfeit money), or (xxiii) s. 462.31 (laundering proceeds of crime,

(b) an offence against s. 354 (possession of property obtained by crime), committed in relation to any property, thing or proceeds obtained or derived directly or indirectly as a result of (i) the commission in Canada of an offence referred to in paragraph (a) or a designated drug offence, or (ii) an act or omission anywhere that, if it had occurred in Canada, would have constituted an offence referred to in paragraph (a) or a designated drug offence,

(c) a conspiracy or an attempt to commit, being an accessory after the fact in relation to, or any counselling in relation to, an offence referred to in paragraph (a), (b) or (b.1) (s. 462.3).

2. Laundering proceeds of crime

Definition of offence — Section 462.31(1)

Every one commits an offence who — uses or transfers the possession of or sends or delivers to any person or place or transports or transmits or alters or disposes of or otherwise deals with, in any manner and by any means — any property or any proceeds of any property — with intent to conceal or convert that property or those proceeds — and knowing that all or a part of that property or of those proceeds — was obtained or derived directly or indirectly as a result of — the commission in Canada of an enterprise crime offence or a designated drug offence or — an act or omission anywhere that, if it had occurred in Canada, would have constituted an enterprise crime offence or a designated drug offence.

Statement of offence — Section 462.31(2)

Every one who — commits an offence under s. 462.31(1) — is guilty of either an indictable offence or an offence punishable on summary conviction.

Intent. Intent to conceal or convert property or proceeds. Knowledge that property or proceeds obtained derived from enterprise crime or designated drug offences.

Limitation period. No proceedings in respect of offences that are declared to be punishable on summary conviction shall be instituted more than 6 months after the time when the subject matter of the proceedings arose (s. 786(2) and s. 785(1)).

Included offences. Attempts (s. 660 and s. 662(1)(b)).

Punishment. On indictment, imprisonment for a term not exceeding 10 years (s. 462.31(2)(a)). On summary conviction, a fine not exceeding $2,000, or 6 months' imprisonment, or both (s. 462.31(2)(b) and s. 787(1)).

Release. Initial decision to release made by peace officer (s. 497).

Election. On indictment, accused may elect trial by judge and jury, judge alone, or provincial court judge (s. 536). On summary conviction, no election.

Informations

A.B., on or about the —— day of ——, 19——, at the —— of ——, in the said (territorial division), did use [OR transfer the possession of OR send (OR deliver) to any person (OR place) OR transport OR alter OR dispose of OR otherwise deal with], in any manner and by any means, any property [OR any proceeds of any property] with intent to conceal [OR convert] that property [OR those proceeds] and knowing that all [OR a part] of that property [OR of those proceeds] was obtained [OR derived] directly [OR indirectly] as a result of the commission in Canada of an enterprise crime offence [OR a designated drug offence OR an act (OR omission) anywhere that, if it had occurred in Canada, would have constituted an enterprise crime offence (OR a designated drug offence)], to wit: (specify the particulars of the offence), contrary to s. 462.31 of the Criminal Code of Canada.

PROCESS. 1. The proceedings in any action or prosecution. 2. In a wide sense, the term may include all the acts of a court from the beginning to the end of its proceedings in a given cause or matter. 3. More specifically, it means the writ, summons, statement of claim or other process used to inform a person of the institution of proceedings against him and to compel his appearance, in either criminal or civil cases. *See also PEACE OFFICER, 2.*

PROCLAMATIONS

1. *Definition of "proclamation"*
2. *Effective day of proclamations*
3. *Judicial notice*
4. *Counterfeit proclamation. See FORGERY AND RELATED OFFENCES, 6.*
5. *Proclamation and related offences. See UNLAWFUL ASSEMBLIES AND RIOTS, 3 and 4.*

1. Definition of "proclamation"

1. A notice publicly given of anything whereof the sovereign thinks fit to advise his subjects (Jowitt's Dictionary of English Law).
2. A written or printed declaration issued by a governmental authority such as the Governor General in Council, a Lieutenant Governor in Council, or a mayor.

2. Effective day of proclamations

A proclamation that is issued under an order of the Governor in Council may purport to have been issued on the day of the order or on any subsequent day, and, if so, takes effect on that day (Interpretation Act, s. 18(3)).

3. Judicial notice

Judicial notice shall be taken of a day for the coming into force of an enactment that is fixed by a regulation that has been published in the Canada Gazette (Interpretation Act, s. 6(3).

PROCURING

1. *Definition of "procuring"*
2. *Procuring offences*
3. *Living on avails of prostitution*
4. *Offence in relation to juvenile prostitution*
5. *Supplying or procuring drugs or instrument. See ABORTION AND MISCARRIAGE, 3.*
6. *Parent or guardian procuring sexual activity. See CORRUPTING MORALS, 15.*

See also COUNSELLING COMMISSION OF OFFENCE WHICH IS NOT COMMITTED.

1. Definition of "procuring"

1. "To procure" means to contrive; to bring about; to effect; to cause; to persuade; to induce; to prevail upon or cause a person to do something.
2. In a sexual content, "procuring" refers to the obtaining of a prostitute for another person.

2. Procuring offences

Section 212(1)(a)

Every one who — procures or attempts to procure or solicits a person — to have illicit sexual intercourse with another person — whether in or out of Canada — is guilty of an indictable offence.

Section 212(1)(b)

Every one who — inveigles or entices — a person who is not a prostitute or a person of known immoral character — to a common bawdy-house or house of assignation — for the purpose of illicit sexual intercourse or prostitution — is guilty of an indictable offence.

Section 212(1)(c)

Every one who — knowingly — conceals a person — in a common bawdy-house or house of assignation — is guilty of an indictable offence.

Section 212(1)(d)

Every one who — procures or attempts to procure a person — to become a prostitute — whether in or out of Canada — is guilty of an indictable offence.

Section 212(1)(e)

Every one who — procures or attempts to procure a person — to leave the usual place of abode of that person in Canada — if that place is not a common bawdy-house — with intent that the person may become an inmate or frequenter of a common bawdy-house — whether in or out of Canada — is guilty of an indictable offence.

Section 212(1)(f)

Every one who — on the arrival of a person in Canada — directs or causes that person to be directed — or takes or causes that person to be taken — to a common bawdy-house or house of assignation — is guilty of an indictable offence.

Section 212(1)(g)

Every one who — procures a person — to enter or leave Canada — for the purpose of prostitution — is guilty of an indictable offence.

Section 212(1)(h)

Every one who — for the purposes of gain — exercises control or direction or influence over the movements of a person — in such manner as to show that he is aiding or abetting or compelling that person to engage in or carry on prostitution with any person or generally — is guilty of an indictable offence.

Section 212(1)(i)

Every one who — applies or administers to a person or causes that person to take — any drug or intoxicating liquor or matter, or thing — with intent to stupefy or overpower that person — in order thereby to enable any person to have illicit sexual intercourse with that person — is guilty of an indictable offence.

Intent. Knowingly (s. 212(1)(c)); intention that person become inmate or frequenter (s. 212(1)(e)); for gain (s. 212(1)(h)); intention to stupefy or overpower for illicit purpose (s. 212(1)(i)).

Included offences. Attempts (s. 660 and s. 662(1)(b)).

Punishment. Imprisonment for 10 years (s. 212(1)).

Release. Initial decision to release made by justice (s. 515(1)).

Election. Accused may elect trial by judge and jury, judge alone, or provincial court judge (s. 536).

Evidence. 1. The husband or wife of a person charged with this offence is a competent and compellable witness for the prosecution without the consent of the person charged (Canada Evidence Act, s. 4(2)).
2. In the case of a female person, prostitution is not confined to acts of sexual intercourse, but will include any form of lewdness for which a woman habitually offers herself for hire. It includes active acts of indecency performed by the woman herself, e.g., masturbation of a male client (Archbold, Pleading Evidence and Practice in Criminal Cases, 39th ed.).
3. To support a conviction for procuring, it must be proven that some active part was played by the accused whereby he was able to cause, or to induce, or to have a persuasive effect upon the alleged misconduct.
4. Where an accused is charged with this offence, no corroboration is required for a conviction and the judge shall not instruct the jury that it is unsafe to find the accused guilty in the absence of corroboration (s. 274).

Informations

A.B., on or about the —— day of ——, 19——, at the —— of ——, in the said (territorial division), did procure [OR attempt to procure OR solicit] C.D., to have illicit sexual intercourse with E.F., to wit: (specify the particulars of the offence), contrary to s. 212(1)(a) of the Criminal Code of Canada.

A.B., on or about the —— day of ——, 19——, at the —— of ——, in the said (territorial division), did inveigle [OR entice] C.D., a person who is not a prostitute or a person of known immoral character, to a common bawdy-house [OR house of assignation] for the purpose of illicit sexual intercourse [OR prostitution], to wit: (specify the particulars of the offence), contrary to s. 212(1)(b) of the Criminal Code of Canada.

A.B., on or about the —— day of ——, 19——, at the —— of ——, in the said (territorial division), did knowingly conceal C.D. in a common bawdy-house or house of assignation, to wit: (specify the particulars of the offence), contrary to s. 212(1)(c) of the Criminal Code of Canada.

A.B., on or about the —— day of ——, 19——, at the —— of ——, in the said (territorial division), did procure [OR attempt to procure] C.D. to become a prostitute, to wit: (specify the particulars of the offence), contrary to s. 212(1)(d) of the Criminal Code of Canada.

A.B., on or about the —— day of ——, 19——, at the —— of ——, in the said (territorial division), did procure [OR attempt to procure] C.D. to leave the usual place of abode of that person with intent that C.D. become an inmate [OR frequenter] of a common bawdy-house, to wit: (specify the particulars of the offence), contrary to s. 212(1)(e) of the Criminal Code of Canada.

A.B., on or about the —— day of ——, 19——, at the —— of ——, in the said (territorial division), on the arrival in Canada of C.D. did direct [OR cause that person to be directed OR take OR cause that person to be taken] to a common bawdy-house [OR house of assignation] to wit: (specify the particulars of the offence), contrary to s. 212(1)(f) of the Criminal Code of Canada.

A.B., on or about the —— day of ——, 19——, at the —— of ——, in the said (territorial division), did procure C.D. to enter [OR leave] Canada, for the purpose of prostitution, to wit: (specify the particulars of the offence), contrary to s. 212(1)(g) of the Criminal Code of Canada.

A.B., on or about the —— day of ——, 19——, at the —— of ——, in the said (territorial division), for the purposes of gain, did exercise control [OR direction OR influence] over the movements of C.D. in such a manner as to show *that A.B. was aiding [OR abetting OR compelling] C.D. to engage in [OR carry on] prostitution with E.F. [OR generally], to wit: (specify the particulars of the offence), contrary to s. 212(1)(h) of the Criminal Code of Canada.*

A.B., on or about the —— day of ——, 19——, at the —— of ——, in the said (territorial division), did apply to C.D. [OR administer to C.D. OR cause C.D. to take] a drug [OR intoxicating liquor OR matter OR thing] with intent to stupefy [OR overpower] C.D. in order thereby to enable E.F. to have illicit sexual intercourse with C.D., to wit: (specify the particulars of the offence), contrary to s. 212(1)(i) of the Criminal Code of Canada.

3. Living on avails of prostitution

Section 212(1)(j)

Every one who — lives wholly or in part — on the avails of prostitution — of another person — is guilty of an indictable offence.

Section 212(2)

Every one who — lives wholly or in part — on the avails of prostitution — of another person who is under the age of 18 years — is guilty of an indictable offence.

Included offences. Attempts (s. 660 and s. 662(1)(b)).

Punishment. Imprisonment for a term not exceeding 10 years (s. 212(1)). Where the prostitution is committed by a person under the age of 18 years, imprisonment for a term not exceeding 14 years (s. 212(2)).

Release. Initial decision to release made by justice (s. 515(1)).

Election. Accused may elect trial by judge and jury, judge alone, or provincial court judge (s. 536).

Evidence. 1. Evidence that a person lives with or is habitually in the company of a prostitute or lives in a common bawdy-house or in a house of assignation is, in the absence of evidence to the contrary, proof that the person lives on the avails of prostitution, for these purposes (s. 212(3)).
2. It is not a defence to a charge under s. 212(2) or (4) that the accused believed that the complainant was 18 years of age or more at the time the offence is alleged to have been committed unless the accused took all reasonable steps to ascertain the age of the complainant (s. 150.1(5)).
3. *See also Evidence under 2, above.*

Informations

A.B., on or about the —— day of ——, 19——, at the —— of ——, in the said (territorial division), did live wholly [OR in part] on the avails of prostitution of C.D., to wit: (specify the particulars of the offence), contrary to s. 212(1)(j), of the Criminal Code of Canada.

4. Offence in relation to juvenile prostitution — Section 212(4)

Every one who — in any place — attempts or attempts to obtain — for consideration — the sexual services of a person who is under the age of 18 years — is guilty of an indictable offence.

Included offences. Attempts (s. 660 and s. 662(1)(b)).

Punishment. Imprisonment for a term not exceeding 5 years (s. 212(4)).

Release. Initial decision to release made by justice (s. 515(1)).

Election. Accused may elect trial by judge and jury, judge alone, or provincial court judge (s. 536).

Evidence. *See Evidence, under* **2***, above, and Evidence, item 2. under* **3***, above.*

PROHIBITED ACT. For the purposes of s. 52, "prohibited act" means an act or omission that either (a) impairs the efficiency or impedes the working of any vessel, vehicle, aircraft, machinery, apparatus or other thing, or (b) causes property, by whomever it may be owned, to be lost, damaged or destroyed (s. 52(2)). *See also SABOTAGE.*

PROHIBITED WEAPONS. A list of weapons expressly prohibited either by the Criminal Code or by Order of the Governor in Council. The latter are known as Prohibited Weapons Orders.

Weapons prohibited by the Criminal Code

1. ***Silencer.*** Any device or contrivance designed or intended to muffle or stop the sound or report of a firearm (s. 84(1)(a)).

2. ***Switch blade.*** Any knife that has a blade that opens automatically by gravity or centrifugal force or by hand pressure applied to a button, spring or other device in or attached to the handle of the knife (s. 84(1)(b)).

3. ***Automatic weapon.*** Any firearm that is capable of, or assembled or designed and manufactured with the capability of, firing projectiles in rapid succession during one pressure of the trigger, whether or not it has been altered to fire only one projectile with one

such pressure, other than a restricted weapon as defined in s. 84(1)(c) or (c.1) of the Criminal Code (s. 84(1)(c)). *See also RESTRICTED WEAPONS.*

4. *Sawed-off shotgun or rifle.* Any firearm adapted from a rifle or shotgun, whether by sawing, cutting or other alteration or modification that, as so adapted, has a barrel that is less than 457 mm (18 inches) in length or that is less than 660 mm (26 inches) in overall length (s. 84(1)(d)). *See also BARREL-LENGTH.*

5. *Weapon prohibited by order of the Governor in Council.* A weapon of any kind, not being an antique firearm or a firearm of a kind commonly used in Canada for hunting or sporting purposes, or a part, component or accessory of such a weapon, or any ammunition, that is declared by order of the Governor in Council to be a prohibited weapon (s. 84(1)(e)).

6. *Large-capacity cartridge magazine.* A large-capacity cartridge magazine prescribed by regulation (s. 84(1)(f)).

Weapons prohibited by Prohibited Weapons Orders

1. *Devices for tear gas or Mace.* Any device designed to be used for the purposes of injuring, immobilizing or otherwise incapacitating any person by the discharge therefrom of either (a) tear gas, Mace or other gas, or (b) any liquid, spray, powder or other substance that is capable of injuring, immobilizing or otherwise incapacitating any person (Prohibited Weapons Order No. 1, C.R.C. 1978, c. 433).

2. *Nunchaku.* Any instrument or device commonly known as "nunchaku", and any similar instrument or device, being hard non-flexible sticks, clubs, pipes or rods linked by a length or lengths of rope, cord, wire or chain (Prohibited Weapons Order No. 2, SOR/78-277, as amended by SOR/83 -182, SOR/85-215).

3. *Shuriken.* Any instrument or device commonly known as "shuriken", being a hard non-flexible plate having three or more radiating points with one or more sharp edges in the shape of a polygon, trefoil, cross, star, diamond or other geometric shape (Prohibited Weapons Order No. 2, SOR/78-277, as amended by SOR/83-182, SOR/85-215).

4. *Manrikigusari or Kusari.* Any instrument or device commonly known as "manrikigusari" or "kusari" and any similar instrument or device being hexagonal or other geometrically shaped hard weights or hand grips linked by a length or lengths of rope, cord wire, or chain (Prohibited Weapons Order No. 2, SOR/78-277, as amended by SOR/83-182, SOR/85-215).

5. ***Finger ring with blades.*** Any finger ring that has one or more blades or sharp objects that are capable of being projected from the surface of the ring (Prohibited Weapons Order No. 2, SOR/78-277, as amended by SOR/83-182, SOR/85-215).

6. ***Taser Public Defender.*** The device known as "Taser Public Defender", being a gun or a device similar to a gun capable of injuring, immobilizing or otherwise incapacitating a person by the discharge therefrom of darts or any other object carrying an electric current or substance; and any other device similar to the "Taser Public Defender" (Prohibited Weapons Order No. 3, SOR/78-278, as amended by SOR/92-428).

7. ***Stun Gun.*** The device known as "Stun Gun", being a device that is designed to be capable of injuring, immobilizing or incapacitating a person or an animal by discharging an electrical charge produced by means of the amplification or accumultation of the electrical current generated by a battery, where the device is designed or altered so that the electrical charge may be discharged when the device is of a length of less than 480 mm; and any other device similar to the "Stun Gun" (Prohibited Weapons Order No. 3, SOR/78-278, as amended by SOR/92-428).

8. ***Constant Companion.*** The device known as the "Constant Companion", being a belt containing a blade capable of being withdrawn from the belt, with the buckle of the belt forming a handle for the blade; and any other device similar to the "Constant Companion" (Prohibited Weapons Order No. 4, SOR/78-279).

9. ***Spiked Wristband.*** The device commonly known as a "Spiked Wristband" being a wristband to which a spike or blade is affixed; and any other device similar to the "Spike Wristband" (Prohibited Weapons Order No. 5, SOR/78-280).

10. ***Yaqua Blowgun.*** The device commonly known as "Yaqua Blowgun", being a tube or pipe designed for the purpose of shooting arrows or darts by the breath; and any other device similar to the "Yaqua Blowgun" (Prohibited Weapons Order No. 6, SOR/78-281).

11. ***Kiyoga Baton or Steel Cobra.*** The device commonly known as a "Kiyoga Baton" or "Steel Cobra" and any similar device consisting of a manually-triggered telescoping spring-loaded steel whip terminated in a heavy calibre striking tip (Prohibited Weapons Order No. 7, C.R.C. 1978, c. 439).

12. ***Morning Star.*** The device commonly known as a "Morning Star" and any similar device consisting of a ball of metal or other heavy material, studded with spikes and connected to a handle by

a length of chain, rope or other flexible material (Prohibited Weapons Order No. 7, C.R.C. 1978, c. 439).

13. ***SSS-1 Stinger.*** The device known as the "SSS-1 Stinger" and any similar device that consists of a single shot weapon of any calibre and is designed or of a size to fit in the palm of the hand or in a cigarette package (Prohibited Weapons Order No. 8, SOR/79-583, as amended by SOR/92-462).

14. ***Brass Knuckles.*** The device known as "Brass Knuckles" and any similar device consisting of a band of metal with finger holes designed to fit over the root knuckles of the hand (Prohibited Weapons Order No. 8, SOR/79-583, as amended by SOR/92-462).

15. ***Device To Operate Trigger Mechanism.*** Any electrical or mechanical device that is designed or adapted to operate the trigger mechanism of a semi-automatic firearm for the purpose of causing the firearm to discharge cartridges in rapid succession (Prohibited Weapons Order No. 9, SOR/92-463).

16. ***Bull-Pup Stock.*** The rifle or carbine stock of the type known as the "bull-pup" design, being a stock that, when combined with a firearm, reduces the overall length of the firearm such that a substantial part of the reloading action or the magazine-well is located behind the trigger of the firearm when the firearm is held in the normal firing position (Prohibited Weapons Order No. 9, SOR/92-463).

17. ***Cartridge Capable of Penetrating Body Armour.*** Any cartridge that is capable of being discharged from a commonly available semi-automatic handgun or revolvere and that is manufactured or assembled with a projectile that is designed, manufactured or altered so as to be capable of penetrating body armour composed of aramid fibre or similar fabric (Prohibited Weapons Order No. 10, SOR/92-464).

18. ***Projectile Designed to Ignite.*** Any projectile that is designed, manufactured or altered to ignite on impact, where the projectile is designed for use in or in conjunction with a cartridge and does not exceed 15 mm in diameter (Prohibited Weapons Order No. 10, SOR/92-464).

19. ***Projectile Designed to Explode.*** Any projectile that is designed, manufactured or altered to explode on impact, where the projectile is designed for use in or in conjunction with a cartridge and does not exceed 15 mm in diameter (Prohibited Weapons Order No. 10, SOR?92-464).

20. ***Flechettes.*** Any cartridge that is capable of being discharged from a shotgun and that contains projectiles known as "flechettes"

or any similar projectiles (Prohibited Weapons Order No. 10, SOR/92-464).

21. ***Franchi SPAS 12 Shotgun.*** The firearm of the design commonly known as the Franchi SPAS 12 shotgun, and any variant or modified version thereof, including the Franchi LAW 12 shotgun (Prohibited Weapons Order No. 11, SOR/92-465).

22. ***Striker Shotgun.*** The firearm of the design commonly known as the Striker shotgun, and any variant or modified version thereof, including the Striker 12 shotgun and the Streetsweeper shotgun (Prohibited Weapons Order No. 11, SOR/92-465).

23. ***USAS-12 Auto Shotgun.*** The firearm of the design commonly known as the USAS-12 Auto Shotgun, and any variant or modified version thereof (Prohibited Weapons Order No. 11, SOR/92-465).

24. ***American 180 Auto Carbine.*** The firearm of the design commonly known as the American 180 Auto Carbine, and any variant or modified version thereof, including the AM-180 Auto Carbine and the Illinois Arms Company Model 180 Auto Carbine (Prohibited Weapons Order No. 11, SOR/92-465).

25. ***Barrett "Light Fifty" Model 82A1 Rifle and the Barrett Model 90 Rifle.*** The firearms of the designs commonly known as the Barrett "Light Fifty" Model 82A1 rifle and the Barrett Model 90 rifle, and any variants or modified versions thereof (Prohibited Weapons Order No. 11, SOR/92-465).

26. ***Calico M-900 Rifle.*** The firearm of the design commonly known as the Calico M-900 rifle, and any variant or modified version thereof, including the M-951 carbine, M-100 carbine and M-105 carbine (Prohibited Weapons Order No. 11, SOR/92-465).

27. ***Iver Johnson AMAC Long-Range Rifle.*** The firearm of the design commonly known as the Iver Johnson AMAC long-range rifle, and any variant or modified version thereof (Prohibited Weapons Order No. 11, SOR/92-465).

28. ***McMillan M87 Rifle.*** The firearm of the design commonly known as the McMillan M87 rifle, and any variant or modified version thereof, including the McMillan M87R and McMillan M88 (Prohibited Weapons Order No. 11, SOR/92-465).

29. ***Pauza Specialties P50 Rifle and P50 Carbine.*** The firearms of the designs commonly known as the Pauza Specialties P50 rifle and P50 carbine, and any variants or modified versions thereof (Prohibited Weapons Order No. 11, SOR/92-465).

30. ***Encom MK-IV Carbine.*** The firearm of the design commonly known as the Encom MK—IV carbine, and any variant or modifield version thereof (Prohibited Weapons Order No. 11, SOR/92-465).

31. ***Encom MP-9 and MP-45 Carbines.*** The firearms of the designs commonly known as the Encom MP-9 and MP-45 carbines, and any variants or modified versions thereof (Prohibited Weapons Order No. 11, SOR/92-465).

32. ***FAMAS Rifle.*** The firearm of the design commonly known as the FAMAS rifle, and any variant or modified version thereof, including the MAS 223, FAMAS Export, FAMAS Civil and Mitchell MAS/22 (Prohibited Weapons Order No. 11, SOR/92-465).

33. ***Feather AT-9 Semi-Auto Carbine.*** The firearm of the design commonly known as the Feather AT-9 Semi-Auto Carbine, and any variant or modified version thereof, including the Feather AT—22 Auto Carbine (Prohibited Weapons Order No. 11, SOR/92-465).

34. ***Federal XC-450 Auto Rifle.*** The firearm of the design commonly known as the Federal XC-450 Rifle, and any variant or modified version thereof, including the Federal XC-900 rifle and Federal XC-220 rifle (Prohibited Weapons Order No. 11, SOR/92-465).

35. ***Gepard Long-Range Sniper Rifle.*** The firearm of the design commonly known as the Gepard long-range sniper rifle, and any variant or modified version thereof (Prohibited Weapons Order No. 11, SOR/92-465).

36. ***Heckler and Koch (HK) Model G11 Rifle.*** The firearm of the design commonly known as the Heckler and Koch (HK) Model G11 rifle, and any variant or modified version thereof (Prohibited Weapons Order No. 11, SOR/92-465).

37. ***Research Armament Industries (RAI) Model 500 Rifle.*** The firearm of the design commonly known as the Research Armament Industries (RAI) Model 500 rifle, and any variant or modified version thereof (Prohibited Weapons Order No. 11, SOR/92-465).

37. ***Spectre Auto Carbine.*** The firearm of the design commonly known as the Spectre Auto Carbine, and any variant or modified version thereof (Prohibited Weapons Order No. 11, SOR/92-465).

38. ***US Arms PMAI "Assault" 22 Rifle.*** The firearm of the design commonly known as the US Arms PMAI "Assault" 22 rifle, and any variant or modified version thereof (Prohibited Weapons Order No. 11, SOR/92-465).

40. ***Weaver Arms Nighthawk Carbine.*** The firearm of the design commonly known as the Weaver Arms Nighthawk Carbine, and any variant or modified version thereof (Prohibited Weapons Order No. 11, SOR/92-465).

41. ***Bushmaster Auto Pistol.*** The firearm of the design commonly known as the Bushmaster Auto Pistol, and any variant or modified version thereof (Prohibited Weapons Order No. 11, SOR/92-465).

42. ***Calico M-950 Auto Pistol.*** The firearm of the design commonly known as the Calico M-950 Auto Pistol, and any variant or modified version thereof, including the M-110 pistol (Prohibited Weapons Order No. 11, SOR/92-465).

43. ***Encom MK-IV Assault Pistol.*** The firearm of the design commonly known as the Encom MK—IV assault pistol, and any variant or modified version thereof (Prohibited Weapons Order No. 11, SOR/92-465).

44. ***Encom MP-9 and MP-45 Assault Pistols.*** The firearms of the designs commonly known as the Encom MP-9 and MP-45 assault pistols, and any variants or modified versions thereof, including the Encom MP-9 and MP-45 mini pistols (Prohibited Weapons Order No. 11, SOR/92-465).

45. ***Federal XP-450 Auto Pistol.*** The firearm of the design commonly known as the Federal XP-450 Auto Pistol, and any variant or modified version thereof, including the XP-900 Auto Pistol (Prohibited Weapons Order No. 11, SOR/92-465).

46. ***Heckler and Koch (HK) SP89 Auto Pistol.*** The firearm of the design commonly known as the Heckler and Koch (HK) SP89 Auto Pistol, and any variant or modified version thereof (Prohibited Weapons Order No. 11, SOR/92-465).

47. ***Intratec TEC-9 Auto Pistol.*** The firearm of the design commonly known as the Intratec TEC—9 Auto Pistol, and any variant or modified version thereof, including the TEC-9S, TEC—9M and TEC-9MS, and all semi-automatic variants, including the TEC-22T and TEC—22TN (Prohibited Weapons Order No. 11, SOR/92-465).

48. ***Iver Johnson Enforcer Model 3000 Auto Pistol and the Iver Johnson Plainfield Super Enforcer Carbine.*** The firearms of the designs commonly known as the Iver Johnson Enforcer Model 3000 Auto Pistol and the Iver Johnson Plainfield Super Enforcer Carbine, and any variants or modified versions thereof (Prohibited Weapons Order No. 11, SOR/92-465).

49. ***Skorpion Auto Pistol.*** The firearm of the design commonly known as the Skorpion Auto Pistol, and any variant or modified version thereof (Prohibited Weapons Order No. 11, SOR/92-465).

50. ***Spectre Auto Pistol.*** The firearm of the design commonly known as the Spectre Auto Pistol, and any variant or modifield version thereof (Prohibited Weapons Order No. 11, SOR/92-465).

51. ***Sterling Mk 7 Pistol.*** The firearm of the design commonly known as the Sterling Mk 7 pistol, and any variant or modified version thereof, including the Sterling Mk 7C4 and Sterling Mk 7C8 (Prohibited Weapons Order No. 11, SOR/92-465).

52. ***Universal Enforcer Model 3000 Auto Carbine.*** The firearm of the design commonly known as the Universal Enforcer Model 3000 Auto Carbine, and any variant or modified version thereof, including the Universal Enforcer Model 3010N, Model 3015G, Model 3020TRB and Model 3025TCO Carbines (Prohibited Weapons Order No. 11, SOR/92-465).

53. ***US Arms PMAIP "Assault" 22 Pistol.*** The firearm of the design commonly known as the US Arms PMAIP "Assault" 22 pistol, and any variant or modified version thereof (Prohibited Weapons Order No. 11, SOR/92-465).

54. ***Goncz High-Tech Long Pistol.*** The firearm of the design commonly known as the Goncz High-Tech Long Pistol, and any variant or modified version thereof (Prohibited Weapons Order No. 11, SOR/92-465).

55. ***Leader Mark 5 Auto Pistol.*** The firearm of the design commonly known as the Leader Mark 5 Auto Pistol, and any variant or modified version thereof (Prohibited Weapons Order No. 11, SOR/92-465).

56. ***Sterling Mk 6 Carbine.*** The firearm of the design commonly known as the Sterling Mk 6 Carbine, and any variant or modified version thereof (Prohibited Weapons Order No. 12, SOR/92-466, as amended by SOR/92-471).

57. ***Steyr AUG Rifle.*** The firearm of the design commonly known as the Steyr AUG rifle, and any variant or modified version thereof (Prohibited Weapons Order No. 12, SOR/92-466, as amended by SOR/92-471).

58. ***UZI Carbine.*** The firearm of the design commonly known as the UZI carbine, and any variant or modified version thereof, including the UZI Model A carbine and the Mini-UZI carbine (Prohibited Weapons Order No. 12, SOR/92-466, as amended by SOR/92-471).

59. ***Ingram M10 and M11 Pistols.*** The firearms of the designs commonly known as the Ingram M10 and M11 pistols, and any variant or modified version thereof, including the Cobray M10 and M11, the RPB M10, M11, SM10 and SM11 pistols and the SWD M10, M11, SM10 and SM11 pistols (Prohibited Weapons Order No. 12, SOR/92-466, as amended by SOR/92-471).

60. ***Partisan Avenger Auto Pistol.*** The firearm of the design commonly known as the Partisan Avenger Auto Pistol, and any variant or modified version thereof (Prohibited Weapons Order No. 12, SOR/92-466, as amended by SOR/92-471).

61. ***UZI Pistol.*** The firearm of the design commonly known as the UZI pistol, and any variant or modified version thereof, including the Micro-UZI pistol (Prohibited Weapons Order No. 12, SOR/92-466, as amended by SOR/92-471).

Prohibited Weapons Offences. *See FIREARMS AND WEAPONS OFFENCES.*

While most prohibited weapons are not in fact firearms, they are nonetheless grouped together in the Criminal Code under the heading "Firearms and Other Offensive Weapons" (Part III).

PROMISE TO APPEAR

1. *Definitions*
2. *Contents of promise to appear*
3. *Attendance for purposes of Identification of Criminals Act*
4. *Valid if issued on a holiday*
5. *Signature of accused*
6. *Period for which appearance notice continues in force*
7. *Failure to comply with promise to appear*

1. Definitions

Promise to appear. A "promise to appear" means a promise in Form 10 given by an officer in charge (s. 493). When completed, the Form constitutes a promise in writing to attend court at a given time and place.

See also OFFICER IN CHARGE.

2. Contents of promise to appear. A promise to appear given to an officer in charge shall (a) set out the name of the accused; (b) set out the substance of the offence that the accused is alleged to have committed; and (c) require the accused to attend court at a time and place to be stated therein and to attend thereafter as required by the court in order to be dealt with according to law (s. 501(1)).

A promise to appear given to an officer in charge shall set out the text of s. 145(5) and (6), which create the offence of failing to comply with a promise to appear, and s. 502, which provides for the issue of a warrant for the arrest of the accused for his failure to appear (s. 501(2)).

3. Attendance for purposes of Identification of Criminals Act. A promise to appear given to an officer in charge may, where the accused is alleged to have committed an indictable offence, require the accused to appear at a time and place stated therein for the purposes of the Identification of Criminals Act, and a person so appearing is deemed, for the purposes only of that Act, to be in lawful custody charged with an indictable offence (s. 501(3)).

4. Valid if issued on holiday. A promise to appear may be issued, executed, given, or entered into on a holiday (s. 20).

5. Signature of accused. An accused shall be requested to sign in duplicate his promise to appear and, whether or not he complies with that request, one of the duplicates shall be given to the accused, but if the accused fails or refuses to sign, the lack of his signature does not invalidate the promise to appear as the case may be (s. 501(4)).

6. Period for which appearance notice continues in force. Where an accused has not been taken into custody or has been released from custody under a promise to appear, the promise to appear given by the accused continues in force, subject to its terms and applies in respect of any new information charging the same offence or an included offence that was received after the promise to appear was given, until his trial is completed. Where the accused is, at his trial, determined to be guilty, it continues in effect until the accused is sentenced, unless the court orders the accused to be taken into custody pending sentencing (s. 523(1)).

7. Failure to comply with promise to appear. It is an offence to fail to comply with the terms of a promise to appear. For particulars of the offence, see *ESCAPES AND RESCUES.*

PROPELLANT. The powder in a cartridge which is ignited by the primer and propels the projectile (Jaffe, A Guide to Pathological Evidence, 2nd ed.).

PROPERTY. 1. For the purposes of the Criminal Code, "property" includes the following: (a) real and personal property of every description and deeds and instruments relating to or evidencing the title or right to property, or giving a right to recover or receive money or goods; (b) property originally in the possession or under the control of any person, and any property into or for which it has been converted or exchanged and anything acquired at any time by the conversion or exchange; and (c) any postal card, postage stamp or other stamp issued or prepared for issue under the authority of Parliament or the legislature of a province for the payment to the Crown or a corporate body of any fee, rate or duty, whether or not it is in the possession of the Crown or of any person (s. 2). 2. For the purposes of Part XI of the Criminal Code (Wilful and Forbidden Acts in Respect of Certain Property), "property" means real or personal corporeal property (s. 428).

PROPRIO MOTU. Of its own motion (Latin).

PROSTITUTION

1. *Definitions* 2. *Offence in relation to prostitution*

See also PROCURING, 3 and 4.

1. Definitions

"Prostitute". A person of either sex who engages in prostitution (s. 197(1)).

"Prostitution". 1. The act or practice of performing an act of sexual intercourse, or providing services for sexual gratification, for hire. 2. In the case of a female person, "prostitution" is not confined to acts of sexual intercourse, but will include any form of lewdness for which a woman habitually offers herself for hire. It includes active acts of indecency performed by the woman herself, e.g., masturbation of a male client (Archbold, Pleading Evidence and Practice in Criminal Cases, 39th ed.).

See also PUBLIC PLACE.

2. Offence in relation to prostitution

Section 213(1)(a)

Every one who — in a public place or in any place open to public view — stops or attempts to stop — any motor vehicle — for the purpose of engaging in prostitution or of obtaining the sexual services of a prostitute — is guilty of an offence punishable on summary conviction.

Section 213(1)(b)

Every one who — in a public place or in any place open to public view — impedes — the free flow of pedestrian or vehicular traffic

or ingress to or egress from — premises adjacent to that place — for the purpose of engaging in prostitution or of obtaining the sexual services of a prostitute — is guilty of an offence punishable on summary conviction.

Section 213(1)(b)

Every one who — in a public place or in any place open to public view — either stops or attempts to stop any person — or in any manner communicates or attempts to communicate with any person — for the purpose of engaging in prostitution or of obtaining the sexual services of a prostitute — is guilty of an offence punishable on summary conviction.

Limitation period. No proceedings in respect of offences that are declared to be punishable on summary conviction shall be instituted more than 6 months after the time when the subject matter of the proceedings arose (s. 786(2) and s. 785(1)).

Included offences. Attempts (s. 660 and s. 662(1)(b)).

Punishment. A fine not exceeding $2,000, or 6 months' imprisonment, or both (s. 213(1) and s. 787(1)).

Release. Initial decision to release made by peace officer (s. 497).

Election. No election, summary conviction offence.

Informations

A.B., on or about the —— day of ——, 19——, at the —— of ——, in the said (territorial division), did stop a motor vehicle [OR attempt to stop a motor vehicle OR (as the case may be)] in a public place [OR in a place open to public view] for the purpose of engaging in prostitution [OR of obtaining the sexual services of a prostitute], to wit: (specify the particulars of the offence), contrary to s. 213(1) of the Criminal Code of Canada.

PROVINCIAL COURT JUDGE. For the purposes of the Criminal Code, "provincial court judge" means a person appointed or authorized to act by or pursuant to an Act of the legislature of a province, by whatever title he may be designated, who has the power and authority of two or more justices of the peace and includes his lawful deputy (s. 2).

PROVISO. 1. "Provided" (Latin). 2. An exception or condition in a document.

PROVOCATION. 1. For the purposes of s. 34 and s. 35, "provocation" includes provocation by blows, words or gestures (s. 36). 2. For the purposes of s. 232, "provocation" means a wrongful act or insult that is of such a nature as to be sufficient to deprive an ordinary person of the power of self-control if the accused acted on it on the sudden and before there was time for his passion to cool (s. 232(2)).

For the purposes of s. 232, the questions (a) whether a particular wrongful act or insult amounted to provocation, and (b) whether the accused was deprived of the power of self-control by the provocation that he alleges he received, are questions of fact, but no one shall be deemed to have given provocation to another by doing anything that he had a legal right to do, or by doing anything that the accused incited him to do in order to provide the accused with an excuse for causing death or bodily harm to any human being (s. 232(3)).

PSYCHOSIS. This term refers to a group of severe mental disorders in which there is loss of contact with reality and which are usually characterized by hallucinations (Jaffe, A Guide to Pathological Evidence, 2nd ed.).

PUBLIC DEPARTMENT. For the purposes of the Criminal Code "public department" means a department of the Government of Canada or a branch thereof or a board, commission, corporation or other body that is an agent of Her Majesty in right of Canada (s. 2).

PUBLIC OFFICER

1. *Definition of "public officer"*
2. *Resisting or obstructing public officer*
3. *Omitting to assist public officer*
4. *Personating a public officer*
5. *Assaulting a public officer. See ASSAULT, 7.*

1. Definition of "public officer"

1. "Public officer" includes any person in the public service of Canada who is authorized by or under an enactment to do or enforce the doing of an act or thing or to exercise a power, or on whom a duty is imposed by or under an enactment (Interpretation Act, s. 2(1)).
2. For the purposes of the Criminal Code, "public officer" includes: (a) an officer of customs or excise, (b) an officer of the Canadian Forces, (c) an officer of the Royal Canadian Mounted Police, and (d) any officer while he is engaged in enforcing the laws of Canada relating

to revenue, customs, excise, trade or navigation (Criminal Code, s. 2).

2. Resisting or obstructing public officer — Section 129(a)

Every one who — resists or wilfully obstructs — either a public officer in the execution of his duty — or any person lawfully acting in aid of such an officer — is guilty of either an indictable offence or an offence punishable on summary conviction.

Intent. Wilfully.

Limitation period. No proceedings in respect of offences that are declared to be punishable on summary conviction shall be instituted more than 6 months after the time when the subject matter of the proceedings arose (s. 786(2) and s. 785(1)).

Included offences. Attempts (s. 660 and s. 662(1)(b)).

Punishment. On indictment, imprisonment for a term not exceeding 2 years (s. 129(d)). On summary conviction, a fine not exceeding $2,000, or 6 months' imprisonment, or both (s. 129(e) and s. 787(1)).

Release. Initial decision to release made by peace officer (s. 497).

Election. On indictment, accused may elect trial by judge and jury, judge alone, or provincial court judge (s. 536). On summary conviction, no election.

Informations

A.B., on or about the —— day of ——, 19——, at the —— of ——, in the said (territorial division), did resist [OR wilfully obstruct] C.D., a public officer, in the execution of his duty, to wit: (specify the particulars of the offence), contrary to s. 129(a) of the Criminal Code of Canada.

3. Omitting to assist public officer — Section 129(b)

Every one who — without reasonable excuse — omits to assist a public officer — in the execution of his duty in arresting a person or in preserving the peace — after having reasonable notice that he is required to do so — is guilty of either an indictable offence or an offence punishable on summary conviction.

Limitation period. No proceedings in respect of offences that are declared to be punishable on summary conviction shall be instituted

more than 6 months after the time when the subject matter of the proceedings arose (s. 786(2) and s. 785(1)).

Included offences. Attempts (s. 660 and s. 662(1)(b)).

Punishment. On indictment, imprisonment for a term not exceeding 2 years (s. 129(d)). On summary conviction, a fine not exceeding $2,000, or 6 months' imprisonment, or both (s. 129(e) and s. 787(1)).

Release. Initial decision to release made by peace officer (s. 497).

Election. On indictment, accused may elect trial by judge and jury, judge alone, or provincial court judge (s. 536). On summary conviction, no election.

4. Personating a public officer

Section 130(a)

Every one who — falsely represents himself — to be a public officer — is guilty of an offence punishable on summary conviction.

Section 130(b)

Every one who — not being a public officer — uses a badge or article of uniform or equipment — in a manner that is likely to cause persons to believe that he is a public officer — is guilty of an offence punishable on summary conviction.

Limitation period. No proceedings in respect of offences that are declared to be punishable on summary conviction shall be instituted more than 6 months after the time when the subject matter of the proceedings arose (s. 786(2) and s. 785(1)).

Included offences. Attempts (s. 660 and s. 662(1)(b)).

Punishment. A fine not exceeding $2,000, or 6 months' imprisonment, or both (s. 130 and s. 787(1)).

Release. Initial decision to release made by peace officer (s. 497).

Election. No election, summary conviction offence.

Sufficiency of count. No count that alleges false pretences, fraud or any attempt or conspiracy by fraudulent means is insufficient by reason only that it does not set out in detail the nature of the false pretence, fraud or fraudulent means (s. 586).

Informations

A.B., on or about the —— day of ——, 19——, at the —— of ——, in the said (territorial division), did falsely represent himself to be a public officer, to wit: (specify the particulars of the offence), contrary to s. 130(a) of the Criminal Code of Canada.

A.B., on or about the —— day of ——, 19——, at the —— of ——, in the said (territorial division), not being a public officer, did use a badge [OR article of uniform OR equipment] in a manner that was likely to cause persons to believe that he was a public officer, to wit: (specify the particulars of the offence), contrary to s. 130(b) of the Criminal Code of Canada.

PUBLIC PLACE. 1. For the purposes of Part V and Part VII of the Criminal Code, and for the purposes of s. 319 (public incitement of hatred), "public place" includes any place to which the public have access as of right or by invitation, express or implied (s. 150, s. 197(1) and s. 319(7)). 2. For the purposes of s. 213 (offence in relation to prostitution), "public place" includes any place to which the public have access as of right or by invitation, express or implied, and any motor vehicle located in a public place or in any place open to public view (s. 213(2)).

PUBLIC STORES

1. Definitions
2. Applying or removing marks without authority
3. Unlawful transactions in public stores
4. Selling defective stores to the government
5. Being a party to the selling of defective stores to the government
6. Unlawful use of military uniforms or certificates
7. Buying military stores from member of Canadian Forces or from deserter
8. Sufficiency of count

1. Definitions

"Public stores". For the purposes of the Criminal Code, this expression includes any personal property that is under the care, supervision, administration or control of a public department or of any person in the service of a public department (s. 2).

See also DISTINGUISHING MARK.

2. Applying or removing marks without authority

Section 417(1)(a)

Every one who — without lawful authority — applies a distinguishing mark to anything — is guilty of an indictable offence.

Section 417(1)(b)

Every one who — with intent to conceal the property of Her Majesty in public stores — removes or destroys or obliterates — a distinguishing mark in whole or in part — is guilty of an indictable offence.

Intent. Intention to conceal (s. 417(1)(b)).

Included offences. Attempts (s. 660 and s. 662(1)(b)).

Punishment. Imprisonment for a term not exceeding 2 years (s. 417(1)).

Release. Initial decision to release made by officer in charge or justice (s. 498).

Election. Accused may elect trial by judge and jury, judge alone, or provincial court judge (s. 536).

Evidence. 1. For the purposes of this offence, the proof of lawful excuse lies on the accused (s. 417(1)(a)).
2. Evidence that a person was at any time performing duties in the Canadian Forces is, in the absence of any evidence to the contrary, proof that his enrolment in the Canadian Forces prior to that time was regular (s. 421(1)).

3. Unlawful transactions in public stores — Section 417(2)

Every one who — without lawful authority — receives or possesses or keeps or sells or delivers — public stores that he knows bear a distinguishing mark — is guilty of either an indictable offence or an offence punishable on summary conviction.

Limitation period. No proceedings in respect of offences that are declared to be punishable on summary conviction shall be instituted more than 6 months after the time when the subject matter of the proceedings arose (s. 786(2) and s. 785(1)).

Included offences. Attempts (s. 660 and s. 662(1)(b)).

Punishment. On indictment, imprisonment for a term not exceeding 2 years (s. 417(2)(a)). On summary conviction, a fine not exceeding $2,000, or 6 months' imprisonment, or both (s. 417(2)(b) and s. 787(1)).

Release. Initial decision to release made by peace officer (s. 497).

Election. On indictment, accused may elect trial by judge and jury, judge alone, or provincial court judge (s. 536). On summary conviction, no election.

Evidence. 1. For the purposes of this offence, the proof of lawful excuse lies on the accused (s. 417(2)).
2. An accused who is charged with this offence shall be presumed to have known that the stores in respect of which the offence is alleged to have been committed bore a distinguishing mark within the meaning of that subsection at the time the offence is alleged to have been committed if he was, at that time, in the service or employment of Her Majesty or was a dealer in marine stores or in old metals (s. 421(2)).
3. *See also Evidence, item 2., under* **2***, above.*

4. Selling defective stores to the government — Section 418(1)

Every one who — knowingly — sells or delivers defective stores to Her Majesty — is guilty of an indictable offence.

Every one who — commits fraud in connection with the sale or lease or delivery of stores to Her Majesty — or commits fraud in connection with the manufacture of stores for Her Majesty — is guilty of an indictable offence.

Intent. Knowingly.

Included offences. Attempts (s. 660 and s. 662(1)(b)).

Punishment. Imprisonment for a term not exceeding 14 years (s. 418(1)).

Release. Initial decision to release made by justice (s. 515(1)).

Election. Accused may elect trial by judge and jury, judge alone, or provincial court judge (s. 536).

Evidence. See Evidence, item 2., under **2***, above.*

Informations

A.B., on or about the —— day of ——, 19——, at the —— of ——, in the said (territorial division), did knowingly sell [OR deliver] to Her Majesty defective stores, to wit: (specify the particulars of the offence), contrary to s. 418(1) of the Criminal Code of Canada.

A.B., on or about the —— day of ——, 19——, at the —— of ——, in the said (territorial division), did commit an act of fraud upon Her Majesty [OR an officer in Her Majesty's service] in connection with the sale [OR lease OR delivery OR manufacture] of certain stores, to wit: (specify the particulars of the offence), contrary to s. 418(1) of the Criminal Code of Canada.

5. Being a party to the selling of defective stores to the government

Section 418(2)(a)

Every one who — being a director or an officer or an agent or an employee of a corporation that commits, by fraud, the offence of selling defective stores to the government — knowingly takes part in the fraud — is guilty of an indictable offence.

Section 418(2)(b)

Every one who — being a director or an officer or an agent or an employee of a corporation that commits, by fraud, the offence of selling defective stores to the government — knows or has reason to suspect that the fraud is being committed or has been or is about to be committed — and does not inform the responsible government, or a department thereof, of Her Majesty — is guilty of an indictable offence.

Included offences. Attempts (s. 660 and s. 662(1)(b)).

Punishment. Imprisonment for a term not exceeding 14 years (s. 418(2)).

Release. Initial decision to release made by justice (s. 515(1)).

Election. Accused may elect trial by judge and jury, judge alone, or provincial court judge (s. 536).

Evidence. See Evidence, item 2., under **2**, above.

6. Unlawful use of military uniforms or certificates

Section 419(a)

Every one who — without lawful authority — wears — either a uniform of the Canadian Forces or any other naval or army or air force — or a uniform that is so similar to the uniform of any of those forces that it is likely to be mistaken therefor — is guilty of an offence punishable on summary conviction.

Section 419(b)

Every one who — without lawful authority — wears — either a distinctive mark relating to wounds received or service performed in war — or a military medal or ribbon or badge or chevron or any decoration or order that is awarded for war services, or any imitation thereof — or any mark or device or thing that is likely to be mistaken for any such mark or medal or ribbon or badge or chevron or decoration or order — is guilty of an offence punishable on summary conviction.

Section 419(c)

Every one who — without lawful authority — has in his possession — a certificate of discharge or certificate of release or statement of service or identity card from the Canadian Forces or any other naval or army or air force — that has not been issued to and does not belong to him — is guilty of an offence punishable on summary conviction.

Section 419(d)

Every one who — without lawful authority — has in his possession — a commission or warrant or a certificate of discharge or certificate of release or statement of service or identity card issued to an officer or a person in or who has been in the Canadian Forces or any other naval or army or air force — that contains any alteration that is not verified by the initials of the officer who issued it, or by the initials of an officer thereto lawfully authorized — is guilty of an offence punishable on summary conviction.

Limitation period. No proceedings in respect of offences that are declared to be punishable on summary conviction shall be instituted more than 6 months after the time when the subject matter of the proceedings arose (s. 786(2) and s. 785(1)).

Included offences. Attempts (s. 660 and s. 662(1)(b)).

Punishment. A fine not exceeding $2,000, or 6 months' imprisonment, or both (s. 419 and s. 787(1)).

Release. Initial decision to release made by peace officer (s. 497).

Election. No election, summary conviction offence.

Evidence. 1. For the purposes of this offence, the proof of lawful excuse lies on the accused (s. 419).
2. *See also Evidence, item 2., under* **2***, above.*

7. Buying military stores from member of Canadian Forces or from deserter — Section 420(1)

Every one who — buys or receives or detains — from a member of the Canadian Forces or a deserter or an absentee without leave therefrom — any military stores that are owned by Her Majesty or for which the member or deserter or absentee without leave is accountable to Her Majesty — is guilty of either an indictable offence or an offence punishable on summary conviction.

Limitation period. No proceedings in respect of offences that are declared to be punishable on summary conviction shall be instituted more than 6 months after the time when the subject matter of the proceedings arose (s. 786(2) and s. 785(1)).

Included offences. Attempts (s. 660 and s. 662(1)(b)).

Punishment. On indictment, imprisonment for a term not exceeding 5 years (s. 420(1)(a)). On summary conviction, a fine not exceeding $2,000, or 6 months' imprisonment, or both (s. 420(1)(b) and s. 787(1)).

Release. Initial decision to release made by peace officer (s. 497).

Election. On indictment, accused may elect trial by judge and jury, judge alone, or provincial court judge (s. 536). On summary conviction, no election.

Evidence. 1. No person shall be convicted of this offence where he establishes that he did not know and had no reason to suspect that the military stores in respect of which the offence was committed were owned by Her Majesty or were military stores for which the member, deserter or absentee without leave was accountable to Her Majesty (s. 420(2)).
2. *See also Evidence, item 2., under* **2***, above.*

8. Sufficiency of count

No count that alleges false pretences, fraud or any attempt or conspiracy by fraudulent means is insufficient by reason only that it does not set out in detail the nature of the false pretence, fraud or fraudulent means (s. 586).

PUBLIC SWITCHED TELEPHONE NETWORK. For the purposes of Part VI of the Criminal Code (Invasion of Privacy), "public switched telephone network" means a telecommunication facility the primary purpose of which is to provide a land line-based telephone service to the public for compensation (s. 183).

PUBLISHING OFFENCES

1. *Publishing evidence of sexual activity*
2. *Publishing report of admission or confession tendered at preliminary inquiry*
3. *Publishing obscene matter. See CORRUPTING MORALS, 2.*
4. *Publishing crime comic. See CORRUPTING MORALS, 4.*
5. *Publishing child pornography. See CORRUPTING MORALS, 6.*
6. *Publishing indecent matter. See CORRUPTING MORALS, 10.*
7. *Publishing particulars of matrimonial proceedings. See CORRUPTING MORALS, 11.*
8. *Publishing or printing the likeness of bank note or security. See CURRENCY OFFENCES. 11.*
9. *Publishing report on proceedings under the Young Offenders Act. See YOUNG OFFENDERS, 9.*

1. Publishing evidence of sexual activity

Prohibition — Section 276.3(1)

No person shall — publish in a newspaper, as defined in s. 297, or in a broadcast either — the contents of an application made under s. 276.1 or — any evidence taken, the information given and the representations made at an application under s. 276.1 or at a hearing under s. 276.2 or — the decision of a judge, provincial court judge or justice under s. 276.1(4), unless the judge provincial court judge or justice, after taking into account the complainant's right of privacy and the interests of justice, orders that the decision may be published or — the determination made and the reasons provided under s. 276.2, unless (i) that determination is that evidence is admissible, or (ii) the judge, provincial court judge or justice, after taking into account the complainant's right of privacy and the interests of justice, orders that the determination and reasons may be published.

Statement of offence — Section 276.3(2)

Every person who — contravenes s. 276.3(1) — is guilty of an offence punishable on summary conviction.

Limitation period. No proceedings in respect of offences that are declared to be punishable on summary conviction shall be instituted

more than 6 months after the time when the subject matter of the proceedings arose (s. 786(2) and s. 785(1)).

Included offences. Attempts (s. 660 and s. 662(1)(b)).

Punishment. A fine not less than $2,000, or 6 months' imprisonment, or both (s. 276.3(2) and s. 787(1)).

Release. Initial decision to release made by peace officer (s. 497).

Election. No election, summary conviction offence.

Definitions. See NEWSPAPER.

2. Publishing report of admission or confession tendered at preliminary inquiry — Section 542(2)

Every one who — publishes in any newspaper or broadcasts — a report that any admission or confession was tendered in evidence at a preliminary inquiry — or a report of the nature of such admission or confession so tendered in evidence — unless either the accused has been discharged — or if the accused has been committed for trial, the trial has ended — is guilty of an offence punishable on summary conviction.

Limitation period. No proceedings in respect of offences that are declared to be punishable on summary conviction shall be instituted more than 6 months after the time when the subject matter of the proceedings arose (s. 786(2) and s. 785(1)).

Included offences. Attempts (s. 660 and s. 662(1)(b)).

Punishment. A fine not less than $2,000, or 6 months' imprisonment, or both (s. 542(2) and s. 787(1)).

Release. Initial decision to release made by peace officer (s. 497).

Election. No election, summary conviction offence.

Definition. See NEWSPAPER.

PUISNE JUDGE. A judge of a superior court other than the Chief Justice. "Puisne" means junior, inferior, or lower in rank.

PUNITIVE DAMAGES. Damages awarded over and above the amount required to compensate a plaintiff for his loss for the purpose of punishing the defendant.

PUTATIVE. Supposed; believed; reputed.

Putative marriage. A marriage believed to be valid.

Putative father. A man believed to be the father of an illegitimate child.

Q

QUA. In the capacity of; as (Latin).

QUAERE. Question; query (Latin).

QUALIFIED MEDICAL PRACTITIONER. For the purposes of ss. 254 to 262, "qualified medical practitioner" means a person duly qualified by provincial law to practise medicine (s. 254(1)).

QUALIFIED TECHNICIAN. For the purposes of ss. 254 to 262 "qualified technician" means (a) in respect of breath samples, a person designated by the Attorney General as being qualified to operate an approved instrument, and (b) in respect of blood samples, any person or class of persons designated by the Attorney General as being qualified to take samples of blood for the purposes of ss. 254, 258 and 262 of the Code (s. 254(1)).

QUANTUM MERUIT. "As much as he has earned" (Latin).

QUASI. As if (Latin).

QUESTION. In law, a point on which there is no agreement that is submitted to a judge or jury for resolution.

Question of fact. An issue involving the resolution of a factual dispute. In general, a jury decides all issues or questions of fact. Exceptions include the following, which are decided by the judge:

(a) a question of fact arising in the course of a trial that is a preliminary to a decision of a point of law, such as the genuineness of a document that is proposed to be admitted in evidence;

(b) a question as to the competence of a witness to be sworn; and

(c) a question as to the law of a foreign country.

Question of law. An issue involving the application or interpretation of a law. A question of law is decided by the judge who determines the question by considering and weighing legal authorities and arguments.

Questions of mixed fact and law. Questions of mixed fact and law arise in matters such as a person's guilt of manslaughter which depends on the facts as to what he did and the question as to whether these facts amounted to manslaughter as the offence is legally defined by the Criminal Code.

QUIA TIMET. 1. "Because it is feared" (Latin). 2. An injunction in anticipation of wrongful conduct.

QUID PRO QUO. 1. "Something for something" (Latin). 2. A consideration.

QUO JURE? "By what right?" (Latin).

QUO WARRANTO. 1. "By what warrant" (Latin). 2. The opening words of a writ to review the right of a person to hold office. 3. A civil action to determine the existence of a civil right.

QUORUM. 1. "Of whom" (Latin). 2. The minimum number needed for a valid meeting.

R

RADIO-BASED TELEPHONE COMMUNICATION. For the purposes of Part VI of the Criminal Code (Invasion of Privacy), "radio-based telephone communication" means any radio communication within the meaning of the Radiocommunication Act that is made over apparatus that is used primarily for connection to a public switched telephone network (s. 183).

RADIOCOMMUNICATION. "Radio" or "radiocommunication" means any transmission, emission or reception of signs, signals, writing, images, sounds or intelligence of any nature by means of electromagnetic waves of frequencies lower than 3,000 Gigacycles per second propagated in space without artificial guide (Interpretation Act, s. 35(1)).

RAPE. The act of having sexual intercourse against a female person's will or without her conscious permission, or where her permission has been extorted by force or fear of immediate bodily harm (Jowitt's Dictionary of English Law). The Criminal Code provisions dealing with the offence of rape have been repealed and replaced by provisions regarding sexual assault.

RATIO DECIDENDI. The reasons or ground of a judicial decision (Latin).

REAL PROPERTY. Lands, tenements, and hereditaments; immovable property which could be covered by a real action (Osborn's Concise Law Dictionary). *See also FRAUD, 9.*

RECOGNIZANCE

1. *Definitions*
2. *Recognizance entered into before an officer in charge*
3. *Recognizance entered into before a justice or a judge*
4. *Contents of a recognizance*
5. *Attendance for purposes of Identification of Criminals Act*
6. *Valid if issued on a holiday*
7. *Acknowledging recognizance using false name*
8. *Failure to comply with the terms of a recognizance*
9. *Recognizance of witness*
10. *Recognizance of appellant*
11. *Recognizance of continuing effect*
12. *Effect of subsequent arrest*
13. *Sureties*
14. *Committal*
15. *Procedure on default*

1. Definitions

Recognizance. A written acknowledgement of a conditional debt to the government that becomes an absolute debt on the happening of certain events.

When used in relation to a recognizance entered into before an officer in charge, the term means a recognizance in Form 11. When used in relation to a recognizance entered into before a justice or a judge, the terms means a recognizance in Form 32 (s. 493).

Surety. A surety is a person who binds himself to satisfy the obligation of another person if that person fails to do something he was obliged to do (Jowitt's Dictionary of English Law).

2. Recognizance entered into before an officer-in-charge

One option available to an officer-in-charge who has a person brought before him by a peace officer is to release the person on his entering into a recognizance without sureties in such amount not exceeding $500 as the officer in charge directs, but without deposit of money or other valuable security (s. 498(1)(g)).

If the person is not ordinarily resident in the province in which the person is in custody or does not ordinarily reside within 200 km of the place in which he is in custody, the peace officer may release the person on his entering into a recognizance before the officer in charge without sureties in such amount not exceeding $500 as the officer in charge directs.

If the officer in charge so directs, he may release also the person on his entering into a recognizance and on his depositing with the officer in charge such sum of money or other valuable security not exceeding in amount or value $500 as the officer in charge directs (s. 498(1)(h)).

3. Recognizance entered into before a justice or a judge

One option available to a justice where an accused is brought before him is to order his release on his entering into a recognizance, either:

1. without sureties, in such amount and with such conditions, if any, as the justice directs but without deposit of money or other valuable security;
2. with sureties in such amount and with such conditions, if any, as the justice directs but without deposit of money or other valuable security;
3. if the accused is not ordinarily resident in the province in which he is in custody or does not ordinarily reside within one hundred kilometres of the place in which he is in custody, with or without sureties in such amount and with such conditions, if any, as the justice directs, and on his depositing with the justice such sum of money or other valuable security as the justice directs (s. 515(2)).

Where a justice, judge or court orders that an accused be released on his entering into a recognizance with sureties, the justice, judge or court may, in the order, name particular persons as sureties (s. 515(2.1)).

4. Contents of recognizance

A recognizance entered into before an officer-in-charge shall: (a) set out the name of accused; (b) set out the substance of the offence that the accused is alleged to have committed; and (c) require the accused to attend court at a time and place to be stated therein and to attend thereafter as required by the court in order to be dealt with according to law (s. 501(1)). A recognizance entered into before an officer in charge shall set out the text of s. 145(5) and (6), which creates the offence of failing to comply with a recognizance, and s. 502, which provides for the issue of a warrant for the arrest of the accused for his failure to appear (s. 501(2)).

A recognizance entered into before a justice or a judge may contain conditions to the effect that the accused shall do any one or more of the following things: (a) report at times to be stated in the order to a peace officer or other person designated in the order; (b) remain within a territorial jurisdiction specified in the order; (c) notify the peace officer or other person designated of any change in his address or his employment or occupation; (d) abstain from communicating with any witness or other person expressly named in the order except in accordance with such conditions specified in the order as the justice deems necessary; (e) where the accused is the holder of a passport, deposit his passport as specified in the order; and (f) comply with such other reasonable conditions specified in the order the justice considers desirable.

5. Attendance for purposes of Identification of Criminals Act

A recognizance entered into before an officer in charge may, where the accused is alleged to have committed an indictable offence, require the accused to appear at a time and place stated therein for the purposes of the Identification of Criminals Act, and a person so appearing is deemed, for the purposes only of that Act, to be in lawful custody charged with an indictable offence (s. 501(3)).

6. Valid if issued on a holiday

A recognizance may be entered into on a holiday (s. 20).

7. Acknowledging recognizance using false name

It is an indictable offence for any one, without lawful authority or excuse, to acknowledge a recognizance of bail before a court or judge or other person authorized to receive the recognizance. Any person convicted of this offence is liable to a term of imprisonment not exceeding 5 years (s. 405).

8. Failure to comply with the terms of a recognizance

It is an offence to fail to comply without lawful excuse with the terms of a recognizance entered into before an officer in charge (s. 145(5)), or the terms of a recognizance entered into before a justice or a judge (s. 145(2) and (3)). *See ESCAPES AND RESCUES.* In addition, the amounts specified in the recognizance are forfeited to the government.

9. Recognizance of witness

Where an accused is ordered to stand trial, the justice who held the preliminary inquiry may require any witness whose evidence is, in his opinion, material to enter into a recognizance to give evidence at the trial of the accused and to comply with such reasonable conditions prescribed in the recognizance as the justice considers desirable for securing the attendance of the witness to give evidence at the trial of the accused (s. 550(1)). The recognizance may be in Form 32, and may be set out at the end of a deposition or be separate therefrom (s. 550(2)). The justice may, for any reason satisfactory to him, require any witness entering into a recognizance pursuant to this section (a) to produce one or more sureties in such amount as he may direct; or (b) to deposit with him a sum of money sufficient in his opinion to ensure that the witness will appear and give evidence (s. 550(3)).

Where a witness does not comply when required to do so by a justice, he may be committed by the justice, by warrant in Form 24, to a prison in the territorial division where the trial is to be held, there to be kept until he does what is required of him or until the trial is concluded (s. 550(4)). Where a witness has been committed to prison, the court before which the witness appears or a justice having jurisdiction in the territorial division where the prison is situated may, by order in Form 39, discharge the witness from custody when the trial is concluded (s. 550(5)).

10. Recognizance of appellant

A person who was the defendant in proceedings before a summary conviction court and by whom an appeal is taken shall, if he is in custody, remain in custody unless the appeal court at which the appeal is to be heard orders that the appellant be released on his entering into a recognizance without sureties in such amount, with such conditions, if any, as the appeal court directs, but without deposit of money or other valuable security, or on his entering into a recognizance with or without sureties in such amount, with such conditions, if any, as the appeal court directs, and on his depositing with that appeal court such sum of money or other valuable security as the appeal court directs, and the person having the custody of the appellant shall, where the appellant complies with the order, forthwith release the appellant (s. 816(1)).

11. Recognizance of continuing effect

Where a person is bound by recognizance to appear before a court, justice or provincial court judge for any purpose and the session or sittings of that court or the proceedings are adjourned or an order is made changing the place of trial, that person and his sureties continue to be bound by the recognizance in like manner as if it had been entered into with relation to the resumed proceedings or the trial at the time and place at which the proceedings are ordered to be resumed or the trial is ordered to be held (s. 763).

Where an accused is bound by recognizance to appear for trial, his arraignment or conviction does not discharge the recognizance, but it continues to bind him and his sureties, if any, for his appearance until he is discharged or sentenced, as the case may be (s. 764(1)).

12. Effect of subsequent arrest

Where an accused is bound by recognizance to appear for trial, his arrest on another charge does not vacate the recognizance, but it continues to bind him and his sureties, if any, for his appearance until he is discharged or sentenced, as the case may be, in respect of the offence to which the recognizance relates (s. 765).

13. Surety

Substitution of surety. Where a surety for a person who is bound by a recognizance has rendered the person into the custody of a court or applies to be relieved of his obligation under the recognizance, the court, justice or provincial court judge, as the case may be, may, instead of committing or issuing an order for the committal of the person to prison, substitute any other suitable person for the surety under the recognizance (s. 767.1(1)). Where a person substituted for a surety under a recognizance signs the recognizance, the original surety is discharged but the recognizance and the order for judicial interim release pursuant to which the recognizance was entered into are not otherwise affected (s. 767.1(2)).

Discharge of surety. A surety for a person who is bound by recognizance to appear may, by an application in writing to a court, justice or provincial court judge, apply to be relieved of his obligation under the recognizance, and the court, justice or provincial court judge shall thereupon issue an order in writing for committal of that person to the prison nearest to the place where he was, under the recognizance, bound to appear (s. 766(1)). The order shall be given to the surety and upon receipt thereof he or any peace officer may arrest the person named in the order and deliver that person with the order to the keeper of the prison named herein, and the keeper shall receive and imprison that person until he is discharged according to law (s. 766(2)).

Where a court, justice or provincial court judge issues such an order and receives from the sheriff a certificate that the person named in the order has been committed to prison, the court, justice or provincial court judge shall order an entry of the committal to be endorsed on the recognizance (s. 766(3)). The endorsement vacates the recognizance and discharges the sureties (s. 766(4)).

A surety for a person who is bound by recognizance to appear may bring that person into the court at which he is required to appear at any time during the sittings thereof and before his trial and the surety may discharge his obligation under the recognizance by giving that person into the custody of the court, and the court shall thereupon commit that person to prison until he is discharged according to law (s. 767).

Rights of surety. Nothing above limits or restricts any right that a surety has of taking and giving into custody any person for whom, under a recognizance, he is a surety (s. 768).

New or additional surety. Notwithstanding the fact that an accused may already be bound by a recognizance, a court, justice or provincial court may require an accused to furnish new or additional sureties for his appearance until he is discharged or sentenced, as the case may be (s. 764(2)).

Sureties to keep the peace. Any person who fears that another person will cause personal injury to him or his spouse or child or will damage his property may lay an information before a justice (s. 810(1)). A justice who receives such an information shall cause the parties to appear before him or before a summary conviction court having jurisdiction in the same territorial division (s. 810(2)).

The justice or the summary conviction court before which the parties appear may, if satisfied by the evidence adduced that the informant has reasonable grounds for his fears, (a) order that the defendant enter into a recognizance, with or without sureties, to keep the peace and be of good behaviour for any period that does not exceed 12 months, and comply with such other reasonable conditions prescribed in the recognizance as the court considers desirable for securing the good conduct of the defendant; or (b) commit the defendant to prison for a term not exceeding 12 months if he fails or refuses to enter into the recognizance (s. 810(3)).

Before making such an order, the justice or the summary conviction court shall consider whether it is desirable, in the interests of the safety of the defendant or of any other person, to include as a condition of the recognizance that the defendant be prohibited from possessing any firearm or any ammunition or explosive substance for any period of time specified in the recognizance and that the defendant surrender any firearms aquisition certificate that the accused possesses and, where the justice or summary conviction court decides that it is not desirable, in the interests of the safety of the defendant or of any other person, for the defendant to possess any of those things, the justice or summary conviction court may add the appropriate condition to the recognizance (s. 810(3.1)).

Any person who fears on reasonable grounds that another person will commit an offence under ss. 151, 152, 155, 159, 160(2), 160(3), 170, 171, 173(2), 271, 272 or 273, in respect of one or more persons who are under the age of 14 years, may lay an information before a provincial court judge, whether or not the person or persons in respect of whom it is feared that the offence will be committed are named (s. 810.1(1)). A provincial court judge who receives such an information shall cause the parties to appear before the provincial court judge (s. 810.1(2)).

The provincial court judge before whom the parties appear may, if satisfied by the evidence adduced that the informant has reasonable grounds for the fear, order the defendant to enter into a recognizance and comply with the conditions fixed by the provincial court judge, including a condition prohibiting the defendant from engaging in any activity that involves contact with persons under the age of 14 years and prohibiting the defendant from attending a public park or public swimming area where persons under the age of 14 years are present or can reasonably be expected to be present, or a daycare centre, schoolground, playground or community centre, for any period fixed by the provincial court judge that does not exceed 12 months (s. 810.1(3)).

A person bound by recognizance who commits a breach of the recognizance is guilty of an offence punishable on summary conviction (s. 811).

14. Committal

Committal by court while bound by recognizance. Notwithstanding the fact that an accused may already be bound by a recognizance, a court, justice or provincial court judge may commit an accused to prison until he is discharged or sentenced, as the case may be (s. 764(2)). The sureties of an accused who is bound by recognizance to appear for trial are discharged if he is committed to prison (s. 764(3)).

Committal when writ not satisfied. Where a writ of *fieri facias* has been issued and it appears from a certificate in a return made by the sheriff that sufficient goods and chattels, lands and tenements cannot be found to satisfy the writ, or that the proceeds of the execution of the writ are not sufficient to satisfy it, a judge of the court may, upon the application of the Attorney General or counsel acting on his behalf, fix a time and place for the sureties to show cause why a warrant of committal should not be issued in respect of them (s. 773(1)).

Seven clear days notice of the time and place fixed for the hearing shall be given to the sureties (s. 773(2)).

The judge shall at the hearing inquire into the circumstances of the case and may in his discretion

(a) order the discharge of the amount for which the surety is liable; or

(b) make an order with respect to the surety and to his imprisonment that he considers proper in the circumstances and issue a warrant of committal in Form 27 (s. 773(3)).

A warrant of committal issued pursuant to this section authorizes the sheriff to take into custody the person in respect of whom the warrant was issued and to confine him in a prison in the territorial division in which the writ was issued or in the prison nearest to the court, until satisfaction is made or until the period of imprisonment fixed by the judge has expired (s. 773(4)).

Application for judicial interim release provisions. Where a surety for a person has rendered him into custody and that person has been committed to prison, the provisions relating to judicial interim release apply, with such modifications as the circumstances require, in respect of him and he shall forthwith be taken before a justice or judge as an accused charged with an offence or as an appellant, as the case may be, for the purposes of those provisions (s. 769).

15. Procedure on default

Where, in proceedings to which this Act applies, a person who is bound by recognizance does not comply with a condition of the recognizance, a court, justice or provincial court judge having knowledge of the facts shall endorse or cause to be endorsed on the back of the recognizance a certificate in Form 33 setting out (a) the nature of the default, (b) the reason for the default, if it is known, (c) whether the ends of justice have been defeated or delayed by reason of the default, and (d) the names and addresses of the principal and sureties (s. 770(1)).

A recognizance that has been endorsed shall be sent to the clerk of the court and shall be kept by him with the records of the court (s. 770(2)).

A certificate that has been endorsed on a recognizance is evidence of the default to which it relates (s. 770(3)).

Where the principal or surety has deposited money as security for the performance of a condition of a recognizance, that money shall be sent to the clerk of the court with the defaulted recognizance (s. 770(4)).

Where a recognizance has been endorsed with a certificate and has been received by the clerk of the court

(a) a judge of the court shall, on the request of the clerk of the court or the Attorney General or counsel acting on his behalf, fix a time and place for the hearing of an application for the forfeiture of the recognizance; and
(b) the clerk of the court shall, not less than 10 days before the time fixed for the hearing, send by registered mail to each principal and surety named in the recognizance, directed to him at the address set out in the certificate, a notice requiring him to appear at the time and place fixed by the judge to show cause why the recognizance should not be forfeited (s. 771(1)).

The judge may, after giving the parties an opportunity to be heard, in his discretion grant or refuse the application and make any order with respect to the forfeiture of the recognizance that he considers proper (s. 771(2)).

Where a judge orders forfeiture of a recognizance, the principal and his sureties become judgment debtors of the Crown, each in the amount that the judge orders him to pay (s. 771(3)). The order may be filed with the clerk of the superior court or, in the Province of Quebec, the prothonotary and, where an order is filed, the clerk or the prothonotary shall issue a writ of *fieri facias* in Form 34 and deliver it to the sheriff of each of the territorial divisions in which the principal or any of his sureties resides, carries on business or has property (s. 771(3.1)).

Where a deposit has been made by a person against whom an order for forfeiture of a recognizance has been made, no writ of *fieri facias* shall issue, but the amount of the deposit shall be transferred by the person who has custody of it to the person who is entitled by law to receive it (s. 771(4)).

Where a writ of *fieri facias* is issued, the sheriff to whom it is delivered shall execute the writ and deal with the proceeds thereof in the same manner in which he is authorized to execute and deal with the proceeds of writs of *fieri facias* issued out of superior courts in the province in civil proceedings (s. 772(1)).

Where this section applies, the Crown is entitled to the costs of execution and of proceedings incidental thereto that are fixed, in the Province of Quebec, by any tariff applicable in the Superior Court in civil proceedings, and in any other province, by any tariff applicable in the superior court of the province in civil proceedings, as the judge may direct (s. 772(2)).

Applications for the forfeiture of recognizances shall be made to the courts of the provinces set out below (s. 762(1)).

Ontario	A judge of the Court of Appeal in respect of a recognizance for the appearance of a person before the Court.	The Registrar of the Court of Appeal.
	The Ontario Court (General Division) in respect of all other recognizances.	A Registrar of the Ontario Court (General Division).
Quebec	The Superior Court, exercising civil jurisdiction.	The Clerk of the Peace.
Nova Scotia	The Supreme Court.	A Prothonotary of the Supreme Court.
New Brunswick	The Court of Queen's Bench.	The Registrar of the Court of Queen's Bench.
British Columbia	The Supreme Court in respect of a recognizance for the appearance of a person before that court or the Court of Appeal.	The District Registrar of the Supreme Court.
	A Provincial Court in respect of a recognizance for the appearance of a person before a judge of that Court or a justice.	The Clerk of the Provincial Court.

Prince Edward Island	The Supreme Court, Trial Division.	The Prothonotary.
Manitoba	The Court of Queen's Bench.	The Registrar or a Deputy Registrar of the Court of Queen's Bench.
Saskatchewan	The Court of Queen's Bench.	The Local Registrar of the Court of Queen's Bench.
Alberta	The Court of Queen's Bench.	The Clerk of the Court of Queen's Bench.
Newfoundland	The Supreme Court.	The Registrar of the Supreme Court.
Yukon Territory	The Supreme Court.	The Clerk of the Supreme Court.
Northwest Territories	The Supreme Court.	The Clerk of the Supreme Court.

RECORD. For the purposes of the Canada Evidence Act, "record" includes the whole or any part of any book, document, paper, card, tape or other thing on or in which information is written, recorded, stored or reproduced, and any copy or transcript received in evidence (Canada Evidence Act, s. 30(12)). *See also CRIMINAL RECORDS and FALSIFICATION OF BOOKS AND DOCUMENTS.*

RECOVERY. Where a person obtains something which has been wrongfully taken or withheld from him, or to which he is entitled. *For Recovery of Goods, see MISLEADING JUSTICE, 9.*

RECRIMINATION. A charge made by an accused person against the accused (Jowitt's Dictionary of English Law).

RECTUM. The terminal portion of the large intestine. It opens to the outside through the anus (Jaffe, A Guide to Pathological Evidence, 2nd ed.).

REGINA. The reigning queen (Latin).

REGULATION. "Regulation" includes an order, regulation, rule, rule of court, form, tariff of costs or fees, letters patent, commission, warrant, proclamation, by-law, resolution or other instrument issued, made or established (a) in the execution of a power conferred by or under the authority of an Act, or (b) by or under the authority of the Governor in Council (Interpretation Act, s. 2(1)).

RELEASE

1. *Release from custody by a peace officer*
2. *Release from custody by either a peace officer or an officer in charge*

3. *Release from custody by an officer in charge*
4. *Release from custody by a justice*
5. *Release from custody by a judge*
6. *Release from imprisonment*

See also APPEARANCE NOTICE, PROMISE TO APPEAR, SUMMONS, RECOGNIZANCE and UNDERTAKING.

1. Release from custody by a peace officer

A peace officer is under an obligation to release as soon as practicable any person that he has arrested without warrant unless:

(i) the peace officer believes on reasonable grounds that it is necessary in the public interest, having regard to all the circumstances including the need to establish the identity of the person, or secure or preserve evidence of or relating to the offence, or prevent the continuation or repetition of the offence or the commission of another offence, that the person be detained in custody or that the matter of his release from custody be dealt with by an officer in charge, or by a judge (s. 497(1)).

(ii) he believes on reasonable grounds that, if the person is released by him from custody, the person will fail to attend court in order to be dealt with according to law (s. 497(1)); or

(iii) the person has been arrested without warrant for an indictable offence alleged to have been committed in Canada outside the province in which he was arrested (s. 497(2) and s. 503(3)).

The peace officer has the choice of either releasing the person from custody with the intention of compelling his appearance by way of summons or issuing an appearance notice to the person and thereupon release him (s. 497(1)).

2. Release from custody by either a peace officer or an officer in charge

Before being taken before a justice. Unless a person has been detained for an offence mentioned in s. 522, a peace officer or an officer in charge who is satisfied that a person should be released from custody, may release a person who is being held in custody for the purpose of being taken before a justice to be dealt with according to law. The person may be released either conditionally or unconditionally (s. 503(1)).

Section 522 provides for interim release only by a judge of a superior court of criminal jurisdiction for the following offences listed in s. 469 of the Criminal Code:

treason (s. 47), attempted treason, conspiracy to commit treason, alarming Her Majesty (s. 49), attempting to or conspiring to alarm Her Majesty,

intimidating Parliament or a legislature (s. 51), attempting to or conspiring to intimidate Parliament or a legislature,

inciting to mutiny (s. 53), attempting to or conspiring to incite to mutiny,

seditious offences (s. 61), attempting to or conspiring to commit seditious offences,

piracy (s. 74) and "piratical offences" and attempting to or conspiring to commit piracy and piratical acts,

murder (s. 235) and conspiracy to commit murder,

being an accessory after the fact to high treason or treason or murder, or

bribery by the holder of a judicial office (s. 119).

Where a peace officer or an officer in charge is satisfied that the person should be released from custody conditionally, he may do one of the following: (i) release the person with the intention of compelling his appearance by way of summons, (ii) release the person on his giving his promise to appear, (iii) release the person on his entering into a recognizance before the officer in charge without sureties in such amount not exceeding five hundred dollars as the officer in charge directs, but without deposit of money or other valuable security, or (iv) if the person is not ordinarily resident in the province in which the person is in custody or does not ordinarily reside within two hundred kilometres of the place in which he is in custody, release the person on his entering into a recognizance before the officer in charge without sureties in such amount not exceeding five hundred dollars as the officer in charge directs and, if the officer in charge so directs, on his depositing with the officer in charge such sum of money or other valuable security not exceeding in amount or value five hundred dollars as the officer in charge directs (s. 503(2)).

Where continued detention no longer necessary to prevent commission of indictable offence. A peace officer in charge having the custody of a person who has been arrested without warrant as a person about to commit an indictable offence shall release that person unconditionally as soon as practicable after he is satisfied that the continued detention of that person in custody is no longer necessary in order to prevent the commission by him of an indictable offence (s. 503).

3. Release from custody by officer in charge

Where person arrested without warrant. Where a person who has been arrested without warrant by a peace officer is taken into custody, or where a person who has been arrested without warrant and delivered to a peace officer is detained in custody for:

(i) an indictable offence mentioned in s. 553,

(ii) an offence for which the person may be prosecuted by indictment or for which he is punishable on summary conviction,

(iii) an offence punishable on summary conviction, or

(iv) any other offence that is punishable by imprisonment for 5 years or less,

and has not been taken before a justice or released from custody, the officer in charge shall, as soon as practicable, do one of the things described below.

Specifically, the officer in charge shall either:

(i) release the person with the intention of compelling his appearance by way of summons,

(ii) release the person on his giving his promise to appear,

(iii) release the person on his entering into a recognizance before the officer in charge without sureties in such amount not exceeding five hundred dollars as the officer in charge directs, but without deposit of money or other valuable security, or

(iv) if the person is not ordinarily resident in the province in which the person is in custody or does not ordinarily reside within two hundred kilometres of the place in which he is in custody, release the person on his entering into a recognizance before the officer in charge without sureties in such amount not exceeding five hundred dollars as the officer in charge directs and, if the officer in charge so directs, on his depositing with the officer in charge such sum of money or other valuable security not exceeding in amount or value five hundred dollars as the officer in charge directs.

An exception to this requirement that the person be released exists when the officer in charge either:

(i) believes on reasonable grounds that it is necessary in the public interest, having regard to all the circumstances including the need to establish the identity of the person, secure or preserve evidence of or relating to the offence, or prevent the continuation or repetition of the offence or the commission of another offence, that the person be detained in custody or that the matter of his release from custody be otherwise dealt with, or

(ii) believes on reasonable grounds that, if the person is released by him from custody, the person will fail to attend court in order to be dealt with according to law (s. 498(1)). This provision does not apply in respect of a person who has been arrested without warrant by a peace officer for an offence described in s. 503(3) (s. 498(2)).

Where person arrested with a warrant. Where a person who has been arrested with a warrant by a peace officer is taken into custody for:

(i) an indictable offence mentioned in s. 553,

(ii) an offence for which the person may be prosecuted by indictment or for which he is punishable on summary conviction,

(iii) an offence punishable on summary conviction, or

(iv) any other offence that is punishable by imprisonment for 5 years or less,

the officer in charge may, if the warrant has been endorsed by a justice, either

(i) release the person on his giving his promise to appear,

(ii) release the person on his entering into a recognizance before the officer in charge without sureties in such amount not exceeding five hundred dollars as the officer in charge directs, but without deposit of money or other valuable security, or

(iii) if the person is not ordinarily resident in the province in which the person is in custody or does not ordinarily reside within two hundred kilometres of the place in which he is in custody, release the person on his entering into a recognizance before the officer in charge without sureties in such amount not exceeding five hundred dollars as the officer in charge directs and, if the officer in charge so directs, on his depositing with the officer in charge such sum of money or other valuable security not exceeding in amount or value five hundred dollars, as the officer in charge directs (s. 499).

Offences mentioned in s. 553. Section 553(a) lists the following offences:

> theft, other than theft of cattle,
> obtaining money or property by false pretences,
> unlawfully having in his possession any property or thing or any proceeds of any property or thing knowing that all or part of the property or thing or of the proceeds was obtained by or derived directly or indirectly from the commission in Canada of an offence

punishable by indictment or an act or omission anywhere that, if it had occurred in Canada, would have constituted an offence punishable by indictment,

having, by deceit, falsehood or other fraudulent means, defrauded the public or any person, whether ascertained or not, of any property, money or valuable security, or

mischief

where the subject-matter of the offence is not a testamentary instrument and where the alleged value of the subject-matter of the offence does not exceed one thousand dollars.

Section 553(c) lists the following offences:

keeping gaming or betting house (s. 201),
betting, pool-selling, book-making, etc. (s. 202),
placing bets (s. 203),
lotteries and games of chance (s. 206),
cheating at play (s. 209),
keeping common bawdy-house (s. 210),
driving while disqualified (s. 259(4)), or
fraud in relation to fares (s. 393).

Section 553(b) also adds to the list counselling or attempting to commit or with being an accessory after the fact to the commission of any offence referred to in s. 553(a), or of any offence referred to in s. 553(c).

Deposit of money or valuable security. Where a person has deposited any sum of money or other valuable security with the officer in charge, the officer in charge shall, forthwith after the deposit thereof, cause the money or valuable security to be delivered to a justice for deposit with the justice (s. 500).

4. Release by a justice

Offences other than those mentioned in s. 469. Where an accused who is charged with an offence other than an offence listed in s. 469 is taken before a justice the justice shall, unless a plea of guilty by the accused is accepted, order, in respect of that offence, that the accused be released on his giving an undertaking without conditions, unless the prosecutor, having been given a reasonable opportunity to do so, shows cause, in respect of that offence, why the detention of the accused in custody is justified or why a different order should be made (s. 515(1)).

The offences listed in s. 469 fall within the exclusive jurisdiction of a superior court of criminal jurisdiction and include the following:

treason (s. 47),
alarming Her Majesty (s. 49),
intimidating Parliament or a legislature (s. 51),
inciting to mutiny (s. 53),
seditious offences (s. 61),
piracy (s. 74),
piratical acts (s. 75),
murder (s. 235),
attempting to commit any one of the above offences except murder or conspiring to commit any of the above offences,
accessory after the fact to high treason or murder, or
bribery by the holder of a judicial offence (s. 119).

Where a justice does not make an order to release the accused on his giving an undertaking without conditions, he shall, unless the prosecutor shows cause why the detention of the accused is justified, order that the accused be released:

(i) on his giving an undertaking with such conditions as the justice directs;

(ii) on his entering into a recognizance before the justice, without sureties, in such amount and with such conditions, if any, as the justice directs but without deposit of money or other valuable security;

(iii) on his entering into a recognizance before the justice with sureties in such amount and with such conditions, if any, as the justice directs but without deposit of money or other valuable security;

(iv) with the consent of the prosecutor, on his entering into a recognizance before the justice, without sureties, in such amount and with such conditions, if any, as the justice directs and on his depositing with the justice such sum of money or other valuable security as the justice directs, or

(v) if the accused is not ordinarily resident in the province in which he is in custody or does not ordinarily reside within one hundred kilometres of the place in which he is in custody, on his entering into a recognizance before the justice with or without sureties in such amount and with such conditions, if any, as the justice directs, and on his depositing with the justice such sum of money or other valuable security as the justice directs (s. 515(2)).

The justice may direct as conditions that the accused shall do any one or more of the following things as specified in the order:

(i) report at times to be stated in the order to a peace officer or other person designated in the order;

(ii) remain within a territorial jurisdiction specified in the order;

(iii) notify the peace officer or other person designated of any change in his address or his employment or occupation;

(iv) abstain from communicating with any witness or other person expressly named in the order, or refrain from going to any place expressly named in the order, except in accordance with the conditions specified in the order that the justice considers necessary;

(v) where the accused is the holder of a passport, deposit his passport as specified in the order; and

(vi) comply with such other reasonable conditions specified in the order as the justice considers desirable (s. 515(4)).

Before making such an order, in the case of an accused who is charged with an offence in the commission of which violence against a person was used, threatened or attempted or an offence described in s. 264 of the Criminal Code or in s. 39(1) or (2) or s. 48(1) or (2) of the Food and Drugs Act or in s. 4(1) or (2) of the Narcotic Control Act, the justice shall consider whether it is desirable, in the interests of the safety of the accused or of any other person, to include as a condition of the order that the accused be prohibited from possessing any firearm or any ammunition or explosive substance for any period of time specified in the order and that the accused surrender any firearms acquisition certificate that the accused possesses, and where the justice decides that it is not desirable, in the interests of the safety of the accused or of any other person, for the accused to possess any of those things, the justice may add the appropriate condition to the order (s. 515(4.1)).

Before making such an order, in the case of an accused who is charged with an offence described in s. 264, or an offence in the commission of which violence against a person was used, threatened or attempted, the justice shall consider whether it is desirable, in the interests of the safety of any person, to include as a condition of the order that the accused abstain from communicating with any witness or other person expressly named in the order, or be prohibited from going to any place expressly named in the order (s. 515(4.2)).

Where an accused who is charged with an indictable offence, other than an offence listed in s. 469 and is not ordinarily resident in Canada, shows cause why the accused's detention in custody is not justified, the justice shall order that the accused be released on giving an undertaking or entering into a recognizance with such conditions as the justice considers desirable (s. 515(8) and s. 515(6)(b)).

Offences mentioned in s. 515. Where an accused who is charged with an offence listed in s. 515(6)(a), (c) or (d), shows cause why the accused's detention in custody is not justified, the justice shall order that the accused be released on giving an undertaking or entering into a recognizance with such conditions (or additional conditions) as the justice considers desirable, unless the accused, having been given a reasonable opportunity to do so, shows cause why such conditions (or additional conditions) should not be imposed (s. 515(7)). The offences listed in s. 515(6)(a), (c) and (d) include:

— an indictable offence, other than an offence listed in s. 469, that is alleged to have been committed while he was at large after being released in respect of another indictable offence.
— with an offence under s. 145(2) to (5) that is alleged to have been committed while he was at large after being released in respect of another offence (i.e. failure to attend court (s. 145(2)), failure to comply with condition of undertaking or recognizance (s. 145(3)), failure to appear or comply with summons (s. 145(4)), and failure to comply with appearance notice or promise to appear (s. 145(5)).
— certain Narcotic Act offences including trafficking (s. 4(1)), possession for the purpose of trafficking (s. 4(2)), importing or exporting (s. 5(1)), and conspiring to commit any one of these offences.

Where, before or at any time during the course of any proceedings under s. 515, the accused pleads guilty and that plea is accepted, the justice may make an order for the release of the accused until the accused is sentenced (s. 518(2)).

Contravention of summons, appearance notice, promise to appear, undertaking or recognizance. A peace officer who believes on reasonable grounds that an accused either:

(i) has contravened or is about to contravene any summons, appearance notice, promise to appear, undertaking or recognizance that was issued or given to him or entered into by him, or

(ii) has committed an indictable offence after any summons, appearance notice, promise to appear, undertaking or recognizance was issued or given

may arrest the accused without warrant (s. 524(2)).

Where the accused who has been arrested with a warrant in these circumstances, is taken before a justice, the justice shall either:

(i) where the accused was released from custody pursuant to an order made under s. 522(3) by a judge of the superior court of criminal jurisdiction of any province, order that the accused be taken before a judge of the court; or

(ii) in any other case, hear the prosecutor and his witnesses, if any, and the accused and his witnesses, if any (s. 524(3)).

Where the accused has been taken before the justice and the justice finds either:

(i) that the accused has contravened or had been about to contravene his summons, appearance notice, promise to appear, undertaking or recognizance, or

(ii) that there are reasonable grounds to believe that the accused has committed an indictable offence after any summons, appearance notice, promise to appear, undertaking or recognizance was issued or given to him or entered into by him, he shall cancel the summons, appearance notice, promise to appear, undertaking or recognizance and order that the accused be detained in custody unless the accused, having been given a reasonable opportunity to do so, shows cause why his detention in custody is not justified (s. 524(8)).

Where the accused is able to show cause why his detention in custody is not justified, the justice shall order that the accused be released on his giving an undertaking or entering into a recognizance with such conditions as the justice considers desirable (s. 524(9)).

Where the justice does not make a finding either:

(i) that the accused has contravened or had been about to contravene his summons, appearance notice, promise to appear, undertaking or recognizance, or

(ii) that there are reasonable grounds to believe that the accused has committed an indictable offence after any summons, appearance notice, promise to appear, undertaking or recognizance was issued or given to him or entered into by him,

the justice shall order the accused be released from custody (s. 524(11)).

5. Release by a judge

Offences mentioned in s. 469. Where an accused is charged with an offence listed in s. 469 no court, judge or justice, other than a judge of or a judge presiding in a superior court of criminal jurisdiction for the province in which the accused is so charged, may release the accused before or after the accused has been ordered to stand trial (s. 522(1)).

The offences listed in (s. 469) include the following:

treason (s. 47),
alarming Her Majesty (s. 49),
intimidating Parliament or a legislature (s. 51),
inciting to mutiny (s. 53),
seditious offences (s. 61),
piracy (s. 74),
piratical acts (s. 75),
murder (s. 235),
conspiring to commit any of the above offences or attempting to commit any of the above offences except murder,
accessory after the fact to high treason or murder, or
bribery by the holder of a judicial office (s. 119).

Where an accused is charged with an offence listed in s. 469, a judge of or a judge presiding in a superior court of criminal jurisdiction for the province in which the accused is charged shall order that the accused be detained in custody unless the accused, having been given a reasonable opportunity to do so, shows cause why his detention in custody is not justified (s. 522(2)).

Where the judge does not order that the accused be detained in custody, he may order that the accused be released on his giving an undertaking or entering into a recognizance with such conditions described as the judge considers desirable (s. 522(3)).

Contravention of summons, appearance, promise to appear, undertaking or recognizance. A peace officer who believes on reasonable grounds that an accused either:

(i) has contravened or is about to contravene any summons, appearance notice, promise to appear, undertaking or recognizance that was issued or given to him or entered into by him, or

(ii) has committed an indictable offence after any summons, appearance notice, promise to appear, undertaking or recognizance was issued or given to him or entered into by him,
may arrest the accused without warrant (s. 524(2)).

Where an accused who has been arrested with a warrant is taken before a justice, the justice shall where the accused was released from custody pursuant to an order made by a judge of the superior court of criminal jurisdiction of any province, order that the accused be taken before a judge of that court (s. 524(3)(a)).

Where the judge does not order that the accused be detained in custody, he may order that the accused be released upon his giving an undertaking or entering into a recognizance with such conditions as the judge considers desirable (s. 524(5)).

Where the judge does not make a finding either:

(i) that the accused has contravened or had been about to contravene his summons, appearance notice, promise to appear, undertaking or recognizance, or

(ii) that there are reasonable grounds to believe that the accused has committed an indictable offence after any summons, appearance notice, promise to appear, undertaking or recognizance was issued or given to him or entered into by him,

he shall order that the accused be released from custody (s. 524(7)).

6. Release from imprisonment

For the purposes of s. 100(1) (mandatory prohibition order) and s. 100(2) (discretionary prohibition order), "release from imprisonment" means release from confinement by reason of expiration of sentence, commencement of mandatory supervision or grant of parole other than day parole (s. 100(3)).

REMAND. 1. Send back into custody. 2. A provincial court judge or justice of the peace before whom a person accused of an indictable offence is brought may release him, or remand him to be brought before him or, if the accused is charged with an offence over which a provincial court judge has absolute jurisdiction and is brought before a justice of the peace, to a provincial court judge and adjourn the proceedings (s. 536 and s. 543).

Unless the accused is on bail and he and his sureties and the prosecutor consent, or he is remanded for observation, the adjournment shall not be for more than 8 days.

A trial of an indictable offence may be adjourned at the discretion of the presiding judge. No time limit is fixed, (s. 571, s. 645 and s. 803). In summary conviction proceedings, the adjournment may not in any case be for more than 8 days unless both the accused and the prosecutor consent (s. 803).

It is to be noted that an adjournment relates to the proceedings and remand relates to the person of the accused during the period of the adjournment.

REMANET. 1. "It remains" (Latin). 2. A case left over in a court list from a previous term.

REPEAL. "Repeal" includes revoke or cancel (Interpretation Act, s. 2(1)).

An enactment that has been replaced, has expired, lapsed or has otherwise ceased to have effect is deemed to have been repealed (Interpretation Act, s. 2(2)).

REPLICATION. In criminal proceedings by indictment, the replication is the pleading following the plea (Jowitt's Dictionary of English Law).

REPORTS. Reports of investigations, arrests, inquests or accidents should be typed or where that is impossible should be carefully written on one side only of the paper. The report should be numbered to show whether it is the first, second or final report, or possible first and final report. Leave a wide margin on the left and arrange the paragraphs under subheadings, noting the heading in the margin, such as is done in the marginal note of statutes. Slang terms and abbreviations should not be used unless to quote exact words. When quoting exact words put the words in "inverted commas" and indent the statement. The heading should indicate the post or detachment to which you are attached and the signature should show the rank of person making the report. Reports should indicate the exact place, the time, what occurred, and in cases of injury in which an automobile is involved, should show the condition of the roadway and of the weather, also whether it was light or dark and if visibility was good. In the case of an arrest or conviction, the report should give the full name, with aliases, the age, nationality, the offence and the penalty imposed.

RES. 1. Thing; matter; substance (Latin). 2. Any physical or metaphysical existence, in which a person may claim a right (Jowitt's Dictionary of English Law). ***Res gestae.*** 1. "Things done". 2. This expression refers to the facts surrounding or accompanying a transaction which is the subject of legal proceedings. The courts have held that, where a person who is involved in or witness to an event makes an uncalculated, spontaneous statement in the nature of an outburst in the heat of the moment, referring to the event, the statement may be admissible as evidence of the truth of what was stated (Thompson v. Trevanion (1693) Skin. 402). Such a statement is admissible against all co-accused (R. v. Klippenstein (1981), 19 C.R. (3d) 56 (Alta. C.A.)). ***Res integra.*** 1. A new or unopened thing or a whole thing. 2. A point of law that has not yet been decided. ***Res inter alios acta (alteri nocere non debet).*** 1. "A transaction between strangers ought not to injure another party". 2. Persons are not to be prejudiced by the acts or words of others, to which they were neither party nor privy, and which they had no power to prevent or control

(Jowitt's Dictionary of English Law). ***Res ipsa loquitur.*** 1. "The thing speaks for itself". 2. In certain cases, one fact raises a prima facie presumption of another fact, unless or until the contrary is proven (Jowitt's Dictionary of English Law). ***Res judicata.*** 1. Thing adjudicated; a finished case. 2. A final judgment rendered by a court of competent jurisdiction on the merits is conclusive as to the rights of the parties. ***Res nova.*** A matter not yet decided. ***Res nullius.*** A thing which has no owner. ***Res perit domino.*** "The owner of a thing bears the risk of its loss".

RESCUE. 1. In general, the voluntary intervention by a person in an attempt to save life or property from being lost. 2. In criminal law, the act of forcibly and knowingly freeing a person from an arrest or imprisonment (Jowitt's Dictionary of English Law). *See also ASSAULT, 10 and ESCAPES AND RESCUES*

RESISTANCE. The act of resisting opposition; the employment of forcible means to prevent the execution of an endeavour in which force is employed; standing against; obstructing (Black's Law Dictionary).

Resistance to the commission of an offence. *See BODILY HARM AND ACTS AND OMISSIONS CAUSING DANGER TO THE PERSON, 4.*

Resisting arrest. *See ASSAULTS, 8.*

Resisting or obstructing peace officer. *See PEACE OFFICER, 3.*

Resisting or obstructing public officer. *See PUBLIC OFFICER, 2.*

RESPONDEAT SUPERIOR. "Let the employer respond" (i.e., be liable) (Latin).

RESTITUTIO IN INTEGRUM. Restoration to the original position (Latin).

RESTRICTED DRUGS

1. *Definitions*
2. *Possession of restricted drug*
3. *Trafficking in a restricted drug*
4. *Possession of restricted drug for trafficking*

1. Definitions

"Restricted drug". For the purposes of Part IV of the Food and Drugs Act, this expression means any drug or other substance included in Schedule H (Food and Drugs Act, s. 46).

At present, Schedule H includes the following drugs:

Lysergic acid diethylamide (LSD) or any salt thereof
N, N-Diethyltryptamine (DET) or any salt thereof
N, N-Dimethyltryptamine (DMT) or any salt thereof
4-Methyl-2, 5-dimethoxyamphetamine (STP(DOM)) or any salt thereof
3, 4-methylenedioxyamphetamine (MDA) or any salt thereof
N-methyl-3-piperidyl benzilate (LBJ) or any salt thereof
2, 3-dimethoxyamphetamine or any salt thereof
2, 4-dimethoxyamphetamine or any salt thereof
2, 5-dimethoxyamphetamine or any salt thereof
2, 6-dimethoxyamphetamine or any salt thereof
3, 4-dimethoxyamphetamine or any salt thereof
3, 5-dimethoxyamphetamine or any salt thereof
4, 9-dihydro-7-methoxy-1-methyl-3H-pyrido (3, 4-b) indole (Harmaline) and any salt thereof
4, 9-dihydro-1-methyl-3H-pyrido (3, 4-b) indol-7-ol (Harmalol) and any salt thereof
4-methoxyamphetamine or any salt thereof
3-[2-(Dimethylamino) ethyl]-4-hydroxyindole (Psilocin) or any salt thereof
3-[2-(Dimethylamino) ethyl]-4-phosphoryloxyindole (Psilocybin) or any salt thereof
2, 4, 5-Trimethoxyamphetamine or any salt, isomer, or salt of isomer, thereof
3, 4-methylenedioxy-N-methylamphetamine or any salt thereof
N-(1-phenycyclohexyl) ethylamine or any salt thereof
4-bromo-2, 5-dimethoxyamphetamine or any salt thereof
1-[1-(2-thienyl) cyclohexyl] piperidine and its salts
1-phenyl-N-propylcyclohexanamine or any salt thereof

3,4,5-trimethoxybenzeneethanamine (Mescaline) or any salt thereof but not including peyote (lophophora)
4-ethoxy-2, 5-dimethoxy-a-methylbenzeneethanamine or any salt, isomer, or salt of isomer, thereof
7-methoxy-a-methyl-1,3-benzodioxole-5-ethanamine (MMDA) or any salt, isomer or salt isomer thereof

N,N-a-trimethyl-1,3 benzodioxole-5-ethanamine or any salt, isomer or salt of isomer thereof

N-ethyl-a-methyl-1,3-benzodioxole-t-ethanamine or any salt, isomer or salt of isomer thereof

4-ethyl-2,5-dimethoxy-a-methylbenzeneethanamine (DOET) or any salt, isomer or salt of isomer thereof

4-ethoxy-a-methylbenzeneethanamine or any salt, isomer or salt of isomer thereof

4-chloro-2,5-dimethoxy-a-methylbenzeneethanamine or any salt, isomer of salt of isomer thereof

4,5-dihydro-4-methyl-5-phenyl-2-oxazolamine (4-methylaminorex) or any salt thereof

N-ethy-a-methylbenzeneethanamine or any salt thereof

a-methyl-N-propyl-1, 3-benzodioxole-5-ethanamine or any salt, isomer or salt of isomer thereof

1-[1-(phenylmethyl)cyclohexyl]piperidine or any salkt, isomer or salt of isomer thereof

1-[1-(4-methylphenyl)]cyclohexylpiperidine or any salt, isomer or salt of isomer thereof

2-methylamino-1-phenyl-1-propanone or any salt thereof

(As amended by SOR/71-357; SOR/71-564; SI/73-36; SOR/74-198; SOR/74-611; SOR/74-670; SOR/76-368; SOR/77-824; SOR/78-425; SOR/78-650; SOR/79-938; SOR/86-90; SOR/86-833; SOR/87-76; SOR/87-406; SOR/87-485; SOR/87-574; SOR/87-653; SOR/89-410; SOR/90-156).

Schedule H is amended by the Governor in Council (Food and Drugs Act, s. 45(2) and s. 51).

See also POSSESSION and TRAFFICKING.

2. Possession of restricted drug — Food and Drugs Act, section 47(1) and (2)

Every one who — except as authorized by Part IV of the Food and Drugs Act or its regulations — has in his possession — a restricted drug — is guilty of either an indictable offence or an offence punishable on summary conviction.

Punishment. On indictment, a fine not exceeding $5,000 or to imprisonment for a term not exceeding 3 years, or to both (Food and Drugs Act, s. 47(2)(b)). On summary conviction, for a first offence, a fine not exceeding $1,000 or to imprisonment for a term not exceeding 6 months, or to both. For a subsequent offence, a fine not exceeding $2,000 or to imprisonment for a term not exceeding one year, or to both (Food and Drugs Act, s. 47(2)(a)).

Release. Initial decision to release made by peace officer (s. 497).

Election. On indictment, accused may elect trial by judge and jury, judge alone, or provincial court judge (s. 536). On summary conviction, no election.

Evidence. 1. No exception, exemption, excuse or qualification prescribed by law is required to be set out or negatived, as the case may be, in an information or indictment for this offence (Food and Drugs Act, s. 50(1)).
2. The burden of proving that an exception, exemption, excuse or qualification prescribed by law operates in favour of the accused is on the accused, and the prosecutor is not required, except by way of rebuttal, to prove that the exception, exemption, excuse or qualification does not operate in favour of the accused, whether or not it is set out in the information or indictment (Food and Drugs Act, s. 50(2)).

Informations

A.B., on or about the —— day of ——, 19——, at the —— of ——, in the said (territorial division), did, without authorization, have in his possession a restricted drug, to wit: (specify the particulars of the offence), contrary to s. 47 of the Food and Drugs Act.

3. Trafficking in a restricted drug — Food and Drugs Act, section 48(1) and (3)

Every one who — traffics — in a restricted drug — or any substance represented or held out by him to be a restricted drug — is guilty of either an indictable offence or an offence punishable on summary conviction.

Punishment. On indictment, imprisonment for a term not exceeding 10 years (Food and Drugs Act, s. 48(3)(b)). On summary conviction, imprisonment for a term not exceeding 18 months (Food and Drugs Act, s. 48(3)(a)).

Release. Initial decision to release made by peace officer (s. 497).

Election. On indictment, accused may elect trial by judge and jury, judge alone, or provincial court judge (s. 536). On summary conviction, no election.

Evidence. *See Evidence under* **2**, *above.*

Informations

A.B., on or about the —— day of ——, 19——, at the —— of ——, in the said (territorial division), did traffic in a restricted drug [OR a substance represented or held out by him to be a restricted drug], to wit: (specify the particulars of the offence), contrary to s. 48 of the Food and Drugs Act.

4. Possession of restricted drug for trafficking — Food and Drugs Act, section 48(2) and (3)

Every one who — has in his possession — any restricted drug — for the purpose of trafficking — is guilty of either an indictable offence or an offence punishable on summary conviction.

Punishment. On indictment, imprisonment for a term not exceeding 10 years (Food and Drugs Act, s. 48(3)(b)). On summary conviction, imprisonment for a term not exceeding 18 months (Food and Drugs Act, s. 48(3)(a)).

Release. Initial decision to release made by peace officer (s. 497).

Election. On indictment, accused may elect trial by judge and jury, judge alone, or provincial court judge (s. 536). On summary conviction, no election.

Evidence. *See Evidence under* **2**, *above.*

Informations

A.B., on or about the —— day of ——, 19——, at the —— of ——, in the said (territorial division), did have in his possession a restricted drug for the purpose of trafficking, to wit: (specify the particulars of the offence), contrary to s. 48 of the Food and Drugs Act.

RESTRICTED WEAPONS

Weapons restricted by the Criminal Code

1. ***One hand action.*** Any firearm designed, altered or intended to be aimed and fired by the action of one hand, other than a prohibited weapon (s. 84(1)(a)).

2. ***Semi-automatic.*** Any firearm that has a barrel that is less than 470 mm (18.5 inches) in length and is capable of discharging centre-fire ammunition in a semi-automatic manner, other than a prohibited weapon (s. 84(1)(b)(i)). *See also BARREL-LENGTH.*

3. ***Folding or telescoping.*** Any firearm that is designed or adapted to be fired when reduced to a length of less than 660 mm (26 inches) by folding, telescoping or otherwise (s. 84(1)(b)(ii)).

4. ***Genuine gun collector.*** Any firearm that is designed, altered or intended to fire bullets in rapid succession during one pressure of the trigger and that, on January 1, 1978, was registered as a restricted weapon and formed part of a gun collection in Canada of a genuine gun collector (s. 84(1)(c)), or any firearm that is assembled or designed and manufactured with the capability of firing projectiles in rapid succession with one pressure of the trigger, to the extent that (i) the firearm is altered to fire only one projectile with one such pressure, (ii) on October 1, 1992, the firearm was registered as a restricted weapon, or an application for a registration certificate was made to a local registrar of firearms in respect of the firearm, and the firearm formed part of a gun collection in Canada of a genuine gun collector, and (iii) s. 109(4.1) and (4.2) (changes that firearm (s. 84(1)(c.1)).

5. ***Weapon restricted by order of Governor in Council.*** A weapon of any kind, not being a prohibited weapon or a shotgun or rifle of a kind that, in the opinion of the Governor in Council, is reasonable for use in Canada for hunting or sporting purposes, that is declared by order of the Governor in Council to be a restricted weapon (s. 84(1)(d)).

6. ***Restricted firearms.*** Firearms which under s. 84(1) become restricted firearms include the following:

Armolite Model AR-180, .223 calibre, 18 1/4" barrel
National Ordinance Model M-1 Carbine, .30 calibre, 18" barrel
P.J.K. Model 68 Carbine, 9 mm calibre, 16 3/16" barrel
Plainfield Model Carbine, .223 or .30 calibre, 18" barrel
Universal Model 1003, .30 calibre, 18" barrel
Universal Model 1002, .30 calibre, 18" barrel
Valmet Model 62S, 7.62 calibre, 16 5/8" barrel
Valmet Model 72S, .223 calibre, 16 5/8" barrel
Eagle Model Apache Carbine, 45 calibre, 16 1/2" barrel
J & R Model 68, 9 mm calibre, 16 1/4" barrel
Universal Model 1000, .30 calibre, 18" barrel
Universal Model 1020, .30 calibre, 18" barrel
Universal Model Enforcer, .30 calibre, 10 1/4" barrel
Cetme Model Sport, .308 calibre, 17 3/4" barrel
Universal Model 1005, .30 calibre, 18" barrel
Barretta Model BM-69, 7.62 calibre, 17" barrel
U.S. Carbine Model M-1, .30 calibre, 18" barrel
U.S. Carbine Model M-1 A-1, .30 calibre, 18" barrel

Heckler & Koch Model HK-93, .223 calibre, 16 1/4" barrel
National Ordinance Model M-1 Tank, 30-06 calibre, 17 1/2" barrel
Plainfield Model Carbine, .30 calibre, 18" barrel

Weapons restricted by Restricted Weapons Order (SOR/92-467 (Gaz. 12/8/92, p. 3450))

1. *High Standard Model 10, Series A Shotgun and High Standard Model 10, Series B Shotgun.* The firearms of the designs commonly known as the High Standard Model 10, Series A shotgun and High Standard Model 10, Series B shotgun, and any variants or modified versions thereof.

2. *AK-47 Rifle.* The firearm of the design commonly known as the AK-47 rifle, and any variant or modified version thereof, including the (i) AK-74; (ii) AK Hunter; (iii) AKM; (iv) AKM-63; (v) AKS-56S; (vi) AKS-56S-1; (vii) AKS-56S-2; (viii) AKS-74; (ix) AKS-84S-1; (x) AMD-65; (xi) AR Model 223; (xii) Dragunov; (xii) Galil; (xiv) KKMPi69; (xv) M60; (xvi) M62; (xvii) M70B1; (xviii) M70AB2; (xix) M76; (xx) M77B1; (xxi) M78; (xxii) M80; (xxiii) M80A; (xxiv) MAK90; (xxv) MPiK; (xxvi) MPiKM; (xxvii) MPiKMS-72; (xxviii) MPiKS; (xxix) PKM; (xxx) PKM-DGN-60; (xxxi) PMKM; (xxxii) RPK; (xxxiii) RPK-74; (xxxiv) RPK-87S; (xxxv) Type 56; (xxxvi) Type 56-1; (xxxvii) Type 56-2; (xxxviii) Type 56-3; (xxxix) Type 56-4; (xl) Type 68; (xli) Type 79; (xlii) American Arms AKY39; (xliii) American Arms AKF39; (xliv) American Arms (AKC47; (xlv) American Arms AKF47; (xlvi) MAM70WS762; (xlvii) MAM70FS762; (xlviii) Mitchell AK-22; (xlix) Mitchell AK-47; (l) Mitchell Heavy Barrel AK-47; (li) Norinco 84S; (lii) Norinco 84S AK; (liv) Norinco 56; (lv) Norinco 56-2; (lvi) Norinco 56-3; (lvii) Norinco 56-4; (lvii) Poly Technologies Inc. AK-47/S; (lix) Poly Technologies Inc. AKS-47/S; (lx) Poly Technologies Inc. AKS-762; (lxi) Valmet Hunter; (lxii) Valmet M76; (lxiii) Valmet M76 carbine; (lxiv) Valmet M78; (lxv) Valmet M78/A2; (lxvi) Valmet MK78 (NATO) LMG; (lxvii) Valmet M82; and (lxviii) Valmet M82 Bullpup.

3. *Armalite AR-180 Sporter Carbine.* The firearm of the design commonly known as the Armalite AR-180 Sporter carbine, and any variant or modified version thereof.

4. *Beretta AR70 Assault Rifle.* The firearm of the design commonly known as the Beretta AR70 assault rifle, and any variant or modified version thereof.

5. *BM59 Rifle.* The firearm of the design commonly known as the BM 59 rifle, and any variant or modified version thereof, including

(i) the Beretta (A) BM 59; (B) BM 59R; (C) BM 59GL; (D) BM 59D; (E) BM 59 Mk E; (F) BM 59 Mk I; (G) BM 59 Mk Ital; (H) BM 59 Mk II; (I) BM 59 Mk III; (J) BM 59 Mk Ital TA; (K) BM 59 Mk Ital Para; (L) BM 59 Mk Ital TP; and (M) BM 60CB; and (ii) the Springfield Armory (A) BM 59 Alpine; (B) BM 59 Alpine Paratrooper; and (C) BM 59 Nigerian Mk IV.

6. ***Bushmaster Auto Rifle.*** The firearm of the design commonly known as the Bushmaster Auto Rifle, and any variant or modified version thereof.

7. ***Cetme Sport Auto Rifle.*** The firearm of the design commonly known as the Cetme Sport Auto Rifle, and any variant or modified version thereof.

8. ***Daewoo K1 Rifle.*** The firearm of the design commonly known as the Daewoo K1 rifle, and any variant or modified version thereof, including the Daewoo K1A1, K2, Max 1, Max 2, AR-100 and AR 110C.

9. ***Demro TAC-1M Carbine.*** The firearm of the design commonly known as the Demro TAC-1M carbine, and any variant or modified version thereof, including the Demro XF-7 Wasp Carbine.

10. ***Eagle Apache Carbine.*** The firearm of the design commonly known as the Eagle Apache Carbine, and any variant or modified version thereof.

11. ***FN-FNC Rifle.*** The firearm of the design commonly known as the FN-FNC rifle, and any variant or modified version thereof, including the FNC Auto Rifle, FNC Auto Paratrooper, FNC-11, FNC-22 and FNC-33.

12. ***FN-FAL (FN-LAR) Rifle.*** The firearm of the design commonly known as the FN-FAL (FN-LAR) rifle, and any variant or modified version thereof, including the FN 308 Model 44, FN-FAL (FN-LAR) Competition Auto, FN-FAL (FN-LAR) Heavy Barrel 308 Match, FN-FAL (FN-LAR) Paratrooper 308 Match 50-64 and FN 308 Model 50-63.

13. ***G3 Rifle.*** The firearm of the design commonly known as the G3 rifle, and any variant or modified version thereof, including the Heckler and Koch (i) HK 91; (ii) HK 91A2; (iii) HK 91A3; (iv) HK G3 A3; (v) HK G3 A3 ZF; (vi) HK G3 A4; (vii) HK G3 SG/1; and (viii) HK PGS1.

14. ***Galil Assault Rifle.*** The firearm of the design commonly known as the Galil assault rifle, and any variant or modified version thereof, including the Galil ARM, Galil AR, Galil SAR, Galil 332 and Mitchell Galil/22 Auto Rifle.

15. *Goncz High-Tech Carbine.* The firearm of the design commonly known as the Goncz High-Tech Carbine, and any variant or modified version thereof.

16. *Heckler and Koch HK 33 Rifle.* The firearm of the design commonly known as the Heckler and Koch HK 33 rifle, and any variant or modified version thereof, including the (i) HK 33A2; (ii) HK 33A3; (iii) HK 33KA1; (iv) HK 93; (v) HK 93A2; and (vi) HK 93A3.

17. *J & R Eng M-68 Carbine.* The firearm of the design commonly known as the J & R Eng M-68 carbine, and any variant or modified version thereof, including the PJK M-68 and the Wilinson "Terry" carbine.

18. *Leader Mark Series Auto Rifle.* The firearm of the design commonly known as the Leader Mark Series Auto Rifle, and any variant or modified version thereof.

19. *M-16 Rifle.* The firearm of the design commonly known as the M-16 rifle, and any variant or modified version thereof, including the: (i) Colt AR-15; (ii) Colt AR-15 SPI; (iii) Colt AR-15 Sporter; (iv) Colt AR-15 Collapsible Stock Model; (v) Colt AR-15 A2; (vi) Colt AR-15 A2 Carbine; (vii) Colt AR-15 A2 Government Model Rifle; (viii) Colt AR—15 A2 Government Model Target Rifle; (ix) Colt AR-15 A2 Government Model Carbine; (x) Colt AR-15 A2 Sporter II; (xi) Colt AR-15 A2 H-BAR; (xii) Colt AR-15 A2 Delta H-BAR; (xiii) Colt AR-15 A2 Delta H-BAR Match; (xiv) Colt AR-15 9mm Carbine; (xv) Armalite AR-15; (xvi) AAI M15; (xvii) AP74; (xviii) EAC J-15; (xix) PWA Commando; (xx) SGW XM15A; (xxi) SGW CAR-AR; (xxii) SWD AR-15; and (xxiii) any 22-calibre rimfire variant, including the (A) Mitchell M-16A-1/22; (B) Mitchell M-16/22; (C) Mitchell CAR-15/22; and (D) AP74 Auto Rifle.

20. *MP5 Submachine Gun and MP5 Carbine.* The firearms of the designs commonly known as the MP5 submachine gun and MP5 carbine, and any variants or modified versions thereof, including the Heckler and Koch (i) HK MP5; (ii) HK MP5A2; (iii) HK MP5A3; (iv) HK MP5K; (v) HK MP5SD; (vi) HK MP5SD1; (vii) HK MP5SD2; (viii) HK MP5SD3; (ix) HK 94; (x) HK 94A2; and (xi) HK 94A3.

21. *PE57 Rifle.* The firearm of the design commonly known as the PE57 rifle, and any variant or modified version thereof.

22. *SG-550 Rifle and SG-551 Carbine.* The firearms of the designs commonly known as the SG-550 rifle and SG-551 carbine, and any variants or modified versions thereof.

23. *SIG AMT Rifle.* The firearm of the design commonly known as the SIG AMT rifle, and any variant or modified version thereof.

24. ***Springfield Armory SAR-48 Rifle.*** The firearm of the design commonly known as the Springfield Armory SAR-48 rifle, and any variant or modified version thereof, including the SAR-48 Bush, SAR-48 Heavy Barrel, SAR-48 Para and SAR-488 Model 22.

25. ***Thompson Submachine Gun.*** The firearm of the design commonly known as the Thompson submachine gun, and any variant or modified version thereof, including the (i) Thompson Model 1921; (ii) Thompson Model 1927; (iii) Thompson Model 1928; (iv) Thompson Model M1; (v) Auto-Ordnance M27A-1; (vi) Auto-Ordnance M27A-1 Deluxe; (vii) Auto-Ordnance M1927A-3; (viii) Auto-Ordnance M1927A-5; (ix) Auto-Ordnance Thompson M1; (x) Commando Arms Mk I; (xi) Commando Arms Mk II; (xii) Commando Arms Mk III; (xiii) Commando Arms Mk 9; and (xiv) Commando Arms Mk 45.

REVENUE PAPER. For the purposes of Part IX of the Criminal Code (Offences Against Rights of Property), "revenue paper" means paper that is used to make stamps, licences or permits or for any purpose connected with the public revenue (s. 321).

REX. The reigning king (Latin). ***Rex non potest peccare.*** "The king can do no wrong".

RIFLE. A firearm, normally fired from the shoulder, the barrel of which has rifling on its inner surface (Jaffe, A Guide to Pathological Evidence, 2nd ed.).

RIFLING. The series of spiral grooves on the inner surface of a firearm barrel, designed to impart a spin to the projectile. The number of grooves and their direction (right or left handed) is one criterion on which a classification of firearms is based (Jaffe, A Guide to Pathological Evidence, 2nd ed.).

RIGOR MORTIS. A stiffening and contraction of the musculature of the body (both voluntary and involuntary after death (Jaffe, A Guide to Pathological Evidence, 2nd ed.).

RIM FIRE. Ammunition in which the primer is located in a rim surrounding the base of the cartridge case (Jaffe, A Guide to Pathological Evidence, 2nd ed.).

ROBBERY AND EXTORTION

1. *Robbery*
2. *Stopping mail with intent to rob or search*
3. *Extortion*

1. Robbery

Definition of offence — Section 343

Every one who — either steals — and for the purpose of extorting whatever is stolen or to prevent or overcome resistance to the stealing — uses violence or threats of violence — to a person or property — or steals from any person — and, at the time he steals or immediately before or immediately thereafter — wounds or beats or strikes or uses any personal violence to that person — or assaults any person — with intent to steal from him — or steals from any person — while armed with an offensive weapon or imitation thereof — commits robbery.

Statement of offence — Section 344

Every one who — commits robbery — is guilty of an indictable offence.

Included offences. Attempts (s. 660 and s. 662(1)(b)); wounding (sometimes); assault causing bodily harm (but not necessarily); assault; theft.

Punishment. Imprisonment for life (s. 344).

Release. Initial decision to release made by justice (s. 515(1)).

Election. Accused may elect trial by judge and jury, judge alone, or provincial court judge (s. 536).

Evidence. 1. The courts have held that s. 344 creates only one offence — robbery — which may be committed in the different ways described in s. 343 (R. v. Johnson (1977), 35 C.C.C. (2d) 439 (B.C.C.A.)).
2. Violence or threats of violence are essential elements of the offence (s. 343). By violence is meant something more than a mere assault (R. v. Lew (1978), 40 C.C.C. (2d) 140 (Ont. C.A.)).
3. A simple purse snatching, where the accused merely snatches the purse before the victim can resist and without violence to the victim, is theft, not robbery (R. v. Picard (1976), 39 C.C.C. (2d) 57 (Que. Sess. Ct.)).

4. To be "armed" means to be equipped with or possessed of an offensive weapon or an imitation of one (R. v. Sloan (1974), 19 C.C.C. (2d) 190 (B.C. C.A.)). Using your hand in such a way as to pretend that you have a gun is insufficient to support a charge of robbery (R. v. Gouchie (1976), 33 C.C.C. (2d) 120 (Que. S.P.)).

Informations

A.B., on or about the —— day of ——, 19——, at the —— of ——, in the said (territorial division), did steal (specify the thing stolen) from C.D., and for the purpose of extorting what was stolen [OR to prevent resistance to the stealing OR to overcome resistance to the stealing] used violence [OR threats of violence] to C.D. [OR to the property of C.D.], and did thereby commit robbery, to wit: (specify the particulars of the offence), contrary to s. 343(a) and s. 344 of the Criminal Code of Canada.

A.B., on or about the —— day of ——, 19——, at the —— of ——, in the said (territorial division), did steal (specify the thing stolen) from C.D., and at the same time [OR immediately before OR immediately thereafter] did wound [OR beat OR strike OR use personal violence to] C.D., and did thereby commit robbery, to wit: (specify the particulars of the offence), contrary to s. 343(b) and s. 344 of the Criminal Code of Canada.

A.B., on or about the —— day of ——, 19——, at the —— of ——, in the said (territorial division), did assault C.D. with intent to steal from him, and did thereby commit robbery, to wit: (specify the particulars of the offence), contrary to s. 343(c) and s. 344 of the Criminal Code of Canada.

A.B., on or about the —— day of ——, 19——, at the —— of ——, in the said (territorial division), did steal from C.D. while armed with an offensive weapon [OR with an imitation of an offensive weapon], and did thereby commit robbery, to wit: (specify the particulars of the offence), contrary to s. 343(d) and s. 344 of the Criminal Code of Canada.

A.B., on or about the —— day of ——, 19——, at the —— of ——, in the said (territorial division), did rob C.D. of (specify the thing), to wit: (specify the particulars of the offence), contrary to s. 344 of the Criminal Code of Canada.

2. Stopping mail with intent to rob or search — Section 345

Every one who — stops a mail conveyance — with intent to rob or search it — is guilty of an indictable offence.

Intent. Intention to rob or search.

Included offences. Attempts (s. 660 and s. 662(1)(b)).

Punishment. Imprisonment for life (s. 345).

Release. Initial decision to release made by justice (s. 515(1)).

Election. Accused may elect trial by judge and jury, judge alone, or provincial court judge (s. 536).

Definitions. A "mail conveyance" means any physical, electronic, optical or other means used to transmit mail (Canada Post Corporation Act, R.S.C. 1985, c. C-10, s. 2(1)).

"Mail" means mailable matter from the time it is posted to the time it is delivered to the addressee thereof (Canada Post Corporation Act, s. 2(1)).

"Mailable matter" means any message, information, funds or goods that may be transmitted by post (Canada Post Corporation Act, s. 2(1)).

Evidence. The charge in connection with mailable matter may describe the article as being the property of the Postmaster General.

Informations

A.B., on or about the —— day of ——, 19——, at the —— of ——, in the said (territorial division), did stop a mail conveyance with intent to rob [OR search] it, to wit: (specify the particulars of the offence), contrary to s. 345 of the Criminal Code of Canada.

3. Extortion

Definition of offence — Section 346(1)

Every one who — without reasonable justification or excuse — and with intent to obtain anything by threats or accusations or menaces or violence — induces or attempts to induce any person (whether or not he is the person threatened or accused or menaced or to whom violence is shown) — to do anything or cause anything to be done — commits extortion.

Statement of offence — Section 346(1.1)

Every one who — commits extortion — is guilty of an indictable offence.

Intent. Intention to obtain anything by threats, accusations, menaces or violence.

Included offences. Attempts (s. 660 and s. 662(1)(b)).

Punishment. A maximum term of imprisonment for life (s. 346(1.1)).

Release. Initial decision to release made by justice (s. 515(1)).

Election. Accused may elect trial by judge and jury, judge alone, or provincial court judge (s. 536).

Definitions. "Menace" means a threat; the declaration or show of a disposition or determination to inflict an evil or injury upon another (Black's Law Dictionary).

Evidence. 1. The extorting of an act of sexual intercourse is an offence (R. v. Bird (1969), 9 C.R.N.S. 1 (B.C. C.A.)).
2. A threat to institute civil proceedings is not a threat for the purposes of this offence (s. 346(2)).

Informations

A.B., on or about the —— day of ——, 19——, at the —— of ——, in the said (territorial division), without reasonable justification or excuse and with intent to obtain (specify the thing sought to be obtained), by threats [OR accusations OR menaces OR violence] did induce [OR attempt to induce] C.D., the person threatened [OR the person accused OR the person menaced OR the person to whom violence was shown OR (specify any other person)], to do [OR cause to be done] (specify the thing done or caused to be done), to wit: (specify the particulars of the offence), contrary to s. 346(1.1) of the Criminal Code of Canada.

ROYAL WARRANT. An instrument or piece of writing under which a tradesman is authorized to conduct his trade for some member of the royal family.

RULE OF LAW. The general principle that no one can be punished for an act unless the conduct in question has been formally expressed in law to be wrongful.

No crime exists and no penalty can be imposed unless the crime and punishment have been specified in laws.

There are a number of important aspects of the general principle:

(i) The laws must be properly passed, i.e., in accordance with all of the specific procedural rules established for our parliamentary institutions.

(ii) It is implicit that criminal laws should not be made to apply retroactively.

(iii) The definition of the offence must be stated with precision.

These concepts are just as applicable to laws relating to procedure and evidence as they are to laws defining specific offences.

The state may only use the criminal process to interfere in the lives of individuals where such interference in specifically authorized in law, and only to that extent (Ratushny, Self-Incrimination in the Canadian Criminal Process).

S

S. 1. An abbreviation for "section". 2. When combined with other letters, as in R.S.C., it means "statute", i.e., the Revised Statutes of Canada. 3. In the Police Officers Manual, it refers to a section of the Criminal Code unless some other statute is expressly referred to.

SABOTAGE

See also PROHIBITED ACT.

Section 52(1)

Every one who — does a prohibited act — for a purpose prejudicial to — either the safety or security or defence of Canada — or the safety or security of the naval or army or air forces of any state other than Canada that are lawfully present in Canada — is guilty of an indictable offence.

Exceptions. 1. No person does a prohibited act by reason only that (a) he stops work as a result of the failure of his employer and himself to agree on any matter relating to his employment, (b) he stops work as a result of the failure of his employer and a bargaining agent acting on his behalf to agree on any matter relating to his employment, or (c) he stops work as a result of his taking part in a combination of workmen or employees for their own reasonable protection as workmen or employees (s. 52(3)).

2. No person does a prohibited act by reason only that he attends at or near or approaches a dwelling-house or place for the purpose only of obtaining or communicating information (s. 52(4)).

Intent. For purpose prejudicial to safety, security or defence.

Included offences. Attempts (s. 660 and s. 662(1)(b)).

Punishment. Imprisonment for a term not exceeding 10 years (s. 52(1)).

Release. Initial decision to release made by justice (s. 515(1)).

Election. Accused may elect trial by judge and jury, judge alone, or provincial court judge (s. 536).

Evidence. In proceedings for this offence, no evidence is admissible of an overt act unless that overt act is set out in the indictment or unless the evidence is otherwise relevant as tending to prove an overt act that is set out therein (s. 55).

SADISM. A form of perversion in which pleasure or sexual satisfaction is derived from the infliction of cruelty or pain on another person or an animal (Jaffe, A Guide to Pathological Evidence, 2nd ed.).

SALE. A transfer of property or of a right from one person to another, in consideration of a sum of money, as opposed to barter exchanges and gifts (Jowitt's Dictionary of English Law). *For the fraudulent sale of real property, see FRAUD, 9. For the sale of automobile master keys, see BREAKING AND ENTERING, 9.*

SCIENTER. 1. Knowingly (Latin). 2. An allegation in a pleading that a defendant or an accused did a thing knowingly (Jowitt's Dictionary of English Law).

SCILICET (SC). "That is to say" (Latin).

SCINTILLA OF EVIDENCE. A very insignificant particle of evidence.

SEARCH AND SEIZURE

1. *Unreasonable search and seizure*
2. *Admissibility of illegally obtained evidence*
3. *Search warrants*
4. *Telewarrants*
5. *Execution of search warrants*
6. *Firearms and other offensive weapons*
7. *Obscene publications*
8. *Timber*
9. *Disorderly houses*
10. *Precious metals*

1. Unreasonable search and seizure

The Canadian Charter of Rights and Freedoms provides that everyone has the right to be secure against unreasonable search or seizure (Charter, s. 8). In the absence of lawful authority, every entry into private property is a trespass, and every removal of the property of another is a tort (B.A.C.M. on Criminal Procedure, p. 19).

A search is unreasonable where there exists no factual basis for the peace officer to say that he has reasonable and probable cause to search a place.

A warrantless search is *prima facie* unreasonable. Prior authorization, usually in the form of a valid search warrant, has been a consistent prerequisite for a valid search and seizure both at common law and under most statutes (Hunter v. Southam Inc. (1984), 14 C.C.C. (3d) 97 (S.C.C.)).

2. Admissibility of illegally obtained evidence

The Canadian Charter of Rights and Freedoms provides that where a court concludes that evidence was obtained in a manner that infringed or denied any rights or freedoms guaranteed by the Charter, the evidence is to be excluded if it is established that, having regard to all the circumstances, the admission of it in the proceedings could bring the administration of justice into disrepute (Charter, s. 24(2) and R. v. Collins (1987), 56 C.R. (3d) 193 (S.C.C.)).

3. Search warrants

Information on Oath. Most search warrants are issued pursuant to s. 487(1) of the Criminal Code, which provides that a justice of the peace or provincial court judge may issue a search warrant in Form 5 based upon an information on oath in Form 1.

Reasonable grounds. The person laying the information must state his grounds for believing that there is evidence of an offence in the building, receptacle or place named. The grounds must be reasonable (s. 487(1)).

Evidence of an offence. A search warrant may be issued for: (a) anything on or in respect of which any Criminal Code offence or any other federal offence has been or is suspected to have been committed; (b) anything that there are reasonable grounds to believe will afford evidence with respect to the commission of a Criminal Code offence or any other federal offence; or (c) anything that there are reasonable grounds to believe is intended to be used for the purpose of committing any offence against the person for which a person may be arrested without warrant (s. 487(1)).

Contents of search warrant. The warrant authorizes the person named therein or a peace officer to search the building, receptacle or place for evidence and to seize it (s. 487(1)(d)).

Steps to be taken after execution of search warrant. As soon as practicable after evidence has been seized, the person or peace officer who seized the evidence must either bring it before a justice or make a report about it to a justice (s. 487(1)(e)).

Where search to be conducted in another territorial jurisdiction. Where the building, receptacle or place to be searched is not in the territorial jurisdiction of the justice issuing the warrant, it must be endorsed in Form 28 by a local justice before it can be enforced (s. 487(2) and (4)).

Information for general warrant. A provincial court judge, a judge of a superior court of criminal jurisdiction or a judge as defined in s. 552 may issue a warrant in writing authorizing a peace officer to, subject to this section, use any device or investigative technique or procedure or do any thing described in the warrant that would, if not authorized, constitute an unreasonable search or seizure in respect of a person or a person's property if (a) the judge is satisfied by information on oath in writing that there are reasonable grounds to believe that an offence against this or any other Act of Parliament has been or will be committed and that information concerning the offence will be obtained through the use of the technique, procedure or device or the doing of the thing; (b) the judge is satisfied that it is in the best interests of the administration of justice to issue the warrant; and (c) there is no other provision in this or any other Act of Parliament that would provide for a warrant, authorization or order permitting the technique, procedure or device to be used or the thing to be done (s. 487.01(1)).

Nothing shall be construed as to permit interference with the bodily integrity of any person (s. 487.01(2)).

A warrant issued shall contain such terms and conditions as the judge considers advisable to ensure that any search or seizure authorized by the warrant is reasonable in the circumstances (s. 487.01(3)).

A warrant issued that authorizes a peace officer to observe, by means of a television camera or other similar electronic device, any person who is engaged in activity in circumstances in which the person has a reasonable expectation of privacy shall contain such terms and conditions as the judge considers advisable to ensure that the privacy of the person or of any other person is respected as much as possible (s. 487.01(4)).

Where an authorization is given under ss. 184.2, 184.3, 186 or 188, a warrant is issued under ss. 487.01, 492.1 or 492.2(1) or an order is made under s. 492.2(2), the judge or justice who gives the authorization, issues the warrant or makes the order may order any person to provide assistance where the person's assistance may reasonably be considered to be required to give effect to the authorization, warrant or order (s. 487.02).

Where a warrant is issued under ss. 487.01, 492.1, or 492.2(1) in one province but it may reasonably be expected that it is to be executed in another province and the execution of the warrant would require entry into or upon the property of any person in the other province or would require that an order under s. 487.02 be made with respect to any person in that other province, a judge or justice, as the case may be, in the other province may, on application, confirm the warrant and when the warrant is so confirmed, it shall have full force and effect in that other province as though it had originally been issued in that other province (s. 487.03).

Seizure of things not specified. Every person who executes a search warrant may seize, in addition to the things mentioned in the warrant, any thing that the person believes on reasonable grounds has been obtained by or has been used in the commission of an offence (s. 489).

4. Telewarrants

Information on oath by telephone. Where a peace officer believes that an indictable offence has been committed and that it would be impracticable to appear personally before a justice to make application for a warrant, the peace officer may submit an information on oath by telephone or other means of telecommunication to a justice designated for the purpose by the chief judge of the provincial court having jurisdiction in the matter (s. 487.1(1)). An information submitted by telephone or other means of telecommunication shall be on oath and shall be recorded verbatim by the justice who shall, as soon as practicable, cause to be filed with the clerk of the court for the territorial division in which the warrant is intended for execution the record or a transcription thereof, certified by the justice as to time, date and contents (s. 487.1(2)). For this purpose the oath may be administered by telephone or other means of telecommunication (s. 487.1(3)).

An information on oath submitted by telephone or other means of telecommunication shall include

(a) a statement of the circumstances that make it impracticable for the peace officer to appear personally before a justice;

(b) a statement of the indictable offence alleged, the place or premises to be searched and the items alleged to be liable to seizure;

(c) a statement of the peace officer's grounds for believing that items liable to seizure in respect of the offence alleged will be found in the place or premises to be searched; and

(d) a statement as to any prior application for a warrant under this section or any other search warrant, in respect of the same matter, of which the peace officer has knowledge (s. 487.1(4)).

A justice who is satisfied that an information on oath submitted by telephone or other means of telecommunication

(a) is in respect of an indictable offence and conforms to the necessary requirements,

(b) discloses reasonable grounds for dispensing with an information presented personally and in writing, and

(c) discloses reasonable grounds for the issuance of a warrant in respect of an indictable offence,

may issue a warrant to a peace officer conferring the same authority respecting search and seizure as may be conferred by a warrant issued by a justice before whom the peace officer appears personally and may require that the warrant be executed within such time period as the justice may order (s. 487.1(5)).

Where a justice issues a warrant by telephone or other means of telecommunication,

(a) a justice shall complete and sign the warrant in Form 5.1, noting on its face the time, date and place of issuance;

(b) the peace officer, on the direction of the justice, shall complete, in duplicate, a facsimile of the warrant in Form 5.1, noting on its face the name of the issuing justice and the time, date and place of issuance; and

(c) the justice shall, as soon as practicable after the warrant has been issued, cause the warrant to be filed with the clerk of the court for the territorial division in which the warrant is intended for execution (s. 487.1(6)).

Steps to be taken after search warrant executed. A peace officer to whom a warrant is issued by telephone or other means of telecommunication shall file a written report with the clerk of the court for the territorial division in which the warrant was intended for execution as soon as practicable but within a period not exceeding seven days after the warrant has been executed, which report shall include

(a) a statement of the time and date the warrant was executed or, if the warrant was not executed, a statement of the reasons why it was not executed;

(b) a statement of the things, if any, that were seized pursuant to the warrant and the location where they are being held; and

(c) a statement of the things, if any, that were seized in addition to the things mentioned in the warrant and the location where they are being held, together with a statement of the peace officer's grounds for believing that those additional things had been obtained by, or used in, the commission of an offence (s. 487.1(9)).

The clerk of the court with whom a written report is filed shall, as soon as practicable, cause the report, together with the information on oath and the warrant to which it pertains, to be brought before a justice to be dealt with, in respect of the things seized referred to in the report, in the same manner as if the things were seized pursuant to a warrant issued, on an information presented personally by a peace officer, by that justice or another justice for the same territorial division (s. 487.1(10)).

Proof of authorization. In any proceeding in which it is material for a court to be satisfied that a search or seizure was authorized by a warrant issued by telephone or other means of telecommunication, the absence of the information on oath, transcribed and certified by the justice as to time, date and contents, or of the original warrant, signed by the justice and carrying on its face a notation of the time, date and place of issuance, is, in the absence of evidence to the contrary, proof that the search or seizure was not authorized by a warrant issued by telephone or other means of telecommunication (s. 487.1(11)).

5. Execution of search warrants

A search warrant shall be executed by day, unless the justice has by the warrant authorized its execution by night (s. 488).

A peace officer who executes a warrant issued by telephone or other means of telecommunication shall, before entering the place or premises to be searched or as soon as practicable thereafter, give a facsimile of the warrant to any person present and ostensibly in control of the place or premises (s. 487.1(7)).

A peace officer who, in any unoccupied place or premises, executes a warrant issued by telephone or other means of telecommunication shall, on entering the place or premises or as soon as practicable thereafter, cause a facsimile of the warrant to be suitably affixed in a prominent place within the place or premises (s. 487.1(8)).

6. Firearms and other offensive weapons

Search and seizure with warrant. Where, on application to a justice made by a peace officer with respect to any person, the justice is satisfied that there are reasonable grounds for believing that it is not desirable in the interests of the safety of that person, or of any other person, that that person possess, or have custody or control of, any firearm or other offensive weapon or any ammunition or explosive substance, the justice may issue a warrant authorizing the search for and seizure of any firearm or other offensive weapon or any ammunition, explosive substance, authorization referred to in s. 90(3.2), firearms acquisition certificate, registration certificate issued under s. 109 or permit issued under s. 110, in the possession, custody or control of that person (s. 103(1)).

However, where, with respect to any person, a peace officer is satisfied that there are reasonable grounds for believing that it is not desirable in the interests of the safety of that person, or of any other person, that that person possess, or have custody or control of, any firearm or other offensive weapon or any ammunition or explosive substance, the peace officer may, where the conditions for obtaining a warrant under subsection (1) exist but by reason of a possible danger to the safety of that person or any other person, it would not be practicable to obtain a warrant, search for and seize any firearm or other offensive weapon or any ammunition, explosive substance, authorization referred to s. 90(3.2), firearms acquisition certificate, registration certificate issued under s. 109 or permit issued under s. 110, in the possession, custody or control of that person (s. 103(2)).

A peace officer who executes a warrant referred to in subsection (1) or who conducts a search without warrant under subsection (2) shall forthwith make a return to the justice by whom the warrant was issued, or if no warrant was issued, to a justice by whom a warrant might have issued showing

(a) in the case of an execution of a warrant, the articles, if any, seized and the date of execution of the warrant; and
(b) in the case of a search without warrant, the grounds on which it was concluded that the peace officer was entitled to conduct the search and the articles, if any, seized (s. 103(3)).

Where a peace officer who performs a seizure under subsection (1) or (2) is unable to seize an authorization referred to in s. 90(3.2), a firearms acquisition certificate, a registration certificate issued under s. 109 or a permit issued under s. 110, the authorization, firearms acquisition certificate, registration certificate or permit is automatically revoked (s. 103(3.1)).

Where any articles have been seized pursuant to subsection (1) or (2), the justice by whom a warrant was issued or, if no warrant was issued, a justice by whom a warrant might have been issued shall, on application for an order for the disposition of the articles so seized made by the peace officer within 30 days after the date of execution of the warrant or of the seizure without warrant, as the case may be, fix a date for the hearing of the application and direct that notice of the hearing be given to such persons or in such manner as the justice may specify (s. 103(4)).

A justice may proceed to hear and determine an application under subsection (4) in the absence of the person against whom the order is sought in circumstances in which a summary conviction court may, pursuant to Part XXVII, proceed with a trial in the absence of the defendant as fully and effectually as if the defendant had appeared (s. 103(4.1)).

At the hearing of an application under subsection (4), the justice shall hear all relevant evidence, including evidence respecting the value of the articles in respect of which the application was made (s. 103(5)).

If, following the hearing of an application under subsection (4) made with respect to any person, the justice finds that it is not desirable in the interests of the safety of that person or of any other person that that person should possess, or have custody or control of, any firearm or other offensive weapon or any ammunition or explosive substance, the justice may

> (a) order that any or all of the articles seized be disposed of on such terms as the justice deems fair and reasonable, and give such directions concerning the payment or application of the proceeds, if any, of the disposition as the justice sees fit; and
> (b) where the justice is satisfied that the circumstances warrant such action,
>> (i) order that the possession by that person of any firearm or other offensive weapon or any ammunition or explosive substance specified in the order, or of all such articles, be prohibited during any period, not exceeding 5 years, specified in the order and computed from the day on which the order is made, and
>> (ii) order that any firearms acquisition certificate issued to the person be revoked and prohibit the person from applying

for a firearms acquisition certificate for any period referred to in subparagraph (i) (s. 103(6)).

Otherwise, the firearms, etc.... are to be returned.

Search and seizure without warrant. Whenever a peace officer believes on reasonable grounds that an offence is being committed or has been committed against any of the provisions of this Act relating to prohibited weapons, restricted weapons, firearms or ammunition and that evidence of the offence is likely to be found on a person, in a vehicle or in any place or premises other than a dwelling-house, the peace officer may, where the conditions for obtaining a warrant exist but, by reason of exigent circumstances, it would not be practicable to obtain a warrant, search, without warrant, the person, vehicle, place or premises, and may seize anything by means of or in relation to which that officer believes on reasonable grounds the offence is being committed or has been committed (s. 101(1)).

A peace officer who finds either

(a) a person in possession of any restricted weapon who fails then and there to produce, for inspection by the peace officer, a registration certificate or permit under which he may lawfully possess the weapon,
(b) a person under the age of 16 years in possession of any firearm who fails then and there to produce, for inspection by the peace officer, a permit under which he may lawfully possess the firearm, or
(c) any person in possession of a prohibited weapon,

may, unless possession of the restricted weapon, firearm or prohibited weapon by the person in the circumstances in which it is so found is authorized by any provision of Part III, seize the restricted weapon, firearm or prohibited weapon (s. 102(1)). A person under the age of 18 years is authorized to be in possession of a firearm where (a) the person is under the direct and immediate supervision of another person who may lawfully possess the firearm; or (b) the person possesses a permit under which the person may lawfully possess the firearm (s. 102(1.1)). Where a person from whom a restricted weapon, firearm or prohibited weapon was seized under subsection (1), within 14 days after the seizure, claims it and produces for inspection by the peace officer by whom it was seized, or any other peace officer having custody thereof, a registration certificate or permit under which the person from whom the seizure was made is lawfully entitled to possess the restricted weapon, firearm or prohibited weapon, the restricted weapon, firearm or prohibited weapon shall forthwith be returned to that person (s. 102(2)). Where any restricted weapon, firearm or prohibited weapon that was seized is not returned, a peace officer shall forthwith take it before a provincial court judge who may, after affording the person from whom it was seized or the owner thereof, if known, an opportunity to establish that he is lawfully entitled to the possession thereof, declare it to be forfeited to Her Majesty, whereupon it shall be disposed of as the Attorney General directs (s. 102(3)).

7. Obscene publications

Warrant of seizure. A judge who is satisfied by information on oath that there are reasonable grounds for believing that (a) any publication, copies of which are kept for sale or distribution in premises within the jurisdiction of the court, is obscene or a crime comic, within the meaning of s. 163, or (b) any representation or written material, copies of which are kept in premises within the jurisdiction of the court, is child pornography within the meaning of s. 163.1, shall issue a warrant authorizing seizure of the copies (s. 164(1)).

Forfeiture proceedings. Within 7 days of the issue of a warrant, the judge shall issue a summons to the occupier of the premises requiring him to appear before the court and show cause why the matter seized should not be forfeited to Her Majesty (s. 164(2)).

The owner and the maker of the matter seized, and alleged to be obscene, a crime comic or child pornography, may appear and be represented in the proceedings in order to oppose the making of an order for the forfeiture of the matter (s. 164(3)).

If the court is satisfied that the publication, representation or written material is obscene, a crime comic or child pornography, it shall make an order declaring the matter forfeited to Her Majesty in right of the province in which the proceedings take place, for disposal as the Attorney General may direct (s. 164(4)).

Restoration of property. If the court is not satisfied that the publication, representation or written material is obscene, a crime comic or child pornography, it shall order that the matter be restored to the person from whom it was seized forthwith after the time for final appeal was expired (s. 164(5)).

8. Timber

A peace officer who suspects, on reasonable grounds, that any lumber owned by any person and bearing the registered timber mark of that person is kept or detained in or on any place without the knowledge or consent of that person, may enter into or on that place to ascertain whether or not it is detained there without the knowledge or consent of that person (s. 339(3)).

9. Disorderly houses

Warrant to search. A justice who receives from a peace officer a report in writing that he believes on reasonable grounds that one of the following offences is being committed at any place within the jurisdiction of the justice may issue a warrant under his hand authorizing a peace officer to enter and search the place by day or night:

keeping gaming or betting house (s. 201)
betting (s. 202)
placing bets (s. 203)
lotteries and games of chance (s. 206 and s. 207) or
keeping common bawdy house (s. 210).

During the search, the peace officer may seize anything that may be evidence that such an offence was being committed at that place, and to take into custody all persons who are found in or at that place and requiring those persons and things to be brought before him or before another justice having jurisdiction, to be dealt with according to law (s. 199(1)).

The Ontario High Court has ruled this section to be of no force and effect by reason of its inconsistency with the protection against unreasonable search and seizure in s. 8 of the Charter (Re Vella (1984), 14 C.C.C. (3d) 513 (Ont. H.C.)).

Search without warrant, seizure and arrest. A peace officer may, whether or not he is acting under a warrant issued pursuant to this section, take into custody any person whom he finds keeping a common gaming house and any person whom he finds therein, and may seize anything that may be evidence that such an offence is being committed and shall bring those persons and things before a justice having jurisdiction, to be dealt with according to law (s. 199(2)).

Disposal of property seized. Except where otherwise expressly provided by law, a court, judge, justice or provincial court judge before whom anything that is seized is brought may declare that the thing is forfeited, in which case it shall be disposed of or dealt with as the Attorney General may direct if no person shows sufficient cause why it should not be forfeited (s. 199(3)). However, no declaration or direction shall be made in respect of anything seized under this section until (a) it is no longer required as evidence in any proceedings that are instituted pursuant to the seizure; or (b) the expiration of 30 days from the time of seizure where it is not required as evidence in any proceedings (s. 199(4)).

The Attorney General may, for the purpose of converting anything forfeited under this section into money, deal with it in all respects as if he were the owner thereof (s. 199(5)).

10. Precious metals

Search. Where an information in writing is laid under oath before a justice by any person having an interest in a mining claim, that any precious metals or rock, mineral or other substance containing precious metals is unlawfully deposited in any place or held by any person contrary to law, the justice may issue a warrant to search any of the places or persons mentioned in the information (s. 395(1)).

Seizure. Where, on search, any unlawfully deposited or held precious metals etc. . . . is found, it shall be seized and carried before the justice who shall order (a) that it be detained for the purposes of an inquiry or a trial; or (b) if it is not detained for the purposes of an inquiry or trial, (i) that it be restored to the owner, or (ii) that it be forfeited to Her Majesty in right of the province in which the proceedings take place if the owner cannot be ascertained (s. 395(2)).

SECOND OFFENCE. There are a number of instances where the punishment provided for the offence, e.g., impaired driving, is greater where the accused has previously been convicted of a similar offence. The fact that a previous conviction may be alleged must not be shown on the information or indictment (s. 664 and s. 789). But notice must be served upon the accused prior to plea that greater punishment will be sought by reason of a previous conviction. If this is done and the accused is convicted as charged, he may be asked whether he was previously convicted. If he denies this, then evidence may be adduced to prove previous convictions (s. 665). Such may be proved by certificate purporting to be signed by the person who made the conviction or the clerk of the court or by a fingerprint examiner (s. 667). If it is intended to prove a previous conviction by a certificate, reasonable notice must be given to the accused, together with a copy of the certificate (s. 667(4)). A fingerprint examiner must be a person specially designated by the Solicitor General of Canada (s. 667(5)).

SECRET COMMISSIONS

Section 426(1)(a) and (3)

Every one who — corruptly — either gives or offers or agrees to give or offer to an agent — or being an agent — demands or accepts or offers or agrees to accept from any person — any reward or advantage or benefit or any kind — as consideration for doing or forbearing to do, or for having done or forborne to do, any act relating to the affairs or business of his principal — or as consideration for showing or forbearing to show favour or disfavour to any person with relation — to the affairs or business of his principal — is guilty of an indictable offence.

Section 426(1)(b) and (3)

Every one who — with intent to deceive a principal — gives to an agent of that principal — or, being an agent — with intent to deceive his principal — uses a receipt of account or other writing — in which the principal has an interest — and that contains any statement that is false or erroneous or defective in any material particular — and that is intended to mislead the principal — is guilty of an indictable offence.

Section 426(2) and (3)

Every one who — knowingly — is privy to the commission of such offence — is guilty of an indictable offence.

Intent. Corruptly (s. 426(1)(a)); intention to deceive (s. 426(1)(b)); knowingly (s. 426(2)).

Included offences. Attempts (s. 660 and s. 662(1)(b)).

Punishment. Imprisonment for a term not exceeding 5 years (s. 426(3)).

Release. Initial decision to release made by officer in charge or justice (s. 498).

Election. Accused may elect trial by judge and jury, judge alone, or provincial court judge (s. 536).

Definitions. For these purposes, "agent" includes an employee and "principal" includes an employer (s. 426(4)).

Evidence. 1. This offence is directed at secret transactions with an agent concerning the affairs of his principal. It is no defence that the

accused believed he had a right to have the thing done by the agent's principal.
2. The intention of corrupt payments may be inferred from proven facts.

SECRETOR. An individual secreting blood group substances in the body fluids and secretions such as milk, saliva and seminal fluid. About 80 per cent of the population are secretors (Jaffe, A Guide to Pathological Evidence, 2nd ed.).

SED QUAERE. "But this is open to question" (Latin).

SEDATIVE. A drug which allays excitement. Sedatives include the barbiturates, bromides and chloral hydrate. In large doses sedatives may act as hypnotics (Jaffe, A Guide to Pathological Evidence, 2nd ed.).

SEDITION

1. *Definitions*
2. *Seditious offences*
3. *Offences in relation to members of military forces*

See also MILITARY FORCES.

1. Definitions

"Seditious conspiracy". An agreement between two or more persons to carry out a seditious intention (s. 59(3)).

"Seditious intention". Without limiting the generality of the meaning of "seditious intention", every one shall be presumed to have a seditious intention who (a) teaches or advocates, or (b) publishes or circulates any writing that advocates, the use, without the authority of law, of force as a means of accomplishing a governmental change within Canada (s. 59(4)).

Notwithstanding the preceding statement, no person shall be deemed to have a seditious intention by reason only that he intends, in good faith,

(a) to show that Her Majesty has been misled or mistaken in her measures;

(b) to point out errors or defects in the government or constitution of Canada or a province, Parliament or the legislature of a province, or the administration of justice in Canada;

(c) to procure, by lawful means, the alteration of any matter of government in Canada; or
(d) to point out, for the purpose of removal, matters that produce or tend to produce feelings of hostility and ill will between different classes of persons in Canada (s. 60).

"Seditious libel". A libel that expresses a seditious intention (s. 59(2)).

"Seditious words". Words that express a seditious intention (s. 59(1)).

2. Seditious offences

Section 61(a)

Every one who — speaks seditious words — is guilty of an indictable offence.

Section 61(b)

Every one who — publishes — a seditious libel — is guilty of an indictable offence.

Section 61(c)

Every one who — is a party to — a seditious conspiracy — is guilty of an indictable offence.

Jurisdiction. Triable only in a superior court of criminal jurisdiction (s. 468 and s. 469(a)(v)).

Included offences. Attempts (s. 660 and s. 662(1)(b)).

Punishment. Imprisonment for a term not exceeding 14 years (s. 61).

Release. Initial decision to release may only be made by superior court judge (s. 522).

Election. Superior court (with jury) exclusive, except where accused elects superior court trial without jury with consent of Attorney General (s. 473) (s. 469).

Sufficiency of count. 1. No count for publishing a seditious libel is insufficient by reason only that it does not set out the words that are alleged to be libellous (s. 584(1)).
2. A count for publishing a libel may charge that the published matter was written in a sense that by innuendo made the publication thereof criminal, and may specify that sense without any introductory assertion to show how the matter was written in that sense (s. 584(2)).

3. It is sufficient, on the trial of a count for publishing a libel, to prove that the matter published was libellous, with or without innuendo (s. 584(3)).

Informations

A.B., on or about the —— day of ——, 19——, at the —— of ——, in the said (territorial division), did speak seditious words [OR did publish a seditious libel OR was a party to a seditious conspiracy], to wit: (specify the particulars of the offence), contrary to s. 61(a) [OR (b) or (c)] of the Criminal Code of Canada.

3. Offences in relation to members of military forces

Section 62(1)(a)

Every one who — wilfully — interferes with or impairs or influences — the loyalty or discipline — of a member of a force — is guilty of an indictable offence.

Section 62(1)(b)

Every one who — wilfully — publishes or edits or issues or circulates or distributes a writing — that advises or counsels or urges insubordination or disloyalty or mutiny or refusal of duty by a member of a force — is guilty of an indictable offence.

Section 62(1)(c)

Every one who — wilfully — advises or counsels or urges or in any manner causes — insubordination or disloyalty or mutiny or refusal of duty by a member of a force — is guilty of an indictable offence.

Intent. Wilfully.

Included offences. Attempts (s. 660 and s. 662(1)(b)).

Punishment. Imprisonment for a term not exceeding 5 years (s. 62(1)).

Release. Initial decision to release made by officer in charge or justice (s. 498).

Election. Accused may elect trial by judge and jury, judge alone, or provincial court judge (s. 536).

Definitions. For these purposes, "member of a force" means a member of the Canadian Forces, or the naval, army or air forces of a state other than Canada that are lawfully present in Canada (s. 62(2)).

Informations

A.B., on or about the —— day of ——, 19——, at the —— of ——, in the said (territorial division), wilfully did interfere with [OR impair OR influence] the loyalty [OR discipline] of a member of the Canadian forces [OR a member of the naval (OR army OR air) forces of (specify a state other than Canada) lawfully present in Canada], to wit: (specify the particulars of the offence), contrary to s. 62(1)(a) of the Criminal Code of Canada.

A.B., on or about the —— day of ——, 19——, at the —— of ——, in the said (territorial division), wilfully did publish [OR edit OR issue OR circulate OR distribute] a writing that advises [OR counsels OR urges] insubordination [OR disloyalty OR mutiny OR refusal of duty] by a member of the Canadian forces [OR a member of the naval (OR army OR air) forces of (specify a state other than Canada) lawfully present in Canada] to wit: (specify the particulars of the offence), contrary to s. 62(1)(b) of the Criminal Code of Canada.

A.B., on or about the —— day of ——, 19——, at the —— of ——, in the said (territorial division), wilfully did advise [OR counsel OR urge OR cause] insubordination [OR disloyalty OR mutiny OR refusal of duty] by a member of the Canadian forces [OR a member of the naval (OR army OR air) forces of (specify a state other than Canada) lawfully present in Canada], to wit: (specify the particulars of the offence), contrary to s. 62(1)(c) of the Criminal Code of Canada.

SEGMENTATION. Numerous transverse interruptions of the blood column in the blood vessels of the eye grounds. It has been regarded as one of the earliest signs of death. Also box-car sign (Jaffe, A Guide to Pathological Evidence, 2nd ed.).

SELF-DEFENCE. A good defence to a charge of crime provided no more violence is used than is necessary for self-preservation. A person attacked may do more than ward off the blow, he may strike back, but an attacked person would not be justified in using a knife against an unarmed assailant. A person is likewise permitted to use force to resist the taking unlawfully of things legally in his possession (ss. 34-42).

SELL. For the purposes of the Criminal Code, "sell" includes offer for sale, expose for sale, have in possession for sale or distribute or advertise for sale (s. 183).

SEMEN. A viscous fluid ejected from the penis during orgasm and consisting of spermatoza derived from the testis and of secretions of the prostate gland and seminal vesicles. Also seminal fluid (Jaffe, A Guide to Pathological Evidence, 2nd ed.).

SEX CHROMATIN. A particle of chromatin present only in cell nuclei of female individuals. It represents one of the X chromosomes and has been used to determine the sex of fragmentary human remains. Chromatin is the carrier of genetic information (Jaffe, A Guide to Pathological Evidence, 2nd ed.).

SEXUAL ASSAULT

1. *Sexual assault*
2. *Sexual assault — With a weapon*
3. *Sexual assault — Threats to a third party*
4. *Sexual assault — Causing bodily harm*
5. *Sexual assault — Party to the offence*
6. *Aggravated sexual assault*
7. *Removal of child from Canada*
8. *Evidence of sexual activity*
9. *Consent*

See also ASSAULT, BINDING OVER TO KEEP THE PEACE, SEXUAL OFFENCES.

1. Sexual assault

Definition of offence — Section 265(1)

A person commits an assault when

(a) without the consent of another person, he applies force intentionally to that other person, directly or indirectly;
(b) he attempts or threatens, by an act or a gesture, to apply force to another person, if he has, or causes that other person to believe on reasonable grounds that he has, present ability to effect his purpose; or
(c) while openly wearing or carrying a weapon or an imitation thereof, he accosts or impedes another person or begs.

This definition applies to all forms of assault, including sexual assault, sexual assault with a weapon, threats to a third party or causing bodily harm and aggravated sexual assault (s. 265(2)).

Statement of offence — Section 271(1)

Every one who — commits a sexual assault — is guilty of either an indictable offence or an offence punishable on summary conviction.

Limitation period. No proceedings in respect of offences that are declared to be punishable on summary conviction shall be instituted more than 6 months after the time when the subject matter of the proceedings arose (s. 786(2) and s. 785(1)).

Included offences. Attempts (s. 660 and s. 662(1)(b)).

Punishment. On indictment, imprisonment for a term not exceeding 10 years (s. 271(1)(a)). On summary conviction, a fine not exceeding $2,000, or 6 months' imprisonment, or both (s. 271(1)(b) and s. 787(1)).

Release. Initial decision to release made by peace officer (s. 497).

Election. On indictment, accused may elect trial by judge and jury, judge alone, or provincial court judge (s. 536). On summary conviction, no election.

Defences. 1. Where an accused is charged with this offence in respect of a complainant under the age of 14 years, it is not a defence that the complainant consented to the activity that forms the subject matter of the charge (s. 150.1(1)).
2. Where an accused is charged with this offence in respect of a complainant who is 12 years of age or more but under the age of 14 years, it is not a defence that the complainant consented to the activity that forms the subject matter of the charge unless the accused (a) is 12 years of age or more but under the age of 16 years; (b) is less than 2 years older that the complainant; and (c) is neither in a position of trust or authority towards the complainant nor is a person with whom the complainant is in a relationship of dependency (s. 150.1(2)).
3. It is not a defence to a charge under this offence that the accused believed that the complainant was 14 years of age or more at the time the offence is alleged to have been committed unless the accused took all reasonable steps to ascertain the age of the complainant (s. 150.1(4)).
4. *See item 2., under* **9**, *below.*

Evidence. 1. No consent is obtained where the complainant submits or does not resist by reason of (a) the application of force to the complainant or to a person other than the complainant; (b) threats or fear of the application of force to the complainant or to a person other than the complainant; (c) fraud; or (d) the exercise of authority (s. 265(3)).
2. Where an accused alleges that he believed that the complainant consented to the conduct that is the subject matter of the charge, a

judge, if satisfied that there is sufficient evidence and that, if believed by the jury, the evidence would constitute a defence, shall instruct the jury, when reviewing all the evidence relating to the determination of the honesty of the accused's belief, to consider the presence or absence of reasonable grounds for that belief (s. 265(4)).
3. Where an accused is charged with this offence, no corroboration is required for a conviction and the judge shall not instruct the jury that it is unsafe to find the accused guilty in the absence of corroboration (s. 274).
4. The rules relating to evidence of recent complaint with respect to sexual assault cases have been abrogated (s. 275).
5. The wife or husband of a person charged with this offence is a competent and compellable witness for the prosecution without the consent of the person charged (Canada Evidence Act, s. 4(2)).
6. A husband or wife may be charged with an offence relating to sexual assault in respect of his or her spouse whether or not the spouses were living together at the time the activity that forms the subject matter of the charge occurred (s. 278).
7. *See also* **8** *and* **9**, *item 1., below.*

Informations

A.B., on or about the —— day of ——, 19——, at the —— of ——, in the said (territorial division), did commit a sexual assault on C.D., to wit: (specify the particulars of the offence), contrary to s. 271(1) of the Criminal Code of Canada.

2. Sexual assault — With a weapon — Section 272(a)

Every one who — in committing a sexual assault — carries or uses or threatens to use — a weapon or an imitation thereof — is guilty of an indictable offence.

Included offences. Attempts (s. 660 and s. 662(1)(b)).

Punishment. Imprisonment for a term not exceeding 14 years (s. 272).

Release. Initial decision to release made by justice (s. 515(1)).

Election. Accused may elect trial by judge and jury, judge alone, or provincial court judge (s. 536).

Defences. 1. *See Defences, items 1. and 3., under* **1**, *above.*
2. *See also item 2., under* **9**, *below.*

Evidence. 1. *See Evidence under* **1**, *above.*

2. *See also* **8** *and* **9**, *item 1., below.*

Informations

A.B., on or about the —— day of ——, 19——, at the —— of ——, in the said (territorial division), while committing a sexual assault on C.D., did carry [OR use OR threaten to use] a weapon [OR an imitation of a weapon], to wit: (specify the particulars of the offence), contrary to s. 272(a) of the Criminal Code of Canada.

3. Sexual assault — Threats to a third party — Section 272(b)

Every one who — in committing a sexual assault — threatens to cause bodily harm — to a person other than the complainant — is guilty of an indictable offence.

Included offences. Attempts (s. 660 and s. 662(1)(b)).

Punishment. Imprisonment for a term not exceeding 14 years (s. 272).

Release. Initial decision to release made by justice (s. 515(1)).

Election. Accused may elect trial by judge and jury, judge alone, or provincial court judge (s. 536).

Definitions. *See BODILY HARM.*

Defences. 1. *See Defences, items 1. and 3., under* **1**, *above.*
2. *See also item 2., under* **9**, *below.*

Evidence. 1. *See Evidence under* **1**, *above.*
2. *See also* **8** *and* **9**, *item 1., below.*

Informations

A.B., on or about the —— day of ——, 19——, at the —— of ——, in the said (territorial division), while committing a sexual assault on C.D., did threaten to cause bodily harm to E.F., to wit: (specify the particulars of the offence), contrary to s. 272(b) of the Criminal Code of Canada.

4. Sexual assault — Causing bodily harm — Section 272(c)

Every one who — in committing a sexual assault — causes bodily harm — to the complainant — is guilty of an indictable offence.

Included offences. Attempts (s. 660 and s. 662(1)(b)).

Punishment. Imprisonment for a term not exceeding 14 years (s. 272).

Release. Initial decision to release made by justice (s. 515(1)).

Election. Accused may elect trial by judge and jury, judge alone, or provincial court judge (s. 536).

Definitions. *See BODILY HARM.*

Defences. 1. *See Defences, items 1. and 3., under* **1**, *above.*
2. *See also item 2., under* **9**, *below.*

Evidence. 1. *See Evidence under* **1**, *above.*
2. *See also* **8** *and* **9**, *item 1., below.*

Informations

A.B., on or about the —— day of ——, 19——, at the —— of ——, in the said (territorial division), while committing a sexual assault on C.D., did cause bodily harm to C.D., to wit: (specify the particulars of the offence), contrary to s. 272(c) of the Criminal Code of Canada.

5. Sexual assault — Party to the offence — Section 272(d)

Every one who — in committing a sexual assault — is a party to the offence — with any other person — is guilty of an indictable offence.

Included offences. Attempts (s. 660 and s. 662(1)(b)).

Punishment. Imprisonment for a term not exceeding 14 years (s. 272).

Release. Initial decision to release made by justice (s. 515(1)).

Election. Accused may elect trial by judge and jury, judge alone, or provincial court judge (s. 536).

Defences. 1. See Defences, items 1. and 3., under **1**, *above.*
2. *See also item 2., under* **9** *below.*

Evidence. 1. *See Evidence under* **1**, *above.*
2. *See also* **8** *and* **9**, *item 1., below.*

6. Aggravated sexual assault

Definition of offence — Section 273(1)

Every one who — in committing a sexual assault — wounds or maims or disfigures or endangers the life of — the complainant — commits an aggravated sexual assault.

Statement of offence — Section 273(2)

SEXUAL ASSAULT 589

Every one who — commits an aggravated sexual assault — is guilty of an indictable offence.

Punishment. Imprisonment for life (s. 273(2)).

The sentence to be pronounced against a person who is to be sentenced to imprisonment for life in respect of a person who has been convicted of this offence shall be that he be sentenced to imprisonment for life with normal eligibility for parole (s. 742(c)).

Release. Initial decision to release made by justice (s. 515(1)).

Election. Accused may elect trial by judge and jury, judge alone, or provincial court judge (s. 536).

Defences. 1. See Defences, items 1. and 3., under **1**, *above.*
2. *See also item 2., under* **9**, *below.*

Evidence. 1. *See Evidence under* **1**, *above.*
2. *See also* **8** *and* **9**, item 1., below.

Informations

A.B., on or about the —— day of ——, 19——, at the —— of ——, in the said (territorial division), did commit an aggravated sexual assault on C.D., to wit: (specify the particulars of the offence), contrary to s. 273(2) of the Criminal Code of Canada.

7. Removal of child from Canada

Prohibition — Section 273.3(1)

No person shall — do anything for the purpose of removing from Canada — a person who is ordinarily resident in Canada and who is — under the age of 14 years, with the intention that an act be committed outside Canada that if it were committed in Canada would be an offence against s. 151 (sexual interference) or s. 152 (invitation to sexual touching) or s. 160(3) (bestiality in presence of or by child) or s. 173(2) (exposure) in respect of that person — or over the age of 14 years but under the age of 18 years, with the intention that an act committed outside Canada that if it were committed in Canada would be an offence against s. 153 (sexual exploitation) in respect of that person — or under the age of 18 years, with the intention that an act committed outside Canada that if it were committed in Canada would be an offence against s. 155 (incest) or s. 159 (anal intercourse) or s. 160(2) (compelling bestiality) or s. 170 (parent or guardian procuring sexual activity) or s. 171 (householder permitting

sexual activity) or s. 267 (assault with a weapon or causing bodily harm) or s. 268 (aggravated assault) or s. 269 (unlawfully causing bodily harm) or s. 271 (sexual assault) or s. 272 (sexual assault with a weapon, threats to a third party or causing bodily harm) or s. 273 (aggravated sexual assault) in respect of that person.

Statement of offence — Section 273.3(2)

Every person who — contravenes s. 273.3 — is guilty of either an indictable offence or an offence punishable on summary conviction.

Limitation period. No proceedings in respect of offences that are declared to be punishable on summary conviction shall be instituted more than 6 months after the time when the subject matter of the proceedings arose (s. 786(2) and s. 785(1)).

Included offences. Attempts (s. 660 and s. 662(1)(b)).

Punishment. On indictment, imprisonment for a term not exceeding 5 years (s. 273.3(2)(a)). On summary conviction, a fine not exceeding $2,000, or 6 months' imprisonment, or both (s. 273.3(2)(b) and s. 787(1)).

Release. Initial decision to release made by peace officer (s. 497).

Election. On indictment, accused may elect trial by judge and jury, judge alone, or provincial court judge (s. 536). On summary conviction, no election.

Informations

A.B., on or about the —— day of ——, 19——, at the —— of ——, in the said (territorial division), did contravene s. 273.3(1), to wit: (specify the particulars of the offence), contrary to s. 273.3(2) of the Criminal Code of Canada.

8. Evidence of sexual activity

1. In proceedings in respect of offences relating to sexual assault, evidence that the complainant has engaged in sexual activity, whether with the accused or with any other person, is not admissible to support an inference that, by reason of the sexual nature of that activity, the complainant (a) is more likely to have consented to the sexual activity that forms the subject-matter of the charge; or (b) is less worthy of belief (s. 276(1)). No evidence shall be adduced by or on behalf of the accused that the complainant has engaged in sexual activity other

than the sexual activity that forms the subject-matter of the charge, whether with the accused or with any other person, unless the judge, provincial court judge or justice determines, in accordance with the procedures set out in ss. 276.1 and 276.2, that the evidence (a) is of specific instances of sexual activity; (b) is relevant to an issue at trial;o and (c) has significant probative value that is not substantially outweighed by the danger of prejudice to the proper administration of justice (s. 276(2)).

In determining whether evidence is admissible under s. 276(2), the judge, provincial court judge or justice shall take into account (a) the interests of justice, including the right of the accused to make a full answer and defence; (b) society's interest in encouraging the reporting of sexual assault offences; (c) whether there is a reasonable prospect that the evidence will assist in arriving at a just determination in the case; (d) the need to remove from the fact-finding process any discriminatory belief or bias; (e) the risk that the evidence may unduly arouse sentiments of prejudice, sympathy or hostility in the jury; (f) the potential prejudice to the complainant's personal dignity and right of privacy; (g) the right of the complainant and of every individual to personal security and to the full protection and benefit of the law; and (h) any other factor that the judge, provincial court judge or justice considers relevant (s. 276(3)).

Application may be made to the judge, provincial court judge or justice by or on behalf of the accused for a hearing under s. 276.2 to determine whether evidence is admissible under s. 276(2) (s. 276.2(1)).

An application referred to in s. 276.1(1) must be made in writing and set out (a) detailed particulars of the evidence that the accused seeks to adduce, and (b) the relevance of that evidence to an issue at trial, and a copy of the application must be given to the prosecutor and to the clerk of the court l(s. 276.1(2)). The judge, provincial court judge or justice shall consider the application with the jury and the public excluded (s. 276.1(3)). Where the judge, provincial court judge or justice is satisfied (a) that the application was made in accordance with s. 276.1(2), (b) that a copy of the application was given to the prosecutor and to the clerk of the court at least 7 days previously, or such shorter interval as the judge, provincial court judge or justice may allow where the interests of justice so require, and (c) that the evidence sought to be adduced is capable of being admissible under s. 276(2), the judge, provincial court judge or justice shall grant the application and hold a hearing under s. 276.2 to determine whether the evidence is admissible under s. 276(2) (s. 276.1(4)).

At a hearing to determine whether evidence is admissible under s. 276(2), the jury and the public shall be excluded (s. 276.2(1)). The complainant is not a compellable witness at the hearing (s. 276.2(2)). At the conclusion of the hearing, the judge, provincial court judge or justice shall determine whether the evidence, or any part thereof, is admissible under s. 276(2) and shall provide reasons for that determination, and (a) where not all of the evidence is to be admitted, the reasons must state the part of the evidence that is to be admitted; (b) the reasons must state the factors referred to in s. 276(3) that affected the determination; and (c) where all or any part of the evidence is to be admitted, the reasons must state the manner in which that evidence is expected to be relevant to an issue at trial (s. 276.2(3)). The reasons provided under s. 276.2(3) shall be entered in the record of the proceedings or, where the proceedings are not recorded, shall be provided in writing (s. 276.2(4)).

No person shall publish in a newspaper, as defined in s. 297, or in a broadcast, any of the following: (a) the contents of an application made under s. 276.1; (b) any evidence taken, the information given and the representations made at an application under s. 276.1 or at a hearing under s. 276.2; (c) the decision of a judge, provincial court judge or justice under s. 276.1(4), unless the judge, provincial court judge or justice, after taking into account the complainant's right of privacy and the interests of justice, orders that the decision may be published; and (d) the determination made and the reasons provided under s. 276.2, unless (i) that determination is that evidence is admissible, or (ii) the judge, provincial court judge or justice, after taking into account the complainant's right of privacy and the interests of justice, orders that the determination and reasons may be published (s. 276.3(1)).

For definitions, see NEWSPAPER. Every person who contravenes s. 276.3(1) is guilty of an offence punishable on summary conviction (s. 276.3(2)).

Where evidence is admitted at trial pursuant to a determination made under s. 276.2, the judge shall instruct the jury as to the uses that the jury may and may not make of that evidence (s. 276.4).

For the purposes of ss. 675 and 676, a determination made under s. 276.2 shall be deemed to be a question of law (s. 276.5).

2. In proceedings in respect of any offence relating to sexual assault, evidence of sexual reputation, whether general or specific, is not admissible for the purpose of challenging or supporting the credibility of the complainant (s. 277).

9. Consent

1. Subject to s. 273.1(2) and s. 265(3), "consent" means, for the purposes of ss. 271, 272 and 273, the voluntary agreement of the complainant to engage in the sexual activity in question (s. 273.1(1)).

No consent is obtained, for the purposes of ss. 271, 272 and 273, where (a) the agreement is expressed by the words or conduct of a person other than the complainant; (b) the complainant is incapable of consenting to the activity; (c) the accused induces the complainant to engage in the activity by abusing a position of trust, power or authority; (d) the complainant expresses, by words or conduct, a lack of agreement to engage in the activity; or (e) the complainant, having consented to engage in sexual activity, expresses, by words or conduct, a lack of agreement to continue to engage in the activity (s. 273.1(2)).

Nothing in s. 273.1(2) shall be construed as limiting the circumstances in which no consent is obtained (s. 273.1(3)).

2. It is not a defence to a charge under s. 271, 272 or 273 that the accused believed that the complainant consented to the activity that forms the subject-matter of the charge, where (a) the accused's belief arose from the accused's (i) self-induced intoxication, or (ii) recklessness or wilful blindness; or (b) the accused did not take reasonable steps, in the circumstances known to the accused at the time, to ascertain that the complainant was consenting (s. 273.2).

SEXUAL OFFENCES

1. *Sexual interference*
2. *Invitation to sexual touching*
3. *Sexual exploitation*
4. *Incest*
5. *Anal intercourse*
6. *Bestiality*
7. *Compulsion to commit bestiality*
8. *Bestiality in presence of or by child*
9. *Order of Prohibition*
10. *Person convicted of sexual offence. See VAGRANCY, 2.*
11. *Parent or guardian procuring sexual activity. See CORRUPTING MORALS, 15.*
12. *Householder permitting sexual activity. See CORRUPTING MORALS, 16.*
13. *Corrupting children. See CORRUPTING MORALS, 17.*

See also BINDING OVER TO KEEP THE PEACE, DISORDERLY HOUSES, PROCURING, PROSTITUTION, SEXUAL ASSAULT AND SOLICITING.

1. Sexual interference — Section 151

Every one who — for a sexual purpose — touches, directly or indirectly — with a part of the body or with an object — any part of the body of a person under the age of 14 years — is guilty of either an indictable offence or an offence punishable on summary conviction.

Intent. For sexual purpose.

Exceptions. No person aged 12 or 13 years shall be tried for this offence unless the person is in a position of trust or authority towards the complainant or is a person with whom the complainant is in a relationship of dependency (s. 150.1(3)).

Limitation period. No proceedings in respect of offences that are declared to be punishable on summary conviction shall be instituted more than 6 months after the time when the subject matter of the proceedings arose (s. 786(2) and s. 785(1)).

Included offences. Attempts (s. 660 and s. 662(1)(b)).

Punishment. On indictment, imprisonment for a term not exceeding 10 years (s. 151). On summary conviction, a fine not exceeding $2,000, or 6 months' imprisonment, or both (s. 151 and s. 787(1)).

Release. Initial decision to release made by peace officer (s. 497).

Election. On indictment, accused may elect trial by judge and jury, judge alone, or provincial court judge (s. 536). On summary conviction, no election.

Defences. 1. Where an accused is charged with this offence in respect of a complainant under the age of 14 years, it is not a defence that the complainant consented to the activity that forms the subject matter of the charge (s. 150.1(1)).
2. Where an accused is charged with this offence in respect of a complainant who is 12 years of age or more but under the age of 14 years, it is not a defence that the complainant consented to the activity that forms the subject matter of the charge unless the accused (a) is 12 years of age or more but under the age of 16 years; (b) is less than 2 years older than the complainant; and (c) is neither in a position of trust or authority towards the complainant nor is a person with whom the complainant is in a relationship of dependency (s. 150.1(2)).
3. It is not a defence to a charge under this offence that the accused believed that the complainant was 14 years of age or more at the

time the offence is alleged to have been committed unless the accused took all reasonable steps to ascertain the age of the complainant (s. 150.1(4)).

Evidence. 1. Where an accused is charged with this offence, no corroboration is required for a conviction and the judge shall not instruct the jury that it is unsafe to find the accused guilty in the absence of corroboration (s. 274).
2. The rules relating to evidence of recent complaint are hereby abrogated with respect to this offence (s. 275).
3. In proceedings in respect of this offence, evidence that the complainant has engaged in sexual activity, whether with the accused or with any other person, is not admissible to support an inference that, by reason of the sexual nature of that activity, the complainant (a) is more likely to have consented to the sexual activity that forms the subject-matter of the charge; or (b) is less worthy of belief (s. 276(1)). No evidence shall be adduced by or on behalf of the accused that the complainant has engaged in sexual activity other than the sexual activity that forms the subject-matter of the charge, whether with the accused or with any other person, unless the judge, provincial court judge or justice determines, in accordance with the procedures set out in ss. 276.1 and 276.2, that the evidence (a) is of specific instances of sexual activity; (b) is relevant to an issue at trial;o and (c) has significant probative value that is not substantially outweighed by the danger of prejudice to the proper administration of justice (s. 276(2)).

In determining whether evidence is admissible under s. 276(2), the judge, provincial court judge or justice shall take into account (a) the interests of justice, including the right of the accused to make a full answer and defence; (b) society's interest in encouraging the reporting of sexual assault offences; (c) whether there is a reasonable prospect that the evidence will assist in arriving at a just determination in the case; (d) the need to remove from the fact-finding process any discriminatory belief or bias; (e) the risk that the evidence may unduly arouse sentiments of prejudice, sympathy or hostility in the jury; (f) the potential prejudice to the complainant's personal dignity and right of privacy; (g) the right of the complainant and of every individual to personal security and to the full protection and benefit of the law; and (h) any other factor that the judge, provincial court judge or justice considers relevant (s. 276(3)).

Application may be made to the judge, provincial court judge or justice by or on behalf of the accused for a hearing under s. 276.2

to determine whether evidence is admissible under s. 276(2) (s. 276.2(1)).

An application referred to in s. 276.1(1) must be made in writing and set out (a) detailed particulars of the evidence that the accused seeks to adduce, and (b) the relevance of that evidence to an issue at trial, and a copy of the application must be given to the prosecutor and to the clerk of the court l(s. 276.1(2)). The judge, provincial court judge or justice shall consider the application with the jury and the public excluded (s. 276.1(3)). Where the judge, provincial court judge or justice is satisfied (a) that the application was made in accordance with s. 276.1(2), (b) that a copy of the application was given to the prosecutor and to the clerk of the court at least 7 days previously, or such shorter interval as the judge, provincial court judge or justice may allow where the interests of justice so require, and (c) that the evidence sought to be adduced is capable of being admissible under s. 276(2), the judge, provincial court judge or justice shall grant the application and hold a hearing under s. 276.2 to determine whether the evidence is admissible under s. 276(2) (s. 276.1(4)).

At a hearing to determine whether evidence is admissible under s. 276(2), the jury and the public shall be excluded (s. 276.2(1)). The complainant is not a compellable witness at the hearing (s. 276.2(2)). At the conclusion of the hearing, the judge, provincial court judge or justice shall determine whether the evidence, or any part thereof, is admissible under s. 276(2) and shall provide reasons for that determination, and (a) where not all of the evidence is to be admitted, the reasons must state the part of the evidence that is to be admitted; (b) the reasons must state the factors referred to in s. 276(3) that affected the determination; and (c) where all or any part of the evidence is to be admitted, the reasons must state the manner in which that evidence is expected to be relevant to an issue at trial (s. 276.2(3)). The reasons provided under s. 276.2(3) shall be entered in the record of the proceedings or, where the proceedings are not recorded, shall be provided in writing (s. 276.2(4)).

No person shall publish in a newspaper, as defined in s. 297, or in a broadcast, any of the following: (a) the contents of an application made under s. 276.1; (b) any evidence taken, the information given and the representations made at an application under s. 276.1 or at a hearing under s. 276.2; (c) the decision of a judge, provincial court judge or justice under s. 276.1(4), unless the judge, provincial court judge or justice, after taking into account the complainant's right of privacy and the interests of justice, orders that the decision may be published; and (d) the determination made and the reasons provided under s. 276.2, unless (i) that determination is that evidence is admissible, or (ii) the judge, provincial court judge or justice, after taking into account the complainant's right of privacy and the interests of justice, orders that the determination and reasons may be published (s. 276.3(1)).

For definitions, see NEWSPAPER. Every person who contravenes s. 276.3(1) is guilty of an offence punishable on summary conviction (s. 276.3(2)).

Where evidence is admitted at trial pursuant to a determination made under s. 276.2, the judge shall instruct the jury as to the uses that the jury may and may not make of that evidence (s. 276.4).

For the purposes of ss. 675 and 676, a determination made under s. 276.2 shall be deemed to be a question of law (s. 276.5).

4. In proceedings in respect of this offence, evidence of sexual reputation, whether general or specific, is not admissible for the purpose of challenging or supporting the credibility of the complainant (s. 277).

5. The wife or husband of a person charged with this offence is a competent and compellable witness for the prosecution without the consent of the person charged (Canada Evidence Act, s. 4(2)).

2. Invitation to sexual touching — Section 152

Every one who — for a sexual purpose — invites or counsels or incites — a person under the age of 14 years — to touch, directly or indirectly — with a part of the body or with an object — the body of any person, including the body of the person who so invites or counsels or incites and the body of the person under the age of 14 years — is guilty of either an indictable offence or an offence punishable on summary conviction.

Intent. For sexual purpose.

Exceptions. *See Exceptions under* **1**, *above.*

Limitation period. No proceedings in respect of offences that are declared to be punishable on summary conviction shall be instituted more than 6 months after the time when the subject matter of the proceedings arose (s. 786(2) and s. 785(1)).

Included offences. Attempts (s. 660 and s. 662(1)(b)).

Punishment. On indictment, imprisonment for a term not exceeding 10 years (s. 152). On summary conviction, a fine not exceeding $2,000, or 6 months' imprisonment, or both (s. 152 and s. 787(1)).

Release. Initial decision to release made by peace officer (s. 497).

Election. On indictment, accused may elect trial by judge and jury, judge alone, or provincial court judge (s. 536). On summary conviction, no election.

Defences. See Defences under **1**, *above.*

Evidence. See Evidence under **1**, *above.*

3. Sexual exploitation

Section 153(1)(a)

Every one who — is in a position of trust or authority towards a young person — or is a person with whom the young person is in a relationship of dependency — and for a sexual purpose — touches, directly or indirectly — with a part of the body or with an object — any part of the body of the young person — is guilty of either an indictable offence or an offence punishable on summary conviction.

Section 153(1)(b)

Every one who — is in a position of trust or authority towards a young person — or is a person with whom the young person is in a relationship of dependency — and for a sexual purpose — invites or counsels or incites a young person — to touch, directly or indirectly — with a part of the body or with an object — the body of any person, including the body of the person who so invites or counsels or incites and the body of the young person — is guilty of either an indictable offence or an offence punishable on summary conviction.

Intent. For sexual purpose.

Limitation period. No proceedings in respect of offences that are declared to be punishable on summary conviction shall be instituted more than 6 months after the time when the subject matter of the proceedings arose (s. 786(2) and s. 785(1)).

Included offences. Attempts (s. 660 and s. 662(1)(b)).

Punishment. On indictment, imprisonment for a term not exceeding 5 years (s. 153(1)). On summary conviction, a fine not exceeding $2,000, or 6 months' imprisonment, or both (s. 153(1) and s. 787(1)).

Release. Initial decision to release made by peace officer (s. 497).

Election. On indictment, accused may elect trial by judge and jury, judge alone, or provincial court judge (s. 536). On summary conviction, no election.

Definitions. For these purposes, "young person" means a person 14 years of age or more but under the age of 18 years (s. 153(2)).

Defences. 1. It is not a defence to a charge under this offence that the accused believed that the complainant was 18 years of age or more at the time the offence is alleged to have been committed unless the accused took all reasonable steps to ascertain the age of the complainant (s. 150.1(5)).
2. *See Defences, item 1., under* **1**, *above.*

Evidence. See Evidence under **1**, *above.*

4. Incest

Definition of offence — Section 155(1)

Every one who — knowing that another person is by blood relationship his or her parent or child or brother or sister or grandparent or grandchild (as the case may be) — has sexual intercourse — with that person — commits incest.

Statement of offence — Section 155(2)

Every one who — commits incest — is guilty of an indictable offence.

Intent. Knowledge of relationship.

Included offences. Attempts (s. 660 and s. 662(1)(b)).

Punishment. Imprisonment for 14 years (s. 155(2)).

Release. Initial decision to release made by justice (s. 515(1)).

Election. Accused may elect trial by judge and jury, judge alone, or provincial court judge (s. 536).

Definitions. 1. For these purposes, "brother" includes half-brother (s. 155(4)).
2. For these purposes, "sister" includes half-sister (s. 155(4)).

Defences. No accused shall be found guilty of incest if the accused was under restraint, duress or fear of the person with whom the accused had the sexual intercourse at the time the sexual intercourse occurred (s. 155(3)).

Evidence. See Evidence under **1**, *above.*

Informations

A.B., on or about the —— day of ——, 19——, at the —— of ——, in the said (territorial division), knowing that C.D. was by blood relationship his [OR her] parent [OR child OR brother OR sister OR grandparent OR grandchild] had sexual intercourse with C.D. and did thereby commit incest, to wit: (specify the particulars of the offence), contrary to s. 155(1) of the Criminal Code of Canada.

5. Anal intercourse — Section 159(1)

Every one who — engages in an act of anal intercourse — is guilty of either an indictable offence or an offence punishable on summary conviction.

Exceptions. This offence does not apply to any act engaged in, in private, between either husband and wife, or any two persons, each of whom is 18 years of age or more, both of whom consent to the act (s. 159(2)).

Limitation period. No proceedings in respect of offences that are declared to be punishable on summary conviction shall be instituted more than 6 months after the time when the subject matter of the proceedings arose (s. 786(2) and s. 785(1)).

Included offences. Attempts (s. 660 and s. 662(1)(b)).

Punishment. On indictment, imprisonment for a term not exceeding 10 years (s. 159(1)). On summary conviction, a fine not exceeding $2,000, or 6 months' imprisonment, or both (s. 159(1) and s. 787(1)).

Release. Initial decision to release made by peace officer (s. 497).

Election. On indictment, accused may elect trial by judge and jury, judge alone, or provincial court judge (s. 536). On summary conviction, no election.

Defences. See Defences, item 2., under **3**, *above.*

Evidence. 1. For these purposes, an act shall be deemed not to have been engaged in in private if it is engaged in in a public place or if more than two persons take part or are present (s. 159(3)(a)).
2. For these purposes, a person shall be deemed not to consent to an act if the consent is extorted by force, threats or fear of bodily harm or is obtained by false and fraudulent misrepresentations

respecting the nature and quality of the act, or if the court is satisfied beyond a reasonable doubt that the person could not have consented to the act by reason of mental disability (s. 159(3)(b)).
3. *See Evidence under* **1**, *above.*

6. Bestiality

Definition of "bestiality". Sexual intercourse with an animal (Jaffe, A Guide to Pathological Evidence, 2nd ed.). The term is not defined in the Criminal Code.

Statement of offence — Section 160(1)

Every one who — commits bestiality — is guilty of either an indictable offence or an offence punishable on summary conviction.

Limitation period. No proceedings in respect of offences that are declared to be punishable on summary conviction shall be instituted more than 6 months after the time when the subject matter of the proceedings arose (s. 786(2) and s. 785(1)).

Included offences. Attempts (s. 660 and s. 662(1)(b)).

Punishment. On indictment, imprisonment for a term not exceeding 10 years (s. 160(1)). On summary conviction, a fine not exceeding $2,000, or 6 months' imprisonment, or both (s. 160(1) and s. 787(1)).

Release. Initial decision to release made by peace officer (s. 497).

Election. On indictment, accused may elect trial by judge and jury, judge alone, or provincial court judge (s. 536). On summary conviction, no election.

Evidence. *See Evidence, item 1., under* **1**, *above.*

Informations

A.B., on or about the —— day of ——, 19——, at the —— of ——, in the said (territorial division), did commit bestiality, to wit: (specify the particulars of the offence), contrary to s. 160(1) of the Criminal Code of Canada.

7. Compulsion to commit bestiality — Section 160(2)

Every one who — compels another — to commit bestiality — is guilty of either an indictable offence or an offence punishable on summary conviction.

Limitation period. No proceedings in respect of offences that are declared to be punishable on summary conviction shall be instituted more than 6 months after the time when the subject matter of the proceedings arose (s. 786(2) and s. 785(1)).

Included offences. Attempts (s. 660 and s. 662(1)(b)).

Punishment. On indictment, imprisonment for a term not exceeding 10 years (s. 160(2)). On summary conviction, a fine not exceeding $2,000, or 6 months' imprisonment, or both (s. 160(2) and s. 787(1)).

Release. Initial decision to release made by peace officer (s. 497).

Election. On indictment, accused may elect trial by judge and jury, judge alone, or provincial court judge (s. 536). On summary conviction, no election.

Evidence. *See Evidence under* **1**, *above.*

8. Bestiality in presence of or by child — Section 160(3)

Every one who — commits bestiality — in the presence of a person who is under the age of 14 years — is guilty of either an indictable offence or an offence punishable on summary conviction.

Every one who — incites a person under the age of 14 years — to commit bestiality — is guilty of either an indictable offence or an offence punishable on summary conviction.

Limitation period. No proceedings in respect of offences that are declared to be punishable on summary conviction shall be instituted more than 6 months after the time when the subject matter of the proceedings arose (s. 786(2) and s. 785(1)).

Included offences. Attempts (s. 660 and s. 662(1)(b)).

Punishment. On indictment, imprisonment for a term not exceeding 10 years (s. 160(3)). On summary conviction, a fine not exceeding $2,000, or 6 months' imprisonment, or both (s. 160(3) and s. 787(1)).

Release. Initial decision to release made by peace officer (s. 497).

Election. On indictment, accused may elect trial by judge and jury, judge alone, or provincial court judge (s. 536). On summary conviction, no election.

Defences. *See Defences, items 1. and 3. under* **1**, *above.*

Evidence. *See Evidence under* **1**, *above.*

9. Order of prohibition — Section 161

Order of prohibition. Where an offender is convicted, or is discharged on the conditions prescribed in a probation order under s. 736, of an offence under ss. 151, 152, 155, 159, 160(2), 160(3), 170, 171, 271, 272 or 273, in respect of a person who is under the age of 14 years, the court that sentences the offender or directs that the accused be discharged, as the case may be, in addition to any other punishment that may be imposed for that offence or any other condition prescribed in the order of discharge, shall consider making and may make, subject to the conditions or exemptions that the court directs, an order prohibiting the offender from (a) attending a public park or public swimming area where persons under the age of 14 years are present or can reasonably be expected to be present, or a daycare centre, schoolground, playground or community centre; or (b) seeking, obtaining or continuing any employment, whether or not the employment is remunerated, or becoming or being a volunteer in a capacity, that involves being in a position of trust or authority towards persons under the age of 14 years. (s. 161(1)).

The prohibition may be for life or for any shorter duration that the court considers desirable and, in the case of a prohibition that is not for life, the prohibition begins on the later of (a) the date on which the order is made; and (b) where the offender is sentenced to a term of imprisonment, the date on which the offender is released from imprisonment for the offence; including release on parole, mandatory supervision or statutory release. (s. 161(2)).

A court that makes an order of prohibition or, where the court is for any reason unable to act, another court of equivalent jurisdiction in the same province, may, on application of the offender or the prosecutor, require the offender to appear before it at any time and, after hearing the parties, that court may vary the conditions prescribed in the order if, in the opinion of the court, the variation is desirable because of changed circumstances after the conditions were prescribed. (s. 161(3)).

Statement of offence — Section 161(4)

Every person who — is bound by an order of prohibition — and who does not comply with the order — is guilty of either an indictable offence or an offence punishable on summary conviction.

Limitation period. No proceedings in respect of offences that are declared to be punishable on summary conviction shall be instituted

more than 6 months after the time when the subject matter of the proceedings arose (s. 786(2) and s. 785(1)).

Included offences. Attempts (s. 660 and s. 662(1)(b)).

Punishment. On indictment, imprisonment for a term not exceeding 2 years (s. 161(4)(a)). On summary conviction, a fine not exceeding $2,000, or 6 months' imprisonment, or both (s. 161(4)(b) and s. 787(1)).

Release. Initial decision to release made by peace officer (s. 497).

Election. On indictment, accused may elect trial by judge and jury, judge alone, or provincial court judge (s. 536). On summary conviction, no election.

Informations

A.B., on or about the —— day of ——, 19——, at the —— of ——, in the said (territorial division), being bound by an order of prohibition, did not comply with the order, to wit: (specify the particulars of the offence), contrary to s. 161(4) of the Criminal Code of Canada.

SHALL. This expression is to be construed as imperative (Interpretation Act, s. 11).

SHIP. For the purposes of s. 78.1, "ship" means every description of vessel not permanently attached to the seabed, other than a warship, a ship being used as a naval auxiliary or for customs or police purposes or a ship that has been withdrawn from navigation or is laid up (s. 78.1(5)).

SHOCK. A condition characterized by pallor, low blood pressure, rapid but shallow pulse and clammy perspiration (Jaffe, A Guide to Pathological Evidence, 2nd ed.).

Primary shock. A transient loss of consciousness due to fear or violent emotion. Also faint; syncope (Jaffe, A Guide to Pathological Evidence, 2nd ed.).

Secondary shock. A state of shock, often progressing to death, caused by a sudden reduction of circulating blood volume. Also oligemic shock; surgical shock; traumatic shock (Jaffe, A Guide to Pathological Evidence, 2nd ed.).

SIC. So; thus (Latin). *[sic]*. This indicates an apparent error in the text. ***Sic utere tuo ut alienum non laedas.*** "Use your own property so that you do not harm another".

SIMPLICITER. Simply (Latin).

SINE DIE. Without a day being named; indefinitely (Latin).

SINE PROLE. Without issue (Latin).

SINE QUA NON. Indispensable condition or qualification (Latin).

SINGEING. An area of burned skin surrounding the entrance wound of a bullet fired at close range and caused by hot gases escaping from the muzzle. Also branding (Jaffe, A Guide to Pathological Evidence, 2nd ed.).

SITUS. Situation; location (Latin).

SLOT MACHINE. For the purposes of s. 198(2), "slot machine" means any automatic machine or slot machine (a) that is used or intended to be used for any purpose other than vending merchandise or services, or (b) that is used or intended to be used for the purpose of vending merchandise or services if (i) the result of one of any number of operations of the machine is a matter of chance or uncertainty to the operator, (ii) as a result of a given number of successive operations by the operator the machine produces different results, or (iii) on any operation of the machine it discharges or emits a slug or token, but does not include an automatic machine or slot machine that dispenses as prizes only one or more free games on that machine (s. 198(3)).

SMUDGING. An area of blackening produced by powder gases and surrounding the entrance wound of a bullet fired at close range (Jaffe, A Guide to Pathological Evidence, 2nd ed.).

SPONTE SUA. Of one's own accord (Latin).

STAMP. For the purposes of s. 376, "stamp" means an impressed or adhesive stamp used for the purpose of revenue by the Government of Canada or of a province or by the government of a state other than Canada (s. 376(3)). *See also FORGERY AND OFFENCES RESEMBLING FORGERY, 9.*

STARE DECISIS. To abide by authorities or cases already adjudicated upon (Latin).

STATEMENTS. For the purposes of s. 319 (public incitement of hatred and wilful promotion of hatred), "statements" includes words spoken or written or recorded electronically or electro-magnetically or otherwise, and gestures, signs or other visible representations (s. 319(7)).

STATUS QUO. The existing state of things at any given date (Latin).

STATUTORY DECLARATIONS. The Canada Evidence Act (s. 41) provides that any judge, notary public, justice of the peace, police or stipendiary magistrate, recorder, mayor or commissioner authorized to take affidavits to be used either in the provincial or federal courts, or any other functionary authorized by law to administer an oath in any matter, may receive the solemn declaration of any person voluntarily making the declaration before him, in the following form, in attestation of the execution of any writing, deed or instrument, or of the truth of any fact, or of any account rendered in writing:

I, ——, solemnly declare that (state the fact or facts declared to), and I make this solemn declaration conscientiously believing it to be true, and knowing that it is of the same force and effect as if made under oath.

Declared before me —— at —— this —— day of ——, 19——.

STEAL. For the purposes of the Criminal Code, "steal" means to commit theft (s. 2).

STILLBIRTH. The birth of a dead infant during the last trimester of pregnancy or at term. An infant is regarded as stillborn if it has not shown any signs of life while completely external to the mother (Jaffe, A Guide to Pathological Evidence, 2nd ed.).

STRANGULATION. Death caused by compression or constriction of the neck. ***Ligature strangulation.*** Strangulation caused by the application of a narrow, constricting object such as a rope, a stocking or a shoe lace around the neck. ***Manual strangulation.*** Strangulation by ~~ or both hands. Manual strangulation often causes injury to the hyoid bone or thyroid cartilage. Also throttling (Jaffe, A Guide to Pathological Evidence, 2nd ed.).

STRYCHNINE. A vegetable alkaloid obtained from the seeds of Strychnos nux vomica. It is a strong nervous system stimulant and convulsant (Jaffe, A Guide to Pathological Evidence, 2nd ed.).

SUB. Under; at; in the power of (Latin). *Sub judice.* In course of trial; under consideration. *Sub modo.* Under condition or restriction; in a qualified sense. *Sub nom.* An abbreviation for "sub nomine" which means "under the name of". *Sub voce.* "Under the title".

SUBPOENA

1. *Subpoena (ad testificandum)*
2. *Subpoena (duces tecum)*
3. *When subpoena issued*
4. *How subpoena issued*
5. *Who may issue subpoena*
6. *Contents of subpoena*
7. *Effect of subpoena*
8. *Service of subpoena*
9. *Proof of service*
10. *Where subpoena effective*

1. Subpoena (ad testificandum)

1. Under penalty (for testifying) (Latin). 2. The opening words of a writ, and hence an order to appear in court.

2. Subpoena (duces tecum)

1. "Under penalty bring with you" (Latin). 2. The opening words of a writ requiring a person to bring evidence to court.

3. When subpoena issued

Where a person is likely to give material evidence in a proceeding to which this Act applies, a subpoena may be issued requiring that person to attend to give evidence (s. 698(1)).

4. How subpoena issued

Where a person is required to attend to give evidence before a superior court of criminal jurisdiction, a court of appeal, an appeal court or a court of criminal jurisdiction other than a provincial court judge acting under Part XIX of the Criminal Code, a subpoena directed to that person shall be issued out of the court before which the attendance of that person is required (s. 699(1)).

5. Who may issue subpoena

Where a person is required to attend to give evidence before a provincial court judge acting under Part XIX, or a summary conviction court under Part XXVII of the Criminal Code or in proceedings over which a justice has jurisdiction, a subpoena directed to that person shall be issued: (a) by a justice or provincial court judge, as the case may be, where the person whose attendance is required is within the province in which the proceedings were instituted; or (b) out of a superior court of criminal jurisdiction or a county or district court of the province in which the proceedings were instituted, where the person whose attendance is required is not within the province. A subpoena shall not be issued pursuant to (b), except pursuant to an order of a judge of the court made on application by a party to the proceedings. The subpoena shall be under the seal of the court and shall be signed by a judge of the court or by the clerk of the court. A subpoena or warrant that is issued by a justice or provincial court judge shall be signed by the justice or provincial court judge. Finally, the subpoena may be in Form 16 (s. 699(2)).

6. Contents of subpoena

A subpoena shall require the person to whom it is directed to attend, at a time and place to be stated in the subpoena, to give evidence and, if required, to bring with him anything that he has in his possession or under his control relating to the subject-matter of the proceedings (s. 700(1))).

7. Effect of subpoena

A person who is served with a subpoena shall attend and shall remain in attendance throughout the proceedings unless he is excused by the presiding judge, justice or provincial court judge (s. 700(2)).

8. Service of subpoena

A subpoena that is issued out of a superior court of criminal jurisdiction or a county or district court of the province in which the proceedings were instituted, must be served personally on the person to whom it is directed (s. 701(2)). Except as just specified, a subpoena shall be served by a peace officer who shall deliver it personally to the person to whom it is directed or, if that person cannot be conveniently found, shall leave it for him at his last or usual place of abode with some inmate thereof who appears to be at least 16 years of age (s. 701(1) and s. 509(2)).

9. Proof of service

Service of a subpoena may be proved by the affidavit of the person who effected service (s. 701(3)).

10. Where subpoena effective

A subpoena that is issued out of a superior court of criminal jurisdiction, a court of appeal, an appeal court or a court of criminal jurisdiction other than a provincial court judge acting under Part XIX has effect anywhere in Canada according to its terms (s. 702(1)).

A subpoena that is issued by a justice or provincial court judge has effect anywhere in the province in which it is issued (s. 702(2)).

SUI GENERIS. Of its own peculiar kind (Latin).

SUI JURIS. Of his own right; of full age and capacity (Latin).

SUMMARY CONVICTION. One of three types of offences created by the Criminal Code. The three types are:

(i) those punishable by summary conviction;
(ii) those punishable by indictment; and
(iii) those punishable by summary conviction or indictment, at the election of the Crown (known as "hybrid offences"). This type of offence is deemed to be an indictable offence unless and until the Crown elects to proceed by way of summary conviction (Interpretation Act, s. 34(1)(a)).

There is no fundamental or conceptual difference between the different types of offences. Resort must be had to the section of the Criminal Code or Act creating the offence to determine the type of offence. Where the Code or Act is silent, the offence is deemed to be a summary conviction offence (Interpretation Act, s. 34(1)(b)).

A summary conviction offence is tried before a provincial court judge without a jury and without a preliminary inquiry. The procedure for such a trial is set out in Part XXVII of the Criminal Code. An indictable offence tried by a provincial court judge with the consent of the accused is not a summary conviction offence, but is a summary trial of an indictable offence.

The maximum penalty for any summary conviction offence, unless otherwise provided, is $2,000, or 6 months' imprisonment, or both (s. 787(1)).

The limitation for all summary conviction offences under the Criminal Code is 6 months after the time when the subject matter of the proceedings arose (s. 786(2)). Offences created by other statutes may have a different limitation period.

SUMMARY CONVICTION COURT. For the purposes of Part XXVII of the Criminal Code (Summary Convictions), "summary conviction court" means a person who has jurisdiction in the territorial division where the subject matter of the proceedings is alleged to have arisen and who (a) is given jurisdiction over the proceedings by the enactment under which the proceedings are taken, (b) is a justice or provincial court judge, where the enactment under which the proceedings are taken does not expressly give jurisdiction to any person or class of persons, or (c) is a provincial court judge, where the enactment under which the proceedings are taken gives jurisdiction in respect thereof to two or more justices (s. 785(1)).

SUMMARY TRIAL. This is the procedure laid down in Part XIX of the Criminal Code (Indictable Offences — Trial Without Jury), whereby certain provincial court judges and other functionaries are given power to try (usually with the consent of the accused) persons charged with indictable offences. The offence is still an indictable offence even though tried by the provincial court judge.

SUMMONS

1. *Definition*
2. *Issue of summons*
3. *Period for which summons continues in force*
4. *Valid if issued on a holiday*
5. *Service of summons on a corporation*
6. *Where summons effective*
7. *Failure to appear or to comply with summons*
8. *Contents of summons*
9. *Service of summons*
10. *Proof of service*

1. Definition

A summons is a written order issued by a justice or a judge to a person charged with an offence to appear in court at a certain time and place in order to be dealt with according to law. The order may also direct the person to attend at a police station at a particular place for the purposes of the Identification of Criminals Act (Form 6).

2. Issue of summons

A justice who receives an information and considers that a case for doing so is made out, may issue either a summons to compel the accused to attend before him or some other justice for the same territorial division to answer to a charge of an offence (s. 507(1)(b)).

No justice shall refuse to issue a summons or a warrant by reason only that the alleged offence is one for which a person may be arrested without warrant (s. 507(2)).

Where the justice considers that a case is made out for compelling an accused to attend before him to answer to a charge of an offence, he shall issue a summons to the accused unless the allegations of the informant or the evidence of any witness or witnesses disclose reasonable grounds to believe that it is necessary in the public interest to issue a warrant for the arrest of the accused (s. 507(4)).

A justice shall not sign a summons or warrant in blank (s. 507(5)).

Where on an appeal from or review of any decision or matter of jurisdiction, a new trial or hearing or a continuance or renewal of a trial or hearing is ordered, a justice may issue either a summons in order to compel the accused to attend at the new or continued or renewed trial or hearing (s. 507(8)).

Where notice of the recommencement of proceedings has been given or an indictment has been filed with the court before which the proceedings are to commence or recommence, the court, if it considers it necessary, may issue (a) a summons addressed to, or (b) a warrant for the arrest of, the accused or defendant, as the case may be, to compel him to attend before the court to answer the charge described in the indictment (s. 578(1)).

Notwithstanding any other law that requires an information to be laid before or to be tried by two or more justices, one justice may receive the information; issue a summons or warrant with respect to the information; and do all other things preliminary to the trial (s. 788(2)).

3. Period for which summons continues in force

Where an accused, in respect of an offence with which he is charged, has not been taken into custody or has been released from custody, the summons issued to the accused continues in force, subject to its terms, and applies in respect of any new information charging the same offence or an included offence that was received after the summons was issued where the accused was released from custody pursuant to an order of a judge until his trial is completed; or in any other case, (i) until his trial is completed, and (ii) where the accused is, at his trial, determined to be guilty of the offence, until a sentence is imposed on the accused unless, at the time the accused is determined to be guilty, the court, judge or justice orders that the accused be taken into custody pending such sentence (s. 523(1)).

Where an accused who has not been taken into custody or who has been released from custody pleads guilty to or is found guilty of an offence but is not convicted, the summons issued to him continues in force, subject to its terms, until a disposition in respect of him is made unless, at the time he pleads guilty or is found guilty, the court, judge or justice orders that he be taken into custody pending such a disposition (s. 736(2)).

4. Valid if issued on a holiday

A summons may be issued on a holiday (s. 20).

5. Service of summons on a corporation

Where any summons, notice or other process is required to be or may be served on a corporation, and no other method of service is provided, service may be effected by delivery: (a) in the case of a municipal corporation, to the mayor, warden, reeve or other chief officer of the corporation, or to the secretary, treasurer or clerk of the corporation; and (b) in the case of any other corporation, to the manager, secretary or other executive officer of the corporation or of a branch thereof (s. 703.2).

6. Where summons effective

A summons may be served anywhere in Canada and, if served, is effective notwithstanding the territorial jurisdiction of the authority that issued the summons (s. 703.1).

7. Failure to appear or to comply with summons

Every one who is served with a summons and who fails, without lawful excuse, the proof of which lies on him, to appear at a time and place stated therein, if any, for the purposes of the Identification of Criminals Act or to attend court in accordance therewith, is guilty of either an indictable offence and is liable to imprisonment for a term not exceeding two years; or an offence punishable on summary conviction (s. 145(4)). *See ESCAPES AND RESCUES.*

8. Contents of summons

A summons issued shall: (a) be directed to the accused; (b) set out briefly the offence in respect of which the accused is charged; and (c) require the accused to attend court at a time and place to be stated therein and to attend thereafter as required by the court in order to be dealt with according to law (s. 509(1)).

A summons may, where the accused is alleged to have committed an indictable offence, require the accused to appear at a time and place stated therein for the purposes of the Identification of Criminals Act, and a person so appearing is deemed, for the purposes only of that Act, to be in lawful custody charged with an indictable offence (s. 509(5)).

Every summons shall contain the text of s. 145(4) (which states that it is an offence to fail to comply with a summons) and s. 510 (which states that a warrant for the arrest of the person may be issued for failure to comply with the summons for the purpose of the Identification of Criminals Act) (s. 509(4)).

9. Service of summons

A summons shall be served by a peace officer who shall deliver it personally to the person to whom it is directed or, if that person cannot conveniently be found, shall leave it for him at his latest or usual place of abode with an inmate thereof who appears to be at least sixteen years of age (s. 509(2)).

10. Proof of service

Service of a summons may be proved by the oral evidence, given under oath, of the peace officer who served it or by his affidavit made before a justice or other person authorized to administer oaths or to take affidavits (s. 509(3)).

SUPERIOR COURT. (a) In the Provinces of Nova Scotia, Prince Edward Island or Newfoundland, the Supreme Court of the Province, (b) in the Province of Ontario, the Court of Appeal for the Province and the Ontario Court (General Division), (c) in the Province of Quebec, the Court of Appeal, and the Superior Court in and for the Province, (d) in the Provinces of New Brunswick, Manitoba, Saskatchewan or Alberta, the Court of Appeal for the Province and the Court

of Queen's Bench for the Province, (e) in the Province of British Columbia, the Court of Appeal and the Supreme Court of the Province, (f) in the Yukon Territory or the Northwest Territories, the Supreme Court thereof,
and includes the Supreme Court of Canada and the Exchequer Court of Canada (Interpretation Act, s. 35(1)).

SUPPRESSIO VERI SUGGESTIO FALSI. "The suppression of truth is the suggestion of falsehood" (Latin).

SUPRA. "Above" (Latin).

SURPLUSAGE. In an information or indictment, assertions of facts which are not essential to successful prosecution and which need not be proved at trial (The Charge Document in Criminal Cases, Law Reform Commission of Canada, Working Paper 55).

T

TELECOMMUNICATION OFFENCES

1. *Definition of "telecommunication"*
2. *Instrument or device to obtain service without payment*
3. *Telegram, cablegram or radio message in false name*
4. *False messages*
5. *Indecent telephone calls*
6. *Harassing telephone calls*
7. *Sufficiency of count*
8. *Theft of telecommunication service. See THEFT, 4.*

See also WIRETAPPING OFFENCES.

1. Definition of "telecommunication"

For the purposes of s. 326 and s. 327, "telecommunication" means any transmission, emission or reception of signs, signals, writing, images or sounds or intelligence of any nature by wire, radio, visual or other electromagnetic system (s. 326(2)).

2. Instrument or device to obtain service without payment — Section 327

Every one who — without lawful excuse — manufactures or possesses or sells or offers for sale or distributes — any instrument or device or any component thereof — the design of which renders it primarily useful for obtaining the use of any telecommunication facility or service — under circumstances that give rise to a reasonable inference that the device has been used or is or was intended to be used to obtain the use of any telecommunication facility or service without payment of a lawful charge therefor — is guilty of an indictable offence.**

Included offences. Attempts (s. 660 and s. 662(1)(b)).

Punishment. Imprisonment for a term not exceeding 2 years (s. 327(1)).

Where a person is convicted of this offence, any instrument or device in relation to which the offence was committed or the possession of which constituted the offence, upon such conviction, in addition to any punishment that is imposed, may be ordered forfeited to Her Majesty, whereupon it may be disposed of as the Attorney General directs (s. 327(2)).

No such order for forfeiture shall be made in respect of telephone, telegraph or other communication facilities or equipment owned by a person engaged in providing telephone, telegraph or other communication service to the public or forming part of the telephone, telegraph or other communication service or system of such a person by means of which this offence has been committed if such person was not a party to the offence (s. 327(3)).

Release. Initial decision to release made by officer in charge or justice (s. 498).

Election. Accused may elect trial by judge and jury, judge alone, or provincial court judge (s. 536).

Evidence. For the purposes of this offence, the proof of lawful excuse lies on the accused (s. 327(1)).

Informations

A.B., on or about the —— day of ——, 19——, at the —— of ——, in the said (territorial division), did manufacture [OR possess OR sell OR offer for sale OR distribute] an instrument [OR device OR component of an instrument OR component of a device] the design of which renders it primarily useful for obtaining the use of a telecommunication service [OR facility], under circumstances that gave rise to a reasonable inference that the device had been used [OR was intended to be used OR had been intended to be used] to obtain the use of any telecommunication service [OR facility] without payment of a lawful charge therefor, to wit: (specify the particulars of the offence), contrary to s. 327 of the Criminal Code of Canada.

3. Telegram, cablegram or radio message in false name — Section 371

Every one who — with intent to defraud — causes or procures a telegram or cablegram or radio message — to be sent or delivered as being sent by the authority of another person — knowing that it is not sent by his authority — and with intent that the message should be acted on as being sent by his authority — is guilty of an indictable offence.

Intent. Intention to defraud; knowledge of being sent by spurious authority; intention that message be acted upon.

Included offences. Attempts (s. 660 and s. 662(1)(b)).

Punishment. Imprisonment for a term not exceeding 5 years (s. 371).

Release. Initial decision to release made by officer in charge or justice (s. 498).

Election. Accused may elect trial by judge and jury, judge alone, or provincial court judge (s. 536).

Evidence. See **7**, *below.*

4. False messages — Section 372(1)

Every one who — with intent to injure or alarm any person — conveys or causes or procures to be conveyed — by letter or telegram or telephone or cable or radio, or otherwise — information that he knows is false — is guilty of an indictable offence.

Intent. Intention to injure or alarm; knowledge of falsity.

Included offences. Attempts (s. 660 and s. 662(1)(b)).

Punishment. Imprisonment for a term not exceeding 2 years (s. 372(1)).

Release. Initial decision to release made by officer in charge or justice (s. 498).

Election. Accused may elect trial by judge and jury, judge alone, or provincial court judge (s. 536).

Evidence. See **7**, *below.*

5. Indecent telephone calls — Section 372(2)

Every one who — with intent to alarm or annoy any person — makes any indecent telephone call to that person — is guilty of an offence punishable on summary conviction.

Intent. Intention to alarm or annoy.

Limitation period. No proceedings in respect of offences that are declared to be punishable on summary conviction shall be instituted more than 6 months after the time when the subject matter of the proceedings arose (s. 786(2) and s. 785(1)).

Included offences. Attempts (s. 660 and s. 662(1)(b)).

Punishment. A fine not exceeding $2,000, or 6 months' imprisonment, or both (s. 372(2) and s. 787(1)).

Release. Initial decision to release made by peace officer (s. 497).

Election. No election, summary conviction offence.

6. Harassing telephone calls — Section 372(3)

Every one who — without lawful excuse — and with intent to harass any person — makes or causes to be made — repeated telephone calls to that person — is guilty of an offence punishable on summary conviction.

Intent. Intention to harass.

Limitation period. No proceedings in respect of offences that are declared to be punishable on summary conviction shall be instituted more than 6 months after the time when the subject matter of the proceedings arose (s. 786(2) and s. 785(1)).

Included offences. Attempts (s. 660 and s. 662(1)(b)).

Punishment. A fine not exceeding $2,000, or 6 months' imprisonment, or both (s. 372(3) and s. 787(1)).

Release. Initial decision to release made by peace officer (s. 497).

Election. No election, summary conviction offence.

7. Sufficiency of count

No count that alleges false pretences, fraud or any attempt or conspiracy by fraudulent means is insufficient by reason only that it does not set out in detail the nature of the false pretence, fraud or fraudulent means (s. 586).

TEMPERATURE PLATEAU. The period immediately after death during which the internal body temperature does not fall. The temperature plateau may last 1 to 5 hours (Jaffe, A Guide to Pathological Evidence, 2nd ed.).

TEMPORARY CAVITY. A momentary cavity created in the tissues by the rapid passage of a projectile. The size of the temporary cavity depends on the energy of the projectile and on its rate of retardation (Jaffe, A Guide to Pathological Evidence, 2nd ed.).

TERRITORIAL DIVISION. For the purposes of the Criminal Code, "territorial division" includes any province, county, union of counties, township, city, town, parish or other judicial division or place to which the context applies (s. 2).

TESTAMENTARY INSTRUMENT. For the purposes of the Criminal Code, "testamentary instrument" includes any will, codicil or other testamentary writing or appointment, during the life of the testator whose testamentary disposition it purports to be and after his death, whether it relates to real or personal property or to both (s. 2).

THEATRE. For the purposes of Part V of the Criminal Code (Sexual Offences, Public Morals and Disorderly Conduct), "theatre" includes any place that is open to the public where entertainments are given, whether or not any charge is made for admission (s. 150).

THEFT AND OFFENCES RESEMBLING THEFT

1. *Theft*
2. *Theft by bailee of things under seizure*
3. *Electricity and gas*
4. *Telecommunications*
5. *Theft by husband or wife*
6. *Assisting theft by husband or wife*
7. *Theft by person required to account*
8. *Theft by person holding power of attorney*
9. *Misappropriation of money held under direction*
10. *Taking motor vehicle or vessel without consent*
11. *Criminal breach of trust*
12. *Public servant refusing to deliver property*
13. *Theft of cattle*
14. *Fraudulently taking cattle or defacing brand*
15. *Lumber and lumbering equipment*
16. *Dealing in marked lumbering equipment*
17. *Destroying documents of title*

18. *Fraudulent concealment*
19. *Theft from mail*
20. *Sufficiency of count*
21. *Credit card offences. See CREDIT CARDS, 2*

1. Theft

Definition of offences

Section 322(1)

Every one who — fraudulently and without colour of right — takes or converts to his use or to the use of another person — anything, whether animate or inanimate — with intent — either to deprive, temporarily or absolutely, the owner of it, or a person who has a special property or interest in it, of the thing or of his property or interest in it — or to pledge it or deposit it as security — or to part with it under a condition with respect to its return that the person who parts with it may be unable to perform — or to deal with it in such a manner that it cannot be restored in the condition in which it was at the time it was taken or converted — commits theft.

Section 322(2)

A person who — with intent to steal anything — moves it or causes it to move or to be moved — or begins to cause it to become movable — commits theft.

Statement of offence — Section 334

— Except where otherwise provided by law — every one who — commits theft — is guilty of an indictable offence where the property stolen is a testamentary instrument or where the value of what is stolen exceeds $1,000 — or where the value of what is stolen does not exceed $1,000 — is guilty of either an indictable offence or an offence punishable on summary conviction.

Intent. Fraudulently with intention to deprive, pledge, deposit, part with or deal with anything (s. 322(1)); intention to steal (s. 322(2)).

Exceptions. 1. A factor or agent does not commit theft by pledging or giving a lien on goods or documents of title to goods that are entrusted to him for the purpose of sale or for any other purpose, if the pledge or lien is for an amount that does not exceed the sum of (a) the amount due to him from his principal at the time the goods or documents are pledged or the lien is given, and (b) the amount of any bill of exchange that he has accepted for or on account of his principal (s. 325).

2. No person commits theft by reason only that he takes, for the purpose of exploration or scientific investigation, a specimen of ore or mineral from land that is not enclosed and is not occupied or worked as a mine, quarry or digging (s. 333).

Jurisdiction. The jurisdiction of a provincial court judge to try an accused charged with theft is absolute and does not depend on the consent of the accused, where the subject matter of the offence is not a testamentary instrument, and where its alleged value does not exceed $1,000 (s. 553(a)(i)).

Limitation period. No proceedings in respect of offences that are declared to be punishable on summary conviction shall be instituted more than 6 months after the time when the subject matter of the proceedings arose (s. 786(2) and s. 785(1)).

Included offences. Attempts (s. 660 and s. 662(1)(b)); obtaining by false pretences.

A charge of the theft of a number of articles includes a charge of the theft of any of the articles. A charge of the theft of a letter containing money includes a charge of the theft of the money.

Punishment. On indictment, imprisonment for a term not exceeding 10 years, where the property stolen is a testamentary instrument or where the value of what is stolen exceeds $1,000 (s. 334(a)). Imprisonment for a term not exceeding 2 years, where the value of what is stolen does not exceed $1,000 (s. 334(b)(i)). On summary conviction, a fine of not more than $2,000, or to imprisonment for 6 months, or to both (s. 334(b)(ii) and s. 787(1)).

Release. Where the property stolen is a testamentary instrument or where the value of what is stolen exceeds $1,000, initial decision to release made by justice (s. 515(1)). Where the value of what is stolen does not exceed $1,000, initial decision to release made by peace officer (s. 497).

Election. On indictment, where the property stolen is a testamentary instrument or where the value of what is stolen exceeds $1,000, accused may elect trial by judge and jury, judge alone, or provincial court judge (s. 536). Where the value of what is stolen does not exceed $1,000, no election, absolute jurisdiction of provincial court judge (s. 553). On summary conviction, no election.

Evidence. 1. A taking or conversion of anything may be fraudulent notwithstanding that it is effected without secrecy or attempt at concealment (s. 322(3)).
2. For these purposes, the question whether anything that is converted is taken for the purpose of conversion, or whether it is, at the time it is converted, in the lawful possession of the person who converts it is not material (s. 322(4)).
3. A person who has a wild living creature in captivity shall be deemed to have a special property or interest in it while it is in captivity and after it has escaped from captivity (s. 322(5)).
4. Where oysters and oyster brood are in oyster beds, layings or fisheries that are the property of any person and are sufficiently marked out or known as the property of that person, that person shall be deemed to have a special property or interest in them (s. 323(1)). An indictment is sufficient if it describes an oyster bed, laying or fishery by name or in some other way, without stating that it is situated in a particular territorial division (s. 323(2)).
5. A person may be convicted of theft notwithstanding that anything that is alleged to have been stolen was stolen (a) by the owner of it from a person who has a special property or interest in it; (b) by a person who has a special property or interest in it from the owner of it; (c) by a lessee of it from his reversioner; (d) by one of several joint owners, tenants in common or partners of or in it from the other persons who have an interest in it; or (e) by the directors, officers or members of a company, body corporate, unincorporated body or of a society associated together for a lawful purpose from the company, body corporate, unincorporated body or society, as the case may be (s. 328).
6. *See also* **20**, *below.*

Informations

A.B., on or about the —— day of ——, 19——, at the —— of ——, in the said (territorial division), did steal (specify what) of the value of (specify the value in dollars), the property of C.D., to wit: (specify the particulars of the offence), contrary to s. 334 of the Criminal Code of Canada.

2. Theft by bailee of things under seizure

Definition of offence — Section 324

Every one who — is a bailee — of anything that is under lawful seizure — by a police officer or public officer in the execution of the duties of his office — and is obliged by law or agreement —

to produce and deliver it — to that officer or to another person entitled thereto — at a certain time and place, or on demand — steals it — if he does not produce and deliver it in accordance with his obligation.

Statement of offence — Section 334

Every one who — commits theft — is guilty of either an indictable offence or an offence punishable on summary conviction.

Exceptions. 1. A bailee does not steal a thing under seizure if his failure to produce and deliver it is not the result of a wilful act or omission by him (s. 324).
2. *See also Exceptions under* **1**, *above.*

Definitions. To "steal" is to commit theft.

See Jurisdiction, Limitation period, Included offences, Punishment, Release and Election under **1**, *above.*

3. Electricity and gas

Definition of offence — Section 326(1)(a)

Every one who — fraudulently or maliciously, or without colour of right — abstracts or consumes or uses electricity or gas — or causes to be wasted or diverted — commits theft.

Statement of offence — Section 334

Every one who — commits theft — is guilty of either an indictable offence or an offence punishable on summary conviction.

Intent. Fraudulently or maliciously.

See Jurisdiction, Limitation period, Included offences, Punishment, Release, Election and Evidence, items 1., 2., and 5., under **1**, *above. See also* **20**, *below.*

Informations

A.B., on or about the —— day of ——, 19——, at the —— of ——, in the said (territorial division), did fraudulently [OR maliciously OR without colour of right] abstract [OR consume OR use] electricity [OR gas] and did thereby commit theft, to wit: (specify the particulars of the offence), contrary to s. 334 of the Criminal Code of Canada.

4. Telecommunications

Definition of offence — Section 326(1)(b)

Every one who — fraudulently or maliciously, or without colour of right — uses any telecommunication facility — or obtains any telecommunication service — commits theft.

Statement of offence — Section 334

Every one who — commits theft — is guilty of either an indictable offence or an offence punishable on summary conviction.

Intent. Fraudulently or maliciously.

Punishment. *See Punishment under* **1**, *above.*
In addition to any punishment that is imposed, the instrument or device in relation to which the offence was committed may be ordered forfeited (s. 327(2)).

Definitions. *See TELECOMMUNICATION OFFENCES, 1.*

See Jurisdiction, Limitation period, Included offences, Release, Election and Evidence, items 1., 2, and 5., under **1**, *above. See also* **20**, *below.*

Informations

A.B., on or about the —— day of ——, 19——, at the —— of ——, in the said (territorial division), did fraudulently [OR maliciously OR without colour of right] use a telecommunication facility [OR obtain a telecommunication service], to wit: (specify the particulars of the offence), and did thereby commit theft contrary to s. 334 of the Criminal Code of Canada.

5. Theft by husband or wife

Definition of offence — Section 329(2)

A husband or wife who — intending to desert or on deserting the other or while living apart from the other — fraudulently takes or converts — anything that is by law the property of the other — in a manner that, if it were done by another person, would be theft — commits theft.

Statement of offence — Section 334

Every one who — commits theft — is guilty of an indictable offence, or an offence punishable on summary conviction.

Intent. Intention to desert; fraudulently.

Evidence. 1. Subject to s. 329(2), no husband or wife, during cohabitation, commits theft of anything that is by law the property of the other (s. 329(1)).
2. The wife or husband of a person charged with this offence is a competent and compellable witness for the prosecution without the consent of the person charged (Canada Evidence Act, s. 4(2)).
3. *See also Evidence under* **1**, *above.*

See Exceptions, Jurisdiction, Limitation period, Included offences, Punishment, Release and Election under **1**, *above.*

Informations

A.B., on or about the —— day of ——, 19——, at the —— of ——, in the said (territorial division), with the intention to desert [OR on deserting OR while living apart from] C.D., the wife [OR husband] of A.B., did fraudulently take [OR convert] (specify what was taken or converted), the property of C.D., to wit: (specify the particulars of the offence), and did thereby commit theft, contrary to s. 334 of the Criminal Code of Canada.

6. Assisting theft by husband or wife

Definition of offence — Section 329(3)

Every one who — during cohabitation of husband and wife — knowingly — either assists either of them in dealing with anything that is by law the property of the other in a manner that would be theft if they were not married — or receives from either of them anything that is by law the property of the other and has been obtained from the other by dealing with it in a manner that would be theft if they were not married — commits theft.

Statement of offence — Section 334

Every one who — commits theft — is guilty of either an indictable offence or an offence punishable on summary conviction.

Intent. Knowingly.

See Exceptions, Jurisdiction, Limitation period, Included offences, Punishment, Release, Election and Evidence under **1**, *above.*
See also Evidence under **5**, *above.*

Informations

A.B., on or about the —— day of ——, 19——, at the —— of ——, in the said (territorial division), during the cohabitation of C.D. and E.F., a husband and wife, knowingly did assist C.D. [OR E.F.] with (specify what), the property of E.F. [OR C.D.], in a manner that would have been theft if C.D. and E.F. were not married, to wit: (specify the particulars of the offence), and did thereby commit theft, contrary to s. 334 of the Criminal Code of Canada.

A.B., on or about the —— day of ——, 19——, at the —— of ——, in the said (territorial division), during the cohabitation of C.D. and E.F., a husband and wife, knowingly did receive from C.D. [OR E.F.] (specify what was received) that is by law the property of E.F. [OR C.D.] and had been obtained from E.F. [OR C.D.] by dealing with it in a manner that would have been theft if C.D. and E.F. were not married, to wit: (specify the particulars of the offence), and did thereby commit theft, contrary to s. 334 of the Criminal Code of Canada.

7. Theft by person required to account

Definition of offence — Section 330(1)

Every one who — having received anything from any person — on terms that require him to account for it or pay it or pay the proceeds of it or pay a part of the proceeds of it to that person or another person — fraudulently — fails to do what the terms require — commits theft.

Statement of offence — Section 334

Every one who — commits theft — is guilty of either an indictable offence or an offence punishable on summary conviction.

Intent. Fraudulently.

Evidence. 1. Where s. 330(1) otherwise applies, but one of the terms is that the thing received or the proceeds or part of the proceeds of it shall be an item in a debtor and creditor account between the person who receives the thing and the person to whom he is to account for or to pay it, and that the latter shall rely only on the liability of the other as his debtor in respect thereof, a proper entry in that account of the thing received or the proceeds or part of the proceeds of it, as the case may be, is a sufficient accounting therefor, and no fraudulent conversion of the thing or the proceeds or part of the proceeds of it thereby accounted for shall be deemed to have taken place (s. 330(2)). 2. *See also Evidence under* **1**, *above.*

See Exceptions, Jurisdiction, Limitation period, Included offences, Punishment, Release and Election under **1**, *above.*

Informations

A.B., on or about the —— day of ——, 19——, at the —— of ——, in the said (territorial division), did receive (specify what was received) from C.D. on terms that required A.B. to account for it [OR pay it OR pay the proceeds of it OR pay a part of the proceeds of it] to C.D. [OR E.F.] and did fraudulently fail to account for it [OR pay it OR pay the proceeds of it OR pay a part of the proceeds of it] accordingly, to wit: (specify the particulars of the offence), contrary to s. 334 of the Criminal Code of Canada.

8. Theft by person holding power of attorney

Definition of offence — Section 331

Every one who — being entrusted, whether solely or jointly with another person, with a power of attorney for the sale or mortgage or pledge or other disposition of real or personal property — either fraudulently sells or mortgages or pledges or otherwise disposes of the property or any part of it — or fraudulently converts the proceeds of a sale or mortgage or pledge or other disposition of the property, or any part of the proceeds, to a purpose other than that for which he was entrusted by the power of attorney — commits theft.

Statement of offence — Section 334

Every one who — commits theft — is guilty of either an indictable offence or an offence punishable on summary conviction.

Intent. Fraudulently.

See Exceptions, Jurisdiction, Limitation period, Included offences, Punishment, Release, Election and Evidence under **1**, *above.*

9. Misappropriation of money held under direction

Definition of offence — Section 332(1)

Every one who — having received, either solely or jointly with another person, money or valuable security or a power of attorney for the sale of real or personal property — with a direction that the money or a part of it, or the proceeds or a part of the proceeds of the security or the property shall be applied to a purpose or paid to a person specified in the direction — fraudulently and contrary

to the direction — applies to any other purpose or pays to any other person — the money or proceeds or any part of it — commits theft.

Statement of offence — Section 334

Every one who — commits theft — is guilty of either an indictable offence or an offence punishable on summary conviction.

Intent. Fraudulently.

Exceptions. 1. This offence does not apply where a person who receives anything mentioned above and the person from whom he receives it deal with each other on such terms that all money paid to the former would, in the absence of any such direction, be properly treated as an item in a debtor and creditor account between them, unless the direction is in writing (s. 332(2)).
2. *See also Exceptions under* **1**, *above.*

See Jurisdiction, Limitation period, Included offences, Punishment, Release, Election and Evidence under **1**, above.

10. Taking motor vehicle or vessel without consent — Section 335

Every one who — without the consent of the owner — takes a motor vehicle or vessel — with intent to drive or use or navigate or operate it — or with intent to cause it to be driven or used or navigated or operated — is guilty of an offence punishable on summary conviction.

Intent. Intention to drive, use, navigate or operate.

Limitation period. No proceedings in respect of offences that are declared to be punishable on summary conviction shall be instituted more than 6 months after the time when the subject matter of the proceedings arose (s. 786(2) and s. 785(1)).

Included offences. Attempts (s. 660 and s. 662(1)(b)).

Punishment. A fine not exceeding $2,000, or 6 months' imprisonment, or both (s. 335 and s. 787(1)).

Release. Initial decision to release made by peace officer (s. 497).

Election. No election, summary conviction offence.

Evidence. Mere presence in a motor vehicle or vessel that has been unlawfully taken is not per se proof that a person was a party to the original taking of it.

Informations

A.B., on or about the —— day of ——, 19——, at the —— of ——, in the said (territorial division), did take a motor vehicle [OR vessel] without the consent of C.D., the owner of the motor vehicle [OR vessel], with intent to drive [OR use OR navigate OR operate] it, to wit: (specify the particulars of the offence), contrary to s. 335 of the Criminal Code of Canada.

A.B., on or about the —— day of ——, 19——, at the —— of ——, in the said (territorial division), did take a motor vehicle [OR vessel] without the consent of C.D., the owner of the motor vehicle [OR vessel], with intent to cause it to be driven [OR used OR navigated OR operated], to wit: (specify the particulars of the offence), contrary to s. 335 of the Criminal Code of Canada.

11. Criminal breach of trust — Section 336

Every one who — being a trustee of anything for the use or benefit, whether in whole or in part, of another person, or for a public or charitable purpose — with intent to defraud and in contravention of his trust — converts that thing or any part of it — to a use that is not authorized by the trust — is guilty of an indictable offence.

Intent. Intention to defraud.

Included offences. Attempts (s. 660 and s. 662(1)(b)).

Punishment. Imprisonment for a term not exceeding 14 years (s. 336).

Release. Initial decision to release made by justice (s. 515(1)).

Election. Accused may elect trial by judge and jury, judge alone, or provincial court judge (s. 536).

Evidence. 1. At common law, a trustee is the owner of trust property and therefore the act of converting such property to his own use or to the use of any other person in breach of the terms of the trust was not a criminal offence. It has been made the subject of a special statute. However, the definition of "theft" in the Criminal Code will cover most, if not all, cases of the fraudulent conversion of trust property.
2. *See also* **20**, *below*.

12. Public servant refusing to deliver property — Section 337

Every one who — being or having been employed in the service of Her Majesty in right of Canada or in right of a province, or in the service of a municipality — and entrusted by virtue of that

employment with the receipt or custody or management or control of anything — refuses or fails to deliver it — to a person who is authorized to demand it and does demand it — is guilty of an indictable offence.

Included offences. Attempts (s. 660 and s. 662(1)(b)).

Punishment. Imprisonment for a term not exceeding 14 years (s. 337).

Release. Initial decision to release made by justice (s. 515(1)).

Election. Accused may elect trial by judge and jury, judge alone, or provincial court judge (s. 536).

13. Theft of cattle — Section 338(2)

Every one who — commits theft of cattle — is guilty of an indictable offence.

Included offences. Attempts (s. 660 and s. 662(1)(b)).

Punishment. Imprisonment for a term not exceeding 10 years (s. 338(2)).

Release. Initial decision to release made by officer in charge or justice (s. 498).

Election. Accused may elect trial by judge and jury, judge alone, or provincial court judge (s. 536).

Evidence. 1. In any such proceedings, evidence that cattle are marked with a brand or mark that is recorded or registered in accordance with any Act is, in the absence of any evidence to the contrary, proof that the cattle are owned by the registered owner of that brand or mark (s. 338(3)).
2. Where an accused is charged with this offence, the burden of proving that the cattle came lawfully into the possession of the accused or his employee or into the possession of another person on behalf of the accused is on the accused, if the accused is not the registered owner of the brand or mark with which the cattle are marked, unless it appears that possession of the cattle by an employee of the accused or by another person on behalf of the accused was without the knowledge and authority, sanction or approval of the accused (s. 338(4)).

14. Fraudulently taking cattle or defacing brand

Section 338(1)(a)

Every one who — without the consent of the owner — fraudulently takes or holds or keeps in his possession or conceals or receives or appropriates or purchases or sells — cattle that are found astray — is guilty of an indictable offence.

Section 338(1)(b)

Every one who — without the consent of the owner — fraudulently — in whole or in part — either obliterates or alters or defaces a brand or mark on cattle — or makes a false or counterfeit brand or mark on cattle — is guilty of an indictable offence.

Included offences. Attempts (s. 660 and s. 662(1)(b)).

Intent. Fraudulently.

Punishment. Imprisonment for a term not exceeding 5 years (s. 338(1)).

Release. Initial decision to release made by officer in charge or justice (s. 498).

Election. Accused may elect trial by judge and jury, judge alone, or provincial court judge (s. 536).

Evidence. 1. *See Evidence under* **13**, *above.*
2. *See also* **20**, *below.*

Informations

A.B., on or about the —— day of ——, 19——, at the —— of ——, in the said (territorial division), without the consent of C.D., did fraudulently take [OR hold OR keep in his possession OR conceal OR receive OR appropriate OR purchase OR sell] cattle owned by C.D. that were found astray, to wit: (specify the particulars of the offence), contrary to s. 338(1)(a) of the Criminal Code of Canada.

A.B., on or about the —— day of ——, 19——, at the —— of ——, in the said (territorial division), without the consent of C.D., did fraudulently, in whole or in part, obliterate [OR alter OR deface] a brand [OR mark] on cattle owned by C.D., to wit: (specify the particulars of the offence), contrary to s. 338(1)(b) of the Criminal Code of Canada.

A.B., on or about the —— day of ——, 19——, at the —— of ——, in the said (territorial division), without the consent of C.D., did fraudulently, in whole or in part, make a false [OR counterfeit] brand [OR mark] on cattle owned by C.D., to wit: (specify the particulars of the offence), contrary to s. 338(1)(b) of the Criminal Code of Canada.

15. Lumber and lumbering equipment

Section 339(1)(a)

Every one who — without the consent of the owner — fraudulently takes or holds or keeps in his possession or conceals or receives or appropriates or purchases or sells — any lumber or lumbering equipment — that is found adrift or cast ashore or lying on or embedded in — the bed or bottom, or on the bank or beach of a river or stream or lake in Canada, or in the harbours or any of the coastal waters of Canada — is guilty of an indictable offence.

Section 339(1)(b)

Every one who — without the consent of the owner — removes or alters or obliterates or defaces a mark or number on — any lumber or lumbering equipment — that is found adrift or cast ashore or lying on or embedded in — the bed or bottom, or on the bank or beach of a river or stream or lake in Canada, or in the harbours or any of the coastal waters of Canada — is guilty of an indictable offence.

Section 339(1)(c)

Every one who — without the consent of the owner — refuses to deliver up — to the owner or to the person in charge — thereof on behalf of the owner or to a person authorized by the owner to receive it — any lumber or lumbering equipment — that is found adrift or cast ashore or lying on or embedded in — the bed or bottom, or on the bank or beach of a river or stream or lake in Canada, or in the harbours or any of the coastal waters of Canada — is guilty of an indictable offence.

Intent. Fraudulently (s. 339(1)(a)).

Included offences. Attempts (s. 660 and s. 662(1)(b)).

Punishment. Imprisonment for a term not exceeding 5 years (s. 339(1)).

Release. Initial decision to release made by officer in charge or justice (s. 498).

Election. Accused may elect trial by judge and jury, judge alone, or provincial court judge (s. 536).

Definitions. For these purposes: "Coastal waters of Canada" includes all of Queen Charlotte Sound, all the Strait of Georgia and the Canadian waters of the Strait of Juan de Fuca (s. 339(6)).
See also LUMBER and LUMBERING EQUIPMENT.

Evidence. 1. A peace officer who suspects, on reasonable grounds, that any lumber owned by any person and bearing the registered timber mark of that person is kept or detained in or on any place without the knowledge or consent of that person, may enter into or on that place to ascertain whether or not it is detained there without the knowledge or consent of that person (s. 339(3)).
2. Where any lumber or lumbering equipment is marked with a timber mark or a boom chain brand registered under any Act, the mark or brand is, in the absence of any evidence to the contrary, proof that it is the property of the registered owner of the mark or brand (s. 339(4)).
3. Where an accused or his servants or agents are in possession of lumber or lumbering equipment marked with the mark, brand, registered timber mark, name or initials of another person, the burden of proving that it came lawfully into his possession or into possession of his servants or agents is on the accused (s. 339(5)).
4. *See also* **20**, *below.*

16. Dealing in marked lumbering equipment — Section 339(2)

Every one who — being a dealer in second-hand goods of any kind — trades or traffics in or has in his possession for sale or traffic — any lumbering equipment — that is marked with the mark or brand or registered timber mark or name or initials of a person — without the written consent of that person — is guilty of an offence punishable on summary conviction.

Limitation period. No proceedings in respect of offences that are declared to be punishable on summary conviction shall be instituted more than 6 months after the time when the subject matter of the proceedings arose (s. 786(2) and s. 785(1)).

Included offences. Attempts (s. 660 and s. 662(1)(b)).

THEFT AND OFFENCES RESEMBLING THEFT 633

Punishment. A fine not exceeding $2,000, or 6 months' imprisonment, or both (s. 339(2) and s. 787(1)).

Release. Initial decision to release made by peace officer (s. 497).

Election. No election, summary conviction offence.

Definitions. *See LUMBERING EQUIPMENT.*

Evidence. *See Evidence items 2. and 3., under* **15**, *above.*

Informations

A.B., on or about the —— day of ——, 19——, at the —— of ——, in the said (territorial division), being a dealer in second-hand goods, did trade in [OR traffic in OR have in his possession for sale (OR traffic)] lumbering equipment that was marked with the mark [OR brand OR registered timber mark OR name OR initials] of C.D., without the written consent of C.D., to wit: (specify the particulars of the offence), contrary to s. 339(2) of the Criminal Code of Canada.

17. Destroying documents of title — Section 340

Every one who — for a fraudulent purpose — destroys or cancels or conceals or obliterates — either a document of title to goods or lands — or a valuable security or testamentary instrument — or a judicial or official document — is guilty of an indictable offence.

Intent. For fraudulent purpose.

Included offences. Attempts (s. 660 and s. 662(1)(b)).

Punishment. Imprisonment for a term not exceeding 10 years (s. 340).

Release. Initial decision to release made by justice (s. 515(1)).

Election. Accused may elect trial by judge and jury, judge alone, or provincial court judge (s. 536).

Evidence. *See* **20**, *below.*

18. Fraudulent concealment — Section 341

Every one who — for a fraudulent purpose — takes or obtains or removes or conceals anything — is guilty of an indictable offence.

Intent. For fraudulent purpose.

Included offences. Attempts (s. 660 and s. 662(1)(b)).

Punishment. Imprisonment for a term not exceeding 2 years (s. 341).

Release. Initial decision to release made by officer in charge or justice (s. 498).

Election. Accused may elect trial by judge and jury, judge alone, or provincial court judge (s. 536).

Evidence. *See* **20**, *below.*

Informations

A.B., on or about the —— day of ——, 19——, at the —— of ——, in the said (territorial division), for a fraudulent purpose, did take [OR obtain OR remove OR conceal] (specify the thing), to wit: (specify the particulars of the offence), contrary to s. 341 of the Criminal Code of Canada.

19. Theft from mail — Section 356(1)(a)

Every one who — steals — either anything sent by post after it is deposited at a post office and before it is delivered — or a bag or sack or other container or covering in which mail is conveyed whether or not it contains mail — or a key suited to a lock adopted for use by the Canada Post Office — is guilty of an indictable offence.

Jurisdiction. *See Jurisdiction under* **1**, *above.*

Included offences. Attempts (s. 660 and s. 662(1)(b)).

Punishment. Imprisonment for a term not exceeding 10 years (s. 356(1)).

Release. Initial decision to release made by justice (s. 515(1)).

Election. Accused may elect trial by judge and jury, judge alone, or provincial court judge (s. 536).

Evidence. 1. It is not necessary to allege in the indictment or to prove on the trial that the thing in respect of which the offence was committed had any value (s. 356(2)).
2. A letter once it is deposited at a Post Office is deemed to be the property of the Postmaster General (s. 588).

Informations

A.B., on or about the —— day of ——, 19——, at the —— of ——, in the said (territorial division), did steal (specify the thing stolen) that had been sent by post, after it had been deposited at a post office and before it was delivered, to wit: (specify the particulars of the offence), contrary to s. 356(1)(a) of the Criminal Code of Canada.

A.B., on or about the —— day of ——, 19——, at the —— of ——, in the said (territorial division), did steal a bag [OR sack OR container OR covering] in which mail is conveyed, to wit: (specify the particulars of the offence), contrary to s. 356(1)(a) of the Criminal Code of Canada.

A.B., on or about the —— day of ——, 19——, at the —— of ——, in the said (territorial division), did steal a key suited to a lock adopted for use by the Canada Post Office, to wit: (specify the particulars of the offence), contrary to s. 356(1)(a) of the Criminal Code of Canada.

20. Sufficiency of count

No count that alleges false pretences, fraud or any attempt or conspiracy by fraudulent means is insufficient by reason only that it does not set out in detail the nature of the false pretence, fraud or fraudulent means (s. 586).

THREATS

1. *Uttering threats relating to persons*
2. *Uttering threats relating to property*
3. *Uttering threats relating to animals*

See also CRIMINAL HARASSMENT.

1. Uttering threats relating to persons — Section 264.1(1)(a) and (2)

Every one who — in any manner — knowingly — utters or conveys or causes any person to receive a threat — to cause death or serious bodily harm to any person — is guilty of an indictable offence.

Intent. Knowingly.

Included offences. Attempts (s. 660 and s. 662(1)(b)).

Punishment. Imprisonment for a term not exceeding 5 years (s. 264.1(2)).

Release. Initial decision to release made by officer in charge or justice (s. 498).

Election. Accused may elect trial by judge and jury, judge alone, or provincial court judge (s. 536).

Informations

A.B., on or about the —— day of ——, 19——, at the —— of ——, in the said (territorial division), did knowingly utter [OR convey OR cause C.D. to receive] a threat to cause death [OR serious bodily harm] to C.D. [OR E.F.], to wit: (specify the particulars of the offence), contrary to s. 264.1(1)(a) and (2) of the Criminal Code of Canada.

2. Uttering threats relating to property — Section 264.1(1)(b) and (3)

Every one who — in any manner — knowingly — utters or conveys or causes any person to receive a threat — to burn or destroy or damage real or personal property — is guilty of either an indictable offence or an offence punishable on summary conviction.

Intent. Knowingly.

Limitation period. No proceedings in respect of offences that are declared to be punishable on summary conviction shall be instituted more than 6 months after the time when the subject matter of the proceedings arose (s. 786(2) and s. 785(1)).

Included offences. Attempts (s. 660 and s. 662(1)(b)).

Punishment. On indictment, imprisonment for a term not exceeding 2 years (s. 264.1(3)(a)). On summary conviction, a fine not exceeding $2,000, or 6 months' imprisonment, or both (s. 264.1(3)(b) and s. 787(1)).

Release. Initial decision to release made by peace officer (s. 497).

Election. On indictment, accused may elect trial by judge and jury, judge alone, or provincial court judge (s. 536). On summary conviction, no election.

Informations

A.B., on or about the —— day of ——, 19——, at the —— of ——, in the said (territorial division), did knowingly utter [OR convey OR cause C.D. to receive] a threat to burn [OR destroy OR damage] real [OR personal] property, to wit: (specify the particulars of the offence), contrary to s. 264.1(1)(b) and (3) of the Criminal Code of Canada.

3. Uttering threats relating to animals — Section 264.1(1)(c) and (3)

Every one who — in any manner — knowingly — utters or conveys or causes any person to receive a threat — to kill or poison or injure an animal or bird that is the property of any person — is guilty of either an indictable offence or an offence punishable on summary conviction.

Intent. Knowingly.

Limitation period. No proceedings in respect of offences that are declared to be punishable on summary conviction shall be instituted more than 6 months after the time when the subject matter of the proceedings arose (s. 786(2) and s. 785(1)).

Included offences. Attempts (s. 660 and s. 662(1)(b)).

Punishment. On indictment, imprisonment for a term not exceeding 2 years (s. 264.1(3)(a)). On summary conviction, a fine not exceeding $2,000, or 6 months' imprisonment, or both (s. 264.1(3)(b) and s. 787(1)).

Release. Initial decision to release made by peace officer (s. 497).

Election. On indictment, accused may elect trial by judge and jury, judge alone, or provincial court judge (s. 536). On summary conviction, no election.

Informations

A.B., on or about the —— day of ——, 19——, at the —— of ——, in the said (territorial division), did knowingly utter [OR convey OR cause C.D. to receive] a threat to kill [OR poison OR injure] an animal [OR a bird] belonging to C.D. [OR E.F.], to wit: (specify the particulars of the offence), contrary to s. 264.1(1)(c) and (3) of the Criminal Code of Canada.

THREE-CARD MONTE. For the purposes of the Criminal Code, "three-card monte" means the game commonly known as three-card monte, including any other game that is similar to it, whether or not the game is played with cards and notwithstanding the number of cards or other things that are used for the purpose of playing (s. 206(2)).

TIME

1. *Computation of time*
2. *Holiday*
3. *Month*
4. *Year*
5. *Standard time*
6. *Local time*

1. Computation of time

Time limits and holidays. Where the time limited for the doing of a thing expires or falls on a holiday, the thing may be done on the day next following that is not a holiday (Interpretation Act, s. 26).

Clear days. Where there is a reference to a number of clear days or "at least" a number of days between two events, in calculating that number of days, the days on which the events happen are excluded (Interpretation Act, s. 27(1)).

Not clear days. Where there is a reference to a number of days, not expressed to be clear days, between two events, in calculating the number of days the day on which the first event happens is excluded and the day on which the second event happens is included (Interpretation Act, s. 27(2)).

Beginning and ending of prescribed periods. Where a time is expressed to begin or end at, on or with a specified day, or to continue to or until a specified day, the time includes that day (Interpretation Act, s. 27(3)).

After specified day. Where a time is expressed to begin after or to be from a specified day, the time does not include that day (Interpretation Act, s. 27(4)).

Within a time. Where anything is to be done within a time after, from, of or before a specified day, the time does not include that day (Interpretation Act, s. 27(5)).

Calculation of a period of months after or before a specified day. Where there is a reference to a period of time consisting of a number of months after or before a specified day the period is calculated by (a) counting forward or backward from the specified day the number of months, without including the month in which that day falls; (b) excluding the specified day; and (c) including in the last month counted under para. (a) the day that has the same calendar number as the specified day or, if that month has no day with that number, the last day of that month (Interpretation Act, s. 28).

Time of the day. Where there is a reference to time expressed as a specified time of the day, the time shall be taken to mean standard time (Interpretation Act, s. 29).

Time when specified age attained. A person shall be deemed not to have attained a specified number of years of age until the commencement of the anniversary, of the same number, of the day of his birth (Interpretation Act, s. 30).

2. Holiday

"Holiday" means any of the following days:

Sunday
New Year's Day
Good Friday
Easter Monday
Christmas Day
the birthday or the day fixed by proclamation for the celebration of the birthday of the reigning Sovereign
Victoria Day
Canada Day
the first Monday in September, designated Labour Day
Remembrance Day
any day appointed by proclamation to be observed as a day of general prayer or mourning or day of public rejoicing or thanksgiving

and any of the following additional days, namely:

(a) in any province, any day appointed by proclamation of the lieutenant governor of the province to be observed as a public holiday or as a day of general prayer or mourning or day of public rejoicing or thanksgiving within the province, and any day that is a non-juridical day by virtue of an Act of the legislature of the province, and

(b) in any city, town, municipality or other organized district, any day appointed as a civic holiday by resolution of the council or other authority charged with the administration of the civic or municipal affairs of the city, town, municipality or district (Interpretation Act, s. 35(1)).

3. Month

"Month" means a calendar month (Interpretation Act, s. 35(1)).

4. Year

"Year" means any period of 12 consecutive months (Interpretation Act, s. 37(1)).

"Calendar year". A period of 12 consecutive months commencing on January 1 (Interpretation Act, s. 37(1)).

"Dominical year" (referred to by number). The period of 12 consecutive months commencing on January 1 of that year (Interpretation Act, s. 37(1)).

"Financial year" or "fiscal year" means, in relation to money provided by Parliament, or the Consolidated Revenue Fund, or the accounts, taxes or finances of Canada, the period beginning on April 1 in one calendar year and ending on March 31 in the next calendar year (Interpretation Act, s. 37(1)).

5. Standard time

Except as otherwise provided by any proclamation of the Governor in Council which may be issued for the purposes of this definition in relation to any province or territory or any part thereof, "standard time" means (a) in relation to the Province of Newfoundland, Newfoundland standard time, being 3 hours and 30 minutes behind Greenwich time, (b) in relation to the Provinces of Nova Scotia, New Brunswick and Prince Edward Island, those parts of the Province of Quebec lying east of the 63rd meridian of west longitude, and those parts of the Northwest Territories lying east of the 68th meridian of west longitude, Atlantic standard time, being 4 hours behind Greenwich time, (c) in relation to those parts of the Province of Quebec lying west of the 63rd meridian of west longitude, and those parts of the Province of Ontario, lying between the 90th and the 68th meridians of west longitude, Southampton Island and the islands adjacent to Southampton Island, and that part of the Northwest Territories lying between the 68th and the 85th meridians of west longitude, eastern standard time, being 5 hours behind Greenwich time, (d) in relation to that part of the Province of Ontario lying west of the 90th meridian of west longitude, the Province of Manitoba, and that part of the Northwest Territories, except Southampton Island and the islands adjacent to Southampton Island, lying between the 85th and the 102nd meridians of west longitude, central standard time, being 6 hours behind Greenwich time, (e) in relation to the Province of Saskatchewan, the Province of Alberta, and that part of the Northwest Territories lying west of the 102nd meridian of west longitude, mountain standard time, being 7 hours behind Greenwich time, (f) in relation to the Province of British Columbia, Pacific standard time, being 8 hours behind Greenwich time, and (g) in relation to the Yukon Territory, Yukon standard time, being 9 hours behind Greenwich time (Interpretation Act, s. 35(1)).

6. Local time

"Local time" in relation to any place, the time observed in that place for the regulation of business hours (Interpretation Act, s. 35(1)).

TRACE EVIDENCE. Evidence based upon the examination of small amounts of biological materials such as blood or on specimens of soil, textile fibers etc. (Jaffe, A Guide to Pathological Evidence, 2nd ed.).

TRADE COMBINATION. For the purposes of the Criminal Code, "trade combination" means any combination between masters or workmen or other persons for the purpose of regulating or altering the relations between masters or workmen, or the conduct of a master or workman in or in respect of his business, employment or contract of employment or service (s. 467(2)).

TRADE-MARK OFFENCES

1. *Definitions*
2. *Forging a trade mark*
3. *Passing off*
4. *Possession of instruments for forging trade-mark*
5. *Defacing, concealing or removing trade-mark*
6. *Using bottle or siphon bearing trade-mark*
7. *Reconditioned goods*
8. *Falsely claiming royal warrant*
9. *Sufficiency of count*

1. Definitions

"Trade-mark". A mark that is used by a person for the purpose of distinguishing or so as to distinguish wares or services manufactured, sold, leased, hired or performed by him, for those manufactured, sold, leased, hired or performed by others. The definition of a trade-mark includes a "certification mark", a "distinguishing guise" and a "proposed trade-mark" (Trade-marks Act, s. 2).

"Certification mark". A mark that is used for the purpose of distinguishing or so as to distinguish wares or services that are of a defined standard with respect to the character or quality of the wares

or services, the working conditions under which the wares have been produced or the services performed, the class of persons by whom the wares have been produced or the services performed, or the area within which the wares have been produced or the services performed, from wares or services that are not of such a defined standard (Trade-marks Act, s. 2).

"Distinguishing guise". A shaping of wares or their containers, or a mode of wrapping or packaging wares, the appearance of which is used by a person for the purpose of distinguishing or so as to distinguish wares or services manufactured, sold, leased, hired or performed by him from those manufactured, sold, leased, hired or performed by others (Trade-marks Act, s. 2).

"Forging trade-mark". For the purposes of Part X of the Criminal Code (Fraudulent Transactions Relating to Contracts and Trade) every one forges a trade-mark who either

(a) without the consent of the proprietor of the trade-mark, makes or reproduces in any manner that trade-mark or a mark so nearly resembling it as to be calculated to deceive, or

(b) falsifies, in any manner, a genuine trade-mark (s. 406).

2. Forging a trade-mark — Section 407 and section 412(1)

Every one who — with intent to deceive or defraud the public or any person (whether ascertained or not) — forges a trade-mark — is guilty of an indictable offence or an offence punishable on summary conviction.

Intent. Intention to deceive or defraud.

Limitation period. No proceedings in respect of offences that are declared to be punishable on summary conviction shall be instituted more than 6 months after the time when the subject matter of the proceedings arose (s. 786(2) and s. 785(1)).

Included offences. Attempts (s. 660 and s. 662(1)(b)).

Punishment. On indictment, imprisonment for a term not exceeding 2 years (s. 412(1)(a)). On summary conviction, a fine not exceeding $2,000, or 6 months' imprisonment, or both (s. 412(1)(b) and s. 787(1)).

Release. Initial decision to release made by peace officer (s. 497).

Election. On indictment, accused may elect trial by judge and jury, judge alone, or provincial court judge (s. 536). On summary conviction, no election.

Evidence. 1. Anything by means of which or in relation to which a person commits this offence is, unless the court otherwise orders, forfeited on the conviction of the person for this offence (s. 412(2)).
2. Where the alleged offence relates to imported goods, evidence that the goods were shipped to Canada from a place outside of Canada is, in the absence of any evidence to the contrary, proof that the goods were made or produced in the country from which they were shipped (s. 414).

3. Passing off — Section 408 and section 412(1)

Every one who — with intent to deceive or defraud the public or any person (whether ascertained or not) — either passes off other wares or services as and for those ordered or required — or makes uses, in association with wares or services, of any description that is false in a material respect as to — either the kind or quality or quantity or composition — or the geographical origin — or the mode of the manufacture, production or performance of such wares or services — is guilty of an indictable offence or an offence punishable on summary conviction.

Intent. Intention to deceive or defraud.

Limitation period. No proceedings in respect of offences that are declared to be punishable on summary conviction shall be instituted more than 6 months after the time when the subject matter of the proceedings arose (s. 786(2) and s. 785(1)).

Included offences. Attempts (s. 660 and s. 662(1)(b)).

Punishment. On indictment, imprisonment for a term not exceeding 2 years (s. 412(1)(a)). On summary conviction, a fine not exceeding $2,000, or 6 months' imprisonment, or both (s. 412(1)(b) and s. 787(1)).

Release. Initial decision to release made by peace officer (s. 497).

Election. On indictment, accused may elect trial by judge and jury, judge alone, or provincial court judge (s. 536). On summary conviction, no election.

Evidence. See Evidence under **2**, above.

Informations

A.B., on or about the —— day of ——, 19——, at the —— of ——, in the said (territorial division), with intent to deceive [OR defraud] the public [OR C.D.], did pass off other wares [OR services] as and for those ordered [OR required], to wit: (specify the particulars of the offence), contrary to s. 408(a) of the Criminal Code of Canada.

A.B., on or about the —— day of ——, 19——, at the —— of ——, in the said (territorial division), with intent to deceive or defraud the public [OR C.D.], did make use, in association with wares [OR with services] of a description that was false in a material aspect as to the kind [OR the quality OR the quantity OR the composition OR the geographical origin OR the mode of manufacture OR the mode of production OR the mode of performance] of such wares [OR services], to wit: (specify the particulars of the offence), contrary to s. 408(b) of the Criminal Code of Canada.

4. Possession of instruments for forging trade-mark — Section 409(1) and section 412(1)

Every one who — makes or has in his possession or disposes of — a die or block or machine or other instrument designed or intended to be used in forging a trade-mark — is guilty of an indictable offence or an offence punishable on summary conviction.

Limitation period. No proceedings in respect of offences that are declared to be punishable on summary conviction shall be instituted more than 6 months after the time when the subject matter of the proceedings arose (s. 786(2) and s. 785(1)).

Included offences. Attempts (s. 660 and s. 662(1)(b)).

Punishment. On indictment, imprisonment for a term not exceeding 2 years (s. 412(1)(a)). On summary conviction, a fine not exceeding $2,000, or 6 months' imprisonment, or both (s. 412(1)(b) and s. 787(1)).

Release. Initial decision to release made by peace officer (s. 497).

Election. On indictment, accused may elect trial by judge and jury, judge alone, or provincial court judge (s. 536). On summary conviction, no election.

Evidence. 1. No person shall be convicted of this offence where he proves that he acted in good faith in the ordinary course of his business or employment (s. 409(2)).
2. While it need not be shown that the trade mark was or is registered, it must be proven to be a trade mark as defined by the Trade-marks Act.
3. *See also Evidence under* **2**, *above.*

Informations

A.B., on or about the —— day of ——, 19——, at the —— of ——, in the said (territorial division), did make [OR have in his possession OR dispose of] a die [OR a block OR a machine OR (specify some other instrument)], designed [OR intended] to be used in forging a trade mark, to wit: (specify the particulars of the offence), contrary to s. 409(1) of the Criminal Code of Canada.

5. Defacing, concealing or removing trade-mark — Section 410(a) and section 412(1)

Every one who — with intent to deceive or defraud — defaces or conceals or removes — a trade-mark or the name of another person from anything (without the consent of that other person) — is guilty of an indictable offence or an offence punishable on summary conviction.

Intent. Intention to deceive or defraud.

Limitation period. No proceedings in respect of offences that are declared to be punishable on summary conviction shall be instituted more than 6 months after the time when the subject matter of the proceedings arose (s. 786(2) and s. 785(1)).

Included offences. Attempts (s. 660 and s. 662(1)(b)).

Punishment. On indictment, imprisonment for a term not exceeding 2 years (s. 412(1)(a)). On summary conviction, a fine not exceeding $2,000, or 6 months' imprisonment, or both (s. 412(1)(b) and s. 787(1)).

Release. Initial decision to release made by peace officer (s. 497).

Election. On indictment, accused may elect trial by judge and jury, judge alone, or provincial court judge (s. 536). On summary conviction, no election.

Evidence. *See Evidence under* **2**, *above.*

Informations

A.B., on or about the —— day of ——, 19——, at the —— of ——, in the said (territorial division), with intent to deceive [OR to defraud] did deface [OR conceal OR remove] a trade mark [OR the name of C.D. from (specify the thing) without the consent of C.D.], to wit: (specify the particulars of the offence), contrary to s. 410(a) of the Criminal Code of Canada.

6. Using bottle or siphon bearing trade-mark — Section 410(b) and section 412(1)

Every one who — with intent to deceive or defraud — being a manufacturer or dealer or trader or bottler — fills any bottle or siphon that bears the trade mark or name of another person — without the consent of that other person — with a beverage or milk or by-product of milk or other liquid commodity — for the purpose of sale or traffic — is guilty of an indictable offence or an offence punishable on summary conviction.

Intent. Intention to deceive or defraud.

Limitation period. No proceedings in respect of offences that are declared to be punishable on summary conviction shall be instituted more than 6 months after the time when the subject matter of the proceedings arose (s. 786(2) and s. 785(1)).

Included offences. Attempts (s. 660 and s. 662(1)(b)).

Punishment. On indictment, imprisonment for a term not exceeding 2 years (s. 412(1)(a)). On summary conviction, a fine not exceeding $2,000, or 6 months' imprisonment, or both (s. 412(1)(b) and s. 787(1)).

Release. Initial decision to release made by peace officer (s. 497).

Election. On indictment, accused may elect trial by judge and jury, judge alone, or provincial court judge (s. 536). On summary conviction, no election.

Evidence. *See Evidence under* **2**, *above.*

7. Reconditioned goods — Section 411 and section 412(1)

Every one who — sells or exposes or has in his possession for sale — or advertises for sale — goods that have been used or reconditioned or remade — and that bear the trade-mark or the trade name of another person — without making full disclosure that the goods have been reconditioned or rebuilt or remade for sale and that they are not in the condition in which they were originally made or produced — is guilty of an indictable offence or an offence punishable on summary conviction.

Limitation period. No proceedings in respect of offences that are declared to be punishable on summary conviction shall be instituted more than 6 months after the time when the subject matter of the proceedings arose (s. 786(2) and s. 785(1)).

Included offences. Attempts (s. 660 and s. 662(1)(b)).

Punishment. On indictment, imprisonment for a term not exceeding 2 years (s. 412(1)(a)). On summary conviction, a fine not exceeding $2,000, or 6 months' imprisonment, or both (s. 412(1)(b) and s. 787(1)).

Release. Initial decision to release made by peace officer (s. 497).

Election. On indictment, accused may elect trial by judge and jury, judge alone, or provincial court judge (s. 536). On summary conviction, no election.

Evidence. *See Evidence, under* **2***, above.*

8. Falsely claiming royal warrant — Section 413

Every one who — falsely represents — that goods are made — by a person holding a royal warrant — or for the service or Her Majesty or a member of the Royal Family or a public department — is guilty of an offence punishable on summary conviction.

Limitation period. No proceedings in respect of offences that are declared to be punishable on summary conviction shall be instituted more than 6 months after the time when the subject matter of the proceedings arose (s. 786(2) and s. 785(1)).

Included offences. Attempts (s. 660 and s. 662(1)(b)).

Punishment. A fine not exceeding $2,000, or 6 months' imprisonment, or both (s. 413 and s. 787(1)).

Release. Initial decision to release made by peace officer (s. 497).

Election. No election, summary conviction offence.

9. Sufficiency of count

No count that alleges false pretences, fraud or any attempt or conspiracy by fraudulent means is insufficient by reason only that it does not set out in detail the nature of the false pretence, fraud or fraudulent means (s. 586).

TRADING STAMP OFFENCES

1. *Definition of "trading stamps"*
2. *Issuing trading stamps*
3. *Giving to purchaser of goods*

1. Definition of "trading stamps"

For the purposes of Part X of the Criminal Code (Fraudulent Transactions Relating to Contracts and Trade) "trading stamps" includes any form of cash receipt, receipt, coupon, premium ticket or other device, designed or intended to be given to the purchaser of goods by the vendor thereof or on his behalf, and to represent a discount on the price of the goods or a premium to the purchaser thereof:

(a) that may be redeemed by any person other than the vendor, the person from whom the vendor purchased the goods or the manufacturer of the goods; by the vendor, the person from whom the vendor purchased the goods or the manufacturer of the goods in cash or in goods that are not his property in whole or in part; or by the vendor elsewhere than in the premises where the goods are purchased; or

(b) that does not show upon its face the place where it is delivered and the merchantable value thereof; or

(c) that may not be redeemed on demand at any time,

but an offer, endorsed by the manufacturer on a wrapper or container in which goods are sold, of a premium or reward for the return of that wrapper or container to the manufacturer is not a trading stamp (s. 379).

2. Issuing trading stamps — Section 427(1)

Every one who — by himself or his employee or agent — directly or indirectly — issues or gives or sells or otherwise disposes of — or offers to issue or give or sell or otherwise dispose — of trading stamps — to a merchant or dealer in goods for use in his business — is guilty of an offence punishable on summary conviction.

Limitation period. No proceedings in respect of offences that are declared to be punishable on summary conviction shall be instituted more than 6 months after the time when the subject matter of the proceedings arose (s. 786(2) and s. 785(1)).

Included offences. Attempts (s. 660 and s. 662(1)(b)).

Punishment. A fine not exceeding $2,000, or 6 months' imprisonment, or both (s. 427(1) and s. 787(1)).

Release. Initial decision to release made by peace officer (s. 497).

Election. No election, summary conviction offence.

Informations

A.B., on or about the —— day of ——, 19——, at the —— of ——, in the said (territorial division), by himself [OR by C.D., his employee, OR by C.D., his agent] directly [OR indirectly] did issue [OR give OR sell OR dispose of OR offer to issue OR offer to sell OR offer to dispose of] trading stamps to E.F., a merchant [OR dealer in goods] for use in his business, to wit: (specify the particulars of the offence), contrary to s. 427(1) of the Criminal Code of Canada.

3. Giving to purchaser of goods — Section 427(2)

Every one who — being a merchant or dealer in goods — by himself or his employee or agent — directly or indirectly — gives or in any way disposes of — or offers to give or in any way dispose of — trading stamps — to a person who purchases goods from him — is guilty of an offence punishable on summary conviction.

Limitation period. No proceedings in respect of offences that are declared to be punishable on summary conviction shall be instituted more than 6 months after the time when the subject matter of the proceedings arose (s. 786(2) and s. 785(1)).

Included offences. Attempts (s. 660 and s. 662(1)(b)).

Punishment. A fine not exceeding $2,000, or 6 months' imprisonment, or both (s. 427(2) and s. 787(1)).

Release. Initial decision to release made by peace officer (s. 497).

Election. No election, summary conviction offence.

Informations

A.B., on or about the —— day of ——, 19——, at the —— of ——, in the said (territorial division), being a merchant [OR a dealer in goods] by himself [OR by C.D., his employee, OR by C.D., his agent] directly [OR indirectly] did give [OR dispose of OR offer to give OR offer to dispose of] trading stamps to E.F., a person who purchased goods from him, to wit: (specify the particulars of the offence), contrary to s. 427(2) of the Criminal Code of Canada.

TRAFFICKING. 1. For the purposes of Part III (Controlled Drugs) and Part IV (Restricted Drugs) of the Food and Drugs Act, to "traffic" means to manufacture, sell, export from or import into Canada, transport or deliver, otherwise than under the authority of Part III or Part IV or the regulations (Food and Drugs Act, s. 38 and s. 46). 2. For the purposes of the Narcotic Control Act, to "traffic" means (a) to manufacture, sell, give, administer, transport, send, deliver or distribute, or (b) to offer to manufacture, sell, give, administer, transport, send, deliver or distribute otherwise than under the authority of the Narcotic Control Act or the regulations (Narcotic Control Act, s. 2).

TREASON AND OTHER OFFENCES AGAINST THE QUEEN'S AUTHORITY AND PERSON

1. *High treason*
2. *Treason*
3. *Alarming Her Majesty the Queen*
4. *Causing bodily harm to Her Majesty the Queen*
5. *Assisting alien enemy to leave Canada*
6. *Omitting to prevent treason*

See also INCITING TO MUTINY.

1. High treason

Definition of offence

Section 46(1)(a)

Every one who — in Canada — kills or attempts to kill Her Majesty — or does her any bodily harm tending to death or destruction — or maims or wounds her — or imprisons or restrains her — commits high treason.

Section 46(1)(b)

Every one who — in Canada — levies war against Canada — or does any act preparatory thereto — commits high treason.

Section 46(1)(c)

Every one who — in Canada — assists an enemy at war with Canada — or any armed forces against whom Canadian Forces are engaged in hostilities — whether or not a state of war exists between Canada and the country whose forces they are — commits high treason.

Section 46(3)(a)

A Canadian citizen or a person who — owes allegiance to Her Majesty — in right of Canada — commits high treason — if he does anything mentioned above — while in or out of Canada.

Statement of offence — Section 47(1)

Every one who — commits high treason — is guilty of an indictable offence.

Jurisdiction. Triable only in a superior court of criminal jurisdiction (s. 468 and s. 469(a)(i)).

Included offences. Attempts (s. 660 and s. 662(1)(b)).

Punishment. Imprisonment for life (s. 47(1)).
For these purposes, the sentence prescribed is a minimum punishment (s. 47(4)).

Release. Initial decision to release may only be made by superior court judge (s. 522).

Election. Superior court (with jury) exclusive, except where accused elects superior court trial without jury with consent of Attorney General (s. 473) (s. 469).

Evidence. 1. No person shall be convicted of this offence on the evidence of only one witness, unless the evidence of that witness is corroborated in a material particular by evidence that implicates the accused (s. 47(3)).
2. Where it is treason to conspire with any person, the act of conspiring is an overt act of treason (s. 46(4)).
3. In proceedings for this offence, no evidence is admissible of an overt act unless that overt act is set out in the indictment or unless the evidence is otherwise relevant as tending to prove an overt act that is set out therein (s. 55).
4. Where an accused is charged with this offence, every overt act that is to be relied upon shall be stated in the indictment (s. 581(4)).
5. The authority of a court to amend indictments does not authorize the court to add to the overt acts stated in an indictment for this offence (s. 601(9)).
6. No person shall be convicted of the offence of high treason unless in the indictment charging the offence he is specifically charged with that offence (s. 582).

Informations

A.B., on or about the —— day of ——, 19——, at the —— of ——, in the said (territorial division), in Canada, did kill Her Majesty [OR did attempt to kill Her Majesty OR did Her Majesty bodily harm tending to death (OR destruction) OR did maim (OR wound) Her Majesty OR did imprison (OR restrain) Her Majesty] and did thereby commit high treason, contrary to s. 47(1) of the Criminal Code of Canada.

2. Treason

Definition of offence

Section 46(2)(a)

Every one who — in Canada — uses force or violence — for the purpose of overthrowing the government of Canada or a province — commits treason.

Section 46(2)(b)

Every one who — in Canada — without lawful authority — communicates or makes available to an agent of a state other than Canada — military or scientific information or any sketch or plan or model or article or note or document of a military or scientific character — that he knows or ought to know may be used by that state for a purpose prejudicial to the safety or defence of Canada — commits treason.

Section 46(2)(c)

Every one who — in Canada — either conspires with any person to commit high treason — or to use force or violence for the purpose of overthrowing the government of Canada or a province — commits treason.

Section 46(2)(d)

Every one who — in Canada — forms an intention — to do anything that is high treason — or uses force or violence for the purpose of overthrowing the government of Canada or a province — and manifests that intention by an overt act — commits treason.

Section 46(2)(e)

Every one who — in Canada — conspires with any person — to, without lawful authority, communicate or make available to an agent of a state other than Canada — military or scientific information of any sketch or plan or model or article or note or document of a military or scientific character — that he knows or ought to know may be used by that state for a purpose prejudicial to the safety or defence of Canada — or forms an intention — to, without lawful authority, communicate or make available to an agent of a state other than Canada — military or scientific information or any sketch or plan or model or article or note or document of a military or scientific character — that he knows or ought to know may be used by that

state for a purpose prejudicial to the safety or defence of Canada — and manifests that intention by an overt act — commits treason.

Section 46(3)(b)

A Canadian citizen or a person who — owes allegiance to Her Majesty — in right of Canada — if he does anything mentioned above — while in or out of Canada — commits treason.

Statement of offence — Section 47(2)

Every one who — commits treason — is guilty of an indictable offence.

Intent. Knowledge of prejudicial nature of information (s. 46(2)(b) and (e)).

Jurisdiction. Triable only in a superior court of criminal jurisdiction (s. 468 and s. 469(a)(i)).

Limitation period. 1. No proceedings for committing treason by using force or violence for the purpose of overthrowing the government of Canada or a province (s. 46(2)(a)) shall be commenced more than 3 years after the time when the offence is alleged to have been committed (s. 48(1)).
2. No proceedings shall be commenced under s. 47 in respect of an overt act of treason expressed or declared by open and considered speech unless (a) an information setting out the overt act and the words by which it was expressed or declared is laid under oath before a justice within 6 days after the time when the words are alleged to have been spoken, and (b) a warrant for the arrest of the accused is issued within 10 days after the time when the information is laid (s. 48(2)).

Included offences. Attempts (s. 660 and s. 662(1)(b)).

Punishment. Imprisonment for life if he is guilty of an offence under s. 46(2)(a), (c) or (d) (s. 47(2)(a)).

Imprisonment for life if he is guilty of an offence under s. 46(2)(b) or (e) committed while a state of war exists between Canada and another country (s. 47(2)(b)).

Imprisonment for a term not exceeding 14 years if he is guilty of an offence under s. 46(2)(b) or (e) committed while no state of war exists between Canada and another country (s. 47(2)(c)).

Release. Initial decision to release may only be made by superior court judge (s. 522).

Election. Superior court (with jury) exclusive, except where accused elects superior court trial without jury with consent of Attorney General (s. 473) (s. 469).

Evidence. See Evidence under **1**, *above.*

Informations

A.B., on or about the —— day of ——, 19——, at the —— of ——, in the said (territorial division), in Canada, did use force or violence for the purpose of overthrowing the government of Canada [OR the government of the Province of ——], to wit: (specify the particulars of the offence), contrary to s. 47(2) of the Criminal Code of Canada.

3. Alarming Her Majesty the Queen — Section 49(a)

Every one who — wilfully — in the presence of Her Majesty — does an act — with intent to alarm Her Majesty — or with intent to break the public peace — is guilty of an indictable offence.

Intent. Wilfully.

Jurisdiction. Triable only in a superior court of criminal jurisdiction (s. 468 and s. 469(a)(ii)).

Included offences. Attempts (s. 660 and s. 662(1)(b)).

Punishment. Imprisonment for a term not exceeding 14 years (s. 49).

Release. Initial decision to release may only be made by superior court judge (s. 522).

Election. Superior court (with jury) exclusive, except where accused elects superior court trial without jury with consent of Attorney General (s. 473) (s. 469).

*Evidence. See Evidence, items 3. to 5., under **1**, above.*

Informations

A.B., on or about the —— day of ——, 19——, at the —— of ——, in the said (territorial division), wilfully, in the presence of Her Majesty the Queen, did an act with intent to alarm Her Majesty [OR did an act with intent to break the public peace], to wit: (specify the particulars of the offence), contrary to s. 49(a) of the Criminal Code of Canada.

TREASON AND OTHER OFFENCES

4. Causing bodily harm to Her Majesty the Queen — Section 49(b)

Every one who — wilfully — in the presence of Her Majesty — does an act — that is intended or is likely to cause bodily harm to Her Majesty — is guilty of an indictable offence.

Intent. Wilfully.

Jurisdiction. Triable only in a superior court of criminal jurisdiction (s. 468 and s. 469(a)(ii)).

Included offences. Attempts (s. 660 and s. 662(1)(b)).

Punishment. Imprisonment for a term not exceeding 14 years (s. 49).

Release. Initial decision to release may only be made by superior court judge (s. 522).

Election. Superior court (with jury) exclusive, except where accused elects superior court trial without jury with consent of Attorney General (s. 473) (s. 469).

Evidence. See Evidence, items 3. to 5., under **1**, *above.*

Informations

A.B., on or about the —— day of ——, 19——, at the —— of ——, in the said (territorial division), wilfully, in the presence of Her Majesty, did an act that was intended to cause bodily harm to Her Majesty [OR that was likely to cause bodily harm to Her Majesty], to wit: (specify the particulars of the offence), contrary to s. 49(b) of the Criminal Code of Canada.

5. Assisting alien enemy to leave Canada

Section 50(1)(a)(i) and (2)

Every one who — incites or wilfully assists — a subject of a state that is at war with Canada — to leave Canada without the consent of the Crown — unless the accused establishes that assistance to the state that is at war with Canada was not intended thereby — is guilty of an indictable offence.

Section 50(1)(a)(ii) and (2)

Every one who — incites or wilfully assists — a subject of a state against whose forces Canadian Forces are engaged in hostilities — whether or not a state of war exists between Canada and the state whose forces they are — to leave Canada without the consent of the Crown — unless the accused establishes that assistance to the forces of that state was not intended thereby — is guilty of an indictable offence.

Intent. Wilfully assists.

Included offences. Attempts (s. 660 and s. 662(1)(b)).

Punishment. Imprisonment for a term not exceeding 14 years (s. 50(2)).

Release. Initial decision to release made by justice (s. 515(1)).

Election. Accused may elect trial by judge and jury, judge alone, or provincial court judge (s. 536).

Evidence. See Evidence, items 3. to 5., under **1**, *above.*

6. Omitting to prevent treason — Section 50(1)(b) and (2)

Every one who — knowing that a person is about to commit high treason or treason — does not, with all reasonable dispatch, inform — a justice of the peace or other peace officer thereof — or does not make other reasonable efforts — to prevent that person from committing high treason or treason — is guilty of an indictable offence.

Intent. Knowledge of act about to be committed.

Included offences. Attempts (s. 660 and s. 662(1)(b)).

Punishment. Imprisonment for a term not exceeding 14 years (s. 50(2)).

Release. Initial decision to release made by justice (s. 515(1)).

Election. Accused may elect trial by judge and jury, judge alone, or provincial court judge (s. 536).

Evidence. See Evidence, items 3. to 5., under **1**, *above.*

TRIAL. In Part XXVII of the Criminal Code (Summary Convictions), "trial" includes the hearing of a complaint (s. 785(1)).

TRIAL COURT. In Part XXI of the Criminal Code (Appeals — Indictable Offences) "trial court" means the court by which an accused was tried and includes a judge or a provincial court judge acting under Part XIX of the Code (s. 673).

TRIAL, PLACE OF. Where the offence is committed on water or on a bridge, between two or more territorial divisions, or committed on the boundary or within 500 metres thereof, or where begun in one and completed in another, the trial may be in either (s. 476(a) and (b)). If committed in or on a vehicle or vessel employed in a journey, or in an aircraft in flight, the trial may be held in any jurisdiction through or over which the conveyance passed (s. 476(c) and (d)).

Where the offence is committed in an unorganized tract of land, the trial may take place in any territorial division or provisional judicial district of the province in which the offence was committed (s. 480(1)).

If a prisoner is in jail or is arrested in one country for trial there and is wanted for offences committed elsewhere in the same province, all the offences may be tried where the prisoner is in custody (s. 470). Where a person in custody signifies in writing an intention to plead guilty to an offence committed elsewhere, he may be tried in the county or district where he is imprisoned (s. 479). If the offence was committed in another province, the Attorney General of that province must consent (s. 478(3)).

Every person charged with the publication of defamatory libel in a newspaper shall be tried in either the province where he resides or the province where the newspaper is published (s. 478(2)).

A prisoner cannot be brought into the county so as to give the court there jurisdiction to try an offence committed outside the county. The ordinary rule which is superseded by the above is that an accused is entitled to trial in the county where the offence was committed.

TRUSTEE. In the Criminal Code, "trustee" means a person who is declared by any Act to be a trustee or is, by the law of a province, a trustee, and without restricting the generality of the foregoing, includes a trustee on an express trust created by deed, will or instrument in writing, or by parol (s. 2).

U

UBERRIMAE FIDEI. Of the fullest confidence; of the utmost good faith (Latin).

UBI JUS, IBI REMEDIUM. "Where there is a right there is a remedy" (Latin).

ULTRA VIRES. 1. "In excess of the authority conferred by law" (Latin). 2. In Canada, Parliament has the exclusive power to enact criminal law (Constitution Act, 1867, s. 91(27)). Provincial legislation that is found by the courts to be criminal law will be found to be ultra vires and will be struck down. Similarly, federal legislation which purports to be criminal law, but which is found by the courts to be within the powers granted to the provincial legislatures and not to be criminal law, will also be found to be ultra vires and will be struck down.

UMBILICAL CORD. The cord connecting the navel of the fetus with the placenta and containing two arteries and one vein (Jaffe, A Guide to Pathological Evidence, 2nd ed.).

UNDERTAKING

1. *Definition*
2. *Undertaking of appellant*
3. *Undertaking of prosecutor other than the Attorney General*
4. *Period for which undertaking continues in force*
5. *Valid if given on a holiday*
6. *Failure to comply with an undertaking*

1. Definition

An undertaking is a promise in writing given by a person charged with an offence that he or she will attend at court on a specified date and place in order to be dealt with according to law (Form 12).

While the usual meaning is that in Form 12, the Criminal Code offers two other types of undertakings:

Form 13 — Undertaking by appellant (defendant).
Form 14 — Undertaking by appellant (prosecutor).

2. Undertaking of appellant

A person who was the defendant in proceedings before a summary conviction court and by whom an appeal is taken under s. 813 shall, if he is in custody, remain in custody unless the appeal court at which the appeal is to be heard orders that the appellant be released on his giving an undertaking to the appeal court, without conditions or with such conditions as the appeal court directs, to surrender himself into custody in accordance with the order, and the person having the custody of the appellant shall, where the appellant complies with the order, forthwith release the appellant (s. 816(1)).

When a notice of appeal is filed pursuant to s. 830, the appeal court may order that the appellant appear before a justice and give an undertaking. This does not apply where the appellant is the Attorney General or counsel acting on behalf of the Attorney General (s. 832).

3. Undertaking of prosecutor other than the Attorney General

The prosecutor in proceedings before a summary conviction court by whom an appeal is taken under s. 813 shall, forthwith after filing the notice of appeal and proof of service thereof, appear before a justice, and the justice shall, after giving the prosecutor and the respondent a reasonable opportunity to be heard, order that the prosecutor give an undertaking as prescribed in this section (s. 817(1)). The condition of the undertaking is that the prosecutor will appear personally or by counsel at the sittings of the appeal court at which the appeal is to be heard (s. 817(2)).

This provision does not apply in respect of an appeal taken by the Attorney General or by counsel acting on behalf of the Attorney General (s. 817(3)).

The undertaking may be in Form 14 and a recognizance under this section may be in Form 32 (s. 817(4)).

4. Period for which undertaking continues in force

Where an accused who has not been taken into custody or who has been released from custody under or by virtue of any provision of Part XVI pleads guilty to or is found guilty of an offence but is not convicted, any undertaking given by him continues in force, subject to its terms, until a disposition in respect of him is made unless, at the time he pleads guilty or is found guilty, the court, judge or justice orders that he be taken into custody pending such a disposition (s. 736(2)).

5. Valid if given on a holiday

An undertaking may be given on a holiday (s. 20).

6. Failure to comply with an undertaking

It is an offence to fail to comply with the terms of an undertaking. This includes both the requirement that the accused attend court at a certain time and place and any conditions that may form part of the undertaking (s. 145(2) and (3)). *See ESCAPES AND RESCUES.*

UNFIT TO STAND TRIAL. For the purposes of the Criminal Code, "unfit to stand trial" means unable on account of mental disorder to conduct a defence at any stage of the proceedings before a verdict is rendered or to instruct counsel to do so, and, in particular, unable on account of mental disorder to (a) understand the nature or object of the proceedings, (b) understand the possible consequences of the proceedings, or (c) communicate with counsel (s. 2).

UNLAWFUL ASSEMBLIES AND RIOTS

1. *Unlawful assembly*
2. *Rioting*
3. *Reading proclamation*
4. *Offences relating to proclamation*
5. *Neglect by peace officer*

1. Unlawful assembly

Definition. An unlawful assembly is an assembly of 3 or more persons who, with intent to carry out any common purpose, assemble in such a manner or so conduct themselves when they are assembled as to cause persons in the neighbourhood of the assembly to fear, on reasonable grounds, that they (a) will disturb the peace tumultuously, (b) will by that assembly needlessly and without reasonable cause provoke other persons to disturb the peace tumultuously (s. 63(1)).

Persons who are lawfully assembled may become an unlawful assembly if they conduct themselves with a common purpose in a manner that would have made the assembly unlawful if they had assembled in that manner for that purpose (s. 63(2)).

Persons are not unlawfully assembled by reason only that they are assembled to protect the dwelling-house of any one of them against persons who are threatening to break and enter it for the purpose of committing an indictable offence therein (s. 63(3)).

Statement of offence — Section 66

Every one who — is a member of an unlawful assembly — is guilty of an offence punishable on summary conviction.

Limitation period. No proceedings in respect of offences that are declared to be punishable on summary conviction shall be instituted more than 6 months after the time when the subject matter of the proceedings arose (s. 786(2) and s. 785(1)).

Included offences. Attempts (s. 660 and s. 662(1)(b)).

Punishment. A fine not exceeding $2,000, or 6 months' imprisonment, or both (s. 66 and s. 787(1)).

Release. Initial decision to release made by peace officer (s. 497).

UNLAWFUL ASSEMBLIES AND RIOTS

Election. No election, summary conviction offence.

Informations

A.B., on or about the —— day of ——, 19——, at the —— of ——, in the said (territorial division), was a member of an unlawful assembly, to wit: (specify the particulars of the offence), contrary to s. 66 of the Criminal Code of Canada.

A.B., on or about the —— day of ——, 19——, at the —— of ——, in the said (territorial division), with other persons to the number of 3 or more, with intent to carry out the common purpose of (specify what the common purpose was), did assemble themselves in such a manner [OR so conduct themselves when assembled] as to cause persons in the neighbourhood to fear on reasonable grounds that the said A.B. with the other persons there assembled, would disturb the peace tumultuously [OR would by such assembly needlessly and without any reasonable cause provoke other persons to disturb the peace tumultuously], to wit: (specify the particulars of the offence), contrary to s. 66 of the Criminal Code of Canada.

2. Rioting

Definition of "riot". A riot is an unlawful assembly that has begun to disturb the peace tumultuously (s. 64).

Statement of offence — Section 65

Every one who — takes part in a riot — is guilty of an indictable offence.

Included offences. Attempts (s. 660 and s. 662(1)(b)).

Punishment. Imprisonment for a term not exceeding 2 years (s. 65).

Release. Initial decision to release made by officer in charge or justice (s. 498).

Election. Accused may elect trial by judge and jury, judge alone, or provincial court judge (s. 536).

Informations

A.B., on or about the —— day of ——, 19——, at the —— of ——, in the said (territorial division), was a member of a lawful assembly that had begun to disturb the peace tumultuously, to wit: (specify the particulars of the offence), and did thereby take part in a riot, contrary to s. 65 of the Criminal Code of Canada.

A.B., on or about the —— day of ——, 19——, at the —— of ——, in the said (territorial division), did take part in a riot, to wit: (specify the particulars of the offence), contrary to s. 65 of the Criminal Code of Canada.

3. Reading proclamation

A justice, mayor or sheriff or the lawful deputy of a mayor or sheriff who receives notice that, at any place within his jurisdiction, twelve or more persons are unlawfully and riotously assembled together, shall go to that place and, after approaching as near as safely he may do, if he is satisfied that a riot is in progress, shall command silence and thereupon make or cause to be made in a loud voice a proclamation in the following words or to the like effect:

Her Majesty the Queen charges and commands all persons being assembled immediately to disperse and peaceably to depart to their habitations or to their lawful business upon the pain of being guilty of an offence for which, upon conviction, they may be sentenced to imprisonment for life. GOD SAVE THE QUEEN (s. 67).

4. Offences relating to proclamation

Section 68(a)

Every one who — opposes or hinders or assaults — wilfully and with force — a person who begins to make or is about to begin to make or is making — the proclamation referred to in s. 67 (reading proclamation) — so that it is not made — is guilty of an indictable offence.

Section 68(b)

Every one who — does not peaceably disperse and depart — from a place where the proclamation referred to above is made — within 30 minutes after it is made — is guilty of an indictable offence.

Section 68(c)

Every one who — does not depart from a place within 30 minutes — when he has reasonable grounds to believe — that the proclamation referred to above would have been made in that place — if some person had not opposed or hindered or assaulted, wilfully and with force, a person who would have made it — is guilty of an indictable offence.

Intent. Wilfully (s. 68(a)).

Included offences. Attempts (s. 660 and s. 662(1)(b)).

Punishment. Imprisonment for life (s. 68).

Release. Initial decision to release made by justice (s. 515(1)).

Election. Accused may elect trial by judge and jury, judge alone, or provincial court judge (s. 536).

5. Neglect by peace officer — Section 69

A peace officer who — receives notice that there is a riot within his jurisdiction — and without reasonable excuse — fails to take all reasonable steps to suppress the riot — is guilty of an indictable offence.

Included offences. Attempts (s. 660 and s. 662(1)(b)).

Punishment. Imprisonment for a term not exceeding 2 years (s. 69).

Release. Initial decision to release made by officer in charge or justice (s. 498).

Election. Accused may elect trial by judge and jury, judge alone, or provincial court judge (s. 536).

UNLAWFUL DRILLING

1. *Orders prohibiting unlawful drilling*
2. *Contravention of orders prohibiting unlawful drilling*

1. Orders prohibiting unlawful drilling

The Governor in Council may by proclamation make orders (a) to prohibit assemblies, without lawful authority, of persons for the purpose of training or drilling themselves, of being trained or drilled to the use of arms, or of practising military exercises; or (b) to prohibit persons when assembled for any purpose from training or drilling themselves or from being trained or drilled (s. 70(1)).

Such an order may be general or may be made applicable to particular places, districts or assemblies to be specified in the order (s. 70(2)).

2. Contravention of orders prohibiting unlawful drilling — Section 70(3)

Every one who — contravenes — an order made under s. 70(1) (prohibiting unlawful drilling) — is guilty of an indictable offence.

Included offences. Attempts (s. 660 and s. 662(1)(b)).

Punishment. Imprisonment for a term not exceeding 5 years (s. 70(3)).

Release. Initial decision to release made by officer in charge or justice (s. 498).

Election. Accused may elect trial by judge and jury, judge alone, or provincial court judge (s. 536).

UNLAWFUL SOLEMNIZATION OF MARRIAGE

1. *Pretending to solemnize marriage*
2. *Solemnizing a marriage contrary to law*

1. Pretending to solemnize marriage

Section 294(a)

Every one who — solemnizes or pretends to solemnize a marriage — without lawful authority — is guilty of an indictable offence.

Section 294(b)

Every one who — procures a person to solemnize a marriage — knowing that he is not lawfully authorized to solemnize the marriage — is guilty of an indictable offence.

Intent. Knowledge of lack of authority (s. 294(b)).

Included offences. Attempts (s. 660 and s. 662(1)(b)).

Punishment. Imprisonment for a term not exceeding 2 years (s. 294).

Release. Initial decision to release made by officer in charge or justice (s. 498).

Election. Accused may elect trial by judge and jury, judge alone, or provincial court judge (s. 536).

Evidence. 1. For the purposes of this offence, the proof of lawful excuse lies on the accused (s. 294(a)).

2. The wife or husband of a person charged with this offence is a competent and compellable witness for the prosecution without the consent of the accused (Canada Evidence Act, s. 4(2)).

Informations

A.B., on or about the —— day of ——, 19——, at the —— of ——, in the said (territorial division), without lawful authority did solemnize [OR pretend to solemnize] a marriage between C.D. and E.F., to wit: (specify the particulars of the offence), contrary to s. 294(a) of the Criminal Code of Canada.

A.B., on or about the —— day of ——, 19——, at the —— of ——, in the said (territorial division), then knowing that C.D. was not lawfully authorized to solemnize a marriage, did procure C.D. to solemnize a marriage between E.F. and G.H., to wit: (specify the particulars of the offence), contrary to s. 294(b) of the Criminal Code of Canada.

2. Solemnizing a marriage contrary to law — Section 295

Every one who — being lawfully authorized to solemnize marriage — knowingly and wilfully — solemnizes a marriage — in contravention of the laws of the province in which the marriage is solemnized — is guilty of an indictable offence.

Intent. Knowingly and wilfully.

Included offences. Attempts (s. 660 and s. 662(1)(b)).

Punishment. Imprisonment for a term not exceeding 2 years (s. 295).

Release. Initial decision to release made by officer in charge or justice (s. 498).

Election. Accused may elect trial by judge and jury, judge alone, or provincial court judge (s. 536).

UNUSQUISQUE SPONDET PERITIAM ARTIS SUAE. "Everyone warrants the skill of his own art" (Latin).

UTTER. For the purposes of Part XII of the Criminal Code (Offences Relating to Currency), "utter" includes sell, pay, tender and put off (s. 448). *See also CURRENCY OFFENCES and FORGERY.*

V

VAGAL INHIBITION. Stoppage of the heart beat through stimulation of the vagus nerve. Also, vagus reflex; vaso-vagal reflex. Vagal inhibition may be caused by pressure on the neck, immersion in cold water and minor surgical procedures (Jaffe, A Guide to Pathological Evidence, 2nd ed.).

VAGINA. The tubular muscular passage in the female connecting the vulva with the cervix (Jaffe, A Guide to Pathological Evidence, 2nd ed.).

VAGRANCY

1. *Supporting oneself by gaming or crime*	2. *Person convicted of sexual offence*

1. Supporting oneself by gaming or crime

Definition of offence — Section 179(1)(a)

Every one who — supports himself in whole or in part — by gaming or crime — and has no lawful profession or calling by which to maintain himself — commits vagrancy.

Statement of offence — Section 179(2)

Every one who — commits vagrancy — is guilty of an offence punishable on summary conviction.

Limitation period. No proceedings in respect of offences that are declared to be punishable on summary conviction shall be instituted more than 6 months after the time when the subject matter of the proceedings arose (s. 786(2) and s. 785(1)).

Included offences. Attempts (s. 660 and s. 662(1)(b)).

Punishment. A fine not exceeding $2,000, or 6 months' imprisonment, or both (s. 179(2) and s. 787(1)).

Release. Initial decision to release made by peace officer (s. 497).

Election. No election, summary conviction offence.

Evidence. 1. It is not enough to prove that an accused has no peaceable profession or calling; it must also be shown that the accused supports himself in one of the ways specified.

2. The wife or husband of a person charged with this offence is a competent and compellable witness for the prosecution without the consent of the person charged (Canada Evidence Act, s. 4(2)).

Informations

A.B., on or about the —— day of ——, 19——, at the —— of ——, in the said (territorial division), having no lawful profession or calling by which to maintain himself, did support himself in whole [OR in part] by gaming [OR crime], and did thereby commit vagrancy, to wit: (specify the particulars of the offence), contrary to s. 179(1)(a) of the Criminal Code of Canada.

2. Person convicted of sexual offence

Definition of offence — Section 179(1)(b)

Every one who — having at any time been convicted of any of the following offences:

- **s. 151 (sexual interference)**
- **s. 152 (invitation to sexual touching)**
- **s. 153 (sexual exploitation)**
- **s. 160(3) (bestiality in presence of or by child)**
- **s. 173(2) (exposure)**
- **s. 271 (sexual assault)**
- **s. 272 (sexual assault with a weapon)**
- **s. 273 (aggravated sexual assault)**

— or having at any time been convicted of an offence under a provision referred to in paragraph (b) of the definition "serious personal injury" in s. 752 as it read before January 4, 1983 — is found loitering — in or near a school ground or playground or public park or bathing area — commits vagrancy.

Statement of offence — Section 179(2)

Every one who — commits vagrancy — is guilty of an offence punishable on summary conviction.

"Serious personal injury" — Section 752. The following is paragraph (b) of the definition of "serious personal injury" in s. 752 as it read before January 4, 1983, referred to above in s. 179(1)(b)):

"Serious personal injury offence" means ... (b) an offence mentioned in section 144 (rape) or 145 (attempted rape) or an offence or attempt to commit an offence mentioned in section 146 (sexual intercourse with a female under fourteen or between fourteen and sixteen), 149 (indecent assault on a female), 156 (indecent assault on a male) or 157 (gross indecency).

Limitation period. No proceedings in respect of offences that are declared to be punishable on summary conviction shall be instituted more than 6 months after the time when the subject matter of the proceedings arose (s. 786(2) and s. 785(1)).

Included offences. Attempts (s. 660 and s. 662(1)(b)).

Punishment. A fine not exceeding $2,000, or 6 months' imprisonment, or both (s. 179(2) and s. 787(1)).

Release. Initial decision to release made by peace officer (s. 497).

Election. No election, summary conviction offence.

Evidence. *See Evidence, item 2., under* **1**, *above.*

Informations

A.B., on or about the —— day of ——, 19——, at the —— of ——, in the said (territorial division), having been convicted of the offence of (specify an offence mentioned in s. 179(1)(b)), was found loitering in [OR near] a school ground [OR playground OR public park OR bathing area], and did thereby commit vagrancy, to wit: (specify the particulars of the offence), contrary to s. 179(1)(b) of the Criminal Code of Canada.

VALUABLE SECURITY. For the purposes of the Criminal Code, "valuable security" includes

(a) an order, exchequer acquittance or other security that entitles or evidences the title of any person to a share or interest in a public stock or fund or in any fund of a body corporate, company or society, or to a deposit in a savings bank or other bank,

(b) any debenture, deed, bond, bill, note, warrant, order or other security for money or for the payment of money,

(c) a document of title to lands or goods wherever situated,

(d) a stamp or writing that secures or evidences title to or an interest in a chattel personal, or that evidences delivery of a chattel personal, and

(e) a release, receipt, discharge or other instrument evidencing payment of money (s. 2).

VEHICLE IDENTIFICATION NUMBER. For the purposes of s. 354(2) (possession of property obtained by crime), "vehicle identification number" means any number or other mark placed on a motor vehicle for the purpose of distinguishing the motor vehicle from other similar motor vehicles (s. 354(3)).

VENIRE DE NOVO. New trial (Latin).

VENIRE FACIAS. 1. "Cause to come" (Latin). 2. The opening words of a writ to summon a jury.

VENUE. The locality in which a crime has been committed or that in which a court has jurisdiction to try the offence (David M. Walker, The Oxford Companion to Law). *See also JURISDICTION.*

Change of venue. A court before which an accused is or may be indicted, or a judge who may hold or sit in that court, may at any time before or after an indictment is found, order the trial to be held in a territorial division in the same province other than that in which the offence would otherwise be tried "if it appears expedient to the ends of justice". The order is made on the application of the prosecutor or the accused (s. 599(1)(a)). A change of venue is justified where there is strong evidence of a general prejudicial attitude in the community as a whole (R. v. Alward (1976), 39 C.R.N.S. 281 (N.B. C.A.).

Such an order may also be made if a competent authority has directed that a jury is not to be summoned at the time appointed in a territorial division where the trial would otherwise by law be held (s. 599(1)(b)).

Authority to remove prisoner. An order for a change in venue is sufficient warrant, justification and authority to all sheriffs, keepers of prisons and peace officers for the removal, disposal and reception of an accused in accordance with the terms of the order and the sheriff may appoint and authorize any peace officer to convey the accused to a prison in the territorial division in which the trial is ordered to be held (s. 600).

VERBA CHARTARUM FORTIUS ACCIPIUNTUR CONTRA PROFERENTEM. "Words of documents are more strongly construed against one who proffers the document" (Latin).

VERBA ITA SUNT INTELLIGENDA UT RES MAGIS VALEAT QUAM PEREAT. "Words are to be understood to give effect to rather than to destroy the transaction or object" (Latin).

VESSELS AND RELATED OFFENCES

1. *Definition of "vessel"*
2. *Dangerous operation of vessel*
3. *Dangerous operation causing bodily harm*
4. *Dangerous operation causing death*
5. *Failure to keep watch on person towed*
6. *Towing person after dark*
7. *Unseaworthy vessel*
8. *Failing to stop at scene of accident*
9. *Operation of vessel while impaired or with more than 80 mgs. of alcohol in blood*
10. *Impaired operation causing bodily harm*
11. *Impaired operation causing death*
12. *Failure or refusal to provide sample*
13. *Operation of vessel while disqualified*
14. *Preventing or impeding the saving of a vessel*
15. *Making fast a vessel or boat to a marine signal*
16. *Altering, removing or concealing marine signal*
17. *Public harbours*
18. *Seizing control of ship or fixed platform*
19. *Endangering safety of ship or fixed platform*
20. *False communication endangering safe navigation*
21. *Threats causing damage or injury on ship or fixed platform*
22. *Taking vessel without consent. See THEFT AND OFFENCES RESEMBLING THEFT, 10*
23. *Setting fire to vessel. See ARSON, 3.*

See also PIRACY; WRECK.

---

1. Definition of "vessel"

1. "Vessel" includes any ship or boat or any other description of vessel used or designed to be used in navigation (Canada Shipping Act, s. 2).

2. For the purposes of Part VIII of the Criminal Code (Offences Against the Person and Reputation), "vessel" includes a machine designed to derive support in the atmosphere primarily from reactions against the earth's surface of air expelled from the machine (s. 214).

2. Dangerous operation of vessel — Section 249(1)(b) and (2)

Every one who — operates a vessel or any water skis or surfboard or water sled or other towed object — on or over any of the internal waters of Canada or the territorial sea of Canada — in a manner that is dangerous to the public — having regard to all the circumstances — including the nature and condition of such waters or sea and the use that at the time is or might reasonably be expected

to be made of such waters or sea — is guilty of either an indictable offence or an offence punishable on summary conviction.

Limitation period. No proceedings in respect of offences that are declared to be punishable on summary conviction shall be instituted more than 6 months after the time when the subject matter of the proceedings arose (s. 786(2) and s. 785(1)).

Included offences. Attempts (s. 660 and s. 662(1)(b)).

Punishment. On indictment, imprisonment for a term not exceeding 5 years (s. 249(2)(a)). On summary conviction, a fine not exceeding $2,000, or 6 months' imprisonment, or both (s. 249(2)(b) and s. 787(1)).

In addition to any other punishment that may be imposed, the court may make an order prohibiting the offender from operating a vessel during any period not exceeding 3 years (s. 259(2)(c)).

Release. Initial decision to release made by peace officer (s. 497).

Election. On indictment, accused may elect trial by judge and jury, judge alone, or provincial court judge (s. 536). On summary conviction, no election.

Informations

A.B., on or about the —— day of ——, 19——, at the —— of ——, in the said (territorial division), did operate [OR navigate] a vessel in a manner dangerous to the public, to wit: (specify the particulars of the offence), contrary to s. 249(1)(b) of the Criminal Code of Canada.

A.B., on or about the —— day of ——, 19——, at the —— of ——, in the said (territorial division), did operate water skis [OR a surf-board OR (as the case may be)] in a manner dangerous to the public, to wit: (specify the particulars of the offence), contrary to s. 249(1)(b) of the Criminal Code of Canada.

3. Dangerous operation causing bodily harm — Section 249(3)

Every one who — commits the offence of dangerous operation of a vessel (s. 249(1)(b)) — and thereby causes bodily harm to any other person — is guilty of an indictable offence.

Included offences. Attempts (s. 660 and s. 662(1)(b)); dangerous operation of vessel.

Punishment. Imprisonment for a term not exceeding 10 years (s. 249(3)).

In addition to any other punishment that may be imposed, the court may make an order prohibiting the offender from operating a vessel during any period not exceeding 10 years (s. 259(2)(b)).

Release. Initial decision to release made by justice (s. 515(1)).

Election. Accused may elect trial by judge and jury, judge alone, or provincial court judge (s. 536).

Informations

A.B., on or about the —— day of ——, 19——, at the —— of ——, in the said (territorial division), did operate [OR navigate] a vessel in a manner dangerous to the public, thereby causing bodily harm to C.D., to wit: (specify the particulars of the offence), contrary to s. 249(3) of the Criminal Code of Canada.

A.B., on or about the —— day of ——, 19——, at the —— of ——, in the said (territorial division), did operate water skis [OR a surf-board OR (as the case may be)] in a manner dangerous to the public, thereby causing bodily harm to C.D., to wit: (specify the particulars of the offence), contrary to s. 249(3) of the Criminal Code of Canada.

4. Dangerous operation causing death — Section 249(4)

Every one who — commits the offence of dangerous operation of a vessel (s. 249(1)(b)) — and thereby causes the death of any other person — is guilty of an indictable offence.

Included offences. Attempts (s. 660 and s. 662(1)(b)); dangerous operation of vessel.

Punishment. Imprisonment for a term not exceeding 14 years (s. 249(4)).

In addition to any other punishment that may be imposed, the court may make an order prohibiting the offender from operating a vessel during any period not exceeding 10 years (s. 259(2)(b)).

Release. Initial decision to release made by justice (s. 515(1)).

Election. Accused may elect trial by judge and jury, judge alone, or provincial court judge (s. 536).

Informations

A.B., on or about the —— day of ——, 19——, at the —— of ——, in the said (territorial division), did operate [OR navigate] a vessel in a manner dangerous to the public, thereby causing the death of C.D., to wit: (specify the particulars of the offence), contrary to s. 249(4) of the Criminal Code of Canada.

A.B., on or about the —— day of ——, 19——, at the —— of ——, in the said (territorial division), did operate water skis [OR a surf-board OR (as the case may be)] in a manner dangerous to the public, thereby causing the death of C.D., to wit: (specify the particulars of the offence), contrary to s. 249(4) of the Criminal Code of Canada.

5. Failure to keep watch on person towed — Section 250(1)

Every one who — operates a vessel — while towing a person on any water skis or surf-board or water sled or other object — when there is not on board such vessel another responsible person keeping watch on the person being towed — is guilty of an offence punishable on summary conviction.

Limitation period. No proceedings in respect of offences that are declared to be punishable on summary conviction shall be instituted more than 6 months after the time when the subject matter of the proceedings arose (s. 786(2) and s. 785(1)).

Included offences. Attempts (s. 660 and s. 662(1)(b)).

Punishment. A fine not exceeding $,2000 or 6 months' imprisonment, or both (s. 250(1) and s. 787(1)).

In addition to any other punishment that may be imposed, the court may make an order prohibiting the offender from operating a vessel during any period not exceeding 3 years (s. 259(2)(c)).

Release. Initial decision to release made by peace officer (s. 497).

Election. No election, summary conviction offence.

Informations

A.B., on or about the —— day of ——, 19——, at the —— of ——, in the said (territorial division), did operate [OR navigate] a vessel while towing a person on water skis [OR (as the case may be)], at which time there was not on board such vessel another responsible person keeping watch on the person being towed, to wit: (specify the particulars of the offence), contrary to s. 250(1) of the Criminal Code of Canada.

6. Towing person after dark — Section 250(2)

Every one who — operates a vessel — while towing a person on any water skis or surf-board or water sled or other object — during

the period from one hour after sunset to sunrise — is guilty of an offence punishable on summary conviction.

Limitation period. No proceedings in respect of offences that are declared to be punishable on summary conviction shall be instituted more than 6 months after the time when the subject matter of the proceedings arose (s. 786(2) and s. 785(1)).

Included offences. Attempts (s. 660 and s. 662(1)(b)).

Punishment. A fine not exceeding $2,000, or 6 months' imprisonment, or both (s. 250(2) and s. 787(1)).

In addition to any other punishment that may be imposed, the court may make an order prohibiting the offender from operating a vessel during any period not exceeding 3 years (s. 259(2)(c)).

Release. Initial decision to release made by peace officer (s. 497).

Election. No election, summary conviction offence.

Informations

A.B., on or about the —— day of ——, 19——, at the —— of ——, in the said (territorial division), did operate [OR navigate] a vessel while towing a person on water skis [OR (as the case may be)], during the period from one hour after sunset to sunrise, to wit: (specify the particulars of the offence), contrary to s. 250(2) of the Criminal Code of Canada.

7. Unseaworthy vessel — Section 251(1)(a)

Every one who — knowingly — either sends or being the master takes a vessel — that is registered or licensed, or for which an identification number has been issued, pursuant to any Act of Parliament — and that is unseaworthy — either on a voyage from a place in Canada to any other place in or out of Canada — or on a voyage from a place on the inland waters of the United States to a place in Canada — and thereby endangers the life of any person — is guilty of an indictable offence.

Intent. Knowingly.

Consent to prosecute. No proceedings shall be instituted under s. 251 without the written consent of the Attorney General of Canada (s. 251(3)).

Included offences. Attempts (s. 660 and s. 662(1)(b)).

Punishment. Imprisonment for a term not exceeding 5 years (s. 251(1)).

In addition to any other punishment that may be imposed, the court may make an order prohibiting the offender from operating a vessel during any period not exceeding 3 years (s. 259(2)(c)).

Release. Initial decision to release made by officer in charge or justice (s. 498).

Election. Accused may elect trial by judge and jury, judge alone, or provincial court judge (s. 536).

Defences. An accused shall not be convicted where he establishes that (i) he used all reasonable means to ensure that the vessel was seaworthy, or (ii) to send or take the vessel while it was unseaworthy was, under the circumstances, reasonable and justifiable (s. 251(2)(a)).

8. Failure to stop at scene of accident — Section 252(1)

Every one who — has the care or charge or control of a vessel — that is involved in an accident with — either another person — or a vehicle or another vessel or an aircraft — and with intent to escape civil or criminal liability — fails to stop his vessel — and fails to give his name and address — and, where any person has been injured or appears to require assistance, fails to offer assistance — is guilty of either an indictable offence or an offence punishable on summary conviction.

Intent. Intention to escape civil or criminal liability.

Limitation period. No proceedings in respect of offences that are declared to be punishable on summary conviction shall be instituted more than 6 months after the time when the subject matter of the proceedings arose (s. 786(2) and s. 785(1)).

Included offences. Attempts (s. 660 and s. 662(1)(b)).

Punishment. On indictment, imprisonment for a term not exceeding 2 years (s. 252(1)). On summary conviction, a fine not exceeding $2,000, or 6 months' imprisonment, or both (s. 252(1) and s. 787(1)).

In addition to any other punishment that may be imposed, the court may make an order prohibiting the offender from operating a vessel during any period not exceeding 3 years (s. 259(2)(b)).

Release. Initial decision to release made by peace officer (s. 497).

Election. On indictment, accused may elect trial by judge and jury, judge alone, or provincial court judge (s. 536). On summary conviction, no election.

Evidence. Evidence that an accused failed to stop his vessel, offer assistance where any person has been injured or appears to require assistance and give his name and address is, in the absence of evidence to the contrary, proof of an intent to escape civil or criminal liability (s. 252(2)).

Informations

A.B., on or about the —— day of ——, 19——, at the —— of ——, in the said (territorial division), having the care [OR charge OR control] of a vessel that was involved in an accident with C.D. [OR a vehicle (OR a vessel OR an aircraft) in the charge of C.D.], did, with intent to escape civil or criminal liability, fail to stop his vessel and give his name and address [and offer assistance to C.D. (OR E.F.), a person who was injured in the accident], to wit: (specify the particulars of the offence), contrary to s. 252(1) of the Criminal Code of Canada.

9. Operation of vessel while impaired or with more than 80 mg of alcohol in blood — Section 253 and section 255(1)

Every one who — either operates a vessel — or has the care or control of a vessel — whether it is in motion or not — either while his ability to operate the vessel is impaired by alcohol or a drug — or having consumed alcohol in such a quantity that the concentration thereof in his blood exceeds 80 mg of alcohol in 100 ml of blood — is guilty of either an indictable offence or an offence punishable on summary conviction.

Limitation period. No proceedings in respect of offences that are declared to be punishable on summary conviction shall be instituted more than 6 months after the time when the subject matter of the proceedings arose (s. 786(2) and s. 785(1)).

Included offences. Attempts (s. 660 and s. 662(1)(b)).

Punishment. On indictment, imprisonment for a term not exceeding 5 years (s. 255(1)(b)). On summary conviction, imprisonment for a term not exceeding 6 months (s. 255(1)(c)).

Whether on indictment or on summary conviction, liable to the following minimum punishment: namely, (i) for a first offence, to a fine of not less than $300; (ii) for a second offence, to imprisonment for not less than 14 days; and (iii) for each subsequent offence, to imprisonment for not less than 90 days (s. 255(1)(a)).

In addition to any other punishment that may be imposed, the court shall make an order prohibiting the offender from operating a vessel (a) for a first offence, during a period of not more than 3 years and not less than 3 months; (b) for a second offence, during a period of not more than 3 years and not less than 6 months; and (c) for each subsequent offence, during a period of not more than 3 years and not less than one year (s. 259(1)).

Release. Initial decision to release made by peace officer (s. 497).

Election. On indictment, accused may elect trial by judge and jury, judge alone, or provincial court judge (s. 536). On summary conviction, no election.

Breath samples. Where a peace officer believes on reasonable and probable grounds that a person is committing, or at any time within the preceding 2 hours has committed, as a result of the consumption of alcohol, an offence under s. 253 (operation of vessel while impaired or with more than 80 mg of alcohol in blood), the peace officer may, by demand made to that person forthwith or as soon as practicable, require that person to provide then or as soon thereafter as is practicable such samples of the person's breath as in the opinion of a qualified technician are necessary to enable proper analysis to be made in order to determine the concentration, if any, of alcohol in the person's blood, and to accompany the peace officer for the purpose of enabling such samples to be taken (s. 254(3)(a)).

Where samples of the breath of the accused have been taken pursuant to a demand under s. 254(3), evidence of the results of the analyses so made is (in the absence of evidence to the contrary) proof of the concentration of alcohol in the blood of the accused at the time of the alleged offence, if the following conditions are met: (i) at the time each sample was taken, the person taking the sample offered to provide to the accused a specimen of the breath of the accused in an approved container for his own use, and, at the request of the accused made at that time, such a specimen was thereupon provided to the accused; (ii) each sample was taken as soon as practicable after the time of the alleged offence and, in the case of the first sample, not later than 2 hours after that time, with an interval of at least 15 minutes between the times when the samples were taken; (iii) each sample was received from the accused directly into an approved container or approved instrument operated by a qualified technician; and (iv) an analysis of each sample was made by means of an approved instrument operated by a qualified technician (s. 258(1)(c)).

However, the result of an analysis of a sample of the breath of the accused (other than a sample taken pursuant to a s. 254(3) demand) may be admitted in evidence notwithstanding that, before the accused gave the sample, he was not warned that he need not give the sample or that the result of the analysis of the sample might be used in evidence (s. 258(1)(b)).

Blood samples. Where a peace officer believes on reasonable and probable grounds that a person is committing, or at any time within the preceding 2 hours has committed, as a result of the consumption of alcohol, an offence under s. 253 (operation of vessel while impaired or with more than 80 mg alcohol in blood), the peace officer may, by demand made to that person forthwith or as soon as practicable, require that person to provide then or as soon thereafter as is practicable, where the peace officer has reasonable and probable grounds to believe that, by reason of any physical condition of the person, (i) the person may be incapable of providing a sample of his breath, or (ii) it would be impracticable to obtain a sample of his breath, such samples of the person's blood as in the opinion of a qualified medical practitioner or qualified technician taking the samples are necessary to enable proper analysis to be made in order to determine the concentration, if any, of alcohol in the person's blood, and to accompany the peace officer for the purpose of enabling such samples to be taken (s. 254(3)(b)).

Samples of blood may be taken pursuant to a s. 254(3) demand only if the samples are taken by or under the direction of a qualified medical practitioner who is satisfied that the taking of such samples would not endanger the life or health of the person from whom those samples are taken (s. 254(4)).

Where a justice is satisfied, on an information on oath in Form 1 or on an information on oath submitted to the justice pursuant to s. 487.1 by telephone or other means of telecommunications, that there are reasonable grounds to believe that (a) a person has, within the preceding 2 hours, committed, as a result of the consumption of alcohol, an offence under s. 253 (operation of vessel while impaired or with more than 80 mg alcohol in blood) and that person was involved in an accident resulting in the death of another person or in bodily harm to himself or herself or to any other person, and (b) a qualified medical practitioner is of the opinion that (i) by reason of any physical or mental condition of the person that resulted from the consumption of alcohol, the accident or any other occurrence related to or resulting from the accident, the person is unable to consent to the taking of samples of his blood and (ii) the taking of samples of blood from the person would not endanger the life or health of the person, the justice may issue a warrant authorizing a peace officer to require a qualified medical practitioner to take, or to cause to be taken by a qualified technician under the direction of the qualified medical practitioner, such samples of the blood of the person as in the opinion of the person taking the samples are necessary to enable a proper analysis to be made in order to determine the concentration, if any, of alcohol in his blood (s. 256(1)). For the purposes of s. 256, an information on oath submitted by telephone or other means of telecommunication shall include a statement of the circumstances that make it impracticable for the peace officer to appear personally before a justice (s. 487.1(4)(a)), a statement setting out the offence alleged to have been committed and identifying the person from whom blood samples are to be taken (s. 256(3)) and a statement as to any prior application for a warrant in respect of the same matter, of which the peace officer has knowledge (s. 487.1(4)(d)). Where a warrant issued pursuant to s. 256(1) is executed, the peace officer shall, as soon as practicable thereafter, give a copy or, in the case of a warrant issued by telephone or other means of telecommunication, a facsimile of the warrant to the person from whom the samples were taken (s. 256(5)).

No qualified medical practitioner or qualified technician is guilty of an offence only by reason of his refusal to take a sample of blood from a person for the purposes of s. 254 or s. 256 and no qualified medical practitioner is guilty of an offence only by reason of his refusal to cause to be taken by a qualified technician under his direction a sample of blood from a person for such purposes (s. 257(1)).

No qualified medical practitioner by whom or under whose direction a sample of blood is taken from a person pursuant to a demand made under s. 254(3) or a warrant issued under s. 256 and no qualified technician acting under the direction of a qualified medical practitioner incurs any criminal or civil liability for anything necessarily done with reasonable care and skill in the taking of such a sample of blood (s. 257(2)).

Where a sample of the blood of the accused has been taken pursuant to a demand under s. 254(3) or otherwise with the consent of the accused or pursuant to a warrant issued under s. 256, evidence of the result of the analysis is (in the absence of evidence to the contrary) proof of the concentration of alcohol in the blood of the accused at the time of the alleged offence if the following conditions are met: (i) at the time the sample was taken, the person taking the sample took an additional sample of the blood of the accused and one of the samples was retained, to permit an analysis thereof to be made by or on behalf of the accused and, at the request of the accused made within 3 months from the taking of the samples, one of the samples was ordered to be released; (ii) both such samples were taken as soon as practicable after the time of the alleged offence and in any event not later than 2 hours after that time; (iii) both such samples were taken by a qualified medical practitioner or a qualified technician under the direction of a qualified medical practitioner; (iv) both samples were received from the accused directly into, or placed directly into, approved containers that were subsequently sealed; and (v) an analysis was made by an analyst of at least one of the samples that was contained in a sealed approved container (s. 258(1)(d)). However, the result of an analysis of a sample of blood of the accused (other than a sample taken pursuant to a s. 254(3) demand) may be admitted in evidence notwithstanding that, before the accused gave the sample, he was not warned that he need not give the sample or that the result of the analysis of the sample might be used in evidence (s. 258(1)(b)).

Other evidence. Physical evidence of impaired operation or impaired care or control should be obtained from the investigating officer and, if possible, one or more civilian witnesses, i.e., that (i) he staggered or was unsteady on his feet, (ii) his breath smelled of an alcoholic beverage, (iii) his speech was slurred, (iv) his eyes were bloodshot, and (v) his operation of the vessel was erratic.

An accused shall be deemed to have had the care or control of a vessel where it is proved that the accused occupied the seat or position ordinarily occupied by a person who operates a vessel, unless the accused establishes that he did not occupy that seat or position for the purpose of setting the vessel in motion (s. 258(1)(a)).

The result of an analysis of the urine or other bodily substance of the accused (other than a sample of breath or blood taken pursuant to a s. 254(3) demand) may be admitted in evidence notwithstanding that, before the accused gave the sample, he was not warned that he need not give the sample or that the result of the analysis of the sample might be used in evidence (s. 258(1)(b)).

Evidence that the accused, without reasonable excuse, failed or refused to comply with a demand for samples made to him by a peace officer under s. 254 is admissible and the court may draw an inference therefrom adverse to the accused (s. 258(3)).

Informations

A.B., on or about the —— day of ——, 19——, at the —— of ——, in the said (territorial division), while his ability to operate a vessel was impaired by alcohol [OR a drug], did operate [OR have the care or control of] a vessel, to wit: (specify the particulars of the offence), contrary to s. 253 of the Criminal Code of Canada.

A.B., on or about the —— day of ——, 19——, at the —— of ——, in the said (territorial division), did operate [OR have the care or control of] a vessel, having consumed alcohol in such a quantity that the concentration thereof in the blood of A.B. exceeded 80 mgs. of alcohol in 100 ml. of blood, to wit: (specify the particulars of the offence), contrary to s. 253 of the Criminal Code of Canada.

10. Impaired operation causing bodily harm — Section 255(2)

Every one who — commits the offence of operation of a vessel while impaired (s. 253(a)) — and thereby causes bodily harm to any other person — is guilty of an indictable offence.

Included offences. Attempts (s. 660 and s. 662(1)(b)); operation of vessel while impaired.

Punishment. Imprisonment for a term not exceeding 10 years (s. 255(2)).

In addition to any other punishment that may be imposed, the court may make an order prohibiting the offender from operating a vessel during any period not exceeding 10 years (s. 259(2)(b)).

Release. Initial decision to release made by justice (s. 515(1)).

Election. Accused may elect trial by judge and jury, judge alone, or provincial court judge (s. 536).

Informations

A.B., on or about the —— day of ——, 19——, at the —— of ——, in the said (territorial division), while his ability to operate a vessel was impaired by alcohol [OR a drug], did operate [OR have the care or control of] a vessel, thereby causing bodily harm to C.D., to wit: (specify the particulars of the offence), contrary to s. 255(2) of the Criminal Code of Canada.

11. Impaired operation causing death — Section 255(3)

Every one who — commits the offence of operation of a vessel while impaired (s. 253(a)) — and thereby causes the death of any other person — is guilty of an indictable offence.

Included offences. Attempts (s. 660 and s. 662(1)(b)); operation of vessel while impaired.

Punishment. Imprisonment for a term not exceeding 14 years (s. 255(3)).

In addition to any other punishment that may be imposed, the court may make an order prohibiting the offender from operating a vessel during any period not exceeding 10 years (s. 259(2)(b)).

Release. Initial decision to release made by justice (s. 515(1)).

Election. Accused may elect trial by judge and jury, judge alone, or provincial court judge (s. 536).

Informations

A.B., on or about the —— day of ——, 19——, at the —— of ——, in the said (territorial division), while his ability to operate a vessel was impaired by alcohol [OR a drug], did operate [OR have the care or control of] a vessel, thereby causing the death of C.D., to wit: (specify the particulars of the offence), contrary to s. 255(3) of the Criminal Code of Canada.

12. Failure or refusal to provide sample — Section 254(5) and section 255(1)

Every one who — without reasonable excuse — fails or refuses to comply with a demand — made to him by a peace officer under s. 254 — is guilty of either an indictable offence or an offence punishable on summary conviction.

Intent. Intentional non-compliance.

Authority to test. Where a peace officer reasonably suspects that a person who is operating a vessel or who has the care or control of a vessel, whether it is in motion or not, has alcohol in his body, the peace officer may, by demand made to that person, require that person to provide forthwith such a sample of his breath as in the opinion of the peace officer is necessary to enable a proper analysis of his breath to be made by means of an approved screening device and, where necessary, to accompany the peace officer for the purpose of enabling such a sample of his breath to be taken (s. 254(2)). Where a peace officer believes on reasonable and probable grounds that a person is committing, or at any time within the preceding 2 hours has committed, as a result of the consumption of alcohol, an offence under s. 253 (operation of vessel while impaired or with more than 80 mg of alcohol in blood), the peace officer may, by demand made to that person forthwith or as soon as practicable, require that person to provide then or as soon thereafter as is practicable (a) such samples of the person's breath as in the opinion of a qualified technician (or (b) where the peace officer has reasonable and probable grounds to believe that, by reason of any physical condition of the person, (i) the person may be incapable of providing a sample of his breath, or (ii) it would be impracticable to obtain a sample of his breath, such samples of the person's blood, as in the opinion of a qualified medical practitioner or qualified technician taking the samples) are necessary to enable proper analysis to be made in order to determine the concentration, if any, of alcohol in the person's blood, and to accompany the peace officer for the purpose of enabling such samples to be taken (s. 254(3)).

Limitation period. No proceedings in respect of offences that are declared to be punishable on summary conviction shall be instituted more than 6 months after the time when the subject matter of the proceedings arose (s. 786(2) and s. 785(1)).

Included offences. Attempts (s. 660 and s. 662(1)(b)).

Punishment. On indictment, imprisonment for a term not exceeding 5 years (s. 255(1)(b)). On summary conviction, imprisonment for a term not exceeding 6 months (s. 255(1)(c)).

Whether on indictment or on summary conviction, liable to the following minimum punishment: namely, (i) for a first offence, to a fine not less than $300; (ii) for a second offence, to imprisonment for not less than 14 days; and (iii) for each subsequent offence, to imprisonment for not less than 90 days (s. 255(1)(a)).

In addition to any other punishment that may be imposed, the court shall make an order prohibiting the offender from operating a vessel (a) for a first offence, during a period of not more than 3 years and not less than 3 months; (b) for a second offence, during a period of not more than 3 years and not less than 6 months, and (c) for each subsequent offence, during a period of not more than 3 years and not less than one year (s. 259(1)).

Release. Initial decision to release made by peace officer (s. 497).

Election. On indictment, accused may elect trial by judge and jury, judge alone, or provincial court judge (s. 536). On summary conviction, no election.

Evidence. With respect to a s. 254(2) demand, proof is necessary that (i) there was in fact a demand, (ii) the accused was either operating a vessel or had the care or control of a vessel, (iii) a peace officer formed a suspicion that the accused had alcohol in his body, and (iv) the suspicion was a reasonable one. A demand, not a request, must be made to the accused and it is usually made in the words of the section itself; for example, "I demand that you provide such a sample of your breath as is necessary to enable a proper analysis of your breath to be made by means of an approved screening device", or "I demand that you accompany me to [specify where] for the purpose of enabling you to provide such a sample of your breath as is necessary to enable a proper analysis of your breath to be made by means of an approved screening device". An "approved screening device" is a device of a kind that is designed to ascertain the presence of alcohol in the blood of a person and that is approved for the purposes of s. 254 by order of the Attorney General of Canada (s. 254(1)).

With respect to a s. 254(3) demand, proof is necessary that (i) there was in fact a demand, (ii) a peace officer formed a belief that the accused was committing or had committed within the 2 preceding hours an offence under s. 253 (operation of vessel while impaired or with more than 80 mg of alcohol in blood), and (iii) the officer had reasonable and probable grounds for his belief. The belief must be formulated within 2 hours after the time of the operation or the care or control. A demand, not a request, must be made to the accused and is usually made in the words of the section itself; for example, "I demand that you accompany me to [specify where] to enable you to provide such samples of your breath as are necessary to enable proper analysis to be made in order to determine the concentration, if any, of alcohol in your blood". That demand must be made forthwith or as soon as practicable after the peace officer has formed the belief referred to above. The words "as soon as practicable" mean that as long as there is reasonable justification for any delay after the belief is formed, the demand will be a proper one.

Before making either a s. 254(2) demand or a s. 254(3) demand, the officer must inform the accused of his right to retain and instruct counsel without delay (Canadian Charter of Rights and Freedoms, s. 10(b)).

Proof is necessary that there was in fact a failure or refusal. There is a significant difference between the words failure and refusal. The qualified technician is entitled to determine what a suitable sample of breath is and anything less than that offered by the accused, such as short puffs of air, can constitute a refusal. The failure or refusal can be to fail or refuse to accompany the officer or to provide a sample or to do both.

What is a reasonable excuse? The burden is on the accused at trial to show that there was a reasonable excuse. A refusal by an officer to give the accused a reasonable opportunity to attempt to communicate with a solicitor in private before complying with the demand may be a reasonable excuse.

Informations

A.B., on or about the —— day of ——, 19——, at the —— of ——, in the said (territorial division), without reasonable excuse, did fail [OR refuse] to comply with a demand made to A.B. by C.D., a peace officer, under s. 254(2) [OR s. 254(3)] of the Criminal Code, to wit: (specify the particulars of the offence), contrary to s. 254(5) of the Criminal Code of Canada.

13. Operation of vessel while disqualified — Section 259(4)

Every one who — operates a vessel in Canada — while he is disqualified from doing so — is guilty of either an indictable offence or an offence punishable on summary conviction.

Limitation period. No proceedings in respect of offences that are declared to be punishable on summary conviction shall be instituted more than 6 months after the time when the subject matter of the proceedings arose (s. 786(2) and s. 785(1)).

Included offences. Attempts (s. 660 and s. 662(1)(b)).

Punishment. On indictment, imprisonment for a term not exceeding 2 years (s. 259(4)(a)). On summary conviction, a fine not exceeding $2,000, or 6 months' imprisonment, or both (s. 259(4)(b) and s. 787(1)).

In addition to any other punishment that may be imposed, the court may make an order prohibiting the offender from operating a vessel during any period not exceeding 3 years (s. 259(2)(c)).

Release. Initial decision to release made by peace officer (s. 497).

Election. On indictment, accused may elect trial by judge and jury, judge alone, or provincial court judge (s. 536). On summary conviction, no election.

Definitions. *See DISQUALIFICATION.*

Informations

A.B., on or about the —— day of ——, 19——, at the —— of ——, in the said (territorial division), did operate a vessel in Canada while he was disqualified from doing so, to wit: (specify the particulars of the offence), contrary to s. 259(4) of the Criminal Code of Canada.

14. Preventing or impeding the saving of a vessel — Section 438(1)

Every one who — wilfully — prevents or impedes — or endeavours to prevent or impede — either the saving of a vessel that is wrecked or stranded or abandoned or in distress — or a person who attempts to save a vessel that is wrecked or stranded or abandoned or in distress — is guilty of an indictable offence.

Included offences. Attempts (s. 660 and s. 662(1)(b)).

Punishment. Imprisonment for a term not exceeding 5 years (s. 438(1)).

Release. Initial decision to release made by officer in charge or justice (s. 498).

Election. Accused may elect trial by judge and jury, judge alone, or provincial court judge (s. 536).

Evidence. No person shall be convicted of this offence where he proves that he acted with legal justification or excuse and with colour of right (s. 429(2)).

Informations

A.B., on or about the —— day of ——, 19——, at the —— of ——, in the said (territorial division), wilfully did prevent or impede [OR wilfully did endeavour to prevent or impede] the saving of a vessel that was wrecked [OR stranded OR abandoned OR in distress], to wit: (specify the particulars of the offence), contrary to s. 438(1)(a) of the Criminal Code of Canada.

A.B., on or about the —— day of ——, 19——, at the —— of ——, in the said (territorial division), wilfully did prevent or impede [OR wilfully did endeavour to prevent or impede] a person who attempted to save a vessel that was wrecked [OR stranded OR abandoned OR in distress], to wit: (specify the particulars of the offence), contrary to s. 438(1)(b) of the Criminal Code of Canada.

15. Making fast a vessel or boat to a marine signal — Section 439(1)

Every one who — makes fast a vessel or boat — to a signal or buoy or other sea-mark that is used for purposes of navigation — is guilty of an offence punishable on summary conviction.

Limitation period. No proceedings in respect of offences that are declared to be punishable on summary conviction shall be instituted

more than 6 months after the time when the subject matter of the proceedings arose (s. 786(2) and s. 785(1)).

Included offences. Attempts (s. 660 and s. 662(1)(b)).

Punishment. A fine not exceeding $2,000, or 6 months' imprisonment, or both (s. 439(1) and s. 787(1)).

Release. Initial decision to release made by peace officer (s. 497).

Election. No election, summary conviction offence.

Evidence. *See Evidence under* **14**, *above.*

Informations

A.B., on or about the —— day of ——, 19——, at the —— of ——, in the said (territorial division), did make fast a vessel [OR boat] to a signal [OR buoy OR (specify other sea-mark)] that was used for purposes of navigation, to wit: (specify the particulars of the offence), contrary to s. 439(1) of the Criminal Code of Canada.

16. Altering, removing or concealing marine signal — Section 439(2)

Every one who — wilfully — alters or removes or conceals — a signal or buoy or other sea-mark that is used for purposes of navigation — is guilty of an indictable offence.

Intent. Wilfully.

Included offences. Attempts (s. 660 and s. 662(1)(b)).

Punishment. Imprisonment for a term not exceeding 10 years (s. 439(2)).

Release. Initial decision to release made by justice (s. 515(1)).

Election. Accused may elect trial by judge and jury, judge alone, or provincial court judge (s. 536).

Evidence. *See Evidence under* **14**, *above.*

Informations

A.B., on or about the —— day of ——, 19——, at the —— of ——, in the said (territorial division), wilfully did alter [OR remove OR conceal] a signal [OR buoy OR specify other sea-mark] that was used for the purposes of navigation, to wit: (specify the particulars of the offence), contrary to s. 439(2) of the Criminal Code of Canada.

17. Public harbours — Section 440

Every one who — wilfully — and without the written permission of the Minister of Transport — removes any stone or wood or earth or other material — that forms a natural bar necessary to the existence of a public harbour — or that forms a natural protection to such a bar — is guilty of an indictable offence.

Intent. Wilfully.

Included offences. Attempts (s. 660 and s. 662(1)(b)).

Punishment. Imprisonment for a term not exceeding 2 years (s. 440).

Release. Initial decision to release made by officer in charge or justice (s. 498).

Election. Accused may elect trial by judge and jury, judge alone, or provincial court judge (s. 536).

Evidence. 1. For the purposes of this offence, the proof of lawful excuse lies on the accused (s. 440).
2. *See also Evidence under* **14**, *above.*

18. Seizing control of ship or fixed platform — Section 78.1(1)

Every one who — seizes or exercises control over a ship or fixed platform — by force or threat of force or by any other form of intimidation — is guilty of an indictable offence.

Included offences. Attempts (s. 660 and s. 662(1)(b)).

Punishment. Imprisonment for life (s. 78.1(1)).

Release. Initial decision to release made by justice (s. 515(1)).

Election. Accused may elect trial by judge and jury, judge alone, or provincial court judge (s. 536).

Definitions. See FIXED PLATFORM; SHIP.

Informations

A.B., on or about the —— day of ——, 19——, at the —— of ——, in the said (territorial division), did seize [OR exercise control over] a ship [OR fixed platform] by force [OR threat of force OR by any other form of intimidation], to wit: (specify the particulars of the offence), contrary to s. 78.1(1) of the Criminal Code of Canada.

19. Endangering safety of ship or fixed platform — Section 78.1(2)(a)

Every one who — commits an act of violence against a person on board a ship or fixed platform — where that act is likely to endanger the safe navigation of a ship or the safety of a fixed platform — is guilty of an indictable offence.

Section 78.1(2)(b)

Every one who — destroys or causes damage to a ship or its cargo or to a fixed platform — where that act is likely to endanger the safe navigation of a ship or the safety of a fixed platform — is guilty of an indictable offence.

Section 78.1(2)(c)

Every one who — destroys or causes serious damage to or interferes with the operation of any maritime navigational facility — where that act is likely to endanger the safe navigation of a ship or the safety of a fixed platform — is guilty of an indictable offence.

Section 78.1(2)(d)

Every one who — places or causes to be placed on board a ship or fixed platform — anything that is likely to cause damage to the ship or its cargo or to the fixed platform — where that act is likely to endanger the safe navigation of a ship or the safety of a fixed platform — is guilty of an indictable offence.

Included offences. Attempts (s. 660 and s. 662(1)(b)).

Punishment. Imprisonment for life (s. 78.1(2)).

Release. Initial decision to release made by justice (s. 515(1)).

Election. Accused may elect trial by judge and jury, judge alone, or provincial court judge (s. 536).

Definitions. See FIXED PLATFORM; SHIP.

Informations

A.B., on or about the —— day of ——, 19——, at the —— of ——, in the said (territorial division), did commit an act of violence against a person on board a ship [OR fixed platform], where that act was likely to endanger the safe navigation of a ship [OR the safety of a fixed platform], to wit: (specify the particulars of the offence), contrary to s. 78.1(2)(a) of the Criminal Code of Canada.

A.B., on or about the —— day of ——, 19——, at the —— of ——, in the said (territorial division), did destroy [OR cause damage] to a ship [OR its cargo OR to a fixed platform], where that act was likely to endanger the safe navigation of a ship [OR the safety of a fixed platform], to wit: (specify the particulars of the offence), contrary to s. 78.1(2)(b) of the Criminal Code of Canada.

A.B., on or about the —— day of ——, 19——, at the —— of ——, in the said (territorial division), did destroy [OR cause serious damage to OR interfere with the operation of] any maritime navigational facility, where that act was likely to endanger the safe navigation of a ship [OR the safety of a fixed platform], to wit: (specify the particulars of the offence), contrary to s. 78.1(2)(c) of the Criminal Code of Canada.

A.B., on or about the —— day of ——, 19——, at the —— of ——, in the said (territorial division), did place [OR cause to be placed] on board a ship [OR fixed platform] anything that was likely to cause damage to the ship [OR its cargo OR to the fixed platform], where that act was likely to endanger the safe navigation of a ship [OR the safety of a fixed platform], to wit: (specify the particulars of the offence), contrary to s. 78.1(2)(d) of the Criminal Code of Canada.

20. False communication endangering safe navigation — Section 78.1(3)

Every one who — communicates information that endangers the safe navigation of a ship — knowing the information to be false — is guilty of an indictable offence.

Intent. Knowledge that information false.

Included offences. Attempts (s. 660 and s. 662(1)(b)).

Punishment. Imprisonment for life (s. 78.1(3)).

Release. Initial decision to release made by justice (s. 515(1)).

Election. Accused may elect trial by judge and jury, judge alone, or provincial court judge (s. 536).

Definitions. See FIXED PLATFORM; SHIP.

Informations

A.B., on or about the —— day of ——, 19——, at the —— of ——, in the said (territorial division), did communicate information that endangered the safe navigation of a ship, knowing the information to be false, to wit: (specify the particulars of the offence), contrary to s. 78.1(3) of the Criminal Code of Canada.

21. Threats causing damage or injury on ship or fixed platform — Section 78.1(4)

Every one who — threatens to commit an offence under s. 78.1(2)(a), (b) or (c) in order to compel a person to do or refrain from doing any act — where the threat is likely to endanger the safe navigation of a ship or the safety of a fixed platform — is guilty of an indictable offence.

Included offences. Attempts (s. 660 and s. 662(1)(b)).

Punishment. Imprisonment for life (s. 78.1(4)).

Release. Initial decision to release made by justice (s. 515(1)).

Election. Accused may elect trial by judge and jury, judge alone, or provincial court judge (s. 536).

Definitions. See FIXED PLATFORM; SHIP.

Informations

A.B., on or about the —— day of ——, 19——, at the —— of ——, in the said (territorial division), did threaten to commit an offence under s. 78.1(2)(a) [OR (b) OR (c)] of the Criminal Code in order to compel a person to do [OR refrain from doing] any act, where the threat is likely to endanger the safe navigation of a ship [OR the safety of a fixed platform], to wit: (specify the particulars of the offence), contrary to s. 78.1(4) of the Criminal Code of Canada.

VI ET ARMIS. By force of arms (Latin).

VIABILITY. As applied to a fetus, the stage of development at which it would be capable of an independent existence. It is variously given as 20 to 28 weeks of gestation (Jaffe, A Guide to Pathological Evidence, 2nd ed.).

VICE VERSA. The other way around (Latin).

VIDE. See (Latin).

VIDELICET (or VIZ). To wit; namely (Latin).

VIEW. Where it appears to be in the interests of justice, a judge may direct the jury to have a view of any place, person or thing. Where a view is ordered, both the accused and the judge attend. In ordering a view, the judge shall give directions respecting the manner in which, and the persons by whom, the place, thing or person is shown to the jury and respecting the prevention of undue communication by persons of the jury (s. 652).

VIGILANTIBUS NON DORMIENTIBUS LEX SUCCURRIT. "The law aids the watchful, not the sleepy" (Latin).

VINCULUM JURIS. 1. Chain of law (Latin). 2. Relevant connection.

VIRTUAL COOLING TIME. The time the internal body temperature takes to fall through the first 85 per cent of the difference between the body temperature at death and that of the environment. The virtual cooling time has been used in the calculation of the time of death (Jaffe, A Guide to Pathological Evidence, 2nd ed.).

VIS MAJOR. Main force (Latin).

VITAL. Characteristic of or essential to life (Jaffe, A Guide to Pathological Evidence, 2nd ed.).

Vital reaction. A reaction in a tissue such as inflammation, occurring during life and used to distinguish pre mortem from post mortem wounds (Jaffe, A Guide to Pathological Evidence, 2nd ed.).

Vital signs. Physical signs such as respiration and pulse indicative of the presence of life (Jaffe, A Guide to Pathological Evidence, 2nd ed.).

VIVE VOICE. By word of mouth (Latin).

VIZ. An abbreviation for "videlicet", which means "namely" or "that is to say" (Latin).

VOIR DIRE. A proceeding in which the judge, in the absence of the jury, hears testimony for the purpose of determining the competency of a witness and his evidence. For example, a voir dire will be held to determine whether a confession was voluntary and therefore admissible, or involuntary and therefore inadmissible.

VOLENTI NON FIT INJURIA. "That to which a man consents cannot be considered an injury" (Latin).

W

WARRANTS

1. *Definition of a "warrant"*
2. *Warrant for the arrest of an accused*
3. *Warrant for the committal of an accused*
4. *Warrant to convey an accused before a justice*
5. *Warrant for a witness*
6. *Warrant to arrest an absconding witness*
7. *Warrant remanding a prisoner*
8. *Warrant of committal of witness for refusing to be sworn or to give evidence*
9. *Warrant of committal on conviction by a judge*
10. *Warrant of committal on conviction by a summary conviction court*
11. *Warrant of committal for failure to furnish recognizance to keep the peace*
12. *Warrant of committal of witness for failure to enter into recognizance*
13. *Warrant of committal for contempt*
14. *Warrant of committal in default of payment of the costs of an appeal*
15. *Warrant of committal on forfeiture of a recognizance*
16. *Warrant for tracking device*
17. *Warrant for number recorder*

1. Definition of a "warrant"

A written authority empowering a person to do some act, particularly to execute an arrest or search (David M. Walker, The Oxford Companion to Law). The Criminal Code provides for a number of specific warrants, most of which are set out below. *See also SEARCH AND SEIZURE.*

2. Warrant for the arrest of an accused

A warrant in Form 7 may be issued in the following circumstances:

— where there are reasonable grounds to believe that it is necessary in the public interest to issue a warrant for the arrest of the accused (s. 507(4); s. 512(1));
— where the accused failed to attend court in accordance with the summons served on him (s. 512(2));

- where either an appearance notice or a promise to appear or a recognizance entered into before an officer in charge was confirmed and the accused failed to attend court in accordance therewith (s. 512(2));
- where it appears that a summons cannot be served because the accused is evading service (s. 512(2));
- where the accused was ordered to be present at the hearing of an application for a review of an order made by a justice and did not attend the hearing (s. 520(5); s. 521(5));
- where there are reasonable grounds to believe that the accused has contravened or is about to contravene (either the promise to appear or undertaking or recognizance) on which he was released (s. 524(1); s. 525(5); s. 679(6));
- where there are reasonable grounds to believe that the accused has since his release from custody on either a promise to appear or an undertaking or a recognizance, committed an indictable offence (s. 524(1); s. 525(5); s. 679(6));
- where the accused was required by either an appearance notice or a promise to appear or a recognizance entered into before an officer in charge or a summons, to attend at a time and place stated therein for the purposes of the Identification of Criminals Act and did not appear at that time and place (s. 502; s. 510);
- where an indictment has been found against the accused and the accused has not appeared or remained in attendance before the court for his trial (s. 597);
- where an accused absconds during the course of his trial (s. 475);
- where a summary conviction court requires the defendant to appear personally and not by counsel or agent (s. 800(2));
- where a defendant to whom an appearance notice that has been confirmed by a justice under s. 508 has been issued or who has been served with a summons does not appear at the time and place appointed for the trial and the issue of the appearance notice or service of the summons within a reasonable time before the appearance was required is proved, or where a defendant does not appear for the resumption of a trial that has been adjourned in accordance (s. 803(2)).

3. Warrant for the committal of an accused

Where an accused who is charged with an offence mentioned in s. 469 is taken before a justice, the justice must order that the accused be detained in custody until he is dealt with according to law and must issue a warrant in Form 8 for the committal of the accused. The offences mentioned in s. 469 include the following: (i) treason (s. 47); (ii) alarming Her Majesty (s. 49); (iii) intimidating Parliament or a legislature (s. 51); (iv) inciting to mutiny (s. 53); (v) seditious offences (s. 61); (vi) piracy (s. 74); (vii) piratical acts (s. 75); (viii) murder (s. 235); (ix) the offence of conspiring to commit one of the offences listed in (i) through (viii); (x) the offence of attempting to commit one of the offences listed in (i) through (vii); (xi) the offence of being an accessory after the fact to high treason or treason or murder; and (xii) bribery (s. 119) by the holder of a judicial office.

A warrant in Form 8 may also be issued in the following circumstances:

— where the prosecutor has shown cause why the detention of the accused in custody is justified (s. 515(5));
— where an order has been made that the accused be released on (giving an undertaking *or* entering into a recognizance) but the accused has not yet complied with the order (s. 519(1); s. 520(9); s. 521(10); s. 524(12); s. 525(8));
— where the application by the prosecutor for a review of the order of a justice in respect of the interim release of the accused has been allowed and that order has been vacated, and the prosecutor has shown cause why the detention of the accused in custody is justified (s. 521);
— where the accused has contravened or was about to contravene his (promise to appear *or* undertaking *or* recognizance) and the same was cancelled, and the detention of the accused in custody is justified or seems proper in the circumstances (s. 524(4); s. 524(8));
— where there are reasonable grounds to believe that the accused has after his release from custody on (a promise to appear *or* an undertaking *or* a recognizance) committed an indictable offence and the detention of the accused in custody is justified or seems proper in the circumstances (s. 524(4); s. 524(8));
— where the accused has contravened or was about to contravene the (undertaking *or* recognizance) on which he was released and the detention of the accused in custody seems proper in the circumstances (s. 525(7); s. 679(6)); and
— where there are reasonable grounds to believe that the accused has after his release from custody on (an undertaking *or* a recognizance) committed an indictable offence and the det-

ention of the accused in custody seems proper in the circumstances (s. 525(7); s. 679(6)).

4. Warrant to convey an accused before a justice

Where an accused is charged with an offence alleged to have been committed out of the limits of the jurisdiction in which he has been charged, the justice before whom he appears or is brought may, at any stage of the inquiry after hearing both parties, order the accused to appear, or if the accused is in custody, issue a warrant in Form 15 to convey the accused before a justice having jurisdiction in the place where the offence is alleged to have been committed, who shall continue and complete the inquiry (s. 543(1)).

5. Warrant for a witness

Evading service of a subpoena. Where it is made to appear that a person who is likely to give material evidence will not attend in response to a subpoena if a subpoena is issued, or is evading service of a subpoena, a court, justice or provincial court judge having power to issue a subpoena to require the attendance of that person to give evidence may issue a warrant in Form 17 to cause that person to be arrested and to be brought to give evidence (s. 698(2)).

Non-compliance with subpoena. Where a person who has been served with a subpoena to give evidence in a proceeding does not attend or remain in attendance, the court, judge, justice or provincial court judge before whom that person was required to attend may, if it is established that the subpoena has been properly served and that the person is likely to give material evidence, issue or cause to be issued a warrant in Form 17 for the arrest of that person (s. 705(1)). The warrant may be executed anywhere in Canada (s. 705(3)).

Non-compliance with recognizance. Where a person who has been bound by a recognizance to attend to give evidence in any proceeding does not attend or does not remain in attendance, the court, judge, justice or provincial court judge before whom that person was bound to attend may issue or cause to be issued a warrant in Form 17 for the arrest of that person (s. 705(2)). The warrant may be executed anywhere in Canada (s. 705(3)).

6. Warrant to arrest an absconding witness

Where a person is bound by recognizance to give evidence in any proceedings, a justice who is satisfied on information being made before him in writing and under oath that the person is about to abscond or has absconded may issue his warrant in Form 18 directing a peace officer to arrest that person and to bring him before the court, judge, justice or provincial court judge before whom he is bound to appear (s. 704(1)).

A person who is arrested under this section is entitled, on request, to receive a copy of the information upon which the warrant for his arrest was issued (s. 704(3)).

7. Warrant remanding a prisoner

A justice may, before or at any time during the course of any proceedings with respect to judicial interim release (s. 515), on application by the prosecutor or the accused, adjourn the proceedings and remand the accused to custody in prison by warrant in Form 19, but no adjournment shall be for more than three clear days except with the consent of the accused (s. 516).

One of the options available to a justice conducting a preliminary inquiry is to remand the accused to custody in a prison by warrant in Form 19, except where the accused is authorized to be at large (s. 537(1)(c)).

8. Warrant of committal of witness for refusing to be sworn or to give evidence

Where a person, being present at a preliminary inquiry and being required by the justice to give evidence, either refuses to be sworn, or having been sworn, refuses to answer the questions that are put to him, or fails to produce any writings that he is required to produce, or refuses to sign his deposition, without offering a reasonable excuse for his failure or refusal, the justice may adjourn the inquiry and may, by warrant in Form 20, commit the person to prison for a period not exceeding eight clear days or for the period during which the inquiry is adjourned, whichever is the lesser period (s. 545(1)).

Where the person is brought before the justice on the resumption of the adjourned inquiry and again refuses to do what is required of him, the justice may again adjourn the inquiry for a period not exceeding 8 clear days and commit him to prison for the period of adjournment or any part thereof, and may adjourn the inquiry and commit the person to prison from time to time until the person consents to do what is required of him (s. 545(2)).

9. Warrant of committal on conviction by a judge

Where an accused who is determined by a judge or provincial court judge to be guilty of an offence on acceptance of a plea of guilty or on a finding of guilt, the judge or provincial court judge, as the case may be, shall endorse the information accordingly and shall sentence the accused or otherwise deal with the accused in the manner authorized by law and, on request by the accused, the prosecutor or a peace officer, shall cause a conviction in Form 35 and a certified copy thereof, or an order in Form 36 and a certified copy thereof, to be drawn up and shall deliver the certified copy to the person making the request (s. 570(1)).

In addition, where an accused other than a corporation is convicted, the judge or provincial court judge, as the case may be, shall issue or cause to be issued a warrant of committal in Form 21 (s. 570(5)).

10. Warrant of committal on conviction by a summary conviction court

Where a defendant is convicted or where an order is made in relation to him, a minute or memorandum of the conviction or order shall be made by the summary conviction court, without fee, indicating that the matter was dealt with and, on request by the defendant or the prosecutor, the court shall cause a conviction or order in Form 35 or 36, as the case may be, and a certified copy thereof to be drawn up and shall deliver the certified copy to the person making the request (s. 806(1)).

Where a defendant is convicted or an order is made against him, the summary conviction court shall issue a warrant of committal in Form 21 or 22 (s. 806(2)).

11. Warrant of committal for failure to furnish recognizance to keep the peace

Any person who fears that another person will cause personal inquiry to him or his spouse or child or will damage his property may lay an information before a justice. The justice who receives the information must cause the parties to appear before him or before a summary conviction court having jurisdiction in the same territorial division. If the justice (or summary conviction court) is satisfied by the evidence adduced that the informant has reasonable grounds for his fears, he may either: order that the defendant enter into a recognizance, with or without sureties, to keep the peace and be of good behaviour for any period that does not exceed 12 months, and comply with such other reasonable conditions prescribed in the recognizance as the court considers desirable for securing the good conduct of the defendant; or commit the defendant to prison for a term not exceeding 12 months if he fails or refuses to enter into the recognizance (s. 810(1)-(3)). Before making such an order, the justice or the summary conviction court shall consider whether it is desirable, in the interests of the safety of the defendant or of any other person, to include as a condition of the recognizance that the defendant be prohibited from possessing any firearm or any ammunition or explosive substance for any period of time specified in the recognizance and that the defendant surrender any firearms acquisition certificate that the accused possesses and, where the justice or summary conviction court decides that it is not desirable, in the interests of the safety of the defendant or of any other person, for the defendant to possess any of those things, the justice or summary conviction court may add the appropriate condition to the recognizance (s. 810(3.1)).

Any person who fears on reasonable grounds that another person will commit an offence under ss. 151, 152, 155, 159, 160(2), 160(3), 170, 171, 173(2), 271, 272 or 273, in respect of one or more persons who are under the age of 14 years, may lay an information before a provincial court judge, whether or not the person or persons in respect of whom it is feared that the offence will be committed are named (s. 810.1(1)). A provincial court judge who receives such an information shall cause the parties to appear before the provincial court judge (s. 810.1(2)). The provincial court judge before whom the parties appear may, if satisfied by the evidence adduced that the informant has reasonable grounds for the fear, order the defendant to enter into a recognizance and comply with the conditions fixed by the provincial court judge, including a condition prohibiting the defendant from engaging in any activity that involves contact with persons under the age of 14 years and prohibiting the defendant from attending a public park or public swimming area where persons under the age of 14 years are present or can reasonably be expected to be present, or a daycare centre, schoolground, playground or community centre, for any period fixed by the provincial court judge that does not exceed 12 months (s. 810.1(3)).

12. Warrant of committal of witness for failure to enter into recognizance

Where a witness whose evidence is material fails to comply with the order of a justice either to produce one or more sureties in such amount as he may direct, or to deposit with him a sum of money to ensure that the witness will appear and give evidence, the witness may be committed by the justice, by warrant in Form 24, to a prison in the territorial division where the trial is to be held, there to be kept until he does what is required of him or until the trial is concluded (s. 550(3) and (4)).

13. Warrant of committal for contempt

A person who, being required by law to attend or remain in attendance for the purpose of giving evidence, fails, without lawful excuse, to attend or remain in attendance accordingly is guilty of contempt of court (s. 708(1)).

A court, judge, justice or provincial court judge may deal summarily with a person who is guilty of contempt of court under s. 708 and that person is liable to a fine not exceeding one hundred dollars or to imprisonment for a term not exceeding 90 days or to both, and may be ordered to pay the costs that are incident to the service of any process and to his detention, if any (s. 708(2)).

A conviction under s. 708 may be in Form 38 and a warrant of committal in respect of a conviction under this section may be in Form 25 (s. 708(3)).

14. Warrant of committal in default of payment of the costs of an appeal

Where the appeal court orders the appellant or respondent to pay costs, the order shall direct that the costs be paid to the clerk of the court, to be paid by him to the person entitled to them, and shall fix the period within which the costs shall be paid (s. 827(1)).

Where costs are not paid in full within the period fixed for payment and the person who has been ordered to pay them has not been bound by a recognizance to pay them, the clerk of the court shall, on application by the person entitled to the costs, or by any person on his behalf, and on payment of any fee to which the clerk of the court is entitled, issue a certificate in Form 42 certifying that the costs or a part thereof, as the case may be, have not been paid (s. 827(2)).

A justice having jurisdiction in the territorial division in which a certificate has been issued may, upon production of the certificate, by warrant in Form 26, commit the defaulter to imprisonment for a term not exceeding one month, unless the amount of the costs and, where the justice thinks fit so to order, the costs of the committal and of conveying the defaulter to prison are sooner paid (s. 827(3)).

15. Warrant of committal on forfeiture of a recognizance

A judge may issue a warrant of committal in Form 27 at a hearing held to inquire into the circumstances where a sheriff cannot find sufficient goods and chattels and lands and tenements to satisfy a writ of *fieri facias* or where the proceeds of the execution of a writ are not sufficient to satisfy it (s. 773(1) and (3)).

The warrant of committal issued on forfeiture of a recognizance authorizes the sheriff to take into custody the person in respect of whom the warrant was issued and to confine him in a prison in the territorial division in which the writ was issued or in the prison nearest to the court, until satisfaction is made or until the period of imprisonment fixed by the judge has expired (s. 773(4)).

16. Warrant for tracking device

A justice who is satisfied by information on oath in writing that there are reasonable grounds to suspect that an offence under this or any other Act of Parliament has been or will be committed and that information that is relevant to the commission of that offence, including the whereabouts of any person, can be obtained through the use of a tracking device, may at any time issue a warrant authorizing a person named therein or a peace officer (a) to install, maintain and remove a tracking device in or on any thing, including a thing carried, used or worn by any person; and (b) to monitor, or to have monitored, a tracking device installed in or on any thing (s. 492.1(1)).

Such warrant is valid for the period, not exceeding 60 days, mentioned in it (s. 492.1(2)).

A justice may issue further warrants under this section (s. 492.1(3)).

For the purposes of this section, "tracking device" means any device that, when installed in or on any thing, may be used to help ascertain, be electronic or other means, the location of any thing or person (s. 492.1(4)).

17. Warrant for number recorder

A justice who is satisfied by information on oath in writing that there are reasonable grounds to suspect that an offence under this or any other Act of Parliament has been or will be committed and that information that would assist in the investigation of that offence could be obtained through the use of a number recorder, may at any time issue a warrant authorizing a person named in it or a peace officer

(a) to install, maintain and remove a number recorder in relation to any telephone or telephone line; and (b) to monitor, or to have monitored, the number recorder (s. 492.2(1)).

When such circumstances exist, a justice may order that any person or body that lawfully possesses records of telephone calls originated from, or received or intended to be received at, any telephone give the records, or a copy of the records, to a person named in the order (s. 492.2(2)).

Such warrant is valid for the period, not exceeding 60 days, mentioned in it. A justice may issue further warrants under this section (s. 492.2(3)).

For the purposes of this section, "number recorder" means any device that can be used to record or identify the telephone number or location of the telephone from which a telephone call originates, or at which it is received or is intended to be received (s. 492.2(4)).

WASCHHAUT. The wrinkling of the skin of the hands and feet caused by prolonged exposure to moisture. Also washerwoman's skin. It may occur before or after death (Jaffe, A Guide to Pathological Evidence, 2nd ed.).

WEAPON. For the purposes of the Criminal Code, "weapon" means (a) anything used, designed to be used or intended for use in causing death or injury to any person, or (b) anything used, designed to be used or intended for use for the purpose of threatening or intimidating any person and, without restricting the generality of the foregoing, includes any firearm as defined in s. 84(1) (s. 2). *See FIREARM AND WEAPON OFFENCES.*

WHIPLASH INJURY. An injury to the tissues of the neck caused by a sudden overextension of the spine. It is common in rear end collisions. The injury usually involves the muscles and spinal ligaments but in severe cases may damage the vertebral discs, esophagus and trachea (Jaffe, A Guide to Pathological Evidence, 2nd ed.).

WILFULLY. For the purposes of Part XI of the Criminal Code (Wilful and Forbidden Acts in respect of Certain Property) which includes s. 433, s. 434, s. 435 and s. 437), every one who causes the occurrence of an event by doing an act or by omitting to do an act that it is his duty to do, knowing that the act or omission will probably cause the occurrence of the event and being reckless as to the whether or not the event occurs, shall be deemed wilfully to have caused the occurrence of the event (s. 429(1)).

WIRED INFORMANT. A party to a communication (either an undercover law enforcement officer or a private citizen) equipped with a concealed transmitter or recorder for the purpose of securing evidence in the form of a recorded conversation.

WIRETAPPING OFFENCES

1. *Interception of private communication*
2. *Interception of radio-based telephone communication*
3. *Possession of devices for interception*
4. *Disclosure of information from private communication*
5. *Disclosure of information from radio-based telephone communication*

1. Interception of private communication — Section 184(1)

Every one who — by means of any electro-magnetic or acoustic or mechanical or other device — wilfully — intercepts a private communication — is guilty of an indictable offence.

Intent. Wilfully.

Exceptions. 1. This offence does not apply to the following lawful interceptions:

(a) a person who has the consent to intercept, express or implied, of the originator of the private communication or of the person intended by the originator thereof to receive it;

(b) a person who intercepts a private communication in accordance with an authorization or pursuant to s. 184.4 or any person who in good faith aids in any way another person who the aiding person believes on reasonable grounds is acting with an authorization or pursuant to s. 184.4;

(c) a person engaged in providing a telephone, telegraph or other communication service to the public who intercepts a private communication, if the interception is necessary for the purpose of providing the service, or in the course of service observing or random monitoring necessary for the purpose of mechanical or service quality control checks, or if the interception is necessary to protect the person's rights or property directly related to providing the service; or

(d) an officer or servant of Her Majesty in right of Canada who engages in radio frequency spectrum management, in respect of a private communication intercepted by that officer or servant for the purposes of identifying, isolating or preventing an unauthorized or interfering use of a frequency or of a transmission (s. 184(2)).

2. An agent of the state may intercept, by means of any electro-magnetic, acoustic, mechanical or other device, a private communication if (a) either the originator of the private communication or the person intended by the originator to receive it has consented to the interception; (b) the agent of the state believes on reasonable grounds that there is a risk of bodily harm to the person who consented to the interception; and (c) the purpose of the interception is to prevent the bodily harm (s. 184.1(1)).

The contents of a private communication that is obtained from such an interception are inadmissible as evidence except for the purposes of proceedings in which actual, attempted or threatened bodily harm is alleged, including proceedings in respect of an application for an authorization under this Part or in respect of a search warrant or a warrant for the arrest of any person (s. 184.1(2)).

The agent of the state who intercepts such a private communication shall, as soon as is practicable in the circumstances, destroy any recording of the private communication that is obtained from such an interception, any full or partial transcript of the recording and any notes made by that agent of the private communication if nothing in the private communication suggests that bodily harm, attempted bodily harm or threatened bodily harm has occurred or is likely to occur (s. 184.1(3)).

For the purposes of this section, "agent of the state" means (a) a peace officer; and (b) a person acting under the authority of, or in cooperation with, a peace officer (s. 184.1(4)).

3. A person may intercept, by means of any electro-magnetic, acoustic, mechanical or other device, a private communication where either the originator of the private communication or the person intended by the originator to receive it has consented to the interception and an authorization has been obtained pursuant to s. 184.2(3) (s. 184.2(1)).

An application for such an authorization shall be made by a peace officer, or a public officer who has been appointed or designated to administer or enforce any federal or provincial law and whose duties include the enforcement of this or any other Act of Parliament, ex parte and in writing to a provincial court judge, a judge of a superior court of criminal jurisdiction or a judge as defined in s. 552, and shall be accompanied by an affidavit, which may be sworn on the information and belief of that peace officer or public officer or of any other peace officer or public officer, deposing to the following matters:

(a) that there are reasonable grounds to believe that an offence against this or any other Act of Parliament has been or will be committed; (b) the particulars of the offence; (c) the name of the person who has consented to the interception; (d) the period for which the authorization is requested; and (e) in the case of an application for an authorization where an authorization has previously been granted under this section or s. 186, the particulars of the authorization (s. 184.2(2)).

An authorization may be given if the judge to whom the application is made is satisfied that (a) there are reasonable grounds to believe that an offence against this or any other Act of Parliament has been or will be committed; (b) either the originator of the private communication or the person intended by the originator to receive it has consented to the interception; and (c) there are reasonable grounds to believe that information concerning the offence referred to in paragraph (a) will be obtained through the interception sought (s. 184.2(3)).

Such an authorization shall (a) state the offence in respect of which private communications may be intercepted; (b) state the type of private communication that may be intercepted; (c) state the identity of the persons, if known, whose private communications are to be intercepted, generally describe the place at which private communications may be intercepted, if a general description of that place can be given, and generally describe the manner of interception that may be used; (d) contain the terms and conditions that the judge considers advisable in the public interest; and (e) be valid for the period, not exceeding 60 days, set out therein (s. 184.2(4)).

4. A peace officer may intercept, by means of any electro-magnetic, acoustic, mechanical or other device, a private communication where (a) the peace officer believes on reasonable grounds that the urgency of the situation is such that an authorization could not, with reasonable diligence, be obtained under any other provision of this Part; (b) the peace officer believes on reasonable grounds that such an interception is immediately necessary to prevent an unlawful act that would cause serious harm to any person or to property; and (c) either the originator of the private communication or the person intended by the originator to receive it is the person who would perform the act that is likely to cause the harm or is the victim, or intended victim, of the harm (s. 184.4).

Included offences. Attempts (s. 660 and s. 662(1)(b)).

Punishment. Imprisonment for a term not exceeding 5 years (s. 184(1)).

Release. Initial decision to release made by officer in charge or justice (s. 498).

Election. Accused may elect trial by judge and jury, judge alone, or provincial court judge (s. 536).

Definitions. *See AUTHORIZATION; ELECTROMAGNETIC, ACOUSTIC, MECHANICAL OR OTHER DEVICE; INTERCEPT; PRIVATE COMMUNICATION.*

Evidence. Where a private communication is originated by more than one person or is intended by the originator thereof to be received by more than one person, a consent to the interception thereof by any one of those persons is sufficient consent (s. 183.1).

Informations

A.B., on or about the —— day of ——, 19——, at the —— of ——, in the said (territorial division), by means of an electro-magnetic [OR an acoustic OR a mechanical OR (specify other device)] device, did wilfully intercept a private communication, to wit: (specify the particulars of the offence), contrary to s. 184(1) of the Criminal Code of Canada.

2. Interception of radio-based telephone communication — Section 184.5(1)

Every person who — intercepts — by means of any electromagnetic, acoustic, mechanical or other device — maliciously or for gain — a radio-based telephone communication — if the originator of the communication or the person intended by the originator of the communication to receive it is in Canada — is guilty of an indictable offence.

Intent. Maliciously or for gain.

Exceptions. *See Exceptions, under* **1**, *above.*

Included offences. Attempts (s. 660 and s. 662(1)(b)).

Punishment. Imprisonment for a term not exceeding 5 years (s. 184.5(1)).

Release. Initial decision to release made by officer in charge or justice (s. 498).

Election. Accused may elect trial by judge and jury, judge alone, or provincial court judge (s. 536).

Definitions. See AUTHORIZATION; ELECTROMAGNETIC, ACOUSTIC, MECHANICAL OR OTHER DEVICE; INTERCEPT; RADIO-BASED TELEPHONE COMMUNICATION.

Evidence. *See Evidence under* **1**, *above.*

Informations

A.B., on or about the —— day of ——, 19——, at the —— of ——, in the said (territorial division), did intercept by means of any electro-magnetic [OR acoustic OR mechanical OR other] device, maliciously [OR for gain], a radio-based telephone communication, the originator of the communication [OR the person intended by the originator of the communication to receive it] was in Canada, to wit: (specify the particulars of the offence), contrary to s. 184.5(1) of the Criminal Code of Canada.

3. Possession of devices for interception — Section 191(1)

Every one who — possesses or sells or purchases — any electro-magnetic or acoustic or mechanical or other device or any component thereof — knowing that the design thereof renders it primarily useful for surreptitious interception of private communications — is guilty of an indictable offence.

Intent. Knowledge of primary use.

Exceptions. This offence does not apply to the following:

(a) a police officer or police constable in possession of such a device or component in the course of his employment;

(b) a person in possession of such a device or component for the purpose of using it in an interception made or to be made in accordance with an authorization;

(c) a person in possession of such a device or component under the direction of a police officer or police constable in order to assist that officer or constable in the course of his duties as a police officer or police constable;

(d) an officer or a servant of Her Majesty in right of Canada or a member of the Canadian Forces in possession of such a device or component in the course of his duties as such an officer, servant or member, as the case may be; and

(e) any other person in possession of such a device or component under the authority of a licence issued by the Solicitor General of Canada (s. 191(2)).

Included offences. Attempts (s. 660 and s. 662(1)(b)).

Punishment. Imprisonment for a term not exceeding 2 years (s. 191(1)).

Release. Initial decision to release made by officer in charge or justice (s. 498).

Election. Accused may elect trial by judge and jury, judge alone, or provincial court judge (s. 536).

Definitions. *See* AUTHORIZATION; ELECTROMAGNETIC, ACOUSTIC, MECHANICAL OR OTHER DEVICE; INTERCEPT; PRIVATE COMMUNICATION.

Evidence. See Evidence, under 1, above.

Informations

A.B., on or about the —— day of ——, 19——, at the —— of ——, in the said (territorial division), did possess [OR sell OR purchase] an electro-magnetic [OR an acoustic OR a mechanical OR (specify another type of device)] device, knowing that the design thereof did render it primarily useful for surreptitious interception of private communications, to wit: (specify the particulars of the offence), contrary to s. 191(1) of the Criminal Code of Canada.

4. Disclosure of information from private communication — Section 193(1)

Every one who — where a private communication has been intercepted by means of an electro-magnetic or acoustic or mechanical or other device without the consent, express or implied, of the originator thereof or of the person intended by the originator thereof to receive it — without the express consent of the originator thereof or of the person intended by the originator thereof to receive it — wilfully — either uses or discloses the private communication or any part thereof or the substance or meaning or purport thereof or of any part thereof — or discloses the existence thereof — is guilty of an indictable offence.

Intent. Wilfully.

Exceptions. 1. This offence does not apply to a person who discloses a private communication or any part thereof or the substance, meaning or purport thereof or of any part thereof or who discloses the existence of a private communication:

(a) in the course of or for the purpose of giving evidence in any civil or criminal proceedings or in any other proceedings in which the person may be required to give evidence on oath;

(b) in the course of or for the purpose of any criminal investigation if the private communication was lawfully intercepted;

(c) in giving notice under s. 189 or furnishing further particulars pursuant to an order under s. 190;

(d) in the course of the operation of either a telephone, telegraph or other communication service to the public, or a department or an agency of the Government of Canada, if the disclosure is necessarily incidental to an interception described in s. 184(2)(c) or (d);

(e) where disclosure is made to a peace officer and is intended to be in the interests of the administration of justice; or

(f) where the disclosure is made to the Director of the Canadian Security Intelligence Service or to an employee of the Service for the purpose of enabling the Service to perform its duties and functions under s. 12 of the Canadian Security Intelligence Service Act (s. 193(2)).

2. In addition, this offence does not apply to a person who discloses a private communication or any part thereof or the substance, meaning or purport thereof or of any part thereof or who discloses the existence of a private communication, where that which is disclosed by him was, prior to the disclosure, lawfully disclosed in the course of or for the purpose of giving evidence in proceedings referred to in s. 193(2)(a) of the Criminal Code (s. 193(3)).

Included offences. Attempts (s. 660 and s. 662(1)(b)).

Punishment. Imprisonment for a term not exceeding 2 years (s. 193(1)).

Release. Initial decision to release made by officer in charge or justice (s. 498).

Election. Accused may elect trial by judge and jury, judge alone, or provincial court judge (s. 536).

Definitions. *See AUTHORIZATION; ELECTROMAGNETIC, ACOUSTIC, MECHANICAL OR OTHER DEVICE; INTERCEPT; PRIVATE COMMUNICATION.*

Evidence. *See Evidence, under* **1**, *above.*

Informations

A.B., on or about the —— day of ——, 19——, at the —— of ——, in the said (territorial division), wilfully did use [OR disclose OR disclose the existence of] a private communication [OR a part of a private communication OR the substance (OR meaning OR purport) of a private communication] that had been intercepted by means of an electro-magnetic [OR an acoustic OR a mechanical

OR (specify other type of device)] device, without the consent, express or implied, of C.D., the originator of the private communication, or E.F., the person intended by C.D. to receive it, to wit: (specify the particulars of the offence), contrary to s. 193(1) of the Criminal Code of Canada.

5. Disclosure of information received from interception of radio-based telephone communications — Section 193.1(1)

Every person who — wilfully — uses or discloses — a radio-based telephone communication — or who — wilfully — discloses the existence of such a communication — if the originator of the communication or the person intended by the originator of the communication to receive it was in Canada when the communication was made — the communication was intercepted by means of an electromagnetic, acoustic, mechanical or other device without the consent, express or implied, of the originator of the communication or of the person intended by the originator to receive the communication and — the person does not have the express or implied consent of the originator of the communication or of the person intended by the originator to receive the communication — is guilty of an indictable offence.

Intent. Wilfully.

Exceptions. *See Exceptions under* **4**, *above.*

Included offences. Attempts (s. 660 and s. 662(1)(b)).

Punishment. Imprisonment for a term not exceeding 2 years (s. 193.1(1)).

Release. Initial decision to release made by officer in charge or justice (s. 498).

Election. Accused may elect trial by judge and jury, judge alone, or provincial court judge (s. 536).

Evidence. *See Evidence under* **1**, *above.*

Definitions. *See AUTHORIZATION; ELECTROMAGNETIC, ACOUSTIC, MECHANICAL OR OTHER DEVICE: INTERCEPT; RADIO-BASED TELEPHONE COMMUNICATION.*

Informations

A.B., on or about the —— day of ——, 19——, at the —— of ——, in the said (territorial division), wilfully did use [OR disclose] a radio-based telephone communication [OR did disclose the existence of such a communication], if the originator of the communication [OR the person intended by the originator of the communication to receive it] was in Canada when the communication was made, the communication was intercepted by means of an electromagnetic [OR acoustic OR mechanical OR other] device without the consent, express or implied, of the originator of the communication [OR of the person intended by the originator to receive the communication] and the person did not have the express [OR implied] consent of the originator of the communication [OR if the person intended by the originator to receive the communication], to wit: (specify the particulars of the offence), contrary to s. 193.1(1) of the Criminal Code of Canada.

WITNESSES

1. *Definition of "witness"*
2. *Appearance before a justice or provincial court judge*
3. *At other trials of indictable offences*
4. *Witness in prison*
5. *Material witness*
6. *Adverse witness*
7. *Previous statements in writing*
8. *Previous oral statements*
9. *Previous conviction*
10. *Incriminating questions and answers to such questions.*

1. Definition of "witness"

For the purposes of Part IV of the Criminal Code (Offences Against the Administration of Law and Justice) "witness" means a person who gives evidence orally under oath or by affidavit in a judicial proceeding, whether or not he is competent to be a witness, and includes a child of tender years who gives evidence but does not give it under oath, because, in the opinion of the person presiding, the child does not understand the nature of an oath (s. 118).

2. Appearance before a justice or provincial court judge

A justice or provincial court judge may issue a subpoena to require the appearance before him of any person within the province who is likely to give material evidence for the prosecution or for the defence (s. 698 and Form 17). Such subpoena may require the witness to bring with him any documents in his possession or under his control.

The subpoena must be served by a constable or other peace officer either personally on the person to whom it is directed, or if such person cannot conveniently be met with, by leaving it for him at his last or most usual place of abode with some inmate apparently not under 16 years of age (s. 701(1)).

Reasonable effort must be made to serve the witness personally before resorting to substitutional service, because if the witness does not appear in answer to the subpoena, the justice may issue a warrant to arrest him.

In default of appearance, a warrant for arrest will only be issued after proof before the justice that the subpoena was served as aforesaid and if satisfied that such person is likely to give material evidence (s. 705). The justice, before issuing a warrant, will want to know that the subpoena came to the attention of the witness and that he is deliberately disobeying it. The warrant so issued may be executed anywhere in the province, but if outside the jurisdiction of the justice, it must be endorsed (*see ARREST*). The witness, when arrested, should be brought at once before the justice, who may order him detained in custody or released on furnishing sureties for his attendance to give evidence. The justice may also, in a summary way, dispose of the charge of contempt. If the justice convicts, he may impose a fine not exceeding $100, or imprisonment for 90 days or both, and may also order him to pay the costs incident to the service and execution of the subpoena and warrant and his detention in custody (s. 708(2)).

Where the witness is in another province, a superior court of criminal jurisdiction or county court or district court of the province may cause a subpoena to be issued under the seal of the court and signed by a judge, or by the clerk of the court pursuant to an order of a judge directing a witness to appear and give evidence before a justice. Service of the subpoena must be personal service but need not be served by a constable or peace officer. Proof of the service of such subpoena may be by affidavit. A subpoena issued by a superior court, a court of appeal or a court of criminal jurisdiction other than a provincial court judge has effect anywhere in Canada (s. 702, s. 699(2) and (3)).

3. At other trials of indictable offences

At other trials of indictable offences, the subpoena is issued out of the court at which the witness is required to attend (s. 699(1)).

4. Witness in prison

An order may be obtained from a judge of a superior or county or district court for a prisoner confined in any prison in Canada to attend before the court to give evidence (s. 527(1)). A provincial court judge has jurisdiction to issue the order if the witness is in a prison within the province (s. 527(2)).

5. Material witness

Where it is made to appear that a person likely to give material evidence will not attend in response to a subpoena or is evading service of a subpoena, the court, justice or provincial court judge may issue a warrant for his arrest (s. 698). The court, justice or provincial court judge may order that he be detained or released on recognizance (s. 706). If a witness is on recognizance and is about to abscond, an information may be laid against him (s. 704) and he may be arrested on warrant.

No formal information for the issue of a warrant for the arrest in the first instance of a witness is prescribed in the Code. S. 698(2) simply requires that it be "made to appear" to the justice that a witness will not attend in answer to a subpoena or is evading service. However, the justice in his discretion may require an information on oath and if so, the following form is suggested:

The informant says that he has reasonable and probable grounds to believe and does believe that A.B. is a person who is likely to give material evidence in the case of Regina vs. C.D. upon a charge that the said C.D. (set out the charge), and who will not attend as a witness in response to a subpoena if a subpoena is issued [OR is evading service of subpoena issued by ——, at ——, on ——]. A Justice of the Peace for ——, [OR as the case may be].

Signature of Informant

When arrested, a witness must not be treated as an ordinary prisoner; it has been laid down that he should not be searched. The only thing required of him is his appearance to give evidence. A person arrested under s. 704 is entitled to demand to receive a copy of the information on which the warrant was issued (s. 704(3)).

6. Adverse witness

A party producing a witness shall not be allowed to impeach his credit by general evidence of bad character, but if the witness, in the opinion of the court, proves adverse, such party may contradict him by other evidence, or, by leave of the court, may prove that the witness made at other times a statement inconsistent with his present testimony; but before such last-mentioned proof can be given, the circumstances of the supposed statement, sufficient to designate the particular occasion, shall be mentioned to the witness, and he shall be asked whether or not he did make such statement (Canada Evidence Act, s. 9(1)).

7. Previous statements in writing

Where the party producing a witness alleges that the witness made at other times a statement in writing, or reduced to writing, inconsistent with his present testimony, the court may, without proof that the witness is adverse, grant leave to that party to cross-examine the witness as to the statement and the court may consider such cross-examination in determining whether in the opinion of the court the witness is adverse (Canada Evidence Act, s. 9(2)).

On any trial a witness may be cross-examined as to previous statements made by him in writing, or reduced to writing, relative to the subject matter of the case, without such writing being shown to him; but, if it is intended to contradict the witness by the writing, his attention must, before such contradictory proof can be given, be called to those parts of the writing that are to be used for the purpose of so contradicting him; the judge, at any time during the trial, may require the production of the writing for his inspection, and thereupon make such use of it for the purposes of the trial as he thinks fit (Canada Evidence Act, s. 10(1)).

A deposition of the witness, purporting to have been taken before a justice on the investigation of a criminal charge and to be signed by the witness and the justice, returned to and produced from the custody of the proper officer, shall be presumed prima facie to have been signed by the witness (Canada Evidence Act, s. 10(2)).

8. Previous oral statements

Where a witness upon cross-examination as to a former statement made by him relative to the subject matter of the case and inconsistent with his present testimony, does not distinctly admit that he did make such statement, proof may be given that he did in fact make it; but before such proof can be given, the circumstances of the supposed statement, sufficient to designate the particular occasion, shall be mentioned to the witness, and he shall be asked whether or not he did make such statement (Canada Evidence Act, s. 11).

9. Previous conviction

A witness may be questioned as to whether he has been convicted of any offence, and upon being so questioned, if he either denies the fact or refuses to answer, the opposite party may prove such conviction (Canada Evidence Act, s. 12(1)).

The conviction may be proved by producing (a) a certificate containing the substance and effect only, omitting the formal part, of the indictment and conviction, if it is for an indictable offence, or a copy of the summary conviction, if for an offence punishable on summary conviction, purporting to be signed by the clerk of the court or other officer having the custody of the records of the court in which the conviction, if upon indictment, was had, or to which the conviction, if summary, was returned; and (b) proof of identity (Canada Evidence Act, s. 12(2)).

10. Incriminating questions and answers to such questions

No witness shall be excused from answering any question upon the ground that the answer to such question may tend to criminate him, or may tend to establish his liability to a civil proceeding at the instance of the Crown or of any person (Canada Evidence Act, s. 5(1)).

Where with respect to any question a witness objects to answer upon the ground that his answer may tend to criminate him, or may tend to establish his liability to a civil proceeding at the instance of the Crown or of any person, and if but for the Canada Evidence Act, or the Act of any provincial legislature, the witness would therefore have been excused from answering such question, then although the witness is by reason of the Canada Evidence Act, or by reason of such provincial Act, compelled to answer, the answer so given shall not be used or receivable in evidence against him in any criminal trial, or other criminal proceeding against him thereafter taking place, other than a prosecution for perjury in the giving of such evidence (Canada Evidence Act, s. 5(2)).

WOUND. A disruption of a tissue caused by violence (Jaffe, A Guide to Pathological Evidence, 2nd ed.).

Defence wound. A wound on the fingers, hands or forearms of the victim of an attack with a sharp weapon, sustained while trying to grasp or ward off the blade (Jaffe, A Guide to Pathological Evidence, 2nd ed.).

Hesitation wound. Tentative stabs or cut made by a suicide prior to the infliction of a lethal wound (Jaffe, A Guide to Pathological Evidence, 2nd ed.).

Penetrating wound. A wound which extends into an organ or tissue, having an entrance opening only (Jaffe, A Guide to Pathological Evidence, 2nd ed.).

Perforating wound. A wound which completely transverses an organ or tissue, having both an entrance and exit opening (Jaffe, A Guide to Pathological Evidence, 2nd ed.).

WOUNDED OFFENDERS. If a person upon arrest requires hospital treatment he should not be kept in the custody of the police officer. Arrangements should be made to have the provincial court judge go to the hospital and remand the accused. The sheriff or jailer (or whoever then becomes the proper custodial officer) is then the responsible officer and he has the authority, which a police officer has not, of incurring expenses for hospital treatment or for extra guards. It it is impossible to have this done, the police officer should obtain instructions from his superior officer or attempt to have the sheriff or jailer assume responsibility for payment. The police officer should be careful in such cases where a prisoner, or other person, requires medical or hospital attention to make it plain that he is not pledging his own credit, otherwise he might make himself liable for payment. Unless he has authority so to do he should also advise that he has no authority to incur expenses on behalf of his employers.

WRECK

1. *Definition of "wreck"*
2. *Offences in relation to wreck*
3. *Preventing or impeding the saving of wreck*

1. Definition of "wreck"

1. In the Criminal Code "wreck" includes the cargo, stores and tackle of a vessel and all parts of a vessel separated from the vessel, and the property of persons who belong to, are on board or have quitted a vessel that is wrecked, stranded or in distress at any place in Canada (s. 2).

2. In the Canada Shipping Act, "wreck" includes (a) jetsam, flotsam, lagan and derelict found in or on the shores of the sea or of any tidal water, or of any of the inland waters of Canada, (b) cargo, stores and tackle of any vessel and of all parts of the vessel separated therefrom, (c) the property of shipwrecked persons, and (d) any wrecked aircraft or any part thereof and cargo thereof (Canada Shipping Act, s. 2).

2. Offences in relation to wreck

Section 415(a)

Every one who — either secretes a wreck — or defaces or obliterates the marks on a wreck — or uses any means to disguise or conceal the fact that anything is a wreck — or in any manner conceals the character of a wreck — from a person who is entitled to inquire into the wreck — is guilty of either an indictable offence or an offence punishable on summary conviction.

Section 415(b)

Every one who — receives a wreck — knowing that it is a wreck — from a person other than the owner thereof or a receiver of the wreck — and does not within 48 hours thereafter inform the receiver of the wreck — is guilty of either an indictable offence or an offence punishable on summary conviction.

Section 415(c)

Every one who — either offers a wreck for sale — or otherwise deals with it — knowing that it is a wreck — and not having a lawful authority to sell or deal with it — is guilty of either an indictable offence or an offence punishable on summary conviction.

Section 415(d)

Every one who — keeps a wreck in his possession — knowing that it is a wreck — without lawful authority to keep it — for any time longer than the time reasonably necessary to deliver it to the receiver of the wreck — is guilty of either an indictable offence or an offence punishable on summary conviction.

Section 415(e)

Every one who — boards a vessel — that is wrecked or stranded or in distress — against the will of the master — unless he is a receiver of the wreck or a person acting under orders of a receiver of the wreck — is guilty of either an indictable offence or an offence punishable on summary conviction.

Intent. Knowledge of being wreck (s. 415(b), (c) and (d)).

Limitation period. No proceedings in respect of offences that are declared to be punishable on summary conviction shall be instituted more than 6 months after the time when the subject matter of the proceedings arose (s. 786(2) and s. 785(1)).

Included offences. Attempts (s. 660 and s. 662(1)(b)).

Punishment. On indictment, imprisonment for a term not exceeding 2 years (s. 415(f)). On summary conviction, a fine not exceeding $2,000, or 6 months' imprisonment, or both (s. 415(g) and s. 787(1)).

Release. Initial decision to release made by peace officer (s. 497).

Election. On indictment, accused may elect trial by judge and jury, judge alone, or provincial court judge (s. 536). On summary conviction, no election.

3. Preventing or impeding the saving of wreck — Section 438(2)

Every one who — wilfully — either prevents or impedes — or endeavours to prevent or impede — the saving of the wreck — is guilty of an offence punishable on summary conviction.

Intent. Wilfully.

Limitation period. No proceedings in respect of offences that are declared to be punishable on summary conviction shall be instituted more than 6 months after the time when the subject matter of the proceedings arose (s. 786(2) and s. 785(1)).

Included offences. Attempts (s. 660 and s. 662(1)(b)).

Punishment. A fine not exceeding $2,000, or 6 months' imprisonment, or both (s. 438(2) and s. 787(1)).

Release. Initial decision to release made by peace officer (s. 497).

Election. No election, summary conviction offence.

Evidence. No person shall be convicted of this offence where he proves that he acted with legal justification or excuse and with colour of right (s. 429(2)).

Informations

A.B., on or about the —— day of ——, 19——, at the —— of ——, in the said (territorial division), wilfully did prevent or impede [OR wilfully did endeavour to prevent or impede] the saving of a wreck, to wit: (specify the particulars of the offence), contrary to s. 438(2) of the Criminal Code of Canada.

WRITING. 1. "Writing", or any term of like import, includes words printed, typewritten, painted, engraved, lithographed, photographed, or represented or reproduced by any mode of representing or reproducing words in visible form (Interpretation Act, s. 35(1)). 2. For the purposes of the Criminal Code, "writing" includes a document of any kind and any mode in which, and any material on which, words or figures, whether at length or abridged, are written, printed or otherwise expressed or a map or plan is inscribed (s. 2).

Y

YOUNG OFFENDERS

1. *Definitions*
2. *Application of the Young Offenders Act*
3. *Application of the Criminal Code*
4. *Procedure on arrest*
5. *Notice to parents, relatives or friends*
6. *Detention of a young person*
7. *Jurisdiction*
8. *Prosecution and trials of young persons*
9. *Dispositions*
10. *Protection of privacy of young persons*

1. Definitions

Young person. A person who is or, in the absence of evidence to the contrary, appears to be 12 years of age or more, but under 18 years of age (Young Offenders Act, s. 2(1)).

Child. A person who is, or in the absence of evidence to the contrary, appears to be under the age of 12 years (Young Offenders Act, s. 2(1)).

2. Application of the Young Offenders Act

A young person who commits any offence created by or under federal legislation, including the Criminal Code, will be dealt with in accordance with the Young Offenders Act. The Act does not apply to provincial and municipal offences.

The Young Offenders Act provides that the Act shall be liberally construed in accordance with the principles that young persons should bear responsibility for their offences, but should not always be held accountable and suffer the same consequences for their behaviour as adult offenders, and that society must be protected from illegal behaviour (Young Offenders Act, s. 3).

3. Application of the Criminal Code

All Criminal Code provisions apply to proceedings under the Young Offenders Act, except to the extent that they are inconsistent with or excluded by the Act (Young Offenders Act, s. 51).

4. Procedure on arrest

When a young person is arrested, the arresting officer must immediately advise him of his right to be represented by counsel and give him an opportunity to obtain counsel (Young Offenders Act, s. 11(2)). No fingerprints or photographs of the young person may be taken unless it would be permissible to do so under the Identification of Criminals Act (Young Offenders Act, s. 44(2)). If a statement is to be taken from the young person, the officer taking the statement must explain to the young person that he is under no obligation to make a statement; that any statement may be used as evidence in proceedings against him; that the young person has the right to consult with counsel, a parent or another appropriate adult prior to making the statement; and that any statement made by him must be made in the presence of the person so consulted, unless the young person desires otherwise (Young Offenders Act, s. 56(2)(b)).

5. Notice to parents, relatives or friends

When a young person is arrested and detained in custody, the officer in charge must, as soon as possible, inform a parent of the young person of the arrest, stating the place of detention and the reason for the arrest (Young Offenders Act, s. 9(1)). When a summons or appearance notice is issued in respect of a young person, or when a young person is released on giving his promise to appear or entering into a recognizance, the officer in charge must, as soon as possible, give written notice to a parent of the young person of the summons, appearance notice, promise to appear or recognizance (Young Offenders Act, s. 9(2)). When notice must be given but the whereabouts of the parents of the young person are not known or it appears that no parent is available, notice may be given to an adult relative of the young person or to another appropriate adult (Young Offenders Act, s. 9(3)). Forms are provided in the Young Offenders Act for this purpose.

6. Detention of a young person

If a young person is detained following his arrest, he shall be detained in a place of temporary detention, designated as such by the Lieutenant Governor in Council of his province (Young Offenders Act, s. 7(1)). No young person may be detained in any place where an adult charged with or convicted of an offence is being detained, unless a youth court judge or justice orders otherwise (Young Offenders Act, s. 7(2)).

7. Jurisdiction

A youth court has exclusive jurisdiction in respect of any offence alleged to have been committed by a person while he was a young person (Young Offenders Act, s. 5(1)). However, when a young person over 14 years old is charged with an indictable offence, other than an offence referred to in s. 553 of the Criminal Code, a youth court judge may order that the young person be proceeded against in ordinary court in accordance with the law ordinarily applicable to an adult (Young Offenders Act, s. 16(1)).

8. Prosecutions and trials of young persons

Prosecutions and trials under the Young Offenders Act shall be governed by the provisions of the Criminal Code relating to summary conviction offences, except to the extent that those provisions are inconsistent with the Act, whether the young person is charged with a summary conviction offence or an indictable offence (Young Offenders Act, s. 52(1)). However, s. 786(2) of the Criminal Code, which prohibits the prosecution of a summary conviction offence more than 6 months after the alleged commission of the offence, does not apply when the young person is charged with an indictable offence (Young Offenders Act, s. 52(4)).

9. Dispositions

When a youth court finds a young person guilty of an offence, the court shall make a disposition, which is analogous to the imposition of a sentence in ordinary court. There are a wide variety of dispositions that may be made, including custody in a juvenile facility, fines, restitution orders and community service orders (Young Offenders Act, ss. 20-26).

10. Protection of privacy of young persons

When a youth court hears an application to transfer proceedings against a young person to ordinary court, it may make an order directing that no information respecting the alleged offence shall be published in any newspaper or broadcast (Young Offenders Act, s. 17). During youth court proceedings, the judge may exclude the public from the courtroom if any evidence presented in court would be harmful or prejudicial to the young person charged with an offence, to a child (under age 12) or young person aggrieved by or who was the victim of the offence or to a young person or child appearing as a witness. The judge may also exclude the public if doing so would be in the interest of public morals, the maintenance of order or the proper administration of justice (Young Offenders Act, s. 39(1)). No person may publish any report on proceedings under the Act disclosing any information identifying the young person charged with the offence, or a young person or child appearing as a witness (Young Offenders Act, s. 38(1)). Everyone who publishes such information is guilty of an indictable offence and liable to imprisonment for a term not exceeding 2 years or is guilty of an offence punishable on summary conviction (Young Offenders Act, s. 38(2)).